Ada *plus*
Data Structures
An Object-Oriented Approach

Nell Dale
University of Texas, Austin

John McCormick
University of Northern Iowa, Cedar Falls

JONES AND BARTLETT PUBLISHERS
Sudbury, Massachusetts
BOSTON   TORONTO   LONDON   SINGAPORE

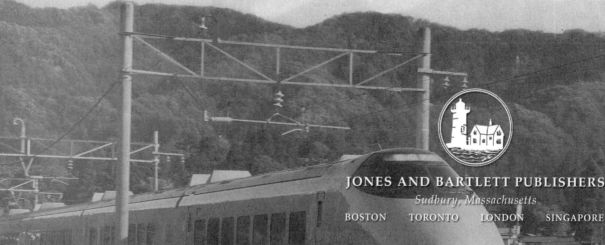

World Headquarters
Jones and Bartlett Publishers
40 Tall Pine Drive
Sudbury, MA 01776
978-443-5000
info@jbpub.com
www.jbpub.com

Jones and Bartlett Publishers
Canada
6339 Ormindale Way
Mississauga, Ontario L5V 1J2
CANADA

Jones and Bartlett Publishers
International
Barb House, Barb Mews
London W6 7PA
UK

Jones and Bartlett's books and products are available through most bookstores and online booksellers. To contact Jones and Bartlett Publishers directly, call 800-832-0034, fax 978-443-8000, or visit our website www.jbpub.com.

> Substantial discounts on bulk quantities of Jones and Bartlett's publications are available to corporations, professional associations, and other qualified organizations. For details and specific discount information, contact the special sales department at Jones and Bartlett via the above contact information or send an email to specialsales@jbpub.com.

Copyright © 2007 by Jones and Bartlett Publishers, Inc.

All rights reserved. No part of the material protected by this copyright may be reproduced or utilized in any form, electronic or mechanical, including photocopying, recording, or by any information storage and retrieval system, without written permission from the copyright owner.

Production Credits
Acquisitions Editor: Tim Anderson
Production Director: Amy Rose
Editorial Assistant: Laura Pagluica
Production Assistant: Jamie Chase
Manufacturing Buyer: Therese Connell
Marketing Manager: Andrea DeFronzo
Composition: Northeast Compositors, Inc.
Interior Design: Anne Spencer
Cover Design: Timothy Dziewit
Cover Image: Images © Thomas Nord/ShutterStock, Inc. & © Jason Cheever/ShutterStock, Inc.
Printing and Binding: Malloy, Inc.
Cover Printing: John Pow Company

ISBN-13: 978-0-7637-3794-8
ISBN-10: 0-7637-3794-1

Library of Congress Cataloging-in-Publication Data
Dale, Nell B.
  ADA plus data structures / Nell Dale and John McCormick. — 2nd ed.
     p. cm.
  Includes bibliographical references and index.
  ISBN-13: 978-0-7637-3794-8 (pbk.)
  ISBN-10: 0-7637-3794-1 (pbk.)
  1. Ada (Computer program language) 2. Data structures (Computer science) 3. Object-oriented programming (Computer science) I. McCormick, John A. (John Ash). II. Title.
  QA76.73.A35D35 2006
  005.13'3—dc22
                                    2006004531
6048

Printed in the United States of America
10 09 08 07 06   10 9 8 7 6 5 4 3 2 1

To Al, my husband and best friend, to our children and our childrens' children, and to our dogs Chrissie and Winston, who round out our family.

N.D.

To Naomi, my wife of 35 years and still my best friend.

J.M.

preface

Welcome to the second edition of *Ada Plus Data Structures: An Object-Oriented Approach*. Historically, a course on data structures has been a mainstay of most computer science departments. Since the first edition of this textbook was published in 1995, the focus of this course has broadened considerably. The topic of data structures has now been subsumed under the broader study of classes of objects whose logical behavior is defined by a set of values and a set of operations.

The term data structures refers to the study of data and how to represent data objects within a program; that is, the implementation of structured relationships. The term abstract data type refers to the separation of the logical properties of a data structure from its implementation. The shift in emphasis is representative of the move toward more abstraction in computer science education. We are now interested in the study of abstract properties of classes of data objects in addition to how the objects might be represented in a program. Johannes J. Martin put it succinctly, "depending on the point of view, a data object is characterized by its type (for the user) or by its structure (for the implementor)."[1] In Ada, an abstract data type is implemented using the class construct, which is easily extended through inheritance and provides run-time polymorphism.

You'll find that all of the familiar topics of strings, sets, stacks, queues, lists, trees, graphs, sorting, searching, Big-O analysis, and recursion are still here, but are now covered from an object-oriented point of view using the features of Ada 2005. We develop generic classes that students can extend via inheritance. While the design of application software is not a major focus of this book, we introduce Class-Responsibility-Collaborator (CRC) Cards and Universal Modeling Language (UML) diagrams to help us model and visualize classes and their interrelationships. We hope that you enjoy this up-to-date approach to the traditional data structures course.

---

[1] Johannes J. Martin, *Data Types and Data Structures*, Prentice-Hall International Series in Computer Science, C.A.R. Hoare, Series Editor, Prentice-Hall International (UK) 1986, p. 1.

Three Levels of Abstraction

The recurring theme throughout this book is *modeling with levels of abstraction*. From simple scalars to complex graphs, we study each class from three different perspectives: their specification, their application, and their implementation. The specification level describes the logical or abstract level. This level is concerned with *what* the operations are and *what* they do. The application perspective, sometimes called the user perspective, is concerned with how the data type might be used to solve a problem. This level is concerned with *why* the operations do what they do. The implementation level is where the operations are actually coded. This level is concerned with the *how* questions.

Using this approach, we stress computer science theory and software engineering principles including information hiding, data encapsulation, data abstraction, stepwise refinement, visual aids, the analysis of algorithms, and software verification methods. We feel strongly that these principles should be introduced to computer science students early in their education so that they can learn to practice good software techniques from the beginning.

An understanding of theoretical concepts helps students put the new ideas they encounter into place, and practical advice allows them to apply what they have learned. To teach these concepts we consistently use intuitive explanations, even for topics that have a basis in mathematics, like the analysis of algorithms. In all cases, our highest goal has been to make sure our explanations are readable and as easily understandable as possible.

Prerequisite Assumptions

In this book, we assume that readers are familiar with the following Ada constructs.

- Built-in simple data types and subtypes: *Character, Float, Integer, Positive, Natural,* and *Boolean.*
- Programmer defined simple data types and subtypes: *enumeration types, integer types,* and *floating point types.*
- Constrained array types, unconstrained array types, and record types.
- Control structures *if, case, loop-exit, for loop,* and *exception handlers.*
- Procedures, functions, and parameter passing modes.
- Input and output using operations in the predefined packages: Ada.Text_IO, Ada.Integer_Text_IO, and Ada.Float_Text_IO.
- Instantiation and use of packages for the input and output of enumeration values and other programmer-defined simple data types.

We have included reviews of some of these topics within the text to refresh students' memory concerning some of the details of these topics.

Changes in the Second Edition

This edition uses *Ada 2005*. All of the Ada examples in the first edition were implemented in Ada 83, a language that did not support inheritance or dynamic polymorphism. Ada 95 added support for object-oriented programming while maintaining the safety that is Ada's hallmark. Many of the improvements made in Ada 2005 are targeted at the real-time and high integrity domains. Features of Ada 2005 that are relevant to first-year students and used in this edition include:

- The object.operation syntax as an alternative to the traditional package.operation(object) syntax for invoking class operations.
- More flexible access types. In particular, the expanded use of anonymous access types simplifies declarations.
- The new reserved word overriding that eliminates the nasty bugs that arise from confusing overloading and overriding of superclass operations.
- Extensions to the standard library.

Object-oriented design is a hard topic for most students, because most people think procedurally. In Chapter 1, we discuss the importance of abstraction and information hiding in design, the use of stepwise refinement and visual aids, and the relationship between functional decomposition and object-oriented design. Chapter 1 introduces a design methodology with four phases: *brainstorming* in which the possible objects in a problem are isolated; *filtering* to remove redundant or unnecessary classes; *scenarios* for asking "what if" questions and assigning responsibilities to classes; and *responsibility algorithms* during which the algorithms for class operations are designed.

Since the first edition of this book, *object-oriented programming* has become part of the first-year curriculum, as demonstrated by its inclusion in all variations of the first year outlined in the Computer Curricula 2001 developed by the Joint Task Force of the IEEE Computer Society and the Association for Computing Machinery. Accordingly, the class concept has moved into the first year. In Chapter 2 we introduce Ada's tagged type and its support for dynamic polymorphism and type extension. All of the data structures are implemented as classes that can be extended with additional data and operations.

We study the *string classes* defined in the standard library rather than define our own string classes. We provide insights to the implementation of these classes.

The introduction to *Big-O* is now delayed until Chapter 5 where we first encounter a data structure with multiple implementations (array based and linked list based stacks).

With the expanded use of anonymous access types available in Ada 2005 we now define *non-generic traversal procedures* in our list classes. Instead of supplying the processing procedure as a generic actual parameter, we pass a pointer to it when we call the traversal procedure.

The *nonlinked representation of a binary tree* is an important concept within its own right, not just as an implementation for a heap. This binary tree implementation is now covered in Chapter 10 with other tree implementation techniques.

Expanded coverage of *hash functions* and *collision resolution* including a discussion on the *performance of hashing*.

Many more *chapter exercises* and *programming problems*.

Content and Organization

Chapter 1 outlines the basic goals of high-quality software, and the basic principles of software engineering for designing and implementing programs to meet those goals. Abstraction, stepwise refinement, functional decomposition, and object-oriented design are discussed. This chapter also addresses what we see to be a critical need in software education: the ability to design and implement correct programs and to verify that they are actually correct. Topics covered include: the concept of "life-cycle" verification; designing for correctness using preconditions, postconditions, and loop invariants; the use of deskchecking and design/code walkthroughs and inspections to identify errors before testing; debugging techniques, data coverage (black-box), and code coverage (clear-box) approaches; test plans, unit testing, and structured integration testing using stubs and drivers. We conclude the chapter with a case study to show how all of these concepts can be applied to the development of a binary search procedure.

Chapter 2 introduces the concepts of data types, data structures, and data abstractions; software engineering concepts that relate to the design of classes. Three perspectives of data are introduced: the abstract or *logical view*, the *application view*, and the *implementation view*. We apply these three perspectives in a comprehensive review of Ada's built-in types. The remainder of the chapter is devoted to Ada's mechanisms for encapsulation (packages and private types) and creation of extendable classes (tagged types and primitive operations). A case study demonstrates the object-oriented design methodology and visual aids introduced in the previous chapter and the Ada features needed to implement the design.

Chapter 3 introduces the discrete set class. The set is first considered from the logical perspective that we describe formally through a package specification. Then, before discussing any implementation details, we use the set specification to implement the Bingo Basket object used in the previous chapter's case study. At this point students can design and implement software that *uses* the set class. Only then do we discuss the third perspective—the implementation of the discrete set class. Chapter 3 also introduces students to the design and implementation of generic units. Motivated by a need for a more general set class, we discuss generic packages, formal types, and formal subprograms. A small case study of the design of a reusable version of Chapter 1's binary search procedure strengthens these concepts. A second case study that uses the set class in a solution to a realistic problem also introduces the nature of a greedy solution.

Chapter 4 discusses the string class. We begin with the terminology and classification of strings: fixed-length, bounded-length, and unbounded-length. We use the package specifications from the standard library to discuss these different string classes at the logical level. We design and implement a string application that rearranges and sorts names. Finally we show how each of the three different string classes might be implemented. The implementation of the unbounded-length string type provides the motivation for access (pointer) types and dynamic allocation and deallocation of memory. We discuss the problems of aliases and memory leaks and introduce the use of controlled types to prevent them.

Chapter 5 is about stacks. Again our order of presentation is logical level (package specifications), application level (a program to evaluate postfix expressions), and implementation level (package bodies). The implementation of the unbounded stack class motivates the need for the linked list. The technique used to link nodes in dynamically allocated memory is described in detail and illustrated with many figures. Protection from stack memory leaks provides a second look at controlled types. The comparison of the two stack implementations motivates our introduction to Big-O. We also analyze the two implementations in the use of storage space, program size, and execution time experiments.

Chapter 6 introduces the FIFO queue. After specifying the FIFO queue class we develop an application to prepare freight train manifests. We use this application to review our approach to object-oriented design. In this chapter, we give a detailed look at the design considerations of selecting among multiple FIFO queue implementation choices. Two array-based implementations are discussed as well as a linked list representation. We analyze our FIFO queue implementations in terms of program size, use of storage space, Big-O, and execution time experiments. The chapter is concluded with a discussion of heterogeneous collections and the Ada constructs (general access types and class wide types) used to implement them.

Chapter 7 introduces linear lists that are ordered according to a key value. After we review constructor, observer, and transformer operations that were defined in Chapter 1, we introduce the iterator. We use our key-ordered list specification in the design and implementation of an electronic address book. Our program uses data retained in a binary file between runs. The key-ordered list class is implemented using both sequential (array-based) and linked (dynamically allocated) representations. These two representations are compared in detail in terms of code size, memory usage, Big-O, and execution time experiments.

Chapter 8 continues the discussion of linked lists with a number of variations: circular linked lists, doubly linked lists, and linked lists with dummy nodes (headers and trailers). We present a version, the linked implementation of the key-ordered list given in Chapter 7, in which the nodes are stored non-sequentially in an array. We compare the Big-O's and execution time experiments for the insert and delete operations for all five linked list implementations. As a final linked list implementation of a key-ordered list class, we store the nodes non-sequentially in a direct access binary file. We explain direct files for students who have never used them. We end this chapter with a brief discussion of key-ordered lists with non-unique keys.

Chapter 9 discusses recursion, giving the student an intuitive understanding of the concept, and then showing how recursion can be used to solve programming problems. Guidelines for writing recursive procedures and functions are illustrated with many examples. After demonstrating that by-hand simulation of a recursive routine can be very tedious, we introduce a simple Three-Question technique for verifying the correctness of recursive procedures and functions. Because many students are wary of recursion, the introduction to this material is deliberately intuitive and nonmathematical. A more detailed discussion of how recursion works leads to an understanding of how recursion can be replaced with iteration and stacks. The case study at the end of this chapter is a recursive solution of a maze problem. We compare this implementation to a nonrecursive (stack-based) approach to demonstrate how recursion simplifies the solution to some kinds of problems.

Chapter 10 introduces binary search trees as a way to arrange data, giving the flexibility of a linked structure with $O(\log_2 N)$ retrieval, insertion, and deletion times. In order to build on the previous chapter and exploit the inherent recursive nature of binary trees, the algorithms are first presented recursively. After all the operations have been implemented recursively, we code them iteratively to show the flexibility of binary search trees. We compare the performances of these two implementations of the binary tree and linear lists. After observing the poor performance of degenerate trees, we present an algorithm for balancing a binary search tree. We also introduce AVL and Balanced Multi-Way trees as alternative search tree implementations. We conclude this chapter with a discussion of a nonlinked representation of binary trees.

Chapter 11 presents a collection of other branching structure classes: priority queues, heaps, and graphs. We show both list and heap implementations of the priority queue and discuss the performance of a variety of implementations. The coverage of graphs includes the specification of a graph class, its use in an airline application (connections between cities), and the implementation of basic graph operations with an adjacency matrix. The graph algorithms make use of stacks, queues, and priority queues, thus both reinforcing earlier material as well as demonstrating just how general these structures are. The chapter also describes and illustrates the use of adjacency list graph representations.

Chapter 12 presents a number of sorting and searching algorithms and asks the question: Which are better? The $O(N^2)$ sorting algorithms that are illustrated, implemented, and compared include selection sort, bubble sort, and insertion sort. The $O(N\log_2 N)$ sorting algorithms include merge sort, quick sort, and heap sort. To illustrate a completely different kind of sorting algorithm (one that does not compare keys), we design, implement, and analyze a generic radix sort. The performance of all of the algorithms are compared using both Big-O and the results of timed experiments. The discussion of algorithm analysis continues in the context of searching. Previously presented searching algorithms are reviewed and new ones are described. The discussion of hashing includes more detailed discussions and examples of collision resolution and key transformation than in the first edition. We introduce perfect hash functions and provide an example of a perfect hash function for the Ada 2005 reserved words. We present analyses of the various hashing techniques.

Additional Features and Resources

Chapter Goals A set of goals presented at the beginning of each chapter helps the students assess what they have learned. The goals are tested in the exercises at the end of each chapter.

Chapter Exercises There are about 40 exercises per chapter organized by sections to make it easy to assign them. They vary in levels of difficulty, including short and long programming problems, the analysis of algorithms, and problems to test the student's understanding of concepts. Approximately one-fourth of the exercises are answered on the Web at *http://www.jbpub.com/catalog/0763737941/supplements*.

Applications and Case Studies We develop an application program to illustrate the use of each particular class presented in the book. These applications are short enough that students can follow them without being overwhelmed by a multitude of details. In addition to these application programs, we present several larger-scale case studies. Program reading is an essential skill for software professionals, but few books include programs of sufficient length for students to get this experience. The case studies provide an opportunity to follow the specification, design, and implementation of a solution to a nontrivial problem. They also provide a base for class discussion on design issues and programming assignments.

Complete Code We include all the Ada code for each class discussed in the text—on the Web at *http://www.jbpub.com/catalog/0763737941/supplements*. The online source code collection also includes the test and analysis programs used to produce the data presented in the text. Having the source code for the classes encourages students to think in terms of reusable code. The source code provided for the application programs and case studies gives students the opportunity to practice modification of programs without having to spend time typing the original programs.

Website Jones and Bartlett has designed a website to support this text. At *http://www.jbpub.com/catalog/0763737941/supplements*, students will find answers to selected exercises and the source code described previously. Instructors will find teaching notes, in-class activity suggestions, answers to those exercises not in the student section, and PowerPoint presentations for each chapter. To obtain a password for the instructor section of this site, please contact Jones and Bartlett at 1-800-832-0034. Please contact John.McCormick@acm.org if you have any questions or have material related to the text that you would like to share.

Compilers and Tools AdaCore, a prominent supplier of Ada compilers and tools to industry, provides the academic community with the *GNAT Academic Package* (GAP) at no cost. This industrial-strength comprehensive toolset and support package is designed to give educators the tools they need to use Ada in their teaching and research. The package includes an integrated binary distribution of the GNAT 2005 tool set and a variety of add-ons and libraries. You may freely distribute these tools to your students. Instructors also receive direct help and support for all academic versions of GNAT including: assistance in using the system, suggestions for workarounds when system issues arise, and help in understanding Ada 2005.

In addition to Ada tools, the GAP community is a place to share knowledge, fresh ideas, resources, and teaching materials such as course materials, slide presentations, papers, and articles related to education, lecture notes, books and videos, and programming exercises. GAP also sponsors the Ada Intern Program, an initiative to connect Universities and AdaCore customers who are seeking Ada-knowledgeable interns. You can read an overview of the resources available and instructions for becoming a member of the GAP community at *http://www.adacore.com/academic_overview.php*.

Professor Martin Carlisle at the U.S. Air Force Academy has developed and made available a number of Ada tools that many of us have found useful in the classroom. *AdaGIDE* is a very easy to use integrated development environment (IDE) for developing Ada software. *RAPID* is a portable Graphical User Interface (GUI) tool. Students can create GUIs for their applications by simply drawing them. RAPID then generates Ada code using a platform-independent GUI library. *A#* is a port of Ada to the Microsoft .NET Platform. These and other Ada tools and utilities may be obtained at

> http://adagide.martincarlisle.com
> http://rapid.martincarlisle.com
> http://asharp.martincarlisle.com

Other Ada Resources *ACM SIGAda*, the *Ada Resource Association*, and other members of the Ada community provide resources on the Web that anyone teaching Ada will find useful.

> http://www.sigada.org
> http://www.adaic.org
> http://www.adapower.com
> http://www.adaworld.com
> http://en.wikipedia.org/wiki/Ada_programming_language

Acknowledgments

We would like to thank the many individuals who have helped us with this project. We are indebted to the adopters of the first edition who took the time to send us their comments. The comments, corrections, and suggestions made by our technical reviewers have enormously improved and enriched this book. We are grateful to the following people who reviewed the manuscript under tight deadlines:

Anthony Ruocco
Roger Williams University

Ricky Sward
United States Air Force Academy

Gail Miles
Lenoir-Rhyne College

Richard Hull
Lenoir-Rhyne College

Bo Sandén
Colorado Technical University

Martin Carlisle
United States Air Force Academy

The staff at Jones and Bartlett Publishers have been very helpful. We particularly thank Tim Anderson for his vision and support of this project and Amy Rose for turning a manuscript into a beautiful book.

Anyone who has written a textbook can appreciate the amount of time and effort involved and anyone related to a textbook author can tell you at whose expense that time is spent. Nell thanks her husband Al, her children, and her childrens' children. John thanks his wife Naomi for her support and understanding.

about the cover

The passengers in this high speed train are probably unaware of the many computers on board and along the track that make their journey possible. Computers control the locomotive power, brakes, and signals. Because an error in any of the programs running on these embedded computers could result in the loss of life and property, such software is called safety-critical. Ada is good at detecting errors in programs early in the programming lifecycle. You submit your code to an Ada compiler and it informs you right away that you made mistakes that a lot of other languages would let slip by. So it is not surprising that Ada is the prime programming language for high-integrity and safety-critical applications, including commercial and defense aircraft avionics, air traffic control, railroad systems, financial services and medical devices.

1 Software Engineering 1

1.1 The Software Process 2
    Goals of Quality Software 4
    Specification: Understanding the Problem 6
    Writing Detailed Specifications 7

1.2 Program Design 8
    Abstraction 8
    Information Hiding 9
    Stepwise Refinement 10
    Visual Aids 12
    Functional Decomposition 13
    Object-Oriented Design 14
    Exceptions 31

1.3 Verification of Software Correctness 32
    Origin of Bugs 34
    Designing for Correctness 37
    Design Review Activities 45
    Program Testing 47
    Debugging with a Plan 51
    Practical Considerations 52
    Problem-Solving Case Study: Testing a Binary Search Operation 53

Summary 62
Exercises 63

2 Data Design and Implementation 77

- 2.1 Different Views of Data 78
  - Data Types 78
  - Data Abstraction 79
  - Data Structures 82
  - Data Levels 83
  - An Analogy 84
- 2.2 Ada's Built-In Types 88
  - Scalar Types 89
  - Composite Types 97
  - Subtypes 105
- 2.3 Packages 108
- 2.4 Child Packages 109
  - Kinds of Packages 109
  - Encapsulation 116
  - Additional Constructs for Object-Oriented Programming 127
  - Problem-Solving Case Study: Bingo Games—How Long Should They Take? 132
- Summary 153
- Exercises 155

3 Sets with an Introduction to Generic Units 163

- 3.1 The Abstract Level 164
  - Set Operations 165
  - A Set Specification 166
- 3.2 The Application Level 169
  - Bingo Number Selection 170
- 3.3 The Implementation Level 172
- 3.4 Programming for Reuse: Generic Units 177
  - Generic Formal Types 183
  - Generic Formal Subprograms 191
  - Problem-Solving Case Study: A Reusable Binary Search Procedure 193
  - Problem-Solving Case Study: Minimizing Translations 200
- Summary 206
- Exercises 207

4 Strings with Introductions to Access Types and Controlled Types 213

- 4.1 String Terminology 214
- 4.2 The Logical Level 215
  - Fixed-Length Strings 215
  - Bounded-Length Strings 221
  - Unbounded-Length Strings 226
- 4.3 The Application Level 226
  - Problem Description 226
  - The Algorithm 227
  - Implementation 227
- 4.4 The Implementation Level 230
  - Fixed-Length Strings 231
  - Bounded-Length Strings 231
  - Unbounded-Length Strings and Access Types 234
  - Organization of Memory 255
- Summary 256
- Exercises 256

5 Stacks with Introductions to Linked Lists and Big-O 273

- 5.1 The Logical Level 274
  - Operations on Stacks 274
  - Exceptions 277
- 5.2 The Application Level 279
  - Evaluating Postfix Expressions 279
  - Other Stack Applications 289
- 5.3 The Implementation Level 290
  - The Implementation of a Stack as a Static Array 290
  - The Implementation of a Stack as a Linked List 294
  - Extending the Stack Class 311
  - Encapsulation Revisited 313
- 5.4 Comparing Implementations 314
  - Space 315

Complexity 315
Time 317
Big-O 318
Summary 324
Exercises 325

6 FIFO Queues with Introductions to General Access Types and Class-Wide Types 343

6.1 The Logical Level 344
Operations on Queues 345
6.2 The Application Level 348
Freight Train Manifests 348
6.3 The Implementation Level 355
The Implementation of a Queue as a Static Array 355
The Implementation of a Queue as a Linked Structure 362
6.4 Comparing the Queue Implementations 370
Complexity 371
Space 371
Big-O 372
Time 373
6.5 Testing the Queue Operations 374
6.6 Heterogeneous Collections 375
General Access Types 375
Class-Wide Types 378
Summary 382
Exercises 382

7 Key-Ordered Lists 403

7.1 The Logical Level 404
Operations 404
A Key-Ordered List Specification 406
Sample Package Instantiations 409
Using the Iterator 411
7.2 The Application Level 413
An Electronic Address Book 413

7.3 The Implementation Level   426
    A Sequential List Implementation   428
    A Linked List Implementation   441
7.4 Analyzing the List Implementations   460
    Complexity   461
    Space   461
    Big-O   462
    Time   463
    Other Factors to Consider   464
7.5 Testing the List Operations   465
    Summary   465
    Exercises   465

8 Lists Plus   481

8.1 Circular Linked Lists   482
    Traversing a Circular List   484
    Finding a List Element in a Circular List   485
    Inserting into a Circular List   488
    Deleting from a Circular List   491
8.2 Doubly Linked Lists   493
    Finding a List Element in a Doubly Linked List   494
    Operations on a Doubly Linked List   496
8.3 Linked Lists with Dummy Nodes   499
    Doubly Linked Lists with Dummy Nodes   502
8.4 The Linked List as an Array of Nodes   504
    Why Use an Array?   504
    How Is an Array Used?   505
    Array Memory Management   516
8.5 Comparison of the Linked Implementations   519
8.6 The Linked List as a File of Nodes   520
    Direct Files   520
    The Abstract Level   522
    The Implementation Level   525
    Analysis of the File-Based List   534

xxii | Contents

       8.7   Lists with Duplicate Keys   534
            Summary   536
            Exercises   536

9 Programming with Recursion 555

       9.1   What Is Recursion?   556
       9.2   The Classic Example of Recursion   557
       9.3   Programming Recursively   560
            Coding the Factorial Function   560
            Comparison to the Iterative Solution   562
       9.4   Verifying Recursive Procedures and Functions   563
            The Three-Question Method   563
       9.5   Writing Recursive Procedures and Functions   564
            Writing a Boolean Function   564
            Multiple Recursive Calls   567
       9.6   Using Recursion to Simplify Solutions—Three Examples   569
            Combinations   569
            Recursive Processing of Linked Lists   571
            Towers of Hanoi   573
       9.7   A Recursive Version of Binary Search   577
       9.8   Debugging Recursive Routines   579
       9.9   How Recursion Works   579
            Static Storage Allocation   580
            Dynamic Storage Allocation   583
            Recursion and Big-O   589
            Parameter Passing   589
     9.10   Removing Recursion   590
            Iteration   590
            Stacking   592
     9.11   Deciding Whether to Use a Recursive Solution   593
            Problem-Solving Case Study: Escape from a Maze   596
            Summary   612
            Exercises   613

10 Binary Search Trees 627

     10.1   Trees   628
            Binary Trees   630

Binary Search Trees 633
Binary Tree Traversals 634
10.2 The Logical Level 636
10.3 The Application Level 640
10.4 The Implementation Level 647
Simple Binary Search Tree Operations 649
Recursive Binary Search Tree Operations 650
Iterative Binary Search Tree Operations 671
Recursion or Iteration 677
10.5 Comparing Binary Search Trees to Linear Lists 678
Big-O and Execution Time Comparisons 678
10.6 Balancing a Binary Search Tree 682
Other Approaches to Balancing 685
10.7 A Nonlinked Representation of Binary Trees 686
Summary 690
Exercises 690

11 Priority Queues, Heaps, and Graphs 707

11.1 Priority Queues 708
The Logical Level 708
The Application Level 710
The Implementation Level 712
11.2 Heaps 713
The Logical Level 713
The Application Level 719
The Implementation Level 721
11.3 Introduction to Graphs 727
The Logical Level 730
The Application Level: Graph Traversals 735
The Implementation Level 746
Summary 754
Exercises 755
Graphs 760

12 Sorting and Searching Algorithms 767

12.1 Sorting 768
12.2 $O(N^2)$ Sorts 769

Straight Selection Sort 769
Bubble Sort 774
12.3 O(N log$_2$ N) Sorts 782
Merge Sort 782
Quick Sort 788
Heap Sort 795
12.4 Radix Sort 800
The Implementation Level 803
Analysis of Radix Sort 805
12.5 Efficiency Considerations 806
When N Is Small 806
Eliminating Calls to Procedures and Functions 806
Removal of Recursion 807
12.6 More Sorting Considerations 808
Sorting in Descending Order 808
Stability 808
Multiple Keys 809
Sorting Pointers 810
12.7 Summary—Sorting 812
12.8 Searching 814
Linear Searching 815
High-Probability Ordering 815
Key Ordering 816
Binary Searching 817
Interpolation Searching 817
12.9 Hashing 818
Handling Collisions 821
Performance of Hashing 831
Deleting Elements 832
Choosing a Good Hash Function 833
Summary—Searching 841
Exercises 841

Glossary 861

Index 869

Software Engineering

Goals

Goals for this chapter include that you should be able to
- describe software life cycle activities
- describe the goals for "quality" software
- explain the following terms: software requirements, software specifications, algorithm, information hiding, abstraction, stepwise refinement, acceptance tests, regression testing, verification, validation, functional domain, black box testing, white box testing
- describe four variations of stepwise refinement
- explain the fundamental ideas of object-oriented design
- explain the relationships among classes, objects, and inheritance
- explain how CRC cards are used to help with software design
- interpret a basic UML class diagram
- identify sources of software errors
- describe strategies to avoid software errors
- specify the preconditions and postconditions of a program segment or method
- develop loop invariants
- show how deskchecking, code walk-throughs, and design and code inspections can improve software quality and reduce effort
- state several testing goals and indicate when each would be appropriate
- describe several integration-testing strategies and indicate when each would be appropriate
- explain how program verification techniques can be applied throughout the software development process

1.1 The Software Process

When we consider computer programming, we immediately think of writing code in some computer language. As a beginning student of computer science, you wrote programs that solved relatively simple problems. Much of your effort went into learning the syntax of a programming language such as Ada, C++, or Java: the language's reserved words, its data types, its constructs for selection and looping, and its input/output mechanisms.

You learned a programming methodology that takes you from a problem description all the way through to the delivery of a software solution. There are many design techniques, coding standards, and testing methods that programmers use to develop high-quality software. Why bother with all that methodology? Why not just sit down at a computer and enter code? Aren't we wasting a lot of time and effort, when we could just get started on the "real" job?

If the degree of our programming sophistication never had to rise above the level of trivial programs (like summing a list of prices or averaging grades), we might get away with such a code-first technique (or, rather, a lack of technique). Some new programmers work this way, hacking away at the code until the program works more or less correctly—usually less!

As your programs grow larger and more complex, you must pay attention to other software issues in addition to coding. If you become a software professional, you may work as part of a team that develops a system containing tens of thousands, or even millions, of lines of code. The activities involved in such a software project's whole "life cycle" clearly go beyond just sitting down at a computer and writing programs. These activities include:

- *Problem analysis:* Understanding the nature of the problem to be solved
- *Requirements definition:* Determining exactly what the program must do
- *Software specification:* Specifying what the program must do (the functional requirements) and the constraints on the solution approach (nonfunctional requirements, such as what language to use)
- *High- and low-level design:* Recording how the program meets the requirements, from the "big picture" overview to the detailed design
- *Implementation of the design:* Coding a program in a computer language
- *Testing and verification:* Detecting and fixing errors and demonstrating the correctness of the program
- *Delivery:* Turning over the tested program to the customer or user (or instructor)
- *Operation:* Actually using the program
- *Maintenance:* Making changes to fix operational errors and to add to or modify the function of the program

Software development is not simply a matter of going through these steps sequentially. Many activities take place concurrently. We may be coding one part of the solution while we're designing another part, or defining requirements for a new version of a program while we're still testing the current version. Often a number of people work on different parts of the same program simultaneously. Keeping track of all these activities requires planning.

We use the term **software engineering** to refer to the discipline concerned with all aspects of the development of high-quality software systems. It encompasses all variations of techniques used during the software life cycle plus supporting activities such as documentation and teamwork. A **software process** is a specific set of interrelated software engineering techniques used by a person or organization to create a system.

> **Software engineering** The discipline devoted to the design, production, and maintenance of computer programs that are developed on time and within cost estimates, using tools that help to manage the size and complexity of the resulting software products.
>
> **Software process** A standard, integrated set of software engineering tools and techniques used on a project by a person or an organization.
>
> **Algorithm** A logical sequence of discrete steps that describes a complete solution to a given problem computable in a finite amount of time and space.

What makes our jobs as programmers or software engineers challenging is the tendency of software to grow in size and complexity and to change at every stage of its development. Part of a good software process is the use of tools to manage this size and complexity. Usually a programmer has several toolboxes, each containing tools that help to build and shape a software product.

- *Hardware:* One toolbox contains the hardware itself: the computers and their peripheral devices (such as monitors, network connections, storage devices, and printers), on which and for which we develop software.
- *Software:* A second toolbox contains various software tools: operating systems, editors, compilers, interpreters, debugging programs, test-data generators, and so on. You've used some of these tools already.
- *Ideaware:* A third toolbox is filled with the knowledge that software engineers have collected over time. This box contains the algorithms that we use to solve common programming problems, as well as data structures for modeling the information processed by our programs. Recall that an **algorithm** is a step-by-step description of the solution to a problem.

Ideaware contains programming methodologies, such as object-oriented design, and software concepts, including information hiding, data encapsulation, and abstraction. It includes aids for creating designs such as Classes, Responsibilities, and Collaborations (CRC) cards and methods for describing designs such as the Unified Modeling Language (UML). It also contains tools for measuring, evaluating, and proving the correctness of our programs. We devote most of this book to exploring the contents of this third toolbox.

Some might argue that using these tools takes the creativity out of programming, but we don't believe that to be true. Artists and composers are creative, yet their innovations are grounded in the basic principles of their crafts. Similarly, the most creative programmers build high-quality software through the disciplined use of basic programming tools.

Goals of Quality Software

Quality software is much more than a program that accomplishes its task. A good program achieves the following goals:

1. It works.
2. It can be modified without excessive time and effort.
3. It is reusable.
4. It is completed on time and within budget.

It's not easy to meet these goals, but they are all important.

Goal 1: Quality Software Works A program must accomplish its task, and it must do it correctly and completely. Thus, the first step is to determine exactly what the program is required to do. You need to have a definition of the program's **requirements**. For students, the requirements often are included in the instructor's problem description. For programmers on a government contract, the requirements document may be hundreds of pages long.

> **Requirements** A statement of what is to be provided by a computer or software product.
>
> **Software specification** A detailed description of the function, inputs, processing, outputs, and special requirements of a software product. It provides the information needed to design and implement the product.

We develop programs that meet the requirements by fulfilling **software specifications**. The specifications indicate the format of the input and output, details about processing, performance measures (How fast? How big? How accurate?), what to do in case of errors, and so on. The specifications tell what the program does, but not how it is done. Sometimes your instructor provides detailed specifications; other times you have to write them yourself, based on a problem description, conversations with your instructor, or intuition.

How do you know when the program is right? A program has to be

- *Complete:* It should "do everything" specified.
- *Correct:* It should "do it right."
- *Usable:* Its user interface should be easy to work with.
- *Efficient:* It should be at least as efficient as "it needs to be."

For example, if a desktop-publishing program cannot update the screen as rapidly as the user can type, the program is not as efficient as it needs to be. If the software isn't efficient enough, it doesn't meet its requirements, and thus, according to our definition, it doesn't work correctly.

Goal 2: Quality Software Can Be Modified When does software need to be modified? Changes occur in every phase of its existence.

Software is changed in the design phase. When your instructor or employer gives you a programming assignment, you begin to think of how to solve the problem. The next time you meet, however, you may be notified of a change in the problem description.

Software is changed in the coding phase. You make changes in your program because of compilation errors. Sometimes you see a better solution to a part of the problem after the program has been coded, so you make changes.

Software is changed in the testing phase. If the program crashes or yields wrong results, you must make corrections.

In an academic environment, the life of the software typically ends when a program is turned in for grading. When software is developed for actual use, however, many changes can be required during the maintenance phase. Someone may discover an error that wasn't uncovered in testing, someone else may want to include additional functionality, a third party may want to change the input format, and a fourth party may want to run the program on another system.

The point is that software changes often and in all phases of its life cycle. Knowing this, software engineers try to develop programs that are easy to modify. Modifications to programs often are not even made by the original authors but by subsequent maintenance programmers. Someday you may be the one making the modifications to someone else's program.

What makes a program easy to modify? First, it should be readable and understandable to humans. Before it can be changed, it must be understood. A well-designed, clearly written, well-documented program is certainly easier for human readers to understand. The number of pages of documentation required for "real-world" programs usually exceeds the number of pages of code. Almost every organization has its own policy for documentation.

Second, it should be able to withstand small changes easily. The key idea is to partition your programs into manageable pieces that work together to solve the problem, yet are relatively independent. The design methodologies reviewed later in this chapter should help you write programs that meet this goal.

Goal 3: Quality Software Is Reusable It takes time and effort to create quality software. Therefore, it is important to receive as much value from the software as possible.

One way to save time and effort when building a software solution is to reuse programs, classes, operations, and so on from previous projects. By using previously designed and tested code, you arrive at your solution sooner and with less effort. Alternatively, when you create software to solve a problem, it is sometimes possible to structure that software so it can help solve future, related problems. By doing this, you are gaining more value from the software created.

Creating reusable software does not happen automatically. It requires extra effort during the specification and design of the software. Reusable software is well documented and easy to read, so that it is easy to tell if it can be used for a new project. It usually has a simple interface so that it can easily be plugged into another system. It is modifiable (Goal 2), in case a small change is needed to adapt it to the new system.

When creating software to fulfill a narrow, specific function, you can sometimes make the software more generally reusable with a minimal amount of extra effort. Therefore, you increase the chances that you will reuse the software later. For example, if you are creating a routine that sorts a list of integers into increasing order, you might generalize the routine so that it can also sort other types of data. Furthermore, you could design the routine to accept the desired sort order, increasing or decreasing, as a parameter.

One of the main reasons for the rise in popularity of object-oriented approaches is that they lend themselves to reuse. Previous reuse approaches were hindered by inappropriate units of reuse. If the unit of reuse is too small, then the work saved is not worth the effort. If the unit of reuse is too large, then it is difficult to combine it with other system elements. Object-oriented classes, when designed properly, can be very appropriate units of reuse. Furthermore, object-oriented approaches simplify reuse through class inheritance, which is described later in this chapter.

Goal 4: Quality Software Is Completed on Time and within Budget You know what happens in school when you turn your program in late. You probably have grieved over an otherwise perfect program that received only half credit—or no credit at all—because you turned it in one day late. "But the network was down for five hours last night!" you protest.

Although the consequences of tardiness may seem arbitrary in the academic world, they are significant in the business world. The software for controlling a space launch must be developed and tested before the launch can take place. A patient database system for a new hospital must be installed before the hospital can open. In such cases, the program doesn't meet its requirements if it isn't ready when needed.

"Time is money" may sound trite, but failure to meet deadlines is expensive. A company generally budgets a certain amount of time and money for the development of a piece of software. If part of a project is only 80% complete when the deadline arrives, the company must pay extra to finish the work. If the program is part of a contract with a customer, there may be monetary penalties for missed deadlines. If it is being developed for commercial sales, the company may be beaten to the market by a competitor and be forced out of business.

Once you know what your goals are, what can you do to meet them? Where should you start? Software engineers use many different tools and techniques. In the next few sections of this chapter, we focus on a review of techniques to help you understand, design, and code programs.

Specification: Understanding the Problem

No matter what programming design technique you use, the first steps are the same. Imagine the following situation: On the third day of class, you are given a 12-page description of Programming Assignment 1, which must be running perfectly and turned in by noon, a week from yesterday. You read the assignment and realize that this program is three times larger than any program you have ever written. Now, what is your first step?

The responses listed here are typical of those given by a class of students in such a situation:

1. Panic and do nothing. 39%
2. Panic and drop the course. 30%
3. Sit down at the computer and begin typing. 27%
4. Stop and think. 4%

Response 1 is a predictable reaction from students who have not learned good programming techniques. Students who adopt Response 2 find their education progressing rather slowly. Response 3 may seem to be a good idea, especially considering the deadline looming. Resist the temptation, though, to immediately begin coding; the first step is to think. Before you can come up with a program solution, you must understand the problem. Read the assignment, and then read it again. Ask questions of your instructor to clarify the assignment. Starting early affords you many opportunities to ask questions; starting the night before the program is due leaves you no opportunity at all.

One problem with coding first and thinking later is that it tends to lock you into the first solution you think of, which may not be the best approach. We have a natural tendency to believe that once we've put something in writing, we have invested too much in the idea to toss it out and start over.

Writing Detailed Specifications

Many writers experience a moment of terror when faced with a blank piece of paper—where to begin? As a programmer, however, you should always have a place to start. Using the assignment description, first write a complete definition of the problem, including the details of the expected inputs and outputs, the processing and error handling, and all the assumptions about the problem. When you finish this task, you have a specification—a definition of the problem that tells you what the program should do. In addition, the process of writing the specification brings to light any holes in the requirements. For instance, are embedded blanks in the input significant or can they be ignored? Do you need to check for errors in the input? On what computer system(s) is your program to run? If you get the answers to these questions at this stage, you can design and code your program correctly from the start.

Many software engineers make use of operational scenarios to understand requirements. A scenario is a sequence of events for one execution of the program. Here, for example, is a scenario that a designer might consider when developing software for a bank's automated teller machine (ATM).

1. The customer inserts a bankcard.
2. The ATM reads the account number on the card.
3. The ATM requests a PIN (personal identification number) from the customer.
4. The customer enters 5683.
5. The ATM successfully verifies the account number and PIN combination.
6. The ATM asks the customer to select a transaction type (deposit, show balance, withdrawal, or quit).

7. The customer selects show balance.
8. The ATM obtains the current account balance ($1,204.35) and displays it.
9. The ATM asks the customer to select a transaction type (deposit, show balance, withdrawal, or quit).
10. The customer selects quit.
11. The ATM returns the customer's bankcard.

Scenarios allow us to get a feel for the behavior expected from the system. A single scenario cannot show all possible behaviors, however, so software engineers typically prepare many different scenarios to gain a full understanding of the requirements.

Sometimes details that are not explicitly stated in the requirements may be handled according to the programmer's preference. In some cases you have only a vague description of a problem, and it is up to you to define the entire software specification; these projects are sometimes called open problems. In any case, you should always document assumptions that you make about unstated or ambiguous details.

The specification clarifies the problem to be solved. However, it also serves as an important piece of program documentation. Sometimes it acts as a contract between a customer and a programmer. There are many ways in which specifications may be expressed and a number of different sections that may be included. Our recommended program specification includes the following sections:

- Processing requirements
- Sample inputs with expected outputs
- Assumptions

If special processing is needed for unusual or error conditions, it also should be specified. Sometimes it is helpful to include a section containing definitions of terms used. It is also useful to list any testing requirements so that verifying the program is considered early in the development process. In fact, a test plan can be an important part of a specification; test plans are discussed later in this chapter in the section on verification of software correctness.

1.2 Program Design

Remember, the specification of the program tells what the program must do, but not how it does it. Once you have clarified the goals of the program, you can begin the design phase of the software life cycle. In this section, we review some ideaware tools that are used for software design and present a review of object-oriented design constructs and methods.

Abstraction

The universe is filled with complex systems. We learn about such systems through models. A model may be mathematical, like equations describing the motion of satellites around the earth. A physical object such as a model airplane used in wind-tunnel tests is another form of model. Only the characteristics of the system that are essential to the problem being studied are modeled; minor or irrelevant details are ignored. For example, although the earth is an oblate ellipsoid, globes (models of the earth) are spheres. The small difference in shape is not important to us in studying the political divisions and physical landmarks on the earth. Similarly, in-flight movies are not included in the model airplanes used to study aerodynamics.

An **abstraction** is a model of a complex system that includes only the essential details. Abstractions are the fundamental way that we manage complexity. Different viewers use different abstractions of a particular system. Thus, whereas we see a car as a means of transportation, the automotive engineer may see it as a large mass with a small contact area between it and the road.

> **Abstraction** A model of a complex system that includes only the details essential to the perspective of the viewer of the system.

What does abstraction have to do with software development? The programs we write are abstractions. A spreadsheet program used by an accountant models the books used to record debits and credits. An educational computer game about wildlife models an ecosystem. Writing software is difficult because both the systems we model and the processes we use to develop the software are complex. One of our major goals is to convince you to use abstractions to manage the complexity of developing software. In nearly every chapter, we make use of abstractions to simplify our work.

Information Hiding

Many design methods are based on decomposing a problem's solution into modules. By "module" we mean a cohesive system subunit that performs a share of the work. In Ada, the primary module mechanisms are the package and the class. Decomposing a system into modules helps us manage complexity. Additionally, the modules can form the basis of assignments for different programming teams working separately on a large system.

> **Information hiding** The practice of hiding the details of a module with the goal of controlling access to the details from the rest of the system.

Modules act as an abstraction tool. The complexity of their internal structure can be hidden from the rest of the system. This means that the details involved in implementing a module are isolated from the details of the rest of the system. Why is hiding the details desirable? Shouldn't the programmer know everything? *No!* **Information hiding** helps manage the complexity of a system so a programmer can concentrate on one module at a time.

Of course, a program's modules are interrelated, because they work together to solve the problem. Modules provide services to each other through a carefully defined interface. The interface in Ada is usually provided through a package specification. Programmers of one module do not need to know the internal details of the modules it interacts with, but they do need to know the interfaces. Consider a driving analogy—you can stop a car without knowing whether it has disk brakes or drum brakes. You don't need to know these lower-level details of the car's brake subsystem in order to stop it. You just have to understand the interface; that is, you only need to know how to press down on the pedal.

Similarly, you don't have to know the details of other modules as you design a specific module. Such a requirement would introduce a greater risk of confusion and error throughout the whole system. For example, imagine what it would be like if every time we wanted to stop our car, we had to think, "The brake pedal is a lever with a mechanical advantage of 10.6 coupled to a hydraulic system with a mechanical advantage of 9.3 that presses a semimetallic pad against a steel disk. The coefficient of friction of the pad/disk contact is. . . ."

Besides helping us manage the complexity of a large system, abstraction and information hiding support our quality goals of modifiability and reusability. In a well-designed system, most modifications can be localized to just a few modules. Such changes are much easier to make than changes that permeate the entire system. Additionally, a good system design results in the creation of generic modules that can be used in other systems.

To achieve these goals, modules should be good abstractions with strong cohesion; that is, each module should have a single purpose or identity and the module should stick together well. A cohesive module usually can be described by a simple sentence. If you have to use several sentences or one very convoluted sentence to describe your module, it is probably *not* cohesive. Each module should also exhibit information hiding so that changes within it do not result in changes in the modules that use it. This independent quality of modules is known as loose coupling. If your module depends on the internal details of other modules, it is *not* loosely coupled.

But what should these modules be and how do we identify them? That question is addressed in the subsection on object-oriented design later in this chapter.

Stepwise Refinement

In addition to concepts such as abstraction and information hiding, software developers need practical approaches to conquer complexity. Stepwise refinement is a widely applicable approach. It has many variations such as top-down, bottom-up, functional decomposition, and even "round-trip gestalt design." Undoubtedly, you have learned a variation of stepwise refinement in your studies, because it is a standard method for organizing and writing essays, term papers, and books. For example, to write a book an author first determines the main theme and the major subthemes. Next, the chapter topics can be identified, followed by section and subsection topics. Outlines can be produced and further refined for each subsection. At some point the author is ready to add detail—to actually begin writing sentences.

In general, with stepwise refinement, a problem is approached in stages. Similar steps are followed during each stage, with the only difference being the level of detail involved. The completion of each stage brings us closer to solving our problem. Let's look at some variations of stepwise refinement:

- *Top-down:* First the problem is broken into several large parts. Each of these parts is in turn divided into sections, then the sections are subdivided, and so on. The important feature is that *details are deferred as long as possible* as we move from a general to a specific solution. The outline approach to writing a book is a form of top-down stepwise refinement.
- *Bottom-up:* As you might guess, with this approach the details come first. It is the opposite of the top-down approach. After the detailed components are identified and designed, they are brought together into increasingly higher-level components. This could be used, for example, by the author of a cookbook who first writes all the recipes and then decides how to organize them into sections and chapters.
- *Functional decomposition:* Functional decomposition is top-down stepwise refinement with an emphasis on functionality. With functional decomposition, the *details of actions* are deferred as long as possible. The main module of the design becomes the main program, and subsections develop into subprograms (procedures and functions). This hierarchy of tasks forms the basis for functional decomposition, with the main program controlling the processing. Functional decomposition is not used for overall system design in the object-oriented world; however, it is used to design the algorithms that implement object operations. The general function of the operation is continually divided into subfunctions until the level of detail is fine enough to code.
- *Round-trip gestalt design:* This confusing term is used to define the stepwise refinement approach to object-oriented design suggested by Grady Booch,[1] one of the early proponents of the Ada language and a leader of the object movement. First, the tangible items and events in the problem domain are identified and assigned to candidate classes and objects. Next, the external properties and relationships of these classes and objects are defined. Finally, the internal details are addressed, and unless these are trivial, the designer must return to the first step for another round of design. This approach is top-down stepwise refinement with an emphasis on objects and data.

---

[1]Grady Booch, *Object Oriented Design with Applications* (Redwood City, CA: Benjamin Cummings, 1991).

Good designers typically use a combination of the stepwise refinement techniques described here.

Visual Aids

Abstraction, information hiding, and stepwise refinement are interrelated methods for controlling complexity during the design of a system. We will now look at some tools that we can use to help us visualize our designs. Diagrams are used in many professions. For example, architects use blueprints, investors use market trend graphs, and truck drivers use maps.

Software engineers use different types of diagrams and tables. Here, we introduce the UML and CRC cards, both of which are used in this text.

UML is used to specify, visualize, construct, and document the components of a software system. It combines the best practices that have evolved over the past several decades for modeling systems, and is particularly well-suited to modeling object-oriented designs. UML diagrams are another form of abstraction. They hide implementation details and allow us to concentrate on only the major design components. UML includes a large variety of interrelated diagram types, each with its own set of icons and connectors. It is a very powerful development and modeling tool.

Covering all of UML is beyond the scope of this text.[2] We use only one UML diagram type, *class diagrams*, to describe some of our designs. Examples are shown beginning on page 17. The notation of the class diagrams is introduced as needed throughout the text.

CRC cards were first described by Beck and Cunningham[3] in 1989 as a means of allowing object-oriented programmers to help identify and describe a set of cooperating classes to solve a problem. A programmer uses a physical 4″ × 6″ index card to represent each class that has been identified as part of a problem solution. Figure 1.1 shows a blank CRC card. It contains room for the following information about a class:

- Class name
- Responsibilities of the class—usually represented by verbs and implemented by public methods
- Collaborations—other classes/objects that are used in fulfilling the responsibilities

Thus the name CRC card. We have added fields to the original design of the card for the programmer to record superclass and subclass information, and the primary responsibility of the class.

CRC cards are a great tool for refining an object-oriented design, especially in a team programming environment. They provide a physical manifestation of the building blocks of a system, allowing programmers to walk through user scenarios, identifying and assigning responsibilities and collaborations. The example in the next subsection demonstrates the use of CRC cards for design.

---

[2] The official definition of the UML is maintained by the Object Management Group. Detailed information can be found at http://www.omg.org/uml/.

[3] Beck and Cunningham: http://c2.com/doc/oopsla89/paper.html.

Class Name:	Superclass:	Subclasses:
Primary Responsibility:		
Responsibilities	Collaborations	

Figure 1.1 *A blank CRC card.*

Functional Decomposition

The development of a computer program by functional decomposition begins with a "big picture" solution to the problem defined in the specification. We then devise a general strategy for solving the problem by dividing it into manageable functional modules. Next, each of the large functional modules is subdivided into several tasks. We do not need to write the top level of a functional design in a programming language; we can write it in English or "pseudocode." Some software development projects even use special design languages that can be compiled. This divide and conquer activity continues until we get down to a level that can easily be translated into lines of code.

Once it has been divided into modules, the problem is simpler to code into a well-structured program. The functional decomposition approach encourages programming in logical units using procedures and functions. The main module of the design becomes the main program and subsections develop into procedures or functions. As an example, let's start the functional design for making a cake.

Make Cake

    Get Ingredients

    Mix Cake Ingredients

    Bake

    Cool

    Apply Icing

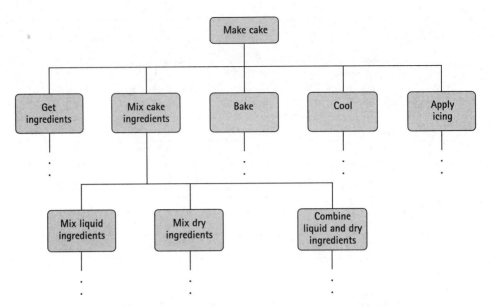

Figure 1.2 *A portion of a functional design for baking a cake.*

The problem now is divided into five logical units, each of which might be further decomposed into more detailed functional modules. Figure 1.2 illustrates the hierarchy of such a functional decomposition.

Object-Oriented Design

Although functional decomposition is suitable for developing solutions to problems small enough to be handled by a single programmer or a small group of programmers, it is generally inadequate for large-scale problems. We believe that the solutions to large-scale problems are better handled with object-oriented design approaches.

The object-oriented paradigm is founded on three interrelated constructs: classes, objects, and inheritance. Objects are the basic run-time entities in an object-oriented system. An object is an instance of a class; or alternately, a class defines the structure of its objects. Classes are organized in an "is-a" hierarchy defined by inheritance. The definition of an object's behavior often depends on its position within this hierarchy. Let's look more closely at each of these constructs, using Ada code to provide a concrete representation of the concepts. Ada reserved words (when used as such), user-defined identifiers, class and operation names, and so on appear in `this font` throughout the entire textbook.

Classes A class describes a set of objects with the same properties, behavior, and relationships. A class definition includes attributes (properties) and operations (actions) that determine the behavior of an object. With object-oriented design, we determine the classes from the things in the problem as described in the specification. We also describe how those classes are related to each other, and how they interact with each other. From this work, we determine a set of properties (attributes) and a set of responsibilities (operations) to associate with each class. With object-oriented design, the function of the program is distributed among a set of collaborating objects.

Let's list some of the classes in our baking problem. There are, of course, all of the various ingredients: eggs, milk, flour, butter, and so on. We also need certain pieces of equipment such as pans, bowls, measuring spoons, and an oven. The baker is another important entity in this problem. All of these entities must collaborate to create a cake. For example, a spoon measures individual ingredients and a bowl holds a mixture of ingredients. The following table illustrates a few of the classes that participate in baking a cake.

Class	Attributes	Responsibilities (Operations)
Oven	Size	Turn on
	Temperature	Turn off
	Number of racks	Set desired temperature
Bowl	Capacity	Add to
	Current amount	Dump
Egg	Size	Crack
		Separate (white from yolk)

Let's look at a simple example. The following Ada code defines a `Date` class that can be used to manipulate `Date` objects, for example, in a course scheduling system. The `Date` class can be used to create `Date` objects and to learn about the year, month, or day of any particular `Date` object.

```
package Date is

   -- Simple types for date class attributes and operations
   ------------------------------------------------------------
   type Month_Type is (January, February, March, April, May, June, July,
                       August, September, October, November, December);
   type Year_Type  is range 1583..Integer'Last;
   type Day_Type   is range 1..31;


   ------------------------------------------------------------
   type Date_Type is tagged private;   -- The type for the date class

   -- operations for date objects
   ------------------------------------------------------------
```

```ada
   function Construct_Date (Month : in Month_Type;
                            Day   : in Day_Type;
                            Year  : in Year_Type) return Date_Type;
   -- Convert three values to a single date

   function Year_Is (Date : in Date_Type) return Year_Type;
   -- Return the year value of this date

   function Month_Is (Date : in Date_Type) return Month_Type;
   -- Return the month value of this date

   function Day_Is (Date : in Date_Type) return Day_Type;
   -- Return the day value of this date

private
   type Date_Type is tagged
      record
         Year  : Year_Type;
         Month : Month_Type;
         Day   : Day_Type;
      end record;
end Date;
```

Don't be concerned if some of the Ada syntax in the Date class example is unfamiliar to you. We will provide the details on each new language feature when needed.

This code is for a package specification. A **package** is a group of logically related entities that may include types and subtypes, objects of those types and subtypes, and subprograms with parameters of those types and subtypes. We write packages in two parts: the package specification and the package body. The **package specification** defines the interface to the package. The specification describes what resources the package can supply to an application. Our date package specification defines the attributes and operations for a date class. The **package body** provides the implementation of the resources defined in the specification. The date package body will contain the actual code to carry out the operations defined in our package specification.

> **Package** A group of logically related entities that may include types and subtypes, objects of those types and subtypes, and subprograms with parameters of those types and subtypes.
>
> **Package specification** The visible portion of a package; specifies what resources are supplied by the package.
>
> **Package body** The implementation of a package.

There are significant advantages to separating the specification of a package from its implementation. A clear interface is important, particularly when a package is used by other members of a programming team. Any ambiguities in an interface will result in problems when the team members' efforts are combined. By separating the specification of the package from its implementation, we have the opportunity to concentrate our efforts on the design of a class without needing to worry about implementation details.

```
┌─────────────────────────────────────────────────────────────┐
│                            Date                             │
├─────────────────────────────────────────────────────────────┤
│ Year   :Year_Type                                           │
│ Month  :Month_Type                                          │
│ Day    :Day_Type                                            │
├─────────────────────────────────────────────────────────────┤
│ Construct_Date(M:Month_Type,D:Day_Type,Y:Year_Type):Date    │
│ Year_Is():Year_Type                                         │
│ Month_Is():Month_Type                                       │
│ Day_Is():Day_Type                                           │
└─────────────────────────────────────────────────────────────┘
```

Figure 1.3 *UML class diagram for the* `Date` *class.*

Now let's look inside the date specification. The simple types provide reasonable ranges for the attributes of our date. We could have used the predefined type `Integer` for our date class's day attribute. However, by modeling the ranges of the attributes we can more easily discover errors in our operations. For example, calling procedure `Construct_Date` with a day value of 42 is surely an error. Our restricted day range allows Ada to find this error without any effort on our part. Similarly, we used `Year_Type` to limit the year of our dates to those of the widely used Gregorian calendar introduced in 1583.

As we will demonstrate in the next section, we use type `Date_Type` to create our date objects. `Date_Type` is the name of our class. `Date_Type` is declared as a tagged private type. Tagged means that another class can inherit the attributes and operations of our type. Private means that the details of the type are not available outside of package `Date`. We use private types to enforce information hiding. The type's details are given in the end of the package specification after the keyword `private`. In our example you can see that the date type is a record. Because this record is private, it is not accessible from outside the package.

The operations in our date class are `Construct_Date`, `Year_Is`, `Month_Is`, and `Day_Is`. `Construct_Date` converts a set of values into a single date object. We classify such an operation as a **constructor**. The remaining three operations are classified as **observer** operations because they "observe" and return the values of an object's attributes. Observer operations do not change the object.

> **Constructor** An operation used to create new values of a class.
>
> **Observer** An operation that returns an observation on the state of an object.

Figure 1.3 shows a UML diagram for the `Date` class. In UML class diagrams, the name of the class appears in the top section of the diagram, the attributes appear in the center section, and the operations are in the bottom section. The diagram includes information about the types of the attributes and parameters for the operations.

At this point we understand what the class `Date` can do. That is the purpose of a package specification and the UML class diagram. Now let's look at its implementation. Here is the package body for our `Date` class:

```ada
package body Date is

   function Construct_Date (Month : in Month_Type;
                            Day   : in Day_Type;
                            Year  : in Year_Type) return Date_Type is
   begin
      return (Year, Month, Day);   -- Return a record aggregate
   end Construct_Date;

   function Year_Is (Date : in Date_Type) return Year_Type is
   begin
      return Date.Year;
   end Year_Is;

   function Month_Is (Date : in Date_Type) return Month_Type is
   begin
      return Date.Month;
   end Month_Is;

   function Day_Is (Date : in Date_Type) return Day_Type is
   begin
      return Date.Day;
   end Day_Is;

end Date;
```

Once a class such as Date has been defined, a program can create and use objects of that class. The effect is similar to expanding the language's set of standard types to include Date_Type. One of the major purposes of this text is to introduce you to a number of classes that are particularly important in the development of software—perhaps the most reusable classes known. These classes often are called abstract data types or data structures. We discuss the concept of the abstract data type in detail in Chapter 2. In the remaining chapters, we fully develop many abstract data types. We describe others and let you to develop them. These classes are fundamental to computer science, and the Ada code for them often can be obtained from a public or private repository or purchased from vendors who market Ada components. If they are already available, why do we spend so much time on their development? Our goal is to teach you how to develop software. As with the development of any skill, you need to practice the fundamentals before you can become a virtuoso.

Objects   Objects are created from classes at run-time. They can contain and manipulate data. You should view an object-oriented system as a set of objects, working together by sending each other messages to solve a problem.

The easiest way to create an object in Ada is to simply declare a variable to be an object of the class type along with a class constructor, as follows:

```
My_Date   : Date_Type := Construct_Date (December, 20, 1948);
Your_Date : Date_Type := Construct_Date (September, 30, 1948);
```

We will show you another way to create objects after we discuss access types (pointers) in Chapter 4.

Ada provides two syntax forms for invoking object operations. The following examples of each form assign the current year of the object `My_Date` to the variable `The_Year`:

```
The_Year := Year_Is(My_Date);      -- Function call form
The_Year := My_Date.Year_Is;       -- Object.Operation form
```

The *Object.Operation* form was introduced in the latest version of Ada. This form may only be used when

1. the type of the objects is *tagged*.
2. the operation is a *primitive operation* for the type.
3. the object is the first parameter of the operation.

We discuss the terms *tagged* and *primitive operation* in Chapter 2.

Inheritance The object-oriented paradigm provides a powerful reuse tool called inheritance, which allows programmers to create a new class that is a specialization of an existing class. In this case, the new class is called a subclass of the existing class, which in turn is the superclass of the new class.

A subclass "inherits" features from its superclass. It adds new features, as needed, related to its specialization. It can also redefine inherited features as necessary. Contrary to the intuitive meaning of super and sub, a subclass usually has more attributes and operations than its superclass. Super and sub refer to the relative positions of the classes in a hierarchy. A subclass is below its superclass, and a superclass is above its subclasses.

Suppose we already have a `Date` class as defined earlier, and we are creating a new application to manipulate `Date` objects. Suppose also that in the new application we are often required to ask if a particular date is a holiday. There are several different ways to obtain this additional functionality:

- Implement the holiday check within the new application. This might appear to be a good approach, because it is the new application that requires the new functionality. However, if future applications also need this functionality, their programmers have to re-implement the solution for themselves. This approach does not support our goal of reusability.
- Add a new attribute and new operations to the existing `Date` specification. This approach is better than the previous approach because it allows any future programs that use the `Date` class to use the new functionality. However, this change presents problems for preexisting programs that use the original `Date` class; for example, an application may maintain a file of date objects. Adding a new attribute to the `Date` class makes it incompatible with the data already stored in the file.

- Use inheritance. Create a new class, called `Holiday_Date`, that inherits all the features of the current `Date` class, but that also adds a new attribute and operations to support holidays. This approach resolves the drawbacks of the previous two approaches. We now look at how to implement this third approach.

We often call the inheritance relationship an *is-a* relationship. In this case we would say that an object of the class `Holiday_Date` is also a `Date` object because it can do anything that a `Date` object can do—and more. This idea can be clarified by remembering that inheritance typically means specialization. `Holiday_Date` is a special case of `Date`, but not the other way around.

To create `Holiday_Date` in Ada we would code the child package specification as follows:

```ada
package Date.Holiday_Date is

   ----------------------------------------------------------------
   -- Type for the holiday date class
   type Holiday_Date_Type is new Date_Type with private;

   ----------------------------------------------------------------

   overriding function Construct_Date
                  (Month   : in Month_Type;
                   Day     : in Day_Type;
                   Year    : in Year_Type) return Holiday_Date_Type;
   -- Convert three values to a single date that is not a holiday


   -- Additional operations for the holiday date class
   ----------------------------------------------------------------
   function Is_Holiday (Date : in Holiday_Date_Type) return Boolean;
   -- Returns True if this Date is a holiday

   procedure Make_Holiday (Date : in out Holiday_Date_Type);
   -- Make this Date a holiday

private
   type Holiday_Date_Type is new Date_Type with
      record
         Holiday : Boolean := False;
      end record;
end Date.Holiday_Date;
```

Inheritance is indicated by the keywords `new` and `with private`, which show that `Holiday_Date_Type` is a new form of `Date_Type` with additional functionality. We say that `Holiday_Date_Type` extends `Date_Type`. The private part of the specification adds a new attribute, Holiday, to our subclass. Our Holiday_Date_Type has four attributes—the three it inherited from Date and the new one, Holiday.

Holiday_Date has an additional field, so we override (replace) Date's constructor with one that creates a Holiday_Date. Type Holiday_Date inherits the remaining three operations (Year_Is, Month_Is, and Day_Is). The other additions to the Holiday_Date class are the Is_Holiday and Make_Holiday operations that provide Holiday_Date's more specialized behavior. Is_Holiday is an observer operation. Make_Holiday is classified as a **transformer** operation, because it changes the internal state of the object. Make_Holiday changes the object's Holiday attribute. The Make_Holiday transformer method may be invoked through either a standard procedure call or the object that it is to transform. For example, the declaration

> **Transformer** An operation that changes the internal state of an object.

```
Our_Date : Holiday_Date_Type := Construct_Date (June, 17, 1971);
```

defines a Holiday_Date object that is turned into a holiday by each of the following statements:

```
Our_Date.Make_Holiday;      -- Object.Operation form
Make_Holiday (Our_Date);    -- Function call form
```

The UML class diagram in Figure 1.4 shows the inheritance relationship. The arrow with the open head is the UML notation for inheritance. The diagram shows that Holiday_Date is a specialized Date. Date is the superclass and Holiday_Date is the subclass.

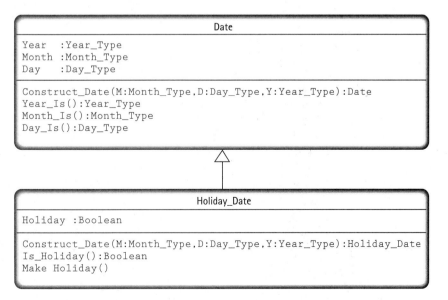

Figure 1.4 *UML class diagram showing inheritance.*

Here is the package body that encapsulates the details of the new operations:

```ada
package body Date.Holiday_Date is

   function Construct_Date (Month : in Month_Type;
                            Day   : in Day_Type;
                            Year  : in Year_Type) return Holiday_Date_Type is
   begin
      return (Year, Month, Day, False);   -- Return a record aggregate
   end Construct_Date;

   function Is_Holiday (Date : in Holiday_Date_Type) return Boolean is
   begin
      return Date.Holiday;
   end Is_Holiday;

   procedure Make_Holiday (Date : in out Holiday_Date_Type) is
   begin
      Date.Holiday := True;
   end Make_Holiday;

end Date.Holiday_Date;
```

Notice that the package name used for our `Holiday_Date` class is prefixed by the name of the package used for its superclass. `Date.Holiday_Date` is a **child package** of `Date`. Child packages provide a hierarchical structure of compilation units (files) that match the hierarchical structure of inheritance. A child package is conceptually part of its parent package, but a child package can be compiled separately without recompiling or modifying the parent. Because it is conceptually part of its parent, a child package may access the resources in both the public and private section of its parent. Access to the details of the tagged private type (the class attributes of the superclass) is needed by the subclass in order to carry out its operations. We always construct a parent–child package hierarchy that matches our inheritance hierarchy.

> **Child package** A package that is conceptually part of its parent. Subclasses are implemented as child packages.

A program with access to both of the date classes can now declare and use both the `Date` and `Holiday_Date` objects. Consider the following program segment:

```ada
My_Date  : Date_Type         := Construct_Date (December, 20, 1948);
Our_Date : Holiday_Date_Type := Construct_Date (June, 17, 1971);


Put_Line ("My_Date day is" & Day_Type'Image (My_Date.Day_Is));
```

```
Put_line ("Our_Date day is" & Day_Type'Image (Our_Date.Day_Is));
Our_Date.Make_Holiday;
if Our_Date.Is_Holiday then
   Put_Line ("Our_Date is a holiday");
end if;
```

This program segment creates and initializes `My_Date` and `Our_Date`, outputs the values of their days, makes `Our_Date` a holiday, and finally checks to see if `Our_Date` is a holiday. You might ask, "How does the system resolve the use of the `Day_Is` method by a `Holiday_Date` object when `Day_Is` is defined in the `Date` class?" Understanding how inheritance is supported provides the answer to this question. The compiler has available to it all the declaration information captured in the extended UML diagram shown in Figure 1.4. Consider the `Day_Is` operation call in the statement:

```
Put_line ("Our_Date day is" & Day_Type'Image (Our_Date.Day_Is));
```

To resolve this operation call, the compiler looks first at the class of the `Our_Date` variable. It does not find a definition for a `Day_Is` operation in the `Holiday_Date` class, so it follows the inheritance link to the superclass `Date`, where it finds, and executes, the `Day_Is` operation. In this case, the `Day_Is` operation returns a `Day_Type` value that represents the day value of the `Our_Date` object. We used the `'Image` operation to convert this whole number into a string for output.

Note that because of the way operation calls are resolved—by searching up the inheritance tree—only objects of the class `Holiday_Date` can use the `Make_Holiday` operation. If you tried to use the `Make_Holiday` operation on an object of the class `Date`, such as the `My_Date` object, there would be no definition available. The compiler would report a syntax error in this situation.

Design The *object-oriented design (OOD)* methodology originated with the development of programs to simulate physical objects and processes in the real world. For example, to simulate an electronic circuit, you could develop a class for simulating each kind of component in the circuit and then "wire-up" the simulation by having the modules pass information among themselves in the same pattern that wires connect the electronic components.

Identifying Classes The key task in designing object-oriented systems is identification of classes. Successful class identification and organization draws upon many of the tools that we discussed earlier in this chapter. Top-down stepwise refinement encourages us to start by identifying the major classes and gradually refine our system definition to identify all the classes we need. We should use abstraction and practice information hiding by keeping the interfaces to our classes narrow and hiding important design decisions and requirements likely to change within our classes. CRC cards can help us identify the responsibilities and collaborations of our classes, and expose holes in our design. UML diagrams let us record our designs in a form that is easy to understand.

When possible, we should organize our classes in an inheritance hierarchy, to benefit from reuse. Another form of reuse is to find prewritten classes, possibly in the standard Ada library, that can be used in a solution.

There is no foolproof technique for identifying classes; we just have to start brainstorming ideas and see where they lead us. A large program is typically written by a team of programmers, so the brainstorming process often occurs in a team setting. Team members identify whatever objects they see in the problem and then propose classes to represent them. The proposed classes are all written on a board. None of the ideas for classes are discussed or rejected in this first stage.

After the brainstorming, the team goes through a process of filtering the classes. First they eliminate duplicates. Then they discuss whether each class really represents an object in the problem. (It's easy to get carried away and include classes, such as "the user," that are beyond the scope of the problem.) The team then looks for classes that seem to be related. Perhaps they aren't duplicates, but they have much in common, and so they are grouped together on the board. At the same time, the discussion may reveal some classes that were overlooked.

Usually it is not difficult to identify an initial set of classes. In most large problems we naturally find entities that we wish to represent as classes. For example, in designing a program that manages a checking account, we might identify checks, deposits, an account balance, and account statements as entities. These entities interact with each other through messages. For example, a check could send a message to the balance entity that tells it to deduct an amount from itself. We didn't list the amount in our initial set of objects, but it may be another entity that we need to represent.

Our example illustrates a common approach to OOD. We begin by identifying a set of objects that we think are important in a problem. Then we consider some scenarios in which the objects interact to accomplish a task. In the process of envisioning how a scenario plays out, we identify additional objects and messages. We keep trying new scenarios until we find that our set of objects and messages is sufficient to accomplish any task that the problem requires. CRC cards help us enact such scenarios.

A standard technique for identifying classes and their methods is to look for objects and operations in the problem statement. Objects are usually nouns and operations are usually verbs. For example, suppose the problem statement includes the sentence: "The student grades must be sorted from best to worst before being output." Potential objects are "student" and "grade," and potential operations are "sort" and "output." We propose that on a printed copy of your requirements you circle the nouns and underline the verbs. The set of nouns are your candidate objects, and the verbs are your candidate operations. Of course, you have to filter this list, but at least it provides a good starting point for design.

Recall that in our discussion of abstraction and information hiding we stated that program modules should display strong cohesion. A good way to validate the cohesiveness of an identified class is to try to describe its main responsibility in a single coherent phrase. If you cannot do this, then you should reconsider your design. Some examples of cohesive responsibilities are:

- Maintain a list of integers.
- Handle file interaction.
- Provide a date type.

Some examples of "poor" responsibilities are:

- Maintain a list of integers and provide special integer output routines.
- Handle file interaction and draw graphs on the screen.

In summation, we have discussed the following approaches to identifying classes:

1. Start with the major classes and refine the design.
2. Hide important design decisions and requirements likely to change within a class.
3. Brainstorm with a group of programmers.
4. Make sure each class has one main responsibility.
5. Use CRC cards to organize classes and identify holes in the design.
6. Walk through user scenarios.
7. Look for nouns and verbs in the problem description.

Design Choices When working on design, keep in mind that there are many different correct solutions to most problems. The techniques we use may seem imprecise, especially in contrast with the precision that is demanded by the computer. But the computer merely demands that we express (code) a particular solution precisely. The process of deciding which particular solution to use is far less precise. It is our human ability to make choices without having complete information that enables us to solve problems. Different choices naturally lead to different solutions to a problem.

For example, in developing a simulation of an air traffic control system, we might decide that airplanes and control towers are objects that communicate with each other. Or we might decide that pilots and controllers are the objects that communicate. This choice affects how we subsequently view the problem, and the responsibilities that we assign to the objects. Either choice can lead to a working application. We may simply prefer the one with which we are most familiar.

Some of our choices lead to designs that are more or less efficient than others. For example, keeping a list of names in alphabetical rather than random order makes it possible for the computer to find a particular name much faster. However, choosing to leave the list randomly ordered still produces a valid (but slower) solution, and may even be the best solution if you do not need to search the list very often.

Other choices affect the amount of work that is required to develop the remainder of a problem solution. In creating a program for choreographing ballet movements, we might begin by recognizing a dancer as the important object and then create a class for each dancer. But in doing so, we discover that all of the dancers have certain common responsibilities. Rather than repeat the definition of those responsibilities for each class of dancer, we can change our initial choice and define a class for an abstract dancer that includes all the common responsibilities and then develop subclasses that add responsibilities specific to each individual.

The point is, don't hesitate to begin solving a problem because you are waiting for some flash of genius that leads you to the perfect solution. There is no such thing. It is better to jump in and try something, step back and see if you like the result, and then either proceed or make changes to your design. Trial and error is appropriate for the design process, and indeed is an advantage of working out a design before you start programming. It is far easier to change a few UML diagrams or CRC cards in a design than it is to change the corresponding code in the program.

Design Example In this section we present a sample object-oriented design process that might be followed if we were on a small team of software engineers. Our purposes are to show the classes that might be identified for an object-oriented system and to demonstrate the utility of CRC cards. We assume that our team of engineers has been given the task of automating an address book. A user should be able to enter and retrieve information from the address book. We have been given a sample physical address book on which to base the product.

First our team studies the problem, inspects the physical address book, and brainstorms that the application has the following potential objects:

| Cover |
| Pages |
| Address |
| Name |
| Home phone number |
| Work phone number |
| E-mail |
| Fax number |
| Pager number |
| Cell phone number |
| Birthday |
| Company name |
| Work address |
| Calendar |
| Time-zone map |
| Owner information |
| Emergency number |
| User |

Then we enter the filtering stage. Our application doesn't need to represent the physical parts of an address book, so we can delete Cover and Pages. However, we need something analogous to a page that holds all the same sort of information. Let's call it an Entry. The different telephone numbers can all be represented by the same kind of object, so we can combine Home, Work, Fax, Pager, and Cell phone into a Phone number class. In consultation with the customer, we find that the electronic address book doesn't need the special pages that are often found in a printed address book, so we delete Calendar, Time-zone map, Owner information, and Emergency number.

Further thought reveals that the User isn't part of the application, although this does point to the need for a User interface that we did not originally list. A Work address is a specific kind of address that has additional information, so we can make it a subclass of Address. Company names are just strings, so there is no need to distinguish them, but Names have a first, last, and middle part. Our filtered list of classes now looks like this:

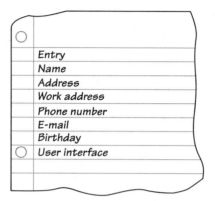

For each of these classes we create a CRC card. In the case of Work address, we list Address as its superclass, and on the Address card we list Work address in its subclasses space.

In doing coursework, you may be asked to work individually rather than in a collaborative team. You can still do your own brainstorming and filtering; however, we recommend that you take a break after the brainstorming and do the filtering once you have let your initial ideas rest for a while. An idea that seems brilliant in the middle of brainstorming may lose some of its attraction after a day or even a few hours.

Initial Responsibilities Once you (or your team) have identified the classes and created CRC cards for them, go over each card and write down its primary responsibility and an initial list of resultant responsibilities that are obvious. For example, a Name class manages a "Name" and has a responsibility to know its first name, its middle name, and its last name. We would list these three responsibilities in the left column of its card, as shown in Figure 1.5. In an implementation, they become methods that return the corresponding part of the name. For many classes, the initial responsibilities include knowing some value or set of values.

A First Scenario Walk-Through To further expand the responsibilities of the classes and see how they collaborate, we must pretend to carry out various processing scenarios by hand. This kind of role playing is known as a *walk-through*. We ask a question such as, "What happens when the user wants to find an address that's in the book?" Then we answer the question by telling how each object is involved in accomplishing this task. In a team setting, the cards are distributed among the team members. When an object of a class is doing something, its card is held in the air to visually signify that it is active.

Class Name: *Name*	Superclass:	Subclasses:
Primary Responsibility: *Manage a Name*		
Responsibilities	Collaborations	
Know first		
Know middle		
Know last		

Figure 1.5 *A CRC card with initial responsibilities.*

With this particular question, we might pick up the User interface card and say, "I have a responsibility to get the person's name from the user." That responsibility gets written down on the card. Once the name is input, the User interface must collaborate with other objects to look up the name and get the corresponding address. What object should it collaborate with? There is no identified object class that represents the entire set of address book entries.

We've found a hole in our list of classes! The Entry objects should be organized into a Book object. We quickly write out a Book CRC card. The User interface card-holder then says, "I'm going to collaborate with the Book class to get the address." The collaboration is written in the right column of the card, and it remains in the air. The owner of the Book card holds it up, saying, "I have a responsibility to find an address in the list of Entry objects that I keep, given a name." That responsibility gets written on the Book card. Then the owner says, "I have to collaborate with each Entry to compare its name with the name sent to me by the User interface."

Now comes a decision. What are the responsibilities of Book and Entry for carrying out the comparison? Should Book get the name from Entry and do the comparison, or should it send the name to Entry and receive an answer that indicates whether they are equal? The team decides that Book should do the comparing, so the Entry card is held in the air, and its owner says, "I have a responsibility to provide the full name as a string. To do that I must collaborate with Name." The responsibility and collaboration are recorded and the Name card is raised.

Name says, "I have the responsibility to know my first, middle, and last names. These are already on my card, so I'm done." And the Name card is lowered. Entry says, "I concatenate the three names into a string with spaces between them, and return the result to Book, so I'm done." The Entry card is lowered.

Book says, "I keep collaborating with Entry until I find the matching name. Then I must collaborate with Entry again to get the address." This collaboration is placed on its card and the Entry card is held up again, saying "I have a responsibility to provide an address. I'm not going to collaborate with Address, but am just going to return the object to Book." The Entry card has this responsibility added and then goes back on the table. Its CRC card is shown in Figure 1.6.

The scenario continues until the task of finding an address in the book and reporting it to the user is completed. Reading about the scenario makes it seem longer and more complex than it really is. Once you get used to role playing, the scenarios move quickly and the walk-through becomes more like a game. However, to keep things moving, it is important to avoid becoming bogged down with implementation details. Book should not be concerned with how the Entry objects are organized on the list. Address doesn't need to think about whether the ZIP code is stored as an integer or a string. Only explore each responsibility far enough to decide whether a further collaboration is needed, or if it can be solved with the available information.

Class Name: *Entry*	Superclass:	Subclasses:
Primary Responsibility: *Manage a "page" of information*		
Responsibilities	Collaborations	
Provide name as a string	*Get first from Name*	
	Get middle from Name	
	Get last from Name	
Provide Address	*None*	

Figure 1.6 *The CRC card for Entry.*

The next step is to brainstorm some additional questions that produce new scenarios. For example, here is list of some further scenarios:

> What happens when the user
> - asks for a name that's not in the book?
> - wants to add an entry to the book?
> - wants to delete an entry from the book?
> - tries to delete an entry that is not in the book?
> - wants a phone number?
> - wants a business address?
> - wants a list of upcoming birthdays?

We walk through each of the scenarios, adding responsibilities and collaborations to the CRC cards as necessary. After several scenarios have been tried, the number of additions decreases. When one or more scenarios take place without adding to any of the cards, then we brainstorm further to see if we can come up with new scenarios that may not be covered. When all of the scenarios that we can envision seem to be doable with the existing classes, responsibilities, and collaborations, then the design is done.

The next step is to implement the responsibilities for each class. The implementation may reveal details of a collaboration that weren't obvious in the walk-through. But knowing the collaborating classes makes it easy to change their corresponding responsibilities. The implementation phase should also include a search of available libraries to see if any existing classes can be used. For example, `Ada.Calendar` contains a date class that can be used directly to implement Birthday.

Enhancing CRC Cards with Additional Information The CRC card design is informal. There are many ways that the card can be enhanced. For example, when a responsibility has obvious steps, we can write them below its name. Each step may have specific collaborations, and we write these beside the steps in the right column. We often recognize that certain data must be sent as part of the message that activates a responsibility, and we can record this in parentheses beside the calling collaboration and the responding responsibility. Figure 1.7 shows a CRC card that includes design information in addition to the basic responsibilities and collaborations.

To summarize the CRC card process, we brainstorm the objects in a problem and abstract them into classes. Then we filter the list of classes to eliminate duplicates. For each class, we create a CRC card and list any obvious responsibilities that it should support. We then walk through a common scenario, recording responsibilities and collaborations as they are discovered. After that we walk through additional scenarios, moving from common cases to special and exceptional cases. When it appears that we have all of the scenarios covered, we brainstorm additional scenarios that may need more

Class Name:	Entry	Superclass:		Subclasses:	
Primary Responsibility:	Manage a "page" of information				
Responsibilities			Collaborations		
Provide name as a string					
get first name			Name		
get middle name			Name		
get last name			Name		
Provide Address			Name		
Change Name (name string)					
Break name into first, middle, last			String		
Update first name			Name, change first (first)		
Update middle name			Name, change middle (middle)		
Update last name			Name, change last (last)		

Figure 1.7 *A CRC card that is enhanced with additional information.*

responsibilities and collaborations. When our ideas for scenarios are exhausted, and all the scenarios are covered by the existing CRC cards, the design is done.

Exceptions

At the design stage, you should plan how to handle **exceptions** in your program. Exceptions are just what the name implies: exceptional situations. They are situations that alter the flow of control of the program, often resulting in a premature end to program execution. Working with exceptions begins at the design phase: What are the unusual situations that the program should recognize? Where in the program can the situations be detected? How should the situations be handled if they occur?

> **Exception** Associated with an unusual, often unpredictable event, detectable by software or hardware, that requires special processing. The event may or may not be erroneous.

Where—indeed whether—an exception is detected depends on the language, the software package design, the design of the libraries being used, and the platform, that is, on the operating system and hardware. Where an exception should be detected depends on the type of exception, on the software package design, and on the platform. Where an exception is detected should be well documented in the relevant code segments.

An exception may be handled any place in the software hierarchy—from the place in the program module where the exception is first detected through the top level of the program. In Ada, as in most programming languages, unhandled built-in exceptions carry the penalty of program termination. Where in an application an exception should be handled is a design decision; however, exceptions should be handled at a level that knows what the exception means.

An exception need not be fatal. For nonfatal exceptions, the thread of execution may continue. Although the thread of execution can continue from any point in the program, the execution should continue from the lowest level that can recover from the exception. When an error occurs, the program may fail unexpectedly. Some of the failure conditions may be anticipated and some may not. All such errors must be detected and managed.

Exceptions can be written in any language. Ada (along with some other languages) provides built-in mechanisms to manage exceptions. All exception mechanisms have three parts:

- Defining the exception
- Generating (raising) the exception
- Handling the exception

Once your exception plan is determined, Ada gives you a clean way of implementing these three phases using raise statements and exception handlers. You are probably already familiar with exception handlers. We cover the raise statement in Chapter 5.

1.3 Verification of Software Correctness

At the beginning of this chapter, we discussed some characteristics of good programs. The first of these was that a good program works—it accomplishes its intended function. How do you know when your program meets that goal? The simple answer is, *test it*.

Let's look at **testing** as it relates to the rest of the software development process. As programmers, we first make sure that we understand the requirements, and then we come up with a general solution. Next we design the solution in terms of a system of classes, using good design principles, and finally we implement the solution, using well-structured code, with classes, comments, and so on.

Once we have the program coded, we compile it repeatedly until the syntax errors are gone. Then we run the program, using carefully selected test data. If the program doesn't work, we say that it has a "bug" in it. We try to pinpoint the error and fix it, a process called **debugging**.

Testing The process of executing a program with data sets designed to discover errors.

Debugging The process of removing known errors.

Notice the distinction between testing and debugging. Testing is running the program with data sets designed to discover errors; debugging is removing errors once they are discovered.

When the debugging is completed, the software is put into use. Before final delivery, software is sometimes installed on one or more customer sites so that it can be tested in a real environment with real data. After passing this **acceptance test** phase, the software can be installed at all of the customer sites. Is the verification process now finished? Hardly! More than half of the total life-cycle costs and effort generally occur after the program becomes operational, in the maintenance phase. Some changes are made to correct errors in the original program; other changes are introduced to add new capabilities to the software system. In either case, testing must be done after any program modification. This is called **regression testing**.

> **Acceptance testing** The process of testing the system in its real environment with real data.
>
> **Regression testing** Reexecution of program tests after modifications have been made in order to ensure the program still works correctly.
>
> **Program verification** The process of determining the degree to which a software product fulfills its specification.
>
> **Program validation** The process of determining the degree to which a software product fulfills its intended purpose.

Testing is useful for revealing the presence of bugs in a program, but it doesn't prove their absence. We can only say for sure that the program worked correctly for the cases we tested. This approach seems somewhat haphazard. How do we know which tests or how many of them to run? Debugging a whole program at once isn't easy. And fixing the errors found during such testing can sometimes be a messy task. Too bad we couldn't have detected the errors earlier—while we were designing the program, for instance. They would have been much easier to fix then.

We know how program design can be improved by using a good design methodology. Is there something similar that we can do to improve our program verification activities? Yes, there is. Program verification activities don't need to start when the program is completely coded; they can be incorporated into the whole software development process, from the requirements phase on. **Program verification** is more than just testing.

In addition to program verification—fulfilling the requirement specifications—there is another important task for the software engineer: making sure the specified requirements actually solve the underlying problem. There have been countless times when a programmer finishes a large project and delivers the verified software, only to be told, "Well, that's what I asked for, but it's not what I need." The process of determining that software accomplishes its intended task is called **program validation**. Program verification asks, "Are we doing the job right?" Program validation asks, "Are we doing the right job?"[4]

---

[4]B. W. Boehm, *Software Engineering Economics* (Englewood Cliffs, NJ: Prentice-Hall, 1981).

Can we really "debug" a program before it has ever been run—or even before it has been written? In this section, we review a number of topics related to satisfying the criterion "quality software works." The topics include:

- Designing for correctness
- Performing code and design walk-throughs and inspections
- Using debugging methods
- Choosing test goals and data
- Writing test plans
- Structured integration testing

Origin of Bugs

When Sherlock Holmes goes off to solve a case, he doesn't start from scratch every time; he knows from experience all kinds of things that help him find solutions. Suppose Holmes finds a victim in a muddy field. He immediately looks for footprints in the mud, for he can tell from a footprint what kind of shoe made it. The first print he finds matches the shoes of the victim, so he keeps looking. Now he finds another, and from his vast knowledge of footprints, he can tell that it was made by a certain type of boot. He deduces that such a boot would be worn by a particular type of laborer, and from the size and depth of the print, he guesses the suspect's height and weight. Now, knowing something about the habits of laborers in this town, he guesses that at 6:30 P.M. the suspect might be found in Clancy's Pub.

In software verification we are often expected to play detective. Given certain clues, we have to find the bugs in programs. If we know what kinds of situations produce program errors, we are more likely to be able to detect and correct problems. We may even be able to step in and prevent many errors entirely, just as Sherlock Holmes sometimes intervenes in time to prevent a crime that is about to take place.

Let's look at some types of software errors that show up at various points in program development and testing, and see how they might be avoided.

Specifications and Design Errors What would happen if, shortly before you were supposed to turn in a major class assignment, you discovered that some details in the professor's program description were incorrect? To make matters worse, you also found out that the corrections were discussed at the beginning of class on the day you got there late, and somehow you never knew about the problem until your tests of the class data set came up with the wrong answers. What do you do now?

Writing a program to the wrong specifications is probably the worst kind of software error. How bad can it be? Most studies indicate that it costs 100 times as much to correct an error discovered after software delivery than it does if it is discovered early in the life cycle. Figure 1.8 shows how fast the costs rise in subsequent phases of software development. The vertical axis represents the relative cost of fixing an error; this cost might be in units of hours, or thousands of dollars, or "programmer months" (the amount of work one programmer can do in a month). The horizontal axis represents the stages in the development of a software product. As

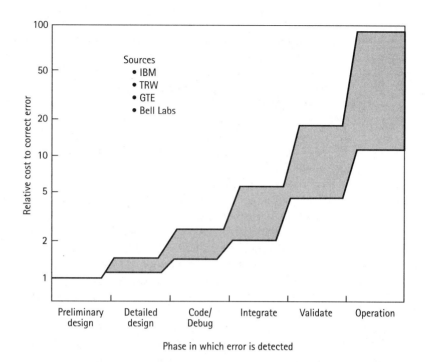

Figure 1.8 *Cost of a specification error based on when it is discovered.*

you can see, an error that would have taken one unit to fix when you first started designing might take a hundred units to correct when the product is actually in operation!

Many specification errors can be prevented by good communication between the programmers (you) and the party who originated the problem (the professor, manager, or customer). In general, it pays to ask questions when you don't understand something in the program specifications. And the earlier you ask, the better.

A number of questions should come to mind as you first read a programming assignment. What error checking is necessary? What algorithm or data structure is supposed to be used in the solution? What assumptions are reasonable? If you obtain answers to these questions when you first begin working on an assignment, you can incorporate them into your design and implementation of the program. Later in the program's development, unexpected answers to these questions can cost you time and effort. In short, in order to write a program that is correct, you must understand precisely what it is that your program is supposed to do.

Compile-Time Errors In the process of learning your first programming language, you probably made a number of syntax errors. These resulted in error messages (for example, "type mismatch," "illegal assignment," "missing semicolon," and so on) when you tried to compile the program. Now that you are more familiar with the programming language, you can save your debugging skills for tracking down important logical errors. Try to get the syntax right the first time. Having your program compile cleanly on the first attempt is a reasonable goal. A syntax error wastes computing time and money, as well as programmer time, and it is preventable.

As you progress in your college career or move into a professional computing job, learning a new programming language is often the easiest part of a new software assignment. This does not mean, however, that the language is the least important part. In this book we discuss data structures and algorithms that we believe are language-independent. This means that they can be implemented in almost any general-purpose programming language. The success of the implementation, however, depends on a thorough understanding of the features of the programming language. What is considered acceptable programming practice in one language may be inadequate in another, and similar syntactic constructs may be just different enough to cause serious trouble.

It is, therefore, worthwhile to develop an expert knowledge of both the control and data constructs and the syntax of the language in which you are programming. In general, if you have a good knowledge of your programming language—and are careful—you can avoid syntax errors. The ones you might miss are relatively easy to locate and correct. Once you have a "clean" compilation, you can execute your program.

Run-Time Errors Errors that occur during the execution of a program are usually harder to detect than syntax errors. Some run-time errors stop execution of the program. When this happens, we say that the program "crashed" or "abnormally terminated."

Run-time errors often occur when the programmer makes too many assumptions. For instance,

```
Result := Dividend / Divisor;
```

is a legitimate assignment statement, if we can assume that `Divisor` is never zero. If `Divisor` is zero, however, a run-time error results.

Run-time errors also occur because of unanticipated user errors. If a user enters the wrong data type in response to a prompt, or supplies an invalid filename to a routine, most simple programs report a run-time error and halt; in other words, they crash. Well-written programs should not crash. They should catch such errors and stay in control until the user is ready to quit.

> **Robustness** The ability of a program to recover following an error; the ability of a program to continue to operate within its environment.

The ability of a program to recover when an error occurs is called **robustness**. If a commercial program is not robust, people do not buy it. Who wants a word processor that crashes if the user says "Save" when the memory stick was removed? We want the program to tell us, "Plug your memory stick into the USB port, and press Enter." For some types of software, robustness is a critical requirement. An airplane's automatic pilot system or an intensive care unit's patient-monitoring program just cannot afford to crash. In such situations, a defensive posture produces good results.

In general, you should actively check for error-creating conditions rather than let them abort your program. For instance, it is generally unwise to make too many assumptions about the correctness of input, especially interactive input from a keyboard. A better approach is to check explicitly for the correct type and bounds of such input. The programmer can then decide how an error should be handled (request new input, print a message, or go on to the next data) rather than leave the decision to the system. Even the decision to quit should be made by a program that is in control of its own execution. If worse comes to worst, let your program die gracefully.

This does not mean that everything that the program inputs must be checked for errors. Sometimes inputs are known to be correct—for instance, input from a file that has been verified. The decision to include error checking must be based upon the requirements of the program.

Some run-time errors do not stop execution but produce the wrong results. You may have incorrectly implemented an algorithm or initialized a variable to an incorrect value. You may have inadvertently swapped two parameters of the same type on a procedure call or used a less-than sign instead of a greater-than sign. These logical errors are often the hardest to prevent and locate. Later in this chapter we talk about debugging techniques to help pinpoint run-time errors. We also discuss structured testing methods that isolate the part of the program being tested. But knowing that the earlier we find an error the easier it is to fix, we turn now to ways of catching run-time errors before run time.

Designing for Correctness

It would be nice if there were some tool that would locate the errors in our design or code without our even having to run the program. That may sound unlikely, but consider an analogy from geometry. We wouldn't try to prove the Pythagorean theorem by proving that it worked on every triangle; that would only demonstrate that the theorem works for every triangle we tried. We prove theorems in geometry mathematically. Can't we do the same for computer programs?

The verification of program correctness, independent of data testing, is an important area of theoretical computer science research. The goal of this research is to establish a method for proving programs that is analogous to the method for proving theorems in geometry. We want to verify a program **statically** (without executing it) rather than **dynamically** (executing it with test data).

> **Static verification** Verifying a program without executing it.
>
> **Dynamic verification** Verifying a program by executing it with a set of test data.

In the past, program proof techniques were considered impractical for all but the smallest of programs. Today, proof techniques have been used successfully with programs containing millions of lines of code.[5] There is now compelling evidence that software development methods based on static verification techniques to focus on bug

---

[5] M. Coxford and J. Sutton, "Breaking Through the V and V Bottleneck," *Lecture Notes in Computer Science*, vol. 1031, 1995, Springer-Verlag, pp. 344–354, ISBN: 3-540-60757-9.

prevention rather than bug detection can raise quality and save time and money. A recent, large avionics project reported a 4-fold increase in productivity, a 10-fold quality improvement, and a 50% reduction in costs through the use of static verification methods.[6,7]

In the following sections we consider several ideas upon which static verification techniques are based. These concepts can help us in our effort to design correctness into our programs. They involve types of assertions that we can make about what our software is trying to do.

Assertions and Program Design An **assertion** is a statement that can be either true or false. We can make assertions about the state of the program. For instance, following the assignment statement

> **Assertion** A statement that is true or false but not both.

```
Sum := Part + 1;    -- Sum and Part are type Integer
```

we might assert: "The value of `Sum` is greater than the value of `Part`." That assertion might not be very useful or interesting by itself, but let's see what we can do with it. We can demonstrate that the assertion is true by making a logical argument: No matter what value `Part` has (negative, zero, or positive), when it is increased by 1, the result is a larger value. Now note what we *didn't* do. We didn't have to run a program containing this assignment statement to verify that the assertion was correct for many different values of `Part`.

The general concept behind formal program verification is that we can make assertions about what the program is intended to do, based on its specifications, and then prove through a logical argument (rather than through execution of the program) that a design or implementation satisfies the assertions. Thus the process can be broken down into two steps: (1) correctly asserting the intended function of the part of the program to be verified, and (2) proving that the actual design or implementation does what is asserted. The first step, making assertions, sounds as if it might be useful to us in the process of designing correct programs whether or not we intend to prove their correctness. After all, we already know that we cannot write correct programs unless we know what they are supposed to do. The second step provides the proof that our implementation was correct.

SPARK[8] is a programming language consisting of a set of annotations and a subset of Ada statements designed specifically for rigorous static analysis. Annotations are assertions that make clear the programmer's intentions. These annotations are read and checked against the Ada code by a static analysis tool called the Examiner. The Examiner alone reports on a wide variety of program errors. The Examiner can also generate conjectures (mathematical statements whose truth values are unknown) based on the

---

[6] P. Amey, "Correctness by Construction: Better Can Also Be Cheaper," *CrossTalk Journal*, vol. 15, no. 3, 2002, pp. 24–28.

[7] http://www.praxis-his.com/sparkada/pdfs/spark_c130j.pdf

[8] J. Barnes, *High Integrity Software: The SPARK Approach to Safety and Security* (London: Addison-Wesley, 2003).

Ada code and annotations. These conjectures can be verified (proven true) by human reasoning or through the use of tools (the Simplifier and the Proof Checker). Conjectures that cannot be verified are indicative of errors in the code.

SPARK proof annotations include preconditions, postconditions, loop invariants, type assertions, and the declaration of proof functions and proof types. We examine some of these forms of assertions in the following sections.

Preconditions and Postconditions Suppose we want to design a module (a logical chunk of the program) to perform a specific operation. To ensure that this module fits into the program as a whole, we must clarify what happens at its *boundaries*—what must be true when we enter the module and what is true when we exit.

To make the task more concrete, picture the design module as it is usually coded, as a procedure or function. To be able to call the procedure or function, we must know its exact interface: the name and the parameter list, which indicates its inputs and outputs. But this isn't enough: We must also know any assumptions that must be true for the operation to function correctly.

We call the assumptions that must be true when invoking the method **preconditions**. The preconditions are like a product disclaimer:

> **Precondition**   Assertions that must be true on entry into an operation for the postconditions to be guaranteed.

For instance, when we said earlier that following the execution of

```
Sum := Part + 1;
```

we can assert that `Sum` is greater than `Part`, there was an assumption—a precondition—that `Part` is not `Integer'Last`. If this precondition were violated, our assertion would not be true.

Previously we discussed the quality of program robustness, the ability of a program to catch and recover from errors. Although creating robust programs is an important goal, it is sometimes necessary to decide at what level errors are caught and handled. Using preconditions for an operation is similar to a contract between the programmer who creates the operation and the programmers who use it. The contract says that the programmer who creates the operation is going to assume that the preconditions hold—he or she will not write the code to check the operation's preconditions. It is up to the programmers who use the operation to ensure that it is never called without meeting the preconditions. In other words, the robustness of the system in terms of the operation's preconditions is the responsibility of the programmers who use it, and not the programmer who creates it. This approach is sometimes called "programming by contract." It can save work because trapping the same error conditions at multiple levels of a hierarchical system is redundant and unnecessary.

We must also know what conditions are true when the operation is complete. The **postconditions** are statements that describe the results of the operation. The postconditions do not tell us how these results are accomplished; they merely tell us what the results should be.

> **Postcondition** Assertions that describe what results are expected at the exit of an operation, assuming that the preconditions were true.

Let's consider what the preconditions and postconditions might be for another simple operation: an operation that deletes the last element from a list. (We are using "list" in an intuitive sense; we formally define it in Chapter 7.) Assuming the operation is defined within a class with the responsibility of maintaining a list, the specification for `Remove_Last` is as follows:

```
procedure Remove_Last (List : in out List_Type;  Value : out Element_Type);
-- Purpose         : Removes and returns the last element in this list
-- Preconditions   : List is not empty
-- Postconditions  : Value is the last element in the original List
--                   List is the original list with the last element removed
```

What do these preconditions and postconditions have to do with program verification? By making explicit statements about what is expected at the interfaces between modules, we can avoid making logical errors based on misunderstandings. For instance, from the precondition we know that we must check *outside* of this operation for the empty condition; this module *assumes* that there is at least one element.

Experienced software developers know that misunderstandings about interfaces to someone else's modules are one of the main sources of program problems. We use preconditions and postconditions at the operation level in this book, because the information they provide helps us to design programs in a truly modular fashion. We can then use the classes we've designed in our programs, confident that we are not introducing errors by making mistakes about assumptions and about what the classes actually do.

We wrote the preconditions and postconditions for procedure `Remove_Last` in English. English is often ambiguous, so when using a static analysis tool such as the SPARK Examiner, preconditions and postconditions must be written in the more formal language of predicates and qualifiers you learned (or will learn) in a course in discrete mathematics or discrete structures. The reward for taking the time to write more formal assertions is that the analysis tools can verify that the Ada code in the procedure body fulfills the stated postconditions.

Loop Invariants Taking our design process down a few more levels, we get into the actual control structures of the design: blocks of statements, branches, and loops. Loops are known troublemakers—sometimes they go on forever and sometimes they don't do what we meant them to do. They also have a bad habit of executing one too many times or one too few times.

Using an assertion called a loop invariant can help you design error-free loops. **Loop invariants** are assertions that must be true at the start of every iteration of the loop body and when the loop terminates. (The loop invariant must always be true; that's why it's called an invariant.) The loop invariant is not the same thing as the exit condition that controls the execution of the loop. The loop invariant also says something about the purpose and semantics (meaning) of the loop.

> **Loop invariant** An assertion of what must be true at the start of each loop iteration and on exit from the loop.

Let's look at an example. The following code fragment specifies a function that sums the values in an array of floating point numbers:

```
type Float_Array is array (Positive range <>) of Float;

function Sum (Numbers : in Float_Array) return Float;
-- Purpose        : Sum all of the elements in Numbers
-- Preconditions  : None
-- Postconditions : Sum is the sum of the elements in Numbers
```

Here is the function body that implements the specification. We have included a loop invariant.

```
function Sum (Numbers : in Float_Array) return Float is
   Result : Float;
begin
   Result := 0.0;
   for Index in Numbers'Range loop
   -- Loop Invariant : Result is the sum of all the elements in
   --                  Numbers(Numbers'First .. Index - 1)
      Result := Result + Numbers(Index);
   end loop;
   return Result;
end Sum;
```

This assertion is true at the beginning of the first iteration of this loop where `Index` is equal to `Numbers'First` because `Result` is 0, which is the sum of the elements in `Numbers(Numbers'First .. Numbers'First - 1)`. The index range in this array slice is a null range, so the array contains no elements. Trivially, the sum of no elements is zero.

This assertion is true at the beginning of the second iteration of this loop because `Result` is the sum of the elements in `Numbers(Numbers'First .. Numbers'First)`. The same logic can be used to reason that the assertion is true at the beginning of the third, fourth, and so on iterations.

After the final iteration of the loop, `Result` is the sum of the elements in `Numbers(Numbers'First .. Numbers'Last)`, which is equal to the sum of all the numbers in the array. The final value of the loop invariant shows that we accomplished what we intended.

Let's look at another example. The following code fragment specifies a function that returns the product of the first `Count` nonzero values in an array of integer numbers:

```
type Int_Array is array (Positive range <>) of Integer;

function Product (Numbers : in Int_Array;
                  Count   : in Positive) return Integer;
-- Purpose          : Calculate the product of the first Count non-zero
--                    elements in the array Numbers
-- Preconditions    : None
-- Postconditions   : If there are Count or more non-zero elements in
--                    Numbers, Product is the product of the first
--                    Count non-zero elements in Numbers.
--                    If there are fewer than Count non-zero elements in
--                    Numbers, Product is the product of all non-zero
--                    elements in Numbers
--                    If there are no non-zero elements in Numbers,
--                    Product is equal to 1
```

Here is the function body that implements the specification. We have not included a loop invariant this time.

```
-- First version
function Product (Numbers : in Int_Array;
                  Count   : in Positive) return Integer is
   Result         : Integer;
   Index          : Positive;
   Non_Zero_Count : Natural;
begin
   Result         := 1;
   Index          := Numbers'First;
   Non_Zero_Count := 0;
   loop
      exit when Non_Zero_Count = Count;
```

```ada
      if Numbers(Index) /= 0 then
         Result := Result * Numbers(Index);
         Non_Zero_Count := Non_Zero_Count + 1;
      end if;
      Index := Index + 1;
   end loop;
   return Result;
end Product;
```

The previous example of summing the values in an array used a `for` loop. Ada's `for` loops are deterministic—they are guaranteed to terminate. The loop in this example is a nondeterministic loop. It may be an infinite loop. Let's see whether the loop terminates. The exit condition says `Non_Zero_Count = Count` (because we want to calculate the product of the first 10 nonzero elements). `Non_Zero_Count` starts out at 0 and is incremented whenever the current list element is not 0. But we don't have any guarantees (no preconditions) that the list actually contains `Count` nonzero elements. If it doesn't, the loop tries to go on looking past the end of the array and raises CONSTRAINT_ERROR. (That's one way of terminating a loop!)

Let's try again, this time writing the invariant first. The invariant consists of all the assertions that must be true on entry into the loop body in order for it to work correctly. For instance, what do we know about `Index`? `Index` tells us how far we have processed in the array; therefore, its value must be within the range of index values on entrance to the loop. But there's nothing in the loop condition of our algorithm that addresses the issue of range! We have forgotten that we need a condition to stop when `Index` gets to the end of the array. The loop invariant is a good reminder: We can keep entering the loop while there are still elements to process. Here's the first part of the loop invariant: *Index may range from 1 .. Numbers'Last + 1.*

Why do we say *Numbers'Last + 1*? Remember that the loop invariant is true on exit from the loop, as well as on entrance to each iteration. The Boolean expression that controls the loop says to `exit when Index > Numbers'Last`. On entrance to each iteration, the loop invariant is true *and* the exit expression is false. Following the execution of the loop (`when Index = Numbers'Last + 1`), the exit expression is true, and the loop invariant is still true.

This part of the loop invariant, as we have phrased it above, is rather wordy. We express this idea (`Index` may range from 1 .. `Numbers'Last + 1`) more concisely as follows:

Loop Invariant Part 1: 1 ≤ `Index` ≤ `Numbers'Last` + 1

What about `Non_Zero_Count`? Before we talk about its range of values, let's ask ourselves what `Non_Zero_Count` means in the loop.

Loop Invariant Part 2: `Non_Zero_Count` = the number of nonzero elements in `Numbers(Numbers'First .. Index - 1)`

Coming into each iteration of the loop body, `Index` tells us which element is about to be processed, so `Non_Zero_Count` is the total number of nonzero elements in `Numbers(1 .. Index - 1)`. `Non_Zero_Count`, however, tells us how many nonzero elements have already been processed at the top of the loop, so when its value is 10 we want to exit the loop body. Here's another part of the loop invariant to indicate that `Non_Zero_Count` may range from 0 to 10:

Loop Invariant Part 3: $0 \leq$ `Non_Zero_Count` ≤ 10

This part of the loop invariant is true on exit from the loop, as well as on entrance to each iteration of the loop body. The associated exit expression, `Non_Zero_Count = 10`, must be false on entrance to each iteration, and is true on exit from the loop (assuming that there are 10 nonzero elements in the list).

Now that we understand the meanings of `Index` and `Non_Zero_Count`, we can also write the part of the loop invariant that defines `Product`.

Loop Invariant Part 4: `Product` = product of the nonzero elements in `Numbers(Numbers'First .. Index - 1)`

The revised function, including our four-part loop invariant, is as follows:

```ada
-- Corrected version
function Product (Numbers : in Int_Array;
                  Count   : in Positive) return Integer is
   Result         : Integer;
   Index          : Positive;
   Non_Zero_Count : Natural;
begin
   Result         := 1;
   Index          := Numbers'First;
   Non_Zero_Count := 0;
   loop
   -- Loop Invariant   Numbers'First <= Index <= Numbers'Last + 1   and
   --                  0 <= Non_Zero_Count <= Count                 and
   --                  Non_Zero_Count = number of non-zero values
   --                       in Numbers(Numbers'First .. Index - 1)    and
   --                  Product is the product of the non-zero
   --                       values in Numbers(Numbers'First .. Index - 1)
      exit when Index > Numbers'Last or Non_Zero_Count = Count;
      if Numbers(Index) /= 0 then
         Result := Result * Numbers(Index);
         Non_Zero_Count := Non_Zero_Count + 1;
      end if;
      Index := Index + 1;
   end loop;
   return Result;
end Product;
```

There still is one potential problem in functions `Sum` and `Product`: We have ignored the possibility that the value of the sum or the product of the numbers in the array might exceed `Float'Last` or `IntegerLast`. We can solve this overflow problem by expanding the loop invariants to include range conditions. This addition is best accomplished by using types with more restrictive ranges than the predefined types `Integer` and `Float`. In the next chapter we discuss how to create such types.

Design Review Activities

When an individual programmer is designing and implementing a program, he or she can find many software errors with pencil and paper. **Deskchecking** the design solution is a very common method of manually verifying a program. The programmer writes down essential data (variables, input values, parameters, and so on) and walks through the design, marking changes in the data on the paper. Known trouble spots in the design or code should be double-checked. A checklist of typical errors (such as loops that do not terminate, variables that are used before they are initialized, and incorrect order of parameters on operation calls) can be used to make the deskcheck more effective. A sample checklist for deskchecking an Ada program appears in Figure 1.9. A few minutes spent deskchecking your designs can save lots of time and eliminate difficult problems that would otherwise surface later in the life cycle (or even worse, would not surface until after delivery).

> **Deskchecking** Tracing an execution of a design or program on paper.
>
> **Walk-through** A verification method in which a team performs a manual simulation of the program or design.
>
> **Inspection** A verification method in which one member of a team reads the program or design line by line and the others point out errors.

Have you ever been really stuck trying to debug a program and showed it to a classmate or colleague who detected the bug right away? It is generally acknowledged that someone else can detect errors in a program better than the original author can. In an extension of deskchecking, two programmers can trade code listings and check each other's programs. Pair programming is an important part of an approach to software engineering called extreme programming. Pair programming teams up two software developers' efforts on a single workstation. One person, the driver, does the typing while the other, the navigator, provides guidance.

Most sizable computer programs are developed by teams of programmers. Two extensions of deskchecking that are effectively used by programming teams are design or code **walk-throughs** and **inspections**. These are formal team activities, the intention of which is to move the responsibility for uncovering bugs from the individual programmer to the group. Because testing is time-consuming and errors cost more the later they are discovered, the goal is to identify errors before testing begins.

In a walk-through, the team performs a manual simulation of the design or program with sample test inputs, keeping track of the program's data by hand on paper or a blackboard. Unlike thorough program testing, the walk-through is not intended to simulate all possible test cases. Instead, its purpose is to stimulate discussion about the way the programmer chose to design or implement the program's requirements.

The Design

1. Does each class in the design have a clear function or purpose?
2. Can large classes be broken down into smaller pieces?
3. Do multiple classes share common code? Is it possible to write more general classes to encapsulate the commonalities and then have the individual classes inherit from that general class?
4. Are all the assumptions valid? Are they well documented?
5. Are the preconditions and postconditions accurate assertions about what should be happening in the method they specify?
6. Is the design correct and complete as measured against the program specification? Are there any missing cases? Is there faulty logic?
7. Is the program designed well for understandability and maintainability?

The Code

1. Has the design been clearly and correctly implemented in the programming language? Are features of the programming language used appropriately?
2. Are operations coded to be consistent with the interfaces shown in the design?
3. Are the actual parameters on operation calls consistent with the parameters declared in the method definition?
4. Is each data object to be initialized set correctly at the proper time? Is each data object set correctly before its value is used?
5. Do all loops terminate?
6. Is the design free of "magic" values? (A magic value is one whose meaning is not immediately evident to the reader. You should use constants in place of such values.)
7. Does each constant, class, variable, and operation have a meaningful name? Are comments included with the declarations to clarify the use of the data objects?

Figure 1.9 *Checklist for deskchecking programs.*

At an inspection, a reader (never the program's author) goes through the requirements, design, or code line by line. The inspection participants are given the material in advance and are expected to have reviewed it carefully. During the inspection, the participants point out errors, which are recorded on an inspection report. Many of the errors have been noted by team members during their pre-inspection preparation. Other errors are uncovered just by the process of reading aloud. As with the walk-through, the chief benefit of the team meeting is the discussion that takes place among team members. This interaction among programmers, testers, and other team members can uncover many program errors long before the testing stage begins.

If you look back at Figure 1.8, you see that the cost of fixing an error is relatively inexpensive up through the coding phase. After that, the cost of fixing an error increases dramatically. Using the formal inspection process can clearly benefit a project.

Program Testing

Eventually, after all the design verification, deskchecking, and inspections have been completed, it is time to execute the code. We are ready to start testing with the intention of finding any errors that may still remain. Even if we have proven that our program matches its specification, we still need to validate it to ensure it fulfills its intended purpose.

The testing process is made up of a set of test cases that, taken together, allow us to assert that a program works correctly. We say "assert" rather than "prove" because testing does not generally provide a proof of program correctness.

The goal of each test case is to verify a particular program feature. For instance, we may design several test cases to demonstrate that the program correctly handles various classes of input errors. Or we may design cases to check the processing when a data structure (such as an array) is empty or when it contains the maximum number of elements.

For each test case we develop, we perform a series of tasks:

1. We determine a goal for a test case.
2. We determine inputs that demonstrate the goal of the test case.
3. We determine the expected behavior of the program for the given input.
4. We run the program and observe the resulting behavior.
5. We compare the expected behavior and the actual behavior of the program. If they are the same, the test case is successful. If not, an error exists, either in the test case itself or in the program. In the latter case, we begin debugging.

For now we are talking about test cases at a class, or operation, level. It's much easier to test and debug modules of a program one at a time, rather than trying to get the whole program solution to work all at once. Testing at this level is called **unit testing**.

> **Unit testing** Testing a class or operation by itself.
> **Functional domain** The set of valid input data for a program or operation.

How do we know what kinds of unit test cases are appropriate, and how many are needed? Determining the set of test cases that is sufficient to validate a unit of a program is in itself a difficult task. There are two approaches to specifying test cases: cases based on testing possible data inputs and cases based on testing aspects of the code itself.

Data Coverage In those limited cases where the set of valid inputs, or the **functional domain**, is extremely small, one can verify a program unit by testing it against every possible input element. This approach, known as *exhaustive testing*, can prove conclusively that the software meets its specifications. For instance, the functional domain of the following function consists of the values 1, 2, 3, 4, and 5:

```
type Door_Range is new Integer range 1..5;

function Odd (Doors : in Door_Range) return Boolean;
-- Determines whether Doors is an odd number
```

It makes sense to apply exhaustive testing to this function, because there are only five possible input values. In most cases, however, the functional domain is very large, so exhaustive testing is almost always impractical or impossible. What is the functional domain of the following method?

```
function Even (Item : in Integer) return Boolean;
-- Determines whether Item is an even number
```

It is not practical to test this function by running it with every possible data input; the number of elements in the set of integer values is clearly too large. In such cases, we do not attempt exhaustive testing. Instead, we pick some other measurement as a testing goal.

You can attempt program testing in a haphazard way, entering data randomly until you cause the program to fail. Guessing doesn't hurt, but it may not help much either. This approach is likely to uncover some bugs in a program, but it is very unlikely to find them all. Fortunately, however, there are strategies for detecting errors in a systematic way.

One goal-oriented approach is to cover general classes of data. You should test at least one example of each category of inputs, as well as boundaries and other special cases. For instance, in our `Even` function there are three basic classes of integer data: negative values, zero, and positive values. So, you should plan three test cases, one for each of these classes. You could try more than one test case in each of these three classes, but these additional cases probably won't find any additional errors. It is also a good idea to check the boundaries of the domain. We should test our `Even` function with `Integer'Last` and `Integer'First` to test the boundaries of the integer domain.

There are other cases of data coverage. For example, if the input consists of commands, you must test each command and varying sequences of commands. If the input is a fixed-sized array containing a variable number of values, you should test the maximum number of values; this is the boundary condition. A way to test for robustness is to try one more than the maximum number of values. It is also a good idea to try an array in which no values have been stored or one that contains a single element. Testing based on data coverage is called **black-box testing**. The tester must know the external interface to the module—its inputs and expected outputs—but does not need to consider what is being done inside the module (the inside of the black box).

Black-box testing Testing a program or operation based on the possible input values, treating the code as a "black box."

Clear (white) box testing Testing a program or operation based on covering all of the branches or paths of the code.

Branch A code segment that is not always executed; for example, a `case` statement has as many branches as there are case alternatives.

Code Coverage A number of testing strategies are based on the concept of code coverage, the execution of statements or groups of statements in the program. This testing approach is called **clear**(or **white**)**box testing**. The tester must look inside the module (through the clear box) to see the code that is being tested.

One approach, called *statement coverage*, requires that every statement in the program be executed at least once. Another approach requires that the test cases cause every **branch**, or code section, in the program to be executed. A single test case can achieve statement coverage of an *if-then* statement, but it takes two test cases to test both branches of the statement.

A similar type of code-coverage goal is to test program **paths**. A path is a combination of branches that might be traveled when the program is executed. In **path testing**, we try to execute all the possible program paths in different test cases.

The code-coverage approaches are analogous to the ways forest rangers might check out the trails through the woods before the hiking season opens. If the rangers wanted to test to

> **Path** A combination of branches that might be traversed during a single execution of a program or operation.
>
> **Path testing** A testing technique whereby the tester tries to execute all possible paths in a program or operation.
>
> **Test plan** A document showing the test cases planned for a program, class, or operation; their goals, inputs, expected outputs, and criteria for success.
>
> **Integration testing** Testing that is performed on combined program modules that already have been independently tested.

make sure that all the trails were clearly marked and not blocked by fallen trees, they would check each branch of the trails (see Figure 1.10[a]). Alternatively, if they wanted to classify each of the various trails (which may be interwoven) according to its length and difficulty from start to finish, they would use path testing (see Figure 1.10[b]).

These strategies lend themselves to measurements of the testing process. We can count the number of paths in a program, for example, and keep track of how many have been covered in our test cases. The numbers provide statistics about the current status of testing; for instance, we could say that 75% of the paths of a program had been executed. When a single programmer is writing a single program, such numbers may be superfluous. In a software development environment with many programmers, however, statistics like these are very useful for tracking the progress of testing. Testing in which goals are based on certain measurable factors is called *metric-based testing.*

Figure 1.10a *Checking out all the branches.*

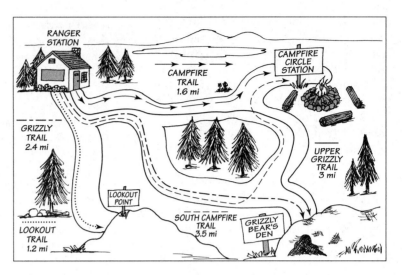

Figure 1.10b *Checking out all the trails.*

Test Plans Deciding on the goal of the test approach—data coverage, code coverage, or (most often) a mixture of the two—precedes the development of a **test plan**. Some test plans are very informal—the goal and a list of test cases, written by hand on a piece of paper. Even this type of test plan may be more than you have ever been required to write for a class programming project. Other test plans (particularly those submitted to management or to a customer for approval) are very formal, containing the details of each test case in a standardized format.

For program testing to be effective, it must be planned. You must design your testing in an organized way, and you must put your design in writing. You should determine the required or desired level of testing, and plan your general strategy and test cases before testing begins. In fact, planning for testing should be done at the same time requirements for the program are developed. Test-driven development (TDD) is an emerging technique for developing software. The first step in TDD is to develop the tests.

Bottom-Up and Top-Down Testing We can test a large, complicated program in a structured way through a method very similar to the approach used to design the program. The central idea is to divide and conquer—to test pieces of the program independently and then to use the parts that have been verified as the basis for the next test. The goal of this type of testing is to integrate the separately tested pieces, so it is called **integration testing**.

Using the bottom-up testing approach we verify the lowest level subprograms first, using **test driver** programs to call them. The test driver gets the test data and calls the operations being tested. It also provides written output about the effects of the operation calls, so that the tester can check the results. Sometimes test drivers are used to test hundreds or thousands of test cases. In such situations, it is best if the test driver reads the test

> **Test driver** A program that sets up the testing environment by declaring and assigning initial values to variables, then calling the operation to be tested.

data from a file and automatically verifies whether the test cases were handled successfully. There are even tools to assist you in writing test drivers. For example, AUnit is a set of Ada packages available under the General Public Licenses (GPL) that facilitates the writing and execution of test drivers.[9]

The test driver does not do any error checking to make sure that the inputs are valid. For instance, it doesn't verify that the input command code is really a legal command. Furthermore, it does not handle possible I/O exceptions; instead it just propagates them out to the run-time environment. Remember that the goal of the test driver is to act as a skeleton of the real program, not to be the real program. Therefore, the test driver does not need to be as robust as the program it simulates.

In top-down testing we check to see whether the overall logical design works and whether the interfaces between modules are correct. At each level of testing, this approach works on the assumption that the lower levels work correctly. We make this assumption by replacing the lower level subprograms with "placeholders" called **stubs**. A stub may consist of a single `Put` call, indicating that we have reached the procedure, or a group of debug `Put` calls, showing the current values of the parameters. It also should assign values to out mode parameters.

> **Stub** A special procedure or function that can be used in top-down testing to stand in for a lower level operation.

By now you probably are protesting that these testing approaches are a lot of trouble and that you barely have time to write your programs let alone "throwaway code" like stubs and drivers. Testing does require extra work. Test drivers and stubs are software items; they must be written and debugged themselves, even though you probably do not turn them in to a professor or deliver them to a customer. These programs are part of a class of software development tools that take time to create but are invaluable in simplifying the testing effort.

Test programs are like the scaffolding that a contractor erects around a building. It takes time and money to build the scaffolding, which is not part of the final product. But without it, the building could not be constructed. In a large program, where verification plays a major role in the software development process, creating these extra tools may be the only way to test the program.

Debugging with a Plan

Testing may indicate that our program contains errors. Debugging is the process of locating those errors. Once we find an error, correcting it may require us to change the program, the design, or even the specification.

Most Ada systems today have online debugging programs that make the debugging process much simpler. These programs usually allow you to execute one statement of your program at a time. This process is called *single stepping*. In addition, debugger programs usually let you set a *break point* at a particular statement in your program.

---

[9] https://libre2.adacore.com/aunit/

Execution of a program with one or more break points halts just before executing a statement that contains a break point. When your program is stopped between single steps or at a break point, the debugger program allows you to examine the value of variables. Learn how to use your debugger.

We find it helpful to develop a top-down debugging plan for each error encountered. Basically, we make a hypothesis (a guess) as to what is causing the error. We then use the debugger or debugging `Put` calls to "prove" or "disprove" our hypothesis. Here is our algorithm for debugging with key words for each step shown in bold:

1. Write down the **symptoms** of the error.
2. Write down your **hypothesis** (best guess) as to what could cause this error. At first this might just be the name of a package or procedure that you think is not functioning correctly. Later it may be a control structure or single statement.
3. Write down a list of **variables to examine** whose values show whether your hypothesis is right or wrong. Also write down where in the program these variables should be examined and what values they should contain. This step is like the test plans we discussed earlier.
4. **Test your hypothesis** by setting break points at the locations determined in step 3. Run the debugger and record the values of variables.
5. **Evaluate the evidence.**
   a. If the evidence indicates that your hypothesis is correct, look for the error at the location you hypothesized. If you can't see the error, start again at step 2 with a more specific guess. Narrow your focus to smaller control structures (from packages to subprograms to control structures to individual statements).
   b. If the evidence indicates that your hypothesis is not correct, you need to focus your attention on another part of the program. Return to step 2 and make another guess. If you can't make another guess, perhaps the error lies in your interpretation of the problem's specification or design. Review them and ask any questions you may have.

A warning about debugging: *Beware of the quick fix!* Program bugs often travel in swarms, so when you find a bug, don't be too quick to fix it and run your program again. Often as not, fixing one bug generates another. A superficial guess about the cause of a program error usually does not produce a complete solution. In general, the time it takes to consider all the ramifications of the changes you are making is time well spent.

If you constantly need to debug, there's a deficiency in your design process. The time spent considering all the ramifications of the design you are making is the best spent time of all.

Practical Considerations

It is obvious from this chapter that program verification techniques are time consuming and, in a job environment, expensive. It would take a long time to do all of the things discussed in this chapter, and a programmer has only so much time to work on any particular program. Certainly not every program is worthy of such cost and effort. How can you tell how much and what kind of verification effort is necessary?

A program's requirements may provide an indication of the level of verification needed. In the classroom, your professor may specify the verification requirements as part of a programming assignment. For instance, you may be required to turn in a written, implemented test plan. Part of your grade may be determined by the completeness of your plan. In the work environment, the verification requirements are often specified by a customer in the contract for a particular programming job. For instance, a contract with a customer may specify that formal reviews or inspections of the software product be held at various times during the development process.

A higher level of verification effort may be indicated for sections of a program that are particularly complicated or error-prone. In these cases, it is wise to start the verification process in the early stages of program development in order to prevent costly errors in the design.

A program whose correct execution is critical to human life is obviously a candidate for a high level of verification. For instance, a program that controls the return of astronauts from a space mission would require a higher level of verification than a program that generates a grocery list. As a more down-to-earth example, consider the potential for disaster if a hospital's patient database system had a bug that caused it to lose information about patients' allergies to medications. A similar error in a database program that manages a Christmas card mailing list, however, would have much less severe consequences.

Problem-Solving Case Study
Testing a Binary Search Operation

This section illustrates how you can use a combination of techniques to develop and verify a procedure to implement the binary search algorithm. As indicated in this chapter, you can apply verification techniques throughout the software development process. In order to test the procedure, we develop a set of test data that is sufficient to verify the procedure, as well as a test driver that inputs this data and calls the search procedure.

A search algorithm was chosen for this case study section because it is a nontrivial algorithm that you probably studied in your first course. Once this procedure has been designed, implemented, and verified, you can use it in other programs. Reusing pieces of software that have already been developed and tested is a very economical way to build programs. In order to use a procedure like this one in your own programs, however, you first must understand its interface—its inputs, outputs, and any assumptions about them. We document this interface with the following procedure specification:

```
type Integer_Array is array (Positive range <>) of Integer;

procedure Binary_Search (List     : in  Integer_Array;
                         Value    : in  Integer;
                         Location : out Natural);
```

```
-- Purpose        : Searches List for Value.  Location is the index of Value
--                  in List if found.  Otherwise returns zero for Location
-- Preconditions  : List is sorted in ascending order
-- Postconditions : List(Location) = Value  or  Location = 0
```

We now know what the procedure does, which is all that the caller of the procedure needs to know. We do not know how the search is done, however. Although this information isn't needed by the caller, it is quite valuable to the programmer, so let's talk a little about searching.

Searching

Given a sorted array of values and a particular value to search for, the first approach that comes to mind is the simplest: Compare `Value` to successive array elements, starting with the first element, and searching until (1) we find `Value`, (2) we pass `Value`'s place in the sorted list without finding it, or (3) there are no more elements in the array to examine. The advantage of this algorithm is its simplicity; you probably have written a similar sequential search procedure. The disadvantage is the need to check every element in the array until `Value` is found. For instance, if `Value` is the last element in a 100,000-element array, this searching algorithm needs to check all 100,000 elements before it finds `Value`.

The Binary Search Algorithm

Can't we do better than that? Think of how you might go about finding a name in a phone book, and you can get an idea of a faster way to search. Let's look for the name "Dale." We open the phone book to the middle and see that the names there begin with M. M is larger than D, so we search the first half of the phone book, the section that contains A to M. We turn to the middle of the first half and see that the names there begin with G. G is larger than D, so we search the first half of this section, from A to G. We turn to the middle page of this section and find that the names there begin with C. C is smaller than D, so we search the second half of this section—that is, from C to G—and so on, until we are down to the single page that contains the name Dale. A similar algorithm is illustrated in Figure 1.11.

Now that we are convinced of how terrific it is, let's design an algorithm for the binary search procedure.

Binary Search
Current Search Area is List(List'First..List'Last)
Found := False
loop
    exit when Current Search Area is empty or Found
    Find Midpoint of Current Search Area
    if Value = List(Midpoint) then
        Found := True
    elsif Value < List(Midpoint) then
        Current Search Area becomes the first half of Current Search Area
    else
        Current Search Area becomes the second half of Current Search Area
    end if

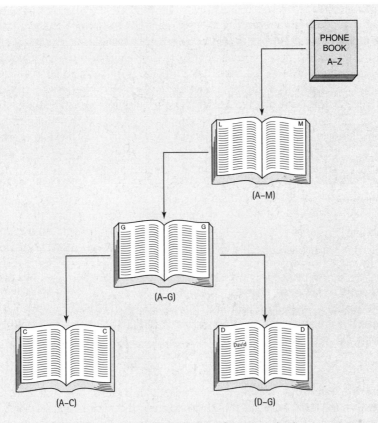

Figure 1.11   *A binary search of the phone book.*

```
end loop
if Found then
    Location := Midpoint
else
    Location := 0
end if
```

What do we mean by "Current Search Area"? We begin our search with the whole list to examine; that is, the current search area goes from List(List'First) to List(List'Last). In each iteration, we split the current search area in half at Midpoint, and if Value is not found there, we search the appropriate half. The part of the list being searched at any time is the current search area. For instance, in the first iteration of the loop, if Value is less than the element at Midpoint, the new current search area goes from index List'First to the Midpoint. If Value is greater than the element at Midpoint, the new search area goes from the Midpoint to index List'Last. Either way, the current search area has been split in half. It looks like we can keep track of the boundaries of the current search area with a pair of indexes, First_Index and Last_Index. In each iteration of the loop, if Value is not found, one of these indexes is reset to shrink the size of the current search area.

How do we know when to quit searching? There are two possible terminating conditions: (1) `Value` isn't in the list, or (2) `Value` has been found.

The first terminating condition, `Value` isn't in the list, occurs when there's no more to search in the current search area. This condition is a function of the values of `First_Index` and `Last_Index`, because these indexes define the current search area. If `First_Index < Last_Index`, there are still elements in the array to be examined. What if `First_Index = Last_Index`? `List(First_Index..Last_Index)` then would describe a range of array positions containing one element. As long as there is an element to examine, we continue the search. If `First_Index > Last_Index`, `List(First_Index..Last_Index)` is a null array; there are no elements in it, so our search is over.

The second terminating condition occurs when `Value` has been found. So the whole exit condition is (`First_Index > Last_Index`) or Found.

Does the loop terminate? Before entering the loop, `First_Index` is initialized to `List'First` and `Last_Index` to `List'Last`. In each iteration of the loop either `First_Index` or `Last_Index` is reset to redefine the current search area. Let's look again at this part of the algorithm.

```
elsif Value < List(Midpoint) then
    Current Search Area becomes the first half of Current Search Area
else
    Current Search Area becomes the second half of Current Search Area
```

If `Value` is less than the list element at `Midpoint`, we want to search the first half of the current search area. We can leave `First_Index` where it is, and move `Last_Index` to the `Midpoint`. Now we've cut the current search area in half. Similarly, if `Value` is greater than the `Midpoint` element, we can leave `Last_Index` where it is and move `First_Index` to the `Midpoint`.

```
elsif Value < List (Midpoint) then
    Last_Index := Midpoint
else
    First_Index := Midpoint
```

`First_Index` is getting bigger and `Last_Index` is getting smaller, so we know that they are heading toward each other. But do they ever pass each other? Uh-oh! What happens when `First_Index = Last_Index`? Now `Midpoint = First_Index = Last_Index`. We keep reassigning `First_Index` or `Last_Index` to the same value, and we find ourselves in an infinite loop!

At this point in the design we realize that, because we already know that `Value /= List(Midpoint)`, `Midpoint` shouldn't be in the new current search area. The correct design for updating the loop control variables is

```
elsif Value < List (Midpoint) then
    Last_Index := Midpoint - 1
else
    First_Index := Midpoint + 1
```

Now `First_Index` is *always* getting larger and `Last_Index` is *always* getting smaller, and eventually they must pass each other, so we know the loop terminates. The design seems to be in pretty good shape, so we're ready to translate our algorithm into Ada.

```ada
-- This procedure contains an error
procedure Binary_Search (List     : in  Integer_Array;
                         Value    : in  Integer;
                         Location : out Natural) is

   Found       : Boolean;   -- Has Value been found yet?
   Midpoint    : Natural;   -- Index of search area's midpoint
   First_Index : Natural;   -- First index in current search area
   Last_Index  : Natural;   -- Last index in current search area

begin
   Found       := False;
   First_Index := List'First;
   Last_Index  := List'Last;

   -- Search until element found or the current search area is empty.
   -- Current search area is List (First_Index..Last_Index)
   loop
      exit when First_Index > Last_Index  or  Found;
      -- Find middle element in the current search area.
      Midpoint := First_Index + Last_Index / 2;
      -- Compare Value to middle element in search area.
      if List(Midpoint) = Value then
         Found := True;
      elsif Value < List(Midpoint) then
         Last_Index := Midpoint - 1;   -- Search area now 1st half
      else
         First_Index := Midpoint + 1;  -- Search area now 2nd half
      end if;
   end loop;
   -- Set value of Location.
   if Found then
      Location := Midpoint;
   else
      Location := 0;
   end if;
end Binary_Search;
```

The Test Plan

Our next step is to determine what kind of inputs thoroughly test our search procedure. Several types of tests come to mind based on the procedure's parameters (data coverage) and from the code we wrote (code coverage). Searching for any `Value` in an empty `List` should result in a `Location` value of zero. There are two cases when searching a `List` containing only one element: Pick the `Value` that is in `List` and another that is not in `List`. Searching a `List` containing a number of elements has a number of different cases to test: `Value` in first list position, `Value` in some middle list position, `Value` in last list position, `Value` smaller than any list element, and `Value` greater than any list element. To make our tests easier to track, we document our planned inputs on a written test plan (see Figure 1.12). When we run the tests, we record the results in the remaining blanks.

The Test Driver

Now that we have decided on the data to test our binary search operation, we need to write a test driver so that we can execute our test plan. An execution of this program assigns values to `List` and `Value`, invokes the search routine, and displays the returned `Location`. Here is our test driver:

```ada
procedure Binary_Search_Test is

   subtype List_Type is Integer_Array (1..10);

   ----------------------------------------------------------------

   procedure Get_List (List  : out List_Type;
                       Count : out Natural) is
   begin
      Put_Line ("Enter number of test elements (0-10).");
      Get (Count);
      Put_Line ("Enter the test elements in order, one per line.");
      for Index in 1..Count loop
         Get (List(Index));
      end loop;
   end Get_List;

   ----------------------------------------------------------------

   Num_Elements : Natural;      -- number of elements to search
   List         : List_Type;    -- list of elements to search
   Search_Value : Integer;      -- value to search for in List
   Location     : Natural;      -- index of Value in List

begin
   Get_List (List => List, Count => Num_Elements);
   Put ("Input value for which to search: ");
   Get (Search_Value);
   Binary_Search (List     => List(1..Num_Elements),
                  Value    => Search_Value,
                  Location => Location);
```

1. Goal: Search of empty List
   Input: List = ( )   Value = 9
   Expected Result: Location = 0
   Actual Result: Location = _____
2. Goal: Successful search of single-element List
   Input: List = (4)   Value = 4
   Expected Result: Location = 1
   Actual Result: Location = _____
3. Goal: Unsuccessful search of single-element List
   Input: List = (4)   Value = 7
   Expected Result: Location = 0
   Actual Result: Location = _____
4. Goal: Successful search for the first element in multi-element List
   Input: List = (3, 5, 7, 9, 11, 13, 15, 17)   Value = 3
   Expected Result: Location = 1
   Actual Result: Location = _____
5. Goal: Successful search for a "middle" element in multi-element List
   Input: List = (3, 5, 7, 9, 11, 13, 15, 17)   Value = 9
   Expected Result: Location = 4
   Actual Result: Location = _____
6. Goal: Unsuccessful search for a "middle" element in multi-element List
   Input: List = (3, 5, 7, 9, 11, 13, 15, 17)   Value = 8
   Expected Result: Location = 0
   Actual Result: Location = _____
7. Goal: Successful search for last element in multi-element List
   Input: List = (3, 5, 7, 9, 11, 13, 15, 17)   Value = 17
   Expected Result: Location = 8
   Actual Result: Location = _____
8. Goal: Unsuccessful search for value less than the first value in multi-element List
   Input: List = (3, 5, 7, 9, 11, 13, 15, 17)   Value = 1
   Expected Result: Location = 0
   Actual Result: Location = _____
9. Goal: Unsuccessful search value greater than first value in multi-element List
   Input: List = (3, 5, 7, 9, 11, 13, 15, 17)   Value = 100
   Expected Result: Location = 0
   Actual Result: Location = _____

Figure 1.12   *Test plan for the binary search operation.*

```
      if Location /= 0 then
         Put ("Search value found at location ");
         Put (Item => Location, Width => 2);
      else
         Put ("Search value not found in list");
      end if;
      New_Line(2);
end Binary_Search_Test;
```

OK, let's run the program! Test cases 1–4 come out as expected. But test 5 goes into an infinite loop. What went wrong? The only loop is in the procedure `Binary_Search`. The exit condition in this loop depends upon the values of `First_Index` and `Last_Index`. The values of these two indices are modified by the calculated `Midpoint`. We need to examine these variables while running the data in test 5. We run the debugger and set a breakpoint on the line just after the value for `Midpoint` is calculated. Figure 1.13 shows the results of our debugging session.

Although the values of our variables seem reasonable during the first two iterations of the loop, clearly `Midpoint` is not being correctly calculated in the third iteration. After the fourth iteration, the three variables never change. Yet somehow test cases 1 through 4 managed to produce correct output! Looking back at the code for procedure `Binary_Search`, we see that the calculation of `Midpoint` indeed is incorrect.

```
Midpoint := First_Index + Last_Index / 2;
```

Ada's precedence levels require that we use parentheses around the addition operation.

```
Midpoint := (First_Index + Last_Index) / 2;
```

Can you see why test cases 1 through 4 produced the correct output despite the error uncovered by test case 5? We make the correction and run the rest of our test plan. We also rerun the tests that previously passed to make sure our correction has not introduced another problem. All of our tests succeed.

Programmers often are surprised to find errors in their programs, especially when they have designed them carefully. However, even with a good design, stupid bugs often are introduced in the coding phase, as we have seen here.

Here is the final, corrected version of procedure `Binary_Search`, which you can use in your programs:

```
-- This procedure no longer contains an error
procedure Binary_Search (List     : in  Integer_Array;
                         Value    : in  Integer;
                         Location : out Natural) is

   Found      : Boolean;    -- Has Value been found yet?
   Midpoint   : Natural;    -- Index of search area's midpoint
```

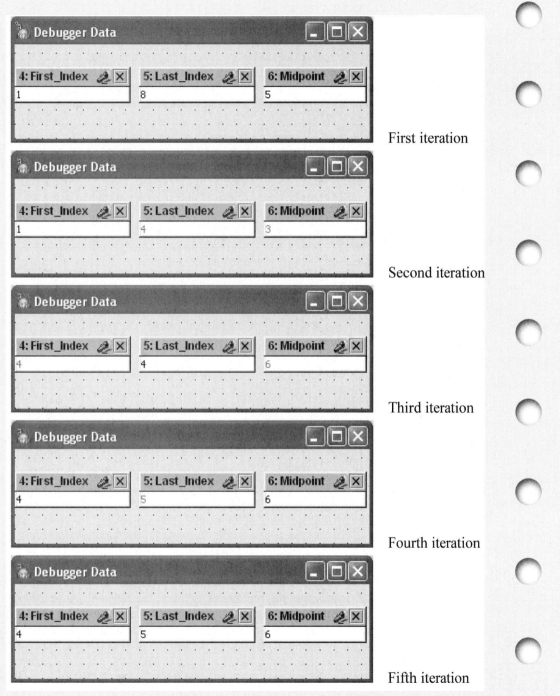

Figure 1.13 *Debugger data for binary search test case 5.*

```ada
      First_Index : Natural;   -- First index in current search area
      Last_Index  : Natural;   -- Last index in current search area

begin
   Found        := False;
   First_Index  := List'First;
   Last_Index   := List'Last;

   -- Search until element found or the current search area is empty.
   -- Current search area is List (First_Index..Last_Index)
   loop
      exit when First_Index > Last_Index  or  Found;
      -- Find middle element in the current search area.
      Midpoint := (First_Index + Last_Index) / 2;
      -- Compare Value to middle element in search area.
      if List(Midpoint) = Value then
         Found := True;
      elsif Value < List(Midpoint) then
         Last_Index := Midpoint - 1;   -- Search area now 1st half
      else
         First_Index := Midpoint + 1;  -- Search area now 2nd half
      end if;
   end loop;
   -- Set value of Location.
   if Found then
      Location := Midpoint;
   else
      Location := 0;
   end if;
end Binary_Search;
```

Summary

How are our quality software goals met by the strategies of abstraction and information hiding? When we hide the details at each level, we make the code simpler and more readable, which makes the program easier to write, modify, and reuse. Object-oriented design processes produce modular units that also are easier to test, debug, and maintain.

One positive side effect of modular design is that modifications tend to be localized in a small set of modules, and thus the cost of modifications is reduced. Remember that whenever we modify a module we must retest it to make sure that it still works correctly in the program. By localizing the modules affected by changes to the program, we limit the extent of retesting needed.

Finally, we increase reliability by making the design conform to our logical picture and delegating confusing details to lower levels of abstraction. By understanding the wide range of activities involved in software development—from requirements analysis through the maintenance of the resulting program—we gain an appreciation of a disciplined software engineering approach. Everyone knows some programming wizard who can sit down and hack out a program in an evening, working alone, coding without a formal design. But we cannot depend on wizardry to control the design, implementation, verification, and maintenance of large, complex software projects that involve the efforts of many programmers. As computers grow larger and more powerful, the problems that people want to solve on them also become larger and more complex. Some people refer to this situation as a software *crisis*. We'd like you to think of it as a software *challenge*.

It should be obvious by now that program verification is not something you begin the night before your program is due. Design verification and program testing go on throughout the software life cycle.

Verification activities begin when we develop the software specifications. At this point, we formulate the overall testing approach and goals. Then, as program design work begins, we apply these goals. We may use formal verification techniques for parts of the program, conduct design inspections, and plan test cases. During the implementation phase, we develop test cases and generate test data to support them. Code inspections give us extra support in debugging the program before it is ever run. Table 1.1 shows how the various types of verification activities fit into the software development cycle. Throughout the life cycle, one thing remains the same: The earlier in this cycle we can detect program errors, the easier (and less costly in time, effort, and money) they are to remove. Program verification is a serious subject; a program that doesn't work isn't worth the disk it's stored on.

Exercises

The Software Process

1. Explain what is meant by "software engineering."
2. Name three computer hardware tools that you have used.
3. Name two software tools that you have used in developing computer programs.
4. Explain what is meant in this chapter by "ideaware."
5. Which of these statements is always true?
    a. All of the program requirements must be completely defined before design begins.
    b. All of the program design must be complete before any coding begins.
    c. All of the coding must be complete before any testing can begin.
    d. Different development activities often take place concurrently, overlapping in the software life cycle.
6. Explain why software might need to be modified
    a. in the design phase.
    b. in the coding phase.

Table 1.1 *Life-Cycle Verification Activities*

Analysis	Make sure that requirements are completely understood.
	Understand testing requirements.
Specification	Verify the identified requirements.
	Perform requirements inspections with your client.
	Write test plan system functionality.
Design	Design for correctness (using assertions such as preconditions, postconditions, and loop invariants).
	Perform design inspections.
	Plan testing approach.
Code	Understand programming language well.
	Perform code inspections.
	Add debugging output statements to the program.
	Write test plan for unit testing of modules.
	Construct test drivers.
Test	Unit test according to test plan.
	Debug as necessary.
	Integrate tested modules.
	Retest after corrections.
Delivery	Execute acceptance tests of complete product.
Maintenance	Execute regression test whenever delivered product is changed to add new functionality or to correct detected problems.

    c. in the testing phase.

    d. in the maintenance phase.

7. Goal 1, "Quality software works," means that the program meets its _____, as documented in the software _____.

8. Name two ways in which you can make your programs meet Goal 2: "Quality software can be modified."

9. Goal 4 says, "Quality software is completed on time and within budget."

    a. Explain some of the consequences of not meeting this goal for a student preparing a class programming assignment.

    b. Explain some of the consequences of not meeting this goal for a team developing a highly competitive new software product.

    c. Explain some of the consequences of not meeting this goal for a programmer who is developing the user interface (the screen input/output) for a spacecraft launch system.

10. What is the first step in developing any software?
11. Software specifications tell exactly _____ a program does, but not _____.
12. Name three sections that you might see detailed in a software specification.
13. You are working on a class programming assignment, and the details of one of the requirements are ambiguous. What are some ways of dealing with this problem?
14. Your professor hands out a programming assignment that is supposed to be turned in at a Tuesday morning class 2 weeks from today. Your sister's wedding is the weekend before your program is due. Make up a schedule that allows you to get your program done without ruining the wedding weekend.

Program Design

15. For each of the following, describe at least two different abstractions for different viewers.
    a. A dress
    b. A key
    c. An aspirin
    d. A saxophone
    e. A carrot
    f. A piece of wood
16. Explain what is meant by "information hiding." Why is the following section of code an example of information hiding?

```
Tax := Rate * Taxable_Income;
Ada.Text_IO.Put ("Your tax liability is ");
Ada.Float_Text_IO.Put (Item => Tax, Fore => 6, Aft => 2, Exp => 0);
```

17. Hiding information is often considered morally wrong. Why is information hiding the right thing to do in software engineering?
18. Briefly describe four different kinds of stepwise refinement.
19. Name two kinds of diagrams that software engineers use to visualize designs.
20. Functional decomposition is based on a hierarchy of _____ whereas object-oriented design is based on a hierarchy of _____.
21. Object-oriented design is based on three inter-related constructs. Name and briefly describe each of these constructs.
22. A class definition includes _____ and _____ that determine the behavior of an object.
23. Write a list of oven attributes that are not relevant to cooking problems. Such attributes would not be included in a package specification for an oven class.

24. What is an Ada package?
25. Why are Ada packages written in two parts?
26. Find a tool that you can use to create UML class diagrams and re-create the diagram of the `Date` class shown in Figure 1.3.
27. a. What is a constructor?
    b. What is an observer?
    c. What is a transformer?
28. What is the difference between an object and a class? Give some examples.
29. Describe the concept of inheritance.
30. Given the `Date` and `Holiday_Date` classes defined in this chapter and the following declarations:

```
Birthday     : Date         := Construct_Date (December, 20, 1948);
Anniversary  : Date         := Construct_Date (June, 17, 1971);
Halloween    : Holiday_Date := Construct_Date (October, 31, 2007);

Day   : Day_Type;
Year  : Year_Type;
```

   indicate which of the following statements are legal and which are illegal. Explain your answers.

   a. `Day := Birthday.Day_Is;`
   b. `Year := Birthday.Day_Is;`
   c. `if Halloween.Is_Holiday then ...`
   d. `if Anniversary.Is_Holiday then ...`
   e. `Birthday := Anniversary;`
   f. `Birthday := Halloween;`

31. Explain how to use the nouns and verbs in the problem description to help identify candidate classes and operations.
32. *True or False?* There is usually one way of solving a problem that is clearly better than any other.
33. Write two additional scenarios for the automated teller machine described in this chapter.
34. Make a list of potential objects from the description of the automated teller machine scenario given earlier in this chapter.
35. The inheritance relationship is called an *is-a* relationship. In object-oriented design, inheritance is used to create more specialized subclasses from a more general superclass. For each of the following superclasses, determine three more specialized subclasses. For one of those subclasses, determine two even more specialized subclasses.
    a. Building
    b. Vehicle

    c. Geometric figure
    d. Cooking utensil
    e. Musical instrument
    f. Music
36. Draw a UML class diagram to illustrate the inheritance relationships between the classes in each of your answers to the previous question. Include only class names in your diagrams—do not include class attributes or operations.

Software Verification

37. *True or False?* (If the statement is false, correct the statement.)
    a. Software verification begins as soon as the program has been completely coded.
    b. "Program verification" and "testing" are the same thing.
    c. Testing is the only way to truly prove that a program is correct.
    d. Compile-time errors are usually easier to detect and to correct than run-time errors.
    e. Logical errors can usually be detected by the compiler.
38. Define the following terms:
    a. Testing
    b. Acceptance testing
    c. Regression testing
39. Explain the difference between program verification and program validation.
40. Have you ever written a programming assignment with an error in the specifications? If so, at what point did you catch the error? How damaging was the error to your design and code?
41. Explain why the cost of fixing an error is higher the later in the software cycle the error is detected.
42. Differentiate between a syntax error and a logical error in a program. When is each type of error likely to be found?
43. Explain how an expert understanding of your programming language can reduce the amount of time you spend debugging.
44. Give an example of a run-time error that might occur as the result of a programmer's making too many assumptions.
45. Define "robustness." How can programmers make their programs more robust by taking a defensive approach?
46. What is meant by "designing for correctness"?
47. Define the following terms:
    a. Static verification
    b. Dynamic verification
    c. Assertion

48. Name two kinds of assertions described in this chapter that can contribute to a correct design.
49. Procedure `Average` takes `Data_List`, a constrained array of floats, and `Element_Count`, an integer that tells how many elements are stored in the array. It returns the float number, `Data_Avg`, which is the average of the data stored in the array. Determine the preconditions and postconditions of this procedure.
50. Given the following preconditions and postconditions for procedure `Add_Element`, determine what would happen if we called `Add_Element` when the list was already full.

    ```
    --Preconditions:    Data_List is not full.

    --Postconditions:   Data_List = original Data_List plus new
                        element added
    ```

51. Define a "loop invariant."
52. Give the loop invariant in the following segments of code:

    ```
    Index := 1;
    Found := False;
    loop
    -- Loop Invariant : _____
        exit when (Index > Element_Count) or Found;
        if Data_List(Index) = Target_Value then
            Found := True;
        else
            Index := Index  1;
        end if;
    end loop;
    ```

    ```
    Quotient := 0;
    loop
        -- Loop Invariant : _____
        exit when Number < 5
        Number := Number - 5;
        Quotient   := Quotient + 1
    end loop;
    ```

```
Largest := Data(1);
Index   := 2;
loop
-- Loop Invariant : _____
   exit when Index > 100;
   if Data(Index) > Largest then
      Largest := Data(Index);
   end if;
   Index : Index + 1;
end loop;
```

53. Explain why the loop invariant contributes more to an understanding of the loop than does the condition on the exit statement alone.

54. Fill in the blanks with "True" or "False."

    On entrance to an iteration of the loop body, the loop invariant must be _____ and the Boolean expression (in the exit statement) may be _____ or _____. To exit from the loop, the loop invariant must be _____ and the Boolean expression (in the exit statement) must be _____.

55. Write the loop that is described by the following loop invariant:

    Loop Invariant: 1 <= Index <= Max_List + 1   and
                      0 is not found in List(1 .. Index - 1) and
                      Sum = Sum of List(1 .. Index - 1)

56. What is the purpose of conducting design and code inspections?

57. The following code fragment is intended to find the first array element with the value 0. It contains a logical error. As a member of the inspection team, you could save the programmer a lot of time by finding the errors during the inspection. Can you help? (Hint: Users of the previous release of this software complained that CONSTRAINT_ERROR was sometimes raised.)

```
Index := List'First;
loop
   exit when Index > List'Last  or  List (Index) = 0;
   Index := Index + 1;
end loop;
```

58. The following code fragment is intended to fill the array List with values from Data_File. The file contains one value per line.

```
Index := 0;
loop
   exit when Ada.Text_IO.End_Of_File (Data_File);
   Index := Index + 1;
   Ada.Integer_Text_IO.Get (File => Data_File,
                            Item => List (Index));
end loop;
```

a. Identify a logical error that could occur due to an incorrect assumption about the input file.

b. Add one line to the code fragment so that the assumption you identified in part (a) need not be made.

59. The following code fragment prints out 37 "good" values and then a screen full of garbage. What's wrong? Correct the problem.

```
for Index in 1 .. Max_List_Size loop
    Ada.Integer_Text_IO.Put (Item => List(Index));
end loop;
```

60. Is there any way a single programmer (for example, a student working alone on a programming assignment) can benefit from some of the ideas behind the inspection process?

61. When is it appropriate to start planning a program's testing?

a. During design or even earlier

b. While coding

c. As soon as the coding is complete

62. Differentiate between unit testing and integration testing.

63. Differentiate between "data coverage" and "code coverage" in program testing. Is one better than the other?

64. *True or False?* It is not a difficult task to test every possible input to a program in order to prove that it works correctly.

65. Describe a realistic goal-oriented approach to data-coverage testing of the procedure specified below:

```
procedure Find_Element (List    : in  Integer_Array;
                        Target  : in  Integer;
                        Index   : out Positive;
                        Found   : out Boolean);

-- Purpose:         Searches List for Target.
--
-- Preconditions:   The elements are in no particular order.
--                  List may be empty.
--
-- Postconditions:  Found = (Target was found in List).
--                  Index = array index of the element if Found
--                  Index = List'Last + 1 if not Found
```

66. A program is to read in a numeric score (0 to 100) and display an appropriate letter grade (A, B, C, D, or F).

a. What is the functional domain of this program?
b. Is exhaustive data coverage possible for this program?
c. Devise a test plan for this program.

67. Explain how paths and branches relate to code coverage in testing. Is 100% path coverage a realistic goal?
68. Differentiate between "top-down" and "bottom-up" integration testing.
69. You are writing a program that contains a loop controlled by a Boolean function Terminate_Loop:

```
loop
    exit when Terminate_Loop (Factor_1, Factor_2);
    -- body of loop action goes here
end loop;
```

You decide to work on testing the loop body, putting off testing the Terminate_Loop function until later. Write a stub for function Terminate_Loop.

70. Explain when a test driver is needed.
71. Explain why the preconditions in the following procedures are not needed:

   a.
   ```
   procedure Assert (Value : in Integer) is
   -- Precondition:  Value is a whole number
   ```

   b.
   ```
   subtype Dozen is Integer range 1..12;
       .
       .
       .
   procedure Eggs (Chicken: in Dozen) is
   -- Precondition:  Chicken is greater than zero
   ```

Programming Problems

72. You are the manager of a team of 10 programmers who have just completed a seminar in software engineering. To prove to your boss that these techniques pay off, you decide to run the following contest: You number the programmers 1 through 10, based on their performance in the seminar (1 is poorest, 10 is best) and monitor their work. As each does his or her part of your project, you keep track of the number of lines of debugged code turned in by each programmer. You record this number as a programmer turns in a debugged module. The winner of the contest is the first person to reach 1000 lines of debugged code. (You hope this is programmer #9 or #10.) As further proof of the value of these new techniques, you want to determine how many poor programmers it takes to surpass the winner's figure; that is, find the smallest k such that programmers 1 through k have turned in more lines than the winner.

Input

The input consists of a sequence of pairs of integers. The first integer in each pair is the programmer's number (an integer from 1 to 10), and the second is the number of lines of code turned in. The pairs occur in the same order as that in which the modules were turned in.

Processing/Output

Read in pairs of integers until someone's total goes over 1000. Display (echo print) each pair as you read it. Ignore any input after someone's total exceeds 1000. Then display a table listing the 10 programmers and their totals, with the winner flagged as shown in the example below. Finally, find the smallest k such that the sum of the totals for programmers $1 - k$ exceeds the winner's total. Print k in an explanatory sentence.

Sample Input

```
10    230
 8    206
 7    111
 3    159
 9    336
 1     51
10    250
 4    101
 9    341
 2    105
 8    256
10    320
 3    150
 5    215
 7    222
 9    400     #9 goes over 1000.
```

Sample Output

```
         PROGRAMMER PROGRESS
Programmer        Lines of Code
    10                  230         Echo print the first 16 pairs.
     .
     .
     9                  400

            FINAL TOTALS
Programmer        Lines of Code
     1                   51
     2                  105
```

```
           3                  309
           4                  101
           5                  215
           6                    0
           7                  333
           8                  462
           9                 1077      *** THE WINNER ***
          10                  800
```

```
It took programmers 1 through 7 to produce more than the
winner.
```

73. You are to design, code, and test a sequential search procedure; then you are to compare this procedure to the binary search that was developed in the Case Study of this chapter.

The Sequential Search

Given an array, `List` (sorted from smallest to largest), and a `Value` to search for, the sequential search uses the following approach: Compare `Value` to successive `List` elements, starting with the first element, and searching until (1) `Value` has been found, (2) we have passed `Value`'s place in the sorted list without finding it, or (3) there are no more elements in the array to examine. You must develop the algorithm using a loop invariant.

When you have finished coding the `Sequential Search` procedure, test it, using the test driver from the Case Study section. (Simply replace the call to `Binary Search` with a call to `Sequential Search`.)

Comparing the Search Procedures

To compare the two searching procedures, you should modify each procedure to count the number of comparisons made before `Value` is found. Using the test driver, search for values in various positions in the array, and for values that are not in the array, using each search procedure. Following each call to a search procedure, the search `Value`, location, and comparison count should be printed. These results should be printed in table format, with the following column headings:

```
                        Comparison Count
Value      Location    Binary Search    Sequential Search
```

Test Data

For more interesting results, you should increase the array size to 100, and fill the array. Remember that the values must be ordered from smallest to largest. Leave some gaps in the values, in order to search for medium-sized values that are not in the array. Because of the large array size, you should modify `Print_List` to print the elements vertically, not horizontally. You only need to print the list once, before you begin to search for values. Modify the test driver to print all data to a file, in addition to the screen. At the end of your experiment, make a hard copy of the file to turn in.

Conclusions

Compare the `Sequential Search` and `Binary Search` procedures in terms of lines of code and number of comparisons. Were the results of your experiment consistent with the discussion in the `Application` section?

Turn In

  a. The design of procedure `Sequential_Search`. (It must contain a loop invariant.)
  b. Listing of procedure `Sequential_Search`.
  c. Output from your comparison test runs.
  d. Your conclusions, in paragraph form.

74. Your assignment is to design, code, and test a sorting procedure that uses the insertion sort algorithm. The procedure sorts the integer elements in an array that has the following declaration:

```
type Int_Array is array (Positive range <>) of Integer;
```

The procedure has the following specifications:

```
procedure Sort List (List : in out Int_Array);
--Purpose:         Sort the elements in List from largest to smallest
                   value
--Preconditions:   1 <= List.Length
--Postconditions:  List(List'Range) are sorted in order of decreasing
                   size
```

The Insertion Sort Algorithm

The basic approach of the insertion sort is as follows: Each successive element in the list is inserted into its proper place relative to the other (already sorted) elements. We begin with the first element. There is only one element in the part of the list being examined, so it must be in its correct place. Now we put the second element in the list into its correct place, so that `List(1)` is larger than `List(2)`. (Note that they are not necessarily in their final positions in the sorted list; they are simply in their correct positions with respect to each other.) Then the value in the third array slot is put into its proper place, with respect to `List(1..3)`. This process continues until all the list elements have been sorted. The changing values of the arrays that follow illustrate the algorithm.

```
List'Length = 5
```

List	List	List	List	List
20	33	33	33	45
33	20	25	25	33
25	25	20	22	25
22	22	22	20	22
45	45	45	45	20

The sorting algorithm involves repeated examination of the elements in a list, which suggests the use of looping constructs. You should develop the design for procedure `Insertion_Sort` using loop invariants, then code the procedure.

Testing the Insertion Sort

Your next step is to create a test plan, showing the various test cases, along with inputs and expected outputs. Your grade is determined, in part, by the design of your test cases.

To test the procedure, you should write a batch test driver. Your test driver should set up the array with values as specified in the test plan and call the `Insertion_Sort` procedure. The values in the array should be printed before and after sorting. The number of times that you need to set up array data and call `Insertion_Sort` depends on the test cases in your test plan. Make sure that the output of each test case clearly identifies it by test number. Write a stub for procedure `Insertion_Sort` to use in testing the test driver.

When your test driver is debugged, you are to comment out the `Insertion_Sort` stub, and replace it with the actual `Insertion_Sort` procedure. Record the results of your tests on the test plan.

Turn In

   a. The design of procedure `Insertion_Sort`. (It must include loop invariants for any loops.)
   b. The test plan, with results recorded.
   c. Listing of the test driver and `Insertion_Sort`. The stub for `Insertion_Sort` and the debugging `Puts` should be in the listing, commented out.

Data Design and Implementation

Goals for this chapter include that you should be able to
- define data type
- explain the difference between an atomic data type and a composite data type
- explain the difference between scalar and discrete types
- understand and use Ada's built-in scalar data types to accurately model scalar objects
- understand and use record discriminants and tagged records
- understand the concepts of information hiding and encapsulation
- use Ada's packages and child packages to create your own classes and subclasses
- define and describe the benefits of using an abstract data type (ADT)
- describe an ADT from three perspectives: logical level, application level, and implementation level
- use Ada's private types to encapsulate the internal details of a class
- explain when an abstract data object (singleton class) is appropriate

This chapter centers on data and the language structures used to organize data. When problem solving, the way you view the data of your problem domain and how you structure the data that your programs manipulate greatly influence your success. In this chapter you learn how to deal with the complexity of your data using abstraction and how to use the Ada language mechanisms that support data abstraction.

We first cover the various data types supported by Ada. We explain why you would want to create your own types beyond those directly provided by language and how to do so. Designing and implementing classes is the essence of object-oriented software development. We also demonstrate the use of Ada's tagged types and packages.

2.1 Different Views of Data

Data Types

> **Data** The representation of information in a manner suitable for communication or analysis by humans or machines.
>
> **Data type** A category of data characterized by the supported elements of the category (its domain) and the supported operations on those elements.
>
> **Scalar data type** A data type in which the values are ordered and each value is atomic.

When we talk about the function of a program, we usually use words like *add*, *read*, *multiply*, *write*, *do*, and so on. The function of a program describes what it does in terms of the verbs in the programming language. The **data** are the nouns of the programming world: the objects that are manipulated, and the information that is processed by a computer program.

Humans have evolved many ways of encoding information for analysis and communication, for example letters, words, and numbers. In the context of a programming language, the term *data* refers to the representation of such information, from the problem domain, by the data types available in the language.

A **data type** can be used to characterize and manipulate a certain variety of data. It is formally defined by describing:

1. The collection of elements that it can represent (the domain)
2. The operations that may be performed on those elements

Most programming languages provide simple data types for representing basic information—types like integers, real numbers, and characters. For example, an integer might represent a person's age; a real number might represent the amount of money in a bank account. An integer data type in a language would be formally defined by listing the range of numbers it can represent and the operations it supports, usually the standard arithmetic operations.

Integer types, real types, and character types have two properties in common. Each is made up of indivisible or atomic elements and each is ordered. Data types with these properties are called **scalar data types**.

When we say atomic, we mean that it has no component parts that can be accessed independently. For example, the string "Good Morning" is not atomic because it is com-

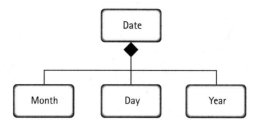

Figure 2.1 *A UML diagram showing composition.*

posed of individual characters that can be accessed through indexing or slicing operations. When we say that the values are ordered, we mean that exactly one of the relations <, >, or = is true for any pair of values.

Integer and character data types have an additional property: Each value (except the first) has a unique predecessor, and each value (except the last) has a unique successor. Types with this property are called **discrete data types**. They are also known as *ordinal data types*.

> **Discrete (ordinal) data type** A scalar data type in which each value (except the first) has a unique predecessor and each value (except the last) has a unique successor.
>
> **Composite data type** A data type whose elements are composed of multiple data items.

Real number types are not discrete because a value has no unique predecessor or successor. Asking what is the next number after 4.2 is meaningless.

Programming languages provide ways for a programmer to combine scalar types into more complex structures, which can capture relationships among the individual data items. For example, a programmer can combine two real values to represent a point in the *x-y* plane or create a list of integer numbers to represent the scores of a class of students on a multiple choice quiz. A data type composed of multiple values is called a **composite type**. Ada's type `String` is a composite data type. It is composed of multiple characters. The array type and record type provide mechanisms for building our own composite types in the Ada language.

The Unified Modeling Language (UML) provides the composition association to show a whole-part relationship. Figure 2.1 shows a UML diagram for the date record we defined in Chapter 1. The solid diamond indicates that Date is *composed of* a Month, a Day, and a Year. We can also read this association the other way—a Year is *part of* a Date. In a composition association, the whole owns its parts. This statement means that if the whole object is copied or deleted, its parts are copied or deleted.

Data Abstraction

In a sense, any data processed by a computer, whether atomic or composite, are just a collection of bits that can be turned on or off. The computer itself needs to have data in this form. Human beings, however, tend to think of information in terms of somewhat larger units like numbers and lists, and thus we want at least the human-readable portions of our programs to refer to data in a way that makes sense to us. To

> **Data abstraction** The separation of a data type's logical properties from its implementation.

separate the computer's view of data from our own, we use **data abstraction** to create another view.

Many people feel more comfortable with things that they perceive as real than with things that they think of as abstract. Thus, data abstraction may seem more forbidding than a more concrete entity like an integer. Let's take a closer look, however, at that very concrete—and very abstract—integer you've been using since you wrote your earliest programs. Just what is an integer? Integers are physically represented in different ways on different computers. In the memory of one machine, an integer may be a binary-coded decimal. In a second machine, it may be a sign-and-magnitude binary. And in a third one, it may be represented in two's-complement binary notation. Although you may not be familiar with these terms, that hasn't stopped you from using integers. (You can learn about these terms in an assembly language or computer organization course, so we do not explain them here.) Figure 2.2 shows some different representations of an integer.

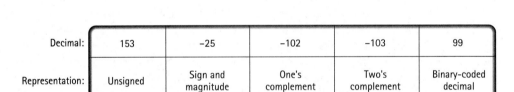

Decimal:	153	−25	−102	−103	99
Representation:	Unsigned	Sign and magnitude	One's complement	Two's complement	Binary-coded decimal

Figure 2.2 *Some decimal equivalents of an 8-bit binary number.*

The way that integers are physically represented determines how the computer manipulates them. As an Ada programmer, however, you don't usually get involved at this level; you simply use integers. All you need to know is how to declare an `Integer` type variable and what operations are allowed on integers: assignment, addition, subtraction, multiplication, division, remainder arithmetic, and so on.

Consider the statement

```
Distance := Rate * Time;
```

It's easy to understand the concept behind this statement. The concept of multiplication doesn't depend on whether the operands are, say, integers or real numbers, despite the fact that integer number multiplication and real number multiplication are implemented in very different ways. Computers would not be very popular if every time we wanted to multiply two numbers we had to get down to the machine-representation level. But we don't have to: Ada has provided the `Integer` data type for us, hiding all the implementation details and giving us just the information we need to create and manipulate data of this type.

We say that Ada has encapsulated integers for us. Think of the capsules surrounding the medicine you get from the pharmacist when you're sick. You don't have to know anything about the chemical composition of the medicine inside to recognize the big blue-and-white capsule as your antibiotic or the little yellow capsule as your decongestant. **Data encapsulation** means that the physical representation of a program's data is hidden by the language. The programmer using the data doesn't see the underlying implementation, but deals with the data only in terms of their logical picture—its abstraction.

Data encapsulation The hiding of the representation of data from the applications that use the data at a logical level; a programming language feature that enforces information hiding.

But if the data are encapsulated, how can the programmer get to them? Operations must be provided to allow the programmer to create, access, and change the data. Let's look at the operations Ada provides for the encapsulated data type Integer. First of all, you can create variables of type Integer using declarations in your program. Then you can assign values to these integer variables by using the assignment operator and perform arithmetic operations on them using +, -, *, /, and rem. Figure 2.3 shows how Ada has encapsulated the type Integer in a nice neat black box.

The point of this discussion is that you have been dealing with a logical data abstraction of integer since the very beginning. The advantages of doing so are clear: You can think of the data and the operations in a logical sense and can consider their use without having to worry about implementation details. The lower levels are still there—they're just hidden from you.

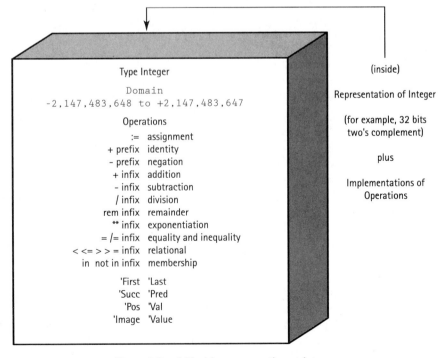

Figure 2.3 *A black box representing an integer.*

> **Abstract data type (ADT)** A data type whose properties (domain and operations) are specified independently of any particular implementation.

Remember that the goal in design is to reduce complexity through abstraction. We extend this goal with another: to protect our data abstraction through encapsulation. We refer to the set of all possible values (the domain) of an encapsulated data "object," plus the specifications of the operations that are provided to create and manipulate the data, as an **abstract data type (ADT)**.

In effect, all of Ada's built-in types are ADTs. An Ada programmer can declare variables of those types without understanding the underlying implementation. The programmer can initialize, modify, and access the information held by the variables using the provided operations.

In addition to the built-in ADTs, Ada programmers can use Ada features such as type extension (inheritance), generic units, and packages to build their own ADTs. For example, the `Date` class defined in Chapter 1 can be viewed as an ADT. Yes, it is true that the programmers who created it need to know about its underlying implementation; for example, they need to know that a `Date` is a record composed of an enumeration field and two integer fields, and they need to know the names of those fields. The application programmers who use the `Date` class, however, do not need this information. They only need to know how to create a `Date` object and how to invoke `Date` operations to use the object.

Data Structures

> **Data structure** A collection of data elements whose logical organization reflects a structural relationship among the elements. A data structure is characterized by accessing operations that are used to store and retrieve the individual data elements.

A single integer can be very useful if we need a counter, a sum, or an index in a program. But generally, we must also deal with data that have many parts and complex interrelationships among those parts. We use a language's composite type mechanisms to build structures, called **data structures**, that mirror those interrelationships. The data elements that make up a data structure can be any combination of atomic types, unstructured composite types, and structured composite types.

When designing our data structures we must consider how the data are used because our decisions about what structure to impose greatly affect how efficient it is to use the data. Computer scientists have developed classic data structures, such as lists, stacks, queues, trees, and graphs, through the years. They form the major area of focus for this textbook.

In languages like Ada, which provide an encapsulation mechanism, it is best to design our data structures as ADTs. We can then hide the detail of how we implement the data structure inside a package that provides operations for using the structure.

As we saw in Chapter 1, the basic operations that are performed on encapsulated data can be classified into categories. We have already seen three of these: constructor, transformer, and observer. As we design operations for data structures, a fourth category becomes important: iterator. Let's take a closer look at what each category does.

- A *constructor* is an operation that creates a new instance (object) of the data type. A constructor that uses the contents of an existing object to create a new object is called a *copy constructor.*
- *Transformers* (sometimes called *mutators*) are operations that change the state of one or more of the data values, such as inserting an item into an object, deleting an item from an object, or making an object empty.
- An *observer* is an operation that allows us to observe the state of one or more of the data values without changing them. Observers come in several forms: *predicates* that ask if a certain property is true, *accessor* or *selector* operations that return a value based on the contents of the object, and *summary* operations that return information about the object as a whole. A Boolean operation that returns True if an object is empty and False if it contains any components is an example of a predicate. An operation that returns a copy of the last item put into a structure is an example of an accessor method. An operation that returns the number of items in a structure is a summary method.
- An *iterator* is an operation that allows us to process all the components in a data structure sequentially. Operations that return successive list items are iterators.

Data structures have a few features worth noting. First, they can be "decomposed" into their component elements. Second, the organization of the elements is a feature of the structure that affects how each element is accessed. Third, both the arrangement of the elements and the way they are accessed can be encapsulated.

Note that although we design our data structures as ADTs, data structures and ADTs are not equivalent. We could implement a data structure without using any data encapsulation or information hiding whatsoever (but we won't!). Also, the fact that a construct is defined as an ADT does not make it a data structure. For example, the Date class defined in Chapter 1 implements a Date ADT, but that is not considered to be a data structure in the classical sense. There is no structural relationship among its three components.

Data Levels

In modeling data in a program, we wear many hats. We must determine the abstract properties of the data, choose the representation of the data, and develop the operations that encapsulate this arrangement. During this process, we consider data from three different perspectives, or levels:

1. *Logical (or abstract) level:* An abstract view of the data values (the domain) and the set of operations to manipulate them. At this level, we define the ADT.
2. *Application (or user) level:* A way of modeling real-life data in a specific context; also called the problem domain. Here the application programmer uses the ADT to solve a problem.
3. *Implementation level:* A specific representation of the structure to hold the data items, and the coding of the operations in a programming language. This is how we

actually represent and manipulate the data in memory: the underlying structure and the algorithms for the operations that manipulate the items on the structure. For the built-in types, this level is hidden from the programmer.

An ADT specifies the logical properties of a data type separate from its implementation. The implementation provides a specific representation for the elements of the data type such as a set of atomic variables, an array, or even another ADT. A third view of an ADT is how it is used in a program to solve a particular problem; that is, its application. If we were writing a program to keep track of student grades, we would need a list of students and a way to record the grades for each student. We might take a by-hand grade book and model it in our program. The operations on the grade book might include adding a name, adding a grade, averaging a student's grades, and so forth. Once we have written a specification for our grade-book data type, we must choose an appropriate data structure to use to implement it and design the algorithms to implement the operations on the structure.

An Analogy

Let's look at a real-life example: a library. A library can be decomposed into its component elements: books. The collection of individual books can be arranged in a number of ways, as shown in Figure 2.4. Obviously, the way the books are physically arranged on the shelves determines how one would go about looking for a specific volume. The particular library we're concerned with doesn't let its patrons get their own books. If you want a book, you must give your request to the librarian, who gets the book for you.

The library "data structure" is composed of elements (books) with a particular interrelationship; for instance, they might be ordered based on the Dewey decimal system. Accessing a particular book requires knowledge of the arrangement of the books. The library user doesn't have to know about the structure because in this example it is encapsulated: Users access books only through the librarian. The physical structure and abstract picture of the books in the library are not the same. The online catalog provides logical views of the library—ordered by subject, author, or title—that are different from its underlying representation.

We use this same approach to data structures in our programs. A data structure is defined by (1) the logical arrangement of data elements, combined with (2) the set of operations we need to access the elements. Let's see what our different viewpoints mean in terms of our library analogy.

At the application level, there are entities like the Library of Congress, the Dimsdale Collection of Rare Books, the Austin City Library, and the Cedar Falls Public Library.

At the logical level, we deal with the "what" questions. What is a library? What services (operations) can a library perform? The library may be seen abstractly as "a collection of books" for which the following operations are specified:

- Check out a book.
- Check in a book.
- Reserve a book that is currently checked out.
- Pay a fine for an overdue book.
- Pay for a lost book.

All over the place (unordered)

Alphabetical order by title

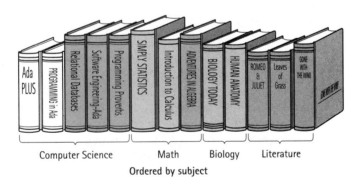
Ordered by subject

Figure 2.4 *A collection of books ordered in different ways.*

How the books are organized on the shelves is not important at the logical level, because the patrons in our library don't actually have direct access to the books. The abstract viewer of library services is not concerned with how the librarian actually organizes the books in the library. The library user only needs to know the correct way to invoke the desired operation. For instance, here is the user's view of the operation to check in a book:

Present the book at the check-in window of the library from which the book was checked out and receive a receipt with a possible overdue fine amount.

At the implementation level, we deal with the answers to the "how" questions. How are the books cataloged? How are they organized on the shelf? How does the librarian process a book when it is checked in? For instance, the implementation information might include the fact that the books are cataloged according to the Dewey decimal system and arranged in four levels of stacks, with 14 rows of shelves on each level. The librarian needs such knowledge to be able to locate a book. This information also includes the details of what happens when each of the operations takes place. For example, when a book is checked back in, the librarian may use the following algorithm to implement the check-in operation:

Check In Book
Examine due date to see whether the book is late.
if book is late
    Calculate fine.
    Issue receipt with amount of fine.
else
    Issue receipt with zero fine.
end if
Update library records.
Check reserve list to see if someone is waiting for the book.
if book is on reserve list
    Put the book on the reserve shelf.
else
    Replace the book on the proper shelf, according to the Dewey decimal system.
end if

All this, of course, is invisible to the library user. The goal of our design approach is to hide the implementation level from the user.

Picture a wall separating the application level from the implementation level, as shown in Figure 2.5. Imagine yourself on one side and another programmer on the other side. How do the two of you, with your separate views of the data, communicate across this wall? Similarly, how do the library user's view and the librarian's view of the library come together? The library user and the librarian communicate through the data abstraction. The abstract view provides the specification of the accessing operations without telling how the operations work. It tells what but not how. For instance, the abstract view of checking in a book can be summarized in the following procedure specification:

```
procedure Check_In_Book (Library : in out Library_Type;
                        Book    : in     Book_Type;
                        Fine    :    out Dollars);
  -- Purpose         : Check in a book, return amount of fine
  -- Preconditions   : Book was checked out of this Library
  -- Postconditions  : Contents of Library are the original contents plus Book
  --                   Fine is amount of money due (may be zero)
  -- Exceptions      : CLOSED is raised if the library is not open
```

2.1 Different Views of Data

Figure 2.5 *Communication between the application level and the implementation level.*

The only communication from the user into the implementation level is in terms of parameter specifications and allowable assumptions—the preconditions of the accessing routines. The only output from the implementation level back to the user is the transformed data structure described by the output specifications, or postconditions, of the routines, or the possibility of an exception being raised. Remember that exceptions are extraordinary situations that disrupt the normal processing of the operation. The abstract view hides the underlying structure but provides functionality through the specified accessing operations.

Although in our example there is a clean separation, provided by the library wall, between the use of the library and the inside organization of the library, there is one way that the organization can affect the users—efficiency. For example, how long does a user have to wait to check out a book? If the library shelves are kept in an organized fashion, as described above, then it should be relatively easy for a librarian to retrieve a book for a customer and the waiting time should be reasonable. On the other hand, if the books are just kept in unordered piles, scattered around the building, shoved into corners and piled on staircases, the wait time for checking out a book could be very long. But in such a library it sure would be easy for the librarian to handle checking in a book—just throw it on the closest pile!

The decisions we make about the way data are structured affect how efficiently we can implement the various operations on that data. One structure leads to efficient implementation of some operations, whereas another structure leads to efficient implementation of other operations. Efficiency of operations can be important to the users of the data. As we look at data structures throughout this textbook we discuss the benefits and drawbacks of various design structure decisions. We often study alternative organizations, with differing efficiency ramifications.

When you write a program as a class assignment, you often deal with data at each of our three levels. In a job situation, however, you may not. Often you may program an application that uses an abstract data type that has been implemented by another programmer. Sometimes you may collaborate with team members to develop the logical view of an abstract data type. Other times you may implement the structure and code the operations defined in a logical view. In this book we ask you to move back and forth between these levels.

2.2 Ada's Built-In Types

Figure 2.6 shows the relationships among Ada's built-in data types. You are probably already familiar with both composite types (array and record) and many of the scalar types. Each type comes with a set of operators (such as :=, <, and +) and a set of attributes (such as 'Image and 'Pos). Attributes are operations that return information about a property of a type. Together the operators and attributes define the set of operations available for the type.

The hierarchy displayed in this figure is similar to a class inheritance hierarchy. Type Boolean *is an* enumeration type. An enumeration type *is a* discrete type, and so on. As we move down the hierarchy, each type becomes more specialized through restrictions in its domain and the availability of additional operations. For example, all atomic types have assignment and equality operations. By adding the property of order to their domains, scalar types are more specialized than atomic types. Scalar types have the operations of atomic types plus the relational operations.

In the following sections, we review many of the built-in types shown in Figure 2.6. We could discuss them from the point of view of all three of the levels defined in the previous section. The application level includes the rules for declaring and using variables of the type, in addition to considerations of what the type can be used to model. You have prior experience with most of the built-in types in the applications you wrote, however, so we spend very little time discussing the application.

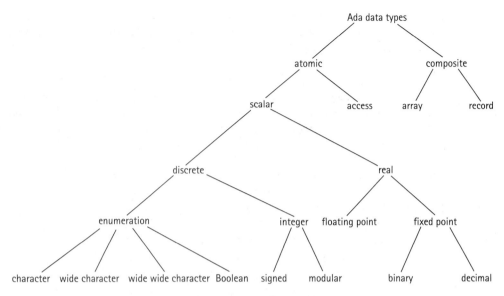

Figure 2.6 *Ada data types.*

We therefore do not look at the implementation level for the built-in types, because the Ada environment hides it and we, as programmers, do not need to understand this level in order to use the built-in types.

We therefore will spend most of our time discussing the logical or abstract level. This level involves understanding the domain of the data type and the operations that can be performed on data of that type.

Scalar Types

We can write a better model of our problem, and thus a better program, if we use data types that accurately reflect the nature of the data in a particular problem. One research study on the nature of costly software faults indicates that poor models of scalar quantities were responsible for nearly 90% of the errors in the cases studied.[1]

One of Ada's greatest strengths is that it allows programmers to create their own scalar data types that accurately model the scalar values in the problem domain. Although we won't say that using well-designed scalar types will eliminate 90% of costly faults, they certainly give us a valuable tool for the production of quality software. We use a **type declaration** to create new data

> **Type declaration** The association of a type identifier with the definition of a new data type.

---

[1]M. Eisenstadt, "My Hairiest Bug War Stories," *Communications of the ACM*, vol. 40, no. 4, 1997, pp. 30–37. An analysis of the war story raw data made available by the author showed that 88% of the "hairy" programming errors studied were due to problems with scalar values.

types. In the type declaration, the programmer describes the domain of the new data type and assigns it a name. A type's operations depend on the kind of type. In the next sections we discuss the kinds of scalar types available to us and their operations.

Signed Integer Types   You are already familiar with the built-in discrete type Integer and have probably used it in applications whenever a whole number type was needed. Type Integer is a signed integer type. Its domain and operations are listed in Figure 2.3 earlier in this chapter. Because the domain of Integer is large and varies from computer to computer, it is usually not a good model for an application. For example, one of the attributes of a car class might be the number of doors. By using type Integer on a computer with an Intel Pentium processor to represent this value, we are saying that a car can have between −2,147,483,648 and +2,147,483,647 doors. No error will be reported when a programmer accidentally creates a car with −3,142 doors. He may spend hours debugging his program to discover this fault.

By defining our own signed integer type with a domain suited to the application, Ada can detect out of range errors. Here is the declaration of a better type for our car application, and an example of using it in the declaration of a variable:

```
type Car_Door_Type is range 2..6;

Doors : Car_Door_Type;
```

The domain of this new type is constrained to the whole numbers 2 through 6. Should we attempt to assign the value −3,142 to variable Doors, Ada will raise the exception CONSTRAINT_ERROR. All signed integer types have the same operations as type Integer.

Our new type not only gives us out of range protection, but also prevents us from performing inappropriate operations. For example, given the additional declarations

```
type Cup_Holder_Type is range 1..30;

Cup_Holders : Cup_Holder_Type;
```

the Ada compiler will generate a syntax error for the assignment statement

```
Cup_Holders := 2 * Cup_Holders + Doors;   -- Type conflict
```

indicating that we are adding two incompatible types.

> **Explicit type conversion**   The conversion of a value from one type to another type. Also called *casting*.

Of course there are times when the incompatibility of different types is not desirable. In such cases we can use an **explicit type conversion** to convert a value from one type to another. For example, suppose we are looking for a new car and want to assign a rating to each model under consideration. Further suppose that we desire a car with a powerful engine, many doors, and few cup holders, resulting in a rating formula expressed by the following assignment statement:

```
Rating := Integer(Horsepower) + 3 * Integer(Doors) - 15 * Integer(Cup_Holders);
```

The numeric values for `Horsepower`, `Doors`, and `Cup_Holders` are each converted to `Integer` and combined using `Integer` multiplication, addition, and subtraction. The result is assigned to the `Integer` variable `Rating`.

Modular Integer Types A signed integer type may include both negative and positive numbers in its domain. The domain of a modular integer type is restricted to non-negative values. Modular integer types are often called *unsigned integer types*. There are three reasons for using a modular integer type instead of a signed integer type. First, we can store larger values in a modular integer type. For example, if we use 32 bits to store our integers, the largest signed integer possible is +2,147,483,647 whereas the largest modular integer is 4,294,967,295.

Second, all arithmetic operations with modular integer types use modular arithmetic. Modular arithmetic is a very handy tool discovered by C.F. Gauss at the beginning of the 19th century. It is extremely important in the field of cryptography. Sometimes called *clock arithmetic*, modular arithmetic is done with numbers on a circle rather than on a number line. As you know, three hours after 11 o'clock is 2 o'clock.

Third, the logical operators `and`, `or`, `xor`, and `not` are available for modular integer types. These operations are carried out on a bit-by-bit basis, using the binary representation of the value of the operands to yield a binary representation for the result, where zero represents `False` and one represents `True`. Bitwise operations are useful when your program needs to interact directly with hardware.

Let's look at some examples. Here are the declarations of two modular integer types and variables:

```ada
type Clock is mod 12;      -- Domain is 0 to 11
type Byte  is mod 256;     -- Domain is 0 to 255

Time     : Clock;
Register : Byte;
```

The number after `mod` in these declarations is called the *modulus*. The modulus must be a positive number. Its upper bound is machine dependent. The domain of a modular integer type is the set of values from 0 to one less than the modulus. Here are some examples of modular arithmetic. The result assigned to each variable is given in the comment.

```ada
Time := 10 + 5;            -- Assigns 3 to Time
Time := 11 * Time;         -- Assigns 9 to Time
Time := 5 - (3 * 5);       -- Assigns 2 to Time

Register := Byte'Last;     -- Assigns 255 (last value in the domain) to Register
Register := Register + 1;  -- Assigns 0 to Register
```

How did we determine what value gets assigned in these examples? Simply do the arithmetic as signed integers and divide the result by the modulus to obtain a remainder. If the remainder is non-negative, it is the final result. If the remainder is negative (as in the third example above) add the modulus to the remainder to get the final result.

Let's look at some examples to illustrate the use of logical operators with modular integers. If you have done any assembly language programming, these operations should look familiar. The `or` operator is used to set bits in a variable to one. The `xor` operator is used to change bits—if a bit is one it is changed to zero and if a bit is zero it is changed to one. The `and` operator is used to clear bits (set them to zero).

```
Register := 170;                      -- 170 base 10 is 10101010 base 2    Register is 10101010
Register := Register or 2#00000110#;  -- Set bits 1-2                      Register is 10101110
Register := Register xor 2#00000111#; -- Change bits 0-2                   Register is 10101001
Register := Register and 2#00111111#; -- Clear bits 6-7                    Register is 00101001
```

> **Bit mask** A pattern of binary values that is combined with some value using bitwise `or`, `and`, or `xor` to set, clear, or change specific bits in the value.

The literal values on the right of our logical operators are used to specify what bits we want to modify in our variable `Register`. They are called **bit masks**. We have expressed our bit masks as base two integer literals to make their effect more obvious. We could have used decimal literals or variables for our bit masks.

Enumeration Types An enumeration type is a discrete type whose domain is an ordered set of identifiers. We define this set by listing (enumerating) the values. Here is the enumeration type we used in the `Date` class in Chapter 1 and a variable declaration:

```
type Month_Type is (January, February, March, April, May, June, July,
                    August, September, October, November, December);
Month : Month_Type;
```

The assignment operator, equality testing operators, and relational operators may all be used with enumeration values. We cannot use the arithmetic operators with enumeration values. It makes no sense to multiply `September` by `December`. Two important attributes for enumeration types are `'Pred` and `'Succ` for determining the predecessor and successor of an enumeration value. Recall that unique predecessors and successors is one of the defining characteristics of discrete types. Here are some examples to illustrate the use of these attributes:

```
Month := April;
Month := Month_Type'Pred(Month);      -- Assigns March to Month
Month := Month_Type'Succ(October);    -- Assigns November to Month
```

The built-in type `Character` is an enumeration type with 256 different values; the built-in type `Wide_Character` is an enumeration type with 65,536 characters. For those needing a character set with even more values, the built-in type `Wide_Wide_Character` provides 2,147,483,648 different values.

The built-in type `Boolean` is an enumeration type with a domain of two values. In addition to the operators available for all enumeration types, `Boolean` types have the logical operators `and`, `or`, `xor`, and `not`.

Real Types Real numbers are far more difficult to use in programs than integer numbers. We need to understand a little about the implementation of these types to use them properly. The basic problem is the great quantity of these numbers. Although there are only 10 whole numbers between 1 and 10, there are an infinite number of real numbers between 1 and 10. What we end up doing is representing and storing only a small fraction of these real numbers exactly. These numbers are called the **model numbers**. The remaining real numbers are rounded or truncated to the closest model number. Thus, for most real numbers we store only an approximation in the computer's memory.

> **Model number** A real number that is represented exactly.
>
> **Absolute error** The difference between the real number and the model number used to represent it.
>
> **Relative error** The absolute error divided by the true value of the real number.

Because the real numbers in our programs are only approximations of the numbers in the application domain, our calculated results will always have some error. The study of these errors is an important part of the discipline of numerical analysis. Famous examples of software failure due to ignoring real number errors include the splashdown of several Mercury space program capsules a considerable distance away from their computed landing points and the 1991 failure of a Patriot missile defense system to recognize an approaching Scud missile that killed 28 soldiers.

We can measure error in two ways. An **absolute error** is the difference between the real number and the model number used to represent it. For example, when we say that our measurement is off by a quarter of an inch, we are expressing an absolute error. A **relative error** is the absolute error divided by the true value of the real number. A relative error describes what fraction of the value is in error. A relative error is often expressed as a percentage. When we say our measurement is off by 3.2% we are expressing a relative error.

In the next sections we discuss the two primary means of representing real numbers: floating point and fixed point. Each method defines a different set of model numbers and therefore yields a different set of errors.

Floating Point Types Floating point is the most common method for representing real numbers in the computer's memory. A floating point type uses a fixed number of digits (the mantissa) and a base raised to a power (the exponent) to approximate a real number. Here is an example:

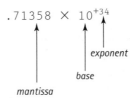

The base need not be 10. In fact, today 2 is nearly universal as the base used for floating point numbers. Scientific notation, a decimal form of floating point, illustrates the origin of the term *floating*. All of the following are representations of the same number:

$$.0512 \times 10^9 \quad .512 \times 10^8 \quad 5.12 \times 10^7 \quad 51.2 \times 10^6 \quad 512. \times 10^5$$

The decimal point may float to any position. When the decimal point floats to the right, we decrease the exponent to compensate. When it floats to the left, we increase the exponent.

The distance between model floating point numbers depends on the value of the exponent. When the exponent is small, the distance between model numbers is small and when the exponent is large, the distance between model numbers is large. Thus the maximum absolute error is small when the exponent is small and large when the exponent is large. However, because it involves a division by the actual value, the maximum relative error is the same throughout the range.

This distribution of model numbers gives us a guideline for selecting floating point for an application. If relative error is more important than absolute error for the real numbers in your application, use floating point types.

Ada's predefined type Float is, as its name implies, a floating point type. Like type Integer, the built-in type Float has a wider range than needed by most applications. We can create our own floating point type to more accurately model our problem. To create our own floating point type, we supply two pieces of information to specify its domain: the number of *digits of precision* and an optional *range*. Here are two examples:

```
type Inches is digits 4 range 0.00..100.00;
type Feet   is digits 6 range 0.00..1000.00;
```

We specified four digits of precision for type Inches and six digits of precision for type Feet.

The computer is limited to a finite number of digits. Thus, floating point values only approximate the real numbers we wish to store. For example, it requires an infinite number of digits to store the value of π exactly. If we need to use π in a problem, we must decide how many digits to use for our approximation of π.

Digits of Precision	Approximation of π
3	3.14
4	3.141
5	3.1416
6	3.14159

Determining the number of digits of precision to use in a floating point type declaration can be a difficult task for beginning programmers. You may learn more about errors and precision of floating point numbers in future courses. Or you may need to ask someone with more expertise in numerical analysis. For now, just use some common sense when selecting the number of digits. Ask yourself, how precise is my data? For example, suppose we need a type for length data. The length measurements are made with a high quality ruler. Realistically, we can expect readings between 00.00 and 12.00 inches and four digits of precision. Why not five digits of precision (00.000 to 12.000 inches)? The human eye can't resolve one one-thousandth of an inch with an ordinary ruler. Using five digits of precision for this data misrepresents the true precision of the measurements; it gives the idea that the measurements are accurate to one one-thousandth of an inch.

Fixed Point Types   Although the point in a floating point number is free to move (with an appropriate change in the exponent), the point in a fixed point number is always in the same place. A consequence of fixing the point is that the distance between model numbers is constant throughout the range. Thus, the maximum absolute error is constant. However, because the relative error involves a division by the actual value, this error varies throughout the range. The maximum relative error decreases with increasing number size.

Again, the distribution of model numbers gives us a guideline for selecting fixed point for an application. If absolute error is more important than relative error in your application, use fixed point types.

As shown in Figure 2.6, Ada provides two kinds of fixed point types: binary fixed point and decimal fixed point. We'll first look at binary fixed point types.

There is one binary fixed point type predefined in Ada. Type `Duration` is used for representing seconds of time. The Ada designers decided to use a fixed point type for time rather than a floating point type because with time measurements, knowing the maximum absolute error is more important than knowing the maximum relative error. `Duration` has a maximum absolute error of 50 microseconds (0.00005 seconds) and a minimum range of $-86{,}400.0$ to $+86{,}400.0$. (86,400 is the number of seconds in 24 hours.)

We can also define our own binary fixed point types. We need to specify a maximum absolute error (the distance between model numbers) called `delta` and a range. Here are two examples:

```
type Meters   is delta 0.001 range -1000.0..1000.0;
type Degrees  is delta 0.25  range 0.0..100.0;
```

`Meters` is a binary fixed point type with an accuracy of at least one one-thousandth of a meter. `Degrees` is a binary fixed point type with an accuracy of at least one quarter of a degree. We say *at least* in each of these descriptions because the Ada compiler may select a smaller error value. In particular, it will pick a value for `delta` that is a power of 2. For `Meters` it will pick a delta of 2^{-10}, which is 1/1024, and for `Degrees` it will pick 2^{-2}, which is 1/4.

Neither floating point numbers nor binary fixed point numbers are appropriate for currency values. Both of these types are based on the binary number system. Certain decimal fractions cannot be represented exactly in binary. For example, we cannot represent 3 cents exactly in binary. Translating this decimal value yields a never-ending binary value.

$$0.03_{10} = 0.0000011110101110000101000111101011100000101\ldots_2$$

There is a second problem with using floating point numbers for currencies. The absolute error of a floating point number depends upon the size of the number. Bigger numbers have bigger absolute errors. Financial calculations require a known absolute error rather than a known relative error. We want our accounts to be balanced to the nearest cent regardless of the amount of money in the account.

Decimal fixed point types provide a known absolute error and exact storage of decimal fractions. These are the types you want to use in financial calculations. There are no predefined decimal fixed point types in Ada. We can, of course, define our own decimal fixed point types. Here are two example declarations:

```
type Euro is delta 0.01 digits 8 range 0.0 ..   100_000.0;
type Peso is delta 0.1  digits 9 range 0.0 ..10_000_000.0;
```

The number after `delta` specifies the precision of the decimal number. This precision must be a power of 10, such as 100.0, 10.0, 1.0, 0.1, 0.01, or 0.001. All values of the type are multiples of this number, so every `Peso` value is a multiple of tenths of a Peso and every `Euro` value is a multiple of hundredths of a Euro. Another way of saying this is that `Peso`s are stored exactly to the nearest tenth and `Euro`s to the nearest hundredth. The number after `digits` specifies the total number of decimal digits used to represent the number.

Together the precision and digits determine the maximum range for the type. With a precision of 0.1 and 9 digits, the maximum range of `Peso` is −99,999,999.9 to +99,999,999.9. With a precision of 0.01 and 8 digits, the maximum range of `Euro` is −999,999.99 to +999,999.99. As illustrated in the above examples, we can include an optional `range` clause in our declaration. The Ada compiler issues an error message if you attempt to specify a `range` that is greater than the maximum allowed by the specified `delta` and `digits`.

After seeing the representational problems present in binary real numbers, why would we choose to use floating point numbers rather than decimal fixed point numbers when we need real numbers in our programs? Historically, floating point representation has been the most common method for storing real numbers. Nearly every programming language uses floating point to represent real numbers. The COBOL programming language, commonly used in financial applications, is a notable exception. Because of the widespread use of floating point types, most of today's CPUs execute floating point operations very quickly. In fact, a common measurement of CPU performance is mega FLOPS (Millions of FLoating point OPerations per Second). Performance of decimal operations depends on the underlying implementation.[2] Ada's decimal operations are typically faster than floating point operations.

---

[2]Binary coded decimal (BCD) and scaled integers are two commonly used methods for representing decimal numbers on a binary computer.

Composite Types

A single integer can be very useful if we need a counter, a sum, or an index in a program, but generally we also must deal with objects that have lots of parts. As we stated earlier in this chapter, such types are called composite types. A composite type gathers together a set of component values. Ada supplies two predefined composite types that contain multiple values: the array and the record.

Arrays   A one-dimensional array is the natural structure for the storage of lists of like data elements such as grocery lists, price lists, lists of phone numbers, and lists of student records. You have probably used one-dimensional arrays in similar ways in some of your programs. You will probably find the review of arrays given in this brief section easier to read if you keep the textbook from which you first learned Ada nearby.

Here is an example showing the declaration of an array of 10 integers indexed from 2 to 11:

```
type Index_Range is range 2..11;
type Number_Array is array(Index_Range) of Integer;

Numbers : Number_Array;
```

A one-dimensional array is a composite data type made up of a finite, fixed-size collection of ordered homogeneous elements to which there is direct access. *Finite* indicates that there is a last element. *Fixed size* means that the size of the array must be known when the array variable is created, but it doesn't mean that all of the slots in the array must contain meaningful values. *Ordered* means that there is a first element, a second element, and so on. (It is the relative position of the elements that is ordered, not necessarily the values stored there.) Because the elements in an array must all be of the same type, they are physically *homogeneous*; that is, they are all of the same data type. In general, it is desirable for the array elements to be logically homogeneous as well—that is, for all of the elements to have the same purpose. (If we kept a list of numbers in an array of integers, with the length of the list—an integer—kept in the first array slot, the array elements would be physically, but not logically, homogeneous.)

The component selection mechanism of an array is *direct access*, which means we can access any element directly, without first accessing the preceding elements. The desired element is specified using an index, which gives its relative position in the collection.

The semantics (meaning) of the component selector is "Locate the element associated with the index expression in the collection of elements identified by the array name." Suppose, for example, we are using an array of integers, called numbers, with 10 elements. The component selector can be used in two ways:

1. It can be used to specify a place into which a value is to be copied, such as

    ```
    Numbers(2) := 5;
    ```

2. It can be used to specify a place from which a value is to be retrieved, such as

    ```
    Value := Numbers(4);
    ```

If the component selector is used on the left-hand side of the assignment statement, it is being used as a transformer: The storage structure is changing. If the component selector is used on the right-hand side of the assignment statement, it is being used as an observer: It returns the value stored in a place in the array without changing it.

Declaring an array and accessing individual array elements are operations predefined in nearly all high-level programming languages. Ada has several additional operations. It allows us to access groups of consecutive elements in an array. These groups of elements are called *slices*. A slice is specified by giving a range rather than a single subscript. For example, the expression

```
Numbers(3..6)
```

specifies an array of four elements. We may use a slice of an array just as we would an entire array.

Other operations predefined by Ada for entire arrays include

Assignment	:=	
Equality testing	= /=	
Relational testing	< <= > >=	Only for arrays with discrete components
Logical	and or xor not	Only for arrays with Boolean components
Attributes (most common)	'First 'Last 'Range 'Length	

Let's look at one more of Ada's array features. *Array aggregates* provide a convenient way to assign values to an array object. The following examples illustrate the use of aggregates in assignment statements:

```
Numbers := (57, 3, 212, 16, 92, 43, 82, 423, 21, 101);

Numbers := (Index_Type => 0);
```

Records Records are very useful for modeling objects that have a number of characteristics. The record data type allows us to collect various types of data about an object and to refer to the whole object by a single name. We also can refer to the different attributes or fields of the object by name. You probably have seen many examples of records used in this way to represent objects.

The record is not available in all programming languages. FORTRAN, for instance, historically has not supported records; newer versions may. However, COBOL, a business-oriented language, uses records extensively. In the C and C++ languages records are called structs.

A record is a composite data type made up of a finite collection of not necessarily homogeneous elements called *fields*. Accessing is done directly through a set of named field *selectors*. The record is an *unstructured* composite type—we select a field by its name, not by its position. We illustrate the syntax and semantics of the component selector within the context of the following declarations:

```
type     Year_Type    is range 1912..2050;
subtype  Maker_String is String (1..10);
type     Dollars      is delta 0.01 digits 8 range 0.00 .. 100_000.00;

type Car_Rec is
   record
      Year  : Year_Type;
      Maker : Maker_String;
      Price : Dollars;
   end record;

My_Car : Car_Rec;
```

The record variable `My_Car` is made up of three components. The first, `Year`, is a signed integer type. The second, `Maker`, is an array data type (`String` is a predefined array of characters). The third component, `Price`, is a decimal fixed point number. The names of the components make up the set of selectors. A picture of `My_Car` appears in Figure 2.7.

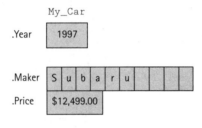

Figure 2.7 `My_Car`.

The syntax of the accessing function is the record variable name, followed by a period, followed by the field selector for the component you are interested in:

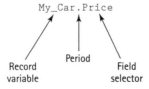

If this expression is on the right-hand side of an assignment statement, a value is being extracted from that place. Such an operation is an observer. For example:

```
Price_Paid := My_Car.Price;
```

If it is on the left-hand side, a value is being stored in that field of the record. This operation is a transformer. For example:

```
My_Car.Price := 12_499.00;
```

The `My_Car.Maker` field is an array whose elements are of type `Character` (Ada's predefined type `String`). You can access that array field as a whole (`My_Car.Maker`), or you can access individual characters or a slice of characters by using an index or range with the field as shown here:

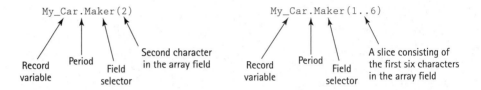

In addition to field selection, Ada provides two other operations for records.

Assignment   :=
Equality testing   = /= Two records are equal if their corresponding fields are equal.

Records are the basic building blocks for data structures. In the next two sections we look at two options that expand the power of the record.

Discriminant A special field in a record declaration that allows us to use the record declaration for different kinds or sizes of objects.

Record Discriminants The declaration of a record type may include one or more discriminants. A **discriminant** is a special field in the record declaration that allows us to use that one record declaration for different kinds of objects. Like any field in a record, the discriminant is declared with a type. The type of a discriminant is restricted; it must be a discrete type.

We develop a simple list data structure to illustrate the use of the discriminant. Here are the necessary declarations:

```
type Array_Type is array (Positive range <>) of Integer;   -- unconstrained array

type List_Type (Max_Size : Positive) is
   record
      List_Count : Natural := 0;                 -- number of slots used
      Elements   : Array_Type (1..Max_Size);     -- constrained array type
   end record;

Small_List  : List_Type (Max_Size => 10);        -- 10 element maximum
Medium_List : List_Type (Max_Size => 100);       -- 100 element maximum
Large_List  : List_Type (Max_Size => 1000);      -- 1000 element maximum
```

The first declaration here is for an unconstrained array type—an array type for which the index range has not been specified. Only the type of the index and the type of the components are given for an unconstrained array type. The symbol <> is called "box."

The identifier Max_Size given in parentheses after the record identifier List_Type is a discriminant. It is declared as Positive, a built-in subtype of Integer. This discriminant is used in the declaration of field Elements. In particular, it is used as the upper bound in the range constraint supplied for the unconstrained type Array_Type.

Now look at the variable declarations of the variables Small_List, Medium_List, and Large_List. Each of these declarations includes a value to be used for Max_Size. The syntax for assigning a value to the discriminant is the same as for associating formal and actual procedure parameters. We use named association here for extra clarity, but you also may use positional association. When these three variable declarations are elaborated, Ada allocates 10 elements for Small_List's array, 100 elements for

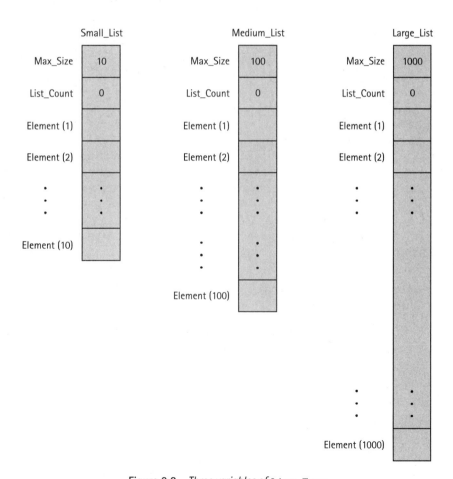

Figure 2.8 *Three variables of* List_Type.

`Medium_List`'s array, and 1000 elements for `Large_List`'s array. We have used one record type to declare three different sizes of objects. Figure 2.8 illustrates these three variables. Notice that each record variable is a different size and that the discriminant, `Max_Size`, is stored as the first field in all of these records.

We could accomplish the same results by declaring three different record types, one with an array of 10 elements, one with an array of 100 elements, and one with an array of 1000 elements. The advantage to using the record with a discriminant is much more than the savings in typing declarations. We can use the record with a discriminant as a formal parameter. This allows us to pass any of the three list variables to the same procedure. Here's an example:

```
procedure Put_List (List : in List_Type) is
begin
   for Index in 1..List.List_Count loop
      Put (List.Elements(Index));
      New_Line;
   end loop;
end Put_List;
   .
   .
   .
Put_List (List => Small_List);      -- Calls to procedure Put_List
Put_List (List => Medium_List);     -- with three different "kinds"
Put_List (List => Large_List);      -- of list records
```

If we declared three different list records rather than one record with a discriminant, we would have to write a separate `Put_List` procedure for each of the three different list types. We use records like this extensively for defining data structures.

One final note on discriminants: The value of a record discriminant may be accessed like any other component in the record. For example, the following statement displays the value 100:

```
Ada.Integer_Text_IO.Put (Item  => Medium_List.Max_Size,
                         Width => 5);
```

However, once you have given the record discriminant a value in the declaration of a record object, you may not change it.[3] Thus, the following statement is illegal:

```
Medium_List.Max_Size := 200;   -- Illegal attempt to change a
                               discriminant
```

---

[3]Ada has a mechanism for declaring and using *unconstrained* record types—records whose discriminants may be changed—that we will not discuss in this book.

Tagged Records Inheritance is a prime feature of object-oriented design. Inheritance allows us to create a new class that is a specialization of an existing class. We create a subclass by extending the superclass with additional attributes (data) and/or operations. The tagged record is the foundation of inheritance in Ada.

Let's look at a simple example. Here is the declaration for a record type and variable that describe the location of a point in two dimensions:

```
type Point_Type is tagged
   record
      X : Float;
      Y : Float;
   end record;

Point : Point_Type;
```

Except for the addition of the word `tagged`, `Point_Type` looks just like the records we discussed earlier. We can use it in just the same ways. Here we assign values to `Point`'s two fields:

```
Point.X := 0.0;
Point.Y := 0.0;
```

The keyword `tagged` allows us to extend the record with additional fields. Let's extend our point into one suitable for displaying on a graph by adding another attribute—the size of the dot used to represent the point on a graph. Here are the declarations:

```
type Dot_Size_Type is range 1..9;

type Plotable_Point_Type is new Point_Type with
   record
      Dot_Size :Dot_Size_Type;
   end record;
```

`Plotable_Point_Type` is a new type based on `Point_Type`. `Plotable_Point_Type` has three fields: `X` and `Y`, which it inherited from `Point_Type`, and `Dot_Size`, which was added in its declaration. The following variable declaration and assignment statements illustrate the use of these three fields:

```
Plot : Plotable_Point_Type;

Plot.X        := 1.5;
Plot.Y        := -6.75;
Plot.Dot_Size := 3;
```

> **Extension aggregate** An aggregate used to specify a value for a type that is a record extension by specifying a value for the ancestor of the type, followed by associations for any components not determined by the ancestor.

We can convert a `Plotable_Point_Type` to a `Point_Type`. This conversion simply removes the extended field. To convert a `Point_Type` into a `Plotable_Point_Type` we must add a value for the additional field. We use an **extension aggregate** to accomplish this conversion. Here are examples of both sorts of conversions:

```
Point := Point_Type(Plot);              -- Discards the Dot_Size field

Plot  := (Point with Dot_Size => 5);    -- Extension aggregate adds
                                        -- a value for Dot_Size
```

`Point_Type` and `Plotable_Point_Type` are different types, but we can still write a single procedure to which we can pass an object of either type. We use the `'Class` attribute to specify that our procedure will accept any object in a class hierarchy. Here is an example of a procedure that displays the X and Y values of either a `Point_Type` or a `Plotable_Point_Type` object:

```
procedure Put_Point (Point : in Point_Type'Class) is
-- This procedure will display the X and Y attributes for any
-- type in the class hierarchy starting at type Point_Type.
begin
   Put ("X is");
   Put (Item => Point.X, Fore => 3, Aft  => 3, Exp  => 0);
   Put ("   ");
   Put ("Y is");
   Put (Item => Point.Y, Fore => 3, Aft  => 3, Exp  => 0);
   New_Line;
end Put_Point;
```

The `'Class` attribute allows the procedure to accept objects of type `Point_Type` *and any subclass* of `Point_Type`. Here are two example calls using the variables of our two tagged types:

```
Point.Put_Point;
Plot.Put_Point;
```

We have now seen how to extend a type with additional data. The second aspect of inheritance—extending the operations—is accomplished by encapsulating our tagged records in packages. We discuss packages and inheritance after we look at one more topic related to types.

Subtypes

By defining our own types, we make our programs easier to read and we get the benefits of automatic range checking. Most importantly, programmer-defined types prevent us from combining values of different types in an expression. This incompatibility of different types can eliminate the possibility of our incorrectly combining values (such as feet and inches) that should not be combined.

In some cases, two types are related so closely that using them together in expressions is common and desired. Although these types can be combined by employing explicit type conversions in expressions, Ada provides a better solution—the subtype.

You may have already used Ada's predefined subtypes Natural and Positive. They are declared within Ada as follows:

```
subtype Natural  is Integer range 0..Integer'Last;   -- These two subtypes are
subtype Positive is Integer range 1..Integer'Last;   -- predefined within Ada
```

Programmer-defined subtypes provide two of the advantages of programmer-defined types (readability and automatic range checking) but without the restrictions on combining values in an expression. As with types, we declare subtypes in the declarative part of the program. Here are some example subtype declarations:

```
subtype Negative      is Integer    range Integer'First..-1;
subtype Uppercase     is Character  range 'A'..'Z';
subtype Lowercase     is Character  range 'a'..'z';
subtype Non_Neg_Float is Float      range 0.00..Float'Last;
subtype Name_String   is String (1..30);
```

With subtypes we can name a subset of the values in a type. The type from which the subset is taken is called the **base type**. All of the operations of the subtype are defined by those of the base type.

The base type of the subtype Negative we declared above is Integer. All of the operations and attributes defined for type Integer are also available for subtype Negative. The operations defined for the sub-

> **Base type** The type from which the operations and values for a subtype are taken.

types Uppercase and Lowercase are the same as those for type Character, their base type. The operations defined for the subtype Non_Neg_Float are the same as those for type Float, its base type. The operations defined for the subtype Non_Neg_Float are the same as those for type Float, its base type. Similarly, the operations defined for the subtype Name_String are identical to those for type String.

We can declare subtypes as subsets of Ada's predefined types, programmer-defined types, or other subtypes. Here are some examples of subtypes declared as subsets of programmer-defined types and subtypes:

```
type     Pounds              is  digits 6    range 0.0..1.0E+06;
subtype  UPS_Weight_Type     is  Pounds      range 0.0..100.0;
subtype  Freight_Weight_Type is  Pounds      range 50.0..10_000.0;

type     Day_Type            is  (Monday, Tuesday, Wednesday, Thursday,
                                  Friday, Saturday, Sunday);
subtype  Week_Day_Type       is  Day_Type    range Monday..Friday;
subtype  Weekend_Day_Type    is  Day_Type    range Saturday..Sunday;

subtype  Grade_Type          is  Uppercase   range 'A'..'E';
subtype  Pass_Grade_Type     is  Grade_Type  range 'A'..'D';
```

`Pounds` is the base type for subtypes `UPS_Weight_Type` and `Freight_Weight_Type`. `Day_Type` is the base type for subtypes `Week_Day_Type` and `Weekend_Day_Type`. When a subtype is a subset of another subtype, it inherits the base type of that subtype. `Grade_Type`'s base is `Character` because `Grade_Type` is a subset of the subtype `Uppercase`, whose base type is `Character`. Because `Pass_Grade_Type` is a subset of `Grade_Type`, its base type is also `Character`.

We can freely combine values of a subtype with any values in its base type or with any values of any other subtype that share that base type. Take, for example, the following variable declarations:

```
Total_Weight    : Pounds;
Package_Weight  : UPS_Weight_Type;
Crate_Weight    : Freight_Weight_Type;
```

Because all three of these variables have the same base type (`Pounds`), the statement

```
Total_Weight := 5.0 * Package_Weight + 2.0 * Crate_Weight;
```

is valid. This statement would not be valid if we had declared `UPS_Weight_Type` and `Freight_Weight_Type` as types instead of subtypes.

The limited range assigned to subtypes ensures that the value of a variable is reasonable. If we attempt to assign a value outside of the subtype's range to a variable, a `CONSTRAINT_ERROR` is raised. Subtype ranges also allow us to test a value ourselves to see whether it is in the domain of the subtype. Such tests are called membership tests. The result of a membership test is type `Boolean`. Ada uses the operators in and not in to perform these tests. Here are some expressions that use membership operators:

Expression	Result
5 in Positive	True
Monday in Week_End_Type	False
102.3 not in UPS_Weight_Type	True

Types or Subtypes? We have illustrated how programmer-defined types and subtypes make our programs easier to understand and debug. Because programmer-defined types and programmer-defined subtypes both limit the domain, how do we decide which to use in our Ada program?

To answer this question, we need to look at the major difference between types and subtypes. We can mix subtype values freely in an expression with values of its base type or with other subtypes that share this base type. In contrast, we may not mix type values in an expression with values of other types; using different types in the same expression requires the use of conversion functions (either explicit type conversions or ones that we write).

We recommend that, given a choice, you use subtypes. Doing so allows you easily to combine variables with different ranges in your expressions. Such expressions are usually easier to read than expressions containing conversion functions. Using subtypes also simplifies input and output. We need only instantiate packages for the base types used in our program. If we use types, we must instantiate a new package for each new type.

Use types for those situations where you want to be sure to prevent the inadvertent mixing of particular variables. For example, weight and mass are two different physical quantities that are sometimes incorrectly thought to be different units for the same quantity. Weight, however, depends on gravitational attraction. This fact explains why you weigh different amounts on different planets even though your mass is constant. Combining a weight and a mass value without applying the correct conversion factor would be disastrous in a satellite navigation program. By declaring different types for these quantities, we help ensure that such a problem is avoided. Types are also more appropriate in team projects.

Whenever you use the predefined types Integer or Float in a variable declaration, ask yourself whether a programmer-defined type or subtype could make your program easier to understand. Also consider whether there is a possibility that you may want to specify a range for that variable sometime in the future.

Many experienced Ada programmers rarely use the predefined types Integer and Float in the declaration of variables. They use types Integer and Float as base types in the declaration of their own subtypes. There is one additional advantage to using types and subtypes to constrain the range of our variables. Static analysis tools such as the SPARK Examiner use the range information to show whether an arithmetic overflow is possible in a program.

2.3 Packages

We introduced information hiding and encapsulation in Chapter 1. We begin this section with a review of these important concepts. Then we show in detail how to use Ada's package to realize them.

Information hiding is the practice of hiding the details of a module with the goal of controlling access to the details from the rest of the system. Information hiding does not mean that information is not available; it is just kept out of sight when not required. Information hiding is not limited to programming. Try to list all of the operations and information required to make a ham and cheese sandwich. We normally don't consider the details of raising hogs and dairy cows; producing cheese; or growing wheat, mustard, tomatoes, and lettuce as part of making a sandwich. Information hiding lets us deal only with the operations and information needed at a particular level in the solution of a problem.

Encapsulation is a programming language feature that lets a compiler enforce information hiding. It is like the case around a watch that prevents us from accessing the works. The case is provided by the watchmaker, who can easily open it when repairs become necessary. Encapsulation lets us use code reliably and with less worry. For example, you call the various predefined `Get` and `Put` procedures without worrying about what the code for these operations looks like.

Ada was designed for developing large programs. Packages, both predefined and programmer-written, are Ada's principal method of encapsulation for complex programs. With packages, we can concentrate our efforts on one level of the problem while our fellow team members concentrate on other levels. The programming process becomes more like making a sandwich. One person concentrates on combining the meat, cheese, and bread; someone else is responsible for raising the pigs.

We write packages in two parts: the package declaration and the package body. The package declaration defines the interface to the package. It is like the face and stems on a watch. The declaration describes what resources the package can supply to the program. Resources supplied by a watch might include the value of the current time and operations to set the current time. In a package, resources can include types, subtypes, constants, and subprograms. The package body provides the implementation of the resources defined in the package declaration (the insides of the watch).

There are significant advantages to separating the declaration of a package from its implementation. A clear interface is important, particularly when a package is used by other members of a programming team. Any ambiguities in an interface will result in problems when the team members' efforts are combined. By separating the declaration of the package from its implementation, we have the opportunity to concentrate our efforts on the design of the interface without needing to worry about implementation details.

By using separate declarations and interfaces for our packages, we can save time during the development of our programs. When we find an error in a body, we need only correct and recompile the package body that contained the error. We do not have to recompile the entire program—a time-consuming process when our programs are large. We discuss the issues of separate compilation in a later section of this chapter.

Another advantage of this separation is that we can change the implementation (the body) at any time without affecting the work done by other programmers. We can make changes when we discover a better algorithm or when there is a change in the environment in which the program is run. For example, suppose we need to render a role-playing game graphic. With the wide variety of video display accelerators available today, the algorithms for efficiently displaying an image often differ from one computer system to another. By defining an interface and encapsulating the algorithms in the package body, we can easily move our program to a different system simply by rewriting one package body. We do not have to change the rest of the program.

2.4 Child Packages

Every Ada compiler vendor provides the many packages defined and required by the Ada standard. These include the packages you have used in your previous Ada programs such as `Ada.Text_IO`, `Ada.Direct_IO`, `Ada.Sequential_IO`, and `Ada.Calendar`. The compiler vendors also provide many other specialized packages that are defined by the standard but not required by it. For example, a vendor who sells Ada compilers to customers who develop financial applications will include the packages defined in the Ada standard's Information Systems annex that provide resources for processing financial data. In addition, compiler vendors, other vendors, and public and private organizations furnish a wide variety of packages to provide a wealth of other resources to Ada programmers. These resources are typically not defined by the Ada standard. You may find hundreds of packages available on the computer system you are using to complete your Ada programming assignments.

Ada provides a hierarchical structure to organize the large numbers of packages found in an Ada development environment. This structure is based on the concept of the child package. All standard packages are organized under three parent packages: `Ada`, `Interfaces`, and `System`. The package named `Ada` serves as the parent of most other standard library packages. Resources for combining Ada statements with statements written in other programming languages in the same program are found in the package `Interfaces` and its children. Finally, package `System` and its children provide the definitions of characteristics of the particular environment in which the program runs.

Child packages can also have children. For example, the standard package `Elementary_Functions` is a child of package `Numerics` which is a child of package `Ada`. The prefixed name of this package is `Ada.Numerics.Elementary_Functions`. We will give some examples of child packages in the next sections.

Kinds of Packages

Although there are many different ways to define and use packages, most packages fall into one of three categories: definition packages, service packages, or data-abstraction packages. We'll take a closer look at each of these in the following sections. This classification system is not strict—its purpose is to give a beginner guidance in the development of packages. Some packages have the properties of more than one of these categories, and a few have properties not found in any of them.

Chapter 2: Data Design and Implementation

Definition Packages A definition package groups related constants and types. Definition packages are useful when the same types must be used in several programs or by different programmers working on different parts of one large program. Specification 2.1 is a simple definition package that defines the SI unit prefixes used in an aircraft system.

Specification 2.1   SI Units

```ada
package SI_Units is

   -- The International System of Units (SI) defines the following prefixes
   -- that are used in the Spruce Goose flight management system

   type Prefix is (Micro, Milli, None, Kilo, Mega);
   -- None means no prefix
end SI_Units;
```

Specification 2.2 is a child package of `SI_Units` and is also a definition package. It defines the basic units for an aircraft flight management system and a temperature constant.

Specification 2.2   SI Base Units

```ada
package SI_Units.Base is

-- This package provides the types used to represent the basic units
-- from the International System of Units (SI) needed for the
-- Spruce Goose flight management system

   type Meters  is digits 12    range -8_000_000.0 .. 8_000_000.0;
   type Grams   is digits 10    range  0.0 .. 250_000_000.0;
   type Seconds is delta  0.001 range  0.0 .. 86_400.0;
   type Kelvin  is digits 6     range  0.0 .. 1_000.0;

   Absolute_Zero : constant Kelvin := 0.0;

end SI_Units.Base;
```

By grouping these declarations into packages shared by the entire programming team, we can eliminate the extra effort involved in typing the declarations over and over again. More importantly, we ensure that all the programmers use the exact same definitions.

Package declarations that contain only subtype, type, and constant declarations are considered a simple form of a package and cannot have a package body. There is nothing to implement; everything is in the package declaration.

Service Packages A service package groups the constants, types, subtypes, and subprograms necessary to provide some particular service. Every Ada compiler comes with a predefined service package called `Elementary_Functions` that contains 29 mathematical subprograms. This package includes functions such as square root, the trigonometric functions (sine, cosine, tangent, and so on), and logarithms for `Float` values. The predefined package `Generic_Elementary_Functions` is a generic template that we instantiate to obtain the same mathematical functions for other real types. We will talk more about generic units in the next chapter.

Specification 2.3 is an example of a service package for our avionics application. This child package of `SI_Units.Base` supplies conversion services. It will scale a quantity to the desired unit prefix and return a string representation of the result suitable for displaying. To save space, we have included only one of the conversion procedures here.

Specification 2.3   SI Conversions

```ada
package SI_Units.Base.String_Conversions is

   procedure Convert_Grams (Item   : in  Grams;
                            Scale  : in  Prefix;
                            Aft    : in  Positive;
                            Value  : out String);
   -- This procedure converts a real value, Item, to a String.
   -- Preconditions  : none
   -- Postconditions : If the scaled Item cannot be represented in the
   --                  Value'Length characters, Value will contain '*'s
   --                  otherwise
   --                  Value will contain a character representation of
   --                  Item with Aft digits after the decimal point.

   -- Similar procedures for the remaining basic units have been omitted

end SI_Units.Base.String_Conversions;
```

Because service packages contain operation declarations, they require a body containing the implementations of the operations. Body 2.1 implements our abbreviated service package.

Body 2.1   SI Conversions: Implements Specification 2.3

```ada
with Ada.Text_IO;
with Ada.IO_Exceptions;
package body SI_Units.Base.String_Conversions is

   procedure Convert_Grams (Item   : in  Grams;
                            Scale  : in  Prefix;
                            Aft    : in  Positive;
                            Value  : out String) is
```

```ada
         package Base_IO is new Ada.Text_IO.Float_IO (Num => Grams'Base);
         Prefix_Exponent : Integer;      -- Value based on SI unit prefixes
         Scaled_Value    : Grams'Base;   -- A larger range than Grams

      begin
         -- Scale Item to the unit specified by the requested prefix
         Prefix_Exponent := Prefix'Pos(Scale) - Prefix'Pos(None);
         Scaled_Value    := Item * 10.0 ** (-3 * Prefix_Exponent);
         -- Convert scaled Item to a String
         Base_IO.Put (To   => Value,
                      Item => Scaled_Value,
                      Aft  => Aft,
                      Exp  => 0);
      exception -- Handle conversion errors by filling with *'s
         when CONSTRAINT_ERROR | Ada.IO_Exceptions.LAYOUT_ERROR =>
            Value := (Value'Range => '*');
      end Convert_Grams;

end SI_Units.Base.String_Conversions;
```

Data Abstraction Packages We defined an abstract data type (ADT) as a data type whose properties (domain and operations) are specified independently of any particular implementation. Because we write a package as two separate parts, it is an ideal mechanism for constructing ADTs. The domain of the data type and the specification of its operations are given in a package specification. The implementation details for the operations are encapsulated in the package body.

Specification 2.4 is for a simple class of railroad cars. Such a class might be used to maintain a database of rolling stock owned by a particular railroad. The specification includes some definitions of domain-specific scalar types and a tagged record to define the domain of our railroad car class. Even though this specification is an extremely simplified model of a railroad car, it provides 909,101,909,101 unique values for type `Car_Type`. The domain of a more realistic model would be far larger.

Specification 2.4 Railroad Cars (exposed version)

```ada
package Railroad_Cars is

   type    Pounds      is range 0..1_000_000;
   subtype Tare_Pounds is Pounds range 1_000..10_000;
   type    Feet        is range 20..120;

   type Car_Type is tagged
      record
         Tare   : Tare_Pounds;   -- Weight of empty car
         Length : Feet;
```

```ada
      Load    : Pounds;
   end record;

   ----------------------------------------------------------------

   function Weight (Car : in Car_Type) return Pounds;
   -- Returns the total weight of a car (load plus tare weight)

   ----------------------------------------------------------------

   procedure Empty_Car (Car   : in out Car_Type);
   -- Sets the load of Car to zero

end Railroad_Cars;
```

Our specification defines five different operations for our railroad car class. In addition to the explicitly defined function `Weight` and procedure `Empty`, there are the three operations implicitly defined for all record types—assignment, equality testing, and field selection.

Package `Railroad_Cars` provides the abstract (logical) view of the class. Here is a code fragment from an application that declares a car class constant and a car class variable and demonstrates calls to the two explicit operations:

```ada
-- Declarations
My_Car : constant Car_Type := (Tare   => 5_530,        -- Assign a record
                               Length => 48,           --   aggregate
                               Load   => 1_240);
Your_Car   : Car_Type;
Car_Weight : Railroad_Cars.Pounds;

   .
   .
   .

-- Executable statements
Your_Car := (Tare    => 6_783,                         -- Assign values to Your_Car
             Length  => 80,
             Load    => 12_350);

Car_Weight := My_Car.Weight;                           -- Display the
Pound_IO.Put (Item => Car_Weight);                     -- values of
New_Line;                                              -- the two
Pound_IO.Put (Item => Your_Car.Weight);                -- cars
New_Line;

Your_Car.Empty_Car;                                    -- Empty Your_Car
```

```
Pound_IO.Put (Item => Your_Car.Weight);   -- Display the values of
New_Line;                                 -- Your_Car again
```

Body 2.2 is the package body containing the bodies for the two subprograms defined in our railroad car class package specification. The package body provides the implementation of the class.

Body 2.2   Railroad Cars: Implements Specification 2.4

```
package body Railroad_Cars is

   -------------------------------------------------------------------
   function Weight (Car : in Car_Type) return Pounds is
   begin
      return Car.Tare + Car.Load;
   end Weight;

   -------------------------------------------------------------------
   procedure Empty_Car (Car  : in out Car_Type) is
   begin
      Car.Load := 0;
   end Empty_Car;

end Railroad_Cars;
```

Specification 2.5 extends our railroad car class to obtain a more specialized car class—tanker cars. We extend the type to include two more attributes (the capacity of the tank and whether the contents are flammable). We also add a new operation that allows us to test whether the car is currently rated as "extremely hazardous." We placed the declarations for our new subclass in a child package. By using child packages, our package hierarchy matches our class hierarchy.

Specification 2.5   Tanker Cars (exposed version)

```
package Railroad_Cars.Tanker is

   type Gallons is range 5_000..50_000;

   type Tank_Car_Type is new Car_Type with
      record
         Capacity  : Gallons;
         Flammable : Boolean;
      end record;

   -------------------------------------------------------------------
```

```ada
   function Extremely_Hazardous (Car         : in Tank_Car_Type;
                                 Danger_Size : in Gallons) return Boolean;
   -- Returns True if the Car carries an especially large amount of
   -- a flammable liquid

end Railroad_Cars.Tanker;
```

The operations available for a `Tank_Car_Type` object include the two defined for `Car_Type` objects (`Weight` and `Empty`) plus the new `Extremely_Hazardous` operation. We cannot use `Extremely_Hazardous` with `Car_Type` objects. Here is a code fragment that demonstrates our new subclass:

```ada
Oil_Car : Tank_Car_Type;

   .
   .
   .

Oil_Car := (Tare      => 4_450,
            Length    => 53,
            Load      => 72_000,
            Capacity  => 10_000,
            Flammable => True);

if Oil_Car.Extremely_Hazardous (Danger_Size => 9_999) then
   Put_Line ("Emptying the car");
   Oil_Car.Empty_Car;
end if;
```

Body 2.3 contains the implementation of our tanker car class.

Body 2.3   Tanker Cars: Implements Specification 2.5

```ada
package body Railroad_Cars.Tanker is

   function Extremely_Hazardous (Car         : in Tank_Car_Type;
                                 Danger_Size : in Gallons) return Boolean is
   begin
      return Car.Flammable and (Car.Capacity >= Danger_Size);
   end Extremely_Hazardous;

end Railroad_Cars.Tanker;
```

Encapsulation

An important goal in designing a class is to protect its content from being damaged by the actions of external code. If the contents of a class can be changed only through a well-defined interface, then it is much easier to use the class and to find errors in the application. Encapsulation provides the means for achieving this goal.

Encapsulation enables us to modify the implementation of a class after its initial development. Perhaps we are rushing to meet a deadline, so we create a simple but inefficient implementation. Later, we can replace the implementation with a more efficient version. The modification is undetectable by the application programmers using the class with the exception that their applications run faster and require less memory.

If we write a class in a manner that exposes implementation details, an application programmer may try to exploit some of those details. If we later change the implementation, that application would stop working. Figure 2.9 illustrates an encapsulated implementation versus one that is exposed to external code.

Encapsulation makes it easier for us to use a class in other applications. An encapsulated class is self-sufficient, so it doesn't depend on declarations in the application. Therefore, it can be used by different applications without requiring changes to either the class or the application.

The data abstraction packages developed in the previous section provide the means to *hide* the details of our abstract data types. The attributes of our classes are hidden within record types and the implementation of the operations are hidden within package bodies.

The package bodies encapsulate the implementation of the operations—the application programmer cannot access anything within a package body. However, the records do not *encapsulate* the attributes. The application programmer can access them directly through record field selectors. We did just that when we set the values of `Tare`, `Length`, `Load`, `Capacity`, and `Flammable` in the previous examples.

What is wrong with the application using these fields directly? Most of the fields in our railroad car and tanker records should not change after a car object is created. The length and tare weight of a railroad car does not change while being loaded or unloaded. Similarly, the capacity of a tank car remains constant for a particular car. By giving the application programmer direct access to these record fields, they may, perhaps unintentionally, change car attributes that should remain constant.

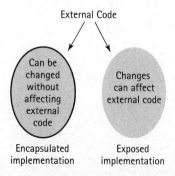

Figure 2.9 *Encapsulated versus exposed implementation.*

Sometimes we want to change the representation of a class's attributes. By giving application programmers direct access to the record fields, they will need to rewrite their code to match our modified fields.

Private Types We need another Ada feature to protect our attributes from external code. That feature is the **private type**.

> **Private type** A type used to encapsulate the attributes (data) of a class.

Let's rewrite our railroad car classes using a private type to prevent external code from accessing the attributes of our point objects. Of course, we will need to provide some additional operations to replace the record assignment and field selection we used in our sample applications. We need to include observers, transformers, and constructors in our interface to give application programmers the power they require to use our class in their programs. Our revised package specification for the railroad car class is given in Specification 2.6.

Specification 2.6 Railroad Cars (encapsulated version)

```ada
package Railroad_Cars is

   type    Pounds      is range 0..1_000_000;
   subtype Tare_Pounds is Pounds range 1_000..10_000;
   type    Feet        is range 20..120;

   type Car_Type is tagged private;

   -- Observers
   ---------------------------------------------------------------------
   function Tare_Weight (Car : in Car_Type) return Tare_Pounds;
   -- Returns the weight of Car with no load

   function Weight (Car : in Car_Type) return Pounds;
   -- Returns the total weight of a car (load plus tare weight)

   procedure Put (Car : in Car_Type);
   -- Displays all the properties of Car

   -- Transformers
   ---------------------------------------------------------------------
   procedure Load_Car (Car  : in out Car_Type;
                       Load : in     Pounds);
   -- Sets the current weight of the load in Car

   -- Constructors
   ---------------------------------------------------------------------
   package Constructors is
      function Construct_Car (Tare   : Tare_Pounds;
                              Length : Feet) return Car_Type;
```

```
         -- Returns a car with the given Tare weight and length
         -- with a zero pound load
   end Constructors;

private
   type Car_Type is tagged
      record
         Tare   : Tare_Pounds;
         Length : Feet;
         Load   : Pounds;
      end record;
end Railroad_Cars;
```

The first difference you will notice between this specification of an encapsulated railroad car class and the specification of an exposed railroad car class in Specification 2.4 is that the declaration for `Car_Type` contains only the words `tagged` and `private`. As before, `tagged` indicates that this type may be extended to create a subclass. The term `private` means that the details of this type are encapsulated—they may not be used by an application programmer. The details are given at the end of the package specification after a line containing only the word `private`. In this package, we can see that `Car_Type` is a record with the three fields `Tare`, `Length`, and `Load`. Even though application programmers can "see" this record in the package specification, they cannot use it in their code.

The line containing only the word `private` marks the boundary between declarations that are exposed to the application programmer and those that are encapsulated and therefore not available to the application programmer. Everything above this line is available to an application. These are the package's *public declarations*. An application can declare variables of type `Car_Type` and use any of the five operations defined in the public part. Everything below it is not available to applications. These are the package's *private declarations*. Applications cannot access the `Tare`, `Length`, or `Load` fields in their `Car_Type` variables. They must use the class's operations to query or modify these fields.

Observers return information on the state of an object. They do not modify objects. In Ada, observer subprograms are easily identified by the use of *in* mode parameters. In mode ensures that the objects are not changed. Here are some examples of using the three observer operations of our railroad car class in an application:

```
Car_Weight := Your_Car.Tare_Weight;       -- Get Your_Car's tare weight
Pound_IO.Put (Item => Car_Weight);
New_Line;
Car_Weight := Your_Car.Weight;            -- Get Your_Car's total weight
Pound_IO.Put (Item => Car_Weight);
New_Line;

Your_Car.Put;                             -- Display all attributes of
                                          -- Your_Car
New_Line;
```

Transformers modify the state of an object. Transformers are always procedures and are easily identified by the use of *in out* mode parameters. Here is an example of using a railroad car class transformer:

```
Your_Car.Load_Car (Load => 12_345);   -- Load Your_Car
```

Constructors are used to create or initialize an object. Even without comments, constructors are easily identified in Ada packages. Functions that return an object are constructors. The value they return is a newly created object. Procedures with *out* mode object parameters are also constructors. The following code fragment illustrates the use of the railroad car class's constructor in some application:

```
-- Initialize a railroad car
Your_Car := Construct_Car (Tare => 6_783, Length  => 80);
```

Our railroad car constructor sets the "constant" tare weight and car length values. The load weight is set to zero (as it would be in a newly manufactured railroad car). Although the encapsulated class has observer operations to return the tare weight and car length values, we have not included any operations to transform these values. Once a railroad car is constructed, it keeps its tare weight and car length. To change these intrinsic car values, we must reconstruct the car.

Primitive Operations and Tagged Types You may have noticed that the constructor declared in Specification 2.6 is within an internal package called `Constructors`. To understand why we used this internal package you need to understand the concept of primitive operations for a type. A **primitive operation** for a type is an operation (function or procedure) that is declared in the same package specification as the type and has a parameter or a return value of the type. Until now, all of the functions and procedures in the package specifications we have given have been primitive operations. The observer and transformer operations defined in Specification 2.6 for type `Car_Type` are all primitive operations for the type. Because the constructor is defined in another package, it is not a primitive operation for type `Car_Type`.

> **Primitive operation** An operation for a type that is declared in the same package specification as the type and has a parameter or a return value of the type.

Each primitive operation defined for a tagged type is inherited by any type that extends the type. For example, the child package given in Specification 2.7 defines type `Tank_Car_Type` as an extension of type `Car_Type`. As we saw earlier, this new type inherits the record fields (`Tare`, `Length`, and `Load`) of its parent and adds the new fields `Capacity` and `Flammable`. `Tank_Car_Type` also inherits the primitive operations of its parent. So we can use the observers and transformers defined for `Car_Type` with `Tank_Car_Type` objects.

Specification 2.7 Tank Cars (encapsulated version)

```ada
package Railroad_Cars.Tanker is

   type Gallons is range 5_000..50_000;

   type Tank_Car_Type is new Car_Type with Private;

   -- Observers
   ---------------------------------------------------------------------
   function Capacity (Car : in Tank_Car_Type) return Gallons;
   -- Returns the maximum number of gallons Car can hold

   function Flammable_Load (Car : in Tank_Car_Type) return Boolean;
   -- Returns whether or not the contents of Car are flammable

   function Extremely_Hazardous (Car         : in Tank_Car_Type;
                                 Danger_Size : in Gallons) return Boolean;
   -- Returns True if the Car carries an especially large amount of
   -- a flammable liquid

   overriding procedure Put (Car : in Tank_Car_Type);
   -- Displays all the properties of tank car

   -- Transformers
   ---------------------------------------------------------------------
   procedure Set_Flammability (Car        : in out Tank_Car_Type;
                               Flammable  : in     Boolean);
   -- Sets whether or not the contents of a tank car are flammable

   -- Constructors
   ---------------------------------------------------------------------
   package Constructors is
      function Construct_Car (Tare     : Tare_Pounds;
                              Length   : Feet;
                              Capacity : Gallons) return Tank_Car_Type;
      -- Returns a tank car with the given Tare weight, Length, and maximum
      -- Capacity with a zero pound non-flammable load
   end Constructors;

private
   type Tank_Car_Type is new Car_Type with
      record
         Capacity : Gallons;
```

```
      Flammable : Boolean;
   end record;
end Railroad_Cars.Tanker;
```

Inheritance is fine for observers and transformers. An application using tank cars will certainly want to inquire about their tare and total weights and change the load weight. However, it does not make sense to use the constructor defined for an ordinary car to construct a tank car. The constructor for an ordinary railroad car requires two parameters (Tare and Length) whereas the constructor for a tank car requires three parameters (Tare, Length, and Capacity). Using a Car_Type constructor for a Tank_Car_Type object would be wrong—only two of its three constant fields would be defined. We need to ensure that the parent's constructor is *not* inherited by its child. Constructors in programming languages such as C++ and Java are not inherited by derived classes. These languages use a syntax that distinguishes constructors from other class operations. In Ada, all primitive operations are inherited by derived types. By making our constructors nonprimitive operations, we ensure that they are not inherited. Declaring our constructors in a nested package is one way to make them nonprimitive operations for the type and therefore not inherited by any child classes. Figure 2.10 shows the inheritance relationship between our two classes. The operations shown for the tank car class are those we added to those available from its superclass.

Package Bodies Although not accessible to applications, the private declarations in a specification may be used by the package body. Bodies 2.4 and 2.5 are the complete package bodies for our encapsulated railroad car and tanker car classes.

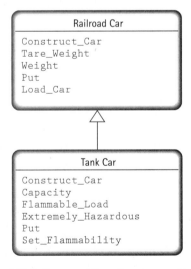

Figure 2.10 *A UML diagram of the railroad car and tank car classes.*

Body 2.4 Railroad Cars: Implements Specification 2.6

```ada
with Ada.Text_IO; use Ada.Text_IO;
package body Railroad_Cars is

   ------------------------------------------------------------------

   function Tare_Weight (Car : in Car_Type) return Tare_Pounds is
   begin
      return Car.Tare;
   end Tare_Weight;

   ------------------------------------------------------------------

   function Weight (Car : in Car_Type) return Pounds is
   begin
      return Car.Tare + Car.Load;
   end Weight;

   ------------------------------------------------------------------

   procedure Put (Car : in Car_Type) is
   begin
      Put ("Tare is" & Pounds'Image(Car.Tare) & " pounds.  ");
      Put ("Load is" & Pounds'Image(Car.Load) & " pounds.  ");
      Put ("Length is" & Feet'Image(Car.Length) & " feet.  ");
   end Put;

   ------------------------------------------------------------------

   procedure Load_Car (Car  : in out Car_Type;
                       Load : in     Pounds) is
   begin
      Car.Load := Load;
   end Load_Car;

   ------------------------------------------------------------------

   package body Constructors is

      function Construct_Car (Tare   : Tare_Pounds;
                              Length : Feet)          return Car_Type is
      begin
         return (Tare, Length, 0);
      end Construct_Car;

   end Constructors;
end Railroad_Cars;
```

Body 2.5   Tank Cars: Implements Specification 2.7

```ada
with Ada.Text_IO;  use Ada.Text_IO;
package body Railroad_Cars.Tanker is

   ------------------------------------------------------------------
   function Capacity (Car : in Tank_Car_Type) return Gallons is
   begin
      return Car.Capacity;
   end Capacity;

   ------------------------------------------------------------------
   function Flammable_Load (Car : in Tank_Car_Type) return Boolean is
   begin
      return Car.Flammable;
   end Flammable_Load;

   ------------------------------------------------------------------
   function Extremely_Hazardous (Car          : in Tank_Car_Type;
                                 Danger_Size : in Gallons) return Boolean is
   begin
      return Car.Flammable and (Car.Capacity >= Danger_Size);
   end Extremely_Hazardous;

   ------------------------------------------------------------------
   procedure Put (Car : in Tank_Car_Type) is
   begin
      Railroad_Cars.Put (Car_Type(Car));   -- Display Tare, Load, and Length
      Put ("Capacity is" & Gallons'Image(Car.Capacity) & " gallons.  ");
      if Car.Flammable then
         Put ("Contents are flammable.");
      end if;
   end Put;

   ------------------------------------------------------------------
   procedure Set_Flammability (Car       : in out Tank_Car_Type;
                               Flammable : in     Boolean) is
   begin
      Car.Flammable := Flammable;
   end Set_Flammability;

   ------------------------------------------------------------------
   package body Constructors is

      function Construct_Car (Tare     : Tare_Pounds;
```

```
                        Length   : Feet;
                        Capacity : Gallons) return Tank_Car_Type is
   begin
      return (Tare, Length, 0, Capacity, False);
   end Construct_Car;

   end Constructors;
end Railroad_Cars.Tanker;
```

Although the code in these two bodies is simple, there are two parts worth noting. The context clause providing access to the library package `Ada.Text_IO` is given in the package bodies rather than in the package declarations. The package declarations have no need for any of the resources in `Ada.Text_IO`. If the specification did require a resource (say `File_Type`) from `Ada.Text_IO`, we would put the context clause in the package declaration. If you include a context clause in a package declaration, you do not need to repeat it in the package body—the body has access to everything in its declaration, including context clauses.

The function `Construct_Car` for tank cars in Body 2.5 returns an aggregate composed of the five fields making up the extended type for `Tank_Car_Type`. `Railroad_Cars.Tanker` is a child package of `Railroad_Cars`, so it has full access to the private aspects of type `Car_Type`. Later we will see the need to extend classes for which we do not have access to the private part of the class, such as when we derive new classes from `Ada.Finalization.Controlled`. In such cases, we must use an extension aggregate to construct a new object. We could use an extension aggregate in our tank car constructor. The following two aggregates contain the same data:

```
(Tare, Length, 0, Capacity, False);

(Railroad_Cars.Constructors.Construct_Car(Tare, Length)  -- Car_Type Constructor
      with Capacity, False);          -- additional fields of extension aggregate
```

For clarity, we have used the fully prefixed form of function `Construct_Car`.

> **Singleton class** A class for which there is only one object. Also called an abstract data object (ADO).

Singleton Classes A **singleton class** is used to encapsulate a class when we need only one object from the class. A singleton class is also called an *abstract data object (ADO)*. With an ADO, the type declarations needed to define the attributes of the class and a variable declaration (to hold one object) are placed inside the package body. The package specification contains only the specifications of the operations available to the application programmer and any type declarations required for parameters in these operations. Returning to our railroad example, Specification 2.8 is the specification for a railroad car ADO.

Specification 2.8   Railroad Car ADO

```ada
package Railroad_Car is

  -- A railroad car with a tare weight of 1,880 pounds and a length of 80 feet

  type    Pounds     is range 0..1_000_000;
  subtype Tare_Pounds is Pounds range 1_000..10_000;
  type    Feet       is range 20..120;

  Length : constant Feet := 80;

  -- Observers
  -----------------------------------------------------------------------
  function Tare_Weight return Tare_Pounds;
  -- Returns the weight of Car with no load

  function Weight return Pounds;
  -- Returns the total weight of Car (load plus tare weight)

  procedure Put;
  -- Displays all the properties of Car

  -- Transformers
  -----------------------------------------------------------------------
  procedure Load_Car (Load : in Pounds);
  -- Sets the current weight of the load in Car

end Railroad_Car;
```

The first thing you should notice in Specification 2.8 is the lack of type declaration for a railroad car type. That declaration is encapsulated in the body and unavailable to the application programmer. We replaced the constructor with a comment describing the values of tare weight and length for the car. We can't construct additional cars, so there is no use for constructor operations. The last change to notice is that the remaining operations do not include a parameter to specify to which railroad car the operation applies. Because there is only one car, we need not say which car we wish to observe or transform.

Body 2.6 contains the implementation of our singleton railroad car class. We moved the type statement that defined our original point class (Specification 2.6) from the private part to the body (Body 2.6). Using the singleton railroad car, the application programmers cannot use Car_Type to declare their own point objects. We declare our one railroad car object in the package body. This variable is used globally by all the operations defined for the ADO.

Body 2.6 Railroad Car ADO: Implements Specification 2.8

```ada
with Ada.Text_IO;  use Ada.Text_IO;
package body Railroad_Car is

-- The railroad car type and one car variable (the object)
-- are encapsulated in this package body

   type Car_Type is
      record
         Tare : Tare_Pounds := 1800;
         Load : Pounds;
      end record;

   The_Car : Car_Type;

   ------------------------------------------------------------------
   function Tare_Weight return Tare_Pounds is
   begin
      return The_Car.Tare;
   end Tare_Weight;

   ------------------------------------------------------------------
   function Weight return Pounds is
   begin
      return The_Car.Tare + The_Car.Load;
   end Weight;

   ------------------------------------------------------------------
   procedure Put is
   begin
      Put ("Tare is" & Pounds'Image(The_Car.Tare) & " pounds.  ");
      Put ("Load is" & Pounds'Image(The_Car.Load) & " pounds.  ");
      Put ("Length is" & Feet'Image(Length) & " feet.  ");
   end Put;

   ------------------------------------------------------------------
   procedure Load_Car (Load : in    Pounds) is
   begin
      The_Car.Load := Load;
   end Load_Car;

end Railroad_Car;
```

We wrote the singleton railroad car class to illustrate the technique with a familiar class. A singleton railroad car class is not very useful to an application programmer who needs a collection of cars. The abstract data type of Specification 2.6 is the appropriate method of encapsulating the details of a railroad car class. However, as we shall show in the case study at the end of this chapter, there are applications in which having more than one object of a particular class is an error. In such cases, the ADO is the better encapsulation method.

Additional Constructs for Object-Oriented Programming

Operation Terminology As you are probably aware, the specification of package `Ada.Text_IO` contains several different procedures called `Put`. Here are the declarations of four of them:

```
procedure Put(File : in  File_Type; Item : in Character);
procedure Put(Item : in  Character);

procedure Put(File : in  File_Type; Item : in String);
procedure Put(Item : in  String);
```

These procedures differ in the number and types of parameters. We say that these four procedures have different **parameter profiles**. The parameter profile is sometimes called the subprogram's *signature*. The use of the same name for subprograms with different parameter profiles is called **overloading**. We could, for example, add a second procedure called `Put` to our railroad car class that had a `File` parameter to allow us to send the output to a file rather than the standard output (screen). By looking at parameter profiles the compiler determines which of the overloaded subprograms to associate with a particular subprogram call.

> **Parameter profile** The distinguishing features of a subprogram—whether the subprogram is a procedure or function, the number of parameters, the type of each parameter, and, if it is a function, the type of the result. Sometimes called the subprogram's *signature*.
>
> **Overloading** The repeated use of a subprogram name with different parameter profiles.
>
> **Overriding** The replacement of a superclass's operation with one defined for the subclass.

The specification of package `Railroad_Cars.Tankers` (Specification 2.7) contains a procedure called `Put` with the *same* parameter profile as the `Put` procedure in the specification of package `Railroad_Cars`. In this case, we say that the function `Put` in package `Railroad_Cars.Tankers` overrides the one in package `Railroad_Cars`. **Overriding** is an important feature of inheritance. A more specialized class (the subclass) can override operations of its superclass. An overridden operation usually implements additional functionality for the more specialized class. In our example, the `Put` for tanker cars displays the values of the attributes for all railroad cars plus the attributes that make a tanker car a more specialized car.

It is common for the body of an overriding operation to call the superclass operation and then carry out the processing of the subclass's specialization. For example, in Body 2.5 the procedure `Put` for tanker cars first calls the `Put` procedure of its parent—a procedure that displays the attributes possessed by all railroad cars: tare weight, load weight, and length. Its parent's `Put` requires a parameter of type `Car_Type`, so we use an explicit type conversion to remove the tank car's extended attributes. After the information for the common attributes has been displayed, the tank car `Put` procedure displays the information unique to tank cars.

In Specification 2.7 the `Put` procedure is declared as

```
overriding procedure Put (Car : in Tank_Car_Type);
-- Displays all the properties of a tank car
```

The reserved word `overriding` that precedes the subprogram declaration tells the Ada compiler that we wish to override the operation of the class's parent. Use of `overriding` is optional. When we use this option, the Ada compiler checks to make sure that the superclass contains an operation with the same parameter profile. If there is no such operation in the superclass, the compiler issues an error message. We use this option to prevent a very common error in object-oriented programming. It is very easy to include an operation in a subclass that we think overrides a superclass's operation but in reality is a new operation. Here are two examples of this error:

```
-- The following two procedure declarations are illegal
overriding procedure Putt (Car : in Tank_Car_Type);

overriding procedure Put (Car  : in    Tank_Car_Type;
                          File : in out Ada.Text_IO.File_Type);
```

We have misspelled the procedure name in the first example and have an erroneous parameter profile in the second. By declaring these as overriding the `Put` procedure in the superclass, the Ada compiler will point out our errors. If we had not declared them as overriding, the compiler would treat both of these operations as *overloaded* operations rather than *overriding* operations. The unsuspecting application programmer who wants to `Put` a tanker car is surprised to find only the basic car information displayed.

Although calls to overloaded subprograms are resolved at compile time, the resolution of calls to overridden subprograms may be done while the program is executing. The resolution of overridden calls is accomplished by searching up the inheritance tree. For example, when the function call

```
My_Tank_Car.Weight
```

is made, the run-time system may first look for a `Weight` operation for tank cars. When it fails to find this operation in the tank car class, it looks at the tank car's superclass and finds the `Weight` operation there.

Abstract Classes Suppose you are given the task of designing a hierarchy of classes for railroad locomotives. Let's assume that there are three fundamental kinds of locomotives—those powered by steam, those powered by diesel engines, and those powered by external electrical sources. Because inheritance should satisfy the *is-a* relationship, we cannot say that one of these classes is a subclass of another. We cannot say that a steam locomotive *is a* diesel locomotive. Nor can we say that an electric locomotive *is a* diesel locomotive. We can say that all three of these classes are locomotives. This thinking suggests the class hierarchy illustrated by the UML diagram in Figure 2.11. This figure also includes two additional kinds of locomotives—a turbocharged locomotive is a specialized diesel locomotive and a Shay locomotive is a specialized steam locomotive.

We created the Locomotive class at the top of the hierarchy of Figure 2.11 to provide the properties common to all locomotives. There are no actual locomotives that are instances of this class. We call a class for which there can be no direct **instances an abstract class**. The three descendents of the abstract Locomotive class are **concrete classes**—we can have instances of Diesel, Steam, and Electric locomotives. In the UML notation an abstract class name is shown in italics.

An abstract class need not always be at the top of an inheritance hierarchy. We could have made Electric an abstract class that inherits the properties and operations of all locomotives. This change would require us to create concrete classes beneath Electric in Figure 2.11 that inherit Electric's properties and operations. An abstract class may not be the descendant of a concrete class. If class Diesel is concrete, then class Supercharged must also be concrete.

> **Instance** An individual entity with its own identity. An object is an *instance* of a class.
>
> **Abstract class** A class that may have no direct instances. You cannot create an object of an abstract class.
>
> **Concrete class** A class that may have instances.

Let's look at some examples of properties and operations that all locomotive's share. All locomotives have a weight. A locomotive's weight is critical in determining how many cars it can pull. All locomotives have throttles and brakes; however, the details of changing the throttle of a steam locomotive are different from those needed to change the throttle of a diesel locomotive. Figure 2.12 shows a more complete UML diagram of the Locomotive class.

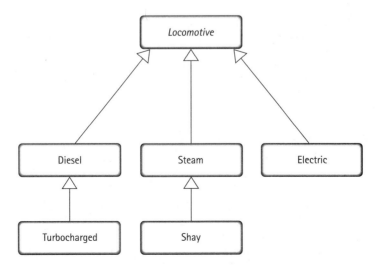

Figure 2.11 *A UML class diagram showing the is-a relationships between different kinds of railroad locomotives.*

All but one of the five operations shown in Figure 2.12 are abstract operations. As with the class name, the use of italics with operation names in a UML diagram indicates that an operation is abstract. Abstract operations have no implementation in the class. The purpose of declaring abstract operations is to ensure that all concrete subclasses provide these operations. We are forcing the Diesel, Steam, and Electric classes to supply these five operations. The single concrete operation to return a locomotive's weight is implemented by the Locomotive class.

Finally, note that Figure 2.12 does not include any constructors for the class. Because Locomotive is an abstract class, we cannot create any Locomotive objects. It does not make any sense to include constructors in abstract classes.

Specification 2.9 shows the Ada package for the abstract Locomotive class. The addition of the reserved word `abstract` to the declaration of type `Locomotive_Type` specifies that this type is for an abstract class. We have included only one field in the private part of `Locomotive_Type`—the value for the weight of the locomotive. This is the only attribute common to all locomotive classes that will be derived from the Locomotive class. The `is abstract` after an operation indicates that the operation is abstract. Function `Weight` is the only concrete operation defined for class Locomotive.

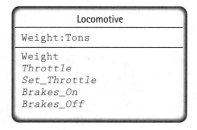

Figure 2.12 *A UML class diagram of locomotive.*

Specification 2.9   Locomotives

```ada
package Locomotives is

    type Percent is range 0..100;
    type Tons    is digits 8 range 0.0..500.0;

    type Locomotive_Type is abstract tagged private;

    -- Observers
    -----------------------------------------------------------------
    function Weight (Loco : in Locomotive_Type) return Tons;
    -- Returns the weight of a Loco

    function Throttle (Loco : in Locomotive_Type) return Percent is abstract;
    -- Returns the current throttle setting of Loco
```

```ada
-- Transformers
------------------------------------------------------------------------
procedure Set_Throttle (Loco  : in out Locomotive_Type;
                        Value : in     Percent) is abstract;
-- Sets the throttle of Loco to the given Value

procedure Brakes_On  (Loco : in out Locomotive_Type) is abstract;
-- Applies Loco's brakes

procedure Brakes_Off (Loco : in out Locomotive_Type) is abstract;
-- Releases Loco's brakes

private
   type Locomotive_Type is abstract tagged
      record
         Weight : Tons;
      end record;
end Locomotives;
```

Body 2.7 implements our abstract class. It is quite short because the class has only one concrete operation. When an abstract class has only abstract operations, we do not write a body.

Body 2.7   Locomotive: Implements Specification 2.9

```ada
package body Locomotives is

   function Weight (Loco : in Locomotive_Type) return Tons is
   begin
      return Loco.Weight;
   end Weight;

end Locomotives;
```

Specification 2.10 is the Diesel class's specification. We have added the field Horsepower and provided a constructor operation that creates a diesel locomotive object from a weight and horsepower rating. We have overridden the parent class's four abstract operations with concrete ones. Our diesel locomotives have two brake systems— air brakes and dynamic brakes. The air brakes are either on or off. The brake operations defined in the abstract Locomotive class are appropriate for the diesel locomotive's air brakes. The level of braking from the dynamic brake system may be set at various levels. As you can see in Specification 2.10, we have overloaded the procedure Brakes_On with another one that takes a percentage that is appropriate for the dynamic braking system. Note that the two procedures have different parameter profiles.

Specification 2.10 Diesel Locomotive

```
package Locomotives.Diesel is

   type Horsepower is range 500..10_000;

   type Diesel Type is new Locomotive_Type with private;

   overriding procedure Set_Throttle (Loco  : in out Diesel_Type;
                                      Value : in     Percent);
   overriding function Throttle (Loco : in Diesel_Type) return percent;

   overriding procedure Brakes_On  (Loco : in out Diesel_Type);
   overriding procedure Brakes_Off (Loco : in out Diesel_Type);
   -- Air brakes

   procedure Brakes_On (Loco  : in out Diesel_Type;
                        Level : in     Percent);
   -- Dynamic brakes

   package Constructors is
      function Construct_Loco (Weight : in Tons;
                               Power  : in Horsepower) return Diesel_Type;
   end Constructors;

private
   type Diesel_Type is new Locomotive_Type with
      record
         Power : Horsepower;
      end record;
end Locomotives.Diesel;
```

Problem-Solving Case Study

Bingo Games—How Long Should They Take?

Your great aunt Elizabeth often asks you to take her to the mall where she plays Bingo. You'd like to visit some other stores while she plays but need to return when she has finished. She doesn't have a cell phone, so you need to determine how long you can shop while she plays. There are several ways to determine how long it should take to complete *N* games of Bingo. You could sit with your aunt for a few evenings and use your watch to time dozens of Bingo games. Then you could calculate how long the average game takes. You prefer not to spend your evenings in the Bingo hall, however, so you reject this empirical approach. If you had taken that course in probability, you could calculate the expected number of Bingo numbers called in an average game of Bingo. It would take only a brief visit to the Bingo hall to determine how quickly numbers are called and the amount of time it takes to start a new game. Given that information you could then calculate the expected time for your aunt's gaming. A third approach is to write a computer program to simulate the game of Bingo. By averaging the number of Bingo numbers called in thousands or hundreds of thousands of simulated Bingo games, you can make a good estimate of how much time you have to shop. That's the approach we take in this case study.

The Design Let's look more at how Bingo is played and then design a program to simulate it. A person, the caller, selects Bingo numbers at random from a basket and announces them to the players. How quickly the caller picks and calls out the numbers varies—callers in Sydney and Melbourne, Australia, are said to be among the fastest. A player has one or more Bingo cards spread out on a table on which they keep track of numbers. Each card has 25 different numbers arranged in five rows and five columns. The five columns are labeled with the letters B, I, N, G, and O. The range of permissible numbers in a given column is:

Column B	1 to 15
Column I	16 to 30
Column N	31 to 45 (and zero)
Column G	46 to 60
Column O	61 to 75

Figure 2.13 shows an example of a Bingo card.

Figure 2.13 *A Bingo card*

When the caller calls out a number, he or she announces both the column letter and the number. Each player looks for that number on their cards. If the number is on a card, they cover it with a token. A player wins the game when one of their cards has five tokens in one row, in one column, or along a diagonal.

To begin our design, let's list the nouns in our problem statement. At this point don't try to be discriminating—just write them down.

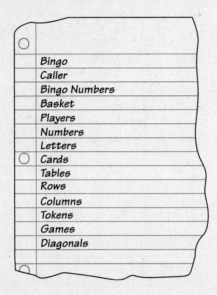

Bingo
Caller
Bingo Numbers
Basket
Players
Numbers
Letters
Cards
Tables
Rows
Columns
Tokens
Games
Diagonals

These nouns are all *potential* classes for our design. Our next task is to discard any unnecessary classes. What classes are unnecessary? Here are a few basic criteria for removing classes from an initial list:

- **Redundant classes:** If two classes are synonyms for the same concept, keep the most descriptive one. In our example *Bingo Numbers* and *Numbers* are synonyms.
- **Irrelevant classes:** If a class has little or nothing to do with our problem, eliminate it. Although *Tables* are certainly important in a real game of Bingo where players need a place to lay out their cards, they are not needed in our computer simulation of the game.
- **Attributes:** Nouns that primarily describe individual objects may be better used as attributes within a class rather than as classes themselves. *Column*, *Row*, and *Diagonal* are properties of a Bingo card. We can also make *Token* a card attribute that indicates that a particular number on the card has been called.
- **Vague classes:** Potential classes that are not specific, are difficult to define, or are too large in scope are candidates for elimination. In our example, *Bingo* and *Games* are too broad in scope so we eliminate them.
- **Derived classes:** Some classes can be determined directly from another class. For example, if we know that the Bingo number is 51, we can easily determine that the letter is *G*. So we eliminate *Letters* from our list of potential classes.

Here is our revised list of classes:

The associations in the UML diagram shown in Figure 2.14 describe collaboration relationships among the classes found in our analysis. The line connecting two classes is labeled with a name that describes the nature of the collaboration. For example, there is a relationship between Bingo players and Bingo cards. A player manages (plays) many cards; a card is managed by a single player. The relationship between player and cards is a *one-to-many* association. The relationship between a Bingo caller and a basket of Bingo numbers is a *one-to-one* association—the caller draws from one basket; a basket is used by only one caller. The association between Bingo numbers and Bingo cards is *many-to-many*. A card has many numbers and a number can be on many cards. We can be more specific by saying that a card has 25 Bingo numbers rather than many Bingo numbers. The numbers on each end of the line connecting two classes indicate the *cardinality* of the association. We can give specific numbers, ranges of numbers, or use * to represent many (zero or more).

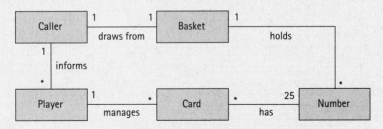

Figure 2.14 *Initial class diagram for Bingo simulation.*

Next we consider the responsibilities of each of our classes. We can determine many of the responsibilities from the game description. A Bingo basket has the obvious responsibility of supplying Bingo numbers to the caller. During a particular game, a number may be supplied only once. At the beginning of each game the basket must contain all 75 numbers. Loading these numbers is a second responsibility for the basket. A CRC card for the basket class is shown in Figure 2.15.

Class Name: **Bingo Basket**	Superclass:	Subclasses:

Primary Responsibility: *Provides random Bingo numbers*

Responsibilities	Collaborations
Draw a random Bingo number	*Used by Caller*
Load with all Bingo numbers	*Uses Numbers*

Figure 2.15 *A CRC card for the Bingo basket.*

Class Name: **Bingo Card**	Superclass:	Subclasses:

Primary Responsibility: *Manages a structure of 25 Bingo Numbers organized in 5 rows and 5 columns*

Responsibilities	Collaborations
Construct	*Used by Player*
Cover a Bingo number with a token	*Uses Numbers*
Clear all the tokens on the card	
Determine whether the pattern of tokens signifies a winner	

Figure 2.16 *A CRC card for a Bingo card.*

In a real Bingo game, the Bingo cards come preprinted with their 25 numbers. In our simulation, each Bingo card abstraction will need a constructor to create a valid collection of numbers. We decided earlier to eliminate the token class by having the cards take responsibility for covering a particular number. We also need to clear all the numbers before starting a new game. Finally, each card has the responsibility of reporting whether it is a winner. A CRC card for the Bingo card class with these four responsibilities is shown in Figure 2.16.

Bingo numbers are a subset of integers. Because integers are built into Ada we won't create a CRC card for them. The only operations we need on these integers are equality and membership testing. We use equality testing to compare called numbers to numbers on a card. The membership tests allow us to derive the column letter from the integer value (recall the relationship between Bingo letters and numbers described earlier).

Now let's work on the responsibilities of the Bingo player. In a real Bingo game, the player is responsible for covering numbers on his or her cards, determining whether one of the cards is a winner, and yelling "Bingo" should one of his or her cards win. Earlier we decided to give the cards the first two of these three responsibilities. In our simulation, we are only interested in knowing how many numbers had to be drawn from the basket before a winner was found. We have no need to determine which person won the game. We therefore have no responsibilities for a player in our Bingo game abstraction. We can eliminate the player class by having the caller give the number drawn from the basket directly to the cards rather than to a player to pass on to the cards. Eliminating the player class simplifies our design without any loss in functionality. Figure 2.17 shows the class diagram with this simplification.

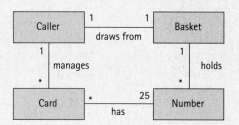

Figure 2.17 *Revised class diagram for Bingo simulation.*

The Bingo caller manages the entire game. The caller collaborates with the basket to obtain a number and with all the cards to cover that number and check for winners. The caller has no internal values to query or update through operations. The CRC card in Figure 2.18 shows that an instance of this class interacts with the Bingo basket and Bingo cards to carry out its single responsibility.

The Logical Level At the logical level we describe the domain and operations for each class. Most of the operations come from the responsibilities listed on our CRC cards. Let's start with our simple types. Specification 2.11 is a definition package that describes the Bingo numbers and letters. In addition to the range of 0 to 75 we defined earlier for Bingo numbers that appear on a card, we define a subtype of the numbers that can be in the basket (1 to 75). We also include ranges for each of the card columns associated with each of the Bingo letters and a type for these letters.

Class Name: *Bingo Caller*	Superclass:	Subclasses:
Primary Responsibility: *Manages the game of Bingo*		
Responsibilities	**Collaborations**	
Conduct Game	*Uses Bingo Basket*	
	Uses Bingo Cards	

Figure 2.18 *A CRC card for Bingo caller.*

Specification 2.11   Bingo Number Definitions

```
package Bingo_Numbers is

-- This package defines Bingo numbers and their associated letters

    -- The range of numbers on a Bingo Card
    type Bingo_Number is range 0..75;

    -- 0 can't be called, it is only for the Free Play square
    subtype Callable_Number is Bingo_Number range 1..75;

    -- Associations between Bingo numbers and letters
    subtype B_Range is Bingo_Number range  1..15;
    subtype I_Range is Bingo_Number range 16..30;
    subtype N_Range is Bingo_Number range 31..45;
    subtype G_Range is Bingo_Number range 46..60;
    subtype O_Range is Bingo_Number range 61..75;

    -- The 5 Bingo letters
    type Bingo_Letter is (B, I, N, G, O);

end Bingo_Numbers;
```

Let's move on to the specification of the Bingo basket. Here we have a class for which having more than one instance in the game is an error. Specification 2.12 shows an appropriate singleton class. While developing this class specification, we discovered a possible error. What happens when the basket is empty and we invoke the Draw operation to remove a number? We decided to declare and raise an exception should this error occur.

Specification 2.12 Bingo Basket Singleton Class

```
with Bingo_Numbers;   use Bingo_Numbers;
package Bingo_Basket is

-- This package implements a single Bingo Basket,
-- an object from which Bingo Numbers are drawn

-- Structure:  An unordered collection of Bingo numbers

    EMPTY : Exception;       -- Raised if an attempt is made to draw a
                             -- number from an empty basket
-------------------------------------------------------------------------
    procedure Load;
    -- Loads all the Bingo numbers into the basket.
    -- Preconditions  : None
    -- Postconditions : All the Bingo numbers are in the Basket

-------------------------------------------------------------------------
    procedure Draw (Letter : out Bingo_Letter;
                    Number : out Callable_Number);
    -- Removes and returns one number at random from the basket
    -- Preconditions  : None
    -- Postconditions : Number is a number not previously drawn from the basket
    --                  Letter is the column in which Number is found
    --                      on a Bingo card
    --                  Basket = Basket with the returned number removed.
    -- Exceptions     : EMPTY  Raised if an attempt is made to draw a
    --                         number from an empty basket.
    --                         The basket remains empty
end Bingo_Basket;
```

Now for the Bingo cards. A singleton class is not appropriate here. We need an abstract data type. Specification 2.13 uses a private type to encapsulate the details of each card. It might be useful to extend this ADT in the future, so we have used a tagged type.

Specification 2.13 Bingo Card Class

```ada
with Bingo_Numbers;  use Bingo_Numbers;
package Bingo_Cards is

   type Bingo_Card_Type is tagged private;  -- The Bingo Card Class

   BAD_NUMBER : exception;    -- Raised for an invalid Bingo number

   ----------------------------------------------------------------------
   procedure Clear (Card : in out Bingo_Card_Type);
   -- Clears the tokens from the Bingo card

   -- Preconditions:  Card is a valid Bingo card (properly constructed)

   -- Postconditions: Only the Free Play number is covered with a token

   ----------------------------------------------------------------------
   procedure Cover_Number (Card   : in out Bingo_Card_Type;
                           Column : in     Bingo_Letter;
                           Number : in     Bingo_Number);
   -- If the given number is on the Bingo card, it is marked as covered.

   -- Preconditions:  Card is a valid Bingo card (properly constructed)

   -- Postconditions: If the given Column and Number is on the Bingo
   --                 card, it is marked.
   --                 Otherwise the Bingo card is unchanged.

   -- Exceptions:     BAD_NUMBER   Raised for invalid Column/Number
   --                              combination

   ----------------------------------------------------------------------
   function Winner (Card : in Bingo_Card_Type) return Boolean;
   -- Returns True if the card has a winning token pattern

   -- Preconditions:  Card is a valid Bingo card (properly constructed)

   -- Postconditions: Returns True if all the numbers in a row, column,
   --                 or diagonal of the card are covered.  False otherwise.

   ----------------------------------------------------------------------
   package Constructors is
      procedure Construct (Card : out Bingo_Card_Type);
      -- Generates a valid Bingo card containing random Bingo numbers
```

```ada
        -- Preconditions:  None

        -- Postconditions: Card is a valid Bingo card.
        --                 The Free Play number is covered with a token.
        --                 All other numbers are cleared of tokens.
    end Constructors;

private
    -- We use a 2-D array with 5 rows and 5 columns to model a Bingo card
    -- Each component in the array consists of a number and a Boolean value
    -- that indicates whether or not that number is covered by a token
    type Component_Type is
        record
            Number  : Bingo_Number;
            Covered : Boolean := False;
        end record;

    subtype Row_Range  is Integer range 1..5;
    type    Card_Array is array (Row_Range, Bingo_Letter) of Component_Type;

    type Bingo_Card_Type is tagged
        record
            Items : Card_Array;
        end record;
end Bingo_Cards;
```

The private part of Specification 2.13 shows the details of this type. You can see that we have used a two-dimensional array to represent a Bingo card. Each component is a record consisting of two fields: the Bingo number and whether it is covered by a token. Although these details are visible to application programmers, they are not accessible to them. Should we decide later to change the two-dimensional array to an array of arrays in order to implement a more efficient winner determination function, the application would give the same answers as before, but more quickly.

Our last class in our design is the Bingo caller. Like the Bingo basket, we require exactly one instance of this class. Specification 2.14 is for a Bingo caller singleton class. It has just a single operation—conduct one game of Bingo. To conduct the game, the caller needs all of the cards it is to manage.

Specification 2.14   Bingo Caller Singleton Class

```ada
with Bingo_Cards;  use Bingo_Cards;
package Bingo_Caller is

-- This package implements a single Bingo caller
-- who obtains Bingo numbers from the basket and
-- manages all the Bingo cards.
```

```
   type Card_Array is array (Positive range <>) of Bingo_Card_Type;

   procedure Conduct_Game (Cards : in out Card_Array;
                           Calls :    out Positive);
   -- Conducts one game of Bingo using the given Cards
   -- Preconditions  : Cards are all valid
   -- Postconditions : Calls is the number of Bingo numbers
   --                  drawn from the Bingo basket for the game

end Bingo_Caller;
```

The Application Level We have now completed the specifications of all the classes in our design. At this point we could assign different programmers to code the implementations of these classes as well as our simulation application. To emphasize that the application can be written with no knowledge of the implementation of the classes, we write it first.

Our problem is to determine how long it will take Aunt Elizabeth to play *N* games of Bingo. The length of one game is directly proportional to how many Bingo numbers are called before a winner is determined. Thus our major goal is to determine the number of calls in an average game. To accomplish this goal, we simulate many games and average the number of numbers drawn from each simulated game. To give us an idea of extreme games, we also calculate the minimum number and maximum number of draws in all our simulations.

The number of calls in an average game is related to the number of cards being played in the game. The more cards there are, the more likely there will be a winner earlier in the game. So our program should allow us to enter the number of cards in play. We now summarize the requirements of our program by listing the inputs and outputs.

Input

The number of Bingo games to simulate

The number of Bingo cards to use in the simulations

Output

The average number of Bingo numbers called

The minimum number of Bingo numbers called in a single game

The maximum number of Bingo numbers called in a single game

Once we have the input values, we can create a collection of Bingo card objects. We can use an array to hold this collection. Then we can play the desired number of games by repeatedly calling the Conduct_Game operation of the Bingo caller. It returns the number of values drawn from the Bingo basket for that game. We add this number to a total and check it against our extremes. After playing all the games, we calculate the average and display the three statistics. The resulting program is given in Body 2.8.

Body 2.8 Bingo Game Simulation

```ada
with Ada.Text_IO;              use Ada.Text_IO;
with Ada.Integer_Text_IO;      use Ada.Integer_Text_IO;
with Ada.Float_Text_IO;        use Ada.Float_Text_IO;
with Bingo_Caller;             use Bingo_Caller;
with Bingo_Cards;              use Bingo_Cards;         use Bingo_Cards.Constructors;
procedure Bingo_Simulation is

   -- Type for Statistics
   type Stat_Rec is
      record
         Average : Float;      -- Average number of calls
         Minimum : Natural;    -- Minimum number of calls
         Maximum : Natural;    -- Maximum number of calls
      end record;

   ----------------------------------------------------------------

   procedure Play_The_Games (Num_Games : in  Positive;
                             Num_Cards : in  Positive;
                             Stats     : out Stat_Rec) is
   -- This procedure simulates Bingo games and keeps track of statistics

      -- Constrained array type for the required number of cards.
      subtype Game_Card_Array is Card_Array (1..Num_Cards);

      Cards       : Game_Card_Array;      -- All the Bingo cards
      Draws       : Natural;              -- Draws for one Bingo game
      Total_Draws : Natural := 0;         -- Total number of draws for all games

   begin
      -- Construct the cards used in all the games
      for Index in Game_Card_Array'Range loop
         Construct (Cards(Index));
      end loop;

      -- Initialize draw extremes
      Stats.Minimum := Positive'Last;
      Stats.Maximum := Positive'First;

      -- Play the games
      for Game_Count in 1.. Num_Games loop
         Bingo_Caller.Conduct_Game (Cards => Cards,
                                    Calls => Draws);

         Total_Draws := Total_Draws + Draws;

         -- Check for new extreme values
```

```ada
            if Draws > Stats.Maximum then
               Stats.Maximum := Draws;
            end if;
            if Draws < Stats.Minimum then
               Stats.Minimum := Draws;
            end if;
         end loop;
         -- Calculate the average number of calls
         Stats.Average := Float(Total_Draws) / Float(Num_Games);
      end Play_The_Games;

------------------------------------------------------------------------

   Num_Games   : Positive;   -- Number of Bingo games to simulate
   Num_Cards   : Positive;   -- Number of Bingo cards used in the games
   Bingo_Stats : Stat_Rec;   -- Game statistics

begin
   -- Get the simulation parameters
   Put ("Enter number of Bingo games to simulate: ");
   Get (Num_Games);
   Put ("Enter number of Bingo cards to use: ");
   Get (Num_Cards);

   -- Carry out the simulation
   Play_The_Games (Num_Games => Num_Games,
                   Num_Cards => Num_Cards,
                   Stats     => Bingo_Stats);

   -- Report the results
   New_Line (2);
   Put ("Average number of draws was ");
   Put (Item => Bingo_Stats.Average, Fore => 3, Aft => 2, Exp => 0);
   New_Line;
   Put ("Minimum number of draws was ");
   Put (Item => Bingo_Stats.Minimum, Width => 3);
   New_Line;
   Put ("Maximum number of draws was ");
   Put (Item => Bingo_Stats.Maximum, Width => 3);
   New_Line;
end Bingo_Simulation;
```

The Implementation Level We are now ready to implement the bodies of our three classes—basket, caller, and card. The Bingo basket is a set of numbers. Because the set is the topic of the next chapter, we defer the implementation of the Bingo basket.

Body 2.9 is the implementation of the Bingo caller. To prepare for the game, the basket is loaded with all of the numbers, and all of the cards are cleared of tokens. Each time through the loop, a number is drawn from the basket. The number is covered on all cards that contain it and cards are checked for winners. After a winner is found, the total number of values drawn from the basket is returned.

Body 2.9 Bingo Caller: Implements Specification 2.14

```ada
with Bingo_Numbers; use Bingo_Numbers;
with Bingo_Basket;
package body Bingo_Caller is


   ------------------------------------------------------------------
   procedure Manage_Cards (Letter      : in      Bingo_Letter;
                           Number      : in      Bingo_Number;
                           Cards       : in out  Card_Array;
                           Have_Winner :     out Boolean) is
   -- Covers the number drawn and checks cards for a winner
      Card_Index  : Positive;    -- Loop control variable

   begin
      -- Process all of the Bingo cards
      -- Each iteration, process one Bingo card
      Card_Index := Cards'First;
      loop
         -- Put a token on the card
         Cover_Number (Card   => Cards(Card_Index),
                       Column => Letter,
                       Number => Number);
         -- Is this card a winner?
         Have_Winner := Winner (Cards(Card_Index));
         exit when Have_Winner or Card_Index = Cards'Last;
         Card_Index := Card_Index + 1;
      end loop;
   end Manage_Cards;


   ------------------------------------------------------------------
   procedure Conduct_Game (Cards : in out Card_Array;
                           Calls :    out Positive) is
      Letter       : Bingo_Letter;    -- The letter and
      Number       : Bingo_Number;    -- number drawn
      Found_Winner : Boolean;         -- True when a winning card is found

   begin
```

```ada
         Calls := 1;
         Bingo_Basket.Load;           -- Put all of the numbers into the basket
         for Index in Cards'Range loop   -- Clear markers from all cards
            Clear (Cards(Index));
         end loop;

         -- Play the game
         -- Each iteration, process one Bingo number call
         loop
            Bingo_Basket.Draw (Letter => Letter, Number => Number);
              -- Cover the number on all the cards and check for a winner
            Manage_Cards (Letter      => Letter,
                          Number      => Number,
                          Cards       => Cards,
                          Have_Winner => Found_Winner);
            exit when Found_Winner;
            Calls := Calls + 1;
         end loop;
      end Conduct_Game;

end Bingo_Caller;
```

Body 2.10 implements the Bingo card class. The Construct operation uses a generic random number generator from the Ada library to fill the card with random Bingo numbers. We discuss generic units in the next chapter. The Clear operation sets the Covered field of all 25 card components to False. It then covers the free play component. The Cover_Number operation searches the given row for the number. If the number is found, it is marked as covered. The Winner operation uses numerous local (helper) procedures to check all of the possible winning patterns.

Body 2.10   Bingo Cards: Implements Specification 2.13

```ada
with Ada.Numerics.Discrete_Random;
package body Bingo_Cards is

   -- Package for generating random Bingo numbers between 1 and 15
   package Random_Num is new Ada.Numerics.Discrete_Random
                         (Result_Subtype => B_Range);
   -- The following object holds the state of a random Bingo number generator
   Bingo_Gen : Random_Num.Generator;

   type    Number_Array is array (Positive range <>) of Callable_Number;
   subtype Column_Array is Number_Array (Row_Range);

   -- Location of the Free Play square
```

```ada
   Free_Play_Row : constant Row_Range   := 3;
   Free_Play_Col : constant Bingo_Letter := N;


   ----------------------------------------------------------------
   -- Local (helper) procedures and functions
   ----------------------------------------------------------------
   function Valid_Number (Column : in Bingo_Letter;
                          Number : in Bingo_Number) return Boolean is
   -- This function returns True if the Bingo number given
   -- is valid for the given Bingo column

      Result : Boolean;

   begin
      case Column is
         when B =>   Result :=  Number in B_Range;
         when I =>   Result :=  Number in I_Range;
         when N =>   Result := (Number in N_Range) or (Number = 0);
         when G =>   Result :=  Number in G_Range;
         when O =>   Result :=  Number in O_Range;
      end case;
      return Result;
   end Valid_Number;


   ----------------------------------------------------------------
   function In_Array (Value : in Callable_Number;
                      List  : in Number_Array) return Boolean is
   -- Returns True if Value is found in List
      Result : Boolean := False;
   begin
      -- Check the entire array
      -- Each iteration, check one element of the array
      for Index in List'Range loop
         if Value = List(Index) then
            Result := True;
         end if;
      end loop;
      return Result;
   end In_Array;


   ----------------------------------------------------------------
   procedure Check_One_Row (Items      : in Card_Array;
                            Row        : in Row_Range;
                            All_Covered : out Boolean) is
   -- Determines whether or not all the numbers in Row are covered
```

```ada
      Column : Bingo_Letter;  -- The column in the row being checked

   begin
      -- Check the Row
      -- Each iteration, check one number in the Row
      Column := Bingo_Letter'First;
      loop
         -- Exit when we find an uncovered number or we reach end of the row.
         exit when not Items (Row, Column).Covered or
                       Column = Bingo_Letter'Last;
         Column := Bingo_Letter'succ (Column);
      end loop;
      -- If we didn't exit the loop because of an uncovered number,
      -- all the numbers in the row are covered
      All_Covered := Items(Row, Column).Covered;
   end Check_One_Row;

   -----------------------------------------------------------------------

   function Row_Winner (Items : in Card_Array) return Boolean is
   -- Returns True if all the numbers in a row are marked

      Row          : Row_Range;     -- The row being checked
      Found_Winner : Boolean;       -- Result of a row check

   begin
      -- Check all the rows
      -- Each iteration, check one row
      Row := 1;
      loop
         Check_One_Row (Items      => Items,
                        Row        => Row,
                        All_Covered => Found_Winner);
         -- Exit when we find a winner or run out of rows
         exit when Found_Winner  or  Row = Row_Range'Last;
         Row := Row + 1;
      end loop;
      return Found_Winner;
   end Row_Winner;

   -----------------------------------------------------------------------

   procedure Check_One_Column (Items       : in  Card_Array;
                               Column      : in  Bingo_Letter;
                               All_Covered : out Boolean) is
   -- Determines whether or not all the numbers in Column are covered
```

```
      Row : Row_Range;      -- The row in the column being checked

begin
   -- Check the column
   -- Each iteration, check one number in the Column
   Row := 1;
   loop
      -- Exit when we find an uncovered number or reach end of column.
      exit when not Items(Row, Column).Covered  or
                Row = Row_Range'Last;
      Row := Row + 1;
   end loop;
   -- If we didn't exit the loop because of an uncovered number,
   -- all the numbers in the column are covered
   All_Covered := Items(Row, Column).Covered;
end Check_One_Column;

-----------------------------------------------------------------

function Column_Winner (Items : in Card_Array) return Boolean is
-- Returns True if all the numbers in a column are marked

   Column        : Bingo_Letter;  -- The column being checked
   Found_Winner  : Boolean;       -- Result of a column check

begin
   -- Check all the columns
   -- Each iteration, check one column
   Column := Bingo_Letter'First;
   loop
      Check_One_Column (Items       => Items,
                        Column      => Column,
                        All_Covered => Found_Winner);
      -- Exit when we find a winner or run out of columns
      exit when Found_Winner  or
               Column = Bingo_Letter'Last;
      Column := Bingo_Letter'succ (Column);
   end loop;
   return Found_Winner;
end Column_Winner;

-----------------------------------------------------------------

function Diagonal_Winner (Items : in Card_Array) return Boolean is
-- Returns True if all the numbers in a diagonal are marked

   Column        : Bingo_Letter;  -- The column being checked
```

```ada
      Row           : Row_Range;        -- The row being checked
      Found_Loser   : Boolean;          -- Result of a number check

begin
   -- First diagonal
   Row := 1;
   Column := Bingo_Letter'First;
   loop
      Found_Loser := not Items(Row, Column).Covered;
      -- Exit if we find an uncovered number (loser) or
      -- reach the end of the diagonal
      exit when Found_Loser  or Row = Row_Range'Last;
      Row := Row + 1;
      Column := Bingo_Letter'succ (Column);
   end loop;

   if Found_Loser then    -- Check the other diagonal
      Row := 1;
      Column := Bingo_Letter'Last;
      loop
         Found_Loser := not Items (Row, Column).Covered;
         -- Exit if we find an uncovered number (loser) or reach the
         -- end of the diagonal
         exit when Found_Loser  or Row = Row_Range'Last;
         Row := Row + 1;
         Column := Bingo_Letter'Pred (Column);
      end loop;
   end if;
   return not Found_Loser;
end Diagonal_Winner;


-------------------------------------------------------------------------
-- Bingo Card Operations
-------------------------------------------------------------------------


procedure Clear (Card : in out Bingo_Card_Type) is
begin
   for Row in Row_Range loop
      for Column in Bingo_Letter loop
         Card.Items (Row, Column).Covered := False;
      end loop;
   end loop;
   -- Cover the Free Play square with a token
```

```ada
      Card.Items (Free_Play_Row, Free_Play_Col) := (Number  => 0,
                                                    Covered => True);
end Clear;

----------------------------------------------------------------
procedure Cover_Number (Card   : in out Bingo_Card_Type;
                        Column : in     Bingo_Letter;
                        Number : in     Bingo_Number) is

   Row : Row_Range; -- Loop control variable

begin
   if not Valid_Number (Column, Number) then
      raise BAD_NUMBER;
   end if;

   Row := 1;
   -- Search the Column for the given Number
   -- Each iteration, one number in Column is checked
   loop
        -- Exit when we find the number or reach the end of the column
        exit when Number = Card.Items (Row, Column).Number  or
                  Row = Row_Range'Last;
      Row := Row + 1;
   end loop;
   -- If we found the number, cover it.
   if Number = Card.Items (Row, Column).Number then
      Card.Items (Row, Column).Covered := True;
   end if;
end Cover_Number;

----------------------------------------------------------------
function Winner (Card : in Bingo_Card_Type) return Boolean is
begin
   return Row_Winner (Card.Items)       or else
          Column_Winner (Card.Items)    or else
          Diagonal_Winner (Card.Items);
end Winner;

----------------------------------------------------------------
package body Constructors is
   procedure Construct (Card : out Bingo_Card_Type) is

      Column_Numbers : Column_Array;   -- One column of numbers
      Row_Index      : Positive;       -- Index for Column_Numbers
```

```ada
            Number : Callable_Number;        -- A Bingo number

         begin
            -- Fill the Bingo card with random Bingo numbers
            -- Each iteration, fill one column with random
            --    numbers appropriate for that column
            for Column in Bingo_Letter loop

               -- Fill one column with random numbers appropriate to it
               -- Each iteration, generate one number for the column
               Row_Index := 1;
               Row_Loop:
               loop
                  -- Generate a random number between 1 and 15
                  Number := Random_Num.Random (Bingo_Gen);
                  -- Scale the value to the range appropriate for the column
                  Number := Number + (Bingo_Letter'Pos(Column) * 15);
                  -- If the number is not already in the column, add it to the column
                  if not In_Array (Value => Number,
                                   List  => Column_Numbers (1..Row_Index-1)) then
                     Column_Numbers (Row_Index) := Number;
                     Row_Index := Row_Index + 1;
                  end if;
                  exit Row_Loop when Row_Index > 5;
               end loop Row_Loop;

               -- Assert : Column_Numbers contains 5 unique Bingo numbers
               --                appropriate for the current Column

               -- Copy the numbers onto the card
               for Row in Row_Range loop
                  Card.Items (Row, Column).Number  := Column_Numbers (Row);
                  Card.Items (Row, Column).Covered := False;
               end loop;
            end loop;
            -- Finally, fill in the free play square
            Card.Items (Free_Play_Row, Free_Play_Col) :=
                     (Number => 0, Covered => True);
         end Construct;
      end Constructors;

   begin
      -- Set the random number generator's seed via the clock
      Random_Num.Reset (Bingo_Gen);
   end Bingo_Cards;
```

Summary

We have discussed how data can be viewed from multiple perspectives. A **data type** describes the collection of elements that it can represent (its domain) and the operations that may be performed on those elements. The separation of a data type's logical properties from its implementation is called **data abstraction**. The hiding of a data type's implementation from the applications that use it is called **data encapsulation**.

Ada provides a variety of predefined scalar and composite data types. Ada encapsulates the implementations of its predefined types so that a programmer rarely needs to understand how each is implemented in hardware. We use Ada's predefined data types to build more complicated data structures. Each **data structure** is a collection of data elements structured to reflect the relationships among the elements. A data structure is characterized by accessing operations that are used to store and retrieve individual data elements.

An **abstract data type** separates the logical properties of a data structure from its implementation (data abstraction) and hides the implementation from the applications that use it (encapsulation). We use Ada packages and private types to create abstract data types.

Object-oriented design is based on modeling a problem with a set of collaborating objects. Objects with similar properties and behaviors are described by a **class**. Inheritance is an important relationship between classes that allows us to easily create more specialized classes (subclasses) from a more general class (superclass). We use tagged records, private types, and packages to create classes in our Ada programs.

Figure 2.19 illustrates the relationships among the concepts discussed in this chapter. The lines between the boxes in a UML diagram are called associations. An **association** shows how two classes are related. We have

> **Association** A relationship between two classes.

already seen two special forms of association—inheritance and composition. Inheritance is shown on a UML diagram as an arrow with an open arrowhead from the subclass to the superclass. Composition shows a whole–part relationship with a solid diamond of the association indicating the whole. Unadorned lines show other relationships or collaborations between classes. The line labeled *encapsulates* indicates that an abstract data type encapsulates a data structure. We can read associations from either direction—a data structure is encapsulated by an abstract data type. The line labeled *instance of* shows that an object is an instance of its class.

The inheritance associations in this UML diagram show that an abstract data type *is a* data type and that a class *is an* abstract data type. The separation of the abstract data type's logical properties from its implementation makes the subclass more specialized than its superclass. By adding inheritance and all of its accompanying properties, class extends the concept of the abstract data type.

The composition associations in Figure 2.19 illustrate that a data structure consists of three components: a collection of elements, a structure among these elements, and operations on these elements. Another composition association shows that, in Ada, a class is implemented as a package declaration and body. A package declaration that implements a class includes tagged records to provide inheritance and private types that encapsulate the logical properties of the class.

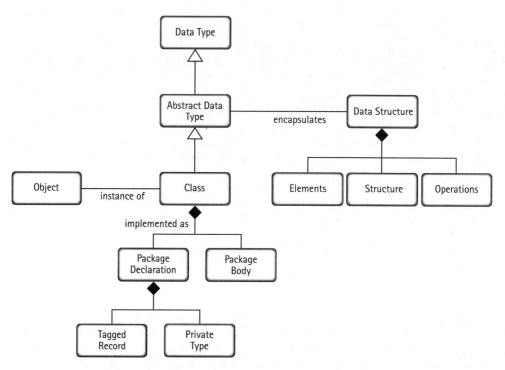

Figure 2.19 *Relationships between data types, abstract data types, data structures, classes, and Ada constructs.*

In the chapters that follow, we extend these ideas to build other data structures: sets, strings, stacks, queues, lists, trees, priority queues, and graphs. We encapsulate these data structures within abstract data types implemented as classes. Although the Ada container library provides many of these data structures, the techniques for building these structures are so important in computer science that we believe you should learn them now.

We consider these classes from the logical view. What is our abstract picture of the data, and what accessing operations can we use to create, assign to, and manipulate the data elements? We express our logical view as an abstract data type (ADT) or an abstract data object (ADO) and record its description in a package specification. So we may easily extend our ADT later, we implement it as a class. Next, we take the application view of the data, using an instance of the class in a short example. Finally, we change hats and turn to the implementation view of the class. We consider the Ada type declarations that represent the data structure, as well as the design of the methods that implement the specifications of the abstract view. Data structures can be implemented in more than one way, so we often look at alternative representations and methods for comparing them. In some of the chapters, we include a longer Case Study in which instances of the ADT are used to solve a problem.

Exercises

Data Types, Data Structures, and Abstract Data Types

1. Define the following terms:
   a. Data type
   b. Scalar data type
   c. Discrete data type
   d. Composite data type
   e. Data abstraction
   f. Data encapsulation
   g. Abstract data type (ADT)
2. Figure 2.3 illustrated the encapsulation of type `Integer`. Create an equivalent illustration for type `Boolean`.
3. How does a data structure differ from a data type?
4. The following terms are used to classify the basic operations performed on encapsulated data. Define each of them.
   a. Constructor
   b. Transformer
   c. Observer
   d. Iterator
5. *True or false?* If a statement if false, explain why it is false.
   a. Data structures may be decomposed into elements.
   b. Data structures and abstract data types are equivalent.
   c. A data structure is characterized by accessing functions that are used to store and retrieve individual data items.
   d. Data structures are scalar types.
6. *True or False?* The arrangement of the elements in a data structure and the way they are accessed can be encapsulated.
7. Name three different perspectives from which we can view an abstract data type. Using the logical data structure "a list of student academic records," give examples of what each perspective might tell us about the data.
8. Consider a Grocery Store.
   a. At the application level, describe Grocery Store.
   b. At the logical (abstract) level, what Grocery Store operations might be defined for the customer?
   c. Specify (at the logical level) the operation Check Out.
   d. Write an algorithm (at the implementation level) for the operation Check Out.
   e. Explain how parts (c) and (d) represent information hiding.

Ada's Built-In Types

9. How does a programmer create a new data type in Ada?
10. Describe three differences between Ada's signed integers and modular integers.
11. Create new scalar data types appropriate for each of the following. You may need to do some research to learn about a particular domain.
    a. The 10 digits on a digital lock used to secure a door
    b. The five letter grades that a student might earn in a course
    c. The distance between the sun and planets in our solar system
    d. The three primary colors (for mixing paints)
    e. The three primary colors (for mixing light)
    f. The value of the Dow Jones Industrial Index
    g. The number of Yen in a Japanese bank savings account
12. What composite types are predefined in the Ada language?
13. Describe the accessing function of an Ada one-dimensional array at the abstract level.
14. What operations does Ada define for the array data type?
15. Given the declarations

    ```
    type B_Array   is array (0..4) of Boolean
    type Grade_Type is (A, B, C, D, F);
    type N_Array   is array (Grade_Type) of Natural;

    X : B_Array  := (0..2 => True, 3..4  => False);
    Y : B_Array  := (2  3 => True, others => False);
    G : N_Array  := (24, 35, 41, 33, 18);
    H : N_Array  := (24, 35, 40, 32, 19);
    ```

    What is the value of each of the following expressions? (Look in an introductory Ada book or the *Ada Language Reference Manual* for any array attributes you are not familiar with.)
    a. X'First
    b. X'Last
    c. X'Length
    d. X'Range
    e. G'First
    f. G'Last
    g. G'Length
    h. G'Range

i. X(2) and Y(2)
j. X and Y
k. X(0..2) & Y(2..3)
l. X(1) = Y(1)
m. X = Y
n. X(1) < Y(1)   Hint: True is greater than False.
o. X < Y
p. G < H
q. G(A..B) < H(D..F)
r. G(A..B) & H(C..F)
s. G(F..F) & G(D..D) & G(C..C) & G (B..B) & G(A..A)
t. G(A..B) & H(C..F) < H(A..B) & G(C..F)

Use the following declarations for Exercises 16 and 17.

```
type Month_Type is (January, February, March, April,
                    May, June, July, August, September,
                    October, November, December);
subtype Year_Range is Integer range 1980..2020;
subtype Degrees    is Integer range -120..160;
subtype Inches     is Float   range 0.0..190.0;
type Weather_Rec is
   record
      Avg_Hi_Temp  : Degrees;
      Avg_Lo_Temp  : Degrees;
      Actual_Rain  : Inches;
      Record_Rain  : Inches;
   end record;
```

16. a. Declare a one-dimensional array type, Weather_Array, of Weather_Rec components, indexed by Month_Type. Declare a variable, Yearly_Weather, of Weather_Array.
    b. Assign the value 1.05 to the actual rainfall field of the July record in Yearly_Weather.

17. a. Declare a two-dimensional array, Decade_Weather, of Weather_Rec components, indexed by Month_Type in the first dimension and by Year_Range in the second dimension.
    b. Draw a picture of Decade_Weather.
    c. Assign the value 26 to the Avg_Lo_Temp field of the March 1989 record.

18. a. Define a three-dimensional array at the logical level.
    b. Suggest some applications for three-dimensional arrays.

158 | Chapter 2: Data Design and Implementation

19. Indicate which predefined Ada types would most appropriately model each of the following (more than one may be appropriate for each):
    a. A chessboard
    b. Information about a single product in an inventory-control program
    c. A list of famous quotations
    d. The casualty figures (number of deaths per year) for highway accidents in Texas from 1954 to 1974
    e. The casualty figures for highway accidents in each of the states from 1954 to 1974
    f. The casualty figures for highway accidents in each of the states from 1954 to 1974, subdivided by month
    g. An electronic address book (name, address, and phone information for all your friends)
    h. A collection of hourly temperatures for a 24-hour period
20. a. What are three advantages of using programmer-defined types?
    b. What are two advantages of using programmer-defined subtypes?
    c. How do you decide whether to use a programmer-defined type or a programmer-defined subtype?
21. What is base type?

Encapsulation

22. What is Ada's principle method for encapsulating data structures?
23. What are the advantages of having separate declarations and implementations of packages?
24. Define the following
    a. Definition package
    b. Service package
    c. Data abstraction package
25. What is the relationship between a package hierarchy and a class hierarchy?
26. What Ada construct is used to encapsulate the attributes (data) of a class?
27. What are public declarations? What are private declarations?
28. What is a primitive operation?
29. What is the relationship between primitive types and inheritance?
30. Why do we declare constructors for a class within a package nested within the package that defines the class?
31. Explain the difference between a singleton class and a class.

32. a. How is the programmer using an ADO package prevented from accessing the details of the object?
    b. How do we prevent the programmer using an ADT package from accessing the details of the type defining the class?
    c. What is the advantage of an abstract data type over an abstract data object?
    d. What is the advantage of an abstract data object over an abstract data type?
33. *True or False?*
    a. The details of a private type can be seen by a programmer using an ADT package.
    b. The details of a private type may be accessed by a programmer using an ADT package.
34. Define the following terms:
    a. Parameter profile
    b. Overloading
    c. Overriding
    d. Instance
    e. Abstract class
    f. Concrete class
    g. Abstract operation
35. Why do abstract classes have no constructors?
36. Write a package declaration for a steam locomotive that extends the locomotive class defined by Specification 2.9. In addition to a weight, all steam locomotives have an attribute that specifies the maximum steam pressure (a value between 90 and 900 pounds per square inch) and the current steam pressure (a value between 0 and 1000 pounds per square inch). Include a new operation for blowing the whistle. Finally, include a constructor for the steam locomotive class.
37. Write a package declaration for a Shay locomotive that extends the locomotive class defined in the previous exercise. In addition to all of the attributes and operations of a steam locomotive, Shay locomotives have an operation to set the gear ratio to either high or low and an operation to query the current value of this gear ratio. Include a constructor for the Shay locomotive class. When a Shay locomotive is constructed, the initial gear ratio is set to low.
38. Using the Bingo card class from Specification 2.13, write
    a. the declaration of two Bingo card objects (variables) called `My_Card` and `Your_Card`.
    b. the declaration of an unconstrained array (type) of Bingo cards.
    c. a specification for a function, `Num_Winners`, that, given an unconstrained array of Bingo cards, returns how many of them are winners.
    d. the body for the function `Num_Winners`.

39. Given the following declarations for "square" matrices

```
type Matrix is array (Positive range <>, Positive range <>) of float;
type Square_Matrix (Size : Positive) is
   record
      Data : Matrix (1..Size, 1..Size);
   end record;
```

   a. Declare the variable `Small_Matrix` to be a 4 × 4 square matrix and the variable `Large_Matrix` to be a 120 × 120 square matrix.
   b. Write the package specification for a square matrix ADT declaring type `Square_Matrix` completely in the visible part of the package (this package should have no private part). Include operations to add two square matrices and to subtract two square matrices and an exception named SIZE_ERROR that is raised if an attempt is made to add or subtract square matrices of different sizes.
   c. Rewrite the package specification you did for part (b) making `Square_Matrix` a private type.
   d. What are the advantages and disadvantages of making `Square_Matrix` a private type?
   e. Using the matrix type defined in the package specification of part (b), declare three 3 × 3 square matrix variables.
   f. Using the variables you declared in part (e) and the package specification of part (b), write a code fragment to read in two 3 × 3 square matrices from the keyboard, add them together, and display the sum.
   g. Write the package body for the declaration you did for part (b). Adding and subtracting is accomplished by adding or subtracting the corresponding components in each matrix.

40. Read over Exercise 41 in the next section.
   a. What are some advantages to declaring the complex type in the visible part of the package declaration rather than as a private type?
   b. If the complex type were declared as a private type, what additional operations would you include in the package specification?

Programming Problems

41. Write an ADT package that defines a type for complex numbers and functions for operators +, -, *, /, <, <=, >, and >=. The type should not be a private type. The package should also include a function that returns the conjugate of a complex number. Also write a service package that provides input and output procedures for these complex numbers. Include `Get` and `Put` procedures that allow for interactive input and output and `Get` and `Put` procedures with a `File` parameter

that allow for file input and output. Finally, write a driver program to test these two packages.

A complex number consists of two parts, a real part and an imaginary part. In algebra a complex number is represented as a quantity of two values often enclosed in parentheses like this:

(5.27 + 17.34i)

where 5.27 is the real part of the complex number and 17.34 is the imaginary part. The i in this notation refers to the imaginary square root of -1. The conjugate of a complex number is obtained by simply changing the sign of the imaginary part of the number. For example, the conjugate of (5.27 + 17.34i) is (5.27 − 17.34i).

Addition and subtraction of complex numbers is done by separately adding and subtracting the real and imaginary parts. For example

(5.27 + 17.34i) + (6.11 − 5.30i) = (11.38 + 12.04i)
(5.27 + 17.34i) − (6.11 − 5.30i) = (−0.84 + 22.64i)

Multiplication of two complex numbers may be done by applying the following formula:

$(a + bi)(c + di) = (e + fi)$

where

$e = ac - bd$
$f = bc + ad$

For example

(5.27 + 17.34i)(6.11 − 5.30i) = (124.10 + 78.02i)

The formula for division of two complex numbers is

$(a + bi) / (c + di) = (e + fi)$

where

$e = (ac + bd) / (c^2 + d^2)$
$f = (bc - ad) / (c^2 + d^2)$

For example

(5.27 + 17.34) / (6.11 − 5.30i) = (−0.91 + 2.05i)

Two complex numbers are equal if, and only if, their real parts are equal and their imaginary parts are equal. Although complex numbers are not ordered like integer and real numbers, we can compare the magnitude of two complex numbers with the relational operators $<$ and $>$. The magnitude of a complex number is calculated by taking the square root of the sum of the squares of its real part and its imaginary part. For example the magnitude of (5.27 + 17.34i) is 18.12 and the magnitude of (6.11 − 5.30i) is 8.09. Thus (5.27 + 17.34i) is greater than (6.11 − 5.30i). In your package, use the square root function from the library that is supplied in `Ada.Numerics.Elementary_Functions`.

The form of input and output values for the service I/O package should be that used in our examples: two numbers separated by a sign enclosed in parentheses. The second number should have an i immediately after it. The `Put` procedure should have an `Aft` parameter to specify the number of decimal places desired for each component in the complex value. Use a default value of 2 for parameter `Aft`.

42. Rewrite your complex number package with the complex type declared as private. Make any necessary modifications and additions to the package specification. What, if any, ramifications does making the type private have on the I/O service package?

43. Write a specification for a program that uses the complex number type to find the roots of a quadratic equation. Design, implement, and test a solution.

44. Extend the Bingo card class to create a class of easy win Bingo cards. In addition to having the free play number covered when a card is constructed or cleared, an easy win card has its four corner numbers covered.

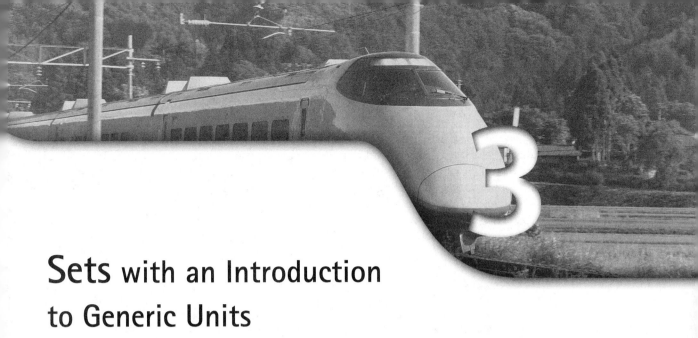

Sets with an Introduction to Generic Units

Goals for this chapter include that you should be able to

- describe a set and its operations at the abstract level.
- determine whether a set is an appropriate data structure for a specific problem.
- use arrays of Boolean components to implement a set class whose elements are discrete objects.
- design and implement generic packages.
- design and implement generic subprograms.
- understand designing for reuse.

Chapter 2 presented the basic principles of designing data structures for data used in computer programs. In this chapter and the ones that follow, we use these principles to build a new range of data structures. These data structures are not predefined by most programming languages, as arrays and records are. However, most of them can be found in the language library. For example, the Ada library packages `Ada.Containers.Hashed_Sets`, `Ada.Containers.Ordered_Sets`, and `Ada.Strings.Maps` provide different set abstractions you can use when you need a set for your application. But, as we said in an earlier chapter, our goal is to teach you how to develop software. You need to practice the fundamentals before you tackle more advanced software development.

We discuss each structure at three levels. First we *define* the abstract class: What does it "look" like and what are the logical operations on it? We write package specifications to specify the structure at this level. Once the package specification for the class is compiled, we can *use* it in applications, so next we look at one or more application examples that use the class. Finally, we *build* one or more implementations of the class as package bodies.

In the second part of this chapter we show you how to write your own generic units. Until the appearance of modern programming languages like Ada, it was common for programmers to implement, verify, and test slightly different versions of a data structure for each application they developed. Even though there were only minor differences between the data structures in the different applications, programmers always "reinvented the wheel." Ada's generic units allow us to design and implement a *template* for a data structure. Then we simply supply some information to the Ada compiler, and it can use our template to generate a data structure customized specifically for our application.

3.1 The Abstract Level

The abstract view of sets comes from discrete mathematics where a set is an *unordered* collection of items called set *members*. An item is either in the set (is a member) or not in the set (is not a member). A set often is written by enclosing the group of items in braces. Here, for example, is how we might write two different sets of fruit:

{ Apple Pear Cherry }   { Orange Cherry Pear Apple Banana }

There are two special types of sets that are important: the **empty set**, which contains no values, and the **universal set**, which contains all the values of the base type. The universal set of fruit would contain all possible fruits. We use { } to indicate an empty set.

> **Empty set** A set with no members.
> **Universal set** A set containing all the values of a component type.

Set Operations

The most commonly used operation for sets is membership testing. Membership testing is simply asking whether an item is in the set. Here are some examples of membership testing:

Membership Test	Answer
Apple in the set { Apple Pear Cherry }	True
Kumquat in the set { Apple Banana Lemon }	False

Union, intersection, and *difference* are three operations that form a new set from two existing sets.

Union: The union of two sets is a set consisting of those components that are in the first set *or* in the second set. The or used here is the inclusive or.

Intersection: The intersection of two sets is a set consisting of those components occurring in the first set *and* in the second set.

Difference: The difference between two sets is the set of components in the first set that are not in the second set.

Here are some examples of these three operations using sets of letters:

First Set	Second Set	Union	Intersection	Difference
{P Q R}	{S}	{P Q R S}	{}	{P Q R}
{S}	{P Q R}	{P Q R S}	{}	{S}
{A B C D}	{B D F}	{A B C D F}	{B D}	{A C}
{L N}	{L M N O P}	{L M N O P}	{L N}	{}
{}	{X Y Z}	{X Y Z}	{}	{}
{X Y Z}	{}	{X Y Z}	{}	{X Y Z}

Another group of operations deals with subsets. A *subset* is a set contained within another set. A set X is a subset of Y if each element of X is an element of Y. If at least one element of Y is not in X, then X is called a *proper subset* of Y. The set {Apple Pear Cherry} is a proper subset of the set {Orange Cherry Pear Peach Apple Banana}.

Here are some examples of subset operations using sets of letters:

First Set	Second Set	First Is Subset of Second	First Is Proper Subset of Second
{A E I O U}	{A B C D E F}	False	False
{A B C D}	{A B C}	False	False
{X Y Z}	{X Y Z}	True	False
{X Y Z}	{W X Y Z}	True	True

Finally, we need some way of adding and removing individual elements from a set. We accomplish this task with operators that take a set and an element as operands. Here are some examples, again using sets of letters:

Set	Element	Addition of Element	Removal of Element
{A E I O U}	B	{A B E I O U}	{A E I O U}
{A B C D}	B	{A B C D}	{A C D}

A Set Specification

Figure 3.1 shows a UML diagram for a set class. Specification 3.1 is a specification for a set class whose members are the callable Bingo numbers (1–75) that we used in Chapter 2.

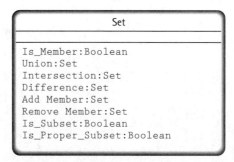

Figure 3.1 *UML class diagram for a set class.*

Specification 3.1 Bingo Number Set

```ada
with Bingo_Numbers; use Bingo_Numbers;
package Bingo_Number_Set is

-- This package implements an object class for a set of Bingo Numbers

   -- Set elements are Bingo numbers (define a synonym)
   subtype Element_Type is Bingo_Numbers.Callable_Number;

   -- The set class
   type Set_Type is private;

   -- A set object with no elements
   Empty_Set : constant Set_Type;    -- A deferred constant (value is assigned
                                     -- in the private part of the package
                                     -- declaration)

   -- A set object with all possible elements
   Universal_Set : constant Set_Type;    -- Another deferred constant


   -----------------------------------------------------------------------
   function Is_Member (Set     : in Set_Type;
                       Element : in Element_Type) return Boolean;
   -- This function determines whether Element is a member of Set

   -----------------------------------------------------------------------
   function "+" (Left : in Set_Type; Right : in Set_Type) return Set_Type;
   -- Returns the union of the two sets
   -- (elements that are in either or both sets)

   -----------------------------------------------------------------------
   function "+" (Left : in Set_Type; Right : in Element_Type) return Set_Type;
   -- Adds an element to a set
   -- (the set is not changed if the element is already a member)

   -----------------------------------------------------------------------
   function "+" (Left : in Element_Type; Right : in Set_Type) return Set_Type;
   -- Adds an element to a set
   -- (the set is not changed if the element is already a member)

   -----------------------------------------------------------------------
```

```ada
    function "*" (Left : in Set_Type; Right : in Set_Type) return Set_Type;
    -- Returns the intersection of the two sets
    -- (elements occurring in both sets)

    ------------------------------------------------------------------------
    function "-" (Left : in Set_Type; Right : in Set_Type) return Set_Type;
    -- Returns the difference of the two sets
    -- (elements in Left and not in Right)

    ------------------------------------------------------------------------
    function "-" (Left : in Set_Type; Right : in Element_Type) return Set_Type;
    -- Removes an element from the set
    -- (the set is not changed if the element is not a member)

    ------------------------------------------------------------------------
    --                    Relational Set Operators
    --              The equality operators (= and /=) are
    --              available for the private type Set_Type
    ------------------------------------------------------------------------

    function "<=" (Left : in Set_Type; Right : in Set_Type) return Boolean;
    -- Returns True if Left is a subset of Right

    function "<" (Left : in Set_Type; Right : in Set_Type) return Boolean;
    -- Returns True if Left is a proper subset of Right

    function ">=" (Left : in Set_Type; Right : in Set_Type) return Boolean;
    -- Returns True if Right is a subset of Left

    function ">" (Left : in Set_Type; Right : in Set_Type) return Boolean;
    -- Returns True if Right is a proper subset of Left

private

    -- We fill this part in later.

end Bingo_Number_Set;
```

Specification 3.1 contains several Ada features worth reviewing. We use the operators +, -, *, and <=, <, >=, and > as function names. In the specification of such a function, the operator symbol is enclosed in quotation marks. When a function name is an operator symbol, we can use it just like we use that operator. For example, we can use the function "+" from our set package to return the union of two sets. If Set_1, Set_2, and Set_3 are all Bingo number sets, the following statement assigns the intersection of Set_2 and Set_3 to Set_1:

```ada
Set_1 := Set_2 + Set_3;
```

The actual parameters, `Set_2` and `Set_3`, in this call to function "+" are associated by position with the formal parameters `Left` and `Right`. We have *overloaded* the function name `"+"`.

We can't use all the operators as function names. Ada does not permit us to use the short circuit operators (`and then` and `or else`) or the membership tests (`in` and `not in`) as function names. The inequality operator (`/=`) cannot be used as a function name. However, the Ada compiler creates a "/=" function for each "=" function that you write.

Specification 3.1 uses a new Ada feature, the deferred constant. `Bingo_Number_Set` contains two deferred constants, `Empty_Set` and `Universal_Set`. These constants, whose types are private, are declared in the visible portion of the package. The actual value of a deferred constant is not given in the visible part; it is deferred to the private part. This means that the package user can use the named constant (because it is declared in the public part), but may not access any of its details (which are declared in the private part).

Here are some example expressions that use our `Bingo_Number_Set` operations:

Expression	Result
Set_1 + Set_2	The union of Set_1 and Set_2
Set_1 + Element	The addition of Element to Set_1
Set_1 * Set_2	The intersection of Set_1 and Set_2
Set_1 - Set_2	The difference of Set_1 and Set_2
Set_1 - Element	The removal of Element from Set_1
Set_1 = Set_2	True if the sets are identical
Set_1 /= Set_2	True if the sets are not identical
Set_1 <= Set_2	True if Set_1 is a subset of Set_2
Set_1 < Set_2	True if Set_1 is a proper subset of Set_2
Set_1 >= Set_2	True if Set_2 is a subset of Set_1
Set_1 > Set_2	True if Set_2 is a proper subset of Set_1

3.2 The Application Level

In Chapter 2 we developed a Bingo game simulation program. We used a Bingo basket object to model the random drawing of Bingo numbers. The basket object must ensure that a number is not called twice in one game—that is, the elements are unique. The numbers can be called in any order, so the collection can be considered unordered. A number either has been called or hasn't been called. We now know a data structure that has these properties and behaviors: a set.

Bingo Number Selection

We can implement the Bingo basket as either a set of numbers that have not been called (those numbers that are still in the basket) or a set of numbers that already have been called (those numbers outside of the basket). Let's choose the first method. (The second is left as an exercise.) The specification of the Bingo basket singleton (Specification 2.12, page 139) contains two operations: `Load` and `Draw`.

We can implement the `Load` procedure, which puts the numbers into the basket, by assigning the universal set to our basket set. Remember that the universal set is the set that contains all the values of the element type. Bingo numbers range from 1 to 75, so the universal set has 75 elements—each of the Bingo values.

The `Draw` procedure requires that we select a number from this set at random. Random selection is not one of our set class operations. We could add such an operation to our set class, but this is not consistent with our mathematical view of this class. It is better for the Bingo number set object to have another object to supply it with a random number. Such objects, which are commonly used in simulation programs, are called *random number generators*. The Ada library contains two different random number generators. `Ada.Numerics.Float_Random` will generate a random floating point number between 0.0 and 1.0. `Ada.Numerics.Discrete_Random` will generate random values of any discrete type we choose. Bingo numbers are integers (and therefore discrete), so we can use `Ada.Numerics.Discrete_Random` to generate the random values needed for our Bingo basket. Body 3.1 implements the Bingo basket singleton class we specified in Chapter 2. It is an application of the set data structure whose specification we developed in the previous section.

Body 3.1   **Bingo Basket Singleton Class: Implements Specification 2.12**

```ada
with Bingo_Number_Set; use Bingo_Number_Set;
with Ada.Numerics.Discrete_Random;
package body Bingo_Basket is

   package Random_Bingo is new Ada.Numerics.Discrete_Random
                              (Result_Subtype => Callable_Number);
   use Random_Bingo;
   -- The following object holds the state of a random Bingo number generator
   Bingo_Gen : Random_Bingo.Generator;

      -- The set of numbers in the Bingo Basket
   The_Basket : Bingo_Number_Set.Set_Type;
```

```ada
   procedure Load is
   begin
      The_Basket := Bingo_Number_Set.Universal_Set;
   end Load;

   -------------------------------------------------------------------------

   procedure Draw (Letter : out Bingo_Letter;
                   Number : out Callable_Number) is
   begin
      if The_Basket = Empty_Set then
         raise EMPTY;
      end if;

      -- Get a number that is still in the Basket
      -- Each iteration, try one number
      loop
         -- "Choose" a number at random.
         Number := Random (Bingo_Gen);

         -- If the number chosen is still in the basket, exit,
         -- otherwise go back and "choose" another number.
         exit when Is_Member (Set     => The_Basket,
                              Element => Number);
      end loop;

      -- Remove the number from the basket
      The_Basket := The_Basket - Number;

      -- Determine the letter using the types in Bingo_Definitions
      case Number is
         when B_Range =>  Letter := B;
         when I_Range =>  Letter := I;
         when N_Range =>  Letter := N;
         when G_Range =>  Letter := G;
         when O_Range =>  Letter := O;
      end case;
   end Draw;
end Bingo_Basket;
```

The `Bingo_Basket` package uses the `Bingo_Number_Set` class without any idea of how it is implemented, just like you have used integers without knowing how they were implemented. The set's specification, given earlier in this chapter, told us what the class is and how to use it, but nothing about how it is implemented. In the next section we look at the details of implementing the `Bingo_Number_Set` class.

The algorithm used to draw a number is not very efficient. Exercise 18 describes a more efficient algorithm and asks you to implement it.

3.3 The Implementation Level

Now that you understand the set class and have seen a simple application that uses it, let's see how to implement it. Earlier we said that a set is an *unordered* collection of items. An item is either in the set (is a member) or not in the set (is not a member). We can use type `Boolean` to model this two-state behavior (`True` if the value is in the set, `False` if it's not). We need one Boolean value for *each* possible item in the set. For example, our set of callable Bingo numbers needs 75 Boolean values.

We can use an array of Boolean components to store all these values. Here are the declarations of such an array and a set variable:

```
type Set_Type is array (Element_Type) of Boolean;

My_Set : Set_Type;
```

The array variable `My_Set` is shown in Figure 3.2. Subtype `Element_Type` was declared in the declaration of package `Bingo_Number_Set` as a synonym of `Bingo_Numbers.Callable_Number`. The indices of the array are the possible set items.

The value of a particular element in the array indicates whether that component is a member of the set. For example, the following code fragment displays whether 4 is a member of `My_Set`:

```
if My_Set(4) then
   Put_Line ("4 is a member of the set");
else
   Put_Line ("4 is not a member of the set");
end if;
```

The empty set is an array in which all components are `False` and the universal set is one in which all components are `True`. We now can fill in the private part of package specification `Bingo_Number_Set`. This part must include the full declarations for type `Set_Type` and deferred constants `Empty_Set` and `Universal_Set`. We use array aggregates to assign values to the two constant arrays.

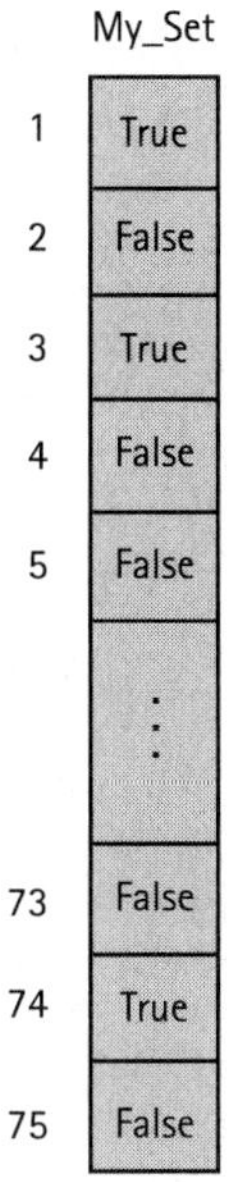

```
                My_Set
           1  │ True  │
           2  │ False │
           3  │ True  │
           4  │ False │
           5  │ False │
                 ⋮
          73  │ False │
          74  │ True  │
          75  │ False │
```

```
if My_Set(4) then
   Put_Line("4 is a member of the set");
else
   Put_Line("4 is not a member of the set");
end if;
```

Figure 3.2 *A set stored as an array of Booleans.*

```
private

   type Set_Type is array (Element_Type) of Boolean;

   -- Completion of deferred constants
   Empty_Set     : constant Set_Type := (Element_Type => False);
   Universal_Set : constant Set_Type := (Element_Type => True);

end Bingo_Number_Set;
```

Because each possible element in the set is represented by a Boolean value, the implementation of most of the set operations in this package use the logical operators and, or, and not. Let's look at an example. Given the declarations

```
Set_One : Set_Type;    -- A set of Bingo_Numbers
Set_Two : Set_Type;    -- Another set of Bingo_Numbers
```

Figure 3.3 shows what the array structures look like if Set_One contains 1, 74, and 3 and Set_Two contains 4, 5, 74, 75, and 3.

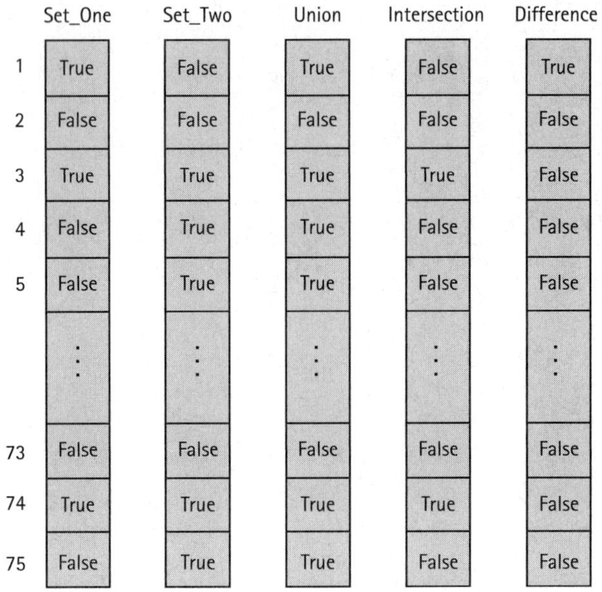

	Set_One	Set_Two	Union	Intersection	Difference
1	True	False	True	False	True
2	False	False	False	False	False
3	True	True	True	True	False
4	False	True	True	False	False
5	False	True	True	False	False
⋮	⋮	⋮	⋮	⋮	⋮
73	False	False	False	False	False
74	True	True	True	True	False
75	False	True	True	False	False

Figure 3.3 *Examples of set operation.*

Note that the elements in the union set are the result of *or*-ing the corresponding elements in the two sets, and the elements in the intersection set are the result of *and*-ing the corresponding elements. The difference set is slightly more complicated. To be in the difference set, an element must be in Set_One but not in Set_Two. Thus each element in the difference array is calculated as

Difference Element := Set_One Element and not (Set_Two Element)

For each of these three operations, we could use a loop to go through the set arrays one element at a time. There is, however, a simpler method. In Chapter 2 we said that Ada's and, or, and not operators may be applied to *entire* arrays of Boolean elements. Operating on the entire array rather than on individual elements eliminates the need for a loop.

The subset operations involve Boolean operations similar to the difference operation. However, the subset operations return a single True or False rather than another set. We can carry out this test with the difference operation. We "subtract" Set_Two from Set_One. Any elements in Set_One that are not in Set_Two are in the difference set. Set_One is not a subset of Set_Two if it contains an element that is not in Set_Two. If all of Set_One's elements are also in Set_Two the difference yields an empty set. Thus our test for subset is a test on whether the difference yields an empty set.

Is a Subset := (Set_One - Set_Two) = Empty_Set

Body 3.2 contains the Ada code for all of these algorithms.

Body 3.2   Bingo Number Set: Implements Specification 3.1

```ada
package body Bingo_Number_Set is

   -------------------------------------------------------------------------
   function Is_Member (Set     : in Set_Type;
                       Element : in Element_Type) return Boolean is
   begin
      return Set(Element);
   end Is_Member;

   -------------------------------------------------------------------------
   function "+" (Left : in Set_Type;  Right : in Set_Type) return Set_Type is
   begin
      return  Left or Right;
   end "+";

   -------------------------------------------------------------------------
   function "+" (Left  : in Set_Type;
                 Right : in Element_Type) return Set_Type is
      Result : Set_Type;
   begin
      Result := Left;
      Result(Right) := True;    -- Add the new element to the set
      return Result;
   end "+";

   -------------------------------------------------------------------------
   function "+" (Left  : in Element_Type;
                 Right : in Set_Type) return Set_Type is
      Result : Set_Type;
   begin
      Result := Right;
      Result(Left) := True;    -- Add the new element to the set
      return Result;
   end "+";

   -------------------------------------------------------------------------
   function "*" (Left : in Set_Type;  Right : in Set_Type) return Set_Type is
   begin
      return  Left and Right;
   end "*";
```

```ada
------------------------------------------------------------
function "-" (Left : in Set_Type; Right : in Set_Type) return Set_Type is
begin
   return Left and not Right;
end "-";

------------------------------------------------------------
function "-" (Left  : in Set_Type;
              Right : in Element_Type) return Set_Type is
   Result : Set_Type;
begin
   Result := Left;
   Result(Right) := False;    -- Remove the element from the set
   return Result;
end "-";

------------------------------------------------------------
function "<=" (Left : in Set_Type; Right : in Set_Type) return Boolean is
   Is_A_Subset : Boolean;
begin
   Is_A_Subset := (Left - Right) = Empty_Set;
   return Is_A_Subset;
end "<=";

------------------------------------------------------------
function "<" (Left : in Set_Type; Right : in Set_Type) return Boolean is
   Result : Boolean;
begin
   if Left = Right then       -- If the sets are equal, not a proper subset
      Result := False;
   else
      Result := Left <= Right;  -- If not equal, test for subset
   end if;                       -- using the function above
   return Result;
end "<";

------------------------------------------------------------
function ">=" (Left : in Set_Type; Right : in Set_Type) return Boolean is
begin
   return  Right <= Left;    -- Reverse the order of the parameters and
                             -- use the operation we've already written
end ">=";

------------------------------------------------------------
```

```
function ">" (Left : in Set_Type; Right : in Set_Type) return Boolean is
begin
   return Right < Left;      -- Reverse the order of the parameters and
                             -- use the operation we've already written
end ">";

end Bingo_Number_Set;
```

The set elements in our package are used as array indexes. Therefore, this implementation technique is limited to sets with discrete elements. We cannot, for example, use this method for a set of real numbers, a set of strings, or a set of student records. In Chapters 7 and 12 we develop data structures that can be used to implement sets with components that are not discrete.

3.4 Programming for Reuse: Generic Units

Designing software modules for reuse is an important aspect of software engineering. The goal of software reuse is to make it possible for a software engineer to develop an application by combining various software modules much like today's hardware engineer develops new circuits by combining standard electronic components. Ada's generic units provide a powerful tool for designing reusable software components.

Looking for things that are familiar is an important problem-solving technique. A good programmer immediately recognizes a problem that he or she has solved before and plugs in the solution. For example, in the previous sections we developed a package to represent a set of Bingo numbers. If you were asked to write a program that required the use of a set of letters (A through Z), you would recognize a similarity with the Bingo number set. It would not take much effort on your part to modify the Bingo number set package to use in your new program.

Ada's **generic units** make reusing previous solutions even easier. We write one general solution to the problem (the generic unit), then we let the compiler modify the general solution to satisfy each particular problem (see Figure 3.4). The specific solution created by the compiler is called an **instance** of our generic solution. We have overloaded the word instance. Earlier we used it to describe the relationship between an object and its class—an object is an instance of a class.

> **Generic unit** A template for a package or subprogram.
>
> **Instance** A package or subprogram created from a generic unit.
>
> **Generic formal parameter** A parameter defined in a generic unit declaration. Used to customize a generic unit for a specific problem.

Generic units allow us to save more than the time and effort it takes to use an editor to modify the solution. Because the Ada compiler makes the modifications without error, we need only test the solution one time. For example, if our generic package works for a set of Bingo numbers, it will also work for a set of letters. Ada's generic contract model guarantees that we do not have to test the set portion of our new program. We can concentrate our testing efforts on the portions of the problem that are new.

But how does the compiler know how to make the specific version of the generic package that we need? **Generic formal parameters** make generic packages flexible so

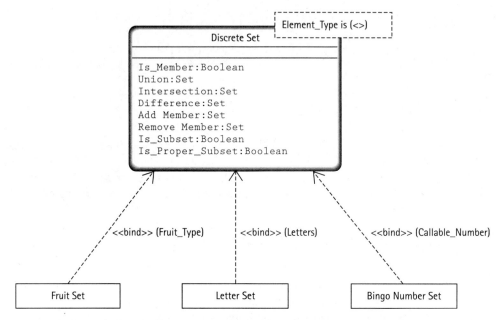

Figure 3.4 *UML diagram of a generic set class and three instances. The Ada compiler can produce specific packages (instances) from a single generic package.*

> **Instantiation** A declaration that creates an instance of a generic unit.

that they can be used in a variety of problems. These parameters give the Ada compiler the information it needs to produce a unit customized for a particular problem from the generic unit. Perhaps without knowing it, you already have used generic parameters. In each **instantiation** of a package for the input and output of enumeration or numeric types you use a generic parameter.

Here is a code fragment to illustrate the use of generic parameters. The instantiation creates a package for the input and output of values of type `Color_Type`.

```
type Color_Type is (Red, Green, Blue, Magenta, Cyan, Yellow);

package Color_IO is new Ada.Text_IO.Enumeration_IO (Enum => Color_Type);
```

Enum is a generic formal parameter of the generic package Enumeration_IO for which we have supplied the actual value of Color_Type. This generic parameter is different than the parameters we use with subprograms—it is a *type*, not a value. When this instantiation is elaborated, the Ada compiler constructs a package called Color_IO from the generic package Enumeration_IO by substituting Color_Type for Enum. It is as though you had a copy of Enumeration_IO and used your program editor to change every occurrence of Enum to Color_Type.

Let's see how we can write a generic set package that we then can use whenever we need a set class in a program. We base this generic package on the Bingo number set package developed earlier in this chapter. Like any package, a generic package consists of two parts: the package specification and the package body. Here is a simplified extended Backus-Naur form (EBNF) definition of a generic package specification:

```
generic_package_declaration    ::=    generic
                                        {generic_parameter_declaration}
                                        package_specification;
```

You can see that the generic formal parameters are declared between the reserved word `generic` and the package specification. The definition of the package specification is exactly the same as with ordinary packages. So to create a generic package we need only precede it with the word *generic* and zero or more generic formal parameters.

The specification for a generic set package is shown in Specification 3.2. Compare this declaration to that of the Bingo number set package (Specification 3.1) on pages 167 and 168.

Specification 3.2   Discrete Set

```ada
generic
   type Element_Type is (<>);  -- This parameter will match any discrete type
package Discrete_Set is

-- This package implements an ADT for a set of discrete elements

   type Set_Type is private;

   Empty_Set     : constant Set_Type; -- A set with no elements
   Universal_Set : constant Set_Type; -- A set with all possible elements

   -----------------------------------------------------------------------
   function Is_Member (Set     : in Set_Type;
                       Element : in Element_Type) return Boolean;
   -- This function determines whether Element is a member of Set

   -----------------------------------------------------------------------
   function "+" (Left : in Set_Type; Right : in Set_Type) return Set_Type;
   -- Returns the union of the two sets
   -- (elements that are in either or both sets)

   -----------------------------------------------------------------------
   function "+" (Left : in Set_Type; Right : in Element_Type) return Set_Type;
   -- Adds an element to a set
   -- (the set is not changed if the element is already a member)
```

```ada
function "+" (Left : in Element_Type; Right : in Set_Type) return Set_Type;
-- Adds an element to a set
-- (the set is not changed if the element is already a member)
```

```ada
function "*" (Left : in Set_Type; Right : in Set_Type) return Set_Type;
-- Returns the intersection of the two sets
-- (elements occurring in both sets)
```

```ada
function "-" (Left : in Set_Type; Right : in Set_Type) return Set_Type;
-- Returns the difference of the two sets
-- (elements in Left and not in Right)
```

```ada
function "-" (Left : in Set_Type; Right : in Element_Type) return Set_Type;
-- Removes an element from the set
-- (the set is not changed if the element is not a member)
```

```ada
--                    Relational Set Operators
--             The equality operators (= and /=) are
--            available for the private type Set_Type
```

```ada
function "<=" (Left : in Set_Type; Right : in Set_Type) return Boolean;
-- Returns True if Left is a subset of Right

function "<" (Left : in Set_Type; Right : in Set_Type) return Boolean;
-- Returns True if Left is a proper subset of Right

function ">=" (Left : in Set_Type; Right : in Set_Type) return Boolean;
-- Returns True if Right is a subset of Left

function ">" (Left : in Set_Type; Right : in Set_Type) return Boolean;
-- Returns True if Right is a proper subset of Left
```

```ada
private

   type Set_Type is array (Element_Type) of Boolean;

   -- Completion of deferred constants
   Empty_Set     : constant Set_Type := (Element_Type => False);
   Universal_Set : constant Set_Type := (Element_Type => True);

end Discrete_Set;
```

The only differences between Specifications 3.1 and 3.2 are the package names and the definitions of `Element_Type`. In package `Discrete_Set`, `Element_Type` is a generic formal parameter. Like any parameters, generic formal parameters are associated with actual parameters. This association is made when a package is instantiated from a generic package. For example, the following code fragment creates a set package for a set of lowercase letters, a set package for fruit, and a set package for Bingo numbers:

```ada
subtype Letters    is Character range 'a'.. 'z';
type    Fruit_Type is (Apple, Banana, Blueberry, Cherry, Plum, Strawberry);

package Letter_Set is new Discrete_Set (Element_Type => Letters);
package Fruit_Set  is new Discrete_Set (Element_Type => Fruit_Type);
package Bingo_Set  is new Discrete_Set (Element_Type => Callable_Numbers);
```

Ada creates the package `Letter_Set` from the generic package `Discrete_Set` by using the generic actual parameter `Letters` in place of the generic formal parameter `Element_Type`. Similarly, Ada creates the package `Fruit_Set` by using the generic actual parameter `Fruit_Type` in place of the generic formal parameter `Element_Type`. Finally, it creates the package `Bingo_Set` by using the generic actual parameter `Callable_Numbers` in place of the generic formal parameter `Element_Type`. Figure 3.4 earlier in the chapter shows the UML diagram of a generic class (called a template class in UML). The generic formal parameters are shown in the dashed box in the upper-right corner of the class icon. Instances are shown as boxes with a dashed arrow pointing to the generic class labeled with «bind» followed by the generic actual parameters.

Ada also allows us to write generic subprograms. These generic units make it easy to reuse a single procedure or function. Like generic packages, generic subprograms may have generic formal parameters that are matched with actual parameters when a subprogram is instantiated from the generic template. Here is a more complete set of EBNF definitions for the declaration of generic units including both packages and subprograms:

generic_declaration	::= generic_subprogram_declaration |
	generic_package_declaration
generic_subprogram_declaration	::= generic_formal_part
	subprogram_specification;

| Chapter 3: Sets

```
generic_package_declaration              ::= generic_formal_part
                                             package_specification;

generic_formal_part                      ::= generic
                                             {generic_formal_parameter_declaration | use_clause}

generic_formal_parameter_declaration     ::= formal_object_declaration        |
                                             formal_type_declaration          |
                                             formal_subprogram_declaration    |
                                             formal_package_declaration

formal_type_declaration                  ::= type defining_identifier[discriminant_part] is
                                             formal_type_definition;

formal_type_definition                   ::= formal_discrete_type_definition           |
                                             formal_signed_integer_type_definition     |
                                             formal_modular_type_definition            |
                                             formal_floating_point_definition          |
                                             formal_ordinary_fixed_point_definition    |
                                             formal_decimal_fixed_point_definition     |
                                             formal_array_type_definition              |
                                             formal_private_type_definition            |
                                             formal_access_type_definition             |
                                             formal_interface_type_definition

formal_discrete_type_definition          ::= (<>)
formal_signed_integer_type_definition    ::= range <>
formal_modular_type_definition           ::= mod <>
formal_floating_point_definition         ::= digits <>
formal_ordinary_fixed_point_definition   ::= delta <>
formal_decimal_fixed_point_definition    ::= delta <> digits <>

formal_array_type_definition             ::= array_type_definition

formal_private_type_definition           ::= [limited] private

formal_subprogram_declaration            ::= with subprogram_specification;

formal_package_declaration               ::=
       with package defining_identifier is new generic_package_name  formal_package_actual_part;
```

This set of EBNF definitions includes definitions of the four different kinds of generic parameters—objects, types, subprograms, and packages. Just as there are rules for subprogram formal and actual parameters, there are rules for generic formal and actual parameters. In this chapter we look at the most commonly used generic formal types. We'll discuss others later as we need them.

Generic Formal Types

Generic formal types allow us to choose the types we want to use in our new package when we instantiate it. The generic formal parameter Element_Type in our discrete set package (Specification 3.2) is an example of a generic formal type. The generic formal parameter Enum in the generic package Enumeration_IO is another example.

Our simplified set of EBNF definitions includes 10 different generic type definitions. Each generic type definition specifies

- What the rules are for matching the actual and formal types
- What operations may be used in the package body with objects of the type

In the following sections we discuss generic type definitions in terms of these two criteria.

Discrete Types   Here is the declaration of Discrete_Set's generic formal parameter Element_Type:

```
type Element_Type is (<>);
```

The (<>) in this declaration means that any discrete type may be used as an actual parameter in an instantiation made from this generic package.[1] Thus we can instantiate set packages for integer types (like Bingo numbers), character types (like lowercase letters), and enumeration types (like Fruit_Type). However, we cannot use type Float, String, any record type, or any array type as a generic actual parameter with our generic set package.

Why did we choose to restrict our set elements to discrete types? In our design of the original Bingo number set package, our algorithms were based on using set elements as array indices. Ada restricts array indices to discrete types, so the type of the set elements must be a discrete type. We use (<>) in the declaration of the generic formal parameter Element_Type to restrict actual parameters to discrete types so that the same algorithms can be used.

In addition to restricting the types of generic actual parameters that can be used, the generic type definition also restricts how the type may be used in the generic package body. For example, the operations permitted in the package body of Discrete_Set on objects of type Element_Type are restricted to those available to *all* discrete types. Thus we may use the assignment operator (:=), equality operators (= and /=), relational operators (>, >=, <, and <=), and the discrete attributes ('First, 'Last, 'Pos, 'Val, 'Pred, and 'Succ) with such objects. We cannot use any arithmetic operators. Arithmetic operators are available for *some* discrete types (integer types and subtypes), not *all* discrete types.

---

[1] We also use the symbol <> (called "box") in the declaration of unconstrained array types.

Body 3.3 is the complete package body for our generic set package. It is nearly identical to the body of our Bingo number set package.

Body 3.3   Discrete Set: Implements Specification 3.2

```ada
package body Discrete_Set is

   ------------------------------------------------------------------
   function Is_Member (Set     : in Set_Type;
                       Element : in Element_Type) return Boolean is
   begin
      return Set(Element);
   end Is_Member;

   ------------------------------------------------------------------
   function "+" (Left : in Set_Type;  Right : in Set_Type) return Set_Type is
   begin
      return Left or Right;
   end "+";

   ------------------------------------------------------------------
   function "+" (Left  : in Set_Type;
                 Right : in Element_Type) return Set_Type is
      Result : Set_Type;
   begin
      Result := Left;
      Result(Right) := True;    -- Add the new element to the set
      return Result;
   end "+";

   ------------------------------------------------------------------
   function "+" (Left  : in Element_Type;
                 Right : in Set_Type) return Set_Type is
      Result : Set_Type;
   begin
      Result := Right;
      Result(Left) := True;    -- Add the new element to the set
      return Result;
   end "+";

   ------------------------------------------------------------------
   function "*" (Left : in Set_Type;  Right : in Set_Type) return Set_Type is
   begin
      return Left and Right;
   end "*";
```

```ada
-------------------------------------------------------------------------------
function "-" (Left : in Set_Type;  Right : in Set_Type) return Set_Type is
begin
   return Left and not Right;
end "-";


-------------------------------------------------------------------------------
function "-" (Left  : in Set_Type;
              Right : in Element_Type) return Set_Type is
   Result : Set_Type;
begin
   Result := Left;
   Result(Right) := False;    -- Remove the element from the set
   return Result;
end "-";


-------------------------------------------------------------------------------
function "<=" (Left : in Set_Type; Right : in Set_Type) return Boolean is
   Is_A_Subset : Boolean;
begin
   Is_A_Subset := (Left - Right) = Empty_Set;
   return Is_A_Subset;
end "<=";


-------------------------------------------------------------------------------
function "<" (Left : in Set_Type; Right : in Set_Type) return Boolean is
   Result : Boolean;
begin
   if Left = Right then    -- If the sets are equal, not a proper subset
      Result := False;
   else
      Result := Left <= Right;   -- If not equal, test for subset
   end if;                       -- using the function above
   return Result;
end "<";


-------------------------------------------------------------------------------
function ">=" (Left : in Set_Type; Right : in Set_Type) return Boolean is
begin
   return  Right <= Left;   -- Reverse the order of the
                            -- parameters and use the operation
                            -- we've already written
end ">=";
```

```ada
   function ">" (Left : in Set_Type; Right : in Set_Type) return Boolean is
   begin
      return Right < Left;       -- Reverse the order of the
                                 -- parameters and use the operation
                                 -- we've already written
   end ">";

end Discrete_Set;
```

Integer Types A formal generic type parameter defined with `range <>` matches an actual parameter of any signed integer type or signed integer subtype. A formal generic type parameter defined with `mod <>` matches an actual parameter of any modular integer type or modular integer subtype. The operations that can be used in the package body with objects of these types include all of the integer operations with which you are familiar. These include assignment, the arithmetic operators, the relational operators, and the attributes defined for integer types (including `'First`, `'Last`, `'Succ`, and `'Pred`).

Let's look at an example. Here's the declaration of a very simple service package that contains three operations for signed integer values: a function that returns the smaller of two values, a function that returns the larger of two values, and a procedure for swapping the values of two integer variables.

```ada
generic
   type Whole_Number_Type is range <>;    -- Generic formal type parameter
package Integer_Ops is

   function Maximum (Left  : in Whole_Number_Type;
                     Right : in Whole_Number_Type) return Whole_Number_Type;
   function Minimum (Left  : in Whole_Number_Type;
                     Right : in Whole_Number_Type) return Whole_Number_Type;
   procedure Swap (Left  : in out Whole_Number_Type;
                   Right : in out Whole_Number_Type);
end Integer_Ops;
```

Here is the body of this generic package:

```ada
package body Integer_Ops is


   function Maximum (Left  : in Whole_Number_Type;
                     Right : in Whole_Number_Type) return Whole_Number_Type is
```

```ada
   begin
      if Left > Right then
         return Left;
      else
         return Right;
      end if;
   end Maximum;
```

```ada
   function Minimum (Left  : in Whole_Number_Type;
                     Right : in Whole_Number_Type) return Whole_Number_Type is
   begin
      if Left < Right then
         return Left;
      else
         return Right;
      end if;
   end Minimum;
```

```ada
   procedure Swap (Left  : in out Whole_Number_Type;
                   Right : in out Whole_Number_Type) is
      Temp : Whole_Number_Type;
   begin
      Temp  := Left;
      Left  := Right;
      Right := Temp;
   end Swap;

end Integer_Ops;
```

And here are some examples of instantiations of packages from this generic package:

```ada
subtype Quiz_Score_Type is Integer range 1..10;
type    Feet            is range 1..25;

package Quiz_Ops is new Integer_Ops (Whole_Number_Type => Quiz_Score_Type);
package Feet_Ops is new Integer_Ops (Whole_Number_Type => Feet);
```

When the package `Quiz_Ops` is instantiated, at every place that `Whole_Number_Type` is used in the generic template `Integer_Ops`, it is replaced with the actual type `Quiz_Score_Type`. Similarly, when the package `Feet_Ops` is instantiated, `Whole_Number_Type` is replaced with the actual type `Feet`.

Real Types A formal generic type parameter defined with `digits <>` matches an actual parameter of any float type or float subtype. A formal generic type parameter defined with `delta <>` matches an actual parameter of any binary fixed point type or binary fixed point subtype. A formal generic type parameter defined with `delta <> digits <>` matches an actual parameter of any decimal fixed point type or decimal fixed point subtype. The operations that can be used in the package bodies for these types include all of the real arithmetic operations with which you are familiar. These include assignment, the arithmetic operators, the relational operators, and the attributes defined for each specific real type.

Here is a code fragment of a generic package declaration with a generic formal float type parameter:

```
generic
   type Number_Type is digits <>;      -- Generic formal type parameter
package Number_Ops is
   .
   .
   .
```

We can use this generic package to instantiate packages for any float type, as illustrated by these examples:

```
type Pounds is digits 8 range 0.0..1000.0;
type Ounces is digits 5 range 0.0..16.0;

package Pound_Ops  is new Number_Ops (Number_Type => Pounds);
package Ounces_Ops is new Number_Ops (Number_Type => Ounces);
```

Array Types The declarations of generic formal array types look just like the declarations that we have used for ordinary array types. Usually, the declaration of a generic formal array type makes use of previously declared generic formal types, as in this example:

```
generic
   type Discrete_Type  is (<>);
   type Int_Type       is range <>;
   type Int_Array      is array (Discrete_Type)          of Int_Type;
   type Discrete_Array is array (Int_Type range <>)      of Discrete_Type;
   type Boolean_Array  is array (Natural range <>)       of Boolean;
   type Char_Array     is array (Int_Type)               of Character;
package Array_Example is
   .
   .
   .
```

In this example, the formal array type `Int_Array` is declared as a constrained array whose index type and bounds are defined by the formal type parameter `Discrete_Type` and whose component type is defined by the formal type parameter `Int_Type`. The formal array type `Discrete_Array` is declared as an unconstrained array whose index type is defined by the formal type parameter `Int_Type` and whose component type is defined by the formal type parameter `Discrete_Type`. The formal array type `Boolean_Array` is declared as an unconstrained array whose index type is `Natural` and whose components are `Boolean` values. Finally, the formal array type `Char_Array` is declared as a constrained array whose index type and bounds are defined by the formal type parameter `Int_Type` and whose components are `Character` values.

The rules for matching actual and formal array types involve the following five conditions:

1. The actual array type and the formal array type must be either both constrained or both unconstrained.
2. The index type of the actual array type and the formal array type must be the same.
3. If the array parameter is constrained, the lower and upper bounds of the actual array type and the formal array parameter must be the same.
4. The component type must be the same for the actual array type as for the formal array type.
5. The actual array type and the formal array type must have the same number of dimensions.

Let's look at an example instantiation of generic package `Array_Example`.

```
subtype Small_Int is Integer range 1..10;

-- Constrained array type
type Small_Array is array (Boolean) of Small_Int;

-- Unconstrained array types
type Truth_Array     is array (Small_Int range <>) of Boolean;
type Falsehood_Array is array (Natural   range <>) of Boolean;

-- Constrained array type
subtype Small_String is String (Small_Int);

package Example is new Array_Example (Discrete_Type   => Boolean,
                                      Int_Type        => Small_Int,
                                      Int_Array       => Small_Array,
                                      Discrete_Array  => Truth_Array,
                                      Boolean_Array   => Falsehood_Array,
                                      Char_Array      => Small_String);
```

For each of the array parameters in this example, go through the five conditions that must be met for a match between an actual and a formal array parameter.

The operations that we can use in the package body with formal array types are the operations available for *any* array type including assignment, indexing, slicing, the relational operators (for one-dimensional arrays whose components are discrete types), and the array attributes (including `'First`, `'Last`, `'Length`, and `'Range`).

Private Types The matching rules for formal private types are simple. A formal generic type parameter defined with `private` matches an actual parameter of any type *except* limited private types. A formal generic type defined with `limited private` matches any type.

The operations that we can use in the body of the generic package or subprogram with objects of a formal private type are restricted to assignment (`:=`) and equality testing (`=` and `/=`). There are no operations available for use in the body of the generic package or subprogram with objects of a formal limited private type. In the next section we show how we can supply the generic body with operations it may use with objects of private and limited private types.

Let's look at an example. Here is the declaration of a generic procedure that swaps the values of its two parameters:

```
generic
    type Swap_Type is private;    -- Matches any type except limited private types
procedure Swap_Values (Left  : in out Swap_Type;
                       Right : in out Swap_Type);
```

We can instantiate a swap procedure for any data type (except limited private types) from this generic procedure. The following instantiations create procedures for swapping the values of two integer variables, two float variables, two character variables, and two student record variables. As with any overloaded procedure call, the Ada compiler uses the type of the actual parameters to determine which of our newly created `Swap` procedures to call.

```
procedure Swap is new Swap_Values (Swap_Type => Integer);
procedure Swap is new Swap_Values (Swap_Type => Float);
procedure Swap is new Swap_Values (Swap_Type => Character);
procedure Swap is new Swap_Values (Swap_Type => Student_Rec);
```

Now let's look at the body of the generic procedure `Swap_Values`. The only operation for which we need to swap two values is assignment.

```
procedure Swap_Values (Left  : in out Swap_Type;
                       Right : in out Swap_Type) is
    Temp : Swap_Type := Left;
```

```
begin
   Left  := Right;
   Right := Temp;
end Swap_Values;
```

Generic Formal Subprograms

As we saw in the previous section, generic formal private types allow us to instantiate generic units for any type. This generality comes with a price—the operations available for values of these types are very restricted. We can use generic subprogram parameters to supply the body with additional operations for private and limited private types. The actual subprograms are supplied by the programmer instantiating the generic unit.

Specification 3.3 shows an example. This procedure sorts an array of values.[2] We can instantiate a sorting procedure from this generic procedure that can sort any array indexed by positive integers. The values in the array can be any type except limited private types. Because `Element_Type` is a formal private type, the only operations permitted in the procedure body are assignment and equality testing. To determine the order of two elements, the procedure requires a relational operation to compare them. We provide that operation as a generic function parameter.

Specification 3.3   Generic Selection Sort

```
generic
   type Element_Type is private;
   type Array_Type  is array (Positive range <>) of Element_Type;
   with function "<" (Left  : in Element_Type;
                      Right : in Element_Type) return Boolean;
procedure Selection_Sort (The_Array : in out Array_Type);
-- Purpose        : Sort an array of elements into ascending order
-- Preconditions  : None
-- Postconditions : The elements in The_Array are in ascending order
```

Before we look at the body of the selection sort procedure, let's look at an example of instantiating a sort procedure for an application where we need to sort an array of inventory records. We want these records to be in ascending order by part number. Here are the declarations for the array we want to sort:

```
type Part_Rec is
   record
      Part_Number : Positive;
      Quantity    : Natural;
   end record;
```

---

[2]The procedure `Ada.Containers.Generic_Array_Sort` in the Ada library provides sorting of arbitrary array types.

```ada
-- The array type that we will sort
type Part_Array is array (Positive range <>) of Part_Rec;
```

We must supply three actual parameters when we instantiate a sort procedure from our generic procedure: the array component type, the array type, and a function for comparing two components. There are no predefined relational operators for records. We need to write our own function to compare two inventory records. The comparison is based on the part number, one of the fields in our inventory record.

```ada
-- A function to compare two inventory records
function "<" (Left  : in Part_Rec;
              Right : in Part_Rec) return Boolean is
begin
   return Left.Part_Number < Right.Part_Number;
end "<";
```

Now we can instantiate an inventory part sorting procedure from our generic selection sort. The three actual generic parameters (`Part_Rec`, `Part_Array`, and "<") are all defined in our application.

```ada
-- The inventory part sorting procedure
procedure Part_Sort is new Selection_Sort (Element_Type => Part_Rec,
                                           Array_Type   => Part_Array,
                                           "<"          => "<");
```

The body of our generic sort procedure is shown in Body 3.4. Notice that this generic procedure body instantiates a procedure to swap two `Element_Type` objects from the generic swap procedure shown on page 190. The `if` statement that compares two array elements uses the "<" function supplied as a generic parameter when the procedure is instantiated.

Body 3.4   Selection Sort: Implements Specification 3.3

```ada
with Swap_Values;
procedure Selection_Sort (The_Array : in out Array_Type) is

   -- Instantiate a procedure to swap two array elements
   procedure Swap is new Swap_Values (Swap_Type => Element_Type);

   Min_Index : Positive;  -- The index of the smallest element

begin
   for Pass_Count in The_Array'First .. The_Array'Last - 1 loop
      Min_Index := Pass_Count;
      for Place_Count in Pass_Count + 1 .. The_Array'Last loop
```

```ada
        if The_Array(Place_Count) < The_Array(Min_Index) then
           Min_Index := Place_Count;
        end if;
     end loop;
     if Min_Index /= Pass_Count then
        Swap (Left  => The_Array(Min_Index),
              Right => The_Array(Pass_Count));
     end if;
  end loop;
end Selection_Sort;
```

We began this last example of a generic unit with a declaration of the unit. When developing a generic unit with generic formal private types, we usually do not know all of the operations needed by the body ahead of time. Therefore we must often develop the body and declaration simultaneously.

Problem-Solving Case Study

A Reusable Binary Search Procedure

When implementing an algorithm it is natural to think in terms of the immediate application. Such an implementation is likely to require modification when the algorithm is needed in a different application. With a little extra effort, we can use Ada's generic units to implement an algorithm or class that we can instantiate for a wide variety of applications.

In Chapter 1 we used a binary search procedure to illustrate testing. The binary search is useful in many applications. We can save a good deal of time in the future by developing a generic binary search procedure that can be instantiated for a wide variety of applications. Here is a nongeneric procedure specification taken from our efforts in Chapter 1:

```ada
-- Final version from Chapter 1
procedure Binary_Search (List     : in  Integer_Array;
                         Value    : in  Integer;
                         Location : out Natural);
-- Purpose         : Searches List for Value.  Location is the index of Value
--                   in List if found.  Otherwise returns zero for Location
-- Preconditions   : List is sorted in ascending order
-- Postconditions  : List(Location) = Value  or  Location = 0
```

The type `Integer_Array` used for this procedure was defined in our test program. It was an unconstrained array of integers indexed by positive integers. We can design a generic version that is not restricted to searching arrays of integers. As we did in the selection sort example, we can include a generic parameter for our element type and the array type. We know from the binary search algorithm we developed in Chapter 1 that we will need to compare our search value to the "middle" array value. We need both equality testing and relational testing. So, like the sort procedure, we can include generic functions to compare the elements. Here is the resulting procedure specification:

```ada
generic   -- Version 1
   type Element_Type is limited private;
   type Array_Type   is array (Positive range <>) of Element_Type;
   with function "<" (Left  : in Element_Type;
                      Right : in Element_Type) return Boolean;
   with function "=" (Left  : in Element_Type;
                      Right : in Element_Type) return Boolean;
   procedure Binary_Search (List     : in  Array_Type;
                            Value    : in  Element_Type;
                            Location : out Natural);
   -- Purpose         : Searches List for Value. Location is the index of Value
   --                   in List if found.  Otherwise returns zero for Location
   -- Preconditions   : List is sorted in ascending order
   -- Postconditions  : List(Location) = Value  or  Location = 0
```

This design allows us to instantiate a binary search procedure for an array of any element type indexed by positive integers. We can do better. Let's generalize the array index type. We can use any discrete type for an array index. Character and enumeration types are commonly used for array indexes. To generalize the index type we add a formal discrete parameter. We use this type in the definition of the formal array parameter and for the Location returned by the procedure.

```ada
generic   -- Version 2  (Do the comments still make sense?)
   type Index_Type is (<>);
   type Element_Type is limited private;
   type Array_Type   is array (Index_Type range <>) of Element_Type;
   with function "<" (Left  : in Element_Type;
                      Right : in Element_Type) return Boolean;
   with function "=" (Left  : in Element_Type;
                      Right : in Element_Type) return Boolean;
   procedure Binary_Search (List     : in  Array_Type;
                            Value    : in  Element_Type;
                            Location : out Index_Type);
   -- Purpose         : Searches List for Value. Location is the index of Value
   --                   in List if found.  Otherwise returns zero for Location
   -- Preconditions   : List is sorted in ascending order
   -- Postconditions  : List(Location) = Value  or  Location = 0
```

This generalization of the array index type has introduced a problem. Look at the comments describing this procedure. They state that if the `Value` is not found in the `List`, `Location` is set to zero. That action was fine when our index was a positive integer type, but now our index can be any discrete type. For many of these types, such as `Character`, zero is not even a valid value.

We used this one parameter for two different purposes—to indicate whether the search was successful and, if it was successful, to indicate the location of `Value` in `List`. To correct this problem, we add a `Boolean` procedure parameter to indicate whether `Value` is found in `List`. Specification 3.4 shows this addition along with appropriate comments describing the procedure's behavior. According to these comments, what is the value of `Location` when `Value` is not in `List`?

Specification 3.4   Generic Binary Search

```
generic
    type Index_Type   is (<>);
    type Element_Type is limited private;
    type Array_Type   is array (Index_Type range <>) of Element_Type;
    with function "<" (Left  : in Element_Type;
                       Right : in Element_Type) return Boolean;
    with function "=" (Left  : in Element_Type;
                       Right : in Element_Type) return Boolean;
procedure Binary_Search (List     : in  Array_Type;
                         Value    : in  Element_Type;
                         Found    : out Boolean;
                         Location : out Index_Type);
-- Purpose        : Search List for Value
-- Preconditions  : List is in ascending order
-- Postconditions : Value is in List and Found and List(Location) = Value
--                  or
--                  Value is not in List and not Found
```

Here are two sample instantiations of this generic procedure:

```
type Month_Type is (January, February, March, April,
                    May, June, July, August, September,
                    October, November, December);

type Nat_Array is array (Month_Type range <>) of Natural;
type Int_Array is array (Positive range <>)   of Integer;

procedure Nat_Search is new Binary_Search (Element_Type => Natural,
```

```ada
                                        Index_Type    => Month_Type,
                                        Array_Type    => Nat_Array,
                                        "<"           => "<",
                                        "="           => "=");

procedure Int_Search is new Binary_Search (Element_Type => Integer,
                                        Index_Type    => Positive,
                                        Array_Type    => Int_Array,
                                        "<"           => Standard."<",
                                        "="           => Standard."=");
```

The first instantiation creates a binary search procedure that searches for a particular natural number in an array whose index type is an enumeration type (`Month_Type`). The "<" and "=" operators for `Month_Type` objects used as actual parameters in the instantiation are defined as part of the declaration of type `Month_Type`. The second instantiation creates a binary search procedure that searches for a particular whole number in an array indexed by a positive integer type. The "<" and "=" operators used as actual parameters in this instantiation are defined in package `Standard` along with all the rest of Ada's built-in types. Although not necessary, we have prefixed these operators with the package name for clarity. Figure 3.5 illustrates two arrays that could be searched by these two procedures.

Let's look at a third instantiation of this generic sort procedure. This time our array components are the inventory records we used earlier.

```ada
type Part_Rec is
   record
      Part_Number : Positive;
      Quantity    : Natural;
   end record;

-- The array type that we will search
type Part_Array is array (Positive range <>) of Part_Rec;
```

(a) An array that procedure `Nat_Search` could search.

March	April	May	June	July	August
0	7	14	19	27	193

(b) An array that procedure `Int_Search` could search.

7	8	9	10	11	12	13	14	15	16	17
-42	-27	-10	0	18	27	182	274	295	507	698

Figure 3.5 *(a) An array that procedure `Nat_Search` could search. (b) An array that procedure `Int_Search` could search.*

Our instantiation requires operations to compare two inventory records. We again write our own function to compare two inventory records based upon the part number field.

```ada
function "<" (Left  : in Part_Rec;
              Right : in Part_Rec) return Boolean is
begin
   return Left.Part_Number < Right.Part_Number;
end "<";
```

Equality operations are defined for records. But these equality operations for records compare all the fields in the record. In our search, we are interested in only a matching part number. So here is a function that determines whether two inventory records have the same part number:

```ada
function Equal_Part_Numbers (Left  : in Part_Rec;
                             Right : in Part_Rec) return Boolean is
begin
   return Left.Part_Number = Right.Part_Number;
end Equal_Part_Numbers;
```

We now have everything to instantiate a procedure to do a binary search on an array of inventory records.

```ada
procedure Part_Search is new Binary_Search (Index_Type   => Positive,
                                            Element_Type => Part_Rec,
                                            Array_Type   => Part_Array,
                                            "<"          => "<",
                                            "="          => Equal_Part_Numbers);
```

Now let's turn to the body of this generic procedure. Obviously, the body on page 60 of Chapter 1 must have its parameters and postconditions changed to match our more general declaration. There are four other changes that we must make.

1. We must change the types of the local variables `Midpoint`, `First_Index`, and `Last_Index` from `Natural` to `Index_Type`.

2. We must calculate `Midpoint` in a manner suitable for any discrete type. When our array indexes were integers, we easily calculated the midpoint through simple algebra.

   Midpoint := (First_Index + Last_Index) / 2;

   However, the array index in our generic version may be any discrete type, so we cannot use arithmetic operators directly. We must make use of the attributes `'Pos` and `'Val` to determine the midpoint.

```
              Midpoint := Index_Type'Val ((Index_Type'Pos (First_Index) +
                                           Index_Type'Pos (Last_Index)) / 2);
```

3. Instead of subtracting or adding one to `Midpoint` to divide the current search area in half we must use `'Succ` and `'Pred`. We replace the lines

```
          elsif Value < List(Midpoint) then
             Last_Index := Midpoint - 1;     --Search 1st half
          else
             First_Index := Midpoint + 1;    --Search 2nd half
```

with

```
          elsif Value < List(Midpoint)  then
             Last_Index := Index_Type'Pred (Midpoint);    --Search 1st half
          else
             First_Index := Index_Type'succ (Midpoint);   --Search 1st half
```

4. If `Midpoint` is equal to `List'First` or to `List'Last`, we may attempt to find the successor of the last value of the type or the predecessor of the first value, thereby raising CONSTRAINT_ERROR. This problem occurs when `Value` is less than any value in the array or greater than any value in the array. We can add a check for these conditions before beginning our search, but first we must make sure that the list is not empty. An attempt to compare `Value` with the first or last values in an empty list also raises CONSTRAINT_ERROR.

Body 3.5 is the complete procedure body reflecting these changes.

Body 3.5   Binary Search Procedure: Implements Specification 3.4

```
procedure Binary_Search (List     : in  Array_Type;
                         Value    : in  Element_Type;
                         Found    : out Boolean;
                         Location : out Index_Type) is
   First_Index : Index_Type; -- First index in current search area
   Last_Index  : Index_Type; -- Last index in current search area
   Midpoint    : Index_Type; -- Index of search area's midpoint
begin
   -- Is the list empty?
   if List'Length = 0 then
      Found := False;
   -- Is the value outside of the range of indices?
   elsif Value < List(List'First)  or  List(List'Last) < Value then
      Found := False;
```

```ada
      else  -- Do the search

         Found       := False;
         First_Index := List'First;
         Last_Index  := List'Last;

         -- Search until element found or the current search area is empty.
         -- Current search area is List (First_Index..Last_Index)
         Search_Loop:
         loop
            exit Search_Loop when First_Index > Last_Index or Found;
            -- Find middle element in the current search area.
            Midpoint := Index_Type'Val ((Index_Type'Pos (First_Index) +
                                         Index_Type'Pos (Last_Index)) / 2);
            -- Compare Value to middle element in search area.
            if List(Midpoint) = Value then
               Found := True;
            elsif Value < List(Midpoint) then
               Last_Index := Index_Type'Pred(Midpoint);   -- Search 1st half
            else
               First_Index := Index_Type'Succ(Midpoint);  -- Search 2nd half
            end if;
         end loop Search_Loop;
         Location := Midpoint;
      end if;
end Binary_Search;
```

Private Types and Generic Formal Private Types

We have used the reserved word *private* in two different contexts: the declaration of private types and the declaration of generic formal types. Private types are used in an ADT package to prevent the program that uses the package from accessing the details of the type. These details are declared in the private part of the package specification and may be used in any way by the package body. By making the types private, we prevent a program that uses the package from accessing the details of the data structure. Then, if we change these details, we can be confident that we won't have to rewrite the application. You have just seen how generic formal private type parameters let us write a generic package that can be instantiated for any type. In this case, it is the package that is restricted in its use of the type. In order to handle any type, we can use only operations that are common to all types. The details of the type are declared outside of the generic package and may not be used in it.

It is easy to confuse these two different uses of private. Just remember that where the details of the type are declared is where they may be fully accessed. With a private type, the details of the type are defined in the ADT package and may be used without restriction by that package. With a generic formal private type parameter, the details of the actual type are defined in the application that instantiates a new package from the generic package. The details of the type are available to that program but not to the generic package.

Problem-Solving Case Study
Minimizing Translations

Let's look at another problem whose solution involves sets. A European conference is being held in Brussels. The conference committee is designing signs to place outside of the different meeting rooms to help delegates find the correct rooms. There is not enough space on a sign to use every language spoken at the conference. Fortunately, the delegates are diplomats so most speak several different languages. The committee must find a small number of languages to put on the signs. These languages must be chosen so that every delegate can read at least one of them. Here is a more formal specification of this problem:

Translations

Purpose: To find a small number of languages of which all delegates can read at least one.

Input: The names of the languages spoken by each delegate. Data are in a text file called delegate.txt. Each line of the file contains the data for one delegate.

Output: A listing of languages of which all delegates can read at least one.

We can model each delegate with a set of languages (a delegate either speaks or does not speak a particular language). To model the collection of delegates, we can use an array of language sets. Here are the declarations needed for this model:

```ada
Max_People : constant := 100;  -- Maximum number of people

type Language_Type is (Dutch, English, Finnish, French, German, Italian,
                       Norwegian, Portuguese, Spanish, Swedish);

-- Create a set class whose components are the languages
package Language_Set is new Discrete_Set (Element_Type => Language_Type);
use Language_Set;   -- Make set operations directly visible

-- A package for I/O of languages
package Language_IO  is new Ada.Text_IO.Enumeration_IO(Enum => Language_Type);
use Language_IO;    -- Make I/O operations directly visible

-- Types for an array of language sets
```

```
subtype Index_Type  is Natural;
subtype Index_Range is Index_Type range 1..Max_People;
type Language_Set_Array is array (Index_Range range <>) of Language_Set.Set_Type;

-- A list of the languages spoken by each delegate.  Each element in the
-- array of this list is a set of languages spoken by one delegate.
Delegate_List  : Language_Set_Array (Index_Range);
Delegate_Count : Index_Type;
```

If there is some common group of languages spoken by all the diplomats, we can find it by taking the intersection of all the language sets. For example, here are the language sets for three diplomats:

{Dutch French German}   {English French German Spanish}   {French Italian German}

The intersection of these three sets is

{French German}

This intersection is the set of languages spoken by all three diplomats. Either of the languages in this intersection could be used alone for the signs. It is, however, likely that there is no language spoken by all the diplomats attending the conference. The following three language sets illustrate this possibility:

{Dutch French German}   {English French Spanish}   {Italian German}

The intersection of these sets is the empty set; there is no language common to these three diplomats.

Upon inspection of these last three sets, we can see that if each sign is written in both French and German, all the diplomats can read it. Such inspections are easy with only a few diplomats. It is much more difficult when there are hundreds of diplomats speaking dozens of languages.

An Optimal Solution

If the intersection of all of the diplomats' language sets yields an empty set, we can test different combinations of languages until we find a set that includes languages spoken by everyone. Start by testing all combinations of two different languages, then all combinations of three different languages, then all combinations of four different languages, and so on until we find a set of languages that satisfies all the diplomats. To test a potential set of languages, we determine the intersection of it with each diplomat's set of languages. If any intersection yields an empty set, that potential set of languages is inadequate. There are two problems with this solution. First, generating the various combinations is not a trivial algorithm. Second, even for a modest number of languages, the number of possible combinations can be very large. For example, the number of possible combinations of languages from a set of 25 is 33,554,431. If the conference has 100 diplomats, our program may need to calculate over 3 billion set intersections.

A Greedy Solution

A greedy algorithm is one that determines a satisfactory, but not necessarily best, solution to a problem in a short amount of time. For example, a greedy algorithm for our language problem might yield a set of five languages whereas the optimal algorithm yields a set of three languages. However, the number of calculations required in the greedy algorithm is much smaller. Here is a greedy algorithm for our language problem:

Find Adequate Set of Languages
Initialize Potential Set to the universal set of languages
L := first language in the universal set
loop
    Remove the Lth language from the Potential Set
    Test the Potential Set against all diplomats
    If the Potential Set does not satisfy some diplomat
        Put the Lth language back in the Potential Set
    end if
    exit loop when all languages have been tested
    Set L to the next language
end loop

In this algorithm we remove one language and test to see if the reduced set still satisfies all the diplomats. If the reduced set is inadequate for a single diplomat, we put that language back in. We do this for each language spoken. If we have 25 languages, the loop iterates 25 times. Testing 100 diplomats then requires the calculation of 2,500 intersections—far fewer than the potential 3 billion intersection calculations in the optimal algorithm. Program 3.1 implements this greedy algorithm.

Program 3.1   Translations

```ada
with Discrete_Set;
with Ada.Text_IO;   use Ada.Text_IO;
procedure Translations is

-- This program finds a "minimum" number of languages needed for an
-- international conference.  Because a greedy algorithm is used, the
-- languages selected may not be the absolute minimum number.

-- Assumptions:   1. The data file delegates.txt exists and contains information
--                   for at least one delegate
--                2. The data file contains one line of data for each delegate
--                3. Each line of the data file contains valid language names
--                4. The last language on a line is followed immediately by
--                   a line terminator

   Max_People : constant := 100;   -- Maximum number of delegates
```

```ada
type Language_Type is (Dutch, English, Finnish, French, German, Italian,
                Norwegian, Portuguese, Spanish, Swedish);

-- Create a set class whose components are the languages
package Language_Set is new Discrete_Set (Element_Type => Language_Type);
use Language_Set;    -- Make set operations directly visible
-- A package for I/O of languages
package Language_IO is new Enumeration_IO(Enum => Language_Type);
use Language_IO;     -- Make I/O operations directly visible

-- Types for an array of language sets
subtype Index_Type  is Natural;
subtype Index_Range is Index_Type range 1..Max_People;
type Language_Set_Array is array (Index_Range range <>)
                    of Language_Set.Set_Type;

-- A list of the languages spoken by each delegate.  Each element in the
-- array of this list is a set of languages spoken by one delegate.
Delegate_List  : Language_Set_Array (Index_Range);
Delegate_Count : Index_Type;

Data_File : Ada.Text_IO.File_Type;     -- Delegate language information
Min_Set   : Language_Set.Set_Type;     -- Set of languages sufficient for all

-------------------------------------------------------------------------
procedure Put_Set (Set : in Language_Set.Set_Type) is
-- Purpose       : Display all of the languages in a given set
-- Preconditions : None
-- Postconditions : Each language in Set is displayed on a separate line
begin
   -- Display all the languages in Set
   -- Each iteration, display one language
   for Language in Language_Type loop
      if Is_Member (Element => Language, Set => Set) then
         Language_IO.Put (Language);
         New_Line;
      end if;
   end loop;
end Put_Set;


-------------------------------------------------------------------------
function Adequate (Delegates : in Language_Set_Array;
                   Set       : in Language_Set.Set_Type) return Boolean is
-- Purpose       : Determines whether the given Set of languages is
--                 adequate for all the Delegates.
-- Preconditions : Delegates'Length > 0
```

```
   -- Postconditions : Returns True if the intersection of every set in
   --                  Delegates with Set is not empty
   Index      : Index_Type;
   Inadequate : Boolean;
begin
   Index      := Delegates'First;
   Inadequate := False;
   -- Check all of the delegates
   -- Each iteration, we check if one delegate speaks a language in Set
   loop
      exit when Inadequate or Index > Delegates'Last;
      -- Set is inadequate if a delegate doesn't speak one of the languages
      Inadequate := Delegates (Index) * Set = Empty_Set;
      Index := Index + 1;
   end loop;
   return not Inadequate;
end Adequate;

---------------------------------------------------------------------

procedure Find_Common (Delegates : in  Language_Set_Array;
                       Common    : out Language_Set.Set_Type) is
-- Purpose        : Determine a set of languages that all Delegates speak
-- Preconditions  : None
-- Postconditions : Common is the intersection of all sets in Delegates
begin
   if Delegates'Length = 0 then
      Common := Empty_Set;
   else
      Common := Universal_Set;
      for Index in Delegates'Range loop
         Common := Common * Delegates(Index);
      end loop;
   end if;
end Find_Common;

---------------------------------------------------------------------

procedure Find_Minimum (List    : in  Language_Set_Array;
                        Min_Set : out Language_Set.Set_Type) is
-- Purpose        : Determines some "small" set of languages that satisfy
--                  the needs of all delegates in the List
-- Preconditions  : List'Length > 0
-- Postconditions : Min_Set is a set of languages spoken by all delegates
--                  in List
   Candidate : Language_Type;              -- One language
begin
   Min_Set:= Language_Set.Universal_Set;   -- Start with all languages
```

```ada
      -- Remove as many languages as possible from the universal set
      -- Each iteration, try to remove languages from the set
      Candidate := Language_Type'First;
      loop
         Min_Set:= Min_Set - Candidate;  -- Remove Candidate language from the set
           -- Is the current set of languages inadequate?
         if not Adequate (Delegates => List, Set => Min_Set) then
            Min_Set:= Min_Set + Candidate;  -- Put the language back in
         end if;
         exit when Candidate = Language_Type'Last;
         Candidate := Language_Type'succ (Candidate);
      end loop;
   end Find_Minimum;

   -------------------------------------------------------------------------

   procedure Get_Delegate_Data (File     : in out Ada.Text_IO.File_Type;
                                Delegate :   out Language_Set.Set_Type) is
   -- Purpose        : Get all the language data for one delegate
   -- Preconditions  : The languages spoken by this delegate are on
   --                  a single line
   --                  The line terminator follows immediately after
   --                  the last language
   -- Postconditions : Delegate is the set of languages from the current
   --                  line of File
   --                  The reading marker is advanced to the next line
      Language : Language_Type;    -- One language spoken by a delegate
   begin
      Delegate := Language_Set.Empty_Set;  -- No languages yet
      -- Get this delegate's set of languages
      -- Each iteration, one language for a delegate is obtained
      loop
         exit when End_Of_Line (File);
           -- Get a language and add it to the delegate's language set
         Get (File => File, Item => Language);
         Delegate := Delegate + Language;
      end loop;
      if not End_Of_File (File) then
         Skip_Line (File);
      end if;
   end Get_Delegate_Data;

   -------------------------------------------------------------------------

begin
   Open (File => Data_File,
         Name => "delegate.txt",
```

```ada
                  Mode => In_File);
Delegate_Count := 0;

-- Get the language data for all the delegates
-- Each iteration, get the language data for one delegate
loop
   exit when End_Of_File (Data_File);
   Delegate_Count := Delegate_Count + 1;
   Get_Delegate_Data (File     => Data_File,
                      Delegate => Delegate_List (Delegate_Count));
end loop;
Close (Data_File);

-- See if there are any languages spoken by ALL delegates by
-- determining the intersection of all their language sets
Find_Common (Delegates => Delegate_List (1..Delegate_Count),
             Common    => Min_Set);

if Min_Set /= Empty_Set then
   Put_Line ("Use any one of the following languages.");
else -- No common language found.
      -- Find some small set that satisfies all delegates
   Find_Minimum (List    => Delegate_List (1..Delegate_Count),
                 Min_Set => Min_Set);
   Put_Line ("Use all of the following languages.");
end if;
New_Line;
Put_Set (Min_Set);
end Translations;
```

Summary

A set is an unordered collection of values. An item is either in the set (is a member) or not in the set (is not a member). Operations for the set come from mathematics. The most common operations are membership, union, intersection, difference, and subsets. We developed a generic set package for sets whose elements are discrete types.

Packages allow us to encapsulate our implementation of a data structure to create an abstract data type (ADT). Generic packages are package templates that can be customized by the user of the ADT when they instantiate a package from our template. Ada also allows us to write generic subprograms. These make it easy to reuse a single procedure or function. We use generic parameters to supply the information necessary for the Ada compiler to carry out the customizing of generic packages and subprograms. The selection of a generic formal parameter type restricts (1) what type of actual parameter can be supplied by the user and (2) what operations the package may use with objects of that type.

Designing a generic package or subprogram for reuse takes more effort than designing it for a specific problem. We must select the most general generic parameters and write the body for the most general case. The benefits gained in reusing well-designed generic units outweigh the original design effort.

Exercises

Sets

1. a. Using the generic discrete set package developed in this chapter, write the necessary declarations to instantiate a set class to contain the months of the year.
   b. Using the package you instantiated in part (a), declare variables `Winter_Months`, `Fall_Months`, and `Cool_Months` to be set objects (variables).
   c. Write a code fragment to assign the appropriate months to `Winter_Months`.
   d. Write a code fragment to assign the appropriate months to `Fall_Months`.
   e. Write a single statement to assign the union of `Winter_Months` and `Fall_Months` to `Cool_Months`.
2. a. Add the following array type and operation to the specification of package `Discrete_Set`:

```
-- An array of set elements may be converted to type Set_Type
type Set_Array is array (Positive range <>) of Element_Type;

function To_Set (Array_Of_Elements : in Set_Array) return Set_Type;
-- This function returns a set consisting of the elements in
-- the given array
```

   b. Implement the function `To_Set` in the body of package `Discrete_Set`.
   c. Use function `To_Set` to write a single Ada statement to assign the appropriate months to the set object `Winter_Months` you declared in the previous question. Hint: Use an array aggregate.
   d. Should type `Set_Array` be declared as a private type like `Set_Type`? Explain your answer.
3. Add a function called `Size` to the specification of package `Discrete_Set` to determine the cardinality of a set (the number of elements in a given set). Implement this operation in the body of package `Discrete_Set`.
4. The complement of set A is the set of all of the elements in the universal set but not in set A.
   a. Using the set constants and operations already defined in package `Discrete_Set`, write a single assignment statement to assign the compliment of set A to set B.

b. Add a function called `Complement` to the specification of package `Discrete_Set` that is given a set and returns the complement of that set.

c. Implement function `Complement` in the body of package `Discrete_Set`. Calculate the complement without calls to other set operations—manipulate the array of Booleans directly. You can do this calculation by applying a single Boolean operator to the array.

5. The symmetric difference of two sets consists of all of the elements belonging to one of the sets but not both of the sets.

   a. Using the set constants and operations already defined in package `Discrete_Set`, write a single assignment statement to assign the symmetric difference of set A and set B to set C. Hint: Look up the definition of symmetric difference for sets in a discrete math book or on the Internet to determine what operations to use.

   b. Add a function called `Symmetric_Difference`, which is given two sets and returns their symmetric difference, to the specification of package `Discrete_Set`.

   c. Implement function `Symmetric_Difference` in the body of package `Discrete_Set`. Calculate the symmetric difference without calls to other set operations—manipulate the array of Booleans directly. You can do this calculation by using a single Boolean operator with the two arrays.

6. Add the following operation to the specification of package `Discrete_Set`:

   `procedure Put_Set (Set : in Set_Type);`
   `-- Display all the elements in Set, one per line`

   Implement the body of this procedure in the body of package `Discrete_Set`. Hint: Use the `'Image` attribute to convert a discrete value to a string and then use `Ada.Text_IO.Put_Line` to display it.

7. A programmer used the following instantiation in a program:

   `package Integer_Set is new Discrete_Set (Element_Type => Integer);`

   The program compiles without error, but when it is run, `STORAGE_ERROR` is raised. Upon single stepping through the program with the debugger, the programmer discovered that this exception is raised by the following variable declaration:

   `Nums : Integer_Set.Set_Type;    -- A set of Integers`

   Explain why `STORAGE_ERROR` is raised here.

8. Why did we choose to implement the set as an abstract data type (ADT) rather than as a singleton (abstract data object)?

Generic Units

9. Explain the difference between a private type and a generic formal private type.
10. Look up the specification of the generic elementary function package

Ada.Numerics.Generic_Elementary_Functions

in the *Ada Language Reference Manual*. Using the following declaration

```
type High_Precision is digits 18;
```

write an instantiation of Ada.Numerics.Generic_Elementary_Functions to provide mathematical operations for these high precision numbers.

11. Look up the specification of the generic discrete random value generating package

    Ada.Numerics.Discrete_Random

    in the *Ada Language Reference Manual*. Using the following declaration

    ```
    type Months is (January, February, March, April, May, June, July,
                    August, September, October, November, December);
    ```

    write an instantiation of Ada.Numerics.Discrete_Random to provide random months for a game application.

12. Look up the specification of the generic sorting procedure

    Ada.Containers.Generic_Constrained_Array_Sort

    in the *Ada Language Reference Manual*. Using the following declarations

    ```
    subtype Lowercase is Character range 'a'..'z';
    type    Natural_Array is array (Lowercase) of Natural;
    ```

    write an instantiation of Ada.Containers.Generic_Constrained_Array_Sort to sort the items in a Natural_Array in ascending order.

13. By changing a single character in the instantiation you wrote for the previous question, you can change the sort so that the array is sorted in descending order rather than in ascending order. What do you need to change to accomplish this task?

14. Look up the specification of the generic sorting procedure

    Ada.Containers.Generic_Array_Sort

    in the *Ada Language Reference Manual*. Using the following declaration

    ```
    type Part_Array is array (Character range <>) of Part_Rec;
    ```

    and the declaration of Part_Rec and the function "<" that compares two Part_Recs on page 192, write an instantiation of Ada.Containers.Generic_Array_Sort to sort the items in Part_Array.

15. a. Write a specification and body for a generic function that is given three discrete values and returns the largest of the three.

    b. Write some declarations to illustrate an instantiation of your function.

16. a. Write a specification and body for a generic function that is given three values of any nonlimited type and returns the largest of the three.

    b. Write everything necessary to instantiate your function to return a copy of the Part_Rec (declared on page 191) with the largest part number.

Programming Problems

17. Write a body for `Bingo_Basket` that uses a set of numbers that has been drawn rather than a set of numbers that has not been drawn.

18. The `Draw` operation of the `Bingo_Basket` ADO we developed does not use a very efficient algorithm. Numbers between 1 and 75 are repeatedly chosen at random until a check reveals that the chosen number is still "in the basket." As the number of numbers remaining in the basket becomes small, this loop may execute many times before a chosen number is found in the basket. Develop a more efficient algorithm. Hint: Use an array of Bingo numbers instead of a set of Bingo numbers and use values from the random number generator to "shuffle" the values in the array.

19. All possible languages spoken at the conference described in the case study at the end of this chapter were coded directly into the Ada program as enumeration literals. Modify this program so that the program reads the names of all the languages spoken as strings before the languages spoken by each delegate are read. One way to accomplish this modification is to associate each language with an integer (the first language entered is 1, the second 2, and so on). After the languages have been entered you can instantiate a set package for sets of the size needed. Why can't you just instantiate a set of `Positive` numbers? Design a package to handle the association between languages and numbers. Think carefully about what operations to include and whether it should be an ADT or an ADO.

20. A local fast food restaurant manager wants you to write a program to analyze the work request days of her employees. She has prepared a data file with one line per employee. The first 10 characters of the line contain an employee name padded with blanks. Following the name are the names of days of the week that the employee would like to work. Here is a short sample data file:

```
Horace     Monday Monday Tuesday wednesday thursday Friday
Mildred    Saturday Sunday Tuesday friday Wednesday Monday Thursday
Elaine     Thursday   Monday Monday Monday Wednesday
Alice      Monday Sunday Tuesday Saturday              Thursday
Ralph      Wednesday Friday
```

Write a program that prompts for the name of the data file and then displays the following information about the employees:

a. The input data (name and requested days for each person).

b. The names of people who requested to work all seven days of the week. There may be none.

c. The names of people who requested to work on the same days (all of them) as the last person in the data file. These people might request more days than the last person. There may be none.

d. The names of people who request to work on the opposite days as the last person in the data file. These people request *all* of the days that the last person in the list does not work and do not request *any* days that the last person in the list works. There may be none.

  e. The names of people who did not request to work Friday, Saturday, or Sunday. There may be none.
  f. The days of the week that everyone requested. There may be none.
  g. The days of the week that no one requested. There may be none.

Assumptions that you may make:
  i. The data in the file are valid.
  ii. There are no trailing spaces on any of the input lines (makes using End_Of_Line easy).
  iii. There are no blank lines in the file (makes using End_Of_File easy).
  iv. There is at least one employee in the data file.
  v. Everyone requests at least one day of work.
  vi. There are no more than 100 employees.

Use operations in the set ADT to calculate your results. You may use any operations you added to the set ADT from any of the previous exercises.

21. Using your knowledge of sets and set operations, implement a program that reads an essay from a text file and computes and displays the following information:
  a. For each line of the essay:
      i. The line number
      ii. The set of vowels used in the line
      iii. The set of consonants used in the line
      iv. The set of punctuation marks used in the line
      v. The set of digits used in the line
  b. For the entire essay:
      i. The set of letters, digits, and punctuation marks not used anywhere in the essay
      ii. The set of characters in the essay that are not letters, digits, or punctuation marks

For our analyses you should assume that

Vowels are {a e i o u y}[3]

Consonants are {b c d f g h j k l m n p q r s t v w x y z}

Digits are {0 1 2 3 4 5 6 7 8 9}

Punctuation marks are {. , ; : ? !}

Advice and additional requirements:

---

[3]Note that the letter *y* is considered both a vowel and a consonant.

- Use the function `Ada.Characters.Handling.To_Lower` to convert any uppercase letters in an essay line to lowercase.
- Use the function `Ada.Text_IO.Line` to determine which line of the essay the reading marker is on. Use an explicit type conversion (cast) to convert a value of type `Positive_Count` to type `Integer` for the output of the line number.
- Write a `Put` procedure to display a set of characters.
- You may only use the `Is_Member` operation in your `Put` procedure.
- Minimize your use of set variables by calculating results that you don't need to save directly in the call to the `Put` procedure. For example, the following call to `Put` displays the union of three sets:

  ```
  Put (Item => First_Set + Second_Set + Third_Set);
  ```

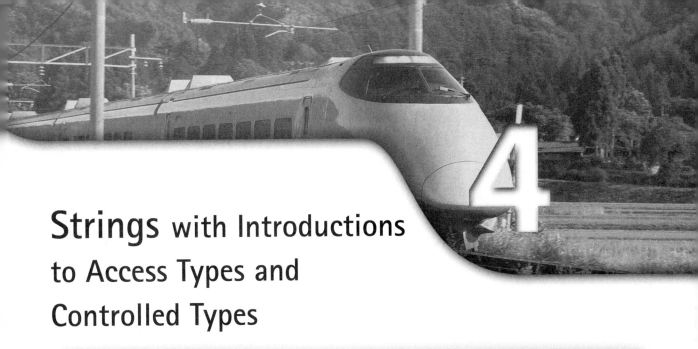

Strings with Introductions to Access Types and Controlled Types

Goals for this chapter include that you should be able to

- differentiate between fixed-length and varying-length string classes.
- differentiate between bounded-length and unbounded-length string classes.
- use the string operations for fixed-length, bounded-length, and unbounded-length strings available in the Ada library.
- implement operations in the different string classes.
- declare and use access variables to designate dynamically created objects.
- use Ada's allocator `new` to create space for a new object at run time.
- understand the difference between an access object and a designated object.
- use procedures instantiated from `Unchecked_Deallocation` to reclaim memory used by a dynamic object.
- understand the purposes of controlled types and their operations.
- create a subclass of a controlled type and override the `Initialize`, `Finalize`, and `Adjust` operations.

4.1 String Terminology

Computers are used extensively to manipulate text. You use an editor program to enter and modify your Ada programs and you use a word processing program to enter, modify, and print essays for your English class. Each of these applications has its own set of operations for manipulating the text. For example, whereas a word processing program wraps the text around to the next line when you reach a right margin, a program editor does not.

We can find many different classes in a typical essay: sections, paragraphs, lines, sentences, words, and characters. What abstractions can we use to model all of the requirements in these different applications? From your previous study of Ada, you are familiar with two useful predefined classes: the character and the string. The declaration of `String` given in package `Standard` is

```
type String is array (Positive range <>) of Character;
```

> **Length**   The number of characters in a string.
>
> **Fixed-length string**   A string that contains a fixed (constant) number of characters.
>
> **Varying-length string**   A string in which the number of characters can change.
>
> **Bounded-length string**   A varying-length string with a fixed maximum number of characters. A bounded-length string has a current length and a maximum length.
>
> **Unbounded-length string**   A varying-length string with no bound on the number of characters.

From this declaration we can see that type `String` is an unconstrained array of characters. Typically, we declare constrained array subtypes from type `String` that we then use to declare string objects. The number of characters in a string object is called the **length**. Because the number of characters in an array object is fixed, string objects based on type `String` are known as **fixed-length strings**. As with any array type, the primitive operations of this string type are meager; we can assign, compare, index, slice, and catenate. Ada provides additional functions and procedures for fixed-length strings in the package `Ada.Strings.Fixed`.

In most problems, the number of characters we need to keep together as a unit is not constant. For example, the number of characters on a line in an Ada program in this book varies from 0 to 80. A string whose length can change is called a **varying-length string**. There are two kinds of varying-length strings. A **bounded-length string** is a varying-length string with a fixed maximum number of characters. A bounded-length string object has both a current length, which can change, and a maximum length, which cannot change. An **unbounded-length string** is a varying-length string with no bound on the number of characters. Like the bounded-length string, the length of an unbounded string object can change over the object's lifetime. Unlike the bounded-length string, there is no maximum size associated with an unbounded-length string object.

The Ada library contains two predefined varying-length string classes. Package `Ada.Strings.Bounded` defines a bounded-length string type. Package `Ada.-Strings.Unbounded` defines an unbounded-length string type. Why would we choose to use a bounded-length string when an unbounded-length string type is available? Generally, unbounded-length strings do not run as efficiently as bounded-length strings; the operations take more time to execute. Later in this chapter we discuss other problems that a programmer must tackle when using unbounded-length strings.

4.2 The Logical Level

What are the basic text string operations? Operations for the set class developed in Chapter 3 come from mathematics. There is widespread agreement on what constitutes the basic operations of this class. There is no such agreement with text strings. There are 35 functions and procedures for fixed-length strings defined in the package `Ada.Strings.Fixed`, 75 functions and procedures for bounded-length strings defined in the package `Ada.Strings.Bounded`, and 68 functions and procedures for unbounded-length strings defined in the package `Ada.Strings.Unbounded`.

In the following sections we'll look at some of these string library operations at the logical level. All three of these packages make use of constants and types in their parent package `Ada.Strings`.

```
package Ada.Strings is
    Space           : constant Character        := ' ';
    Wide_Space      : constant Wide_Character   := ' ';
    Wide_Wide_Space : constant Wide_Wide_Character := ' ';

    LENGTH_ERROR, PATTERN_ERROR, INDEX_ERROR, TRANSLATION_ERROR : exception;

    type Alignment  is (Left, Right, Center);
    type Truncation is (Left, Right, Error);
    type Membership is (Inside, Outside);
    type Direction  is (Forward, Backward);
    type Trim_End   is (Left, Right, Both);
end Ada.Strings;
```

Fixed-Length Strings

The basic model for the operations defined in `Ada.Strings.Fixed` is that a fixed-length string consists of *significant* characters and *padding* characters. Let's look at an example:

```
subtype Name_String is String (1..10);

Name : Name_String;   -- A fixed-length string
```

`Name` is a fixed-length string object. It always contains 10 characters. Now suppose we want to assign the name Mildred to this variable. Do you see why the following assignment statement will raise CONSTRAINT_ERROR?

```
Name := "Mildred";    -- Raises CONSTRAINT_ERROR
```

The object has a fixed length of 10, so we must always assign 10 characters to Name. We can accomplish this by adding three padding characters to our seven significant characters. Padding characters may be added to either or both ends of the significant characters. The space character is the most commonly used padding character. Here are three examples that successfully assign the name Mildred to our fixed-length string variable:

```
Name := "Mildred   ";   -- Padding on right end
Name := "   Mildred";   -- Padding on left end
Name := " Mildred  ";   -- Padding on both ends
```

Manually counting significant characters to determine the required number of padding characters is a time-consuming and error-prone task. Package `Ada.-Strings.Fixed` contains a procedure called `Move` that automatically adds the padding characters. Here is the specification of `Move`:

```
procedure Move (Source  : in  String;
                Target  : out String;
                Drop    : in  Truncation := Error;  -- Types are defined in
                Justify : in  Alignment  := Left;   -- the package Ada.Strings
                Pad     : in  Character  := Space);
```

Procedure `Move` puts a copy of `Source` into `Target`. We use the parameters `Drop`, `Justify`, and `Pad` to describe what we want the `Move` procedure to do if `Source` and `Target` are different size strings. Here are descriptions of these three parameters:

- Pad: Tells what character is stripped or added when copying strings of different sizes. The default value is the space character.

- Justify: Tells how to justify the significant characters in `Target`. Possible values are `Left`, `Right`, and `Center`. The default is to left justify the significant characters by stripping padding from or adding padding to the right side of the string.

- Drop: Tells from which end to strip *significant* characters if necessary. Possible values are `Left`, `Right`, and `Error`. The default is to raise the exception `LENGTH_ERROR` if the significant characters in `Source` won't all fit in `Target`.

Here are some examples to illustrate the use of procedure `Move` for copying fixed-length strings:

```
subtype Name_String  is String (1..10);
subtype Short_String is String (1..4);

Name  : Name_String;     -- Holds 10 characters
Short : Short_String;    -- Holds 4 characters
```

```
Move (Source => "Horace",        -- Name becomes "Horace    " which includes
      Target => Name);            -- 4 padding (space) characters after the e

Move (Source => "Horace         ", -- There are 9 trailing spaces in Source
      Target => Name);            -- Same results as previous example

Move (Source  => "Horace",        -- Name becomes "  Horace  " which includes
      Target  => Name),           -- 2 padding characters before the H
      Justify => Center);         -- and 2 padding characters after the e

Move (Source  => "Horace",        -- Name becomes "$$Horace$$"
      Target  => Name),
      Justify => Center,
      Pad     => '$');

Move (Source => "Horace",         -- Exception Length_Error raised
      Target => Short);

Move (Source => "Horace",         -- Short becomes "Hora"
      Target => Short),
      Drop   => Right);

Move (Source => "Horace",         -- Short becomes "race"
      Target => Short),
      Drop   => Left);
```

In order to make it easier to understand the behavior of the `Move` procedure, we used a string literal as the actual parameter for `Source` in all these examples. It is more common that the source is a fixed-length string variable.

Searching Strings Package `Ada.Strings.Fixed` contains a number of different functions for searching a standard string. We discuss three of these in this section, but there are many more in the library.

The following function searches for a substring within a string. It returns the location (the index) of the first character of a substring (`Pattern`) within a string (`Source`). If `Pattern` does not exist within `Source`, a value of zero is returned.

```
function Index (Source  : in String;
                Pattern : in String;
                Going   : in Direction := Forward;
                Mapping : in Character_Mapping := Identity)
         return Natural;
```

The type `Character_Mapping` and the constant `Identity` are defined in the library package `Ada.Strings.Maps`. This library package contains set and map classes that are very useful in processing strings. You are already familiar with sets. A character map is a lookup table used to translate one character to another. The identity map translates a character to itself. An uppercase to lowercase map translates an uppercase character to a lowercase character. `Ada.Strings.Maps` provides the operations to create character maps.

Here are some example calls to function `Index` that use the default parameter values:

```
Location : Natural;             -- Result of a string search


Location := Index (Source  => "Mildred",     -- Returns 5
                   Pattern => "red");

Location := Index (Source  => "Mildred",     -- Returns 0
                   Pattern => "Red");

Location := Index (Source  => "Mildred",     -- Returns 4
                   Pattern => "d");
```

The parameters `Going` and `Mapping` give us additional control over the search.

> Going: Tells in what direction to perform the search. The default is a forward search (left to right).
>
> Mapping: Tells how to translate characters in the `Pattern` before comparing the `Pattern` to the `Source`. The default (`Identity`) is to do no translation. Package `Ada.Strings.Maps` contains the declarations and operations for character mapping.

Here are some more examples with values supplied for `Going` and `Mapping`:

```
Location       : Natural;              -- Result of a string search
Upper_To_Lower : Character_Mapping;    -- A mapping variable


Location := Index (Source  => "Mildred",           -- Returns 7
                   Pattern => "d",
                   Going   => Backward);

Upper_To_Lower := Ada.Strings.Maps.To_Mapping        -- Create a mapping
        (From => "ABCDEFGHIJKLMNOPQRSTUVWXYZ",        -- from uppercase
         To   => "abcdefghijklmnopqrstuvwxyz");       -- to lowercase

Location := Index (Source  => "Mildred",           -- Returns 5
                   Pattern => "Red",
                   Mapping => Upper_To_Lower);
```

The exception PATTERN_ERROR is raised if Pattern is a null string (contains zero characters). We defined our own mapping for these examples. Package Ada.Strings.Maps.Constants contains predefined maps for mapping between uppercase and lowercase letters.

The second search function we examine searches for one of several characters within a string. It returns the location (the index) of the first character it finds in Source that is in Set. If it can't find one of the set elements in the string, it returns a value of zero. Here is the specification of this function:

```ada
function Index (Source : in String;
                Set    : in Character_Set;
                Test   : in Membership := Inside;   -- Types are defined in
                Going  : in Direction  := Forward)  -- package Ada.Strings
         return Natural;
```

Here are some example calls using the default values of Test and Going:

```ada
-- Create a set of vowels
Vowel_Set := Ada.Strings.Maps.To_Set (Sequence => "AEIOUaeiou");

-- Find first vowel in the string
Location := Index (Source => "Mildred",       -- Returns 2
                   Set    => Vowel_Set);
-- Find first vowel in the string
Location := Index (Source => "Mnppls",        -- Returns 0
                   Set    => Vowel_Set);
```

The parameters Test and Going give us additional control over the search.

Test: Tells whether to search for characters that are inside the set or outside the set.

Going: Tells in what direction to perform the search. The default is a forward search (left to right).

Here are some more examples with values supplied for Test and Going:

```ada
-- Find last vowel in the string
Location := Index (Source => "Mildred",       -- Returns 6
                   Set    => Vowel_Set,
                   Going  => Backward);
-- Find first non-vowel in the string
Location := Index (Source => "Mildred",       -- Returns 1
                   Set    => Vowel_Set,
                   Test   => Outside);
```

The last search operation we examine is a procedure that is similar to the previous function. Instead of searching for one of several characters within a string, it looks for the first contiguous sequence of these characters. It returns the locations (the indexes) of the `First` and `Last` character in the sequence it finds in `Source`. If it can't find such a group of set elements in the string, it returns values of `Source'First` for `First` and zero for `Last`. Here is the specification of this procedure:

```
procedure Find_Token (Source : in  String;
                      Set    : in  Character_Set;
                      Test   : in  Membership;
                      First  : out Positive;
                      Last   : out Natural);
```

Here are some example calls:

```
-- Create a set of vowels
Vowel_Set := Ada.Strings.Maps.To_Set (Sequence => "AEIOUaeiou");

-- The following call returns 2 and 4 for First and Last
Ada.Strings.Fixed.Find_Token (Source => "Beautiful",
                              Set    => Vowel_Set,
                              Test   => Inside,
                              First  => Start_Of_Vowel_String,
                              Last   => End_Of_Vowel_String);

-- The following call returns 1 and 0 for First and Last
Ada.Strings.Fixed.Find_Token (Source => "Mnppls",
                              Set    => Vowel_Set,
                              Test   => Inside,
                              First  => Start_Of_Vowel_String,
                              Last   => End_Of_Vowel_String);

-- Create a set with a single element - the space character
Blank_Set := Ada.Strings.Maps.To_Set (Singleton => ' ');

-- The following call finds the location of the first word of Source.
-- It returns 3 and 7 for First and Last
Ada.Strings.Fixed.Find_Token (Source => "  Hello Mildred  ",
                              Set    => Blank_Set,
                              Test   => Outside,
                              First  => Start_Of_Word,
                              Last   => End_Of_Word);

-- The following call finds the location of the first word of Source.
-- It returns 1 and 7 for First and Last
```

```
Ada.Strings.Fixed.Find_Token (Source => "Mildred",
                              Set    => Blank_Set,
                              Test   => Outside,
                              First  => Start_Of_Word,
                              Last   => End_Of_Word);
```

Other Operations Package `Ada.Strings.Fixed` contains many other operations for fixed-length strings including the following:

- Additional search operations including `Index_Non_Blank`, `Count`, and additional versions of `Index`
- Translation operations that use character maps to change characters in a fixed-length string
- Transformation operations that trim, insert, delete, replace, and overwrite portions of a fixed-length string
- Selector operations that return portions of a fixed-length string including `Head` and `Tail`
- Constructors to create strings by replicating a character or a string multiple times

With an understanding of the examples we have presented and the succinct descriptions given in Section A.4.3 of the *Ada Language Reference Manual*, you should have little difficulty understanding the behaviors of these operations.

Finally, we note that the library packages `Ada.Strings.Wide_Fixed` and `Ada.Strings.Wide_Wide_Fixed` provide equivalent operations for fixed-length wide character strings and fixed-length wide wide character strings.

Bounded-Length Strings

Package `Ada.Strings.Bounded` contains a generic package for a bounded-length string class. Each instantiation of this generic package includes a value for the upper bound of the resulting bounded-length string. Here are two example instantiations:

```
-- Create a bounded-length string class with an upper bound of 10
package Name_Strings is new
        Ada.Strings.Bounded.Generic_Bounded_Length (Max => 10);
use Name_Strings;

-- Create a bounded-length string class with an upper bound of 8
package Postal_Code_Strings is new
        Ada.Strings.Bounded.Generic_Bounded_Length (Max => 8);
use Postal_Code_Strings;
```

Each instantiated bounded-length string package includes the private type `Bounded_String` and operations for this type. Here are two variable declarations that illustrate the use of the types from our two instantiations:

Chapter 4: Strings

```
Name : Name_Strings.Bounded_String;        -- Holds between 0 and 10
                                              characters
Code : Postal_Code_Strings.Bounded_String; -- Holds between 0 and 8 characters
```

The operations for bounded-length strings include most of those available for fixed-length strings, modified as needed to reflect the variability in length. `Bounded_String` is a private type, so additional constructor and selector operations are provided.

Because the varying length eliminates the need for padding characters, there is no bounded-length equivalent to the fixed-length string `Move` procedure. Instead we use the assignment operator to copy bounded-length strings. Another ramification of varying length is the need for an operation to return the number of characters currently in the string. This operation is accomplished by the `Length` function as

```
Char_Count := Length (Name);   -- Returns the number of characters in Name
```

To obtain the upper bound of a particular instantiation of the bounded-length generic package we can use the constant `Max_Length` defined in the package.

```
Largest := Name_Strings.Max_Length; -- Returns the string type's upper bound
```

In the following sections we examine some of the operations available for bounded-length strings. For a complete list see Section A.4.4 in the *Ada Language Reference Manual*.

Conversion The bounded-length strings package contains the following two functions for converting between fixed-length and bounded-length strings:

```
function To_Bounded_String (Source : in String;
                            Drop   : in Truncation := Error)
                            return Bounded_String;

function To_String (Source : in Bounded_String) return String;
```

The `Drop` parameter in the first conversion function allows us to specify what is to be done if the number of characters in `Source` exceeds the upper bound of the bounded-length string. We can choose to raise the exception `LENGTH_ERROR` (the default) or drop enough characters from the left or right side of the source to fit within the bound. Recall that type `Truncation` is defined in package `Ada.Strings`. Here are some examples of conversion function use:

```
Fixed_Name : String(1..10);

Name : Name_Strings.Bounded_String;
Code : Postal_Code_Strings.Bounded_String;
```

```ada
-- Fixed-length to bounded-length.
Name := To_Bounded_String ("Mildred");

-- This conversion raises LENGTH_ERROR
Name := To_Bounded_String ("Hello Mildred");

-- This conversion puts "Mildred Sm" into Name
Name := To_Bounded_String (Source => "Mildred Smedley",
                           Drop   => Right);

-- Set up a bounded-length string with a value for the next examples
Name := To_Bounded_String ("Mildred");

-- Bounded-length to fixed-length.  Notice use of slicing.
Fixed_Name (1..7) := To_String (Name);

-- Usually we need to calculate the range of the slice.
Fixed_Name (1..Length(Name)) := To_String (Name);

-- For complete control, use the fixed-length string Move
-- operation instead of the assignment operator when converting
-- a bounded-length string to a fixed-length string.
Ada.Strings.Fixed.Move (Source  => To_String (Name),
                        Target  => Fixed_Name,
                        Justify => Left,
                        Drop    => Error,
                        Pad     => ' ');

-- Convert one bounded-length string type to another bounded-length
-- string type by first converting it to a fixed-length string type
Code := Postal_Code_Strings.To_Bounded_String (Name_Strings.To_String(Name));
```

The final example in this group shows how to convert one type of bounded-length string to a different bounded-length string type by first converting it to a fixed-length string type. For clarity, we have prefixed each of the function names used in this conversion with the package in which they are defined.

Comparison Package `Ada.Strings.Bounded.Generic_Bounded_Length` contains a full set of equality testing and relational operators for comparing strings. Operators are defined for comparing bounded-length strings to bounded-length strings and bounded-length strings to fixed-length strings.

When using different types of bounded-length strings, comparisons can be made by first converting the values to fixed-length strings and then using the built-in array operators available for type `String`. Here is an example:

```ada
            if To_String (Code) < To_String (Name) then
               .
               .
               .
```

Catenation Package `Ada.Strings.Bounded.Generic_Bounded_Length` contains operators, functions, and procedures for catenating bounded-length strings. There are versions to catenate two bounded strings into a bounded-length string and versions to catenate a fixed-length and a bounded-length string into a bounded-length string. As with fixed-length strings, catenation operators are also available with character parameters. The functions and procedures provide a `Drop` parameter to specify what to do when the combined string exceeds the bound of the bounded-length string.

Here are the specifications of catenation operations for combining two bounded-length strings. The specifications for mixed string type operations are similar.

```ada
-- A new string is constructed by appending Right to Left
function Append (Left  : in Bounded_String;
                 Right : in Bounded_String;
                 Drop  : in Truncation  := Error)   return Bounded_String;

-- Source is modified by the appending of New_Item
procedure Append (Source   : in out Bounded_String;
                  New_Item : in     Bounded_String;
                  Drop     : in     Truncation := Error);

-- This function is analogous to that for fixed-length strings
function "&" (Left  : in Bounded_String;
              Right : in Bounded_String)   return Bounded_String;
```

Selection We use array operations (indexing and slicing) to get and change individual characters and substrings in fixed-length strings. Package `Ada.Strings.Bounded.Generic_Bounded_Length` provides the same functionality for bounded-length strings with the following subprograms:

```ada
function Element (Source           : in Bounded_String;    -- Get a character
                  Index            : in Positive)  return Character;

procedure Replace_Element (Source : in out Bounded_String; -- Change a character
                           Index  : in     Positive;
                           By     : in     Character);

function Slice (Source             : in Bounded_String;    -- Fixed-length slice
                Low                : in Positive;
                High               : in Natural) return String;
```

```
function Bounded_Slice (Source : in Bounded_String;     -- Bounded-length slice
                        Low    : in Positive;
                        High   : in Natural) return Bounded_String;

procedure Replace_Slice (Source : in out Bounded_String;   -- Replace a slice
                         Low    : in     Positive;
                         High   : in     Natural;
                         By     : in     String;
                         Drop   : in     Truncation := Error);
```

Package `Ada.Strings.Bounded.Generic_Bounded_Length` also contains the functions `Head` and `Tail` for getting slices from the beginning and ends of the string. In these functions you give the number of characters you want to slice out rather than the indices of the first and last characters in the slice.

Other Operations Package `Ada.Strings.Bounded.Generic_Bounded_Length` contains search, translation, selector, and constructor operations equivalent to those in `Ada.Strings.Fixed`.

Although input and output of fixed-length strings is provided through operations in the package `Ada.Text_IO`, there are no input or output operations in the Ada library for bounded-length strings. Input and output with bounded-length strings is easily accomplished through the use of conversion functions and the operations in package `Ada.Text_IO`.

```
-- Declare a fixed-length string.
-- Max_Length is a constant in the package Name_Strings
Input_Name : String (1..Name_Strings.Max_Length);
Last       : Natural;


-- Get a bounded-length string
Ada.Text_IO.Get_Line (Item => Input_Name,          -- Get a fixed-length string
                      Last => Last);
Name := To_Bounded_String (Input_Name(1..Last));   -- Convert the slice

-- Put a bounded-length string
Ada.Text_IO.Put_Line (To_String(Name));
```

The library packages `Ada.Strings.Wide_Bounded` and `Ada.Strings.Wide_Wide_Bounded` provide equivalent operations for bounded-length wide character strings and bounded-length wide wide character strings.

Unbounded-Length Strings

An unbounded string is a varying-length string with no upper bound on its length. In practice, the length of an unbounded-length string is limited by memory constraints. Package `Ada.Strings.Unbounded` provides a private unbounded-length string type whose length can vary between 0 and `Natural'Last`. Here are the declarations of two unbounded-length string variables:

```
Part_Name        : Ada.Strings.Unbounded.Unbounded_String;
Part_Description : Ada.Strings.Unbounded.Unbounded_String;
```

Package `Ada.Strings.Unbounded` has operations equivalent to those in package `Ada.Strings.Bounded.Generic_Bounded_Length`. The unbounded-length package has fewer variations of each operation; for example, there are eight variations of the `Append` procedure for bounded-length strings, but only three variations for unbounded-length strings. For a complete list of unbounded-length operations see Section A.4.5 of the *Ada Language Reference Manual*.

The package `Ada.Text_IO.Unbounded_IO` provides routines for input and output of unbounded-length strings. These are detailed in Section A.10.11 of the *Ada Language Reference Manual*. Here are two simple examples:

```
Ada.Text_IO.Unbounded_IO.Get_Line (Part_Name);
Ada.Text_IO.Unbounded_IO.Put_Line (Part_Description);
```

4.3 The Application Level

As we noted earlier, there are many applications for strings. We use a simple problem to illustrate the use of a string class—alphabetizing names. We'll describe the problem, design a solution, and provide one implementation.

Problem Description

A user enters names (one per line) at the keyboard. After all the names are entered, our program displays them in alphabetical order. Names may be entered in one of two forms: a first name followed by a last name or a last name followed by a first name. In the first case, first and last names are separated by one or more spaces. When a last name is entered first, it is separated from the first name by a comma and one or more spaces. There are no spaces between the last name and the comma. Finally, there may be zero or more spaces before the name and after the name. Here is an example of each of our two forms without any extraneous blanks:

   Mildred Smedley
   Beasley, Horace

The program should alphabetize and display all names in the second form (last name first). The user indicates that all names have been entered by entering a null name, a line with no characters or only blank characters. We make the following assumptions:

1. The format of the input is correct.
2. There are no more than 200 names.

The Algorithm

Here is the algorithm we developed to solve this problem:

Sort Names
Num Names := 0
loop
    Get Name
    Remove extraneous space characters from Name
    exit when the length of Name is 0
    Convert Name to last name first form
    Increment Num Names
    Name List (Num Names) := Name
end loop
Sort Name List
Display Name List

Remove Extraneous Space Characters (Name : in out)
Remove leading blanks
Remove trailing blanks
Replace multiple blanks with a single blank

Convert to Last Name First (Name : in out)
Find the blank in Name
if the character before the blank is not a comma
    Name := Portion of Name after blank & ", " & Portion of Name before blank
end if

Implementation

We developed a generic selection sort procedure in Chapter 3 that we can use to sort our array of names. We can implement the names in this algorithm as fixed-length, bounded-length, or unbounded-length strings. We gave few examples in our discussions of Ada's unbounded-length string class, so we decided to use them in our implementation. This decision also eliminates the need to assume a maximum length for an input line.

Ada's string library contains a number of operations that simplify our work. The `Trim` procedure allows us to remove spaces from both sides of a name string. The `Index` function may be used to find occurrences of multiple blanks between the first and last name, and the `Replace_Slice` procedure may be used to replace these blanks with a single blank. The final result is shown in Program 4.1.

Program 4.1 Sort Names

```ada
with Ada.Strings.Unbounded;      use Ada.Strings.Unbounded;
with Ada.Text_IO.Unbounded_IO;   use Ada.Text_IO.Unbounded_IO;
with Ada.Text_IO;
with Selection_Sort;
procedure Sort_Names is

-- This program reads names from the keyboard and displays them in alphabetical
-- order.  Names may be entered one per line in one of two forms:
--
--              First_Name Last_Name    or   Last_Name, First_Name
--
-- The comma is required in the second form.
-- End of input is indicated with a null or blank name.
--
-- Assumptions:  1.  Format of input is correct.
--               2.  There are no more than 200 names.

   Max_Names : constant := 200; -- Maximum number of names

   -- Array type for holding all the names
   subtype Index_Type is Positive;
   type Name_Array is array (Index_Type range <>)
                     of Ada.Strings.Unbounded.Unbounded_String;

   ---------------------------------------------------------------------------
   -- Instantiate a procedure to sort an array of names
   procedure Sort_Names is new Selection_Sort
                       (Element_Type => Unbounded_String,
                        Array_Type   => Name_Array,
                        "<"          => Ada.Strings.Unbounded."<");


   ---------------------------------------------------------------------------
   procedure Remove_Extra_BLanks (Item : in out Unbounded_String) is
   -- Purpose        : Removes all extraneous blanks from Item
   -- Preconditions  : None
   -- Postconditions : Item has no leading or trailing blanks
   --                  All tokens in item are separated by exactly one blank
      Double_Blank    : constant String := "  "; -- Two blanks
      Double_Location : Natural;
```

```ada
begin
   -- Remove both leading and trailing blanks
   Trim (Source => Item,
         Side   => Ada.Strings.Both);
   -- Remove all extra blanks between "words"
   -- Each iteration, replace one pair of blanks with a single blank
   loop
      -- Find the first pair of blanks in item
      Double_Location := Index (Source  => Item,
                                Pattern => Double_Blank);
      -- Exit when no pair of blanks is found
      exit when Double_Location = 0;
      -- Replace the pair of blanks with a single blank
      Replace_Slice (Source => Item,
                     Low    => Double_Location,
                     High   => Double_Location + 1,
                     By     => " ");
   end loop;
end Remove_Extra_Blanks;
```

```ada
procedure Last_Name_First (Name : in out Unbounded_String) is
-- Purpose        : Convert Name to the form "Last_Name, First_Name"
-- Preconditions  : There is exactly one blank between the first
--                  and last names.
--                  If last name is first, it is followed immediately
--                  by a comma.
-- Postconditions : Name is in the form Last_Name, First_Name

   Blank_Position : Natural;

begin
   -- Determine the position of the blank
   Blank_Position := Index (Source  => Name,
                            Pattern => " ");
   -- Is the first name first?  No comma indicates it is.
   if Element (Source => Name,
               Index  => Blank_Position - 1) /= ',' then
      -- Reorganize into last name first form
      Name := Unbounded_Slice (Source => Name,           -- The last name
                               Low    => Blank_Position + 1,
                               High   => Length(Name))
           & ", "                                         -- A comma and blank
           & Slice (Source => Name,                       -- The last name
                    Low    => 1,
                    High   => Blank_Position - 1);
```

```ada
        end if;
    end Last_Name_First;

-------------------------------------------------------------------------

    Name      : Unbounded_String;               -- One name
    Name_List : Name_Array (1..Max_Names);      -- List of names entered
    Num_Names : Natural;                        -- Number of names entered

begin
    Num_Names  := 0;
    -- Get all the names
    -- Each iteration, one name is processed
    loop
        Ada.Text_IO.Put_Line ("Enter a name (blank name to end)");
        Get_Line (Name);
        Remove_Extra_BLanks (Name);
        -- Is this a null name?
        exit when Length (Name) = 0;
        -- Make sure the last name comes before the first name
        Last_Name_First (Name);
        -- Put the name into the list
        Num_Names := Num_Names + 1;
        Name_List (Num_Names) := Name;
    end loop;

    -- Sort the names in the array of names
    Sort_Names (Name_List (1..Num_Names));

    -- Display the sorted names
    for Index in 1..Num_Names loop
        Put_Line (Name_List (Index));
    end loop;

end Sort_Names;
```

4.4 The Implementation Level

In this section we look at possible approaches to implementing the string classes in the Ada library. Obviously, we will use the library operations rather than implement our own. However, understanding the inner workings of these strings will make you a better user of them.

Fixed-Length Strings

Fixed-length strings are simply arrays of characters, so there is no more to discuss regarding their storage. The code to implement the operations is basic array processing. Here, for example, is a possible implementation of the function to find the index of the first nonblank character in the string:

```ada
function Index_Non_Blank (Source : String;
                         Going  : Direction := Forward) return Natural is
begin
   if Going = Forward then
      for Index in Source'Range loop
         if Source (Index) /= ' ' then
            return Index;
         end if;
      end loop;
   else
      for Index in reverse Source'Range loop
         if Source (Index) /= ' ' then
            return Index;
         end if;
      end loop;
   end if;

   -- If we get here, we did not find a nonblank character
   return 0;
end Index_Non_Blank;
```

Bounded-Length Strings

A bounded-length string has a current length that can vary and a maximum length that cannot vary. The following code fragment shows one way that the library package `Ada.Strings.Bounded.Generic_Bounded_Length` might be implemented:

```ada
generic
   Max : Positive;   -- Maximum length of a Bounded_String
package Generic_Bounded_Length is

   Max_Length : constant Positive := Max;

   subtype Length_Range is Natural range 0..Max_Length;

   type Bounded_String is private;
```

```ada
        Null_Bounded_String : constant Bounded_String;

        -- All of the bounded-length string operation declarations go here

private

        subtype Index_Range  is Length_Range range 1..Max_Length;
        subtype String_Array is String (Index_Range);

        type Bounded_String is
           record
              Length : Length_Range := 0;  -- The number of characters
              Data   : String_Array;       -- The characters in the string
           end record;

        Null_Bounded_String : constant Bounded_String := (0, (others => ' '));

end Generic_Bounded_Length;
```

We show only four of the many public declarations in the Ada library package: the constants `Max_Length` and `Null_Bounded_String`, the subtype `Length_Range`, and the private type `Bounded_String`. The value of `Max_Length` is the upper bound on the length of this string class. The details of the private type `Bounded_String` and the value of the deferred constant `Null_Bounded_String` are supplied in the private part of the package declaration.

The declarations shown in the private part are one approach to storing a bounded-length string. The bounded-length string type is a record with two fields. Figure 4.1 illustrates this record type. `Length` contains the number of characters currently in the string, and `Data` is a fixed-length string that holds the characters. Only the characters from position 1 to `Length` in this array contain valid data. The remaining characters in the fixed-length string field are undefined. A record aggregate is used to assign a zero-length string to the constant `Null_Bounded_String`.

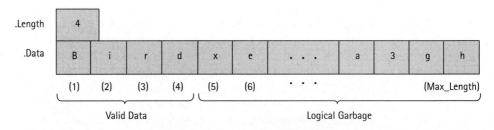

Figure 4.1 *A bounded-length string.*

Let's look at the implementations for some of the bounded-length string operations. The length and conversion to fixed-length string operations are trivial—we simply return the value of the length field or a slice of the data field.

```
function Length (Source : in Bounded_String) return Natural is
begin
   return Source.Length;
end Length;

function To_String (Source : in Bounded_String) return String is
begin
   return Source.Data(1..Source.Length);
end To_String;
```

Here is code that might be used in the bounded-length string library to compare two bounded-length strings:

```
function "<" (Left  : in Bounded_String;
              Right : in Bounded_String) return Boolean is
begin
   return  Left.Data(1..Left.Length) < Right.Data(1..Right.Length);
end "<";
```

This code slices the valid data from each data field using standard array slicing and compares the two subarrays with the less-than operator available for any array whose components are discrete values. The following Boolean expression shows the details of this comparison.

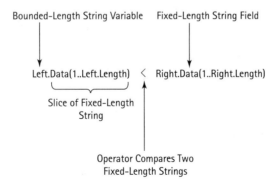

The same approach may be used for the equality operator as well as the remaining relational operators.

As a final example, here is code that might be used in the bounded-length string library to catenate a bounded-length string and a fixed-length string:

```
   function "&" (Left  : in Bounded_String;
                 Right : in String)            return Bounded_String is
      Result : Bounded_String;
begin
   if Left.Length + Right'Length > Max_Length then
      raise LENGTH_ERROR;
   end if;

   Result.Length := Left.Length + Right'Length;
   Result.Data(1..Left.Length)                  := Left.Data(1..Left.Length);
   Result.Data(Left.Length+1..Result.Length) := Right;
   return Result;
end "&";
```

This code builds its return value in a local record. We first check to make sure that the length of the resulting string does not exceed the bound. To calculate the resulting length we add the length field of the bounded-length string parameter to the number of characters in the fixed-length string parameter. The number of characters in the bounded-length string parameter is determined through the record field `Length`. The number of characters in the array attribute parameter is determined through the array attribute `'Length`.

Unbounded-Length Strings and Access Types

In previous sections we defined and showed how we might implement a bounded-length string class. An obvious problem with this class is the necessity to establish an upper bound on the length of string objects. Choosing too small a bound may limit an application and choosing too large a bound may waste memory. The unbounded-length string class offers a solution to this problem. But before we can implement an unbounded-length string class, we must take some time to teach you about another Ada feature, access types. Access types allow us to change the amount of memory used by objects while the program is running.

During the elaboration of an object (variable or constant), Ada finds and allocates the memory necessary for that object. We take advantage of elaboration to declare local variables whose size cannot be determined until the procedure is called. Here is an example:

```
procedure Demonstrate_Elaboration (Item : in out String) is
   Local : String (Item'Range);
begin
   . . .
```

Elaboration   The run-time processing of a declaration. Allocation of memory space for variables and initialization of variables are two common elaboration activities.

The size of the variable `Local` is not known until the procedure is called. During the **elaboration** of `Local`, the size of the parameter `Item` is used to determine how much memory to allocate to `Local`. The elaboration of the declaration in this procedure demonstrates one kind of **dynamic storage allocation**. If Ada can create dynamic variables, why can't we? The answer is: We can. Ada allows a program to allocate space for data dynamically, during the course of its execution.

Access Types To allocate space dynamically in Ada, we use **access type variables**. The value of an access type variable (the access value) contains *information on the location* of an unnamed object of a designated type. Exactly what constitutes an access value is not specified by Ada. An access value might be as simple as the actual memory address of the unnamed object or an offset into a pool of memory locations. It also may include information on the object's size, number of dimensions, and so on. The details of an access value are not important. We picture an access variable as a variable that points to an object (see Figure 4.2). In fact, other languages use the term *pointer variable* instead of access variable.[1]

> **Dynamic allocation** Creation of storage space in memory for a variable during run time.
>
> **Access type variable** A variable that provides access to an object of a designated type.
>
> **Dereferencing** The process of accessing the data in an object designated by an access variable.
>
> **Null** An access value literal that designates no object.

Three phrases commonly are used to describe the association between an access variable and its object. We can say that the access variable *designates* an object, *points to* an object, or *references* an object. The process of accessing the data in an object designated by an access variable is called **dereferencing**.

Let's start with a very simple example. The following type declaration defines an access type that designates `Integer` objects. The declarations for variables A and B define variables that contain access values; that is, information needed to locate an `Integer` object.

```
type Integer_Ptr is access Integer;   -- An access type

A : Integer_Ptr;      -- The value of each of these variables provides
B : Integer_Ptr;      -- access to a memory location containing an Integer

C : Integer;          -- An ordinary Integer;
```

For each access type, there is a literal, `null`, that is an access value designating no object at all. When access type variables such as A and B are elaborated, they are given

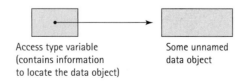

Access type variable   Some unnamed
(contains information   data object
to locate the data object)

Figure 4.2 *An access type variable and its referenced object.*

---

[1] The term *pointer* usually refers to a memory address. Because Ada's access types may contain additional information or are implemented as offsets rather than addresses, the term *pointer* is not accurate for these types.

Figure 4.3 *Access variables with initial values of null—right now they don't access anything.*

an initial value of `null`, indicating that currently the access variable points to no object. Figure 4.3 illustrates the variables A and B after their elaboration.

Allocating Memory An **allocator** is an operation that creates space for an object during the execution of the program. The predefined allocator operation in Ada is named `new`. This allocator has two forms, which we illustrate in the following assignment statements:

> **Allocator** An operation that creates space for an object during the execution of a program.

```
A := new Integer;        -- Allocate space for an integer
B := new Integer'(17);   -- Allocate space and assign a value of 17
```

Do you remember exactly how an assignment statement is executed? First the expression on the right side is evaluated, and then the result is assigned to the variable. Evaluation of the `new` operation allocates enough memory for the object (whose type is given after the word `new`) and yields an access value that identifies the location of this memory. This access value then is assigned to the access variable on the left side of the assignment operator. Figure 4.4 illustrates the state of variables A and B after these two assignment statements have been executed. We use arrows to represent the access values stored in the two variables. Each arrow points to the object designated by the access type variable. Only the `Integer` object designated by variable B contains a value. This value was specified in the allocator expression. The object that variable A designates is undefined.

The syntax of an allocator is

```
allocator            ::=  new subtype_indication|
                          new qualified_expression

qualified_expression ::=  type_mark'(expression)|
                          type_mark'aggregate
```

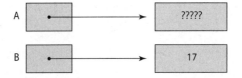

Figure 4.4 *Access variables with non-null access values.*

As we saw, the value of the qualified expression is assigned as an initial value to the newly allocated memory.

Dereferencing We cannot access data in storage obtained through a new operation by name because they have a declared name. Figure 4.4 illustrates the lack of names. There is no name given for the object with the value of 17. We access these data through an access variable that designates them. We access the object designated by an access variable, using a dot notation similar to that used to access the fields of a record variable. To access the object designated by an access variable we use the variable name followed by .all. As we mentioned earlier, this process is called *dereferencing*. Here are some examples of dereferencing access variables A and B. We prefixed the input and output procedure names to clearly show that we are doing output and input with integer values, not access values.

```
Ada.Integer_Text_IO.Put (Item => B.all);
Ada.Integer_Text_IO.Get (Item => A.all);
C := A.all + B.all;
```

The first statement calls procedure Put to display the Integer object designated by B. In the second statement, an integer is obtained from the user and assigned to the object designated by A. The third statement assigns the sum of the two objects designated by A and B to the integer variable C. Figure 4.5 shows the results of these statements (assuming the user entered a value of 3) on the variables and designated objects. Note that A and B are access variables that designate unnamed data by location, and C is a named variable that contains integer data.

An access variable name with .all refers to the object designated by the access variable. An access variable name by itself refers to the access value (location information) it contains. To emphasize the difference between access variables and the objects they designate, consider the following two assignment statements:

```
A.all := B.all;
A     := B;
```

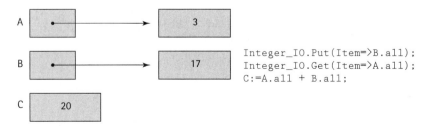

Figure 4.5 *Values after executing the three statements (assuming the user enters 3).*

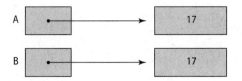

Figure 4.6 *After executing* `A.all := B.all;`.

In the first assignment statement the object designated by A is assigned the value of the object designated by B. Figure 4.6 shows the results: The two objects have identical values and the two access variables have different values (they designate different objects).

The second assignment statement assigns a copy of the access value (information about the *location* of an object) stored in B to A. A and B contain identical values. What does it mean when two access variables have identical values? It means that both designate the same object. Figure 4.7 shows the results of this assignment. An access variable that designates the same object as another access variable is an **alias** of the other access variable. Figure 4.7 shows that A is an alias of B. The use of aliases can result in undesirable side effects. For example, if we assign 0 to A.all, the value of B.all is also changed to 0. Such side effects can be prevented by avoiding aliases. However, as we show later, temporary aliases are often necessary to manipulate data structures based on access variables.

> **Alias** One of several access variables that designate the same object.

Unchecked Deallocation of Memory Figure 4.7 illustrates another problem encountered when assigning a value to an access variable. The object that A originally designated is no longer accessible; it has no name and is not designated by any access variable. This object is lost forever! More importantly, the memory used by this object is lost. Programs that lose memory in this manner are said to have *memory leaks*. The Ada standard allows an implementation to reclaim the memory used by objects that are no longer accessible. The reclaimed memory is then recycled for future allocation operations. This process is colorfully called *garbage collection*. However, we are not aware of any Ada system that has implemented garbage collection.

The Ada standard requires an implementation to supply a generic procedure called `Unchecked_Deallocation` that our programs can use to explicitly recycle the memory used by unwanted objects. Here is the declaration for this generic procedure:

```
generic
   type Object(<>) is limited private;
   type Name       is access Object;
procedure Ada.Unchecked_Deallocation(X : in out Name);
```

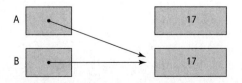

Figure 4.7 *After executing* `A := B;` *the object originally designated by A is lost.*

As with any generic procedure, we use `Unchecked_Deallocation` to create (via an instantiation) a procedure tailored to our needs. This generic function has two generic formal parameters: `Object` and `Name`. We have not yet seen the second of the generic formal types used here. Recall that the designation of `limited private` means that the formal type `Object` matches any type of actual parameter. Type `Name` matches any actual access type that designates type `Object`. The following instantiation uses our declarations for `Integer` objects given on page 235.

```
procedure Free is new Ada.Unchecked_Deallocation (Object => Integer,
                                                  Name   => Integer_Ptr);
```

As with any instantiation, we can choose any name we like; we chose to name our procedure `Free`. Procedure `Free` has a single parameter, X, whose type is `Integer_Ptr` (the type of the actual generic parameter associated with the formal generic parameter `Name`). Here are two example calls of this procedure:

```
Free (X => A);     -- Call using named parameter association
Free (B);          -- Call using positional parameter association
```

In both cases, the memory used by the object designated by the given access variable is reclaimed by the system and the access variable is assigned the value of `null`; it no longer points to any object.

Why is the procedure called `Unchecked_Deallocation`? One of the goals of the Ada language designers was that the language be suitable for writing reliable programs. Use of procedures to explicitly reclaim memory can be dangerous. This danger is a direct result of the side effects of aliases. Let's look at an example using our access variables A and B and the procedure `Free` we instantiated from `Unchecked_-Deallocation`.

```
A := B;            -- Make A an alias of B
Free (A);          -- Recycle the memory used by the object designated by A
B.all := 0;        -- Cannot say what happens
```

Figure 4.7 shows the result of executing the first assignment statement. Figure 4.8 shows the result of calling `Free (A)`. After this call to `Free`, A contains `null`; it no longer points to any object. B is not changed by the call to procedure `Free`; its value still designates some object, although the state of this object is undefined. Attempting to use the object designated by B will in the best case raise some exception and in the worst case (if the memory has been allocated again) change some other dynamic object.

The name `Unchecked_Deallocation` is a warning for anyone who uses it. This procedure does not check to see whether any other access variables are aliases of the parameter designating the memory we want to reclaim. It is up to the programmer to make sure that any aliases are assigned a value of `null`.

Figure 4.8 *After executing* `A := B;` *and* `Free (A);`.

Exceptions and Access Types CONSTRAINT_ERROR is raised whenever an attempt is made to dereference an access variable that contains a null access value. Because an access variable is assigned `null` when it is elaborated, this error is commonly associated with trying to access a designated object before it has been allocated. Procedures instantiated from Unchecked_Deallocation do not raise CONSTRAINT_ERROR when passed a null access value. Here are some examples illustrating the raising of CONSTRAINT_ERROR:

```
Free (A);                                 -- Recycle the memory (A is now null)
Free (A);                                 -- CONSTRAINT_ERROR not raised here
Ada.Integer_Text_IO.Put (Item => A.all);  -- CONSTRAINT_ERROR is raised here

B := null;                                -- B's object now lost
Ada.Integer_Text_IO.Put (Item => B.all);  -- CONSTRAINT_ERROR is raised here
```

The exception STORAGE_ERROR is raised when the system runs out of memory to allocate. This exception might be raised anytime a variable is elaborated or the allocator `new` is used. If you see this exception, look for an infinite loop. If programs with memory leaks (remember Figure 4.7) run long enough, the available memory becomes exhausted. Such programs are difficult to debug because they may have to run for days or weeks before exhausting memory. It is best to design your program to avoid memory leaks. One way to prevent memory leaks is to encapsulate all access variable dereferencing in packages so that memory recycling is confined to one place. We take this approach in all of the classes we implement with access types.

Access of Composite Types All of our previous examples of access variables designated integer objects. We used integer objects to keep our examples as simple as possible. There is no reason why you should use access types instead of simple integer variables. The real power of access types comes when the objects they designate are composite types such as records and arrays. For example, later in this chapter we see how access types that designate unconstrained arrays can be used to implement an unbounded-length string class. Throughout the remainder of this book we use access types that designate records to implement a wide variety of classes. But first, we look at examples of the use of the allocator operation with some simple composite types.

```
subtype Name_String is String (1..20);   -- A constrained array subtype
type Name_Ptr is access Name_String;

First  : Name_Ptr;
Middle : Name_Ptr;
Last   : Name_Ptr;
```

All three of these variables are access variables that designate objects that are arrays of 20 characters. As with all access variables, these three variables have an initial value of null (see Figure 4.9[a]). We use the allocator operation, new, to obtain memory for objects designated by these access variables.

```
First  := new Name_String;                          -- No initial value
Middle := new Name_String'(1..20 => 'A');           -- An array aggregate
Last   := new Name_String'("This string has 20 C"); -- A string literal
```

Figure 4.9(b) shows the results of these three assignment statements. The characters in the string designated by First are undefined. The string designated by Middle contains 20 A's, and the string designated by Last contains the string "This string has 20 C".

(a) Initial values of First, Middle, and Last

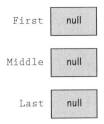

(b) First, Middle, and Last after allocating memory

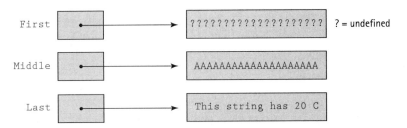

Figure 4.9 *Access variables that designate string objects: (a) Initial values of* First, Middle, *and* Last. *(b)* First, Middle, *and* Last *after allocating memory.*

We can operate on these string objects as we do on any string object. We can, for example, index and slice them.

```
Ada.Text_IO.Put (Item => Last.all);        -- The entire 20-character string
Ada.Text_IO.Put (Item => Last.all(1..4));  -- A 4-character slice
Ada.Text_IO.Put (Item => Last.all(1));     -- The first character

Middle.all(1..5) := "Hello";               -- Replace the first 5 characters
Middle.all(6)    := 'B';                   -- Replace the 6th character
```

When access types are used to designate arrays, Ada permits us to leave out the .all when dereferencing an element or slice in a designated array. Using this shorthand syntax, the previous statements can be rewritten as follows:

```
Ada.Text_IO.Put (Item => Last.all);        -- The entire 20-character string
Ada.Text_IO.Put (Item => Last(1..4));      -- A 4-character slice
Ada.Text_IO.Put (Item => Last(1));         -- The first character

Middle(1..5) := "Hello";                   -- Replace the first 5 characters
Middle(6)    := 'B';                       -- Replace the 6th character
```

Because the first statement in this group dereferences the entire array rather than a slice or individual element, we must include .all. You probably noticed that the shorthand syntax makes it appear as though Last and Middle were array variables rather than access type variables. In fact, some Ada programmers prefer the shorthand form because it allows them to easily change their implementation from access variables to array variables and vice versa. We believe that such decisions should be made during program design rather than during program implementation. Some programmers also prefer the shorthand syntax because it makes it easier to enter their programs from the keyboard. We believe that the extra documentation provided by .all is well worth the extra time it takes to type the four characters. Because of the extra documentation provided, nearly all of the examples in this text use the .all form. You (or your professor) can decide which form is best for your programs.

We can instantiate a procedure from Unchecked_Deallocation that can be used to recycle the 20 character string objects designated by variables of type Name_Ptr. Here is a code fragment that creates an instance of Unchecked_Deallocation and frees the memory designated by First:

```
procedure Free is new Ada.Unchecked_Deallocation (Object => Name_String,
                                                  Name   => Name_Ptr);
   .
   .
   .
Free (First);     -- Reclaim the memory designated by First
```

As a general practice we take advantage of Ada's overloading abilities and use the name `Free` for every procedure that we instantiate from `Unchecked_Deallocation`. Because each one has a different access type for a parameter, the Ada compiler is able to determine which `Free` procedure to use.

A Simple Unbounded-Length String Class Access types also may designate unconstrained arrays and records. We use this capability to implement a simple unbounded-length string class.

```
type Unbounded_String_Type is access String;

W : Unbounded_String_Type;
X : Unbounded_String_Type;
Y : Unbounded_String_Type;
Z : Unbounded_String_Type;
```

Each of these four access variables can designate a string of any size. The size of the designated object is established by the allocator operator, `new`. The size can be specified as a range constraint on the subtype indication (as in the first line below) or through an initial value (as in the last three lines below).

```
W := new String(1..20);              -- String of 20 characters, no initial value
X := new String'("Hello");           -- String of 5 characters with initial value
Y := new String'(1..10 => 'J');      -- String of 10 J's
Z := new String'(X.all & ' ' & "Mildred"); -- String containing "Hello Mildred"
```

Figure 4.10 shows the result of these four allocation operations.

The algorithms for implementing the operations for these simple unbounded-length strings are very similar to those used for bounded-length strings. On the next page is the code for four of those modified for this simple unbounded-length type:

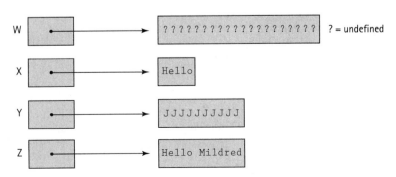

Figure 4.10 *Access variables that designate unconstrained string objects.*

```ada
function Length (Source : in Unbounded_String_Type) return Natural is
begin
   return Source.all'Length;   -- Return length of designated array
end Length;


function To_String (Source : in Unbounded_String_Type) return String is
begin
   return Source.all;   -- Return designated array
end To_String;


function "<" (Left  : in Unbounded_String_Type;
              Right : in Unbounded_String_Type) return Boolean is
begin
   return Left.all < Right.all;   -- Compare designated arrays
end "<";


function "&" (Left  : in Unbounded_String_Type;
              Right : in String)                return Unbounded_String_Type is
-- Catenate an unbounded-length and a fixed-length string
   Result : Unbounded_String_Type;
begin
   Result := new String'(Left.all & Right);
   return Result;
end "&";
```

In all of these functions, we dereference the arrays designated by the parameters and then use standard array operations to process them.

The potential for aliases and memory leaks presents additional problems in this implementation. For example, we normally think of the assignment operator as one that creates copies of objects. This concept certainly is valid for every data type we have encountered before access types. As we saw earlier, normal assignment with access types creates an alias rather than a copy. For example, the assignment statement

```ada
W := X;      -- Failed attempt to assign a COPY of string X to string W
```

makes W an alias of X rather than a copy. Both access variables now designate the same object, the string containing "Hello". This assignment also leaks memory. The string of 20 characters originally designated by W can no longer be accessed. Figure 4.11 shows the results of this assignment statement. To make W a copy of X, we first must reclaim the memory designated by W and then allocate new memory for the copy. The following two statements accomplish this "assignment":

4.4 The Implementation Level | 245

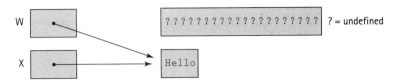

Figure 4.11 *After executing* W := X;, W *and* X *are aliases and memory is lost.*

```
Free (W);                    -- Reclaim memory
W := new String'(X.all);     -- Allocate a new object with an initial value
                             -- equal to the string designated by X
```

Figure 4.12 shows the results of this two-statement "assignment."

Using this two-step assignment does not solve all the problems with memory leaks associated with assignment. The assignment statement

```
X := X & " Horace";     -- Assigns "Hello Horace" to X with memory leak
```

makes the desired assignment with a memory leak like that shown in the previous example. However, this time calling `Free` to deallocate the memory designated by X before the assignment statement is not possible. We need the value designated by X in the evaluation of the expression on the right side of the assignment statement. One way to solve this problem is to use another access variable to designate the memory lost in the previous attempt. The following code uses the variable W to accomplish this task:

```
Free (W);               -- Deallocate any memory designated by W
W := X;                 -- W is now an alias of X
X := X & " Horace";     -- Assigns "Hello Horace" to X
Free (W);               -- Deallocate the memory originally designated by X
```

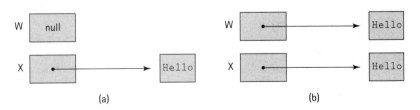

Figure 4.12 *After executing (a)* Free(W); *and (b)* W := new String'(X.all);.

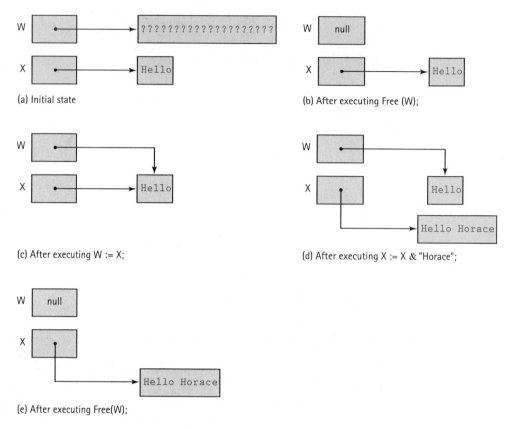

Figure 4.13 *Safely appending "* `Horace`*" to the simple unbounded-length string* `X`.

Notice that we call procedure `Free` twice to recycle the memory originally designated by `W` and `X`. Figure 4.13 illustrates the actions of this sequence of statements.

Writing an application using this simple implementation of an unbounded-length string class requires a great deal of care to avoid aliases and memory leaks. What we need is a mechanism to safely carry out the recycling of dynamic memory. The use of garbage collection discussed earlier in this chapter is one way to eliminate the memory leak problem. The next section presents another solution: Ada's controlled types.

A Controlled Unbounded-Length String Class Ada provides a way of automating the recycling of dynamic memory for specific classes. The package `Ada.Finalization` defines two tagged types from which we can inherit automatic recycling properties. Here is a slightly simplified specification of this package:

```
package Ada.Finalization is

   type Controlled is abstract tagged private;
```

```
procedure Initialize (Object : in out Controlled) is null;
procedure Adjust     (Object : in out Controlled) is null;
procedure Finalize   (Object : in out Controlled) is null;


type Limited_Controlled is abstract tagged limited private;

procedure Initialize (Object : in out Limited_Controlled) is null;
procedure Finalize   (Object : in out Limited_Controlled) is null;

private
    ... -- not specified by the language (left to the compiler vendor)
end Ada.Finalization;
```

The two tagged types, `Controlled`, and `Limited_Controlled`, are referred to as **controlled types**. These types provide the programmer complete control over the initialization, assignment, and finalization of objects.

Recall from our discussion of features of object-oriented programming in Chapter 2 that an abstract type is a tagged type intended for use as an ancestor of other types, but which is not allowed to have objects of its own. Thus, although we cannot declare variables of type `Controlled`, we can declare objects of types derived from `Controlled`. The use of `is null` in the specification of the five procedures in the package `Ada.Finalization` defines them as **null procedures**. Calling a null procedure has no effect. Generally we override null procedures with ones that are meaningful in a more specialized class.

> **Controlled type** A tagged type that provides the programmer with explicit control over initialization, assignment, and finalization of objects.
>
> **Null procedure** A procedure that has no effect.

By overriding these controlled procedures, the implementation programmer has complete control of each controlled object. The usual use of procedure `Initialize` is, as you might expect, to ensure that each object is properly initialized. The usual use of procedure `Finalize` is to ensure that any memory that was dynamically allocated to an object is reclaimed before that object ceases to exist. It is through procedure `Finalize` that we prevent memory leaks. The usual use of procedure `Adjust` is to ensure that when one object is assigned to another object, a copy is made rather than an alias.

The interaction of the three procedures `Initialize`, `Finalize`, and `Adjust` is subtle. Exercise 31 at the end of this chapter provides an opportunity to experiment and become familiar with the implicit calls to these procedures. Here are the common situations when these procedures are called.

Procedure `Initialize` is called

- upon the elaboration of a declaration of a controlled object, if the declaration does not specify an initial value.

- upon the evaluation of an allocator (`new`) creating a controlled object, if the allocator does not specify an initial value.

Procedure `Finalize` is called for a controlled object

- when a controlled object is a target variable of an assignment statement. `Finalize` is called just before the new value is copied into that variable.
- when a controlled object declared in a subprogram body ceases to exist. The object ceases to exist when the subprogram returns.
- when a controlled object declared in a block statement ceases to exist. The object ceases to exist when the execution of the block is finished.
- when a dynamically allocated controlled object ceases. The object ceases to exist when an instance of `Ada.Unchecked.Deallocation` is called.

Procedure `Adjust` is called for a controlled object

- when a controlled object is a target variable of an assignment statement. `Adjust` is called just after the new value is copied into that variable.

There are additional rules for cases in which a controlled object is a component of another object, which we will not discuss.

Let's look at an example to help understand these new concepts. Specification 4.1 is for an unbounded-length string class with just a few operations. It is based on controlled types.

Specification 4.1   Unbounded-Length Strings Based on Controlled Types

```ada
with Ada.Finalization;
package Unbounded_Strings is

-- A package to demonstrate the use of controlled types to implement an
-- unbounded-length string class.  Only a few operations are specified.

   type Unbounded_String_Type is private;

   Null_Unbounded_String : constant Unbounded_String_Type;

   function To_Unbounded (Source : in String) return Unbounded_String_Type;
   function To_String    (Source : in Unbounded_String_Type) return String;

   function Length (Source : in Unbounded_String_Type) return Natural;

   function "=" (Left  : in Unbounded_String_Type;
                 Right : in Unbounded_String_Type) return Boolean;

   function "&" (Left  : in Unbounded_String_Type;
                 Right : in String)                return Unbounded_String_Type;
   -- Catenate an unbounded-length string and a fixed-length string
```

```ada
private

   type String_Ptr is access String;

   type Unbounded_String_Type is new Ada.Finalization.Controlled with
      record
         Reference : String_Ptr;
      end record;

   overriding procedure Initialize (Object : in out Unbounded_String_Type);
   overriding procedure Finalize   (Object : in out Unbounded_String_Type);
   overriding procedure Adjust     (Object : in out Unbounded_String_Type);

   Null_String_Ptr       : constant String_Ptr := new String'("");
   Null_Unbounded_String : constant Unbounded_String_Type :=
            (Ada.Finalization.Controlled with Reference => Null_String_Ptr);

end Unbounded_Strings;
```

In this specification, we declared Unbounded_String_Type as a private type. Recall from Chapter 2 that the operations available for private types are those defined in the package plus assignment and equality testing. We have overridden the equality testing operator with our own.

In the private part you can see that Unbounded_String_Type extends the tagged type Controlled with the addition of Reference, an access type that designates an unconstrained array of characters. Reference is equivalent to the simple unbounded-length string type we presented in the last section. Here is a diagram to illustrate the storage of the Unbounded_String_Type variable, Part_Name:

Part_Name is a record with one field, Reference, that is an access type that designates an unconstrained array of characters. In this example our unbounded-length string is the name of a sewing machine part. The private part also contains the specifications of three procedures that override the null procedures for controlled types.

The completion of the deferred constant Null_Unbounded_String is accomplished by assigning the location of a null string (created in the initialization of the access constant Null_String_Ptr) to its Reference field. This assignment demonstrates the use of an *extension aggregate* to specify the value for a type that is a record extension. Recall from Chapter 2 that an extension aggregate consists of a value or subtype for an ancestor of the type, followed by associations for the additional fields. In our example, the ancestor type is `Controlled` and the additional field is `Reference`.

Now let's look at the operations from our superclass that we need to override for our class. Procedure `Initialize` is called whenever an object of type `Unbounded_String_Type` is created *without* an initial value. For example, when the declaration

```
Name : Unbounded_String_Type;
```

is elaborated, procedure `Initialize` is automatically called with `Name` as its parameter.

Procedure `Finalize` is called just before an object of type `Unbounded_String_Type` is destroyed when it goes out of scope (for example when control leaves the block in which it is declared). With the following code fragment

```
procedure Skip_Word is
   Word : Unbounded_String_Type;
begin
   .
   .
   .
```

procedure `Initialize` is automatically called with `Word` as its parameter when that declaration is elaborated. Procedure `Finalize` is automatically called with `Word` as its parameter when control returns from procedure `Skip_Word` back to where it was called.

Procedure `Adjust` is more complicated. Its purpose is to give programmers complete control over the *assignment* of objects. It is commonly used when we want an assignment statement to create a copy rather than an alias. Let's start with an example.

```
A : Unbounded_String_Type := To_Unbounded ("Hello Horace");
B : Unbounded_String_Type := To_Unbounded ("Goodbye Mildred");

A := B;   -- A becomes a copy of B
```

This assignment statement is carried out in three steps.

1. Procedure `Finalize` is called with `A` as its parameter.
2. The value of `B` (a record containing an access value) is copied into `A`. At this point `A.Reference` is an alias of `B.Reference`.
3. Procedure `Adjust` is called with `A` as its parameter.

Now that you know *when* each of the three procedures is called, let's look at *what* they do for our unbounded-length string class. Body 4.1 includes the code for our very limited set of operations as well as the code to override the procedures of the superclass.

Body 4.1 Unbounded_Strings: Implements Specification 4.1

```ada
with Ada.Unchecked_Deallocation;
package body Unbounded_Strings is

   procedure Free is new Ada.Unchecked_Deallocation (Object => String,
                                                     Name   => String_Ptr);

   -------------------------------------------------------------------------
   function To_String (Source : in Unbounded_String_Type) return String is
   begin
      return Source.Reference.all;
   end To_String;

   -------------------------------------------------------------------------
   function Length (Source : in Unbounded_String_Type) return Natural is
   begin
      return Source.Reference.all'Length;
   end Length;

   -------------------------------------------------------------------------
   function "=" (Left  : in Unbounded_String_Type;
                 Right : in Unbounded_String_Type) return Boolean is
   begin
      return Left.Reference.all = Right.Reference.all;
   end "=";

   -------------------------------------------------------------------------
   function To_Unbounded (Source : in String) return Unbounded_String_Type is
      Result : Unbounded_String_Type;
   begin
      Result.Reference := new String'(Source);
      return Result;
   end To_Unbounded;

   -------------------------------------------------------------------------
   function "&" (Left  : in Unbounded_String_Type;
                 Right : in String)              return Unbounded_String_Type is
      Result : Unbounded_String_Type;
   begin
      Result.Reference := new String'(Left.Reference.all & Right);
      return Result;
   end "&";
```

```ada
procedure Initialize (Object : in out Unbounded_String_Type) is
begin
   Object.Reference := Null_Unbounded_String.Reference;
end Initialize;
```

```ada
procedure Finalize (Object : in out Unbounded_String_Type) is
begin
   -- Do not recycle memory for the null string
   if Object.Reference /= Null_Unbounded_String.Reference then
      Free (Object.Reference);
      Object.Reference := Null_Unbounded_String.Reference;
   end if;
end Finalize;
```

```ada
procedure Adjust (Object : in out Unbounded_String_Type) is
begin
   -- Do not copy the null string, leave it as an alias
   if Object.Reference /= Null_Unbounded_String.Reference then
      Object.Reference := new String'(Object.Reference.all);
   end if;
end Adjust;
end Unbounded_Strings;
```

Procedure `To_String` is nearly identical to the one for the simple unbounded-length string operation we presented earlier. The only change is the addition of the record field name `Reference`. The same additions were made to create the bodies of functions `Length` and `"="` in this package.

Let's look next at the bodies of the procedures `Initialize` and `Finalize`. We have elected to initialize every unbounded-length string to a null string (a string of length zero). Each time a variable of type `Unbounded_String_Type` is created without an initial value, this procedure is called to initialize it to a null string. Procedure `Initialize` assigns the location of the null string created in the package specification to the `Reference` field of the object. All newly created unbounded-length strings reference the same null string; they are, in effect, aliases.

We do not want to leak memory when an unbounded-length string variable goes out of scope and is destroyed, so in the body of procedure `Finalize` we deallocate the memory designated by the `Reference` field. Then we assign it the location of the null string. Notice that if the `Reference` field already designates the null string, we do nothing.

Function `To_Unbounded` declares the local variable `Result`. Procedure `Initialize` is called when this local variable is elaborated. `Initialize` will set the `Reference`

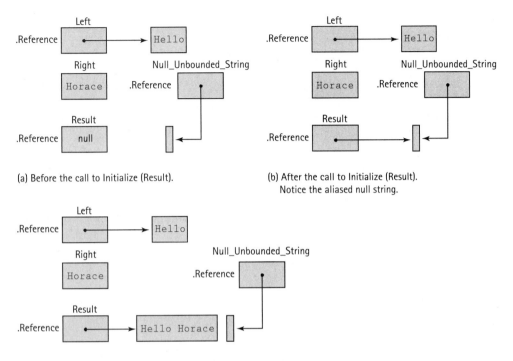

(a) Before the call to Initialize (Result).

(b) After the call to Initialize (Result).
Notice the aliased null string.

(c) After obtaining new memory for combined parameters.

Figure 4.14 *Tracing a Call to Function "&"*.

field of Result to designate our aliased null string. In the execution of the body of this function, new memory is obtained to hold a copy of the parameter Source. At first it may appear that this assignment statement leaks memory; however, because at this point the Reference field is an alias to the null string designated by the constant Null_String_Ptr, no memory is lost. Function "&" is written in a similar manner.

Figure 4.14 illustrates the execution of a call to function "&". Left is an unbounded-length string with the value "Hello" and Right is a fixed-length string with the value " Horace". Figure 4.14(a) shows the values of the two parameters and the local variable before the call to procedure Initialize(Result). Figure 4.14(b) shows the effects of that procedure call. Figure 4.14(c) shows the effect of the first line of the function where we obtain new memory to hold the catenation of the two parameters. Result is then returned.

The Adjust procedure is called as the last step when an assignment is made involving a controlled type. Let's look at a simple example in detail. We'll trace the example we gave earlier. We repeat the code here:

```
A :    Unbounded_String_Type := To_Unbounded("Horace");
B :    Unbounded_String_Type := To_Unbounded("Mildred");
```

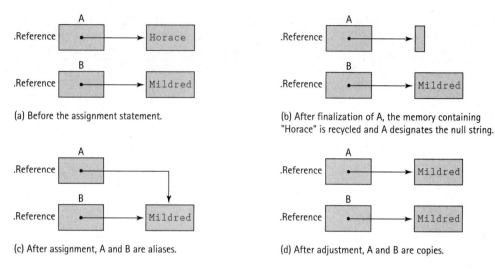

Figure 4.15 *Tracing the assignment statement* A := B;.

The following assignment statement makes A a copy of B:

```
A := B;
```

Figure 4.15 shows the three steps that occur during this assignment of a controlled type. Figure 4.15(a) shows the two unbounded-length strings before execution of the assignment statement. Each of the two objects designates a separate string. The first step in executing an assignment of controlled variables is the finalization of the variable on the left side of the assignment statement. Procedure `Finalize` in our package recycles the memory designated by the variable and sets it to designate the null string, as shown in Figure 4.15(b). The second step is the actual assignment of B to A. This copying results in our two variables designating the same string, as shown in Figure 4.15(c). The last step of the process is the execution of procedure `Adjust` for variable A. In our package, this procedure allocates memory for a copy of the alias and then sets the target variable to designate that copy. The final results are shown in Figure 4.15(d).

Using access types requires a good deal of care. Because they are so error prone, access types are often not allowed in safety-critical software (programs whose failure might result in death, injury, loss of equipment, or environmental harm). This is not to say that access types should never be used. Through packages and private types, Ada allows us to encapsulate all access variable dereferencing. By limiting the manipulation of access-based data structures to a few well-tested or proven packages, we can markedly reduce the inherent risks of access types. The use of controlled types further minimizes risk by eliminating the chances of memory leaks.

In the implementation of data structures in the following chapters we use controlled types and encapsulate our access type operations within package bodies. As a result, the application programmer can use these classes without having to deal directly with the access types used in their implementation.

Organization of Memory

Where does the allocator actually find the memory requested by our program? When a program is running, its memory space is divided into a number of regions. Named variables (the ones we declare within a procedure or function) and parameters are allocated memory in a region called the *stack*. When we use the allocator `new` to obtain memory for an object, the system allocates memory in a region usually called the *heap*. The actual code (the machine-language version of our Ada statements) is stored in another region often called the *code* segment. Global variables declared within package specification or bodies, such as those we used in our ADO packages, are also stored in this region. Figure 4.16 illustrates the memory used by a typical program.

When our program calls a subprogram, memory for its parameters and local variables is allocated on the stack. In Figure 4.16, the boundary between the stack and the unused memory moves upward to add this memory to the stack. When control is returned, this memory is deallocated by moving the boundary back down. When our Ada program uses the allocator `new` to obtain memory, the run-time system allocates it from the heap. This memory may come from recycled memory somewhere in the middle of the heap or from extending the heap into the unused memory region. In Figure 4.16, the boundary between the heap and unused memory moves downward. When the unused memory region becomes exhausted and our program requests additional memory (from the stack or heap), `STORAGE_ERROR` is raised.

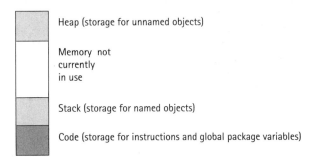

Figure 4.16 *Memory used by a running program.*

Summary

Strings are used extensively to manipulate text. There are three different string classes: fixed-length strings, bounded-length strings, and unbounded-length strings. Ada provides the unconstrained array type `String` with the standard set of array operations to implement fixed-length strings. The library package `Ada.Strings.Fixed` contains a rich collection of additional operations for fixed-length strings. `Ada.Strings.Bounded.Generic_Bounded_Length` is a generic package from which we can specify an upper bound and instantiate our own bounded-length string classes. `Ada.Strings.Unbounded` provides us with an unbounded-length class. Although you will probably never need to design and implement your own string classes, we gave some insight into the implementation of bounded-length and unbounded-length strings.

Access types allow a programmer to allocate memory for objects while the program is executing. All access variables are initialized with the null access value. A null access value indicates that the access variable currently designates no object. Ada's allocator operation `new` is used to allocate memory for an object. The allocation may include an initial value. Once memory for an object has been allocated it is accessed through an access variable.

Access types are most useful when they designate composite types. We showed how an unbounded-length string class might be implemented using access types that designate unconstrained arrays of characters (type `String`).

Two problems with using access variables are aliasing and memory leakage. An alias is an access variable that designates the same object as another access variable. Memory leaks occur when the only access variable designating an object is changed without reclaiming the memory used by the object. Memory is reclaimed by calling a procedure instantiated from the generic procedure `Ada.Unchecked_Deallocation`.

You should encapsulate all classes implemented with access types (as we did in our controlled unbounded-length string class) so that anyone using them is not aware that access types are used. We can eliminate aliases in our applications by deriving our class from one of Ada's controlled types. By overriding the superclass's `Initialize`, `Finalize`, and `Adjust` procedures we can also effectively eliminate memory leaks.

Access types and controlled types provide a highly flexible mechanism for implementing data structures. We will use them throughout the remainder of this book. But these constructs come with a price. Developing access-based code is usually complicated and therefore prone to error. When designing classes that use access types, draw "box and arrow" pictures to help you implement the operations. Allocating and deallocating memory takes time, so programs that use access types are usually less efficient than those that do not. Efficiency is why bounded-length strings are often used rather than unbounded-length strings.

Exercises

String Terminology

1. a. What is a fixed-length string?
   b. What is a varying-length string?

c. What is a bounded-length string?

d. What is an unbounded-length string?

2. Draw a UML diagram to illustrate the relationship among the classes of strings you defined in the previous question. Introducing an abstract class into the diagram may make this task simpler.

3. a. Why would you choose to use a bounded-length string class rather than an unbounded-length string class?

   b. Why would you choose to use an unbounded-length string class rather than a bounded-length string class?

Fixed-Length Strings

4. What is the difference between the literals `'G'` and `"G"`?

5. Declare a subtype for a fixed-length string that holds 45 characters.

Use the following declarations for questions 6 through 9:

```
with Ada.Strings;          use Ada.Strings;
with Ada.Strings.Fixed;    use Ada.Strings.Fixed;
with Ada.Strings.Maps;     use Ada.Strings.Maps;
with Ada.Text_IO;          use Ada.Text_IO;
with Ada.Integer_Text_IO;  use Ada.Integer_Text_IO;
  .
  .
  .

subtype Pome_String   is String (1..12);
subtype Citrus_String is String (1..15);

Apple  : Pome_String;
Pear   : Pome_String;
Orange : Citrus_String;
Lemon  : Citrus_String;

Chars  : Ada.Strings.Maps.Character_Set;
Code   : Ada.Strings.Maps.Character_Mapping;
```

6. Which of the following assignments raise CONSTRAINT_ERROR?

   a. `Pear   := "I like pears";`
   b. `Lemon  := "Lemons are sour";`
   c. `Orange := "Oranges are sweet";`
   d. `Apple  := "Rome";`
   e. `Apple  := Orange;`

f. `Apple  := Pear;`

g. `Lemon  := Pear;`

7. What is the value of `Apple` after the execution of each of the following code segments? Specify the name of any exceptions raised. Show all 12 characters in your answers, using the symbol ▫ to indicate a blank character. You may need to study Section A.4.3 of the *Ada Language Reference Manual* to learn the effects of the fixed-length string operations used.

   a.
   ```
   Move(Source => "McIntosh",
        Target => Apple);
   ```
   b.
   ```
   Move(Source  => "McIntosh",
        Target  => Apple,
        Justify => Right);
   ```
   c.
   ```
   Move (Source  => "McIntosh",
         Target  => Apple,
         Justify => Center);
   ```
   d.
   ```
   Move (Source  => "McIntosh",
         Target  => Apple,
         Justify => Left);
   ```
   e.
   ```
   Move (Source  => "McIntosh",
         Target  => Apple,
         Pad     => '=',
         Justify => Center);
   ```
   f.
   ```
   Move (Source => "McIntosh is my favorite",
         Target => Apple);
   ```
   g.
   ```
   Move (Source => "McIntosh            ",
         Target => Apple);
   ```
   h.
   ```
   Move (Source => "McIntosh is my favorite",
         Target => Apple,
         Drop   => Right);
   ```
   i.
   ```
   Move (Source => "McIntosh is my favorite",
         Target => Apple,
         Drop   => Left);
   ```

j.
```
   Apple := 12 * 'A';
```
k.
```
   Apple := 6 * "AB";
```
l.
```
   Apple := Apple'Length * 'A';
```

8. What is displayed by each of the following code fragments? Use the symbol □ to indicate each blank character. You may need to study Sections A.4.2, A.4.3, and A.4.6 of the *Ada Language Reference Manual* to learn the effects of the fixed-length string operations used.

   a.
```
Pear := "abc ABC aBcD";
Put (Index (Source  => Pear,
            Pattern => "BC"));
```
   b.
```
Pear := "abc ABC aBcD";
Put (Index (Source  => Pear,
            Pattern => "BC",
            Mapping => Ada.Strings.Maps.Constants.Upper_Case_Map));
```
   c.
```
Pear := "abc ABC aBcD";
Put (Index (Source  => Pear,
            Pattern => "BC",
            Mapping => Ada.Strings.Maps.Constants.Upper_Case_Map,
            Going   => Backward));
```
   d.
```
Orange := 5 * ' ' & "Juice" & 5 * ' ';
Put (Index_Non_Blank (Source => Orange));
```
   e.
```
Orange := 5 * ' ' & "Juice" & 5 * ' ';
Put (Index_Non_Blank (Source => Orange ,
                      Going  => Backward));
```

9. What is displayed by each of the following code fragments? Use the symbol □ to indicate each blank character. You may need to study Sections A.4.2, A.4.3, and A.4.6 of the *Ada Language Reference Manual* to learn the effects of the fixed-length string operations used.

   a.
```
   Lemon := "Lemons are sour";
   Put_Line (Head (Source => Lemon,
                   Count  => 5));
```

b.
```
Lemon := "Lemons are sour";
Put_Line (Tail (Source => Lemon,
                Count  => 7));
```
c.
```
Lemon := "Lemons are sour";
Put (Count (Source  => Lemon,
            Pattern => "s"));
```
d.
```
Lemon := "Lemons are sour";
Chars := Ada.Strings.Maps.To_Set ("sour");
Put (Count (Source => Lemon,
            Set    => Chars));
```
e.
```
Pear := "abc ABC aBcD";
Put (Count (Source  => Pear,
            Pattern => "ABC"));
```
f.
```
Pear := "abc ABC aBcD";
Put (Count (Source => Pear,
            Mapping =>
   Ada.Strings.Maps.Constants.Upper_Case_Map,
            Pattern => "ABC"));
```
g.
```
Lemon := "Lemons are sour";
Put_Line (Insert (Source   => Lemon,
                  Before   => 12,
                  New_Item => "nice and "));
```
h.
```
Lemon := "Lemons are sour";
Code  := Ada.Strings.Maps.To_Mapping (From => "aeiou",
                                      To   => "12345");
Put_Line (Translate(Source  => Lemon,
                    Mapping => Code));
```
i.
```
Lemon := "Lemons are sour";
Code  := Ada.Strings.Maps.To_Mapping (From => "aeiou",
                                      To   => "12345");
Put_Line (Translate (Source  => Insert (Source   => Lemon,
                                        Before   => 12,
                                        New_Item => "nice and "),
                     Mapping => Code));
```

10. Read Section A.16 in the *Ada Language Reference Manual* to learn about the operations available for querying and modifying files and directories within a file system. Most of the operations have fixed-length string parameters.

    Write a code fragment that prompts the user for a filename and displays whether that file exists. If the file does exist, display what kind of file it is (as defined by type `File_Kind` in package `Ada.Directories`) and its size.

11. Write the code for the body of the following search function, a simplified version of the `Index` function found in `Ada.Strings.Fixed`:

```
function Index (Source : in String; Pattern : in String) return Natural;
```

Bounded-Length Strings

12. a. Instantiate a package from `Ada.Strings.Bounded.Generic_Bounded_Length` for bounded-length strings with a bound of 100 characters. Call your new package `File_Names`.

    b. Instantiate a package from `Ada.Strings.Bounded.Generic_Bounded_Length` for bounded-length strings with a bound of 120 characters. Call your new package `Directory_Names`.

    c. Given the following two string variable declarations,

    ```
    File_Name   : File_Names.Bounded_String;
    Folder_Name : Directory_Names.Bounded_String;
    ```

    write a single assignment statement that assigns the value of `File_Name` to `Folder_Name`. You will need to convert one kind of bounded-length string to another kind of bounded-length string.

    d. Is it possible for the assignment statement you wrote for part (c) to raise the string exception `LENGTH_ERROR`? Explain why or why not. You may wish to study Section A.4.4 of the *Ada Language Reference Manual* to answer this question.

    e. Using the declarations from part (c), write a single assignment statement that assigns the value of `Folder_Name` to `File_Name`. You will need to convert one kind of bounded-length string to another kind of bounded-length string.

    f. Is it possible for the assignment statement you wrote for part (e) to raise the string exception `LENGTH_ERROR`? Explain why or why not. You may wish to study Section A.4.4 of the *Ada Language Reference Manual* to answer this question.

13. Given the following declarations of three bounded-length string variables and an index variable, complete parts (a)–(e) on the following page.

    ```
    Name      : File_Names.Bounded_String;
    Base_Name : File_Names.Bounded_String;
    Extension : File_Names.Bounded_String;
    Location  : Natural;
    ```

a. Complete the following procedure, which gets a line of input from the standard input file:

```
procedure Get_Line (Item : out File_Names.Bounded_String) is
- This procedure has the same effect as Ada.Text_IO.Get_Line.
- Since it returns a varying-length string, there is no need
- to include an equivalent to the parameter Last.
```

b. Write an example call of procedure `Get_Line` to get a value for `Name`.

c. Write an Ada statement that calls function `Index` to search for a period in `Name` and assigns its location to `Location`.

d. Using the value of `Location` that you determined in part (c), write an Ada statement that uses the slice function to copy the portion of the string before the period in `Name` to `Base_Name`. Do not copy the period.

e. Using the value of `Location` that you determined in part (c), write an Ada statement that uses the slice function to copy the portion of the string after the period in `Name` to `Extension`. Do not copy the period.

14. Given the following declaration of a bounded-length string variable,

    ```
    Reptile : Reptile_Strings.Bounded_String;
    ```

    using bounded-length string operations, implement the following algorithm to replace all of the occurrences of the word *snake* with the word *turtle* in the string `Reptile`.

    Translate all of the uppercase characters in Reptile to lowercase characters
    loop
        Search Reptile for the word snake
        Exit the loop when snake is not found
        Replace the word snake with the word turtle
    end loop

15. Delete the first step of the algorithm in the previous question and then modify it so that the case of the first letter of the word *snake* is preserved upon replacement with *turtle*. That is, the case of the first letter of turtle is the same as the case of the first letter of the word snake it replaces. Implement the revised algorithm. Package `Ada.Characters.Handling`, described in Section A.3.2 of the *Ada Language Reference Manual*, has useful operations for testing and changing the case of characters.

16. Given the following declaration of a bounded-length string variable,

    ```
    Command : Command_Strings.Bounded_String;
    ```

    using bounded-length string operations, implement the following algorithm to display all of the words in the string `Command`. Each word is displayed on a separate line. A token is defined as a sequence of characters delimited by spaces.

    Trim all leading and trailing blanks from Command
    loop
        Exit the loop when Command is a null string

```
         Locate the first token in Command
         Display the first token in Command
         Delete the first token from Command
         Trim any leading blanks from Command
      end loop
```

17. Write the code for the body of the following search function, a simplified version of the `Index` function found in `Ada.Strings.Bounded.Generic_Bounded_Length`. Use the type definition of `Bounded_String` given on pages 231 and 232.

    ```
    function Index (Source  : in Bounded_String;
                    Pattern : in Bounded_String) return Natural;
    ```

Unbounded-Length Strings

18. Solve Exercise 14 using the following declaration of `Reptile`:

    ```
    Reptile : Ada.Strings.Unbounded.Unbounded_String;
    ```

19. Solve Exercise 15 using the following declaration of `Reptile`:

    ```
    Reptile : Ada.Strings.Unbounded.Unbounded_String;
    ```

20. Solve Exercise 16 using the following declaration of `Command`:

    ```
    Command : Ada.Strings.Unbounded.Unbounded_String;
    ```

21. Using unbounded-length string operations, complete the following procedure:

    ```
    procedure Comp (Item : in out Ada.Strings.Unbounded.Unbounded_String) is
    -- This replaces a sequence of 5 blanks in Item
    -- with a sequence of two blanks
    ```

22. The following is a specification of a generic function that converts a bounded-length string to an unbounded-length string. It contains a type of generic formal parameter that we have not discussed—a formal package. A formal package parameter is used to pass an entire package to a generic unit.

    ```
    with Ada.Strings.Bounded;
    with Ada.Strings.Unbounded;
    generic
       with package Strings is new
                  Ada.Strings.Bounded.Generic_Bounded_Length (<>);
    function To_Unbounded (Item : in Strings.Bounded_String)
            return Ada.Strings.Unbounded.Unbounded_String;
    ```

    In this example, the formal package name is `Strings`. The actual package supplied when we create an instance of this generic function must be an instance of the generic package `Ada.Strings.Bounded.Generic_Bounded_Length`. Here is a sample instantiation of function `To_Unbounded`:

```ada
package Name_Strings is new
      Ada.Strings.Bounded.Generic_Bounded_Length (Max => 100);

function Convert is new To_Unbounded (Strings => Name_Strings);
```

The body of function `To_Unbounded` may use any of the resources (types, constants, operations, etc.) defined in package `Strings`. Fill in the blank line to complete the body of generic function `To_Unbounded`.

```ada
function To_Unbounded (Item : in Strings.Bounded_String)
      return Ada.Strings.Unbounded.Unbounded_String is
   use Strings;
   use Ada.Strings.Unbounded;
begin
   return _____ ;
end To_Unbounded;
```

Access Types and Controlled Types

23. What is the difference between an access object (variable) and a designated object?
24. What is the initial value that Ada assigns to all access variables when they are elaborated?
25. Define the following terms:
    a. Elaboration
    b. Dynamic allocation
    c. Dereference
    d. Null access value (or null pointer)
    e. Allocator
    f. Alias
    g. Memory leak
26. Given the following declarations,

```ada
   subtype Name_Type is String (1..10);
subtype GPA_Type is Float range 0.0..4.0;
type Student_Rec is
   record
      First_Name    : Name_Type;
      Last_Name     : Name_Type;
      ID            : Positive;
      GPA           : GPA_Type;
      Current_Hours : Natural;
      Total_Hours   : Natural;
   end record;
```

```
type List_Type is array (1..100) of Student_Rec;

type List_Ptr is access List_Type;

Student_List : List_Ptr;
```

      assume that an access variable takes 6 bytes of memory, an integer or floating point variable takes 4 bytes of memory, and a character variable takes 1 byte of memory. Also assume that the fields in the record are in contiguous memory locations with no gaps.

    a. How much memory (number of bytes) is allocated to the variable `Student_List` when it is elaborated?

    b. How much space is allocated at run time by the following statement?
`Student_List := new List_Type;`
Assume that `new` allocates exactly the number of bytes needed by the data type.

    c. Write an assignment statement to set the ID of the first student in the list array to 1000.

    d. Write a loop to print out the ID's of all the students in the list. Assume that all array positions are in use.

    e. Write a loop to add the `Current_Hours` field of each student to the `Total_Hours` field, and to reset each `Current_Hours` to zero.

    f. Write the necessary declaration to instantiate a procedure called `Free` that reclaims the memory of an object of an access variable of type `List_Ptr`.

    g. Use the procedure `Free` you created in part (f) to reclaim the memory designated by `Student_List`. What is the value of the variable `Student_List` after calling procedure `Free`?

27. Given the following declarations

```
type Frequency_Array is array (Character range <>) of Natural;

type Frequency_Ptr is access Frequency_Array;

A : Frequency_Ptr;
B : Frequency_Ptr;
C : Frequency_Ptr;
```

    a. Write a statement that allocates space for an array with an index range of `'a'..'g'` that is designated by access variable A. The elements in the array should not be given initial values.

    b. Write a loop to assign the value of 100 to all elements in the array designated by access variable B.

    c. Write a statement that allocates space for an array with an index range of `'h'..'n'` that is designated by access variable B. Each element in the array should be given an initial value of zero.

d. Draw a picture to illustrate the value of B after the statement you wrote for part (c) is executed.
e. Write a statement that allocates space for an array with an index range of `'a'..'n'` that is designated by access variable C. Each element in the array should be given an initial value corresponding to the values in the arrays designated by access variables A and B.
f. Write the necessary declaration to instantiate a procedure called Free that reclaims the memory of an object of an access variable of type Frequency_Ptr.
g. Use the procedure Free you created in part (f) to reclaim the memory designated by C.

28. Using the declarations given in the previous question and the procedure Free you instantiated in part (f) of that question, which of the following code fragments raise CONSTRAINT_ERROR? Which result in memory leakage? Assume that before each code fragment is executed, the three access variables A, B, and C designate different objects.

    a.
    ```
    Free(A);
    Free(A);
    ```
    b.
    ```
    Free(A);
    A.all('c') := 52;
    ```
    c.
    ```
    A := null;
    ```
    d.
    ```
    A := null;
    A.all('c') := 52;
    ```
    e.
    ```
    A := B;
    B.all('f') := 96;
    ```
    f.
    ```
    A := B;
    Free(B);
    A := null;
    ```
    g.
    ```
    A.all := C.all('a'..'g');
    ```
    h.
    ```
    A.all := C.all;
    ```
    i.
    ```
    A := null;
    B := A;
    ```

29. Write the code for the body of the following search function, a simplified version of the Index function found in Ada.Strings.Unbounded. Use the type

definition of the simple (not controlled) `Bounded_String_Type` given on page 243.

```
function Index (Source  : in Unbounded_String_Type;
                Pattern : in Unbounded_String_Type) return Natural;
```

30. Controlled types provide the procedures `Initialize`, `Finalize`, and `Adjust` to prevent unwanted aliases and memory leaks.

    a. If `Maple` and `Oak` are objects of some controlled type, tell *when* the procedures `Initialize`, `Finalize`, and `Adjust` are called during the execution of the following assignment statement:

    `Oak := Maple;`

    b. What is the usual use of procedure `Initialize`?
    c. What is the usual use of procedure `Finalize`?
    d. What is the usual use of procedure `Adjust`?

31. The following program demonstrates controlled types. The output statements included in `Initialize`, `Finalize`, and `Adjust` provide an explicit trace of the calls made to them. Because these procedures are not called directly, this demonstration program can help you understand their use.

    a. What is the output of this program?
    b. Type in the following program or copy it from the publisher's website. Run the program to check you answers from part (a).
    c. The object `Elm` was given an initial value of 127. We can see the finalization of `Elm` but there is no apparent call to procedure `Initialization` for `Elm`. Why not?

```
with Ada.Finalization; use Ada.Finalization;
with Ada.Text_IO;      use Ada.Text_IO;
procedure Demo_Controlled is

  Global_Count : Natural := 0;

  type My_Controlled is new Ada.Finalization.Controlled with
    record
        Count : Natural;
    end record;

  overriding
  procedure Initialize (Object : in out My_Controlled);
  overriding
  procedure Finalize (Object : in out My_Controlled);
  overriding
  procedure Adjust (Object : in out My_Controlled);

  -- Primitive operations must be defined before any bodies
```

```ada
-- Here are the bodies for the 3 primitive operations

procedure Initialize (Object : in out My_Controlled) is
begin
   Global_Count := Global_Count + 1;
   Object.Count := Global_Count;
   Put_Line ("Initialized  " & Natural'Image(Object.Count));
end Initialize;

procedure Finalize (Object : in out My_Controlled) is
begin
   Put_Line ("Finalized    " & Natural'Image(Object.Count));
end Finalize;

procedure Adjust (Object : in out My_Controlled) is
begin
   Global_Count := Global_Count + 1;
   Object.Count := Global_Count;
   Put_Line ("Adjusting    " & Natural'Image(Object.Count));
end Adjust;

Oak   : My_Controlled;
Maple : My_Controlled;
                           -- Use of extension aggregate
Elm   : My_Controlled := (Controlled with Count => 127);
begin
   Put_Line ("Assigning Maple to Oak");
   Oak := Maple;
   Put_Line ("Incrementing Elm.Count");
   Elm.Count := Elm.Count + 1;
   Put_Line ("All done with executable statements");
end Demo_Controlled;
```

32. Draw pictures like those used in Figures 4.14 and 4.15 to trace a call of function `To_Unbounded` whose implementation is given in Body 4.1.

Programming Problems

33. The following package declaration specifies a new kind of file type—a file of words. A word is defined as a group of characters delimited by spaces. `Word_IO` is a generic package with a single generic formal parameter. The actual parameter for `Word_Strings` must be an instance of `Generic_Bounded_Length` from `Ada.Strings.Bounded`. Procedures `Open` and `Close` are the `Word_IO` counterparts of the same procedures in `Ada.Text_IO`. Procedure `Get` returns the next available word in the `File`. The word returned is a bounded-length string. Function `End_Of_File` returns true when there are no words remaining in the file.

Procedure Unget moves the reading marker back one word, which has the effect of making it the next word that procedure Get will return. In this package, the application programmer may only unget one word. Procedure Unget raises exception UNGET_OVERFLOW if a second call is made to Unget before getting the previous ungot word.

```ada
with Ada.Strings.Unbounded;
with Ada.Strings.Bounded;   use Ada.Strings.Bounded;
with Ada.Text_IO;
generic
   -- Must supply a bounded-length string package for
   -- processing words in the file.
   with package Word_Strings is new Generic_Bounded_Length (<>);

package Word_IO is

   -- This package implements a File type whose components are "words"

   -- A word is defined as a sequence of characters delimited by blanks
   -- and end of line markers

   type File_Type is limited private;   -- A file of words

   UNGET_OVERFLOW : exception;  -- potentially raised by procedure Unget
   END_ERROR      : exception;  -- potentially raised by procedure Get


   ---------------------------------------------------------------
   procedure Open (File : in out File_Type;
                   Name : in     String);
   -- Purpose        : Prepares File for input
   -- Preconditions  : None
   -- Postconditions : The File with name Name is prepared for input
   -- Exceptions     : Ada.Text_IO.STATUS_ERROR
   --                    raised if File is already open


   ---------------------------------------------------------------
   procedure Close (File : in out File_Type);
   -- Purpose        : Terminates use of File
   -- Preconditions  : None
   -- Postconditions : The connection between file and the input
   --                    device is terminated
```

```ada
-- Exceptions      : Ada.Text_IO.STATUS_ERROR
--                      raised if File is NOT open


-------------------------------------------------------------------
procedure Get (File : in out File_Type;
               Item :    out Word_Strings.Bounded_String);
-- Purpose         : Gets the next word from the file
-- Preconditions   : None
-- Postconditions  : Item is the next word in File.
--                      Reading marker is moved to the delimiter that
--                      marked the end of the word
-- Exceptions      : END_ERROR
--                      raised if there are no more words in File
--                  Ada.Text_IO.STATUS_ERROR
--                      raised if File is not open
--                  Word_Strings.LENGTH_ERROR
--                      raised if the length of the next word
--                      exceeds the bound of a Word_String


-------------------------------------------------------------------
procedure Unget (File : in out File_Type;
                 Word : in     Word_Strings.Bounded_String);
-- Purpose         : Returns the Word to the File so the next call to get
--                      returns Word.  Only one word can be ungot before
--                      the next call to Get
-- Preconditions   : None
-- Postconditions  : The Word is returned to the File and the reading
--                      marker is set to the beginning of the Word
-- Exceptions      : UNGET_OVERFLOW
--                      raised if an attempt is made to unget a second word
--                      before getting the first ungot word


-------------------------------------------------------------------
function End_Of_File (File : in File_Type) return Boolean;
-- Purpose         : Returns True if there are no more words
--                      remaining in the file
-- Preconditions   : None
-- Postconditions  : Returns True if there are no more words in the file.
--                      Otherwise, returns False
```

```
--  Exceptions      : Ada.Text_IO.STATUS_ERROR
--                    raised if File was not open

private

   type File_Type is
      record
         File   : Ada.Text_IO.File_Type;                  -- The text file
         Ungot  : Word_Strings.Bounded_String;            -- The ungot word
         Buffer : Ada.Strings.Unbounded.Unbounded_String; -- File buffer
      end record;

end Word_IO;
```

In the private part of package `Word_IO`, we can see that a word file type is built from three components: a text file, an ungot word, and a buffer. The ungot word is used to store the word returned by the application programmer through a call to procedure `Unget`. The key to this abstraction is the read-ahead buffer maintained for each file. This buffer always contains the next words to be read. When this buffer is empty, the file is exhausted.

Type in the package specification `Word_IO` or copy it from the publisher's website. Your task is to write and test the package body. Here are some hints to get you started:

Function `End_Of_File` returns true when there are no words remaining in the word file. There are no words left when both the file buffer and the ungot word are empty.

Function `Close` simply closes the text file from which we are getting words. Procedure `Open` does two things. It opens the text file. Then it gets the first nonblank line from the text file and stores it in the buffer.

Procedure `Unget` first checks that there is not already a word in the file's ungot field. It then either raises the exception or assigns its parameter to the file's ungot field.

There are three possible paths in procedure `Get`. If there is an ungot word, it returns that word and assigns a null string to the ungot field. If there is not an ungot word, it removes the first word from the file buffer and returns that word. Should the word removed be the last one in the buffer, the procedure needs to refill the buffer with the next nonblank line from the text file. Recall that the buffer always contains the next words to be read. When the buffer is empty, our word file is exhausted.

34. Modify the specification and implementation of the previous question. Instead of saving the ungot word in its own field, add it to the buffer. This modification no

longer has a limit on the number of words you can unget, so remove the exception UNGET_OVERFLOW.

35. Write an Ada program that reads the text of a newspaper story from an unformatted text file and produces a formatted text file. Your program should prompt for and obtain the following information from the user:

   a. The name (no more than 80 characters) of a text file containing a newspaper story

   b. The name (no more than 80 characters) of a text file in which to place the formatted newspaper story

   c. The maximum number of lines on a page in the formatted story (between 10 and 65 lines)

   d. The number of characters on a line in the formatted story (between 10 and 80 characters)

   You may assume that all information entered by the user is valid. Your program should use the information supplied by the user to format the input story. There may be many blank lines in the input file. There may be many blanks between words in the input file. All of these blanks are to be ignored in the output.

   Other requirements:

   - Each line of the formatted output should contain as many words as possible.
   - There should be exactly one blank between words on a line in the output file.
   - No word is to be split between lines.
   - Each line must be padded on the right with blanks so each line contains the exact number of characters requested by the user.
   - Use the package `Word_IO` that you implemented for Exercise 33. You will find a good use for the unget operation. Use fixed-length string variables only for filenames.
   - Each output line must be written to the output file with a single call to `Ada.Text_IO.Put_Line`.

Stacks with Introductions to Linked Lists and Big-O

Goals for this chapter include that you should be able to

- describe a stack and its operations at an abstract level.
- determine when a stack is an appropriate data structure for a specific problem.
- design and implement the solution to a problem for which a stack is an appropriate data structure.
- evaluate a postfix expression.
- show how stacks can be used to evaluate postfix expressions.
- use a static array to implement a stack class.
- use a linked structure to implement a stack class.
- explain the difference between static and dynamic allocation of the space in which a stack is stored.
- extend a class defined in a generic package.
- explain the use of Big-O notation to describe the amount of work done by an algorithm.
- compare stack implementations in terms of source code length, use of storage space, and Big-O approximations of the stack operations.
- choose between a static and a dynamic linked stack structure.

In Chapter 3 we looked at the set, an *unordered* collection of items. In this chapter and the next chapter we examine two data structures (the stack and the queue) that are collections of items *ordered by time* of their entry into the structure.

5.1 The Logical Level

What is a stack? Consider the items pictured in Figure 5.1. Although the objects are all different, each illustrates a common concept: the **stack**. At the logical level, a stack is an ordered group of elements. The removal of existing elements and the addition of new elements can take place only at the top of the stack. For instance, if your favorite blue shirt is underneath a faded, old red one in a stack of shirts, you first must remove the red shirt (the top element) from the stack. Only then can you remove the desired blue shirt, which is now the top element in the stack. The red shirt may then be replaced on the top of the stack or thrown away.

> **Stack** A structure in which elements are added and removed from only one end; a "last in, first out" (LIFO) structure.

The stack is considered an "ordered" group of items because elements occur in a sequence according to how long they've been in the stack. The items that have been in the stack the longest are at the bottom; the most recent are at the top. At any time, given any two elements in a stack, one is higher than the other. (For instance, the red shirt was higher in the stack than the blue shirt.)

Because items are added and removed only from the top of the stack, the last element to be added is the first to be removed. There is a handy mnemonic to help you remember this rule of stack behavior: A stack is a LIFO (last in, first out) structure.

The accessing operation of a stack is summarized as follows: Both to retrieve elements and to assign new elements, access only the top of the stack.

Operations on Stacks

The logical picture of the structure is only half the definition of a class. The other half is a set of operations that allows the user to access and manipulate the elements stored in

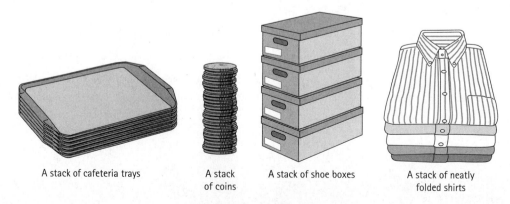

A stack of cafeteria trays   A stack of coins   A stack of shoe boxes   A stack of neatly folded shirts

Figure 5.1 *Real-life stacks.*

the structure. Given the abstract structure of a stack, what kinds of operations do we need in order to use a stack?

The operation that adds an element to the top of a stack is usually called *Push*, and the operation that takes the top element off the stack is referred to as *Pop*. We also must be able to tell whether a stack contains any elements before we pop it, so we need a Boolean operation *Empty*. As a logical data structure, a stack is never conceptually "full," but for a particular implementation you may need to test whether a stack is full before pushing. We'll call this Boolean operation *Full*. We also might want an operation that destroys a stack, getting rid of all the elements left in it and leaving the stack empty. We'll call this operation *Clear*. Figure 5.2 shows how a stack, envisioned as a stack of building blocks, is modified by several Push and Pop operations.

Let's formalize the stack operations we have described. We use a package specification to accurately describe our class. We'll make this a generic package so that our stack abstraction can be easily reused in different applications. We then can instantiate stack

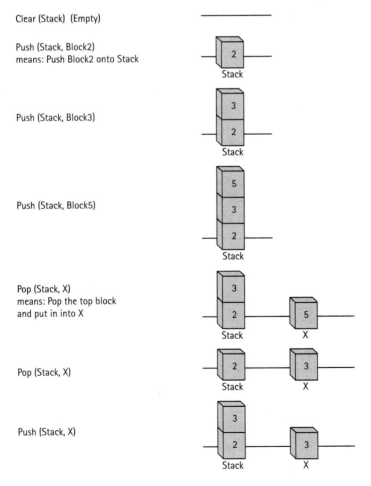

Figure 5.2 *The effects of* Push *and* Pop *operations.*

packages for stacks containing any type of objects. Our generic stack specification is given in Specification 5.1.

Specification 5.1   Bounded Stack

```
generic
   type Element_Type is private;   -- The stack element type
package Stack is

-- This package implements a stack, a data structure in which
-- elements are added and removed from only one end.
-- A "last in, first out" (LIFO) structure.

   type Stack_Type (Max_Size : Natural) is tagged limited private;

   UNDERFLOW : exception;
   OVERFLOW  : exception;


   -------------------------------------------------------------------
   procedure Clear (Stack : in out Stack_Type);
   -- Purpose        : Remove all elements from the stack
   -- Preconditions  : None
   -- Postconditions : Stack is empty; it contains no elements


   -------------------------------------------------------------------
   function Empty (Stack : in Stack_Type) return Boolean;
   -- Purpose        : Tests whether a stack is empty (contains no elements)
   -- Preconditions  : None
   -- Postconditions : Empty = (stack is empty)


   -------------------------------------------------------------------
   function Full (Stack : in Stack_Type) return Boolean;
   -- Purpose        : Tests whether a stack is full. A stack is full
   --                  when no more elements can be pushed on it
   -- Preconditions  : None
   -- Postconditions : Full = (no more elements can be pushed onto Stack)


   -------------------------------------------------------------------
   procedure Push (Stack       : in out Stack_Type;
                   New_Element : in     Element_Type);
   -- Purpose        : Adds New_Element to the top of Stack
   -- Preconditions  : None
   -- Postconditions : Stack = original Stack with New_Element added on top
   -- Exceptions     : OVERFLOW  Raised on attempt to Push a new element onto
   --                            a full stack. Stack is unchanged.
   -------------------------------------------------------------------
```

```
procedure Pop (Stack          : in out Stack_Type;
               Popped_Element :    out Element_Type);
-- Purpose        : Removes the top element from Stack and returns it
-- Preconditions  : None
-- Postconditions : Stack         = original Stack with top element removed
--                  Popped_Element = top element of original Stack
-- Exceptions     : UNDERFLOW Raised on attempt to Pop an element from an
--                            empty stack. Stack remains empty.

private

   -- We'll fill this in later

end Stack;
```

Comparing two stacks for equality and copying stacks are operations not commonly associated with stack classes. Therefore we have declared Stack_Type to be limited private—the only operations permitted on stack objects are the five defined in the package specification. We have also declared Stack_Type as a tagged type to allow an application programmer to use the *object.method* syntax for invoking stack operations and to extend the stack class. This type declaration also includes the discriminant Max_Size. As its name suggests, we supply a value for this discriminant to specify an upper bound on the number of elements a particular stack object can contain. The following code fragment illustrates the creation of a stack class whose elements are unbounded-length strings and two stack objects with different bounds:

```
package Name_Stack is new Stack
                (Element_Type => Ada.Strings.Unbounded.Unbounded_String);

Short_Stack : Name_Stack.Stack_Type (Max_Size => 4);
Big_Stack   : Name_Stack.Stack_Type (Max_Size => 1000);
```

Exceptions

In addition to the stack operations we discussed earlier, our stack package contains the declarations for two exceptions. If a stack is empty when we try to pop an element from it, the resulting error condition is called **stack underflow**. The exception comments for procedure Pop indicate that the exception UNDERFLOW is raised if this condition is detected. **Stack overflow** is the condition resulting from trying to push a new element onto a stack that is already full. Procedure Push raises the exception OVERFLOW if this condition is detected.

> **Stack underflow** The condition resulting from trying to pop an empty stack.
>
> **Stack overflow** The condition resulting from trying to push an element onto a full stack.

Figure 5.3 demonstrates how exceptions are shown on a UML diagram. The dashed line labeled with the stereotype «raise» drawn from the Push operation indicates that this operation may raise the exception OVERFLOW. The diagram also shows that the Pop operation may raise the exception UNDERFLOW. An alternative method for relating

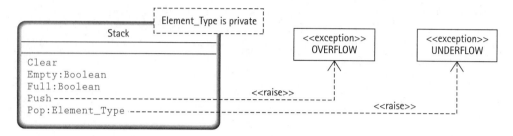

Figure 5.3 *UML diagram of a generic stack class and the exceptions it raises.*

exceptions to a class is to simply list them in the class diagram in a separate box following the operations. This style is illustrated in Figure 5.4. The advantage of this alternative method is that it takes less space. Its disadvantage is that there is no association between individual operations and the exceptions.

Why bother declaring these exceptions in the stack package? Why not just display an error message? For example, instead of raising UNDERFLOW when the Pop operation detects an erroneous condition, Pop could display an error message on the console such as

Error! The stack is empty, you can't remove an item at this time.

One problem with this approach is that the error message we choose when we write the stack package body probably has little meaning in the context of the application program that uses a stack. Imagine the confusion if the above message were displayed when someone running a word processing program clicks their mouse on the "undo" command. A more meaningful error message in this situation would be "There are no more actions to undo."

Part of the task of writing a reusable component is to allow errors that are detected by the component to be dealt with at the *appropriate level of abstraction*. Ada's exceptions are the perfect tool for this job. When the stack package detects a problem, it raises an exception that is propagated back to the client program to deal with. Exception propagation also ensures that the error condition is not ignored. If the client has no

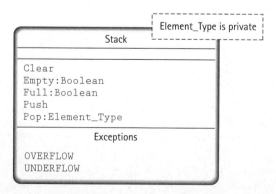

Figure 5.4 *Alternative UML diagram of a generic stack class and the exceptions it raises.*

handler for the exception, it is propagated back to the operating system which ends execution of the program and displays a (usually cryptic) error message.

Exceptions and Postconditions   Postconditions are assertions that state what results are to be expected at the exit of an operation or procedure. Our style of commenting postconditions for package operations is to divide the exit assertions into two groups. The assertions in the group labeled "Postconditions:" are true if the operation terminates normally; that is, when no exception is raised. The comment section labeled "Exceptions:" contains assertions that are true if the package operation terminates abnormally by raising an exception. Notice how our exception comments specify exactly what the state of the stack is after the package raises the exception. Other people prefer to have just a single postcondition comment section that includes the exit assertions found in both of our comment sections.

5.2 The Application Level

Now let's look at an example of how the operations in the stack package might be used in a program. Since you were in elementary school you have written arithmetic expressions using a format known as *infix* notation. This same notation is used for writing arithmetic expressions in Ada. The operator in an infix expression is written in between its operands. When an expression contains multiple operations such as

$$5 + 2 \times 6$$

we need to use a set of rules to determine which operation to carry out first. You learned in your mathematics classes that multiplication is done before addition. You learned Ada's operator precedence rules in your first programming class. In both situations, we use parentheses to override the normal ordering rules. It is easy to make a mistake writing or interpreting an infix expression containing multiple nested sets of parentheses.

Evaluating Postfix Expressions

Postfix notation[1] is another format for writing arithmetic expressions. In this notation, the operator is written after the two operands. Here are some simple postfix expressions and their results.

---

[1]Postfix notation is also known as reverse Polish notation (RPN), so named after the Polish logician Jan Lukasiewicz (1875–1956) who developed it.

Postfix Expression	Result
4 5 +	9
9 3 /	3
17 8 -	9

The rules for evaluating postfix expressions with multiple operators are much simpler than those for evaluating infix expressions; simply evaluate the operators from left to right. There are no precedence rules to learn and parentheses are never needed. Because of this simplicity, some popular handheld calculators use postfix notation to avoid the complications of the multiple parentheses required in nontrivial infix expressions (see Figure 5.5).

Let's look at a postfix expression containing two operators:

$$6\ 2\ /\ 5\ +$$

We evaluate the expression by scanning from left to right. The first item, 6, is an operand so we go on. The second item, 2, is also an operand so again we continue. The third item is the division operator. We now apply this operator to the two previous operands. Which of the two saved operands is the divisor? The one we saw most

Figure 5.5 *A calculator that evaluates postfix expressions.*

recently. We divide 6 by 2 and substitute 3 back into the expression, replacing 6 2 /. Our expression now looks like this:

$$3\ 5\ +$$

We continue our scanning. The next item is an operand, 5, so we go on. The next (and last) item is the operator +. We apply this operator to the two previous operands, giving a result of 8.

Here's another example explained in slightly different terms:

$$4\ 5\ +\ 7\ 2\ -\ *$$

Scanning from left to right, the first operator encountered is +. This is applied to the two preceding operators giving us the expression

$$9\ 7\ 2\ -\ *$$

The next operator encountered is − so we subtract 2 from 7 giving us

$$9\ 5\ *$$

Finally, the last operator, *, is applied to its two preceding operands, giving our final answer of 45.

Here are some more examples of postfix expressions containing multiple operators and the results of evaluating them. See if you get the same results when you evaluate them.

Postfix Expression	Result
4 5 7 2 + - *	−16
3 4 + 2 * 7 /	2
5 7 + 6 2 - *	48
4 2 3 5 1 - * + *	56
4 2 + 3 5 1 - * +	18

Now suppose we need to write a program that evaluates postfix expressions entered interactively from the keyboard. We can use the same approach as we did by hand. We get items one at a time from the line. When the item we get is an operator, we apply it to the last two operands. A stack is the ideal place to store the previous operands because the top item is always the most recent operand and the next item on the stack is always the second most recent operand; just the two operands are required when we find an operator. Here is an algorithm that uses a stack in this manner to evaluate a postfix expression:

Postfix Evaluation
loop
    exit when no more Items left in the expression
    get Item from expression
    if Item is an operator
        pop last two values from the stack
        perform the operation with the two values
        push the result onto the stack
    else
        push Item onto the stack
    end if
end loop
pop the stack to obtain the final result

Each iteration of this loop processes one operator or one operand from the expression. When an operand is found, there is nothing to do with it (we haven't yet found the operator to apply to it) so we save it on the stack till later. When an operator is found, we get the two operands from the stack, do the operation, and put the result back on the stack; the result may be an operand for a future operator.

Let's trace this algorithm. Before we enter the loop, the expression that has not yet been processed and the stack look like this:

5 7 + 6 2 - *

After one iteration of the loop, we have processed the first operand and pushed it onto the stack. Here is what the remaining expression and stack look like now:

7 + 6 2 - *

5

After the second iteration of the loop, the stack contains two operands.

+ 6 2 - *

7
5

The + operator is encountered in the third iteration. We pop the two operands from the stack, perform the operation, and push the result onto the stack.

```
6 2 - *     |   |
            |   |
            |12 |
            |___|
```

In the next two iterations of the loop, two operands are pushed onto the stack.

When the − operator is found, the top two operands are popped and subtracted, and the result is pushed onto the stack.

When the * operator is found, the top two operands are popped and multiplied, and the result is pushed onto the stack.

```
   |    |
   |    |
   | 48 |
   |____|
```

Now that we have processed all of the items on the input line, we exit the loop. The final result, 48, is popped from the stack.

Invalid Expressions Every valid postfix expression must (1) have exactly one more operand than it has operators and (2) have two operands preceding each operator. Here are some examples of invalid postfix expressions that break one of these two rules.

Invalid Postfix Expression	Reason Why Invalid
5 6	Too many operands
5 6 * 7	Too many operands
/ 6 2	/ not preceded by two operands
6 / 2	/ not preceded by two operands
6 2 / * 4	* not preceded by two operands

What happens if the user enters an invalid postfix expression? Let's trace our algorithm using the first invalid expression in the list above. In the first loop iteration, 5 is pushed onto the stack. Then 6 is pushed on during the second iteration. The stack now looks like this:

Because there are no more items remaining in the expression, we exit the loop and pop the final result. Here is what things look like at the end of the algorithm trace:

Although the algorithm is complete, a number remains on the stack. When we use our algorithm to evaluate any postfix expression with excess operands we always find one or more values remaining on the stack when our algorithm is complete. So anytime we find that the stack is not empty when our algorithm is complete, we know that the expression is invalid. The second example also has too many operands (three operands and only one operator). Try tracing our algorithm with this invalid postfix expression. Again we find that there still is an operand on the stack when we reach the end of the algorithm. Note that we did not need to count the number of operators or operands to determine that these postfix expressions are invalid. All we need to do is check whether the stack is empty after completing the loop.

Let's trace the third example in our list of invalid expressions. After determining that / is an operator, we try to pop two values from the stack. There is nothing on the stack, however, so the first call to `Pop` raises `UNDERFLOW`. In the fourth example, our algorithm first pushes 6 onto the stack. Then it finds the / and attempts to pop its two operators from the stack. The second call to `Pop` raises `UNDERFLOW`. In our last example, `Pop` raises `UNDERFLOW` when it is called to get the second operand for *. Anytime that `UNDERFLOW` is raised, our postfix expression must be invalid—there are not two operands preceding some operator.

Is `OVERFLOW` ever raised by our postfix evaluation algorithm? This exception is raised when we attempt to push another value onto a full stack. Our algorithm pushes operands onto the stack until an operator is encountered. `OVERFLOW` is raised when there are more operands preceding an operator than there is space in the stack. The valid postfix expression

$$1\ 2\ 3\ 4\ 5\ 6\ +\ +\ -\ +\ *$$

would thus overflow a stack that holds only five elements.

Program 5.1 uses our algorithm to evaluate postfix expressions. The main program loop prompts for and obtains a postfix expression. This expression is passed to function `Evaluate`, which implements our algorithm. This function raises the exception `INVALID_EXPRESSION` when the postfix expression is not valid. This exception is also raised by the function when the number of operands in the expression is larger than its stack can hold.

In addition to the stack, our postfix evaluation program makes use of two other data structures we have discussed—strings and sets. We chose to store the expression entered by the user in an unbounded-length string. Procedure `Take_Item` removes and returns the first item from the string. To accomplish this action, it uses the `Find_Token` operation to locate the first sequence of nonblank characters in our expression string, the `Unbounded_Slice` operation to make a copy of this sequence, and the `Delete` operation to remove the sequence from the expression string.

The parameters `Set` and `Test` of the `Find_Token` operation define the details of the token search. Together, these two parameters specify what characters can make up a token. `Set` is a set of characters whose type is defined in the library package `Ada.Strings.Maps`. We used the set constructor `To_Set` to create the set constant `Blank_Set`, which contains a single element—the space character. We use this constant as the actual parameter for `Set`. By using a value of `Outside` for `Test`, we specify that tokens may contain any characters outside of `Blank_Set`. In other words, our tokens are sequences of any characters other than blanks. Blanks separate tokens in these strings.

Program 5.1 Postfix Evaluation

```
with Ada.Integer_Text_IO;      use Ada.Integer_Text_IO;
with Ada.Strings.Maps;         use Ada.Strings.Maps;
                               use Ada.Strings;
with Ada.Strings.Unbounded;    use Ada.Strings.Unbounded;
```

```ada
with Ada.Text_IO.Unbounded_IO; use Ada.Text_IO.Unbounded_IO;
                               use Ada.Text_IO;
with Stack;
procedure Postfix is

-- This program gets a postfix expression, evaluates it, and displays
-- the result. An error message is displayed for invalid expressions.
--
-- Assumption  All operands and operators are separated with at least one blank
--
-- Limitation  This program will handle no more than 50 operands in a row

   Operand_Bound : constant := 50; -- Maximum number of saved operands

   INVALID_EXPRESSION: exception;

   package Integer_Stack is new Stack (Element_Type => Integer);

   -------------------------------------------------------------------------
   procedure Take_Item (Source : in out Unbounded_String;
                        Item   :    out Unbounded_String) is
   -- Purpose        : Find and remove the first blank delimited item
   --                  from Source
   -- Preconditions  : None
   -- Postconditions : If Source is a null string or a blank string then
   --                     Item is the null string
   --                  Else Item is the first sequence of non-blank characters
   --                     in Source.
   --                  Item is removed from Source

      -- A set of characters with just a single character - the space character
      Blank_Set : constant Ada.Strings.Maps.Character_Set := To_Set (' ');

      First : Positive;   -- Indices of the first and last
      Last  : Natural;    -- characters in a sequence of non-blank characters
   begin
      -- Determine the indices of the item within Source
      Find_Token (Source => Source,
                  Set    => Blank_Set,
                  Test   => Outside,
                  First  => First,
                  Last   => Last);
      -- Copy the item found
      Unbounded_Slice (Source => Source,
                       Target => Item,
                       Low    => First,
                       High   => Last);
```

```ada
      -- Remove the item from Source
   Delete (Source  => Source,
           From    => First,
           Through => Last);
end Take_Item;

-------------------------------------------------------------------------

function Is_Operator (Item : in Unbounded_String) return Boolean is
-- Purpose      : Determines whether Item is an arithmetic operator
-- Preconditions  : None
-- Postconditions : Returns True if Item is an arithmetic operator and
--                  False otherwise
begin
   return Item = "+" or Item = "-" or Item = "*"  or Item = "/";
end Is_Operator;


-------------------------------------------------------------------------

function Evaluate_Operation (Left  : in Integer;
                             Op    : in Unbounded_String;
                             Right : in Integer) return Integer is
-- Purpose      : Carries out the one arithmetic operation
-- Preconditions  : Op is a valid arithmetic operator
-- Postconditions : Result is Left Op Right
begin
   if Op = "+" then
      return Left + Right;
   elsif Op = "-" then
      return Left - Right;
   elsif Op = "*" then
      return Left * Right;
   else
      return Left / Right;
   end if;
end Evaluate_Operation;


-------------------------------------------------------------------------

function Evaluate (Expression : in Unbounded_String) return Integer is
-- Purpose        : Evaluate a postfix expression
-- Preconditions  : All operands and operators in Expression are
--                  separated by one or more blanks
-- Postconditions : Returns the evaluation of Expression
-- Exceptions     : INVALID_EXPRESSION raised when Expression is not valid
--                                or Expression has too many operands
--                                for this procedure to handle
```

```ada
      Operand_Stack : Integer_Stack.Stack_Type (Max_Size => Operand_Bound);

   Result : Integer;              -- The answer returned
   Buffer : Unbounded_String;     -- Local copy of expression
   Item   : Unbounded_String;     -- An operator or an operand
   Left   : Integer;              -- First operand
   Right  : Integer;              -- Second operand
begin
   Buffer := Expression;   -- Make a local copy of Expression
   Result := 0;
   -- Evaluate the postfix expression in Buffer
   -- Each iteration, process one token (operand or operator) in Buffer
   loop
      Trim (Source => Buffer, Side => Ada.Strings.Left);
      exit when Length (Buffer) = 0;
      -- Remove the first item from the buffer
      Take_Item (Source => Buffer, Item => Item);
      if Is_Operator (Item) then
         -- Obtain the two previous operands from the stack
         Operand_Stack.Pop(Right);
         Operand_Stack.Pop(Left);
         -- Do the operation and put the result back on the stack
         Result := Evaluate_Operation (Left, Item, Right);
         Operand_Stack.Push (Result);
      else
         -- Convert the token to an integer and push it onto the stack.
         -- If Item is not a valid integer, the conversion will
         -- raise CONSTRAINT_ERROR.
         Result := Integer'Value(To_String (Item));
         Operand_Stack.Push(Result);
      end if;
   end loop;

   -- Pop the result from the stack
   Operand_Stack.Pop(Result);
   -- If the stack is not empty at this point, the Expression is invalid
   if not Operand_Stack.Empty then
      raise INVALID_EXPRESSION;
   else
      return Result;
   end if;
exception
   when CONSTRAINT_ERROR =>          -- An operand was not a valid integer
      raise INVALID_EXPRESSION;
   when Integer_Stack.UNDERFLOW => -- An operator not preceded by 2 operands
```

```ada
         raise INVALID_EXPRESSION;
   end Evaluate;

----------------------------------------------------------------------

   Expression : Unbounded_String;   -- A postfix expression
   Result     : Integer;            -- Result of evaluating an expression

begin
   -- Process a sequence of postfix expressions
   -- Each iteration, evaluate one postfix expression
   loop
      -- Get an expression
      Put_Line ("Enter a postfix expression.");
      Get_Line (Expression);

      -- Trim off leading and trailing blanks
      Trim (Source => Expression, Side => Both);
      exit when Length (Expression) = 0;

      -- Echo the input expression
      Put (Expression);

      -- Determine and display the result of evaluating Expression
      Exception_Block:
      begin
         Result := Evaluate (Expression);
         Put (" = ");
         Put (Item => Result, Width => 1);
      exception
         when INVALID_EXPRESSION =>
            Put (" is an invalid postfix expression" &
                 " (or too large for this program)");
      end Exception_Block;
      New_Line(2);
   end loop;
end Postfix;
```

Other Stack Applications

You have just seen an application in which stacks are used to evaluate a postfix arithmetic expression. Stacks also are used extensively in the evaluation of the infix arithmetic expressions you write in your Ada programs. The example of program Postfix hints at the types of applications that use a stack. A stack is the appropriate data structure when information must be saved and then later retrieved in reverse order. A situation requiring you to backtrack to some earlier position may be a good one in which to use a stack. For instance, in trying to find the way out of a maze, you may end up against a wall and need to backtrack to another exit. If you use a stack to save the alternative paths as you pass them, you can retrace your route to an earlier position.

Have you ever wondered how a program determines where to continue executing when it gets to the end of a procedure or function? Many systems use a stack to keep track of the return addresses, parameter values (or their addresses), and other information used by subprograms. For example, when Procedure A is called, its calling information is pushed onto a "run-time stack." Then when Procedure B is called from A, B's calling information is pushed onto the top of the stack. B then calls Procedure C, and C's calling information is pushed onto the stack. When C finishes executing, the stack is popped to retrieve the information needed to return to Procedure B. Then B finishes executing, and its calling information is popped from the stack. Finally Procedure A completes, and the stack is popped again to return to the main program. Because it can grow and shrink throughout execution, according to the level of subprogram nesting, a stack is a good structure for storing data on the order of procedure calls within a program. We return to this topic in Chapter 9 when we discuss recursion.

5.3 The Implementation Level

We now consider the implementation of our stack class. We first look at how a stack can be stored within an array. Then we see how stacks can be stored in dynamically allocated memory.

The Implementation of a Stack as a Static Array

Because all the elements of a stack are of the same type, an array seems like a reasonable structure to contain them. We can put elements in sequential slots in the array, placing the first element pushed in the first array position, the second element pushed in the second array position, and so on. The floating "high-water" mark is the top element in the stack.

Before we can implement our stack as an array, we need to know how to find the top element when we want to pop and where to put the new element when we push. Remember, although we can access any element of an array directly, we have agreed to use the accessing function "last in, first out" for a stack. So we access the stack elements only through the top, not through the bottom or the middle. Recognizing this distinction from the start is important. Even though the implementation of the stack may be a random-access structure such as an array, the stack itself as a logical entity is not randomly accessed. We can use only its top element.

One way to keep track of the top position in the array containing stack elements is to declare another variable, Top. However, the specifications of the stack operations only show the entity Stack passed in and out, not two entities, Stack and Top. We can bundle the array and the top indicator into a single entity, however, by using a record.

In order to declare the array variable that contains the stack, we must decide on its maximum size. We could declare a constant in our stack package to set this size; however, this is not very flexible. The user of our stack class should be able to determine the maximum size of the stack. One way to do so is to include the maximum size as a generic parameter, as is done for bounded-length strings. Users then could supply a value for the maximum stack size when they instantiate a stack package from our generic template. This solution still imposes some limitations on our users. All of the stack objects they declare will have the same maximum size. We have used a better way—an unconstrained array type and a record with a discriminant. The users must supply a value for the record discriminant in the declaration of each different stack object. This value is used to set the size of the array of elements. Here, then, are the declarations for the private part of our stack package:

```
private

   type Stack_Array is array (Positive range <>) of Element_Type;
   type Stack_Type (Max_Size : Natural) is tagged limited
      record
         Top      : Natural := 0;
         Elements : Stack_Array (1..Max_Size);
      end record;

end Stack;
```

When we include a discriminant in the complete declaration in the private section of the package, we also must include it in the incomplete declaration in the visible part of the package. We did include Max_Size in the public type declaration in Specification 5.1.

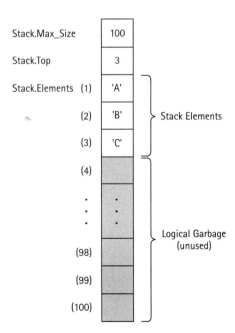

Figure 5.6 *The array implementation of a stack containing three elements—C is the top element.*

Figure 5.6 illustrates the data structure resulting from the following declarations:

```
-- Package for a character stack class
package Char_Stack is new Stack (Element_Type => Character);

-- One stack of characters
Stack : Char_Stack.Stack_Type (Max_Size => 100);
```

In this data structure, Top is the index of the top element in the stack, not the index of the next free slot in the array.

Finally, notice that in our declaration of Stack_Type we have supplied an initial value of 0 for the field Top in our stack record type. This value ensures that all stack objects declared are initially empty. It isn't necessary to blank out the whole array; instead, we simply set the top indicator to 0, as pictured in Figure 5.7. It doesn't matter how much garbage is in the array. If the stack's top indicator says that the stack is empty, none of the array slots can be accessed. Because each stack is initially empty, we did not supply any constructor operations.

Body 5.1 contains the array-based function and procedure bodies that implement the stack operations defined in Specification 5.1. All of these operations are quite short. Procedure Clear simply sets the top indicator back to zero. Because a zero value for Top indicates an empty stack, function Empty tests to see whether the top indicator is zero.

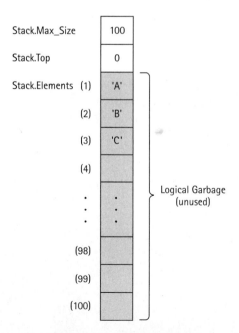

Figure 5.7 *An empty stack.*

Body 5.1 Array-Based Stack: Implements Specification 5.1

```ada
package body Stack is

   procedure Clear (Stack : in out Stack_Type) is
   begin
      Stack.Top := 0;
   end Clear;

   -------------------------------------------------------------------------

   function Empty (Stack : in Stack_Type) return Boolean is
   begin
      return Stack.Top = 0;
   end Empty;

   -------------------------------------------------------------------------

   function Full (Stack : in Stack_Type) return Boolean is
   begin
      return Stack.Top = Stack.Max_Size;
   end Full;

   -------------------------------------------------------------------------

   procedure Push (Stack       : in out Stack_Type;
                   New_Element : in     Element_Type) is
   begin
      if not Full (Stack) then
         Stack.Top := Stack.Top + 1;
         Stack.Elements (Stack.Top) := New_Element;
      else
         raise OVERFLOW;
      end if;
   end Push;

   -------------------------------------------------------------------------

   procedure Pop (Stack          : in out Stack_Type;
                  Popped_Element :    out Element_Type) is
   begin
      if not Empty (Stack) then
         Popped_Element := Stack.Elements (Stack.Top);
         Stack.Top := Stack.Top - 1;
      else
         raise UNDERFLOW;
      end if;
   end Pop;
end Stack;
```

Recall that a stack as an abstract data structure cannot be full; however, a particular implementation may make a test for a full stack necessary. The array implementation of a stack requires the programmer to choose an upper limit for the size of each stack via a value supplied for the discriminant. Our package uses the value of the discriminant to declare the size of the array. Therefore, we have an operation for the stack class to check for a full stack. To make this test, we compare the top indicator to the stack record discriminant Max_Size. We can access record discriminants like any other field in a record.

To add, or push, an element onto the top of the stack is a two-step task. We first increment the top indicator and then assign the new element to the location indicated by the top indicator. First, however, we must check for the possibility that there is no room left in the stack for the new element. We can use the Full operation for this check. If the stack is not already full, we assign the new element to the proper location in the array. If, however, the stack is full, we raise the exception OVERFLOW. Because we have no exception handler associated with procedure Push, this exception is propagated back to the caller of Push. As specified in the exception comments in our stack package declaration, the stack is not changed by the raising of this exception.

Let's take a look at the effect of a push operation on the stack in Figure 5.8(a). We want to Push (Stack => Stack, New_Element => 'L'). To do so we need to increment the top indicator from 3 to 4 and then put our new element, 'L', into the fourth element place. The result is shown in Figure 5.8(b).

To remove, or pop, an element from the stack, we perform the reverse of the push operation. First we check for stack underflow. If the stack is not empty, we assign the top element to our out parameter and then we decrement the top indicator. Figure 5.9 shows how the pop operation would affect a stack. In Figure 5.9(a), the value in Stack.Top tells us that the top element is stored in Stack.Elements(3). We assign the value of the top element, 'Y', to Popped_Element. Then the top indicator is decremented, giving us the stack shown in Figure 5.9(b). Note that after popping, 'Y' still is stored in the third element slot in the array, but we cannot access it through the stack. The 'Y' is now logical garbage, because the stack contains only two elements.

The Implementation of a Stack as a Linked List

The implementation of a stack in an array is very simple, but it has a serious drawback: The amount of storage space for a stack must be known when the stack object is elaborated. When we declare a variable of Stack_Type, memory is allocated to contain the number of stack elements specified by the discriminant. If we use fewer elements at run time, space is wasted; if we need to push more elements than the array can hold, we cannot. It would be nice if we could just get space for stack elements as we need it.

Chapter 4 introduced the concept of dynamic storage allocation, the ability to allocate memory for the program's data at run time. Let's see how we might use this concept to build a stack.

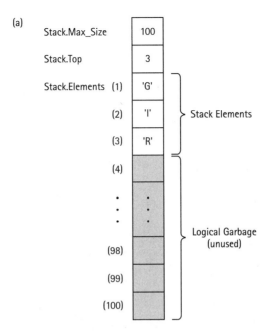
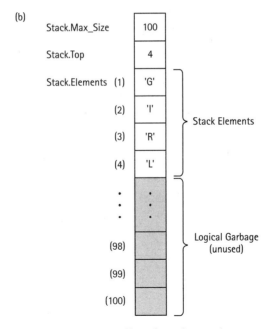

Figure 5.8 *The effect of a push operation.*

296 | Chapter 5: Stacks

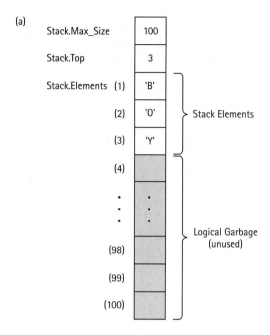

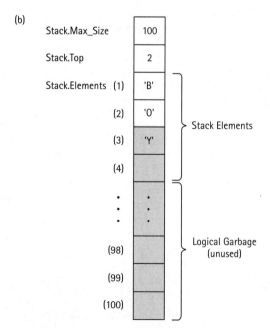

Figure 5.9 *The effect of a pop operation.*

Figure 5.10   *An empty stack.*

We can modify procedure `Push` to allocate space for each new element dynamically. One seemingly apparent way to do so is to implement a stack object as an access type variable.

```
type Stack_Type is access Element_Type;

Top : Stack_Type;   -- Designates the top element on the stack
```

Figure 5.10 illustrates what such an empty stack would look like. When we want to push a new element onto our stack, we use the new allocator to obtain some memory for one element.

```
Top := new Element_Type'(New_Element);
```

Figure 5.11 illustrates what this stack would look like after pushing a value of `'E'`. Although everything looks fine so far, there is a major flaw in this implementation. Determine what happens after you push three more elements onto this stack using the same algorithm. Space is allocated for each new element, and the stack is assigned a value that designates the latest element. However, because our access variable can des-

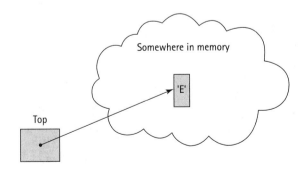

Figure 5.11   *After pushing the first element, `'E'`, onto the stack.*

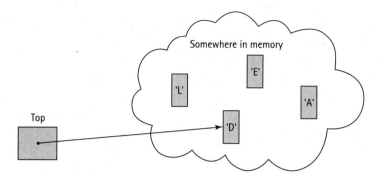

Figure 5.12 *After pushing* `'E'`, `'L'`, `'A'`, *and* `'D'` *onto the stack.*

ignate only a single object, access to the earlier three elements is lost. Figure 5.12 illustrates the situation.

> **Node** A record containing data and an access value that designates another node.

Somehow we must have an access value stored for each element in our stack. One possibility that comes to mind is to declare our stack as an array of access types and to have each element of this array designate an element in the stack, as shown in Figure 5.13. This solution would keep track of the pointers to all the elements in the correct order, but it wouldn't solve our original problem: We still need to declare an array of a particular size. Where else can we put the access values?

We need to be able to allocate memory to store each new stack element *and* allocate memory to store a new access value. We can accomplish this task by allocating a record containing both the new stack element and an access value. Records containing both data and access values are called **nodes**. We use the access value in the node to designate the

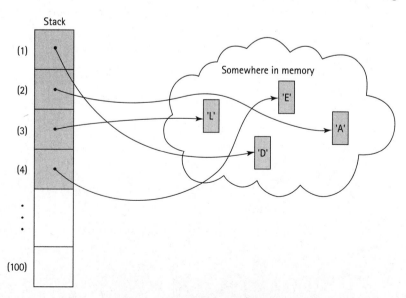

Figure 5.13 *One way to keep track of the access values.*

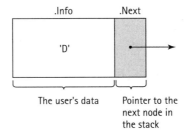

Figure 5.14 *A single node.*

next node in the stack. Figure 5.14 illustrates a single node, a record containing the fields `Info` and `Next`. Figure 5.15 illustrates how nodes can be linked to make a stack containing the values `'A'`, `'L'`, and `'E'`. In this stack, `'A'` is on the top and `'E'` is on the bottom. This chain of nodes is called a **linked list**. The diagonal line in the `Next` field of the last node in the chain represents `null`. There is no node following the last node in the chain.

`Top` is an access variable that designates the top node in the stack. `Top` is an example of an **external pointer**—a pointer from *outside* a linked list that designates a node in that list. Each node in the linked list contains an access value that designates the node "underneath." This access value is an example of an **internal pointer**—a pointer within a node that designates the next node in the linked list.

> **Linked list** A collection of data where each item in the collection includes an access value that designates the next item in the collection.
>
> **External pointer** A pointer outside of a linked list that designates a node in that list.
>
> **Internal pointer** A pointer within a node that designates the next node in the linked list.

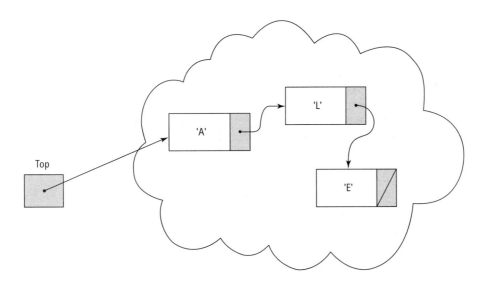

Figure 5.15 *A stack composed of linked nodes.*

The Ada syntax for dereferencing a record object is exactly the same as it is for dereferencing any object: the access variable name, followed by .all. To dereference a particular field of the record, we use normal record syntax (dot notation) after the .all. The following examples illustrate the dereferencing of the nodes in the stack as shown in Figure 5.15.

Expression	Dereferences	Value (from Figure 5.15)
Top.all	Entire record	First (top) node in the stack
Top.all.Info	The Info field	'A'
Top.all.Next	The Next field	Pointer to second node
Top.all.Next.all.Info	The Info field of the second node	'L'

When access types are used to designate records, Ada permits us to leave out the .all when dereferencing a field in a designated record. Using this shorthand syntax, the previous statements can be rewritten as follows:

Expression	Dereferences	Value (from Figure 5.15)
Top.all	Entire record	First (top) node in the stack
Top.Info	The Info field	'A'
Top.Next	The Next field	Pointer to second node
Top.Next.Info	The Info field of the second node	'L'

Because the first statement dereferences the entire record rather than a field, we must include .all. This shorthand syntax makes it appear as though Top was a record variable rather than an access type variable. As with the designated array syntax we described in Chapter 4, some Ada programmers prefer the shorthand form because it allows them to easily change their implementation from access variables to record variables and vice versa. Again, we believe that such decisions should be made during program design rather than during program implementation and that the extra documentation provided by .all is well worth the extra time it takes to type the four characters. Because of the extra documentation provided, most of the examples in this text use the .all form. You (or your professor) can decide which form is best for your programs. The exercises at the end of this chapter give you practice with both forms.

Let's see how to push a new element onto our linked stack. Figure 5.16 shows the result of pushing 'D' onto the stack illustrated in Figure 5.15. Notice what has changed between these two figures.

1. Memory for a new node has been allocated.
2. Values have been assigned to the Info and Next fields of the new node. The Info field contains the new value, 'D'. The Next field designates the node previously designated by Top.
3. Top now designates the new node.

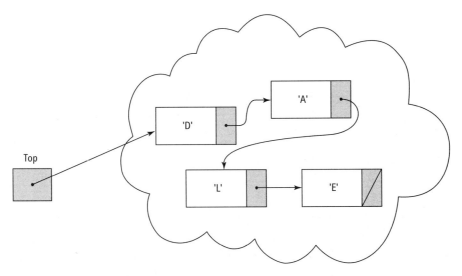

Figure 5.16 *Result of pushing* `'D'` *onto the stack of Figure 5.15.*

All of these changes are carried out by the following Ada statement.

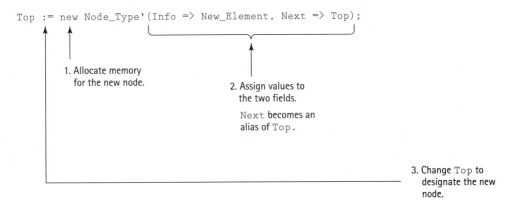

This single statement is all that is required to push a new value onto our linked stack. When working with linked data structures such as this stack, it is important to draw pictures such as we have done in Figures 5.15 and 5.16 before attempting to write the Ada statements to carry out an operation on the structure.

Now let's look at the pop operation. A first attempt at the algorithm for pop is

Pop -- *initial attempt*
    Popped Element := Info in top node
    Unlink the top node from the stack
    Deallocate the memory used by the old top node

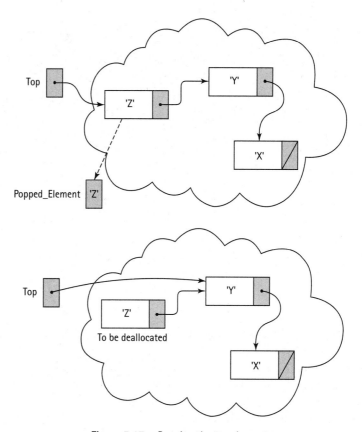

Figure 5.17 *Popping the top element.*

Let's try this algorithm with the stack in Figure 5.17. We first put the value from the top node into `Popped_Element`. How do we "unlink" the top node from the stack? If we reset `Top` to point to the node following the top node, the resulting stack should be correct. Now we can deallocate the memory occupied by the old top node by calling a procedure instantiated from `Unchecked_Deallocation`.

Whoops! The problem with this algorithm is that it leaves the old top node inaccessible—we no longer have an access variable that designates the node. When we code this procedure, let's add a local access variable to designate the old top node before we reset `Top`. Here's the complete algorithm:

Pop
    Popped Element := Info in top node
    Node to Recycle := Top   *-- Alias of top node*
    Top := Next of top element   *-- Stack now designates "2nd" node*
    Deallocate the memory designated by Node to Recycle

Let's trace this algorithm, using the stack in Figure 5.18. `Popped_Element` is set to the value of the `Info` field in the first (top) node (Figure 5.18[a]). We save an access value to the first node, so that we can access it later for recycling (Figure 5.18[b]). Then `Top` is advanced to jump over the first node, making the second node the new top element. How can we get the access value that designates the second node? We get it from the `Next` field of the first node. This access value is assigned to `Top` to complete the unlinking task (Figure 5.18[c]). Finally, we deallocate the memory occupied by the old top node by calling a procedure `Free` that was instantiated from `Unchecked_Deallocation`, using the access value we saved in `Node_To_Recycle` (Figure 5.18[d]).

Does this algorithm work if there is only one node in the stack when `Pop` is called? Let's trace the algorithm using the stack in Figure 5.19. `Popped_Element` is assigned the value in the `Info` field in the top (and only) node in the stack (Figure 15.19[a]). We save an access value to this node (Figure 15.19[b]). Now we unlink this node from the stack. We save an access value to the node, as before, and then assign the value of the `Next` field in the first (and only) node to `Top`. What is the value of this `Next` field? Because this is the last node in the list, its `Next` field contains `null`. This value is assigned to `Top`, which is exactly what we want, because a `null` value for `Top` means that the stack is empty. Finally, we deallocate the memory used by the old top node (Figure 5.19[c]). So the procedure works for a stack of one element.

Our algorithms for push and pop did not consider the possibilities of stack overflow or stack underflow. Because we are using Ada's `new` allocator to obtain memory for a new node, our stack will overflow only when the memory available for dynamic allocation is exhausted. The exception `STORAGE_ERROR` is raised when there is no memory available to allocate to the new node. Underflow occurs when we attempt to pop an item off an empty stack. We can use the empty operation to test for underflow in the `Pop` procedure.

The stack is empty when the stack variable does not designate a node. Figure 5.10 shows an empty stack. Function `Empty` simply needs to check whether `Top` has the value `null`. What about function `Full`? Using dynamically allocated nodes rather than an array, we no longer have an explicit limit on the stack size. We can continue to get more nodes until we run out of memory. In this rare case, the Ada run-time system raises the exception `STORAGE_ERROR`. So we decide to simply return `False` for the `Full` operation.

In the array implementation, the `Clear` procedure simply set `Top` to zero. In the linked implementation, we could set `Top` to `null` to leave the stack empty—but that leaks all the memory occupied by the nodes. It's better to recycle the memory used by all the nodes.

Our `Clear` operation loops through all the elements in the stack, removing them one by one, and disposing of the space.

Clear
    loop
        exit when stack is empty
        Unlink the top node
        Free the node
    end loop

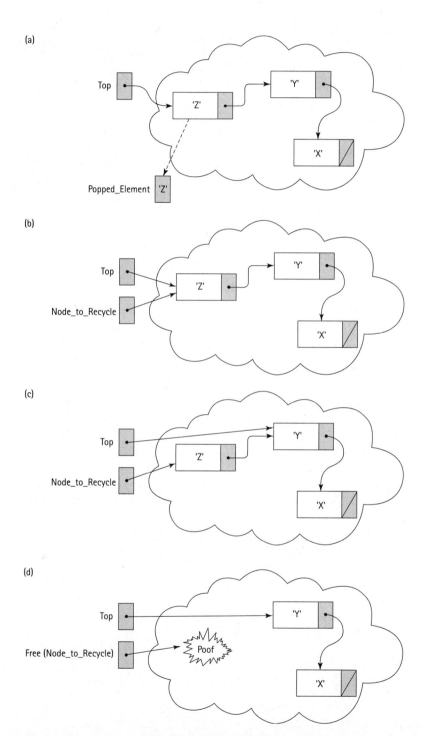

Figure 5.18 *Popping the stack.*

(a)

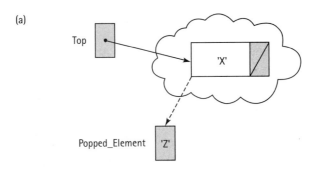

(b)

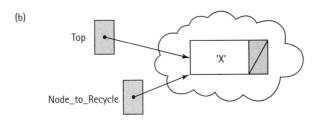

(c)

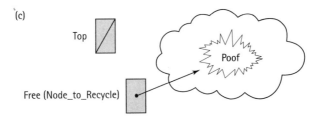

Figure 5.19 *Popping the last element in the stack.*

This process is very much like putting procedure `Pop` inside a loop. In fact, we could just write the loop as

```
loop
   exit when Top = null;
   Pop (Stack, Dummy_Value);
end loop;
```

But for the sake of efficiency (avoiding all the procedure and function calls), not to mention getting some extra practice using access variables, we write the procedure from scratch.

Now that we have the basic algorithms for the operations in our linked stack, we can look in more detail at the types. We require two declarations: one for the node and another for an access type that designates a node in our list. Here is how we might declare these types in the private part of our stack package declaration:

```
type Node_Ptr is access Node_Type;     -- This declaration does not compile

type Node_Type is
   record
      Info : Element_Type;
      Next : Node_Ptr;
   end record;
```

A problem here is that the declaration of `Node_Ptr` uses type `Node_Type` before `Node_Type` has been declared. Well, let's just swap the order of these two declarations.

```
type Node_Type is
   record
      Info : Element_Type;
      Next : Node_Ptr;                  -- This declaration does not compile
   end record;

type Node_Ptr is access Node_Type;
```

> **Incomplete type declaration** A type declaration that gives only the name of the type.

There is still a problem. The access type `Node_Ptr` is used in the declaration of type `Node_Type` before `Node_Ptr` has been declared. With what we know, this problem seems impossible to fix. Ada provides a solution to this "chicken and egg" problem—the incomplete type declaration. An **incomplete type declaration** contains only the name of the type being declared. It may include an optional discriminant. Eventually, every incomplete type declaration must be followed by a full type declaration.

Here are the declarations using an incomplete type declaration for our node:

```ada
type Node_Type;                             -- Incomplete type declaration
type Node_Ptr is access Node_Type;          -- Refers to the incomplete type

type Node_Type is                           -- Full type declaration
   record
      Info : Element_Type;
      Next : Node_Ptr;
   end record;
```

When we developed our algorithms for the linked stack implementation we showed the stack object as a pointer that was `null` for an empty stack and designated the top node in a nonempty stack. Any time we use access types to implement a class, there is a possibility of memory leaks within the application using that class. In Chapter 4 we introduced controlled types to eliminate such memory leaks for the unbounded-length string class we developed. We can derive our linked stack type from a controlled type to prevent memory leaks in applications that use this class. You can see the details of this type in Specification 5.2.

Specification 5.2   Unbounded Stack

```ada
with Ada.Finalization;
generic
   type Element_Type is private;   -- The stack element type
package Unbounded_Stack is

-- This package implements a stack, a data structure in which
-- elements are added and removed from only one end.
-- A "last in, first out" (LIFO) structure.

   type Stack_Type is new Ada.Finalization.Limited_Controlled with private;

   UNDERFLOW : exception;
   OVERFLOW  : exception;
```

```
-------------------------------------------------------------------
procedure Clear (Stack : in out Stack_Type);
-- Purpose        : Remove all elements from the stack
-- Preconditions  : None
-- Postconditions : Stack is empty; it contains no elements

-------------------------------------------------------------------
function Empty (Stack : in Stack_Type) return Boolean;
-- Purpose        : Tests whether a stack is empty (contains no elements)
-- Preconditions  : None
-- Postconditions : Empty = (stack is empty)

-------------------------------------------------------------------
function Full (Stack : in Stack_Type) return Boolean;
-- Purpose        : Tests whether a stack is full. A stack is full when
--                  no more elements can be pushed on it
-- Preconditions  : None
-- Postconditions : Full = (no more elements can be pushed onto Stack)

-------------------------------------------------------------------
procedure Push (Stack       : in out Stack_Type;
                New_Element : in     Element_Type);
-- Purpose        : Adds New_Element to the top of Stack
-- Preconditions  : None
-- Postconditions : Stack = original Stack with New_Element added on top
-- Exceptions     : OVERFLOW  Raised on attempt to Push a new element onto
--                            a full stack.  Stack is unchanged.
-------------------------------------------------------------------
procedure Pop (Stack         : in out Stack_Type;
               Popped_Element :    out Element_Type);
-- Purpose        : Removes the top element from Stack and returns it
-- Preconditions  : None
-- Postconditions : Stack = original Stack with top element removed
--                  Popped_Element = top element of original Stack
-- Exceptions     : UNDERFLOW  Raised on attempt to Pop an element from an
--                             empty stack. Stack remains empty.

private

   type Node_Type;                            -- Incomplete type declaration
   type Node_Ptr is access Node_Type;         -- Refers to the incomplete type
   type Node_Type is                          -- Full type declaration
      record
         Info : Element_Type;
         Next : Node_Ptr;
      end record;
```

```
type Stack_Type is new Ada.Finalization.Limited_Controlled with
   record
      Top : Node_Ptr;    -- Designates first node in the linked list
   end record;

overriding procedure Finalize (Object : in out Stack_Type) renames Clear;

end Unbounded_Stack;
```

The declaration of Stack_Type in the public part of this specification does not have a discriminant to specify an upper bound on the number of elements that the stack object can contain. We have no need to set such an upper bound in our linked version (that's its advantage!).

Let's look at the details of Stack_Type given in the private part of this package. This type extends the type Ada.Finalization.Limited_Controlled with the single field Top. Limited controlled types come with two procedures: Initialize and Finalize. Limited types have no assignment, so there is no need for the Adjust procedure we used in our implementation of unbounded-length strings. Figure 5.20 shows the naming details of a controlled stack object.

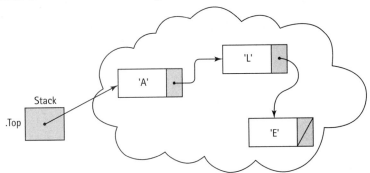

Figure 5.20   *A stack of linked nodes (controlled implementation).*

When a stack object comes into existence, it should be initialized to be empty. As we discussed earlier, an empty stack is one in which Top is null. Because all access values are automatically initialized to null, we do not need to override the Initialize procedure of our stack class's parent with additional object initialization code. Finalization of stack objects is a different matter. When a linked stack object goes out of scope in an application, the memory for the linked list of nodes that it designates must be recycled to prevent memory leaks. We already have a stack operation to accomplish this task—the Clear procedure. The private part of Specification 5.2 shows a new Ada feature—renaming. We declared that the procedure Finalize used to override its superclass's operation is just a new name for our Clear procedure. The parameter profiles of each of these procedures must be identical. We cannot, for example, say that Finalize renames Push. These two procedures have different parameter profiles.

Body 5.2 contains the complete implementation of this unbounded stack class. The operations discussed earlier have been modified slightly for the addition of the inheritance from the controlled class.

Body 5.2   Unbounded Stack: Implements Specification 5.2

```ada
with Ada.Unchecked_Deallocation;
package body Unbounded_Stack is
   -- Instantiate a procedure to recycle nodes
   procedure Free is new Ada.Unchecked_Deallocation (Object => Node_Type,
                                                     Name   => Node_Ptr);
   ----------------------------------------------------------------------
   procedure Clear (Stack : in out Stack_Type) is
      To_Recycle : Node_Ptr;        -- Designates a node for recycling
   begin
      loop
         exit when Stack.Top = null;          -- Exit when stack is empty
         To_Recycle := Stack.Top;             -- Unlink the
         Stack.Top  := Stack.Top.all.Next;    --    top node
         Free (To_Recycle);                   -- Recycle the node
      end loop;
   end Clear;

   ----------------------------------------------------------------------
   function Empty (Stack : in Stack_Type) return Boolean is
   begin
      return Stack.Top = null;
   end Empty;

   ----------------------------------------------------------------------
   function Full (Stack : in Stack_Type) return Boolean is
   begin
      return False;
   end Full;

   ----------------------------------------------------------------------
   procedure Push (Stack       : in out Stack_Type;
                   New_Element : in     Element_Type) is
   begin
      Stack.Top := new Node_Type'(Info => New_Element,
                                  Next => Stack.Top);
   exception
      when STORAGE_ERROR =>         -- Stack is full if no memory is available
         raise OVERFLOW;
   end Push;

   ----------------------------------------------------------------------
   procedure Pop (Stack          : in out Stack_Type;
                  Popped_Element :    out Element_Type) is
```

```
         To_Recycle : Node_Ptr;         -- Designates a node for recycling
   begin
      if not Empty (Stack) then
         Popped_Element := Stack.Top.all.Info;   -- Return the top information
         To_Recycle     := Stack.Top;            -- Unlink the top
         Stack.Top      := Stack.Top.all.Next;   -- node of the stack
         Free (To_Recycle);                      -- Recycle the node
      else
         raise UNDERFLOW;
      end if;
   end Pop;
end Unbounded_Stack;
```

Extending the Stack Class

Both our bounded and unbounded stack classes were implemented as tagged types. There are two advantages to using tagged types to implement a class: We can use the *object.method* syntax to invoke operations, and we can create subclasses to extend our original classes. Extending a class defined within a generic package requires a little more work than for classes defined within nongeneric packages. We'll illustrate the extra steps with an example. We would like to extend our stack class to include a new operation, Top. Top returns a copy of the top element in the stack without removing that element. Specification 5.3 defines a subclass of our bounded stack class with this additional operation.

Specification 5.3   A Bounded Stack with an Additional Operation

---

```
generic
package Stack.Extended is

   type Extended_Stack_Type is new Stack_Type with null record;

   function Top (Stack : in Extended_Stack_Type) return Element_Type;
   -- Purpose         : Return a copy of the top item on Stack
   -- Preconditions   : None
   -- Postconditions  : Value returned is a copy of the top item on Stack
   -- Exceptions      : UNDERFLOW Raised if the stack is empty
   --                             Stack remains empty.

end Stack.Extended;
```

The package Stack.Extended with our extended stack subclass is a child of the package Stack containing the superclass. Because package Stack is a generic package, its children must also be generic packages. Our extended stack does not require any parameters other than the one (Element_Type) that is available through its parent, so

Specification 5.3 has no generic formal parameters. The declaration of type `Extended_Stack_Type` introduces some new Ada syntax. This extension of our stack does not require any additional class attributes. All we need are the `Max_Size`, `Top`, and `Elements` fields in the record defined for the parent `Stack_Type`. We use the clause `with null record` to indicate that our subclass does not add any fields to the parent's record. Because there is nothing to add to the record, our specification does not need a private section. Body 5.3 gives the implementation of this new subclass.

Body 5.3   Extended Stack: Implements Specification 5.3

```ada
package body Stack.Extended is

   function Top (Stack : in Extended_Stack_Type) return Element_Type is
   begin
      if Stack.Top > 0 then
         return (Stack.Elements(Stack.Top));
      else
         raise UNDERFLOW;
      end if;
   end Top;

end Stack.Extended;
```

Program 5.2 is a simple application that uses our extended stack class. To use our generic child package requires two package instantiations. We first instantiate our superclass. In our demonstration code we have created the package `My_Stack`, which is a bounded stack of integers. We create our extended stack of integers by instantiating the child package `My_Extended_Stack` from the child generic package `My_Stack.Extended`.

The stack object, `Short_Stack`, is an extended stack with an upper bound of eight elements. Our demonstration program uses the `Push` operation inherited from the superclass to add eight values to our stack of integers. The second loop uses the inherited `Empty` and `Pop` operations and the `Top` operation defined in our extended class.

Program 5.2 Demonstration of the Extended Stack Class

```ada
with Stack.Extended;
with Ada.Text_IO;  use Ada.Text_IO;
procedure Stack_Extended_Test is

   package My_Stack          is new Stack (Element_Type => Integer);
   package My_Extended_Stack is new My_Stack.Extended;

   Short_Stack : My_Extended_Stack.Extended_Stack_Type (Max_Size => 8);

   X : Integer;
```

```
begin
    for Count in 1..Short_Stack.Max_Size loop
        Short_Stack.Push(Count);
    end loop;
    loop
        exit when Short_Stack.Empty;
        X := Short_Stack.Top;
        Put_Line (Integer'Image(X));
        Short_Stack.Pop(X);
    end loop;
end Stack_Extended_Test;
```

Encapsulation Revisited

We use private types to encapsulate a class. A private type prevents application programmers from accessing the details of the data structure used to implement the class. They can use only the operations given in the package, equality testing (= and /=), and assignment (:=). A limited private type restricts application programmers even further by limiting operations to those defined in the package; they may not use assignment or equality operators with limited private type objects.

Why is encapsulation desirable? Why not let the application programmers have full access to the details of the data structure used to implement our class? There are two major benefits of encapsulation. First, a great deal of work can be saved later if we decide to change the implementation of our class. Suppose instead of declaring our array-based stack as a private type, we declare it in the public part of our specification. The application programmers are now free to access and modify the record fields and array components. By directly referencing the data structure's details, the application programmers have bound their program to this particular implementation. If at a later time we decide to change our stack to a linked implementation, the application programmers have to change every array references in their program to pointer references. Such changes might even require major modifications of their design which, as we discussed in Chapter 1, can be an expensive undertaking.

A second advantage of encapsulation is reliability. Because the state of an object is modified only through operations defined in the package, we have confidence that our objects are always valid. For example, the state of an array-based stack object is determined by the record field Top. With our encapsulation, only the Push, Pop, and Clear operations can modify this field. We need only apply the lengthy verification and testing methods discussed in Chapter 1 to these three operations to ensure every stack object's validity. The amount of effort required to verify every direct access of a stack object by an application that has full access to the data structure makes it less likely that every access is verified.

Private or Limited Private? In Specifications 5.1 and 5.2 we declared Stack_Type as a limited private type. This declaration prevents the programmers using our stack class from comparing two stacks with the equality operators (= and /=) and from using the assignment statement to make copies of stack objects. These operations are rarely used with stacks, so we chose not to include them in our specifications. Several exercises at the end of this chapter ask you to implement these operations.

5.4 Comparing Implementations

As we have shown in this chapter, there is more than one way to solve most problems. If you were asked for directions to Joe's Diner (see Figure 5.21), you could give either of two equally correct answers:

1. "Go east on the big highway to the Y'all Come Inn, and turn left."
2. "Take the winding country road to Honeysuckle Lodge, and turn right."

The two answers are not the same, but because following either route gets the traveler to Joe's Diner, both answers are functionally correct.

If the request for directions contained special requirements, one solution might be preferable to the other. For instance, "I'm late for dinner. What's the quickest route to Joe's Diner?" calls for the first answer, whereas "Is there a scenic road that I can take to get to Joe's Diner?" suggests the second. If no special requirements are known, the choice is a matter of personal preference—which road do you like better?

In this chapter, we have presented two functionally equivalent stack classes. How we choose between two classes that do the same task often depends on the requirements of a particular application. If no relevant requirements exist, the choice may be based on the programmer's own style. The comparison of implementations often comes down to comparisons of efficiency of space (memory needs) and time. Because programmer

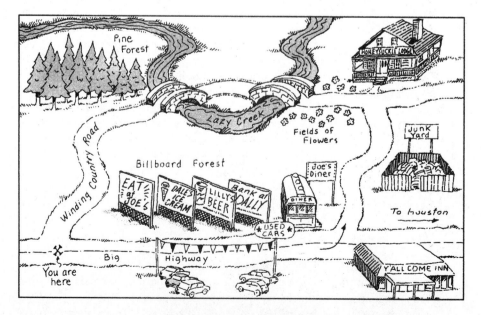

Figure 5.21   *Map to Joe's Diner.*

time is often more valuable than computer time, the complexity of an algorithm from a human's point of view is another factor to consider when making comparisons.

Space

Our first stack class (Specification and Body 5.1) was bounded in size whereas the second (Specification and Body 5.2) was not. If your need is for a stack that can use all available memory, then the choice seems obvious. But does this implementation use its space efficiently? Let's calculate the memory used for the stacks of characters that we used to illustrate each implementation (see Figures 5.6 and 5.20).

The array-based stack is stored in a record with three fields: `Max_Size`, `Top`, and `Elements`. The first two fields are integers and the last is an array of characters. We can use the following formula to calculate the minimum amount of storage required for this record:

Array-Based Stack Storage = 2 × (storage needed for one integer)

+ Max_Size × (storage needed for one character)

If an integer uses 4 bytes of memory and a character uses 1 byte of memory, a total of 108 bytes is required for the stacks illustrated in Figures 5.6 and 5.7. The array implementation uses the same amount of storage whether the stack is empty or full. This is the minimum storage needed for our stack. Unless we choose to restrict it, the Ada compiler is free to add padding to a record so that its fields can be accessed more quickly.

The amount of memory used by the linked stack implementation depends on the current size of the stack. It includes the storage needed for the external pointer (`Stack.Top` in Figure 5.20) and for all of the nodes in the linked list. Each node is a record with the two fields `Info` and `Next`.

Linked Stack Storage = storage needed for one pointer

+ current stack size × (storage needed for one node)

Node Storage = storage needed for one character + storage needed for one pointer

If a character uses 1 byte of memory and a pointer uses 4 bytes of memory, an empty linked stack requires only 4 bytes of storage. A linked stack of 100 elements requires 504 bytes. The pointers in the linked version of this particular example take more memory than our data. Figure 5.22 compares the memory requirements for these two stack implementations. You can see that the linked version exceeds the memory requirements of the array version once the size goes beyond 20.

Complexity

Complexity is the degree to which a system or component has a design or implementation that is difficult to understand and verify.[2] Researchers have devised many measures of complexity for analyzing programs. Halstead's complexity measures are based on the number of operands and operators in an algorithm. Cyclomatic (McCabe's) complexity is based on the number of possible paths through an algorithm.

---

[2] Institute of Electrical and Electronics Engineers, *IEEE Standard Computer Dictionary: A Compilation of IEEE Standard Computer Glossaries* (New York, NY: IEEE, 1990).

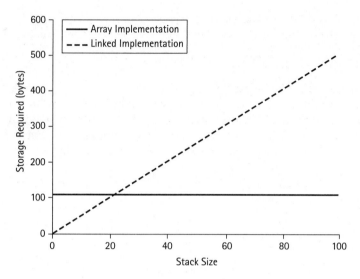

Figure 5.22 *Comparison of space requirements for two stack implementations.*

Simply counting the number of lines is a simple approach that may give some insight to compare the complexity of different implementations of a class. We are assuming that the longer a program is, the more difficult it is to understand. This is not always a valid assumption. A programmer may use some clever trick to reduce many lines of code into a few. Often the trick is more difficult for someone to understand than the longer code it replaces. Here are some line counts from our two stack implementations:

Comparison of Lines of Code

	Array Implementation	Linked Implementation
Declarations (Private Part)	6	10
Clear	4	10
Empty	4	4
Full	4	4
Push	10	9
Pop	10	13
Total	38	50

As you can see from the table, the array implementation code is shorter than the linked code by about 25%. Does this difference reflect your opinion of the relative complexities?

Time

Often the choice between algorithms comes down to a question of time efficiency: Which one takes the least amount of computing time? Which one does the job with the least amount of work? Time efficiency refers to the amount of work that the computer does. Complexity compares algorithms in regard to how much work the programmer does. (One is often minimized at the expense of the other.)

To compare the work done by competing algorithms, we must first define a set of objective measures that can be applied to each algorithm. The analysis of algorithms is an important area of theoretical computer science; in advanced courses students undoubtedly see extensive work in this area. In this text you learn about a small part of this topic, enough to let you determine which of two algorithms requires less work to accomplish a particular task.

How do programmers measure the work that two algorithms perform? The first solution that comes to mind is simply to run the code and then compare the execution times. We have done just that with our different stack operations. We pushed and then popped 100,000 fixed-length strings containing 64 characters onto our stacks and recorded the time it took. We also timed how long it took to clear a stack containing 100,000 of these strings. As we mentioned in our discussion of strings, the unbounded operations are generally less efficient than their bounded equivalents. This statement is certainly supported by our stack timing experiments.

Time for Stack Operations (Milliseconds)

	Array Implementation	Linked Implementation
Push	5.19	54.01
Pop	4.56	44.06
Clear	0.00[3]	43.52

The one with the shorter execution time is clearly the better implementation. Or is it? Using this technique, we really can determine only that implementation A is more efficient than implementation B on a particular computer at a particular time. Execution times are specific to a *particular computer*, because different computers run at different speeds. Sometimes they are dependent on what else the computer is doing in the background. Of course, we could test the operations on many possible computers at various times, but that would be unrealistic and too specific (new computers are becoming available all the time). We want a more general measure.

A second possibility is to count the number of instructions or statements executed. This measure, however, varies with the programming language used, as well as with the style of the individual programmer. To standardize this measure somewhat, we could count the number of passes through a critical loop in the algorithm. If each iteration involves a constant amount of work, this measure gives us a meaningful yardstick of efficiency.

---

[3] Too small to measure

Another idea is to isolate a particular operation fundamental to the algorithm and count the number of times that this operation is performed. Suppose, for example, that we are summing the elements in an integer list. To measure the amount of work required, we could count the integer addition operations. For a list of 100 elements, there are 99 addition operations. Note, however, that we do not actually have to count the number of addition operations; it is some function of the number of elements (N) on the list. Therefore, we can express the number of addition operations in terms of N: For a list of N elements, there are $N - 1$ addition operations. Now we can compare the algorithms for the general case, not just for a specific list size.

Sometimes an operation so dominates an algorithm that the other operations fade into the background "noise." If we want to buy elephants and goldfish, for example, and we are considering two pet suppliers, we only need to compare the prices of elephants; the cost of the goldfish is trivial in comparison. Suppose we have two files of integers, and we want to create a new file of integers based on the sums of pairs of integers from the existing files. In analyzing an algorithm that solves this problem, we could count both file accesses and integer additions. However, file accessing is so much more expensive than integer addition in terms of computer time that the integer additions could be a trivial factor in the efficiency of the whole algorithm; we might as well count only the file accesses, ignoring the integer additions. In analyzing algorithms, we often can find one operation that dominates the algorithm, effectively relegating the others to the "noise" level.

Big-O

We have been talking about work as a function of the size of the input to the operation (for instance, the number of elements on the list to be summed). We can express an approximation of this function using a mathematical notation called order of magnitude, or **Big-O notation**. (This is a letter O, not a zero.) The order of magnitude of a function is identified with the term in the function that increases fastest relative to the size of the problem. For instance, if

Big-O notation A notation that expresses computing time as a term in a function that increases most rapidly relative to the size of a problem.

$$f(N) = 25N^4 + 100N^2 + 10N + 50$$

then $f(N)$ is of order N^4 or, in Big-O notation, $O(N^4)$. That is, for large values of N, some multiple of N^4 dominates the function for sufficiently large values of N.

How is it that we can just drop the low-order terms? Remember the elephants and goldfish that we talked about earlier? The price of the elephants was so much greater that we could just ignore the price of the goldfish. Similarly, for large values of N, N^4 is so much larger than 50, $10N$, or even $100N^2$ that we can ignore these other terms. This doesn't mean that the other terms do not contribute to the computing time; it only means that they are not significant in our approximation when N is "large." Our Big-O notation also ignores the 25 in front of N^4. In terms of our pet example, it does not matter how many elephants we need to buy; the cost of an elephant is the deciding factor in our choice of pet store.

What is this value N? N represents the size of the problem. Most of the problems in this book involve data structures—lists, stacks, queues, and trees. Each structure is composed of elements. We develop algorithms to add an element to the structure and to modify or delete an element from the structure. We can describe the work done by these operations in terms of N, where N is the number of elements in the structure. Yes, we know. We have called the number of characters in a string the length of the string. However, mathematicians talk in terms of N, so we use N for the length when we are comparing algorithms using Big-O notation.

Suppose that we want to write all the elements in a list into a file. How much work is that? The answer depends on how many elements are on the list. Our algorithm is

Write to File
    Create the file
    loop
        Exit when we have processed all the elements in the list
        Put the next element into the file
    end loop

This algorithm is $O(N)$ because the time required to perform the task is proportional to the number of elements (N) plus a little to create the file. How can we ignore the creation time in determining the Big-O approximation? If we assume that the time necessary to create a file is constant, this part of the algorithm is our goldfish. If the list has only a few elements, the time needed to create the file may be significant, but for large values of N, writing the elements is an elephant in comparison with creating the file.

The order of magnitude of an algorithm does not tell you how long in milliseconds the solution takes to run on your computer. Sometimes we need that kind of information. For instance, the requirements for software that controls the fuel flowing into an automobile engine may specify that the fuel flow rate be calculated 20 times a second. To meet this requirement, the calculations solving the differential equations that model the engine must be completed in less than 50 milliseconds. For information like this, we do not use Big-O analysis; we use other measurements. We can compare different implementations of a data structure by coding them and then running a test, recording the time on the computer's clock before and after. This kind of "benchmark" test tells us how long the operations take on a particular computer, using a particular compiler. The Big-O analysis, however, allows us to compare algorithms without reference to these factors.

Common Orders of Magnitude $O(1)$ is called *bounded time*. The amount of work is bounded by a constant and is not dependent on the size of the problem. Assigning a value to the *i*th element in an array of N elements is O(l) because an element in an array can be accessed directly through its index. Although bounded time is often called constant time, the amount of work is not necessarily constant. It is, however, bounded by a constant.

$O(\log_2 N)$ is called *logarithmic time*. The amount of work depends on the log of the size of the problem. Algorithms that successively cut the amount of data to be processed in half at each step typically fall into this category. Finding a value in a list of sorted elements using the binary search algorithm is $O(\log_2 N)$.

$O(N)$ is called *linear time*. The amount of work is some constant times the size of the problem. Printing all the elements in a list of N elements is $O(N)$. Searching for a particular value in a list of unsorted elements is also $O(N)$ because you must potentially search every element on the list to find it.

$O(N \log_2 N)$ is called (for lack of a better term) $N \log_2 N$. Algorithms of this type typically involve applying an $O(N)$ algorithm $\log_2 N$ times. The better sorting algorithms (such as Quicksort, Heapsort, and Mergesort, which are discussed in Chapter 12) have $N \log_2 N$ complexity. That is, these algorithms can transform an unsorted list into a sorted list in $O(N \log_2 N)$ time.

$O(N^2)$ is called *quadratic time*. Algorithms of this type typically involve applying a linear algorithm N times. Most simple sorting algorithms such as Insertion sort and Selection sort are $O(N^2)$ algorithms. (See Chapter 12.) Cubic time, $O(N^3)$, quartic time, $O(N^4)$, and higher polynomial times are rarer than quadratic times.

$O(2^N)$ is called exponential time. These algorithms are extremely costly. An example of a problem for which the best known solution is exponential is the traveling salesman problem—given a set of cities and a set of roads that connect some of them, plus the lengths of the roads, find a route that visits every city exactly once and minimizes total travel distance. As you can see in the following table, exponential times increase dramatically in relation to the size of N.

Comparison of Rates of Growth

N	$\log_2 N$	$N \log_2 N$	N^2	N^3	2^N
1	0	1	1	1	2
2	1	2	4	8	4
4	2	8	16	64	16
8	3	24	64	512	256
16	4	64	256	4,096	65,536
32	5	160	1,024	32,768	4,294,697,296
64	6	384	4,096	262,114	18,446,744,073,709,551,616
128	7	896	16,384	2,097,152	340,282,366,920,938,463,463,374,607,431,768,211,456
256	8	2,048	65,536	16,777,216	115,792,089,237,316,195,423,570,985,008,687,907,853,269,984,665,640,564,039,457,584,007,913,129,639,936

It is interesting to note that the values in the last column grow so quickly that the computation time required for problems of this order may exceed the estimated life span of the universe!

Note that throughout this discussion we have been talking about the amount of work the computer must do to execute an algorithm. This determination does not necessarily relate to the size of the algorithm, say, in lines of code. Consider the following three program fragments, all of which initialize to zero every element in an N-element array:

Algorithm Init1
    Item(1) := 0;
    Item(2) := 0;
    Item(3) := 0;
    Item(4) := 0;
    Item(5) := 0;
    .
    .
    .
    Item(N) := 0;

Algorithm Init2
    for Index in 1..N loop
        Item (Index) := 0;
    end loop;

Algorithm Init3
    Item := (1..N => 0);

All three algorithms are $O(N)$, even though they greatly differ in the number of lines of code.

Now let's look at two different algorithms that calculate the sum of the integers from 1 to N. Algorithm Sum1 is a simple `for` loop that adds successive integers to keep a running total:

Algorithm Sum1
    Sum := 0;
    for Count in 1..N loop
        Sum := Sum + Count;
    end loop;

That seems simple enough. The second algorithm calculates the sum by using a formula. To understand the formula, consider the following calculation when $N = 9$:

$$\begin{array}{c} 1 + 2 + 3 + 4 + 5 + 6 + 7 + 8 + 9 \\ + 9 + 8 + 7 + 6 + 5 + 4 + 3 + 2 + 1 \\ \hline 10 + 10 + 10 + 10 + 10 + 10 + 10 + 10 + 10 = 10 * 9 = 90 \end{array}$$

We pair up each number from 1 to N with another, such that each pair adds up to $N + 1$. There are N such pairs, giving us a total of $(N + 1) \times N$. Now, because each number is included twice, we divide the product by 2. Using this formula, we can solve the problem: $((9 + 1) \times 9) / 2 = 45$. Now we have a second algorithm:

Algorithm Sum2
    Sum := ((N + 1) * N) / 2;

Both of the algorithms are short pieces of code. Let's compare them using Big-O notation. The work done by Sum1 is a function of the magnitude of N; as N gets larger, the amount of work grows proportionally. If N is 50, Sum1 works 10 times as hard as when N is 5. Algorithm Sum1, therefore, is $O(N)$.

To analyze Sum2, consider the cases when $N = 5$ and $N = 50$. They should take the same amount of time. In fact, whatever value we assign to N, the algorithm does the same amount of work to solve the problem. Algorithm Sum2, therefore, is $O(1)$.

Does this mean that Sum2 is always faster? Is it always a better choice than Sum1? That depends. Sum2 might seem to do more "work," because the formula involves multiplication and division, whereas Sum1 is a simple running total. In fact, for very small values of N, Sum2 actually might do more work than Sum1. (Of course, for very large values of N, Sum1 does a proportionally larger amount of work, whereas Sum2 stays the same.) So the choice between the algorithms depends in part on how they are used, for small or large values of N.

Another issue is the fact that Sum2 is not as obvious as Sum1, and thus it is harder for the programmer (a human) to understand. Sometimes a more efficient solution to a problem is more complicated; we may save computer time at the expense of the programmer's time.

So, what's the verdict? As usual in the design of computer programs, there are tradeoffs. We must look at our program's requirements and then decide which solution is better. Throughout this text we examine different choices of algorithms and data structures. We compare them using Big-O, but we also examine the program's requirements and the "elegance" of the competing solutions. As programmers, we design software solutions with many factors in mind.

Family Laundry: An Analogy

How long does it take to do a family's weekly laundry? We might describe the answer to this question with the function

$$f(N) = c \times N$$

where N represents the number of family members and c is the average number of minutes that each person's laundry takes. We say that this function is $O(N)$ because the total laundry time depends on the number of people in the family. The "constant" c may vary a little for different families—depending on the size of their washing machine and how fast they can fold clothes, for instance. That is, the time to do the laundry for two different families might be represented with these functions:

$$f(N) = 100 \times N$$
$$g(N) = 90 \times N$$

But overall, we describe these functions as O(*N*).

Now what happens if Grandma and Grandpa come to visit the first family for a week or two? The laundry time function becomes

$$f(N) = 100 \times (N + 2)$$

We still say that the function is O(*N*). How can that be? Doesn't the laundry for two extra people take any time to wash, dry, and fold? Of course it does! If *N* is small (the family consists of Mother, Father, and Baby), the extra laundry for two people is significant. But as *N* grows large (the family consists of Mother, Father, 8 kids, and a dog named Waldo), the extra laundry for two people doesn't make much difference. (The family's laundry is the elephant; the guest's laundry is the goldfish.) When we compare algorithms using Big-O, we are concerned with what happens when *N* is "large."

If we are asking the question "Can we finish the laundry in time to make the 7:05 train?" we want a precise answer. The Big-O analysis doesn't give us this information. It gives us an approximation. So, if $100 \times N$, $90 \times N$, and $100 \times (N + 2)$ are all O(*N*), how can we say which is better? We can't—in Big-O terms, they are all roughly equivalent for large values of *N*. Can we find a better algorithm for getting the laundry done? If the family wins the state lottery, they can drop all their dirty clothes at a professional laundry 15 minutes' drive from their house (30 minutes round trip). Now the function is

$$f(N) = 30$$

This function is O(1). The answer is not dependent on the number of people in the family. If they switch to a laundry 5 minutes from their house, the function becomes

$$f(N) = 10$$

This function is also O(1). In terms of Big-O, the two professional-laundry solutions are equivalent: No matter how many family members or houseguests you have, it takes a constant amount of the family's time to do the laundry. (We aren't concerned with the professional laundry's time.)

Stack Operations We can compare the relative "efficiency" of the two stack implementations in terms of Big-O notation. In both implementations, the `Full` and `Empty` operations are clearly O(1). They always take a constant amount of work. What about `Push` and `Pop`? Does the number of elements in the stack affect the amount of work done by these operations? No, it does not. In both implementations, we directly access the top of the stack, so these operations also take a constant amount of work. They too are O(1). Only the `Clear` operation differs from one implementation to the other. The array implementation simply sets the Top field to 0, so it is clearly an O(1) operation. The linked implementation must process every node in the stack in order to recycle the node space. This operation, therefore, is O(N), where N is the number of nodes in the stack. Overall, the two stack implementations are roughly equivalent in terms of the amount of work they do, only differing in one of the five operations. Note that if the difference had been in the Push or Pop operation, rather than the less frequently called Clear, it would be more significant. Recall also that we made the controlled Finalize operation a synonym of Clear. The next table summarizes the Big-O comparison of the stack operations.

Big-O Comparison of Stack Operations

	Array Implementation	Linked Implementation
Clear	O(1)	O(N)
Empty	O(1)	O(1)
Full	O(1)	O(1)
Push	O(1)	O(1)
Pop	O(1)	O(1)

So which implementation is better? The answer, as usual, is: It depends on the situation. The linked implementation certainly gives more flexibility, and in applications where the number of stack elements can vary greatly, it wastes less space when the stack is small. In situations where the stack size is totally unpredictable, the linked implementation is preferable, because size is largely irrelevant. Why, then, would we ever want to use the array implementation? Because it is short, simple, and efficient. When Max_Size is small, and we can be sure that we will not need to exceed the declared stack size, the array implementation is a good choice. Also, if you are programming in a language that does not support dynamic storage allocation, an array implementation may be the only good choice.

Summary

We have defined a stack at the logical level as an abstract data type, and we have discussed two implementations of a stack class. In the first implementation, an array is used to store the stack elements. In the second implementation, the stack elements are stored in dynamically allocated memory and linked using access values. By isolating the procedures and functions that operate on the actual representation of the stack in a package and declaring the stack type as a private type, we encapsulate the data structure. No matter which implementation we select, we keep the use of the data structure limited to the interfaces recorded in the stack specification.

The independence of implementation from interface resulting from our encapsulation simplifies program maintenance. We don't have to make changes throughout the program whenever we change the stack body.

Although our logical picture of a stack is a linear collection of data elements with the newest element (the top) at one end and the oldest element at the other end, the physical representation of the stack class does not have to re-create our mental image. The implementation of the stack class must support the last in, first out (LIFO) property; how this property is supported, however, is another matter. For instance, the push operation could "time stamp" the stack elements, and put them into an array in any order. To pop, we would have to search the array, looking for the newest time stamp. This representation is very different from either of the stack implementations we developed in this chapter, but to the user of the stack class they are all functionally equivalent. The implementation is transparent to the program that uses the stack because the stack is encapsulated by the operations in the package that surround it.

Exercises

Logical Level

1. How are the items in a stack ordered?
2. Describe the operations of a stack at the abstract level.
3. Show what is written by the following segments of code, given that Stack is a stack of integer elements and X, Y, and Z are integer variables.

    a.
    ```
    Stack.Clear;
    X := 1;
    Y := 0;
    X := 4;
    Stack.Push(Y);
    Stack.Push(X);
    Stack.Push(X + Z);
    Stack.Pop(Y);
    Stack.Push(Z**2);
    Stack.Push(Y);
    Stack.Push(3);
    Stack.Pop(X);
    Put(X);
    Put(Y);
    Put(Z);
    New_Line;
    loop
       exit when Stack.Empty;
       Stack.Pop(X);
       Put(X);
       New_Line;
    end loop;
    ```

b.
```
Stack.Clear;
X := 4;
Z := 0;
Y := X + 1;
Stack.Push(Y);
Stack.Push(Y + 1);
Stack.Push(X);
Stack.Pop(Y):
X := Y + 1;
Stack.Push(X);
Stack.Push(Z);
loop
   exit when Stack.Empty;
   Stack.Pop(Z);
   Put(Z);
   New_Line;
end loop;
Put(X);
Put(Y);
Put(Z);
```

4. Given the following declarations:

```
subtype Name_String is String (1..20);

type Name_Rec is
  record
     First : Name_String;
     Last  : Name_String;
  end record;
```

a. Instantiate a bounded stack package whose elements are `Name_Rec`s.

b. Using the package you just instantiated, declare a stack object that holds a maximum of 250 names.

c. Instantiate an unbounded stack package whose elements are `Name_Rec`s.

5. *Multiple choice.* The statements
```
Stack.Push(X + 1);
Stack.Pop(X + 1);
```
in an application program

a. would cause a syntax error at compile time.

b. would cause a run-time error.

c. would be legal, but would violate the encapsulation of the stack.

d. would be perfectly legal and appropriate.

Application Level

6. Write a segment of code to perform each of the following operations. You may call any of the operations specified for the Stack class. You may declare additional stack objects as needed.

    a. Set the variable Second_Element equal to the second element in the stack, leaving the stack without its top two elements.

    b. Set the variable Bottom equal to the bottom element in the stack, leaving the stack empty.

    c. Set the variable Bottom equal to the bottom element in the stack, leaving the stack unchanged.

    d. Remove all the zero elements from a stack, leaving all the other elements in the stack.

    e. Make a copy of a stack, leaving the original stack unchanged.

7. In each plastic container of Pez candy, the colors are stored in random order. Your little brother only likes the yellow ones, so he painstakingly takes out all the candies, one by one, eats the yellow ones, and keeps the others in order, so that he can return them to the container in exactly the same order as before—minus the yellow candies, of course. Write the algorithm to simulate this process. You may use any of the operations defined in the stack class, but may not assume any knowledge of how the stack is implemented.

8. Indicate whether a stack would be a suitable data structure for each of the following applications.

    a. A program is to evaluate arithmetic expressions according to the specific order of operators.

    b. A bank wants to simulate its teller operation to see how waiting times would be affected by adding another teller.

    c. A program is to receive data that will be saved and processed in the reverse order.

    d. An address book is to be maintained.

    e. A word processor is to have a PF key that causes the preceding command to be redisplayed. Every time the PF key is pressed, the program is to show the command that preceded the one currently displayed.

    f. A dictionary of words used by a spelling checker is to be built and maintained.

    g. A program is to keep track of patients as they check into a medical clinic, assigning patients to doctors on a first-come, first-served basis.

    h. A data structure is used to keep track of the return addresses for nested procedures while a program is running.

9. Write the body for procedure Print_Reverse, given the following declaration. Your solution should use a stack. You may use any of the operations defined for the stack class.

```
procedure Print_Reverse (Data : in Ada.Text_IO.File_Type);
- This procedure reads a string of characters terminated by a
- blank from file Data and displays the characters in reverse
- order on the console.

- Preconditions  : File Data is open for input
- Postconditions : The screen contains characters from file Data,
-                  from the original reading marker position up to
-                  but not including the first blank, displayed in
-                  reverse order.
```

10. Write the body for the application procedure `Replace_Element`, with the following specification:

```
procedure Replace_Element (Stack  : in out Stack_Type;
                           Old_El : in     Element_Type;
                           New_El : in     Element_Type);
- Replace all occurrences of Old_El in the stack with New_El.
- Preconditions  : None
- Postconditions : Stack = original Stack with any occurrence of
-                  Old_El changed to New_El
```

    You may use any of the operations defined for a bounded stack class. You can declare any local variables you need, including additional stack objects.

11. Write a code segment to read in a string of characters and determine whether they form a palindrome. A palindrome is a sequence of characters that reads the same both forward and backward, for example:

    ABLE WAS I ERE I SAW ELBA

    The character ' . ' ends the string. Write a message indicating whether the string is a palindrome. You may assume that the data are correct and that the maximum number of characters is 80.

12. Evaluate the following postfix expressions:

    a. 6 4 + 1 - 3 /
    b. 1 4 18 6 / 3 + + 5 / +
    c. 1 16 8 4 2 / / / + 5 *

13. The following program contains two loops. In the first loop a counter goes from 1 to 5. During each iteration, the count is either displayed or pushed onto a stack depending on whether True or False is returned by a random Boolean function. In the second loop, any numbers pushed onto the stack are popped and displayed.

```
with Stack;
with Ada.Integer_Text_IO; use Ada.Integer_Text_IO;
with Ada.Numerics.Discrete_Random;
```

```
procedure Random_Stack is

    package Positive_Stack is new Stack (Element_Type => Positive);
    use Positive_Stack;
    package Random_Boolean is new Ada.Numerics.Discrete_Random (Boolean);
    use Random_Boolean;

    Max_Values : constant := 5;

    -- An object that generates random Boolean values
    Generator : Random_Boolean.Generator;

        Stack  : Stack_Type(Max_Values);
        Number : Positive;

begin
    Reset(Generator); -- Initialize the random generator from the system clock
    for Count in 1..Max_Values loop
        if Random(Generator) then   -- Pick a random Boolean
            Put (Item => Count, Width => 3);
        else
            Stack.Push(Count);
        end if;
    end loop;
    loop
        exit when Stack.Empty;
        Stack.Pop(Number);
        Put (Item => Number, Width => 3);
    end loop;
end Random_Stack;
```

Because of the logical properties of a stack, the program cannot display certain sequences of the values of the loop counter. For each of the following sequences of numbers, state whether the sequence is a possible output of program Random_Stack or is not a possible output of the program.

a. 1 2 3 4 5
b. 5 4 3 2 1
c. 1 3 5 2 4
d. 1 3 5 4 2
e. 2 3 4 5 1
f. 1 5 2 3 4

Bounded Stack Implementations

14. A stack is implemented as a record containing the discriminant `Max_Size`; a field to indicate the index of the top element, `Top`; and an array of character `Elements` as discussed in this chapter. `Letter` is a `Character` variable. In each of the following exercises, show the result of the stack operation. For each part of the exercise, the left side of the figure represents the state of things before the specified operation. Show the result of the stack operation on the right side of the figure. For the boxes labeled OVERFLOW or UNDERFLOW, write *yes* or *no* to indicate whether the exception is raised.

(a) `Stack.Push(Letter);`

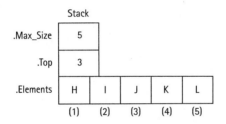
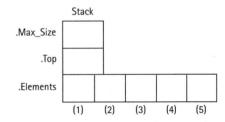

OVERFLOW _____ UNDERFLOW _____

(b) `Stack.Push(Letter);`

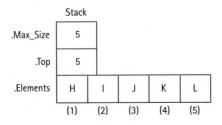
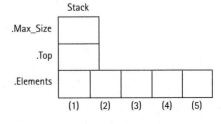

OVERFLOW _____ UNDERFLOW _____

(c) `Stack.Push(Letter);`

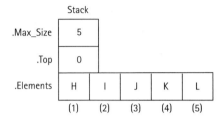

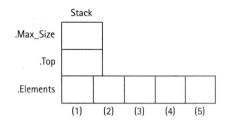

OVERFLOW   UNDERFLOW
———   ———

(d) `Stack.Pop(Letter);`

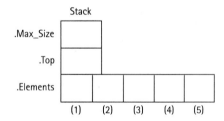

OVERFLOW   UNDERFLOW
———   ———

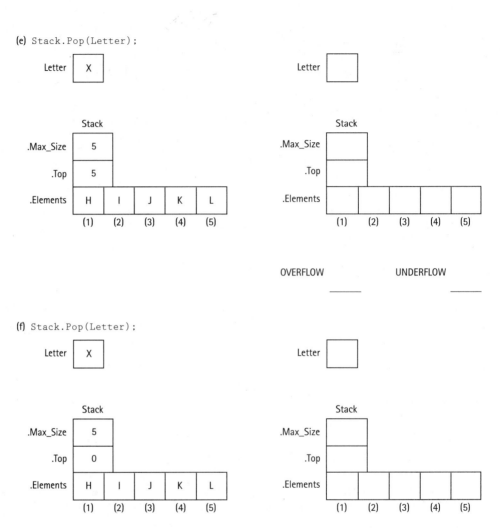

15. *Multiple choice.* If the array implementation of a stack were used, the statement
    Stack.Elements(1) := Stack.Elements(2);

    (setting the bottom element equal to the second to the bottom element) in an application program that uses the stack class

    a. would cause a syntax error at compile time.

    b. would cause a run-time error.

    c. would not be considered an error by the computer, but would violate the encapsulation of the stack data type.

d. would be a perfectly legal and appropriate way to accomplish the intended task.

16. Two stacks of positive integers are needed, both containing integers less than or equal to 1000. One stack contains even integers; the other contains odd integers. The total number of elements in the combined stacks is never greater than 200 at any one time, but we cannot predict how many are in each stack. All the elements could be in one stack, they could be evenly divided, both stacks could be empty, and so on. Can you think of a way to implement both stacks in one array?

    a. Draw a diagram of how the array storage for the double-stack data structure might look.

    b. Write the declarations for such a double-stack data structure.

    c. Implement the Push operation; it should assign the new element to the correct stack according to its value (even or odd).

    d. Implement the Pop operation; it should include a parameter to indicate from which stack to pop (even or odd).

17. Here is an operation we could add to Specification 5.1 that compares two bounded stacks for equality. Two stacks are equal if and only if they contain the same elements in the same order.

```
function "=" (Left  : in Stack_Type;
              Right : in Stack_Type) return Boolean;
```

Write the body for this function as if you were including it in Body 5.1.

18. Here is an operation we could add to Specification 5.1 that makes one bounded stack object a copy of another. This operation provides a way to assign one bounded stack to another.

```
procedure Copy (Target : out Stack_Type;
                Source : in  Stack_Type);
-- Target is a copy of Source
```

Write the body for this procedure as if you were including it in Body 5.1.

19. Here is an operation we could add to Specification 5.1 that removes a given number of items from a stack.

```
procedure Cut_Back (Stack : in out Stack_Type;
                    By    : in     Positive);
-- Remove By items from Stack
-- Exceptions  : UNDERFLOW raised if By is greater than the number of
--               elements currently in Stack.
--               Stack is unchanged
```

Write the body for this procedure as if you were including it in Body 5.1. Be sure that you leave the stack unchanged should the stack contain fewer values than the number in the cut back request.

20. In compiler construction, we need an inspector operation for our stack so that we can examine stack elements based on their location in the stack (the top of the stack is considered location 1, the second element from the top is considered location 2, etc.). This is sometimes called a "glass stack" or "traversable stack." The definition of the stack is exactly as we specify in this chapter, except we add the operation named Inspect with the following specification to Specification 5.1:

```
function Inspect (Stack    : in Stack_Type;
                  Position : in Positive := 1) return Element_Type;
-- Return a copy of an element in the stack without removing it
-- Preconditions  : None
-- Postconditions : Inspect = Stack element at Position, where position 1
--                            is the top element, position 2 is the element
--                            under the top element, etc.
-- Exceptions : UNDERFLOW         Raised on attempt to obtain a value from
--                                an empty stack.
--              CONSTRAINT_ERROR  Raised on attempt to return an element
--                                from a position not in the stack.
```

Write the body for this procedure as if you were including it in Body 5.1.

Linked Lists and Unbounded Stacks

Use the following declarations for Exercises 21 through 23:

```
type Node_Type;
type Ptr_Type is access Node_Type;
type Node_Type is
  record
      Info : Integer;
      Next : Ptr_Type;
  end record;

subtype Stack_Type is Ptr_Type;


type Info_Array is array (1..10) of Integer;
```

```
type List_Data_Type is
  record
     Length : Positive;
     Info   : Info_Array;
  end Record;

type List_Type is access List_Data_Type;

Stack : Stack_Type;
List  : List_Type;
Ptr   : Ptr_Type;
Count : Natural;
```

21. Mark each statement as syntactically valid or invalid.
    a. `Stack := 2;`
    b. `Stack.all.Info := 2;`
    c. `Stack.Info := 2;`
    d. `Stack.Info := List.Info;`
    e. `Stack.Info := List.Info(3);`
    f. `Ptr := Stack.Next;`
    g. `Stack.Info := '2';`
    h. `Ptr.Next := Stack;`
    i. `List.Length := List.Length + 1;`
    j. `Ptr := List;`
    k. `Ptr := Ptr.Next;`
    l. `List.Info (Ptr.Info) := Stack.Info;`

22. Describe each of the following as a pointer, an array, a record, or an integer:
    a. `Stack`
    b. `List`
    c. `List.Info`
    d. `Stack.Info`
    e. `Stack.Next`
    f. `Ptr.Next`
    g. `List.Info(Ptr.Info)`
    h. `Stack.Next.Next.all`

23. What is the output of the following code fragment? Hint: Draw a box and arrow picture as you trace the code.

```
Stack := null;
for Count in reverse 1..5 loop
   Stack := new Node_Type'(Info => Count, Next => Stack);
end loop;
Ptr := Stack;
Count := 0;
loop
   exit when Ptr = null;
   Count := Count + 1;
   Ptr := Ptr.all.Next;
end loop;
Put (Count);
```

24. Here is a fragment of a procedure written by an application programmer that uses our implementation of an unbounded stack:

```
package My_Stack is new Unbounded_Stack (Element_Type => Character);

procedure Exercise (Expression : in out Unbounded_String) is
                   First  : My_Stack.Stack_Type;
                   Second : My_Stack.Stack_Type;
                   Count  : Natural;
begin
   -- Statements that assign values to Count, push values onto
   -- First and Second, and pop values from First and Second.

   -- At the end of this procedure, the stacks
   -- First and Second may or may not be empty.
end Exercise;
```

a. The local variable Count uses 4 bytes of memory. How is this memory recycled when this procedure completes its execution and control is returned to the caller?

b. The local variable First uses 12 bytes of memory. How is this memory recycled when this procedure completes its execution and control is returned to the caller?

c. A maintenance programmer observes that a linked list of nodes is used in the implementation of the unbounded stack. Because the two local stacks may or may not be empty when this procedure completes, he believes that procedure Exercise can leak memory (the nodes in the linked lists making up the stacks). He asks the original author of the code to add calls to the Clear procedure to recycle all of the nodes in the linked lists before the procedure returns. She informs him that there are no memory leaks in procedure Exercise. Who is correct? Explain your answer.

25. A stack is kept in a record (`Stack_Rec`) that has three fields: `Max_Size` (a discriminant used to set the upper bound of the stack array), `Elements` (an array that contains the stack elements), and `Top` (the index of the current top element). The record variable is not declared, but rather it is allocated dynamically when a stack is needed. Here are the declarations:

```
type Stack_Array is array (Positive range <>) of Element_Type;

type Stack_Rec (Max_Size : Positive) is
   record
      Top : Positive;
      Elements : Stack_Array (1..Max_Size);
   end record;

type Stack_Type is access Stack_Rec;

Stack : Stack_Type;
```

   a. Is the space for this array-based data structure statically or dynamically allocated?
   b. How much space is reserved for the variable `Stack`?
   c. Write the `Clear` and `Empty` operations, using the specifications in the `Stack` class.
   d. Is a `Full` operation for this representation meaningful? Write the `Full` operation. (If the operation is not meaningful for this implementation, you should simply return False.)
   e. If you could write the `Push` and `Pop` procedures by modifying the source code of one of the stack implementations in the chapter, which one would you choose to modify? Write the `Push` and `Pop` operations, using the specifications in the Stack class.

26. Here is an operation we could add to Specification 5.2 that compares two unbounded stacks for equality. Two stacks are equal if and only if they contain the same elements in the same order.

```
function "=" (Left  : in Stack_Type;
              Right : in Stack_Type) return Boolean;
```

   Write the body for this function as if you were including it in Body 5.2.

27. Here is an operation we could add to Specification 5.2 that makes one unbounded stack object a copy of another. This operation provides a way to assign one unbounded stack to another.

```
procedure Copy (Target : out Stack_Type;
                Source : in  Stack_Type);
-- Target is a copy of Source
```

   Write the body for this procedure as if you were including it in Body 5.2. Be sure you create a copy of the stack and not an alias of the stack.

28. Here is an operation we could add to Specification 5.2 that removes a given number of items from a stack.

```
procedure Cut_Back (Stack : in out Stack_Type;
                    By    : in     Positive);
-- Remove By items from Stack
-- Exceptions  : UNDERFLOW raised if By is greater than the number of
--                         elements currently in Stack.
--                         Stack is unchanged
```

Write the body for this procedure as if you were including it in Body 5.2. Be sure that you leave the stack unchanged should the stack contain fewer values than the number in the cut back request.

29. In compiler construction, we need an inspector operation for our stack so that we can examine stack elements based on their location in the stack (the top of the stack is considered location 1, the second element from the top is considered location 2, etc.). This is sometimes called a "glass stack" or "traversable stack." The definition of the stack is exactly as we specify in this chapter, except we add the operation named Inspect with the following specification to Specification 5.2:

```
function Inspect (Stack    : in Stack_Type;
                  Position : in Positive := 1) return Element_Type;
-- Return a copy of an element in the stack without removing it
-- Preconditions  : None
-- Postconditions : Inspect = Stack element at Position, where position 1
--                            is the top element, position 2 is the element
--                            under the top element, etc.
-- Exceptions : UNDERFLOW        Raised on attempt to obtain a value from
--                               an empty stack.
--              CONSTRAINT_ERROR Raised on attempt to return an element
--                               from a position not in the stack.
```

Write the body for this procedure as if you were including it in Body 5.2.

Comparing Implementations

30. Assuming that data of Element_Type take 12 bytes, integers take 4 bytes, access types take 4 bytes, and Max_Stack = 100, compare the space requirements of static array-based versus dynamic linked stack implementations. (In calculating the space requirements of the linked implementation, don't forget to count the external pointer.)

Number of Elements	Space for Static Array-Based Stack	Space for Dynamic Linked Stack
0	_____	_____
10	_____	_____
50	_____	_____
100	_____	_____

31. Why is the cyclomatic (McCabe's) complexity of an algorithm a good measure of the amount of effort required for white box (clear box) testing of that algorithm?

32. Many integrated development environments (IDEs) that programmers use to edit, compile, test, and debug software have options to calculate one or more complexity measures. Typically you highlight a section of code and click to show a complexity report. Check to see if your IDE provides such measures. If it does, use it to compare the complexities of the two stack implementations given in this chapter. You can download the source code from the publisher's website.

33. A routine to calculate the sum of the square roots of some values in array Data contains the following code segment:

```
Sum_of_Sqr_Rt := 0.0;
Index := 1;
loop
    exit when Index > Num_Elements;
    SR := Square_Root(Value => Data(Index));
    Sum_of_Sqr_Rt := Sum_of_Sqr_Rt + SR;
    Index : Index  1;
end loop;
```

Identify the "goldfish" and the "elephant" operations inside the loop.

34. Algorithm 1 does a particular task in a "time" of N^3 where N is the number of elements processed. Algorithm 2 does the same task in a "time" of $3N + 1000$.

   a. What are the Big-O requirements of each algorithm?
   b. Which algorithm is more efficient by Big-O standards?
   c. Under what conditions, if any, would the "less efficient" algorithm execute more quickly than the "more efficient" algorithm?

35. A good way to understand the differences in orders of magnitudes for the Big-O notation is to graph functions of the same magnitude. For example, $O(1)$ would be represented by the function $f(x) = 1$, $O(N)$ would be represented by the function $f(x) = x$, $O(\log_2 N)$ would be represented by the function $f(x) = \log_2 x$, $O(N \log_2 N)$ would be represented by the function $f(x) = x \log_2 x$, $O(N^2)$ would be represented by the function $f(x) = x^2$, and $O(2^N)$ would be represented by the function $f(x) = 2^N$.

   a. Graph the functions for $O(1)$, $O(\log_2 N)$, and $O(N)$ on the same coordinate system and compare the rates at which they increase for large values of x. Pick a coordinate system appropriate to show the full range of the most rapidly growing function of the group.

b. Graph the functions for O(N) and O(N log₂N) on the same coordinate system and compare the rates at which they increase for large values of x. Pick a coordinate system appropriate to show the full range of the most rapidly growing function of the group.

c. Graph the functions for O(N), O(N^2), and O(2^N) on the same coordinate system and compare the rates at which they increase for large values of x. Pick a coordinate system appropriate to show the full range of the most rapidly growing function of the group.

36. Describe the order of magnitude of each of the following functions using Big-O notations:

    a. $N^2 + 3N$
    b. $3N^2 + N$
    c. $N^5 + 100N^3 + 245$
    d. $3N \log_2 N + N^2$
    e. $1 + N + N^2 + N^3 + N^4$
    f. $(N \times (N - 1)) / 2$

37. Describe the order of magnitude of each of the following code fragments using Big-O notation:

    a.
    ```
    Count := 0;
    for Orange in 1..N loop
       Count := Count + 1;
    end loop;
    ```

    b.
    ```
    Count := 0;
    for Orange in 1..1_000 loop
       Count := Count + 1;
    end loop;
    ```

    c.
    ```
    Count := 0;
    for Pear in 1..N loop
       for Apple in 1..N loop
          Count := Count + 1;
       end loop;
    end loop;
    ```

    d.
    ```
    Count := 0;
    Value := N;

    loop
       exit when Value <= 1;
       Count := Count + 1;
       Value := Value / 2;
    end loop;
    ```

e.
```
Count := 0;
for Pear in 1..N loop
   Value := N;
   loop
      exit when Value <= 1;
      Count := Count + 1;
      Value := Value / 2;
   end loop;
end loop;
```

38. Three algorithms do the same task. Algorithm 1 is $O(\sqrt{N})$, Algorithm 2 is O(N), and Algorithm 3 is O(log$_2$N). Which algorithm should execute the fastest for large values of N? Which one should execute the slowest? You'll need to figure out where $O(\sqrt{N})$ fits into the growth rate table given on page 320.

39. Search the Internet for an example of an algorithm (other than the examples discussed in the chapter) for each of the common orders of magnitude given in the growth rate table on page 320.

40. *True or False?*

   a. The two pop implementations developed in the chapter are both O(1), so they take the same amount of time to execute.

   b. The array-based stack implementation uses more space than the linked implementation, no matter how many elements are actually in the stack.

   c. If the elements in a stack are stored in an array, then the stack is necessarily a static variable.

Programming Problems

41. Create a subclass of `Unbounded_Stack.Stack_Type`. Your class should extend the original unbounded stack class with all of the operations described in Exercises 26 through 29. Also, add the following function that returns the number of elements in an unbounded stack:

```
function Size (Stack : in Stack_Type) return Natural;
 — Purpose         : Returns the number of elements in Stack
 — Preconditions   : None
 — Postconditions  : The number of elements in Stack is returned
```

   This function may be implemented with an O(N) algorithm or an O(1) algorithm. You will need to add an additional field to the subclass and override some of the superclass's operations to obtain O(1).

   Write a complete test plan and test program to test your stack subclass.

42. Write a program to convert an infix expression to a postfix expression. Your main program should contain a loop that does the following (exit the loop when the user enters a blank infix expression):

a. Prompt the user and read an infix expression into an unbounded-length string.
b. Call a function that is given the infix expression and returns an unbounded-length string containing an equivalent postfix expression.
c. Display the postfix expression.

For example, if the user enters: a+b*c-(d/e+f)*g

your program should display: a b c * + d e / f + g * -

To make things simpler, you may assume that all operands are single characters; that the only operators are +, -, *, and /; and that all infix expressions entered by the user are valid. With these assumptions, we can process the input expression one character at a time. Here is what to do with each character:

When an operand is encountered, it is immediately appended to the result string.

When a left parenthesis is encountered, it is pushed onto the stack.

When a right parenthesis is encountered, the stack is repeatedly popped, appending the popped operators to the result string. It stops popping when a left parenthesis is encountered on the stack. Throw this left parenthesis away.

When an operator is encountered, operators are repeatedly popped from the stack and appended to the result string. It stops popping when the stack is empty, an operator of lower priority than the operator encountered in the infix string is found (+ and - have lower priority than * and /), or a left parenthesis is found. The lower priority operator (it should not have been appended to the result string) or left parenthesis is returned to the stack. Finally, the encountered operator is pushed onto the stack.

When all of the characters in the infix string have been processed, the stack is popped until it is empty, appending operators to the result string.

Practice this algorithm by hand until you thoroughly understand the approach.

Additional Requirements

Your program should handle any length infix expression (limited only by the amount of memory on your computer).

The infix expression may contain any number of blanks before and after operands and operators. You should ignore these blanks. The resulting postfix expression should have exactly one blank after each operand and operator. Put a blank line after displaying the postfix expression.

43. Solve the previous problem without the assumption that all operands are single characters. You may assume that operands are separated by one or more blanks.

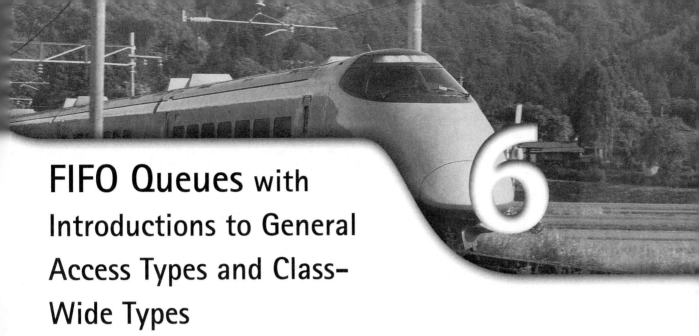

FIFO Queues with Introductions to General Access Types and Class-Wide Types

Goals for this chapter include that you should be able to

- describe the structure of a FIFO queue and its operations at the abstract level.
- determine when a FIFO queue is an appropriate data structure for a specific problem.
- design and implement the solution to a problem for which a FIFO queue is an appropriate data structure.
- use a static array to implement a FIFO queue class.
- use a linked structure to implement a FIFO queue class.
- compare FIFO implementations in terms of source code length, use of storage space, and Big-O approximations of the queue operations.
- choose between a static and a dynamic linked FIFO queue structure.
- differentiate between pool-specific and general access types.
- create a heterogeneous collection of objects with class-wide types.

In Chapter 5 we talked about a stack, a collection class with the special property that elements are always added to and removed from the top. We know from experience that many collections of data elements operate in a different manner: Elements are added at one end and removed from the other. This structure, called a FIFO (First In, First Out) queue, has many uses in computer programs. In this chapter we consider the FIFO queue data structure at three levels: logical, application, and implementation. In the rest of this chapter, "queue" refers to a FIFO queue. (Another queue-type data structure, the priority queue, is discussed in Chapter 11. The accessing function of a priority queue is different from that of a FIFO queue.)

6.1 The Logical Level

What is a **queue**? A queue (pronounced like the letter Q) is an ordered, homogeneous group of elements in which new elements are added at one end (the "rear") and elements are removed from the other end (the "front"). As an example of a queue, consider a line of students waiting to pay for their textbooks at a university bookstore (see Figure 6.1). In theory, if not in practice, each new student gets in line at the rear. When the cashier is ready for a new customer, the student at the front of the line is served.

> **Queue** A structure in which elements are added to the rear and removed from the front; a "first in, first out" (FIFO) structure.

To add elements to a FIFO queue we access the rear of the queue; to remove elements we access the front. The middle elements are logically inaccessible. It is convenient to picture the queue as a linear structure with the front at one end and the rear at

Figure 6.1 *A FIFO queue.*

the other end. However, we must stress that the "ends" of the queue are abstractions; they may or may not correspond to any physical characteristics of the class's implementation. The essential property of the queue is its FIFO access.

Like the stack, the queue is a holding structure for data that we will use later. We put a data element onto the queue, and then when we need it we remove it from the queue. If we want to change the value of an element, we must take that element off the queue, change its value, and then return it to the queue. We do not directly manipulate the values of elements that are currently in the queue.

Operations on Queues

The bookstore example suggests two operations that can be applied to a queue. First, we can add new elements to the rear of the queue, an operation that we call Enqueue. We also can take elements off the front of the queue, an operation that we call Dequeue. Unlike the stack operations Push and Pop, the adding and removing operations on a queue do not have standard names. Enqueue is sometimes called add or insert; Dequeue also is called deque, remove, or serve.

Another useful queue operation is checking whether the queue is empty. The Empty function returns True if our queue is empty and False otherwise. We can only dequeue when the queue is not empty. Theoretically we can always enqueue, because in principle a queue is not limited in size. We know from our experience with stacks, however, that certain implementations (an array representation, for instance) have an upper limit on the number of elements that a particular collection class object can hold. This real-world consideration applies to queues as well, so we define a Full operation. As with stacks, we also might want an operation to destroy the whole structure, leaving it empty. We call this operation Clear. Figure 6.2 shows how a series of these operations would affect a queue.

Next we must formalize the queue operations that we have described. As with the stack class, we'll make this a generic package so that our queue abstraction can be easily reused in different applications. We can instantiate queue packages for queues containing any type of objects. The declaration of our queue class is given in Specification 6.1.

Specification 6.1   A Bounded FIFO Queue

```
generic
   type Element_Type is private;
package Queue is

   -- This package implements a FIFO queue, a data structure in which
   -- elements are added to the rear and removed from the front;
   -- a "first in, first out" (FIFO) structure.

   type Queue_Type (Max_Size : Positive) is tagged limited private;
```

346 | Chapter 6: FIFO Queues

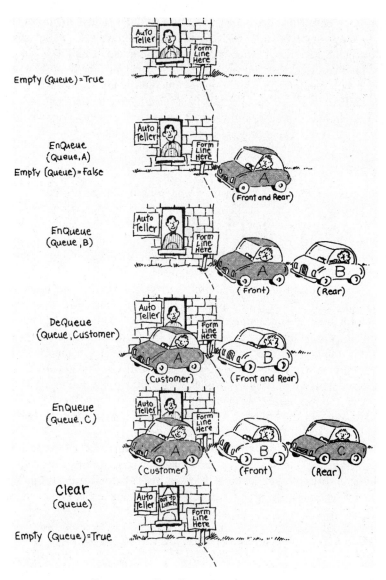

Figure 6.2 *The effects of queue operations.*

```
OVERFLOW  : exception;
UNDERFLOW : exception;
```

```
procedure Clear (Queue : in out Queue_Type);
  -- Purpose        : Remove all elements from the queue
  -- Preconditions  : None
  -- Postconditions : Queue is empty; it contains no elements
```

```
  procedure Enqueue (Queue : in out Queue_Type;
                     Item  : in     Element_Type);
  -- Purpose         : Adds Item to the rear of Queue
  -- Preconditions   : None
  -- Postconditions  : Queue = original Queue with Item added to its rear
  -- Exceptions      : OVERFLOW  Raised on attempt to Enqueue an element onto
  --                             a full queue.  Queue is unchanged.

  -------------------------------------------------------------------------

  procedure Dequeue (Queue : in out Queue_Type;
                     Item  :    out Element_Type);
  -- Purpose         : Removes the front element from Queue and returns it
  -- Preconditions   : None
  -- Postconditions  : Queue = original Queue with front element removed
  --                   Item  = front element of original Queue
  -- Exceptions      : UNDERFLOW  Raised on attempt to dequeue an element from
  --                              an empty Queue.  Queue remains empty.

  -------------------------------------------------------------------------

  function Full (Queue : in Queue_Type) return Boolean;
  -- Purpose         : Tests whether a queue is full.  A queue is full when
  --                   no more elements can be enqueued into it
  -- Preconditions   : None
  -- Postconditions  : Full = (no more elements can be enqueued into Queue)

  -------------------------------------------------------------------------

  function Empty (Queue : in Queue_Type) return Boolean;
  -- Purpose         : Tests whether a queue is empty (contains no elements)
  -- Preconditions   : None
  -- Postconditions  : Empty = (Queue is empty)

private

  -- We'll fill this in later

end Queue;
```

Like our stack package in Chapter 5, this package contains the declarations for two exceptions. If a queue is empty when we try to dequeue an element from it, the resulting error condition is called queue underflow. The exception comments for procedure `Dequeue` indicate that the exception UNDERFLOW is raised if this condition is detected. Queue overflow is the condition resulting from trying to enqueue a new element onto a

Chapter 6: FIFO Queues

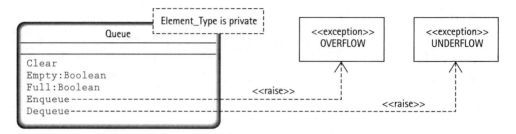

Figure 6.3 *UML diagram of a generic queue class and the exceptions it raises.*

queue that is already full. Procedure `Enqueue` raises the exception OVERFLOW if this condition is detected. Our exception comments specify exactly what the state of the queue is after the package raises the exception. Figure 6.3 shows a Unified Modeling Language (UML) class diagram of this generic queue class.

6.2 The Application Level

FIFO queues are commonly used as "waiting lines." Such waiting lines are common on networked systems of workstations. If you are using a networked computer system, you probably share a printer with other users. When you request a printout of a file, your request is added to a print queue. When your request gets to the front of the print queue, your file is printed. The print queue ensures that only one person at a time has access to the printer and that they get this access on a first come, first serve basis. Operating systems often maintain a FIFO queue of processes that are ready to execute or that are waiting for a particular event (such as a mouse click) to occur. The programmer who creates the operating system can use a queue to implement a waiting line of processes.

Another application area in which queues figure as the prominent data structure is the computer simulation of real-world situations. A branch of mathematics, called queueing theory, studies the phenomena of standing, waiting, and serving. Queueing theory is the primary tool for studying problems of congestions. Given its name, it should come as no surprise that the queue class is important in developing applications based on queueing theory. For instance, consider a supermarket that needs to schedule employees to check out shoppers. There should be enough checkers to service each customer within a "reasonable" wait time, but not too many checkers for the number of customers. The supermarket may want to run a computer simulation of typical customer transactions to determine how to best schedule its employees.

Freight Train Manifests

The DCT railroad provides service for Canadian companies shipping goods into the United States. At Rouses Point, New York, the railroad operates a facility called a

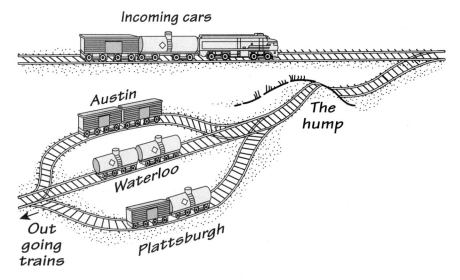

Figure 6.4 *The Rouses Point hump yard.*

hump yard for organizing incoming cars into outgoing trains. In such a rail yard, cars are released on the top of a hill (the hump). As they roll down the hill, they are switched into the section of track in which cars going to the same destination are collected.

Figure 6.4 illustrates a portion of the Rouses Point hump yard. Cars destined for Austin, Texas, are collected on one track, for Waterloo, Iowa, on the second track, and for Plattsburgh, New York, on the third track. Each of these track sections can hold up to 50 cars. In this yard, a locomotive takes cars one at a time from the incoming car track to the top of the hill and releases them. As they roll down the hill, the cars are switched into the proper section of track. After the locomotive has transferred all of the incoming cars to the yard a different locomotive is coupled to each group of cars going to the same destination. Each engineer of the three outgoing locomotives is given a list of cars in their train (a manifest). Our problem is to print a manifest for each of the engineers taking trains out of the yard. Here is a more complete specification.

Freight Train Manifests

Purpose

Print a manifest (list of cars) for each train leaving the Rouses Point hump yard. The program should terminate when there are no more cars remaining on the incoming car track. An outgoing train is complete when its track section is filled or there are no more cars remaining on the incoming car track.

> ### Input
> A text file, `cars.txt`, contains a car identification number (a five-digit number between 10,000 and 99,999), car class (box, flat, hopper, tank), and destination (Austin, Waterloo, or Plattsburgh) of all cars on the incoming car track. There is one line in the file for each car.
>
> ### Output
> The destination and a list of car identification numbers and car classes for each outgoing train is provided. The cars should be listed in order starting at the locomotive.
>
> ### Assumptions:
> 1. Each track section in the hump yard can hold up to 50 cars.
> 2. Car classes and destinations given in the data file are all valid.

The obvious objects in this problem are the yard, cars, locomotives, trains, track sections, and manifests. A car can be modeled as a record with three fields: ID, car type, and destination. Here are the necessary type declarations:

```ada
type Car_Class_Type   is (Box, Flat, Hopper, Tank);
type Destination_Type is (Austin, Waterloo, Plattsburgh);
subtype Car_ID_Type   is Integer range 10000..99999;

-- Type for railroad cars
type Car_Rec is
   record
      ID          : Car_ID_Type;
      Class       : Car_Class_Type;
      Destination : Destination_Type;
   end record;
```

Track sections contain groups of cars. Because the data file contains all the information for the cars on the incoming car track, we use `Ada.Text_IO.File_Type` to model the incoming car track. How about the sections of track in the hump yard? We could use an array of car records to model a hump yard track section. However, because the elements in an array can be accessed in any order, the array is not an accurate model of a section of track. We can add cars to a track section only from one end (the end nearest the hump) and remove them only from the other end. A track section is like a waiting line—the first car in is the first car out. A queue is therefore a more accurate model of a track section. Here are the necessary declarations:

```ada
package Car_Queue is new Queue (Element_Type => Car_Rec);

Section_Size : constant := 50;              -- Maximum cars per section
subtype Track_Section is Car_Queue.Queue_Type (Max_Size => Section_Size);
```

The yard itself is a collection of track sections. Because we need to access the various sections randomly, an array of track sections is an appropriate model. There is one track section in the yard for each of the destinations. We can use the destination as an index for the array. Here are the declarations for the yard class and a single yard object:

```
type Yard_Array is array (Destination_Type) of Track_Section;

Yard : Yard_Array;        -- The hump yard
```

The manifests are the output of the program. We can use the standard output file for the manifests. Locomotives and trains were mentioned in the problem statement; however, they are not necessary for our model of the train yard. Eliminating objects that are not essential in a model is an important aspect of object-oriented design.

Algorithm Design   Now we are ready to design the algorithm for the program. We base the algorithm on the actual operation of the yard. Cars are taken one at a time from the incoming car track and sent onto the appropriate track section in the hump yard. If a track section is filled, an outgoing train is ready to depart so a manifest is printed and the track section is emptied. When the incoming track is empty, all cars in the yard are sent out. Here is the algorithm in top-down form:

Hump Yard
    Open Input File
    loop
        exit when Input File is empty
        Get Car from Input File
        Add Car to Appropriate Track Section
        if the Track Section is full
            Print Manifest and remove cars
        end if
    end loop
    Close Input File
    for each non-empty Track Section
        Print Manifest and remove cars
    end loop

Add Car to Appropriate Track Section
    Enqueue (Queue   => Yard (Destination),
             Item   => Car)

Print Manifest (Destination, Track Section)
    Put Destination
    loop
        exit when Track Section is empty
        Dequeue Car from Track Section
        Display Car information
    end loop

Note how the destination of a car is used as an array index to select the appropriate track section (queue) to add (enqueue) the car. Program 6.1 implements this algorithm.

Program 6.1 Rouses Point Hump Yard

```ada
with Queue;
with Ada.Integer_Text_IO; use Ada.Integer_Text_IO;
with Ada.Text_IO;         use Ada.Text_IO;
procedure Hump_Yard is

-- This program prints manifests (lists of cars) for trains
-- leaving the Rouses Point hump yard.

   Data_File_Name : constant String := "cars.txt";

   -- Types for car attributes
   type Car_Class_Type   is (Box, Flat, Hopper, Tank);
   type Destination_Type is (Austin, Waterloo, Plattsburgh);
   subtype Car_ID_Type   is Integer range 10000..99999;

   -- Input and output of car attributes
   package Class_IO is new Ada.Text_IO.Enumeration_IO (Car_Class_Type);
   use Class_IO;
   package City_IO  is new Ada.Text_IO.Enumeration_IO (Destination_Type);
   use City_IO;

   -- Type for railroad cars
   type Car_Rec is
      record
         ID          : Car_ID_Type;
         Class       : Car_Class_Type;
         Destination : Destination_Type;
      end record;

   -- Types for track sections in the rail yard
   package Car_Queue is new Queue (Element_Type => Car_Rec);
   use Car_Queue;

   Section_Size : constant := 50;          -- Maximum cars per section
   subtype Track_Section is Car_Queue.Queue_Type (Max_Size => Section_Size);

   -- Type for the yard (a collection of track sections)
   type Yard_Array is array (Destination_Type) of Track_Section;
```

```ada
procedure Print_Manifest (Destination : in      Destination_Type;
                          Track       : in out Track_Section)     is
-- Purpose      : Displays information on the cars on the given track.
-- Preconditions  : None
-- Postconditions : The information for the cars on Track is displayed
--                  Track is empty.
   Car : Car_Rec;    -- Information on one car
begin
   -- Display headings
   Put ("Manifest for train going to ");
   Put (Destination);
   New_Line(2);
   Put ("Car ID");
   Ada.Text_IO.Set_Col (To => 10);
   Put ("Car Class");
   New_Line(2);

   loop  -- Each iteration, the information for one car is displayed
      exit when Track.Empty;
      -- Assertion:  The queue Track is not empty
      Track.Dequeue(Car);
      Put (Item => Car.ID,  Width => 5);
      Set_Col (To => 10);
      Put (Car.Class);
      New_Line;
   end loop;
   Ada.Text_IO.New_Page;
end Print_Manifest;
```

```ada
   Yard     : Yard_Array;              -- The hump yard
   Car      : Car_Rec;                 -- A single railroad car
   Incoming : Ada.Text_IO.File_Type;   -- Cars on the incoming car track

begin
   Open (File => Incoming,
         Mode => Ada.Text_IO.In_File,
         Name => Data_File_Name);

   -- Assertion: No queue is full.
```

```ada
-- Process all of the cars in the file
-- Each iteration, one car is moved to the appropriate section of the yard
loop
   exit when End_Of_File (Incoming);
   -- Get the information for a car
   Get (File => Incoming,  Item => Car.ID);
   Get (File => Incoming,  Item => Car.Class);
   Get (File => Incoming,  Item => Car.Destination);
   if not End_Of_File (Incoming) then
      Skip_Line (Incoming);   -- Advance reading marker
   end if;

   -- Add the car to the appropriate track section
   Enqueue (Queue => Yard (Car.Destination),
            Item  => Car);
   -- Check to see if the track section for this destination is now full
   if Full (Yard (Car.Destination)) then
      Print_Manifest (Destination => Car.Destination,
                      Track       => Yard (Car.Destination));
   end if;

   -- Assertion:  No queue is full.
end loop;
Close (Incoming);
-- Display manifests for all trains (from non-empty track sections)
for Destination in Destination_Type loop
   if not Empty (Yard (Destination)) then
      Print_Manifest (Destination => Destination,
                      Track       => Yard (Destination));
   end if;
end loop;
end Hump_Yard;
```

This program does not have any exception handlers for queue OVERFLOW or UNDERFLOW. *There is no chance of these exceptions being raised!* How can we write this statement with such confidence? Let's look at the assertion comments we included in this program. These assertions were derived through careful design and reading of the code. Using a static analysis tool such as the SPARK Examiner would allow us to prove these assertions. The first assertion in the main program is true because the queues were created empty, they have a maximum size greater than zero, and we have not enqueued any values into any queue at this point. Therefore there is no possibility that the first call to procedure Enqueue can raise OVERFLOW. The second assertion in the main program is always true because if the call to Enqueue a few lines earlier filled a queue, the call to Print_Manifest empties it. Therefore there is no possibility that the next call to Enqueue can raise OVERFLOW. Only procedure Dequeue raises UNDERFLOW. This operation is only called in Print_Manifest. Do you see why the assertion made in this procedure is true? This assertion guarantees that UNDERFLOW is never raised in this program.

The assertions in this program are based on the results of explicit tests of a queue's state through the Full and Empty operations. Why did we explicitly test for full and empty queues in this application instead of writing exception handlers as we did in the postfix expression evaluation application in Chapter 5? In this problem, full and empty queues are expected to occur; testing for these states is part of the algorithm. The postfix expression application of Chapter 5 expects the stack to be empty at only one point—the end of the evaluation where we did test it by calling Empty. A full or empty stack at other times is not expected; such an occurrence is considered an exceptional event. We reserve exception handlers for such unexpected events and use explicit tests when they are part of the processing algorithm.

Now you might raise the question of why we bothered to include the exceptions OVERFLOW and UNDERFLOW in our FIFO queue package specification when our application does not use them. When we design a class, we try to make it as general as possible so that we can reuse it in many different applications. In the stack and FIFO queue classes, we have supplied both exceptions and explicit operations that return the state of the class so that the application designer can choose the method most appropriate for their problem.

6.3 The Implementation Level

Now that we've had the opportunity to be queue users, let's take a look at how the body of the FIFO queue might be implemented. As with a stack, the queue can be stored in a static variable—an array—or in dynamically allocated memory in a linked structure. We look at both implementations in this chapter. Note that the application programmer using our queue should not have to be concerned about which implementation is used, because the interfaces to all the queue operations are the same.

The Implementation of a Queue as a Static Array

Like a stack, a queue can be stored in a record with the elements in an array and other information in separate fields.

```
type Queue_Array is array (Positive range <>) of Element_Type;
type Queue_Type (Max_Size : Positive) is tagged limited
   record
      Items : Queue_Array (1..Max_Size);   -- The element array
         .
         .           -- Other information goes here
         .
   end record;
```

We need to determine the relationship between the location of an item in the queue (the logical view) and the location of the item in the array (the implementation view). There are several alternatives we can consider. This design decision is interrelated with the approaches we use for implementing the queue operations.

Fixed-Front Design   In implementing the stack, we began by inserting an element into the first array position and then we let the top float with subsequent `Push` and `Pop` operations. The bottom of the stack, however, was fixed at the first slot in the array. Can we use a similar solution for a queue, keeping the front of the queue fixed in the first array slot and letting the rear move down as we add new elements?

Let's see what happens after a few enqueues and dequeues if we insert the first element in the first array position, the second element in the second position, and so on. After four calls to `Enqueue`, the queue array would look like this:

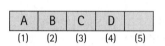

Enqueue 'A'
Enqueue 'B'
Enqueue 'C'
Enqueue 'D'

Remember that the front of the queue is fixed at the first slot in the array, whereas the rear of the queue moves down with each enqueue. Now we dequeue the front element in the queue:

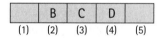

Dequeue
(first step)

This operation deletes the element in the first array slot and leaves a hole. To keep the front of the queue fixed at the first element of the array shown in this picture, we need to move every element in the queue left one slot:

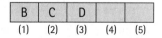

Dequeue
(second step)

Let's summarize the queue operations corresponding to this queue design. The `Enqueue` operation is the same as `Push`. The `Dequeue` operation is more complicated than `Pop`, because all the remaining elements of the queue have to be shifted in the array, to move the new front of the queue up to the first array slot.

Before we go any further, we want to stress that this design would work. It may not be the best design for a queue, but it could be successfully implemented. There are multiple functionally correct ways to implement the same abstract data structure. One design may not be as good as another (because it uses more space in memory or takes longer to execute) and yet still may be correct.

Now let's evaluate this design. Its strength is its simplicity and ease of coding; it is almost exactly like the package of stack routines that we wrote in Chapter 5. Although the queue is accessed from both ends rather than just one (as in the stack), we only have to keep track of the rear, because the front is fixed. Only the `Dequeue` operation is more complicated. What is the weakness of the design? The need to move all the elements up every time we remove an element from the queue increases the amount of work needed to `Dequeue`.

How serious is this weakness? To make this judgment, we have to know something about how the queue will be used. If this queue will be used for storing large numbers of elements at one time, or if the elements in the queue will be large (records with many fields, for instance), the processing required to move up all the elements after the front element has been removed makes this solution a poor one. On the other hand, if the queue generally contains only a few elements and they are small (integers, for instance), all this data movement may not amount to much processing. Further, we need to consider whether performance—how fast the program executes—is of importance in the application that will use the queue. Thus the complete evaluation of the design depends on the requirements of the program.

In the real programming world, however, you don't always know the exact uses or complete requirements of programs. For instance, you may be working on a very large project with a hundred other programmers. Other programmers may be writing the specific programs for the project while you are producing some packages that will be used by all the different applications. If you don't know the requirements of the various users of your queue package, you must design it for the most general case. In this situation the design described above is not the best one possible.

Floating-Front Design The need to move the elements in the array was created by our decision to keep the front of the queue fixed in the first array slot. If we keep track of the index of the front as well as the rear, we can let both ends of the queue float in the array. We use the integer variables `Front` and `Rear` to keep track of these indexes. Because they contain information on the *locations* of particular elements in our queue, we often refer to them as pointers.

Figure 6.5 shows how several `Enqueue` and `Dequeue` operations would affect the queue. (For simplicity, these figures show only the elements that are in the queue. The other slots contain logical garbage, including values that have been dequeued.) The `Enqueue` operations have the same effect as before; they add elements to subsequent slots in the array and increment the index of the `Rear` indicator. The `Dequeue` operation is simpler, however. Instead of moving elements up to the beginning of the array, it merely increments the `Front` indicator to point to the next slot.

Letting the queue elements float in the array creates a new problem when `Rear` gets to the end of the array. In our fixed-front design, this situation told us that the queue was full. Now, however, it is possible for the rear of the queue to reach the end of the (physical) array when the (logical) queue is not yet full (Figure 6.6[a]).

358 | Chapter 6: FIFO Queues

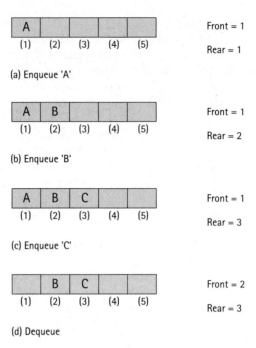

Figure 6.5 *The effects of* Enqueue *and* Dequeue.

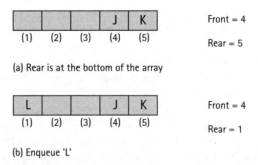

Figure 6.6 *Wrapping the queue around.*

Because there may still be space available at the beginning of the array, the obvious solution is to let the queue "wrap around" the end of the array. In other words, the array can be treated as a circular structure, in which the last slot is followed by the first slot (Figure 6.6[b]). To get the next position for Rear, we can use an if statement.

```
if Rear = Max_Size then
   Rear := 1;
else
   Rear := Rear + 1;
end if;
```

Using the remainder operator, rem, the logic expressed in this if statement can be done with the following single assignment:[1]

```
Rear := (Rear rem Max_Size) + 1;
```

Let's move on to implementing the Empty and Full functions. There would appear to be some relationship between the values of Front and Rear that could indicate when the queue is empty or full. Figure 6.7(a) shows a queue that contains a single element. Figure 6.7(b) shows that same queue after carrying out a dequeue operation—the queue is now empty. Looking at the values of Front and Rear, it looks like we can say that a queue is empty when the Front pointer is just ahead of the Rear pointer. We say "just ahead of" rather than "one greater than" because of the wrap-around feature of our array. The location 1 is just ahead of location 5.

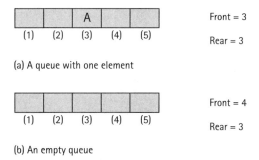

(a) A queue with one element

(b) An empty queue

Figure 6.7 *An empty queue.*

---

[1]Ada provides two very similar operations, rem and mod, either of which could be used here. The rem operator provides the classic remainder of a signed integer division and is defined by the expression A = (A / B) * B + (A rem B), where (A rem B) has the same sign as A. The mod operator is defined by a slightly different form of signed integer division, A = ⌊A / B⌋ * B + (A mod B), where ⌊ ⌋ is the floor function. (A mod B) always has the same sign as B. When A and B have the same sign, the rem and mod operators produce identical results.

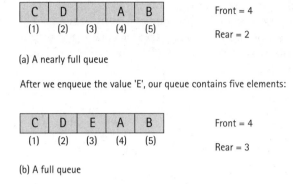

(a) A nearly full queue

After we enqueue the value 'E', our queue contains five elements:

(b) A full queue

Figure 6.8 *A full queue.*

Now let's look at the `Full` operation. Figure 6.8(a) shows a queue that is one element away from being full. Figure 6.8(b) shows that same queue after carrying out an enqueue operation—the queue is now full. Notice that the values of `Front` and `Rear` are identical to that of the empty queue of Figure 6.7!

Programmers have devised many ingenious solutions that solve the problem of differentiating a full queue from an empty one. A simple solution that comes to mind is to add another field to our queue record, in addition to `Front` and `Rear`—a count of the elements in the queue. When `Count` is 0, the queue is empty; when `Count` is equal to the maximum number of array slots, the queue is full. Of course, we must remember to increment `Count` in the `Enqueue` operation and decrement it in the `Dequeue` operation.

Here are the declarations for the private part of Specification 6.1 (page 347) using our solution of array wrap-around and a count field:

```
private

    type Queue_Array is array (Positive range <>) of Element_Type;
    type Queue_Type (Max_Size : Positive) is tagged limited
       record
          Count : Natural  := 0;          -- Number of items in the queue
          Front : Positive := 1;          -- Pointer to first item in the queue
          Rear  : Positive := Max_Size;   -- Pointer to last item in the queue
          Items : Queue_Array (1..Max_Size);  -- The element array
       end record;

end Queue;
```

Notice the initial values assigned to the three scalar fields in the record. The initial value assigned to `Rear` ensures that the element for the first call to `Enqueue` is placed into the first location of the array. Other initial values are possible as long as `Rear` indicates the array slot just before `Front`.

Body 6.1 contains the code that implements our floating-front queue algorithms. Note that `Dequeue`, like the stack `Pop` operation, does not actually remove the value of the element from the array. The value that has just been dequeued still physically exists in the array. It no longer exists in the queue, however, and cannot be accessed because of the change in `Front`.

Body 6.1   Array-Based Queue: Implements Specification 6.1

```ada
package body Queue is

   ----------------------------------------------------------------------

   procedure Enqueue (Queue : in out Queue_Type;
                      Item  : in      Element_Type) is
   begin
      if Queue.Count = Queue.Max_Size then
         raise OVERFLOW;
      else
         Queue.Rear := Queue.Rear rem Queue.Max_Size + 1;
         Queue.Items(Queue.Rear) := Item;
         Queue.Count := Queue.Count + 1;
      end if;
   end Enqueue;

   ----------------------------------------------------------------------

   procedure Dequeue (Queue : in out Queue_Type;
                      Item  :    out Element_Type) is
   begin
      if Queue.Count = 0 then
         raise UNDERFLOW;
      else
         Item := Queue.Items(Queue.Front);
         Queue.Front := Queue.Front rem Queue.Max_Size + 1;
         Queue.Count := Queue.Count - 1;
      end if;
   end Dequeue;

   ----------------------------------------------------------------------

   function Full (Queue : in Queue_Type) return Boolean is
   begin
      return Queue.Count = Queue.Max_Size;
   end Full;
```

```
-------------------------------------------------------------------
function Empty (Queue : in Queue_Type) return Boolean is
begin
   return Queue.Count = 0;
end Empty;

-------------------------------------------------------------------
procedure Clear (Queue : in out Queue_Type) is
begin
   Queue.Count := 0;
   Queue.Front := 1;
   Queue.Rear  := Queue.Max_Size;
end Clear;

end Queue;
```

Comparing Array Implementations   The solution implemented in Body 6.1 is not nearly so simple or intuitive as our first queue design with the fixed front. What did we gain by adding some amount of complexity to our design? By using a more efficient `Dequeue` algorithm, we achieved better performance. To find out how much better, let's analyze the fixed-front design. Because the amount of work to move all the remaining elements is proportional to the number of elements, this version of `Dequeue` is an $O(N)$ operation. The second array-based queue design only requires `Dequeue` to change the values of the `Front` indicator and to decrement `Count`. The amount of work never exceeds some fixed constant, no matter how many elements are in the queue, so the algorithm is $O(1)$.

All of the other operations, for both array-based designs, are $O(1)$. No matter how many elements are in the queue, they do (essentially) a constant amount of work. This does not mean that the two `Enqueue` operations will be the same in terms of lines of code or time of execution. It only means that the amount of work done by both of them does not depend on the number of items in a queue.

The Implementation of a Queue as a Linked Structure

The major weakness of the array-based implementation is the need to declare an array big enough for a structure of the maximum expected size. This size is set when the queue object is elaborated. If a much smaller number of elements is needed, we have wasted a lot of space. If a larger number of elements is unexpectedly needed, we are in trouble. We cannot extend the size of the array after it has been elaborated.

We know, however, from our discussion of stacks in Chapter 5, that we can get around this problem by using dynamic storage allocation to get space for queue ele-

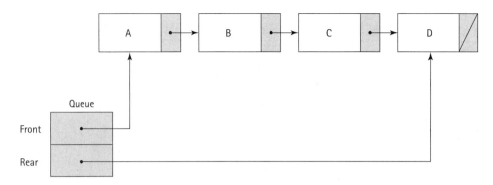

Figure 6.9 *A linked queue representation.*

ments at run time. This implementation relies on the idea of linking the elements one to the next to form a chain.

In a linked representation we store the elements in a linked list of nodes. Each node contains one element and a pointer to the node containing the next element in the queue. We used two integer pointers to keep track of the front and rear elements in our array-based queue. With a linked representation, we use two access variables to designate the front item and the rear item of the queue.

Figure 6.9 shows a queue of four elements implemented as a linked list of four nodes. Front and Rear are external pointers to the first and last nodes in this linked list. Because by now you realize that dynamically allocated nodes in linked structures exist "somewhere in memory," rather than in adjacent locations like array slots, we are going to show the nodes arranged linearly for clarity. The declarations for this data structure are given in the private part of Specification 6.2. As we did for the linked stack, we use a controlled type to ensure that no memory is leaked when a queue object goes out of scope.

Specification 6.2   An Unbounded Queue Class

```
with Ada.Finalization;
generic
   type Element_Type is private;
package Unbounded_Queue is

   -- This package implements a FIFO queue, a data structure in which
   -- elements are added to the rear and removed from the front;
   -- a "first in, first out" (FIFO) structure.

   type Queue_Type is new Ada.Finalization.Limited_Controlled with private;
```

```ada
    OVERFLOW  : exception;
    UNDERFLOW : exception;

    ----------------------------------------------------------------
    procedure Clear (Queue : in out Queue_Type);
    -- Purpose        : Remove all elements from the queue
    -- Preconditions  : None
    -- Postconditions : Queue is empty; it contains no elements

    ----------------------------------------------------------------
    procedure Enqueue (Queue : in out Queue_Type;
                       Item  : in      Element_Type);
    -- Purpose        : Adds Item to the rear of Queue
    -- Preconditions  : None
    -- Postconditions : Queue = original Queue with Item added to its rear
    -- Exceptions     : OVERFLOW  Raised on attempt to Enqueue an element onto
    --                            a full queue.  Queue is unchanged.

    ----------------------------------------------------------------
    procedure Dequeue (Queue : in out Queue_Type;
                       Item  :    out Element_Type);
    -- Purpose        : Removes the front element from Queue and returns it
    -- Preconditions  : None
    -- Postconditions : Queue = original Queue with front element removed
    --                  Item  = front element of original Queue
    -- Exceptions     : UNDERFLOW  Raised on attempt to dequeue an element from
    --                             an empty Queue.  Queue remains empty.

    ----------------------------------------------------------------
    function Full (Queue : in Queue_Type) return Boolean;
    -- Purpose        : Tests whether a queue is full.  A queue is full when
    --                        no more elements can be enqueued into it
    -- Preconditions  : None
    -- Postconditions : Full = (no more elements can be enqueued into Queue)

    ----------------------------------------------------------------
    function Empty (Queue : in Queue_Type) return Boolean;
    -- Purpose        : Tests whether a queue is empty (contains no elements)
    -- Preconditions  : None
    -- Postconditions : Empty = (Queue is empty)

private

    type Node_Type;
    type Node_Ptr is access Node_Type;
```

```
   type Node_Type is
      record
         Info : Element_Type;
         Next : Node_Ptr;
      end record;

   type Queue_Type is new Ada.Finalization.Limited_Controlled with
      record
         Front : Node_Ptr;   -- Designates first item in the queue
         Rear  : Node_Ptr;   -- Designates last item in the queue
      end record;

   overriding procedure Finalize (Object : in out Queue_Type) renames Clear;

end Unbounded_Queue;
```

Box and arrow pictures like that shown in Figure 6.9 are important aids in the design of algorithms that manipulate linked lists. Many linked structures require our algorithms to handle special cases. Two common special cases are adding an element to an empty structure and deleting the last element from a structure. When developing our algorithms, it is therefore useful to draw pictures of the linked structure when it is empty and when it contains a single element. Figure 6.10 shows what our queue looks like when it is empty. Figure 6.11 shows what it looks like with a single element.

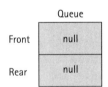

Figure 6.10 *An empty queue.*

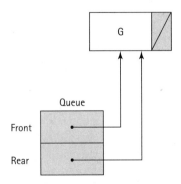

Figure 6.11 *A queue containing one element.*

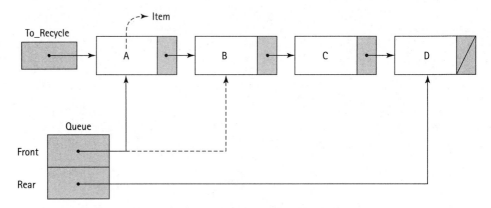

Figure 6.12 *The dequeue operation.*

Our queue is empty when there are no nodes in the queue structure (Figure 6.10). To test for an empty queue, we need only check if `Queue.Front` is null. An alternative method is to check to see if `Queue.Rear` is null. The `Full` operation for a linked queue is identical to the one we used for a linked stack—we simply return `False`.

We can dequeue elements from the queue using an algorithm similar to our stack `Pop` algorithm, with `Queue.Front` designating the first node in the queue. Figure 6.12 illustrates this algorithm for a queue containing more than one element. As in `Pop`, we need to keep a local access variable to designate the node being removed so its memory may be recycled.

Notice that the only access values changed as a result of the dequeue operation are `Queue.Front` and the temporary variable `To_Recycle`, used to designate the node whose memory is recycled. Are these two changes adequate when we dequeue an element in a queue that contains only one element, as shown in Figure 6.11? No! Once we have recycled the last node, `Queue.Rear` no longer contains a valid access value. When we dequeue the last element, we must be sure to also set `Queue.Rear` to `null`.

We can clear the queue using an algorithm similar to our stack clear algorithm, with `Queue.Front` designating the first node in the queue. This algorithm contains a loop that recycles all the nodes. The loop terminates when `Queue.Front` becomes `null`. To match our picture of an empty queue, we then must set `Queue.Rear` to `null`.

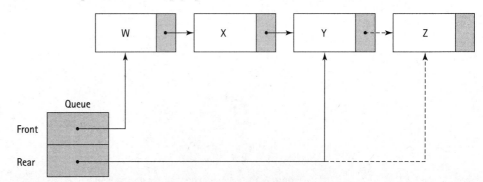

Figure 6.13 *The enqueue operation. The dashed arrow shows the value of the pointer after the enqueue operation is complete.*

We add new elements to the queue by inserting after the last node. Figure 6.13 shows that we need to acquire memory for a new node and change two access values to link the new node into our linked structure. We can accomplish all three of these changes with the following assignment statement:

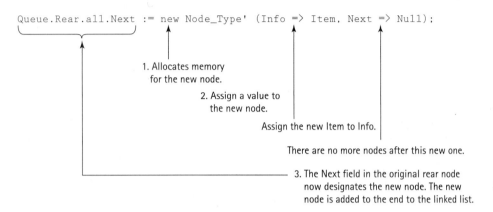

By assigning the result of the allocation operator `new` to the `Next` field of the original rear node, we link the new node after it. We need a second assignment statement to change `Queue.Rear` so it designates our newly added node.

```
Queue.Rear := Queue.Rear.all.Next;
```

Are these two assignment statements adequate for adding an element to an empty queue? Again the answer is no. The first assignment statement raises CONSTRAINT_ERROR because `Queue.Rear` is null; it is not designating a node. Adding an element to an empty queue is a special case. This case is included in the following code for the enqueue operation:

```
if Queue.Front = null then     -- Is the queue empty?
   -- Yes, Front and Back should both designate the new node
   Queue.Front := new Node_Type'(Info => Item,  Next => null);
   Queue.Rear  := Queue.Front;
else
   -- No, link a new node to the rear of the existing queue.
   Queue.Rear.all.Next := new Node_Type'(Info => Item,  Next => null);
   Queue.Rear := Queue.Rear.all.Next;
end if;
```

This logic and that of the previous linked queue operations are incorporated into Body 6.2.

Body 6.2   An Unbounded Queue: Implements Specification 6.2

```
with Unchecked_Deallocation;
package body Unbounded_Queue is
```

```ada
   -- Instantiate a procedure to recycle node memory
   procedure Free is new Unchecked_Deallocation (Object => Node_Type,
                                                 Name   => Node_Ptr);


procedure Clear (Queue : in out Queue_Type) is
   To_Recycle : Node_Ptr;                   -- For recycling nodes
begin
   loop
      exit when Queue.Front = null;
      To_Recycle := Queue.Front;            -- Unlink the
      Queue.Front := Queue.Front.all.Next;  --    front node
      Free (To_Recycle);                    -- Recycle the node
   end loop;
   Queue.Rear := null;                      -- Clean up Rear pointer
end Clear;


procedure Enqueue (Queue : in out Queue_Type;
                   Item  : in     Element_Type) is
begin
   if Queue.Front = null then               -- Is the queue empty?
      -- Yes, Front and Back should both designate the new node
      Queue.Front := new Node_Type'(Info => Item, Next => null);
      Queue.Rear  := Queue.Front;
   else
      -- No, link a new node to the rear of the existing queue.
      Queue.Rear.all.Next := new Node_Type'(Info => Item, Next => null);
      Queue.Rear := Queue.Rear.all.Next;
   end if;
end Enqueue;


procedure Dequeue (Queue : in out Queue_Type;
                   Item  :    out Element_Type) is
   To_Recycle : Node_Ptr;                   -- For recycling nodes
begin
   Item := Queue.Front.Info;                -- Get the value from the front node
   To_Recycle  := Queue.Front;              -- Save access to old front
   Queue.Front := Queue.Front.Next;         -- Change the front
   Free (To_Recycle);                       -- Recycle the memory
   if Queue.Front = null then               -- Is the queue now empty?
      Queue.Rear := null;                   -- Set Rear to null as well
   end if;
end Dequeue;
```

```
function Full (Queue : in Queue_Type) return Boolean is
begin
   return False;
end Full;


function Empty (Queue : in Queue_Type) return Boolean is
begin
   return Queue.Front = null;
end Empty;

end Unbounded_Queue;
```

Our initial picture of the linked queue structure (Figure 6.9) showed that the nodes were linked from front to rear. What if they had been reversed as in Figure 6.14? We then could use an algorithm similar to our stack push algorithm for the enqueue operation. But how could we dequeue? To delete the last node of the linked queue, we need to be able to reset Queue.Front to designate the node preceding the deleted node. Because our access values all point forward, we can't get back to the preceding node. To accomplish this task, we either would have to start at the rear of the queue and traverse the whole list (an O(N) solution—very inefficient, especially if the queue is long) or else keep a linked structure with access values that point in both directions. Use of this kind of doubly linked structure is not necessary if we set up our queue access variables correctly to begin with.

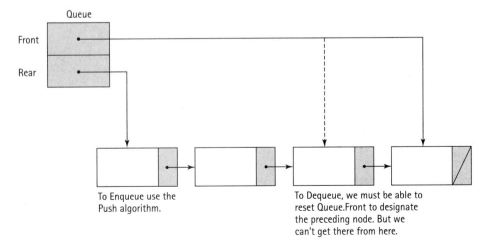

Figure 6.14 *A bad queue design.*

A Circular Linked Queue Design Our `Queue_Type` record contains two pointers, one to each end of the queue. This design is based on the linear structure of the linked queue: Given only an access value that points to the front of the queue, we could follow the pointers to get to the rear, but this technique makes accessing the rear (to enqueue) an O(*N*) operation. With an access value that points to the rear of the queue, we could not access the front because the access values only point from the front to the rear.

However, we could access both ends of the queue from a single pointer, if we made the queue circularly linked; that is, the `Next` field of the rear node would point to the front node of the queue (see Figure 6.15). Now the `Queue_Type` record contains a single external pointer, rather than two. One interesting thing about this queue implementation is that it differs from the logical picture of a queue as a linear structure with two ends. This queue is a circular structure with no ends. What makes it a queue is its support of FIFO access.

In order to enqueue, we access the rear node directly through the access variable `Queue.Rear`. To dequeue, we must access the front node of the queue. We don't have an external access value pointing to this node, but we do have one pointing to the node preceding it—`Queue.Rear`. The access value to the front node of the queue is in `Queue.Rear.all.Next`. An empty queue would be represented by `Queue.Rear` having a value of `null`. Designing and coding the queue operations using a circular linked implementation is left as an exercise.

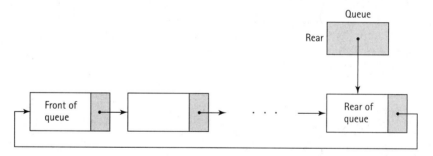

Figure 6.15 *A circular linked queue.*

6.4 Comparing the Queue Implementations

We now have looked at several different implementations of the FIFO queue class. How do they compare? As when we compared stack implementations in Chapter 5, we look at several different factors: the length of the source code required to implement the solutions, the amount of memory required to store the structure, and the amount of "work" the solution requires, as expressed in Big-O notation. We compare the two implementations that are completely coded in this chapter.

Complexity

The size of the source code of the private part declarations, procedures, and functions for each implementation is summarized in the table that follows. As you can see from the table, there are fewer lines of code to develop and to maintain in the array implementation. Now that you are more familiar with Ada access type syntax and use, you may find that the linked implementation of a queue is more intuitive than the array implementation. Deciding which design is easier to understand is very subjective, but it is often a factor in selecting one approach over another.

Comparison of Lines of Code

	Array Implementation	Linked Implementation
Declarations (private part)	8	13
Clear	6	11
Empty	4	4
Full	4	4
Enqueue	11	11
Dequeue	11	12
Total	44	55

Space

The storage requirements for our two queue implementations are similar to those of our two stack implementations. An array variable takes the same amount of memory, no matter how many array slots actually are used; we need to reserve space for the maximum possible number of elements. The linked implementation using dynamically allocated storage space requires space only for the number of elements actually in the queue at run time, plus space for the external access variable(s). Note, however, that the node elements are larger, because we must store the link (the Next field) as well as the user's data.

Let's see how these implementations compare if the queue contains fixed-length strings of 64 characters. The array-based queue is stored in a record with five fields: Max_Size, Count, Front, Rear, and Items. The first four fields are integers and the last is an array of strings. We can use the following formula to calculate the minimum amount of storage required for this record:

$$\text{Array-Based Queue Storage} = 4 \times (\text{storage needed for one integer})$$
$$+ \text{Max\_Size} \times (\text{storage needed for 64 characters})$$

If an integer uses 4 bytes of memory and a character uses 1 byte of memory, a total of 6416 bytes is required for an array-based queue of strings with a Max_Size of 100.

Chapter 6: FIFO Queues

The amount of memory used by the linked queue implementation depends on the current size of the queue. It includes the storage needed for the two external pointers, Front and Rear, and for all of the nodes in the linked list. Each node is a record with the two fields Info and Next.

Linked Queue Storage = 2 × (storage needed for one pointer)
+ current queue size × (storage needed for one node)

Node Storage = storage needed for 64 characters + storage needed for one pointer

If a character uses 1 byte of memory and a pointer uses 4 bytes of memory, an empty linked queue requires 8 bytes of storage. A linked queue of 100 elements requires 6808 bytes. The pointers in the linked version of this particular example take a far smaller portion of the node storage than our linked stack example in Chapter 5. Figure 6.16 compares the memory requirements for these two queue implementations.

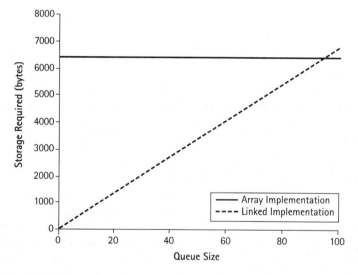

Figure 6.16 *Comparison of space requirements for two queue implementations.*

Big-O

We also can compare the relative "efficiency" of the two implementations, in terms of Big-O. In both implementations, the Full and Empty operations are clearly O(1). They always take a "constant" amount of work. What about Enqueue and Dequeue? Does the number of elements in the queue affect the amount of work performed by these operations? No, it does not; in both implementations, we can directly access the front and rear of the queue. The amount of work done by these operations is independent of the queue size, so these operations are also O(1). Only the Clear operation differs from one implementation to the other. The array-based implementation merely sets Count and the `Front` and `Rear` indexes, so it is clearly an O(1) operation. The linked implementation must process every node in the queue in order to free the node space. This operation, therefore, is O(N), where N is the number of nodes in the queue. As with the array-based and linked implementations of stacks, these two queue implementations are roughly equivalent in terms of the amount of work they do, only differing in one of the six operations. The following table summarizes the Big-O comparison of the queue operations.

Big-O Comparison of Queue Operations

	Array Implementation	Linked Implementation
Clear	O(1)	O(N)
Empty	O(1)	O(1)
Full	O(1)	O(1)
Enqueue	O(1)	O(1)
Dequeue	O(1)	O(1)

Time

Finally, let's look at an actual timed test case, with real numbers. The following table shows how long it takes one particular computer to enqueue and dequeue 100,000 fixed-length strings containing 64 characters. We also timed how long it took to clear a queue containing 100,000 of these strings. Here are the results:

Time for Queue Operations (Milliseconds)

	Array Implementation	Linked Implementation
Enqueue	7.46	53.11
Dequeue	6.97	44.52
Clear	0.00[2]	40.79

Remember that the results of timing tests like these depend on the compiler used to convert the Ada program to machine language and the computer on which the tests are run. As with the stack, the amount of time needed to clear an array-based queue is significantly less than the time required to clear a linked queue.

So which is better? Go back to the comparison of stack implementations in Chapter 5 and read the bottom line. The answer is the same for the two queue implementations: It depends on the requirements of your application. Some of the kinds of issues to consider when choosing an implementation are listed in the next table.

---

[2]Too small to measure

Considerations for Selecting a Queue Implementation

Situation	Recommended Implementation
The number of elements in the queue varies greatly from one program execution to the next.	Linked with access types
The maximum number of elements cannot be predicted.	Linked with access types
The maximum number of elements is known, and the usual number is close to the maximum.	Array
The maximum number of elements is known and is small.	Array
The maximum number of elements is large and the element size is large.	Linked with access types
The system or programming language does not support dynamic storage allocation.	Array
The program requirements specify a static implementation.	Array
The program requirements specify the use of dynamic allocation.	Linked with access types

6.5 Testing the Queue Operations

You can test the FIFO queue class independently of the program that will use it with a test driver. Although it is possible to write a complicated interactive test driver that allows the tester to specify actions (such as enqueue and dequeue), the simplest test driver merely sets up a scenario that executes the various test cases. To make sure that you have tested all the necessary cases, make a test plan, listing all the queue operations and the tests needed for each. (For example, to test function Empty, you must call it at least twice—once when the queue is empty and once when it is not.)

We want to enqueue elements until the (array-based) queue is full; then we need to call functions Full and Empty to see whether they correctly judge the state of the queue. Next we can dequeue all the elements in the queue, printing them out as we go, to make sure that they are correctly dequeued. At this point we can call the queue status functions again to see if the empty condition is correctly detected.

We also want to test out the "tricky" part of the array-based algorithm: enqueue until the queue is full, dequeue an element, then enqueue again, forcing the operation to circle back to the beginning of the array. At each point in the test, you should print out text explaining what the test driver is doing.

We can use the same test driver to test both queue implementations; we merely name the appropriate generic package in a with clause and instantiate an appropriate new package. Note that we get different results for the Full function, depending on the implementation.

Because the type of data stored in the queue has no effect on the operations that manipulate the queue, you can choose Element_Type to simplify the test driver. Suppose that the queue in your application contains a maximum of 1000 record-type elements, each with many fields (a queue of student information records, for instance). You don't need to enqueue actual student records, because the queue element type is not relevant to how `Enqueue` works. For the test driver, you can declare `Element_Type` to be `Character` to simplify setting up the test. You also don't need to test a queue of 1000 elements. Knowing that the code works the same whether `Max_Size` is 10 or 1000, you can set `Max_Size` to 10 for the test.

6.6 Heterogeneous Collections

All of the applications using the queue classes we developed in this chapter and the stack classes we developed in Chapter 5 used homogeneous collections of elements. Although we can instantiate a queue or stack package for nearly any element type, for that instance, all of the elements must be of the given type. We now look at how we can create a stack or a queue that contains a variety of different element types.

General Access Types

We introduced access types in Chapter 4 as a mechanism to implement unbounded-length strings. In Chapter 5 and this chapter we used access types to build linked list implementations of stacks and queues. In all of these applications we used the `new` operator to obtain memory. The Ada run-time system is responsible for locating the amount of memory requested. Figure 6.17 is a review of what you learned in Chapter 4 about the storage of objects in memory.

Stack storage is used for named objects. Whenever a subprogram is called, the top of the system stack is raised to make space for that subprogram's parameters and local variables. When control is returned to the caller of the subprogram, this memory is reclaimed by lowering the stack top to its position prior to the call.

Heap storage is used for unnamed objects. When our program uses the `new` operator, the run-time system searches the system heap for an adequately sized chunk of memory that had been recycled through an unchecked deallocation. If no recycled memory is available, the run-time system increases the size of the heap by moving the

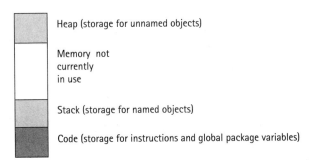

Figure 6.17 *Memory used by a running program.*

boundary shown in Figure 6.17 downward. Should the stack and heap memory boundaries meet, a further request for memory will raise the STORAGE_ERROR exception.

An access value contains the location of an object. The access types with which we have been working are called pool-specific access types. A **pool-specific access type** designates an object in the heap. Ada sets up a separate pool of available storage for each different pool-specific access type.[3] Ada also provides general access types. A **general access type** can designate an object stored in either the heap or the stack. Here are example declarations of these two kinds of access types followed by some variable declarations:

> **Pool-specific access type** An access type whose values can designate only the elements of its associated storage pool.
>
> **General access type** An access type whose values can designate the elements of any storage pool, as well as aliased objects created by declarations (named objects).

```
-- Declaration of three access types
type A_Ptr is access String;            -- A pool-specific access type
type B_Ptr is access all String;        -- A general access type
type C_Ptr is access constant String;   -- Another general access type

-- Declaration of three access variables
Apple   : A_Ptr;
Apricot : A_Ptr;
Banana  : B_Ptr;
Cherry  : C_Ptr;
```

`A_Ptr` is an example of a pool-specific access type. Until now, all of the access types you have seen have been pool-specific. Values of access type `A_Ptr` designate strings stored in heap memory. `B_Ptr` is an example of a general access type. Values of access type `B_Ptr` may designate strings stored in heap memory or strings stored in stack memory. `C_Ptr` is also an example of a general access type. However, the string designated by `C_Ptr` is considered a constant. As with any constant, we may use the value of the designated string but we cannot change its value.

General access values of type `B_Ptr` or `C_Ptr` cannot designate *any* named string variable or constant. Ada requires us to indicate explicitly that a named object is intended to be accessed through a pointer variable. Thus the string variable `Course` declared as

```
Course : String := "Data Structures";
```

cannot be designated by an access value, but the string variable `Name` declared as

```
Name : aliased String := "Mildred";
```

can be designated by an access value. In Chapter 4 we defined *alias* as one of several access variables that designate the same object. The reserved word `aliased` applied to a

---

[3]Ada provides a mechanism through which we can control the size of a storage pool as well as what objects are stored in it. Details are given in Section 13.11 of the *Ada Language Reference* manual.

6.6 Heterogeneous Collections

named variable indicates that the variable's value may be accessed either through its name or by dereferencing any access variable that designates it.

An access variable contains information on the location of an object. How do we obtain a location to assign to an access variable? In Chapter 4 we showed two ways to assign a value to a pool-specific access variable. When we create unnamed space for an object using a call to the allocation operator `new`, the location of the new object is returned. The second way is to copy the value of another access variable, creating an alias.

```
Apple   := new String'("Hello");   -- Obtain memory for a 5-character string
Apricot := Apple;                  -- Apricot and Apple now designate the same string
```

We can use the same two ways to assign a location value to a general access type variable. In addition, we can use the `'Access` attribute to obtain the location of an aliased named object and assign that location to a general access type variable. Here are examples of the use of `'Access`:

```
Banana := Name'Access;    -- The location of Name is assigned to Banana
Cherry := Name'Access;    -- The location of Name is assigned to Cherry
Banana.all(1) :='m';      -- Change the first letter of Name to 'm'
```

`Banana.all`, `Cherry.all`, and `Name` are all aliases for a string object with the value "Mildred". The last statement above accesses and changes the first letter of variable `Name`. Because `Cherry` designates a constant string, the Ada compiler will give a syntax error for the following attempt to change the second letter of `Name`:

```
Cherry.all(2) :='e';      -- Attempt to change a constant will not compile
```

Program 6.2 illustrates general access types. Three named string variables are declared as aliased. The array `Names` contains five general access values that designate strings. The first four assignment statements assign the location of named strings to the first four array components. The fifth array component designates an unnamed string whose memory is allocated dynamically in the heap. Figure 6.18 shows the values of all the named and unnamed objects in this program.

Program 6.2 General Access Types

```
with Ada.Text_IO; use Ada.Text_IO;
procedure Demo_General_Access is

   type String_Ptr       is access all String;            -- General access type
   type String_Ptr_Array is array (1..5) of String_Ptr;

   -- Named variables are allocated space in "stack" memory
   First  : aliased String := "George";
```

Chapter 6: FIFO Queues

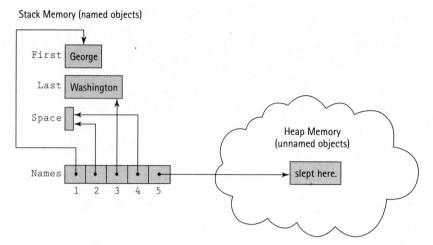

Figure 6.18 *Variables in Program 6.2.*

```
   Last  : aliased String := "Washington";
   Space : aliased String := " ";

   Names : String_Ptr_Array;   -- An array of general access values

begin
   -- Assign values (locations) to the 5 array components
   Names(1) := First'Access;
   Names(2) := Space'Access;
   Names(3) := Last'Access;
   Names(4) := Names(2);   -- The 2nd and 4th component both designate Space
   Names(5) := new String'("slept here.");   -- Allocate "heap" memory

   -- Display all 5 strings on one line
   for Index in Names'range loop
      Put (Item => Names(Index).all);   -- Note the pointer dereferencing
   end loop;
   New_Line;
end Demo_General_Access;
```

Class-Wide Types

We introduced the tagged type in Chapter 2. We can declare access types to designate tagged types. Here are some declarations of access types that designate some of the locomotive classes we defined in Chapter 2:

```
   type Steam_Ptr  is access Steam_Type;
   type Diesel_Ptr is access Diesel_Type;
   type Turbo_Ptr  is access Turbocharged_Type;
```

Here is the declaration of a variable that designates the steam locomotive owned by a small railroad:

```
Locomotive : Steam_Ptr;   -- Designates a steam locomotive
```

And here is an assignment statement that creates a steam locomotive instance and places its location in the access variable `Locomotive`:

```
Locomotive := new Steam_Type'(Construct_Loco (Weight            => 573.3,
                                              Max_Boiler_Pressure => 450.0));
```

Suppose our small railroad decides to trade in its steam locomotive for a diesel. This change requires us to change the type of our `Locomotive` variable from `Steam_Ptr` to `Diesel_Ptr`. And of course we would need to use the diesel locomotive constructor to create our diesel locomotive object.

Now suppose our railroad expands and purchases seven additional locomotives; some are steam, others are diesel, and one is a turbocharged diesel. It seems like we could use an array of eight locomotive pointers to create a collection of locomotives. But there is a major problem with this approach. An array is a homogeneous composite type. All of the components of an array must be the same type. Yet we need our array to hold three different kinds of pointers.

The solution to our problem is the class-wide type. All of our locomotive types are descendants of the tagged type `Locomotive_Type`. (See Figure 2.11 on page 129 for the relationship of all our locomotive classes.) Ada provides the attribute `'Class` for all tagged types. We use this attribute to create a new subtype that represents an entire class hierarchy. Such subtypes are called **class-wide types**. For example, `Locomotive_Type'Class` represents all six classes rooted at the abstract class `Locomotive` and `Diesel_Type'Class` represents the two classes rooted at class Diesel.

> **Class-wide type**   A type consisting of the set of all types in an inheritance hierarchy.
>
> **Indefinite type**   A type for which we cannot declare an object without an initial value or explicit constraint.

Like unconstrained array types, class-wide types may not be used alone in the declarations of named variables. Both of the following declarations are invalid:

```
My_Loco    : Locomotive_Type'Class;    -- Illegal attempts to declare named
First_Name : String;                   -- variables with indefinite subtypes
```

In both of these cases, the compiler cannot determine the amount of memory required for the object. Types that cannot be used in the declaration of named variables are called **indefinite types**. By supplying bounds through an explicit constraint or initial value, we can use an indefinite type in the declaration of a variable, as in the following examples:

```
-- Examples of legal uses of indefinite types in object declarations
My_Loco    : Locomotive_Type'Class := Construct_Loco (Weight => 233.3,
                                                      Power  => 7500);
```

```
First_Name : String := "Mildred";
Last_Name  : String (1..30);
```

In all cases, the constraints supplied in the declaration cannot be changed later. We used the `Diesel` class constructor, so `My_Loco` is always constrained to a `Diesel_Type`. Because the initial value supplied contained seven characters, `First_Name` is always constrained to a seven-character string. `Last_Name` is always constrained to a 30-character string.

The most common uses of indefinite types are in the declarations of parameters and pointers. For example, the following declaration defines an access type that can designate an object of any type in our inheritance hierarchy of locomotives:

```
type Loco_Ptr is access Locomotive_Type'Class;
```

A call to the following procedure will stop any type of locomotive by setting its throttle to zero and applying its brakes:

```
procedure Stop (Loco : in out Locomotive_Type'Class) is
begin
   Loco.Set_Throttle(Value => 0);
   Loco.Brakes_On;
end Stop;
```

There are five different `Set_Throttle` procedures and five different `Brakes_On` procedures in our hierarchy of locomotives. Which ones does procedure `Stop` call? Of course, it depends on what type of locomotive is passed to procedure `Stop`. The `Set_Throttle` and `Brakes_On` that are appropriate for the given locomotive are called. This automatic selection of the appropriate operation while our program is running is called **dynamic dispatching**. The correct `Set_Throttle` and `Brakes_On` are said to be *dispatched*. Dynamic dispatching is an extremely important aspect of object-oriented programming. Dynamic dispatching applies only to primitive operations. Both `Set_Throttle` and `Brakes_On` are primitive operations of `Locomotive_Type` and all of the types derived from `Locomotive_Type`.

> **Dynamic dispatching** The automatic selection at execution time of the appropriate operation in a class hierarchy.

We can now create an array for our small company to hold its collection of eight locomotives.

```
type Loco_Array is array (1..8) of Loco_Ptr;
```

Figure 6.19 illustrates the structure of such an array.

We are now ready to instantiate a queue of heterogeneous elements. The following statement creates a queue class whose elements are access values that designate the class-wide type for locomotives:

```
package Loco_Queue is new Unbounded_Queue (Element_Type => Loco_Ptr);
```

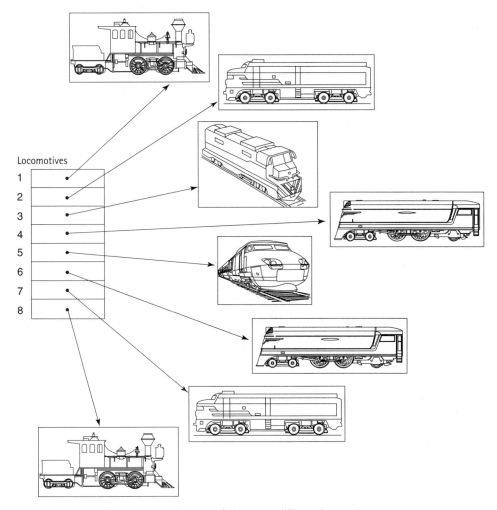

Figure 6.19   *An array of pointers to different locomotive types.*

There is a danger of memory leaks in this approach. The Clear operation for our unbounded-length queue class deallocates only the memory used for the nodes in its linked list. It does not deallocate the memory used by the designated locomotive objects. Switching to an array-based queue class does not resolve this problem—no memory is deallocated in the array-based Clear operation. A simple approach to this problem is to clear a queue by dequeuing each locomotive access value and deallocating the object it designates. A safer but more complex approach is to make our element type extend Ada.Finalization.Controlled with a pointer to our locomotive class-wide type. We can write Finalize operations that deallocate a locomotive object when the access value that designates it is no longer used.

Summary

In this chapter we examined the definition and operations of a FIFO queue. We also discussed some of the design considerations encountered when an array is used to contain the elements of a queue. Although the array itself is a random-access structure, our logical view of the queue as a FIFO structure limits us to accessing only the elements in the front and rear positions of the queue stored in the array. As with stacks, the problem with a static array-based implementation is the need to determine the maximum queue size before compilation. The queue is logically a dynamic structure, but the array is physically a static structure.

The linked implementation of a FIFO queue allows us to allocate space for queue elements as needed. Now that you are getting used to Ada's access types, this implementation will become more intuitive—perhaps more intuitive, even, than the array implementation that we developed.

There usually is more than one functionally correct design for the same class. When multiple correct solutions exist, the requirements and specifications of the problem may determine which solution is the best design.

In the design of data structures and algorithms, you will find that there are often tradeoffs. A more complex algorithm may result in more efficient execution; a solution that takes longer to execute may save memory space. As always, we must base our design decisions on what we know about the problem's requirements.

In this chapter we expanded our knowledge of access types. All of the access types we used in previous chapters were pool-specific access types. The unnamed objects that these access values designate are stored in heap memory. General access values may designate named objects stored in stack memory or unnamed objects stored in heap memory.

Class-wide types are indefinite types that include the set of all types within an inheritance hierarchy. Class-wide types allow us to write functions and procedures that can process any type within the hierarchy. These subprograms can use dynamic dispatching to select the appropriate operation for a particular class.

Although inheritance through the extension of a tagged type and dynamic dispatching are powerful tools for the rapid development of software, they come at a price. The operations are spread among many different class files, so debugging and testing are often complicated. Making a change at the top of a hierarchy can have huge ripple effects for the highly coupled descendants. Dynamic dispatching requires more resources than static linking of a call to a subprogram, as in the abstract data type approach used frequently in this book. Finally, when access types are used at the application level, there is always the danger of aliases and memory leaks.

Exercises

Logical Level

1. How are the items in a FIFO queue ordered?
2. Describe the operations of a FIFO queue at the abstract level.

3. Show what is written by the following segments of code, given that Queue is a FIFO queue of integers; Stack is a stack of integers; and X, Y, and Z are integer variables.

   a.
   ```
   X := 0;
   Y := 1;
   Queue.Enqueue(X);
   Queue.Enqueue(Y);
   Dequeue (Queue, Y);
   Z := Y + 5;
   Queue.Enqueue(Z);
   Queue.Enqueue(7);
   Queue.Dequeue(X);
   Queue.Enqueue(Y);
   loop
       exit when Queue.Empty;
       Queue.Dequeue(Z);
       Put(Z);
       New_Line;
   end loop;
   ```

   b.
   ```
   X := 1;
   Y := 0;
   Z := 4;
   Queue.Enqueue(Y);
   Queue.Enqueue(X);
   Queue.Enqueue(X + Z);
   Queue.Dequeue(Y);
   Queue.Enqueue(Z**2);
   Queue.Enqueue(Y);
   Queue.Enqueue(3);
   Queue.Dequeue(X);
   Put(X);
   Put(Y);
   Put(Z);
   loop
       exit when Queue.Empty;
       Queue.Dequeue(Z);
       Put(Z);
       New_Line;
   end loop;
   ```

   c.
   ```
   X := 0;
   Y := 1;
   ```

```
Z := X + Y;
loop
   exit when Z >= 10;
   if Z rem 2 = 0 then
      Stack.Push(Z);
   else
      Queue.Enqueue(Z);
   end if;
   X := Y;
   Y := Z;
   Z := X + Y;
end loop;

Put ("Stack contains: ");
loop
   exit when Stack.Empty;
   Stack.Pop(Z);
   Put (Z);
end loop;
New_Line;

Put ("Queue contains: ");
loop
   exit when Queue.Empty;
   Queue.Dequeue(Z);
   Put (Z);
end loop;
```

4. Given the following declarations:

   ```
   subtype Name_String is String (1..20);

   type Name_Rec is
      record
         First : Name_String;
         Last  : Name_String;
      end record;
   ```

   a. Instantiate a bounded queue package whose elements are `Name_Recs`.
   b. Using the package you just instantiated, declare a queue object that holds a maximum of 250 names.

5. *Multiple choice.* The statements
   ```
   Queue.Enqueue(X + 1);
   Queue.Dequeue(X + 1);
   ```
   in an application program
   a. would cause a syntax error at compile time.

b. would cause a run-time error.
   c. would be legal, but would violate the encapsulation of the queue.
   d. would be perfectly legal and appropriate.
6. *True or False.* All data structures that are called "queues" have the first in, first out accessing function.

Application Level

7. Write a segment of code to perform each of the following operations. You may call any of the operations specified for the Queue class. You may declare additional queue objects as needed.
   a. Set the variable `Second_Element` to the second element in the queue, leaving the queue without its first two elements.
   b. Set the variable `Last` equal to the last element in the queue, leaving the queue empty.
   c. Set the variable `Last` equal to the last element in the queue, leaving the queue unchanged.
   d. Remove all the zero elements from a queue, leaving all the other elements in the queue.
   e. Make a copy of a queue, leaving the original queue unchanged.
   f. Reverse the elements in the queue. You may declare a stack object.
8. Indicate whether each of the following applications would be suitable for a FIFO queue.
   a. An ailing company wants to evaluate employee records in order to lay off some workers on the basis of service time (the most recently hired employees will be laid off first).
   b. A program is to keep track of patients as they check into a clinic, assigning them to doctors on a first-come, first-served basis.
   c. A program to solve a maze is to backtrack to an earlier position (the last place where a choice was made) when a dead-end position is reached.
   d. An inventory of parts is to be processed by part number.
   e. An operating system is to process requests for computer resources by allocating the resources in the order in which they are requested.
   f. A grocery chain wants to run a simulation to see how average customer wait time would be affected by changing the number of checkout lines in the stores.
   g. A dictionary of words used by a spelling checker is to be created.
   h. Customers are to take numbers at a bakery and be served in order when their numbers come up.
   i. Gamblers are to take numbers in the lottery and win if their numbers are picked.

9. Write the body for the application procedure `Replace_Element`, with the following specification:

```ada
procedure Replace_Element (Queue  : in out Queue_Type;
                           Old_El : in     Element_Type;
                           New_El : in     Element_Type);
-- Replace all occurrences of Old_El in Queue with New_El.
-- Preconditions  : None
-- Postconditions : Queue = original Queue with any occurrence of
--                  Old_El changed to New_El
```

You may use any of the operations defined for a bounded queue class. You can declare any local variables you need, including additional queue objects.

10. The following program contains two loops. In the first loop a counter goes from 1 to 5. During each iteration, the count is either displayed or put into a queue depending on whether true or false is returned by a random Boolean function. In the second loop, any numbers in the queue are removed and displayed.

```ada
with Queue;
with Ada.Integer_Text_IO; use Ada.Integer_Text_IO;
with Ada.Numerics.Discrete_Random;
procedure Random_Queue is

   package Positive_Queue is new Queue (Element_Type => Positive);
   use Positive_Queue;
   package Random_Boolean is new Ada.Numerics.Discrete_Random (Boolean);
   use Random_Boolean;

   Max_Values : constant := 5;

   -- An object that generates random Boolean values
   Generator : Random_Boolean.Generator;

   Queue  : Queue_Type(Max_Values);
   Number : Positive;

begin
   Reset(Generator); -- Initialize the random generator from the system clock
   for Count in 1..Max_Values loop
      if Random(Generator) then  -- Pick a random Boolean
         Put (Item => Count, Width => 3);
      else
         Queue.Enqueue(Count);
      end if;
```

```
      end loop;
      loop
         exit when Queue.Empty;
         Queue.Dequeue(Number);
         Put (Item => Number, Width => 3);
      end loop;
   end Random_Queue;
```

Because of the logical properties of a queue, the program cannot display certain sequences of the values of the loop counter. For each of the following sequences of numbers, state whether the sequence is a possible output of program Random_Queue.

a. 1 2 3 4 5
b. 5 4 3 2 1
c. 1 3 5 2 4
d. 1 3 5 4 2
e. 2 3 4 5 1
f. 2 3 4 1 5

11. The Rouses Point hump yard application discussed in this chapter had track sections for cars going to Austin, Plattsburgh, and Waterloo. Cars bound for other destinations are left coupled to the end of a string of cars attached to the locomotive moving cars from the incoming track to the hump. What data structure is most suitable for modeling the string of cars attached to this locomotive?

12. A particular operating system queues the user jobs that are waiting to be executed according to a priority scheme.

   - There are 10 priority levels based on user ID numbers according to the following scheme:

     | Users 000–099 | Highest (for example, company executives) |
     | Users 100–199 | Next to highest (for example, executive secretaries) |
     | Users 200–299 | Next highest (for example, technical leaders) |

     .
     .
     .

     | Users 800–899 | Next to lowest (for example, regular programmers) |
     | Users 900–999 | Lowest (those whose jobs only run when there are no others) |

   - Within each priority level the jobs execute in the order in which they arrive in the system.
   - If there is a highest priority job queued, it executes before any other job; if not, if there is a next to highest priority job queued, it runs before any lower priority jobs; and so on. That is, a lower priority job runs only when there are no higher priority jobs waiting.

- The system has an array of FIFO queues to hold the queues for the various priority levels. Here are the declarations for the ID type and 10 FIFO queues:

```
type ID_Type is range 0..999;

type Job_Token is . . .              -- Details of the type and constant are
Default_Job : constant Job_Token :=  -- not needed for this exercise
package Job_Queues is new Queue (Element_Type => Job_Token);
use Job_Queues;

-- The following array type provides one queue for each of
-- the ten different priorities in the system
type Job_Array is array (0..9) of Queue_Type (Max_Size => 100);

JOB_OVERFLOW : exception;
```

In completing the following procedures, you may call any of the queue operations specified in the FIFO queue package.

a. Complete the procedure Add_Job, which receives a user ID and a token (representing the job to be executed) and adds the token to the appropriate queue for that user's priority level. Raise the exception JOB_OVERFLOW if the FIFO queue appropriate for this ID is already full.

```
procedure Add_Job (New_Job : in     Job_Token;
                   ID      : in     ID_Type;
                   Jobs    : in out Job_Array) is
-- Adds New_Job to the appropriate job queue based on ID
-- Exceptions : JOB_OVERFLOW if the FIFO queue for this
--              ID is full
```

b. Complete the procedure Get_Next_Job, which returns the token for the highest priority job that is queued for execution. (The token should be removed from the queue.)

```
procedure Get_Next_Job (Jobs     : in out Job_Array;
                        Next_Job :    out Job_Token) is
-- Removes and returns the first job in the highest priority job queue
-- that is not empty.
-- If all job queues are empty, Default_Job is returned.
```

c. The system is going down for maintenance. All jobs that are waiting to be executed have to be purged from the job queues. Fortunately this system is very friendly; it notifies users when their jobs are being cancelled so that the users know to resubmit the jobs later. Complete the procedure Clean_Up_Jobs that sends notification to each of the users with queued jobs. Call procedure Notify to send the notification. The highest priority users should be notified first, of course. Do not write the code for procedure Notify.

```
procedure Notify (User : in Job_Token) is . . .
-- Sends a message to the user informing them
-- that their job has been cancelled

procedure Clean_Up_Jobs (Jobs : in out Job_Array) is
-- Removes all jobs from all job queues.  Notifies each
-- user that their job was cancelled.
```

Bounded Queue Implementations

13. A FIFO queue is implemented as a record containing the discriminant Max_Size; a field to indicate the number of items currently in the queue, Count; a field to indicate the index of the first element in the queue, Front; a field to indicate the index of the last element in the queue, Rear; and an array of character Items, as discussed in this chapter. Letter is a Character variable. In each exercise below, show the result of the queue operation. For each part of the exercise, the left side of the figure represents the state of things before the specified operation. Show the result of the queue operation on the right side of the figure. For the boxes labeled OVERFLOW or UNDERFLOW, write *yes* or *no* to indicate whether the exception is raised.

    a. Queue.Enqueue(Letter):

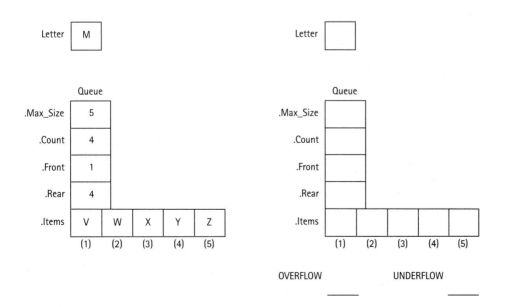

Chapter 6: FIFO Queues

b. `Queue.Enqueue(Letter);`

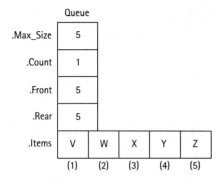

OVERFLOW _____   UNDERFLOW _____

c. `Queue.Enqueue(Letter);`

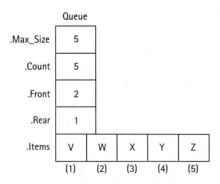
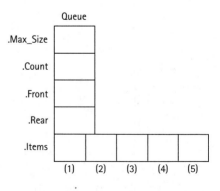

OVERFLOW _____   UNDERFLOW _____

Exercises | 391

d. `Queue.Enqueue(Letter);`

Letter: S

Queue	
.Max_Size	5
.Count	4
.Front	4
.Rear	2
.Items	V W X Y Z
	(1) (2) (3) (4) (5)

Letter: [ ]

Queue	
.Max_Size	
.Count	
.Front	
.Rear	
.Items	
	(1) (2) (3) (4) (5)

OVERFLOW _____   UNDERFLOW _____

e. `Queue.Enqueue(Letter);`

Letter: F

Queue	
.Max_Size	5
.Count	1
.Front	3
.Rear	3
.Items	V W X Y Z
	(1) (2) (3) (4) (5)

Letter: [ ]

Queue	
.Max_Size	
.Count	
.Front	
.Rear	
.Items	
	(1) (2) (3) (4) (5)

OVERFLOW _____   UNDERFLOW _____

f. `Queue.Dequeue(Letter);`

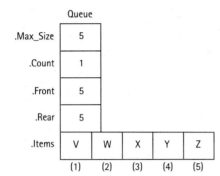
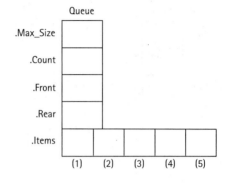

g. `Queue.Dequeue(Letter);`

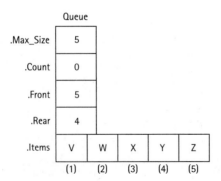
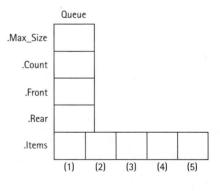

h.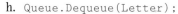

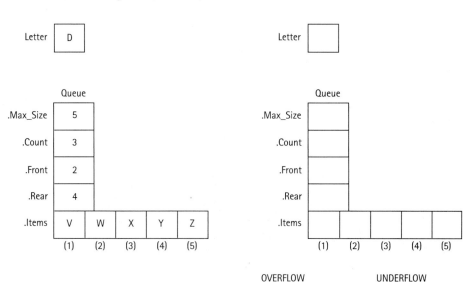

OVERFLOW UNDERFLOW

14. We used the `rem` operator to calculate the next available index in the "circular" array of our bounded queue class implementation. The `mod` operator produces the same results as `rem` when the operands have the same sign; however, the results differ when the operands have different signs. The following program (available from the publisher's website) demonstrates the difference between the `mod` and `rem` operators. What is the output?

```
with Ada.Text_IO;          use Ada.Text_IO;
with Ada.Integer_Text_IO;  use Ada.Integer_Text_IO;
procedure Modulo is

   procedure Display (Dividend : in Integer; Divisor : in Integer) is
   begin
      Put (Item => Dividend, Width => 2);
      Put (" / ");
      Put (Item => Divisor, Width => 2);
      Set_Col(To => 12);
      Put (" = ");
      Put (Item => Dividend / Divisor, Width => 2);
      New_Line;

      Put (Item => Dividend, Width => 2);
      Put (" rem ");
      Put (Item => Divisor, Width => 2);
```

```
      Set_Col(To => 12);
      Put (" = ");
      Put (Item => Dividend rem Divisor, Width => 2);
      New_Line;

      Put (Item => Dividend, Width => 2);
      Put (" mod ");
      Put (Item => Divisor, Width => 2);
      Set_Col(To => 12);
      Put (" = ");
      Put (Item => Dividend mod Divisor, Width => 2);
      New_Line;
   end Display;

begin
   Display ( 51,  14);
   New_Line;
   Display (-51,  14);
   New_Line;
   Display ( 51, -14);
   New_Line;
   Display (-51, -14);
   New_Line;
end Modulo;
```

15. *Multiple choice.* If the array implementation of a queue were used, the statement

    ```
    Queue.Items(Queue.Front) := Queue.Items(Queue.Rear);
    ```

    (setting the first element equal to the last element) in an application program that uses the queue class

    a. would cause a syntax error at compile time.

    b. would cause a run-time error.

    c. would not be considered an error by the computer, but would violate the encapsulation of the queue data type.

    d. would be a perfectly legal and appropriate way to accomplish the intended task.

16. Here is an operation we could add to Specification 6.1 that compares two bounded queues for equality. Two queues are equal if and only if they contain the same elements in the same order.

    ```
    function "=" (Left  : in Queue_Type;
                  Right : in Queue_Type) return Boolean;
    ```

    Write the body for this function as if you were including it in Body 6.1.

17. Here is an operation we could add to Specification 6.1 that makes one bounded queue object a copy of another. This operation provides a way to assign one bounded queue to another.

    ```
    procedure Copy (Target : out Queue_Type;
                    Source : in  Queue_Type);
    -- Target is a copy of Source
    ```
    Write the body for this procedure as if you were including it in Body 6.1.

18. Here is an operation we could add to Specification 6.1 that removes a given number of items from a queue.

    ```
    procedure Cut_Back (Queue : in out Queue_Type;
                        By    : in     Positive);
    -- Remove By items from Queue
    -- Exceptions   : UNDERFLOW raised if By is greater than the number
    --               of elements currently in Queue.
    --               Queue is unchanged
    ```
    Write the body for this procedure as if you were including it in Body 6.1. Be sure that you leave the queue unchanged should the queue contain fewer values than the number in the cut back request.

19. Here is an operation we could add to Specification 6.1 that returns the number of items in a bounded queue.

    ```
    function Size (Queue : in Queue_Type) return Natural;
    -- Purpose        : Returns the number of elements in Queue
    -- Preconditions  : None
    -- Postconditions : The number of elements in Queue is returned
    ```
    Write the body for this procedure as if you were including it in Body 6.1.

20. For some simulation programs we need an inspector operation for our queue so that we can examine queue elements based on their location in the queue (the front of the queue is considered location 1, the second element from the front is considered location 2, etc.). The definition of the queue is exactly as we specify in this chapter, except we add the operation named Inspect with the following specification to Specification 6.1:

    ```
    function Inspect (Queue    : in Queue_Type;
                      Position : in Positive := 1) return Element_Type;
    -- Return a copy of an element in the queue without removing it
    -- Preconditions  : None
    -- Postconditions : Inspect = Queue element at Position, where position 1
    --                  is the front element, position 2 is the
    --                  element after the front element, etc.
    ```

```
-- Exceptions : UNDERFLOW         Raised on attempt to obtain a value from
--                                an empty queue.
--              CONSTRAINT_ERROR  Raised on attempt to return an element
--                                from a position not in the queue.
```
Write the body for this procedure as if you were including it in Body 6.1.

Linked Lists and Unbounded Queues

21. Given the following declarations:
    ```
    type Node-_-Type;
    type Node_Ptr is access Node_Type;
    type Node_Type is
       record
          Info : Integer;
          Next : Node_Ptr;
       end record;

    Start   : Node_Ptr;
    Current : Node_Ptr;
    ```

    a. What is the output of the following program fragment? Hint: Draw a box and arrow picture.
    ```
    Start   := new Node_Type'(Info => 5, Next => null);
    Current := Start;

    for Count in 7..9 loop
       Current.all.Next := new Node_Type'(Info => Count, Next => Start);
       Current          := Current.all.Next;
    end loop;

    for Count in 1..7 loop
       Put (Item => Current.all.Info, Width => 3);
       Current := Current.all.Next;
    end loop;

    Put (Item  => Current.all.Next.all.Next.all.Next.all.Info,
         Width => 3);
    ```

    b. What is the output of the following program fragment? Hint: Draw a box and arrow picture.
    ```
    Start := new Node_Type'(Info => 5, Next => null);
    Start.all.Next := new Node_Type'(Info => 16, Next => null);
    Start.all.Next.all.Next := new Node_Type'(Info => 27, Next => null);
    ```

```
Start.all.Next.all.Next.all.Next := new Node_Type'(Info => 38,
                                                   Next => null);
Current := Start;
loop
   exit when Current.all.Next = null;
   Put (Item => Current.all.Info, Width => 3);
   Current := Current.all.Next;
end loop;
```

22. A queue is implemented as a circular linked structure, as described in the chapter, with the external pointer accessing the "rear" element.

    a. Draw a sketch of a queue with one node.

    b. Draw a sketch of an empty queue.

    c. Write the `Clear` and `Empty` procedure bodies.

    d. Write the `Enqueue` and `Dequeue` procedure bodies.

23. Here is an operation we could add to Specification 6.2 that compares two bounded queues for equality. Two queues are equal if and only if they contain the same elements in the same order.

```
function "=" (Left  : in Queue_Type;
              Right : in Queue_Type) return Boolean;
```

    Write the body for this function as if you were including it in Body 6.2.

24. Here is an operation we could add to Specification 6.2 that makes one bounded queue object a copy of another. This operation provides a way to assign one bounded queue to another.

```
procedure Copy (Target : out Queue_Type;
                Source : in  Queue_Type);
-- Target is a copy of Source
```

    Write the body for this procedure as if you were including it in Body 6.2.

25. Here is an operation we could add to Specification 6.2 that removes a given number of items from a queue.

```
procedure Cut_Back (Queue : in out Queue_Type;
                    By    : in     Positive);
-- Remove By items from Queue
-- Exceptions  : UNDERFLOW raised if By is greater than the number
--               of elements currently in Queue.
--                  Queue is unchanged
```

    Write the body for this procedure as if you were including it in Body 6.2. Be sure that you leave the queue unchanged should the queue contain fewer values than the number in the cut back request.

26. Here is an operation we could add to Specification 6.2 that returns the number of items in a bounded queue.

```
function Size (Queue : in Queue_Type) return Natural;
-- Purpose        : Returns the number of elements in Queue
-- Preconditions  : None
-- Postconditions : The number of elements in Queue is returned
```
    Write the body for this procedure as if you were including it in Body 6.2.

27. For some simulation programs we need an inspector operation for our queue so that we can examine queue elements based on their location in the queue (the front of the queue is considered location 1, the second element from the front is considered location 2, etc.). The definition of the queue is exactly as we specify in this chapter, except we add the operation named Inspect with the following specification to Specification 6.2:

```
function Inspect (Queue    : in Queue_Type;
                  Position : in Positive := 1) return Element_Type;
-- Return a copy of an element in the queue without removing it
-- Preconditions  : None
-- Postconditions : Inspect = Queue element at Position, where position 1
--                            is the front element, position 2 is the
--                            element after the front element, etc.
-- Exceptions : UNDERFLOW        Raised on attempt to obtain a value from
--                               an empty queue.
--              CONSTRAINT_ERROR Raised on attempt to return an element
--                               from a position not in the queue.
```
Write the body for this procedure as if you were including it in Body 6.2.

Comparing Implementations

28. a. Does the circular linked list implementation described in the chapter and in Exercise 22 change the storage requirements of the queue, as compared with the linear linked queue?

    b. Does it change the Big-O approximations of the work required to do each operation?

29. A queue contains 12-byte elements. Assuming that an access value takes 4 bytes and an integer takes 2 bytes, and that the maximum queue size is 80 elements:

    a. Fill in the chart showing the storage requirements, using the implementations developed in the chapter.

Number of Elements	Space for Static Array-Based Queue	Space for Dynamic Linked Queue
0	_____	_____
20	_____	_____
40	_____	_____
60	_____	_____
80	_____	_____
100	_____	_____
120	_____	_____

b. At what point does the linked implementation take more space than the array-based implementation?

Programming Problems

30. A deque (pronounced "deck") is what you get when you cross a stack with a schizophrenic queue. You can add to and delete from either end of a deque. Maybe it should be called a FOLIFOLO (First Or Last In, First Or Last Out) structure.

    a. Using an array to contain the elements in the deque, write a generic package specification for a deque class. Your specification should include

        i. An extensible limited private type to define the deque class. When you complete this type in the private part of the package specification, include initial values so that every deque object starts off empty.

        ii. Underflow and overflow exceptions.

        iii. An operation to add an element to the front or the rear of the deque.

        iv. An operation to remove an element from the front or the rear of the deque.

        v. Operations to determine whether the deque is empty or full.

        vi. An operation to clear the deque.

        vii. Additional scalar types to support the above operations.

    b. Write the package body that implements the deque class.

    c. Write a complete test plan and test program to test your deque class.

31. a. Why is the linked queue implementation developed in this chapter inadequate for solving the Rouses Point hump yard application?

b. Extend the unbounded queue class defined in this chapter to obtain a queue class that is suitable for the Rouses Point hump yard application. The only things that you should need to change in the application are the `with` and `use` clauses and the queue instantiation.

32. The local medical clinic has decided to automate its scheduling services. You have been assigned to design a prototype version of the scheduler. The basic functions that the clinic has in mind are doctor check-in and check-out and patient check-in and check-out.

    A doctor checks in by telling the scheduler his or her name, an examination room number, and a medical specialty code. Each doctor has a favorite room. The scheduler checks to see whether the room is free. If so, it assigns this doctor to the room; if not, it rejects the request with a message, and the doctor can try again to check in. When a doctor checks out, the examination room is freed.

    A patient checking in gives a name, age, specialist code, and emergency indication. The scheduler tries to match up the patient with a doctor according to a set of rules that will be described below. If there is a match, the patient is seen by the assigned doctor. If this doctor is currently seeing a patient, the new patient is queued to see the doctor according to the emergency indicator. Usually there is no emergency, and the patient is put at the end of the doctor's waiting list; if there is an emergency, however, the patient is put at the front of the waiting list ahead of any other patients.

    The rules for assigning doctors to patients are as follows:

    a. Any patient under age 16 is assigned to see a pediatrician.

    b. Patients age 16 and older are assigned a doctor according to the specialty requested. If there is no doctor in the clinic with the requested specialty, the patient is assigned to a general practitioner (GP). If there is no GP, the patient can be assigned to any doctor.

    c. If there is more than one doctor of the requested specialty, the patient is assigned to the doctor with the shortest waiting list.

    When a patient checks out, the doctor he or she was assigned to is available to see the next patient if there is anyone on the waiting list.

    Input

    Because this is a prototype we will use simple text-based input and output. Your program should prompt the users to input the correct information. The initial prompt is

    ```
    Type D for Doctor or P for Patient:
    ```

    The next prompt is

    ```
    Type I for check-in or O for check-out:
    ```

    According to the request, your program should prompt the user for any other needed information, as indicated in the following table:

Action	Additional Information
Doctor check-in	Doctor's name Room number Specialty code
Doctor check-out	Doctor's name
Patient check-in	Patient's name Age Specialty (code requested) Emergency flag
Patient check-out	Patient's name Room number

You may define the format for the input processed by your program.

Output

The output for each request is in the form of messages to the user, according to the request, as indicated in the following table:

Action	Message
Doctor check-in	Confirmation that room is available or error message if room is in use
Doctor check-out	Goodbye message
Patient check-in	Message telling patient which room to go to and which doctor has been assigned; if no doctor available, apologetic message
Patient check-out	Goodbye message; at a later time we may add billing information at this point

In addition to printing the messages on the screen, you should also write the requests and messages to a transaction file (TRANSACT.OUT), to be turned in with your program listing.

Details and Assumptions

- There are 100 examination rooms at the clinic, each with a waiting room attached.
- Specialty codes are as follows:
    - PED   Pediatrics
    - GEN   General practice
    - INT   Internal medicine
    - CAR   Cardiology

SUR	Surgeon
OBS	Obstetrics
PSY	Psychiatry
NEU	Neurology
ORT	Orthopedics
DER	Dermatology
OPT	Ophthalmology
ENT	Ear, nose, and throat

- You may assume that no patient leaves without checking out. (That is, every doctor becomes free eventually.)
- No one leaves before he or she sees the assigned doctor. (That is, no one has to be taken out of the waiting queue.) The clinic is open 24 hours a day, 7 days a week.
- If a doctor checks out while there is still a waiting list of patients assigned to him or her, the patients must be reassigned to other doctors.

Examination rooms are major objects in this problem. Each examination room may have a doctor, a patient, and a waiting list.

The clinic is a collection of examination rooms. The number of rooms is fixed, so you may use an array of records to represent it.

Develop scenarios and use CRC cards to investigate the collaborations of the objects in this problem. You will discover additional objects as you run through various scenarios.

Key-Ordered Lists

Goals for this chapter include that you should be able to

- describe the structure of a key-ordered list and its operations at the abstract level.
- describe the categories of operations for container classes.
- describe how a key-ordered list may be implemented as a sequential or a linked structure.
- implement the following list operations for both sequential and linked implementations:
  - Determine whether the list is empty or full.
  - Clear a list.
  - Insert an element.
  - Retrieve an element.
  - Modify an element.
  - Delete an element.
  - Traverse the list elements in order.
- contrast the sequential and linked implementations of a list in terms of the Big-O approximations of their operations.

We all know intuitively what a "list" is; in our everyday lives we use lists all the time—grocery lists, lists of things to do, lists of addresses, lists of party guests. In this chapter and the next we look at the list class from our three perspectives.

7.1 The Logical Level

In computer programs, lists are very useful and common data structures. From a programming point of view, a list is a *homogeneous* collection of elements, with a linear relationship between the elements. This definition means that, at the logical level, each element in the list except the first one has a unique predecessor and each element except the last one has a unique successor. (At the implementation level, there is also a relationship between the elements, but the physical relationship may not be the same as the logical one.) Lists can be unordered—their elements may be placed into the list in no particular order. Lists also can be ordered in different ways. For instance, stacks and queues are lists that are ordered according to the time when their elements were added.

Lists also can be ordered *by value*; for instance, a list of strings can be ordered alphabetically, or a list of grades can be ordered numerically. Often a value-ordered list is called a **sorted list**. When the elements in a value-ordered list are records, rather than scalar data, their logical (and often physical) order is determined by one of the fields in the record, the record **key**. For example, we can order a list of students on the dean's list alphabetically by name or numerically by student ID. In the first case, the Name field of the record is the key; in the second case, the ID field is the key. Such value-ordered lists also are called **key-ordered lists**.

> **Sorted list** A list in which the elements are ordered by their value.
>
> **Key** A field in a record whose values are used to determine the logical order of records in a list.
>
> **Key-ordered list** A list in which the elements are records and are ordered according to the value of a key field of each element.
>
> **Container class** A class that consists of a collection of components organized by a data structure.

If a list cannot contain records with duplicate keys, it is considered to have *unique keys*. To generalize our list nomenclature, we can consider a list of scalar values to be a list whose elements are keys. This chapter deals with lists of elements with unique keys, ordered from smallest to largest key value.

Operations

Designing a class to be used by many applications is not the same as designing an application to solve a specific problem. In the latter case we can use CRC cards to enact scenarios of the application's use, allowing us to identify and fix holes in our design before turning to implementation. Identifying scenarios for use of a general class is not as straightforward. We must stand back and consider what operations every user of the data type would want it to provide.

In this text we concentrate on classes that consist of collections of components organized by some data structure. Such classes are called **container classes** or collection classes. Stacks, queues, and key-ordered lists are all examples of container classes. The

Ada library contains a number of container classes (including sets, maps, vectors, and lists) rooted at package `Ada.Containers`.

In Chapter 1 we described three categories of operations: constructors, observers, and transformers. We begin this section by reviewing each of those categories from the perspective of a container class. We introduce two additional categories for container classes: destructors and iterators.

A **constructor** is used to initialize the structure of a collection class. In Ada, an object is generally constructed during the elaboration of a variable. We often supply information to initialize the object for our application. For example, when declaring bounded stack and queue objects, we specified a maximum size for the collection. Because this information varies from application to application, it is logical for the client to have to provide it. At the implementation level we supplied default values to ensure that the structure of each new stack and queue was initialized to empty. Procedures and functions that return a new object are also constructors. For example, in Chapter 1 we used the function `Construct_Date` to initialize a new instance of a `Date_Type` object. The `Replicate` and `"*"` operations available for Ada's three string classes are also constructors.

> **Constructor** An operation used to initialize the structure of an instance of a collection class.
>
> **Destructor** An operation used to destroy the structure of an instance of a container class.
>
> **Transformer** An operation that changes the structure of an instance of a collection class.

Some suggest that it is a good idea to include a copy constructor when defining a class. A *copy constructor* accepts an instance of the class as a parameter and creates a copy of it. Although there are situations in which a copy constructor can be helpful for an application programmer who is using a container class such as a stack, queue, or list, these situations are rare. We did not define any copy constructors for our stack or queue classes—they were left as exercises.

Ada's controlled types give us more control over the creation, copying, and destruction of objects. We can override the `Initialize` operation to define what we want to happen when an object is created. Objects are created either by the elaboration of an object declaration or through dynamic allocation. We can override the `Adjust` operation to define what we want to happen when an assignment statement assigns a new value to an object. `Adjust` is commonly used to create copies of linked structures rather than aliases. We used `Initialize` and `Adjust` in our unbounded-length string class developed in Chapter 4.

With controlled types we can also override the `Finalize` operation to define what happens when an object goes out of scope. `Finalize` is an example of a **destructor**. Destructors typically undo things a constructor has done. Our unbounded stack and queue classes developed in the previous chapters used `Finalize` to recycle all the nodes in the linked list that we used to store the collection of elements.

Transformers (also called *mutators*) are operations that change the content of an object's structure in some way. We need transformers to put an item into the structure or to remove a specific item from the structure. Our stack operations `Push` and `Pop` and our queue operations `Enqueue` and `Dequeue` are all examples of transformers. Another transformer is one that makes the structure empty. Our stack and queue classes provided a `Clear` operation to do just that. String operations such as `Trim`, `Delete`, `Insert`,

`Overwrite`, `Replace_Slice`, and `Translate` also are examples of transformers. A transformer that takes two objects and combines them into one is a *binary transformer*. The `Append` and `"&"` operations available for strings are binary transformers.

Observers also come in several forms. They ask true/false questions[1] about the object. (Is the structure empty?) They select or access a particular item. (Give me a copy of the last item.) Or they return a property of the structure. (How many items are in the structure?) Our stack and queue classes had two observer operations: `Empty` and `Full`. In the exercises we asked you to implement the observer operation `Size`. The string classes have many observers including `Length`, `Slice`, `Element`, `Index`, `Find_Token`, and `Count`.

> **Observer** An operation that returns an observation on the state of an instance of a collection class.
>
> **Iterator** An operation that allows us to process all of the components of a data structure.

If a container class has limits on the type of its components, we could define other observers. For example, if we know that our class is a list of numerical values, we could define statistical observers such as minimum, maximum, and average. Here at the logical level, we are interested in generality; we know nothing about the type of the items in the collection, so we use only general observers.

An **iterator** is an operation that allows us to process all the components of the data structure within the collection class in sequence. Iterators do not alter the data structure; however, they may alter individual elements within the data structure. An operation that prints all the elements in a queue is an iterator. So is an operation that adds 10 to the final exam score for each student in a list of students.

A Key-Ordered List Specification

Specification 7.1 defines a key-ordered list class with a small collection of basic list operations. The transformers are operations to add a new element, to delete an element, to modify an element, and to clear the list. The observers are operations to determine whether a list is empty or full, to determine the number of elements in the list, and to retrieve a copy of an element given its key. We include an iterator, which the application programmer may use to process all of the elements in the list in ascending order by key.

Specification 7.1   Key-Ordered List Class

```
generic
   type Element_Type is private;       -- The type of element in the list
   type Key_Type     is limited private;  -- The type of key

   -- The user must supply a function that returns the Key of an Element
   with function Key_Of (Element : in Element_Type) return Key_Type;
   -- The user must supply functions for comparing Keys
   with function "=" (Left : in Key_Type; Right : in Key_Type) return Boolean;
   with function "<" (Left : in Key_Type; Right : in Key_Type) return Boolean;
package Key_Ordered_List is
```

---

[1]An operation that returns a Boolean value defined on a set of objects is sometimes called a *predicate*.

```ada
-- This package implements a key-ordered list class.

-- Each element in a list has a unique key.

-- The elements in a list are ordered from smallest to largest using the "<"
-- function supplied as a generic parameter.  The key value of the predecessor
-- of an element is less than the key value of the element, which is less than
-- the key value of the successor of the element.

   type List_Type (Max_Size : Positive) is tagged limited private;

   DUPLICATE_KEY  : exception;
   KEY_ERROR      : exception;
   OVERFLOW       : exception;

-- Transformers

   ------------------------------------------------------------------------
   procedure Clear (List : in out List_Type);
   -- Purpose         : Removes all elements from List.
   -- Preconditions   : None
   -- Postconditions  : List is empty.


   ------------------------------------------------------------------------
   procedure Insert (List : in out List_Type;
                     Item : in      Element_Type);
   -- Purpose         : Adds Item to List.
   -- Preconditions   : None
   -- Postconditions  : List = original list + Item
   -- Exceptions      : OVERFLOW       If there is no room for Item.
   --                                  List is unchanged.
   --                   DUPLICATE_KEY  If an element already exists in the list
   --                                  with the same key as Item.
   --                                  List is unchanged.


   ------------------------------------------------------------------------
   procedure Delete (List : in out List_Type;
                     Key  : in      Key_Type);
   -- Purpose         : Deletes the element containing Key from List.
   -- Preconditions   : None
   -- Postconditions  : List = original list without element identified by Key
   -- Exceptions      : KEY_ERROR  If there is no element with Key in List.
   --                              List is unchanged.


   ------------------------------------------------------------------------
```

```
procedure Modify (List    : in out List_Type;
                  Element : in     Element_Type);
-- Purpose        : Replaces existing list element.
-- Preconditions  : None
-- Postconditions : List = original list with value of Element replacing
--                         like-keyed original element
-- Exceptions     : KEY_ERROR  If there is no element with the key of
--                             Element in List.  List is unchanged.


-- Observers

-----------------------------------------------------------------------
procedure Retrieve (List    : in     List_Type;
                    Key     : in     Key_Type;
                    Element :    out Element_Type);
-- Purpose        : Gets a copy of the element that contains Key.
-- Preconditions  : None
-- Postconditions : Element = copy of element containing Key
--                  List is unchanged.
-- Exceptions     : KEY_ERROR  If there is no element with the
--                             Key in List.  List is unchanged.

-----------------------------------------------------------------------
function Full (List : in List_Type) return Boolean;
-- Purpose        : Tests whether List is full.  List is full when
--                  no more elements can be inserted into it.
-- Preconditions  : None
-- Postconditions : Full = (List is full)

-----------------------------------------------------------------------
function Empty (List : in List_Type) return Boolean;
-- Purpose        : Tests whether List is empty (contains no elements).
-- Preconditions  : None
-- Postconditions : Empty = (List is empty)

-----------------------------------------------------------------------
function Length (List : in List_Type) return Natural;
-- Purpose        : Determines the number of elements in List.
-- Preconditions  : None
-- Postconditions : Length = number of elements in List


-- Iterator

-----------------------------------------------------------------------
```

```ada
   procedure Traverse
        (List    : in out List_Type;
         Process : not null access procedure (Element : in out Element_Type));
   -- Purpose         : To process all the elements in List in ascending order
   -- Preconditions   : Procedure Process does not change the key of an element
   -- Postconditions  : Every element in List is passed to a call of
   --                   procedure Process
   --                   Elements processed in ascending order

private

   -- We will fill this in later

end Key_Ordered_List;
```

Sample Package Instantiations

This generic list package has the most elaborate set of generic formal parameters that we have used. To instantiate a list we must supply two types and three functions. These five parameters allow us to use the generic list package for many different key-ordered lists; our list package is very reusable. Let's look at some examples that instantiate list packages from this generic declaration.

Example 1: A List of Inventory Records First let's examine a list whose elements are simple inventory records. Each inventory record contains a part name (a string containing no more than 40 characters) and the number in stock. The part name is the key for our inventory record. Using a bounded string type for the part name, here are the necessary declarations for our list element:

```ada
-- Instantiate a bounded-length string class for part names
package Part_Names is new Ada.Strings.Bounded.Generic_Bounded_Length(40);
use     Part_Names;

-- Declare a synonym for clarity
subtype Name_String is Part_Names.Bounded_String;

-- A simple inventory record
type Part_Rec is
   record
      Name            : Name_String;
      Number_In_Stock : Natural := 0;
   end record;
```

We now have the types for our list element (`Part_Rec`) and key (`Name_String`). The functions for comparing keys are available from package `Part_Names`. We must, however, write our own function that returns the key of an element. This function simply returns the value of the `Name` field of our part record.

```
function Name_Of (Part : in Part_Rec) return Name_String is
begin
   return Part.Name;
end Name_Of;
```

Here, then, is the code necessary to instantiate a package for a key-ordered list of part records:

```
-- Instantiate an ADT for an ordered list of inventory records
package Part_List is new Key_Ordered_List (Element_Type => Part_Rec,
                                           Key_Type     => Name_String,
                                           Key_Of       => Name_Of,
                                           "="          => Part_Names."=",
                                           "<"          => Part_Names."<");
```

Example 2: A List of Integers Now let's look at an instantiation of a list whose elements are integer values. In a simple list like this one, the integer element is the key. We supply `Integer` for both formal generic type parameters, `Element_Type` and `Key_Type`. The functions (`"="` and `"<"`) for comparing integer values are predefined by Ada in package `Standard`. That leaves only one more generic parameter: the function that returns the key of an element. Again, we must write that function ourselves. Because the key and element of this simple list of integers are the same, this function just needs to return the element. We call this function `Identity`. Here is the code for it:

```
function Identity (Element : in Integer) return Integer is
begin
   return Element;
end Identity ;
```

Now that we know all of the actual parameter values to supply, we can write the instantiation for our simple list of integers. The use of the prefix `Standard` is optional; we include it to document that these operators are predefined in the language rather than in our application or by another class.

```ada
-- Instantiate an ADT for a sorted list of Integers
package Integer_List is new Key_Ordered_List (Element_Type => Integer,
                                              Key_Type     => Integer,
                                              Key_Of       => Identity,
                                              "="          => Standard."=",
                                              "<"          => Standard."<");
```

Using the Iterator

Procedure `Traverse`, the iterator in Specification 7.1, has two parameters. `List` is an instance of the key-ordered list class to which we wish to apply the iterator. `Process` is a pointer to the procedure that `Traverse` will call for each element in `List`. Until now the only access types that we have used are designated objects. This parameter is our first example of an access value that designates a subprogram. Here is an EBNF (Extended Backus-Naur Form) definition of access type that describes the commonly used options.

access_type_definition	::=	[**not null**] access_to_object_definition |
		[**not null**] access_to_subprogram_definition
access_to_object_definition	::=	**access** [general_access_modifier] subtype_indication
general_access_modifier	::=	**all** | **constant**
access_to_subprogram_definition	::=	**access procedure** parameter_profile |
		access function parameter_and_result_profile

In Chapter 6 you learned that the optional word `all` is used in the declaration of an access type that can designate memory for either named or unnamed objects. The optional word `constant` is used when we wish to treat the designated object as a constant. An attempt to modify such an object through the access value will be caught by the compiler or the run-time system.

The optional words `not null` indicate that an access object cannot be given the value null. This modifier is often used for access types used as formal subprogram parameters to ensure that the actual parameter is not `null`. Our use of `not null` for parameter `Process` requires that the application programmer pass a pointer to a procedure with the given parameter profile. An attempt to use `null` as an actual parameter will be flagged by the compiler.

The declaration of parameter `Process` illustrates a use of an anonymous access type. `Process` is an access type that designates a procedure with a single `in out` mode parameter, `Element`. We use `in out` mode so that the process procedure can modify the element. When we call procedure `Traverse`, our actual access parameter must designate a procedure with the same parameter profile.

Let's look at how an application programmer can use the iterator. Here are the declarations for a list of auto parts using the key-ordered part list class instantiated on page 410.

```
-- Declare a list object
Auto_Part_List : Part_List.List_Type (Max_Size => 500);
```

Suppose, for reordering purposes, we would like to display the name of every part in this inventory list for which there are less than 10 in stock. This requires that we go through our entire list of parts. For each part we check to see if there are less than 10 in stock. If there are less than 10, we display the part name. We write the code for *processing one part* in a procedure whose parameter profile matches that defined for the formal parameter `Process`. Here is a procedure for checking the number in stock of *one* particular part:

```
procedure Check_One_Part (Part : in out Part_Rec) is
begin
   if Part.Number_In_Stock < 10 then
      Put_Line (To_String (Part.Name));
   end if;
end Check_One_Part;
```

Because the procedure is not modifying `Part`, we wouldn't normally use `in out` mode for this parameter. However, in order to pass this procedure to our iterator, `Traverse`, we must match the parameter profile given for the access to procedure type used in the declaration of the formal parameter `Process`.

We now have everything we need to call procedure `Traverse` to iterate through all of the elements in our list to check the amount in stock of each part and display a message should the quantity in stock be under 10. We can use the normal procedure call syntax

```
Traverse (List    => Auto_Part_List,
          Process => Check_One_Part'Access);
```

or use the object.method syntax

```
Auto_Part_List.Traverse (Process => Check_One_Part'Access);
```

In Chapter 6 we used `'Access` to obtain the location of an aliased named object. As you can see in the above calls, we can also use `'Access` to obtain the location of a subprogram.

Let's look at a second example of calling `Traverse`. This time we want to display all of the negative numbers in a list of type `Integer_List.List_Type`. Here is such a list:

```
-- Declare a list object
Number_List : Integer_List.List_Type (Max_Size => 100);
```

We need to write a procedure to process one element of our list. This procedure checks that the element is negative and prints it if it is:

```
procedure Put_If_Negative (Element : in out Integer) is
begin
   if Element < 0 then
      Put (Item => Element, Width => 6);
      New_Line;
   end if;
end Put_If_Negative;
```

Finally, we display all of the negative numbers in `Number_List` by using its `Traverse` operation and our procedure to display a number if it is negative.

```
Number_List.Traverse (Process => Put_If_Negative'Access);
```

We give additional examples of using `Traverse` in the application developed in the next section.

7.2 The Application Level

We can use the list specification presented in the previous section in a variety of applications that need a collection of key-ordered elements. In this section we look at one application in detail.

An Electronic Address Book

You just purchased the latest model portable digital assistant, a pocket-sized computer that helps you keep notes, schedule appointments, and look up important information. This model is so new that the software for the address book has not been released yet. Because you already have a generic key-ordered list package available, you decide that you can easily write your own address book software to keep track of all your friends. You'd like to use this address book in several different applications.

The Specification   Each friend has several pieces of data associated with them:

1. A name
2. An address
3. A phone number
4. A birthday

This description of a friend suggests a record with four fields—one for each of the four pieces of data. All of these pieces of data have subdata associated with them. A name consists of a first name and a last name. A record is a good way to keep track of these two different parts of a name. Likewise, a record is a good way to store the four parts that make up an address (street, city, state, and ZIP). For simplicity, we assume that all our friends are in the United States. What about the phone number? We could store it as a single 10-digit number or as a record with a 3-digit area code and 7-digit number. Because it is possible in the future that we may want to process friends by area code, let's use a record to separate the area code from the number. A birthday seems like an excellent candidate for using a record; there are three numeric fields—day, month, and year. We could make up our own subtypes to limit the ranges of these fields, but there is an alternative. The library package `Ada.Calendar` contains useful types, subtypes, and operations for dealing with time and dates. It includes appropriate numeric subtypes for calendar days, months, and years.

Next let's consider what you should be able to do with an address book. Of course you should be able to look up a name, add a new name (along with relevant information), and delete a name. You also should be able to change the information when a friend moves or changes their phone number. And there is another type of change our program should handle. Our friend Suzanne Pawlan was married last July 3 and became Suzanne Levy. So our address book had better allow us to change a person's name. Let's also make it possible to find out if any of our friends have a birthday coming up this month. Finally, let's make it possible to print out address labels.

One more thing—because we want to keep all our data between runs of our program, we need to be able to save our list information in a file. Specification 7.2 describes a generic ADO for our address book. We can create an address book for any application by instantiating an address book from this generic package.

Specification 7.2   Address Book ADO

```ada
with Ada.Strings.Bounded;
with Ada.Calendar;
generic
   -- The upper bound on the number of entries in the address book
   Max_Friends : in Positive;
   -- Name of a sequential binary file to store the address book between runs
   Friend_File_Name : in String;
   -- A bounded-length string package used for names and addresses
   with package Strings is new Ada.Strings.Bounded.Generic_Bounded_Length (<>);
package Address_Book is

   -- This abstract data object models an address book.

   -- Bounded String Type synonyms for clarity
   subtype Name_String    is Strings.Bounded_String;
   subtype Address_String is Strings.Bounded_String;
```

```ada
subtype State_String is String (1..2);

subtype Digit      is character range '0'..'9';
type Digit_String is array (Positive range <>) of Digit;

subtype Zip_String        is Digit_String (1..5);
subtype Area_Code_String is Digit_String (1..3);
subtype Phone_Num_String is Digit_String (1..7);

type Name_Rec is                    -- Name data
   record
      First : Name_String;
      Last  : Name_String;
   end record;

type Address_Rec is                 -- Address data
   record
      Street : Address_String;
      City   : Address_String;
      State  : State_String;
      Zip    : Zip_String;
   end record;

type Phone_Rec is                   -- Phone number data
   record
      Area   : Area_Code_String;
      Number : Phone_Num_String;
   end record;

type Date_Rec is
   record
      Year  : Ada.Calendar.Year_Number;
      Month : Ada.Calendar.Month_Number;
      Day   : Ada.Calendar.Day_Number;
   end record;

type Friend_Rec is                  -- Friend data
   record
      Name    : Name_Rec;
      Address : Address_Rec;
      Phone   : Phone_Rec;
      Birthday : Date_Rec;
   end record;

-- Exceptions
```

```ada
    DUPLICATE_NAME : Exception;
    MISSING_NAME   : Exception;
    OVERFLOW       : Exception;
```

-- *Transformers*

---

procedure Add (Friend : **in** Friend_Rec);
-- *Purpose   : Add a friend to the address book.*
-- *Preconditions : None*
-- *Postconditions : Address Book = Original Address Book + Friend*
-- *Exceptions   : DUPLICATE_NAME raised when the name of Friend*
--   *is already in the address book.*
--   *The address book is not changed.*
--   *OVERFLOW raised when attempting to add a name to*
--   *an address book with Max_Friends names.*
--   *The address book is not changed.*

---

procedure Delete (Name : **in** Name_Rec);
-- *Purpose   : Delete a friend from the address book.*
-- *Preconditions : None*
-- *Postconditions : Address Book = Original Address Book - friend with Name*
-- *Exceptions   : MISSING_NAME raised when Name is not found in*
--   *the address book.*
--   *The address book is not changed.*

---

procedure Change (Friend : **in** Friend_Rec);
-- *Purpose   : Replace information on a friend with new information*
-- *Preconditions : None*
-- *Postconditions : The information in Friend replaces the information*
--   *for the friend in the address book.*

-- *Exceptions   : MISSING_NAME raised when the name in Friend is not found*
--   *in the address book.*
--   *The address book is not changed.*

---

procedure Change_Name (Old_Name : **in** Name_Rec;
                       New_Name : **in** Name_Rec);
-- *Purpose   : Changes a friend's name.*
-- *Preconditions : None*
-- *Postconditions : The New_Name replaces Old_Name in the address book*
-- *Exceptions   : MISSING_NAME raised when Old_Name is not found in the*

```ada
--                             address book.
--                             The address book is not changed.
--                  DUPLICATE_NAME raised when New_Name is already in the
--                             address book.
--                             The address book is not changed.

-- Observers

-------------------------------------------------------------------------------
procedure Lookup (Name   : in  Name_Rec;
                  Friend : out Friend_Rec);
-- Purpose        : Return information on the friend associated with Name
-- Preconditions  : None
-- Postconditions : Friend = Information associated with Name.
--                  The address book is not changed.

-- Exceptions     : MISSING_NAME raised when Name is not found in the
--                               address book.
--                               The address book is not changed.

-------------------------------------------------------------------------------
procedure Labels (File_Name : in String);
-- Purpose        : Creates labels for all friends in the address book
-- Preconditions  : None
-- Postconditions : A text file is created with the given name containing
--                  mailing labels for all friends in the address book.
--                  Labels are in alphabetical order by name.

-------------------------------------------------------------------------------
procedure Birthdays (Month : in Ada.Calendar.Month_Number);
-- Purpose        : Display the names of all friends having a birthday in
--                  the given Month.
-- Preconditions  : None
-- Postconditions : The names of all friends with birthdays in Month are
--                  displayed in alphabetical order by name.

-------------------------------------------------------------------------------
procedure Save;
-- Purpose        : Save the current address book to disk.
-- Preconditions  : None
-- Postconditions : The current address book is saved for a future run.

end Address_Book;
```

We need to specify three actual parameters when we instantiate this generic package. The first two are simple values—the upper bound on the number of friends we can store in the address book and the name of the file in which we want to store our address book data between runs. The third parameter is one we have not yet discussed—it is a generic formal package. Generic formal package parameters allow us to pass an instance of another generic package to our generic unit. In Specification 7.2, our actual generic parameter must be an instance of the generic bounded-length string package we examined in Chapter 4. Looking at the record type declarations in the specification you can see that this string class is used for all the varying-length strings needed in our address book. First and last names, street addresses, and cities are all stored as bounded-length strings defined by the actual package parameter.

Here is a code fragment from an application that supplies an actual package parameter to create a specific instance of this address book:

```
-- Instantiate a bounded-length string class from the Ada library
package My_Strings is new Ada.Strings.Bounded.Generic_Bounded_Length(20);

-- Create an instance of an address book
package My_Book is new Address_Book(Max_Friends      => 250,
                                    Friend_File_Name => "friends.seq",
                                    Strings          => My_Strings);
```

This code fragment creates an address book with an upper bound of 250 entries. Each entry stores its names, street addresses, and city names as bounded-length strings defined in the package `My_Strings`.

An alternative design is to pass an upper bound for our varying-length string parameter rather than pass a bounded-length string package. With this approach we would instantiate the string class within the address book specification rather than in the application. There is no significant advantage of one approach over the other. We chose the package parameter to illustrate a new type of generic formal parameter.

The Implementation You probably have noted the similarity between this address book object and the key-ordered list class we developed earlier in this chapter. The address book is a kind of key-ordered list. In this application, we can use our list class as the foundation for our address book object. Figure 7.1 shows the relationship between the address book abstract data object (ADO) and the key-ordered list class.

Body 7.1 contains the code to implement the `Address_Book` ADO. The first set of declarations in this body instantiates a key-ordered list package whose elements are type `Friend_Rec` and whose keys are type `Name_Rec`. We wrote functions to return the name portion of a `Friend_Rec` and compare two names. We used these functions as actual generic subprogram parameters in our instantiation of package `Friend_List`. The package variable, `The_Book`, is the list object used globally by all of the address book operations.

7.2 The Application Level | 419

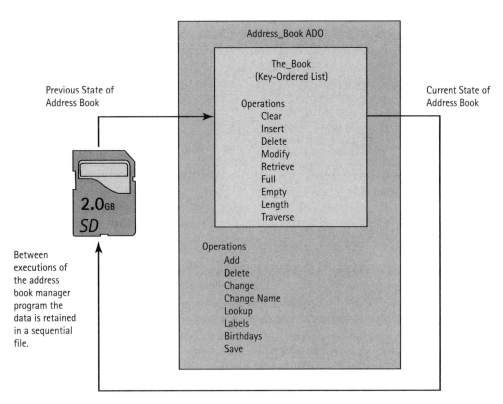

Figure 7.1 *The program data (a key-ordered list) and retained data (sequential file).*

Body 7.1   **Address Book ADO: Implements Specification 7.2**

```
with Ada.Sequential_IO;
with Ada.Text_IO;
with Ada.Integer_Text_IO;
with Ada.IO_Exceptions;
with Key_Ordered_List;
package body Address_Book is

   use Strings;      -- Bounded string package provided as generic parameter
   use Ada.Text_IO;
   use Ada.Integer_Text_IO;

   --------------------------------------------------------------------------
   -- Everything needed to instantiate a key-ordered list of friends
   --------------------------------------------------------------------------
   function Name_Of (Friend : in Friend_Rec) return Name_Rec is
   begin
```

```ada
      return Friend.Name;
end Name_Of;

function "<" (Left : in Name_Rec; Right : in Name_Rec) return Boolean is
begin
   return (Left.Last < Right.Last) or
          (Left.Last = Right.Last and Left.First < Right.First);
end "<";

package Friend_List is new Key_Ordered_List (Element_Type => Friend_Rec,
                                             Key_Type     => Name_Rec,
                                             Key_Of       => Name_Of,
                                             "="          => "=",
                                             "<"          => "<");
-- The address book object
The_Book : Friend_List.List_Type (Max_Size => Max_Friends);


-------------------------------------------------------------------------------
-- Resources for saving address book between program runs
-------------------------------------------------------------------------------
package Friend_IO is new Ada.Sequential_IO (Element_Type => Friend_Rec);
Friend_File : Friend_IO.File_Type;    -- File of Friend records
Friend      : Friend_Rec;             -- One file element (used during initialization)



-------------------------------------------------------------------------------
-- Operation Bodies
-------------------------------------------------------------------------------
procedure Add (Friend : in Friend_Rec) is
begin
   The_Book.Insert (Friend);
exception
   when Friend_List.DUPLICATE_KEY =>
      raise DUPLICATE_NAME;      -- Name already in address book
   when Friend_List.OVERFLOW =>
      raise OVERFLOW;            -- Address book is full
end Add;


-------------------------------------------------------------------------------
procedure Delete (Name : in Name_Rec) is
begin
   The_Book.Delete (Name);
exception
   when Friend_List.KEY_ERROR =>
      raise MISSING_NAME;    -- Name not in address book
```

```ada
end Delete;
```

```ada
procedure Lookup (Name   : in  Name_Rec;
                  Friend : out Friend_Rec) is
begin
   The_Book.Retrieve (Key     => Name,
                      Element => Friend);
exception
   when Friend_List.KEY_ERROR =>
      raise MISSING_NAME;  -- Name not in address book

end Lookup;
```

```ada
procedure Change (Friend : in Friend_Rec) is
begin
   The_Book.Modify (Friend);
exception
   when Friend_List.KEY_ERROR =>
      raise MISSING_NAME;  -- Name not in address book
end Change;
```

```ada
procedure Change_Name (Old_Name : in Name_Rec;
                       New_Name : in Name_Rec) is
   Friend : Friend_Rec;
begin
   -- Retrieve the old information
   The_Book.Retrieve (Key     => Old_Name,
                      Element => Friend);
         -- Change the name
   Friend.Name := New_Name;
   -- Add the new name to the address book
   The_Book.Insert (Friend);
   -- Delete the old name from the address book
   The_Book.Delete (Old_Name);
exception
   when Friend_List.KEY_ERROR =>
      raise MISSING_NAME;    -- Old Name not in address book
   when Friend_List.DUPLICATE_KEY =>
      raise DUPLICATE_NAME;  -- New Name already in address book
end Change_Name;
```

```ada
procedure Put_Digits (File : in File_Type; Item : Digit_String) is
-- Put an array of digits into File
begin
   -- Each iteration, display one character in the array of digits
   for Index in Item'Range loop
      Ada.Text_IO.Put (File => File, Item => Item(Index));
   end loop;
end Put_Digits;
```

```ada
procedure Labels (File_Name : in String) is
   Label_File : Ada.Text_IO.File_Type;

   -- Local procedure for printing one label
   procedure Put_One_Label (Friend : in out Friend_Rec) is
   begin
      Put_Line (File => Label_File,
                Item => To_String(Friend.Name.First) & ' ' &
                        To_String(Friend.Name.Last));
      Put_Line (File => Label_File,
                Item => To_String(Friend.Address.Street));
      Put_Line (File => Label_File,
                Item => To_String(Friend.Address.City) & ", " &
                        Friend.Address.State & ' ');
      Put_Digits (File => Label_File,
                  Item => Friend.Address.Zip);
      New_Line(File => Label_File, Spacing => 2);
   end Put_One_Label;

begin
   Ada.Text_IO.Create (File => Label_File,
                       Name => File_Name);
   The_Book.Traverse (Put_One_Label'Access);
   Ada.Text_IO.Close (Label_File);
end Labels;
```

```ada
procedure Birthdays (Month : in Ada.Calendar.Month_Number) is
   use Ada.Calendar;  -- For the two constant declarations
   Current_Date_Time : constant Time        := Ada.Calendar.Clock;
   Current_Year      : constant Year_Number := Year(Current_Date_Time);

   -- Local procedure for examining one friend's birthday
   procedure Check_One_Birthday (Friend : in out Friend_Rec) is
   begin
```

```ada
         if Month = Friend.Birthday.Month then
            Put (To_String (Friend.Name.First) & ' ' &
                 To_String (Friend.Name.Last)  & " is ");
            Put (Item  => Current_Year - Friend.Birthday.Year,
                 Width => 1);
            Put_Line (" years old");
         end if;
      end Check_One_Birthday;

   begin
      The_Book.Traverse (Check_One_Birthday'Access);
   end Birthdays;

   ---------------------------------------------------------------------------

   procedure Save is

      -- Local procedure to write one friend to the file
      procedure Write_One_Friend (Friend : in out Friend_Rec) is
      begin
         Friend_IO.Write (File => Friend_File, Item => Friend);
      end Write_One_Friend;

   begin
      Friend_IO.Create (File => Friend_File, Name => Friend_File_Name);
      The_Book.Traverse (Write_One_Friend'Access);
      Friend_IO.Close (Friend_File);
   end Save;

   ---------------------------------------------------------------------------

begin  -- Initialize the Address Book

   Friend_IO.Open (File => Friend_File,
                   Mode => Friend_IO.In_File,
                   Name => Friend_File_Name);
   -- Get all of the friends from the disk file
   -- Each iteration, one friend is read from the file and added to the book
   loop
      exit when Friend_IO.End_Of_File (Friend_File);
      Friend_IO.Read (File => Friend_File, Item => Friend);
      The_Book.Insert (Friend);
   end loop;
   Friend_IO.Close (Friend_File);

exception
   when Ada.IO_Exceptions.NAME_ERROR =>
```

```
                  -- Handles first run of program where there is no saved address book
                  Put_Line ("Creating the initial Address Book");
               when Friend_List.OVERFLOW =>
                  -- A smaller value of Max_Friends was used for this run
                  -- than the run that created the file
                  Put_Line ("More friends in file than space in the address book.");
                  raise OVERFLOW;
            end Address_Book;
```

> **Consultation** An implementation mechanism in which an object forwards an operation to another object.

Many of the address book operations are carried out through **consultation**, an implementation mechanism in which an object forwards an operation to another object.[2] For example, the address book `Add` operation simply invokes the key-ordered list's `Insert` operation to place the new `Friend` into `The_Book`. Should the insertion raise a key-ordered list exception, `Add` handles it by raising an address book-specific exception.

Because the key-ordered list class has no operation for changing the key of an element in the list, the `Change_Name` operation is done in four steps. First we retrieve the record for the old name from `The_Book`. Then we change the name field of the record. Next we insert this "new" record into `The_Book`. At this point `The_Book` contains two records for our friend—one keyed by the old name and the other keyed by the new name. Finally we delete the element keyed with the old name from `The_Book`. Two things could go wrong in this sequence of steps. There may be no entry in `The_Book` keyed to the old name. In this case the key-ordered list operation `Retrieve` raises its `KEY_ERROR` exception, which `Change_Name` handles by raising the exception `MISSING_NAME`. Should the new name be the key for another friend already in `The_Book`, the ordered list `Insert` operation raises its `DUPLICATE_KEY` exception, which `Change_Name` handles by raising the exception `DUPLICATE_NAME`. In both error cases, the original address book is left unchanged.

The `Labels`, `Birthdays`, and `Save` operations each require processing of all of the elements in `The_Book`. So it should come as no surprise that their implementation makes use of `Traverse`.

The declarative part of procedure `Labels` contains two items: a file variable for the text file to which we want the labels to be written and the local procedure `Put_One_Label` that puts one label into the file. Procedure `Labels` creates the text file and calls the `Traverse` procedure to process all of the elements in `The_Book`. We have passed the location of the local procedure, `Put_One_Label`, to the traversal procedure, which calls it for every friend in the address book. Why did we nest procedure `Put_One_Label` within procedure `Labels`? Notice that procedure `Put_One_Label` accesses the global variable `Label_File`. Had we not done this nesting, we would have had to make the variable `Label_File` global to the entire package. By nesting, we can restrict the scope of this variable and still give our processing procedure access to it.

---

[2] In the past, this mechanism was called *delegation*.

Procedure `Birthdays` also uses nesting. This time the nesting is used so that the processing procedure can access the parameter `Month` to compare to each friend's birthday month. We need to know the current year in order to calculate each person's age. Function `Ada.Calendar.Clock` returns a value containing the current date and time. Function `Ada.Calendar.Year` extracts the year from that value.

One important feature of the address book is that it must be stored in a file between runs. When our application starts, the retained data in the file automatically is brought into the address book. The retained data is the same information contained in the address book but stored in some kind of file format. Figure 7.1 earlier in the chapter illustrates the relationship between the retained data and our address book.

What sort of file should we use for this data? One approach is to keep the data in a text file, reading and writing all the record fields one at a time. Using a text file requires you to convert back and forth between the way data is formatted in the text file and the way the data are stored in a record. A simpler alternative is to use a binary file. Package `Ada.Sequential_IO` allows us to read and write records without these conversions.

The `save` operation for the address book ADO is implemented by calling the iterator that writes a copy of each list element to the file. But how can we automatically bring this data into our program when the program starts? To solve this problem, we make use of a feature of Ada that you probably have not seen before. Here is a simplified EBNF definition of a package body:

```
package_body    ::=     package body package_simple_name is
                            declarative_part
                        [begin
                            sequence_of_statements
                        [exception
                            exception_handler
                            {exception_handler} ] ]
                        end package_simple_name;
```

Note the optional sequence of statements and the optional exception handlers at the end of a package body. Until now, our package bodies consisted only of the declarative part. Here we declared local types, constants, variables, and subprograms for our package body as well as the bodies for the subprograms declared in the package declaration. The statements in the optional sequence are executed when the package body is elaborated. Because the package body is elaborated before any of its subprograms are called, we can use this code to initialize an abstract data object. For our address book, this initialization consists of reading the retained data from the disk.

We have included two exception handlers in our initialization code. The binary file with our saved data does not exist the first time our program is run. Attempting to open a nonexistent file will raise a `NAME_ERROR` exception. The exception handler simply displays a message informing the user that it is creating the initial address book. Because the list object is initialized to empty when `The_Book` is elaborated, no other action is necessary in our exception handler. The second handler is executed when the sequential data file contains more records than the `Max_Size` given for this instantiation of an address book.

An alternative to our use of package initialization code is to make `The_Book` a controlled object and override the `Initialize` and `Finalize` operations with the code to read the file after `The_Book` is created by elaboration and write `The_Book` to the file before it is destroyed by program termination. Of course, we still need to implement our `Save` operation as given in our specification to permit an application to save the address book at any time.

7.3 The Implementation Level

In our address book ADO we have made calls to the list operations specified for the key-ordered list class, creating and modifying lists without even knowing how the list is implemented. At an application level, these are logical operations on a list. At a lower level, these operations are implemented as Ada procedures or functions that manipulate an array or other data-storing medium holding the list's elements. As we have seen with stacks and queues, there are multiple functionally correct ways to implement an abstract data type. Between the application picture and the eventual representation in the computer's memory, there are intermediate levels of abstractions and design decisions. For instance, how will the logical order of the list elements be reflected in their physical ordering? Will the list be represented as a sequential or a linked structure? If a linked structure is chosen, will its elements be stored in statically or dynamically allocated memory?

We said earlier that the logical order of the list elements may or may not be mirrored in the way that they are physically stored in a data structure. However, the way that the list elements are arranged physically affects the way that we access the elements in the list. This arrangement may have implications on the efficiency of the list operations. For instance, there is nothing in the specification of the key-ordered list class that requires us to implement the list with the elements stored in order. If we stored the elements in an array, completely unordered, we still could implement all the list operations. With this list representation, the insert algorithm could be an O(1) operation, because we do not care about the order of the elements. (If the elements were ordered, the insert operation would be O(N), as we shall discuss later.) However, the traverse operation, which requires that the elements be processed in order, would be $O(N^2)$ (or at best, $O(N\log_2 N)$, as we see in Chapter 12). For a list whose elements are physically sorted, this operation is O(N).

In this section we develop two list representations that preserve the order of the list elements; that is, the elements are physically stored in such a way that, from one list element, we can access its logical successor directly. We first look at a sequential list representation. The distinguishing feature of a sequential implementation is that the elements are stored sequentially, in adjacent slots in an array. The order of the elements is implicit in their placement in the array.

Array-based list implementations are so common that many people refer to an "array" of data when they really mean a "list," as if the two were interchangeable. Of course, we know this to be a misnomer; an array is one place to store list elements, but it is not the only implementation choice.

The second approach that we discuss is a linked list representation. In a linked implementation, the data elements are not constrained to be stored in physically contiguous, sequential order; rather, the individual elements are stored "somewhere in memory," and their order is maintained by explicit links between them.

We want to emphasize that the choice between sequential and linked list representations is not the same as the choice between static and dynamic storage allocation. These are separate issues. We typically store arrays in named variables, as illustrated in Figure 7.2(a). But an array-based implementation does not necessarily use static storage. The whole array could exist in a dynamically allocated area of memory; that is, we could get space for the whole structure at once using the new allocator, as illustrated in Figure 7.2(b). In Chapter 4 we used this approach to implement unbounded-length strings.

We tend to think of linked structures as being in dynamically allocated storage, as illustrated in Figure 7.3(a), but we can implement linked lists without dynamic allocation. A linked list can be implemented in an array; the elements might be stored in the

(a) A Sequential List in Static Storage

```
type Float_Array is array (Positive range <>) of Float;
List : Float_Array(1..5);
```

(b) A Sequential List in Dynamic Storage

```
type Float_Array is array (Positive range <>) of Float;
type Float_Array_Ptr is access Float_Array;

List : Float_Array_Ptr := new Float_Array(1..5);
```

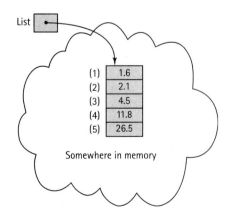

Figure 7.2 *Array-based lists in static and dynamic storage.*

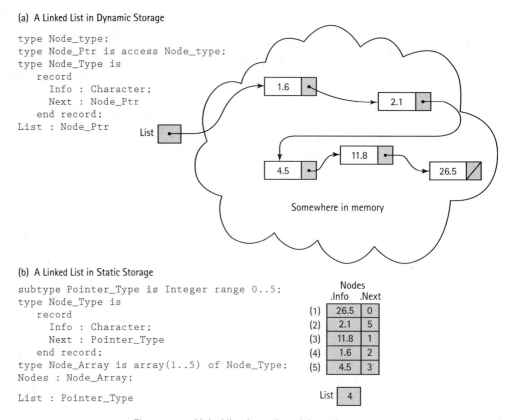

Figure 7.3 *Linked lists in static and dynamic storage.*

array in any order and "linked" by their indexes, as illustrated in Figure 7.3(b). We examine the storage of linked structures in static storage in Chapter 8.

In the next two sections, we develop sequential and linked implementations of a key-ordered list. In each of these implementations we use the generic formal function `Key_Of` to obtain the key of an element. Keys then are compared with the generic formal functions `"="` and `"<"`. All three of these functions are supplied by the user of our generic list package when they instantiate it.

A Sequential List Implementation

The elements in our sequential list implementation are stored in an array. What makes this a sequential representation is not the array itself but the *arrangement* of the elements within the array. The first (smallest key value) element is stored in the first array slot, the second (next smallest key value) element in the second slot, and so on. Now we know where the list begins—in the first array slot. Where does the list end? The array ends at the slot with index `Max_Size`, but the list may not fill the whole array. Therefore, we keep track of the number of list elements; we call this value length. Now we know that the last (largest key value) element in the list is in the array slot with index Length. As we did for stacks and queues, we bundle together the array and its supporting data in a discriminated record type. Here are the necessary declarations for the private part of Specification 7.1 (page 406).

```
private

   type Element_Array is array (Positive range <>) of Element_Type;

   type List_Type (Max_Size : Positive) is tagged limited
      record
         Length : Natural := 0;
         Items  : Element_Array (1..Max_Size);
      end record;

end Key_Ordered_List;
```

Figure 7.4 depicts a sequential list containing five elements. The elements are ordered by their keys. For simplicity, only the key values (names in this example) are shown in the figure. The element whose key comes first alphabetically is in List.Items(1), the next element is in List.Items(2), and so on. The element whose key comes last alphabetically is in List.Items(List.Length).

The Length, Empty, Clear, *and* Full *Operations*   Now let's look at the operations we have specified for our list class. Because of the structural resemblance of this implementation to the array-based stack, several of the operations will seem familiar to

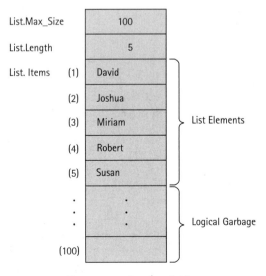

Figure 7.4   *A sequential list.*

you. The length of a list is the number of elements it contains. The Length operation for our array-based list simply returns the value of the Length field. An empty list is one whose Length field is zero. Thus function Empty and procedure Clear merely check or set the value of the Length field.

Like the array-based implementations of stacks and queues, this list implementation requires a full operation to make sure that we do not try to insert another element when all the array slots are full. Because the array has Max_Size slots, the full operation simply compares the list's Length to the record discriminant Max_Size.

Finding a List Element The list operations to retrieve, modify, insert, and delete an element all require searching the list to find the element to process or to find the appropriate place to insert. To support these operations, let's write a procedure Search_Array. This procedure takes a *slice* of the list's array field and a key value as inputs. It searches the array slice for the element with this key. The array slice we pass to Search_Array is the portion of the list array containing list elements; the logical garbage is not passed (Figure 7.4).

If the element is found, Search_Array returns the index of the desired element's location (a value between 1 and Max_Size). What if the element with the specified key is not found, as in the case when we are inserting a new element? If the element is not found, the procedure could return a value of 0 for the location. However, as long as we're searching the array, it would be useful to know where an element with this key would belong if it were in the array. Therefore, Search_Array also returns the index of the array where this key would be inserted. Specification 7.3 defines this search procedure.

Specification 7.3   Array Search

```
procedure Search_Array (The_Array : in  Element_Array;
                        Key       : in  Key_Type;
                        Found     : out Boolean;
                        Location  : out Positive) is
-- Purpose        : Searches for the location of a Value in the The_Array
-- Preconditions  : The_Array is sorted in ascending order
-- Postconditions : If Key is in The_Array
--                      Found is True
--                      Location is the index of the element with Key
--                  else
--                      Found is False
--                      Location is the index of where Key should be inserted
```

We can implement this search using a sequential or a binary algorithm. In either case, we use the generic formal function Key_Of to obtain the key of a list element. In a linear search, we start at the beginning of the array and check each element in order. Sequential searches are often called linear searches because they are O(*N*). We discussed the binary search algorithm in Chapter 1. Each key comparison in a binary search reduces the search array size by half, so the binary search is O(log$_2$N). Because it is more efficient, we decided to use a binary search in our key-ordered list class.

The specification of Search_Array is not quite the same as that of the binary search we developed in Chapter 1—Search_Array includes an additional postcondition. If the Key is not in the array, this operation returns the index of the array where that Key should be placed. Figure 7.5 shows the results of three searches in which the Key is not found in The_Array. The Location returned is the index of the array where the name searched for should go.

If you trace the binary search code given in Chapter 1, you will see that when the search is *not* successful, the local variable First_Index contains the index of the array where the value should go. This observation holds when the array is empty (index range

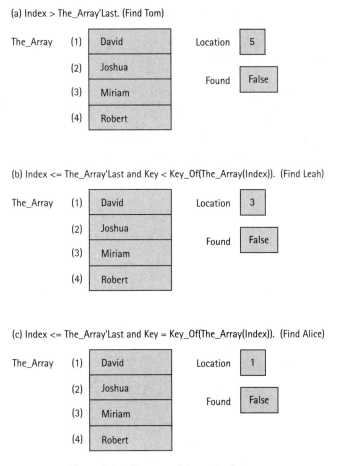

Figure 7.5 *Unsuccessful search of an array.*

is `1..0`) as well as when it contains elements. Using this observation, we set `Location` to `Midpoint` when the search is successful and we set `Location` to `First_Index` when it is not.

```
if Found then
   Location := Midpoint;
else
   Location := First_Index;
end if;
```

Note that procedure `Search_Array` is not included in our key-ordered list package declaration (Specification 7.1). Should we add it? No—this procedure is provided for the use of the list operations, not for the application programmer using the package. It is logically internal to the key-ordered list class. If we do not want the list user to know anything about how the list is stored, there is no reason to provide information about the inner workings (array indexes, pointers, or whatever) of the list implementation. Our goal is information hiding; therefore, this procedure is off-limits to the application programmer.

The `Retrieve` and `Modify` Operations The `Retrieve` operation allows the list user to obtain a copy of the list element with a specified key, if that element exists in the list. To do so, we simply search the list's array with `Search_Array`. If the search is successful, we return a copy of the element whose array index is given by `Location`. If the search is not successful, we raise the `KEY_ERROR` exception. The `Retrieve` operation is illustrated in Figure 7.6.

The `Modify` operation allows the user to replace an element with another with the same key. As with `Retrieve`, we use `Search_Array` to find the `Location` of the element to change. Then we copy the replacement element into this array slot. If the search is not successful, we raise the `KEY_ERROR` exception. The `Modify` operation is illustrated in Figure 7.7.

The Insert Operation To add an element to a value-ordered list, we first must find the place where the new element belongs. Unlike a stack (where we always add to the top)

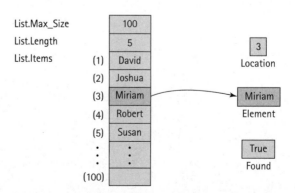

Figure 7.6 *The `Retrieve` operation.*

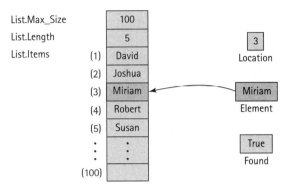

Figure 7.7 The `Modify` operation.

or a queue (where we always add to the rear), the list's insertion location is not fixed. Where the element belongs depends on the value of its key field.

We'll use an example to illustrate the insertion operation. Let's say we wish to add an element for Leah to our list. To add it to the sequential list pictured in Figure 7.8(a), maintaining the alphabetic ordering, we use the following algorithm:

Insert
    Find the place where the new element belongs
    Create space for the new element
    Put the new element into the list

The first task involves searching the list to find the location in the array (in this case, 3). `Search_Array` does this task for us.

Now that we know where the element belongs, we need to create space for it. Because the list is sequential, the element Leah must be put into the slot between its alphabetic predecessor (at index `Location - 1`) and successor (at index `Location`). But this slot is occupied. To "create space" for the new element, we must move down all the list elements that follow it, from `Location` to `List.Length`. We can move these elements with a loop or with a single assignment statement using array slices. We prefer the assignment method because array slice assignment usually executes faster than a loop.[3] Then we increment the `Length` field of the list. Here's the algorithm:

Create space for the new element
    List.Items (Location + 1 .. List.Length + 1) := List.Items (Location .. List.Length)
    List.Length := List.Length + 1

---

[3]When the hardware permits, most Ada compilers translate array or array slice assignment into a single machine language instruction that moves a block of memory. Although such assignment is still O(N), the actual execution time is less than that of a loop.

434 | Chapter 7: Key-Ordered Lists

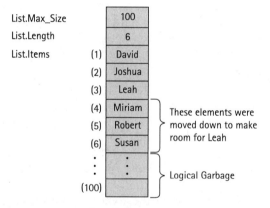

Figure 7.8 *Inserting into a sequential list.*

Now that the array slot at index Location is free, we put the new element in the list in this position. Figure 7.8(b) shows the resulting list.

What if Search_Array returns True for Found? This result means that there is already an element in our list with the same key as the one we are trying to insert. Our specification requires us to raise DUPLICATE_KEY and leave the list unchanged.

Our example involved inserting a new element into the middle of the list array. Does this procedure work if the new element belongs at the beginning or end of the list? Draw yourself a picture to see how the procedure works in each of these cases.

The Delete *Operation* As with Insert, the Delete operation takes two inputs: the list and the key of the element that is to be deleted. We use the following algorithm:

Delete Element
    Find the element in the list
    Remove the element from the list

The first part of the algorithm is easy; we can call procedure `Search_Array`. If on return from `Search_Array`, Found is True, Location contains the index of the element with the key we wish to remove from the list. If Found is returned as False, there is no element in the list with the given key. Our specification requires us to raise KEY_ERROR.

How do we "remove" the element from the list? Let's look at a list example (Figure 7.9[a]). Removing Susan from the list is easy, for hers is the last element in the list (see Figure 7.9[b]). If we then remove David from the list, we need to move up all the elements that follow to fill in the space (see Figure 7.9[c]). In the sequential implementation, we do not actually remove the element; instead we cover it up with the element that previously followed it. Each successive element must be moved to cover up its predecessor. As we did in the `insert` operation, we can use an assignment statement with array slices to move a group of elements. Finally, we decrement the length of the list.

Remove the element from the list
    List.Items (Location .. List.Length - 1) := List.Items (Location + 1 .. List.Length)
    List.Length := List.Length - 1

What happens when we are trying to remove the last element in the list, that is, the element at `List.Items(List.Length)`? There are no elements following it in the list, so the value in this slot doesn't get "covered up." Because in this situation Location + 1 is greater than List.Length, the range Location + 1 .. List.Length is a null range. Location .. List.Length - 1 is also a null range. An array slice with a null range contains no elements. Therefore, no elements are copied by our assignment statement. Decrementing List.Length, in effect, implements the deletion of the element from the list. The deleted element's value is still in the array, but it is no longer in the list. For instance, Susan is still in array slot 6 in Figure 7.9(b), but there are only five elements in the list. This element is logically (though not physically) inaccessible.

The Traverse Operation   Procedure Traverse calls Process (a procedure passed as a parameter from the application) for every element in the list. Because we know how many elements are in the list (List.Length), we can use a `for` loop to traverse the array of elements in our list record.

Traverse
    for Index in 1..List.Length loop
        Process (Element => List.Items(Index))
    end loop

436 | Chapter 7: Key-Ordered Lists

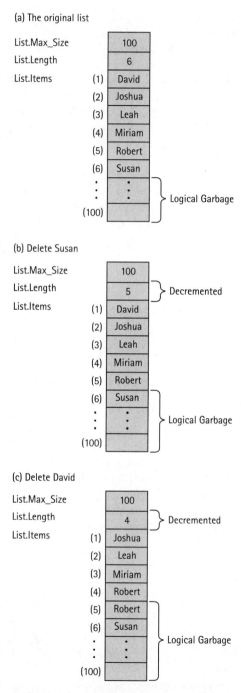

Figure 7.9 *Deleting from a sequential list.*

To allow an application programmer to modify elements in the list, the parameter `Element` for procedure `Process` has a mode of `in out`. There is a danger here. Although the precondition for procedure `Traverse` states that the element processing procedure supplied as an actual parameter does not change the key of any elements, an application programmer could change the key of the element. Making this change would destroy the order of the list.

Encapsulation Revisited In many of the list operations, we declared a local variable `Location`, which contains the array index of the list element being processed. The values of array indexes never get outside of the set of list operations; this information is internal to the implementation of our `List` class. If the application programmer wants a record in the list, procedure `Retrieve` does not give him or her the index of the record; instead it returns a copy of the record itself. If the application programmer changes values in this record, those changes are not reflected in the list unless they call `Modify`. The list user is never allowed to see or manipulate the physical structure in which the list is stored. These details of the list implementation are hidden; the List class is encapsulated by the ADT.

Body 7.2 contains the complete body for our sequential array-based implementation of a key-ordered list.

Body 7.2   Sequential Array-Based List: Implements Specification 7.1

```
package body Key_Ordered_List is

  -- Local procedure
  --------------------------------------------------------------------------
  procedure Search_Array (The_Array :  in Element_Array;
                          Key       :  in Key_Type;
                          Found     :  out Boolean;
                          Location  :  out Positive) is
  -- Purpose        : Searches for the location of a Value in the The_Array.
  -- Preconditions  : The_Array is sorted in ascending order
  -- Postconditions : If Key is in The_Array
  --                     Found is True
  --                     Location is the index of the element with Key
  --                  else
  --                     Found is False
  --                     Location is the index of where Key should be inserted

    First_Index : Integer;   -- First index in current search area
    Last_Index  : Integer;   -- Last index in current search area
    Midpoint    : Integer;   -- Index of search area's midpoint
  begin
    First_Index := The_Array'First;
    Last_Index  := The_Array'Last;
```

```ada
      Found          := False;
      -- Search until Key is found or the current search area is empty.
      -- Current search area is The_Array(First_Index..Last_Index)
      loop
         exit when First_Index > Last_Index or Found;
         Midpoint := (First_Index + Last_Index) / 2;
         -- Compare Key to middle element in search area.
         if Key = Key_Of (The_Array(Midpoint)) then
            Found := True;
         elsif Key < Key_Of (The_Array(Midpoint)) then
            Last_Index := Midpoint - 1;    -- Search area now 1st half
         else
            First_Index := Midpoint + 1;   -- Search area now 2nd half
         end if;
      end loop;
      if Found then
         Location := Midpoint;
      else
         Location := First_Index;
      end if;
   end Search_Array;


   -- Operations defined in the specification
   -------------------------------------------------------------------------
   procedure Clear (List : in out List_Type) is
   begin
      List.Length := 0;
   end Clear;

   -------------------------------------------------------------------------
   procedure Insert (List : in out List_Type;
                     Item : in      Element_Type) is
      Have_Duplicate : Boolean;
      Location       : Positive;
   begin
      if Full (List) then
         raise OVERFLOW;
      else
         Search_Array (The_Array => List.Items(1..List.Length),
                       Key       => Key_Of (Item),
                       Found     => Have_Duplicate,
                       Location  => Location);
         if Have_Duplicate then
            raise DUPLICATE_KEY;
```

```ada
      else  -- Insert the new item into the array
         List.Items(Location+1 .. List.Length+1) :=
                              List.Items(Location .. List.Length);
         List.Items(Location) := Item;
         List.Length := List.Length + 1;
      end if;
   end if;
end Insert;

------------------------------------------------------------------------

procedure Delete (List : in out List_Type;
                  Key  : in     Key_Type) is
   Found    : Boolean;
   Location : Positive;
begin
   Search_Array (The_Array => List.Items(1..List.Length),
                 Key       => Key,
                 Found     => Found,
                 Location  => Location);
   if not Found then
      raise KEY_ERROR;
   else
      List.Items(Location .. List.Length-1) :=
                         List.Items(Location+1 .. List.Length);
      List.Length := List.Length - 1;
   end if;
end Delete;

------------------------------------------------------------------------

procedure Modify (List    : in out List_Type;
                  Element : in     Element_Type) is
   Found    : Boolean;
   Location : Positive;
begin
   Search_Array (The_Array => List.Items(1..List.Length),
                 Key       => Key_Of (Element),
                 Found     => Found,
                 Location  => Location);
   if not Found then
      raise KEY_ERROR;
   else
      List.Items(Location) := Element;
   end if;
end Modify;
```

```ada
   procedure Retrieve (List    : in      List_Type;
                       Key     : in      Key_Type;
                       Element :     out Element_Type) is
      Found    : Boolean;
      Location : Positive;
   begin
      Search_Array (The_Array => List.Items(1..List.Length),
                    Key       => Key,
                    Found     => Found,
                    Location  => Location);
      if not Found then
         raise KEY_ERROR;
      else
         Element := List.Items(Location);
      end if;
   end Retrieve;

   ----------------------------------------------------------------

   function Full (List : in List_Type) return Boolean is
   begin
      return List.Length = List.Max_Size;
   end Full;

   ----------------------------------------------------------------

   function Empty (List : in List_Type) return Boolean is
   begin
      return List.Length = 0;
   end Empty;

   ----------------------------------------------------------------

   function Length (List : in List_Type) return Natural is
   begin
      return List.Length;
   end Length;

   ----------------------------------------------------------------

   procedure Traverse
       (List    : in out List_Type;
        Process : not null access procedure (Element : in out Element_Type)) is
   begin
      for Index in 1..List.Length loop
         Process (List.Items(Index));   -- Call user's procedure to process the
      end loop;                          -- element
   end Traverse;
end Key_Ordered_List;
```

Figure 7.10 *A linked list.*

A Linked List Implementation

In a linked list representation, the data elements are not constrained to be stored in sequential order; rather, the individual elements are stored "somewhere" in memory. The order of the elements is maintained by explicit links between them. Figure 7.10 shows pictorially how a key-ordered list would be represented as a linked list. An empty list contains no nodes; the external pointer (Head in Figure 7.10) is null.

We construct the linked list structure much like the linked versions of the stack and FIFO queues. Each node contains both data and an explicit link to the next node in the list. Because the list is linear, the link field of the last node contains null, the special access value that says, "This doesn't designate anything." An external access variable (e.g., Head) tells us where the list starts. You cannot access nodes in a linked list directly or randomly; that is, you cannot get directly to the twenty-fifth element in the list, as you can with a sequential array-based representation. Rather, you access the first node through the external pointer, the second node through the first node's "next" pointer, the third node through the second node's "next" pointer, and so on, to the end of the list.

In discussing the advantages of the linked stack and queue representations, we focused on the issue of dynamic storage allocation. Because the nodes were created dynamically, we did not have to declare an array variable large enough to store the maximum number of elements, thus saving space when the list was smaller. There are, however, other advantages to a linked implementation, unrelated to the issue of storage allocation.

Using a linked structure streamlines the algorithms that manipulate the elements of a key-ordered list. For instance, we can avoid all of the data movement that was necessary to insert and delete in our sequential implementation. With a linked representation, the existing elements stay where they are as others are added and deleted. What changes are the links that establish the order of the elements.

Specification 7.4 describes an unbounded key-ordered list. The declarations in the private part of this specification define the same node and link types we used in our unbounded stack and queue specifications. List_Type extends Ada.Finalization.Limited_Controlled so that we can recycle any memory used by a list object that goes out of scope. This recycling is accomplished by overriding the Finalize procedure.

Specification 7.4   Unbounded Key-Ordered List

```
with Ada.Finalization;
generic
   type Element_Type is private;        -- The type of element in the list
   type Key_Type     is limited private; -- The type of key

   -- The user must supply a function that returns the Key of an Element
   with function Key_Of (Element : in Element_Type) return Key_Type;
```

```ada
   -- The user must supply functions for comparing Keys
   with function "=" (Left : in Key_Type; Right : in Key_Type) return Boolean;
   with function "<" (Left : in Key_Type; Right : in Key_Type) return Boolean;
package Unbounded_List is

-- This package implements a key-ordered list class.

-- Each element in the list has a unique key.

-- The elements in the list are ordered from smallest to largest using the "<"
-- function supplied as a generic parameter.  The key value of the predecessor
-- of an element is less than the key value of the element, which is less than
-- the key value of the successor of the element.

   type List_Type is new Ada.Finalization.Limited_Controlled with private;

   DUPLICATE_KEY  : exception;
   KEY_ERROR      : exception;
   OVERFLOW       : exception;


   -- Transformers

   -------------------------------------------------------------------------
   procedure Clear (List : in out List_Type);
   -- Purpose        : Removes all elements from List.
   -- Preconditions  : None
   -- Postconditions : List is empty.


   -------------------------------------------------------------------------
   procedure Insert (List : in out List_Type;
                     Item : in     Element_Type);
   -- Purpose        : Adds Item to List.
   -- Preconditions  : None
   -- Postconditions : List = original list + Item
   -- Exceptions     : OVERFLOW      If there is no room for Item.
   --                                List is unchanged.
   --                  DUPLICATE_KEY If an element already exists in the list
   --                                with the same key as Item.
   --                                List is unchanged.


   -------------------------------------------------------------------------
   procedure Delete (List : in out List_Type;
                     Key  : in     Key_Type);
   -- Purpose        : Deletes the element containing Key from List.
```

```
-- Preconditions  : None
-- Postconditions : List = original list without element identified by Key
-- Exceptions     : KEY_ERROR  If there is no element with Key in List.
--                             List is unchanged.


------------------------------------------------------------------------
procedure Modify (List    : in out List_Type;
                  Element : in     Element_Type);
-- Purpose        : Replaces existing list element.
-- Preconditions  : None
-- Postconditions : List = original list with value of Element replacing
--                         like-keyed original element
-- Exceptions     : KEY_ERROR  If there is no element with the key of
--                             Element in List.  List is unchanged.


-- Observers

------------------------------------------------------------------------
procedure Retrieve (List    : in     List_Type;
                    Key     : in     Key_Type;
                    Element :    out Element_Type);
-- Purpose        : Gets a copy of the element that contains Key.
-- Preconditions  : None
-- Postconditions : Element = copy of element containing Key.
--                  List is unchanged.
-- Exceptions     : KEY_ERROR  If there is no element with the
--                             Key in List.  List is unchanged.

------------------------------------------------------------------------
function Full (List : in List_Type) return Boolean;
-- Purpose        : Tests whether List is full.  List is full when
--                         no more elements can be inserted into it.
-- Preconditions  : None
-- Postconditions : Full = (List is full)

------------------------------------------------------------------------
function Empty (List : in List_Type) return Boolean;
-- Purpose        : Tests whether List is empty (contains no elements)
-- Preconditions  : None
-- Postconditions : Empty = (List is empty)


------------------------------------------------------------------------
function Length (List : in List_Type) return Natural;
-- Purpose        : Determines the number of elements in List.
```

```
       -- Preconditions  : None
       -- Postconditions : Length = number of elements in List


  -- Iterator

  -------------------------------------------------------------------------
       procedure Traverse
            (List    : in out List_Type;
             Process : not null access procedure (Element : in out Element_Type));
       -- Purpose        : To process all the elements in List in ascending order
       -- Preconditions  : Procedure Process does not change the key of an element
       -- Postconditions : Every element in List is passed to a call of
       --                    procedure Process
       --                  Elements processed in ascending order

private

     type Node_Type;
     type Node_Ptr is access Node_Type;
     type Node_Type is
        record
           Info : Element_Type;
           Next : Node_Ptr;
        end record;

     type List_Type is new Ada.Finalization.Limited_Controlled with
        record
           Head : Node_Ptr;   -- Designates first node in the linked list
        end record;

     overriding procedure Finalize (List : in out List_Type) renames Clear;

end Unbounded_List;
```

Because we are using a linked list to implement an unbounded key-ordered list, the `List_Type` discriminate `Max_Size` used in the bounded key-ordered list (Specification 7.1) is no longer needed. This deletion is the only change we need to make to the public portion of our package declaration.

The Empty, Full, and Clear Operations Because Ada initializes every access variable to null, every list object we declare is initialized to empty—there is no need to override the `Initialize` method of `List_Type`'s superclass. We can use the knowledge that an empty list is one whose external access value is `null` to write a short `Empty` function. The `Full` operation for a linked list is identical to the one we used for a linked stack and a linked queue—it simply returns false.

The `Clear` operation for a linked list is more complicated than its sequential list counterpart, because the dynamically allocated space used by the elements must be freed. The easiest approach is to unlink each successive node in the list and free it. This algorithm is exactly like the clear operation for stacks developed in Chapter 5, so we'll reuse the code, changing "Top" references to "Head."

The Traverse Operation The algorithm for the `Traverse` operation that we developed for the sequential list early in this chapter used an array index to access each element in the array that stored the list's elements. A for loop allowed us to easily move from one element to the next. In the linked implementation, we must use the `Next` field of a node to locate the next node in the list. How do we know when we have processed all of the elements in the list? The end of the list is marked by a null value, so we stop when we reach `null`. Here is the algorithm:

Traverse
```
Location := List.Head;           -- Location designates 1st node of list
loop
    exit when Location is null
    Process (Location.all.Info)  -- Process info in node designated by Location
    Location := Location.all.Next --Advance Location to the next node
end loop;
```

The implementation has changed, but the basic algorithm to traverse a list stayed the same. Trace this algorithm using the list shown in Figure 7.10. Does this algorithm work correctly when the list is empty?

The Length Operation Our linked list `List_Type` does not contain a `Length` field as our sequential one did. To determine the number of elements in the list we must traverse the list, counting each node as we go. The algorithm is nearly identical to the one we developed for the traverse operation.

Length
```
Count    := 0
Location := List.Head
loop
    exit when Location is null
    Count := Count + 1
    Location := Location.all.Next
end loop;
return Count
```

Finding a List Element The rest of the list operations (retrieve, modify, insert, and delete) require searching the list to find the element to process. As we did for the sequential list implementation, we write a procedure to simplify these other operations. This time we call it `Search_Linked_List`. This procedure takes the list and a key value as inputs and searches the list for the element with the specified key. If the element is found, the output parameter `Location` (an access variable) designates the node with the desired key. If the element is not found, `Location` designates the node that would come immediately after the node containing the desired key, if that key were in the list. We are going to add another `out` parameter to this procedure. In the linked list implementation, an access variable that designates the node that precedes the one designated by `Location` is useful both in inserting and in deleting elements. We will call this parameter `Pred_Loc` (predecessor location). Specification 7.5 defines this search procedure.

Specification 7.5   Linked List Search

```
procedure Search_Linked_List (List     : in  List_Type;
                              Key      : in  Key_Type;
                              Found    : out Boolean;
                              Pred_Loc : out Node_Ptr;
                              Location : out Node_Ptr) is
-- Purpose        : Searches for the location of Key in the List
-- Preconditions  : The nodes in List are in ascending order
-- Postconditions : If Key is in List
--                      Found is True
--                      Location designates the element with Key
--                      Pred_Loc designates the predecessor of the node
--                               designated by Location.  If Location
--                               designates the first node in the list,
--                               Pred_Loc is null.
--                  else
--                      Found is False
--                      Location designates the node that would follow a node
--                               containing Key.  If Key's node would follow
--                               the last node in the list, Location is null.
--                      Pred_Loc designates the predecessor of the node
--                               designated by Location.  If Location
--                               designates the first node in the list,
--                               Pred_Loc is null.
```

This specification contains the most complex set of postconditions we have presented. Figure 7.11 shows different cases indicated in the postconditions for procedure `Search_Linked_List`. Spend some time looking at each of these cases to make sure that you understand exactly what this search procedure returns.

We use a sequential search algorithm to locate the desired key. We start at the beginning of the linked list and loop through it until (1) we have found an element with the desired key; (2) we have passed all the elements in the list whose keys are smaller than `Key`; or (3) we have reached the end of the list. Here is the basic loop structure using `Location` to designate the node we currently are looking at:

7.3 The Implementation Level | 447

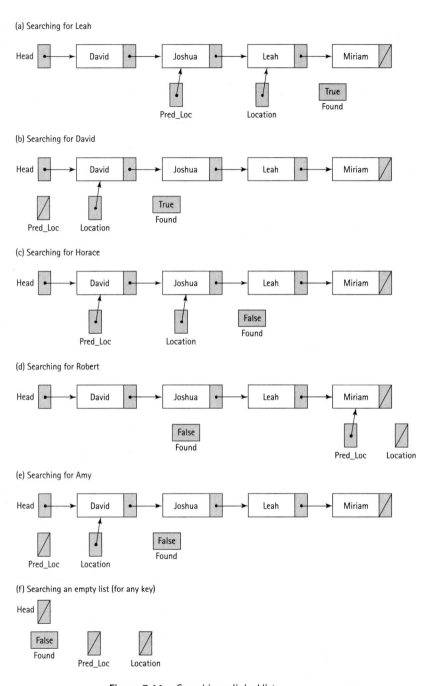

Figure 7.11 *Searching a linked list.*

```
-- Version 1 (sometimes raises CONSTRAINT_ERROR)
Location := List.Head;    -- Start at the beginning of the linked list
-- Search the linked list
-- Each iteration, check one node
loop
    exit when Key = Key_Of (Location.all.Info) or     -- Found it
             Key < Key_Of (Location.all.Info) or     -- Passed by
             Location = null;                         -- Reached the end
    Location := Location.all.Next;     -- Move to the next node
end loop;
```

A problem occurs with this loop structure when `Key` is larger than any of the keys in the linked list. In this case, `Location` becomes `null` when it moves past the last node in the list. Attempting to dereference this null pointer to check the key in the node that it designates raises CONSTRAINT_ERROR. Rearranging the order of the conditions in the exit statement is not the complete solution. CONSTRAINT_ERROR is still raised in the following exit statement:

```
-- Still raises constraint error when we run off the end of the list
exit when Location = null                          or   -- Reached the end
         Key = Key_Of (Location.all.Info) or;           -- Found it
         Key < Key_Of (Location.all.Info);              -- Passed by
```

When using the `and` or `or` operators, *all* of the terms in a Boolean expression are evaluated. Thus, even when the first term in the above exit statement evaluates to `True`, the remaining two terms still are evaluated; CONSTRAINT_ERROR is raised. Ada has other logical operators, called *short-circuit operators*, that stop the evaluation of additional terms in a Boolean expression as soon as the result is known. The two short-circuit operators are `and then` and `or else`.

How can we determine the result of a Boolean expression without evaluating all of the terms? The `and` operator requires both operands to be true in order for the overall result to be true. If either or both of the operands are false, this makes the entire result false. Thus, if the first operand is false, we don't even need to look at the second term. We already know that the expression is false. If either of the operands with an `or` operator is true, then the expression is true. So if the first operand is true, we don't need to look at the second operand. This logic is exactly what the `and then` and `or else` operators perform. The following tables summarize these two logical operators. The question marks under Y are used to indicate that we have not yet looked at Y's value.

X	Y	X and then Y
False	????	False
True	False	False
True	True	True

X	Y	X or else Y
True	????	True
False	True	True
False	False	False

Here is our loop using an exit statement with short-circuit operators. When `Location` becomes `null`, the remaining terms in the exit statement's Boolean expression are not evaluated; `CONSTRAINT_ERROR` is not raised.

```
-- Version 2
Location := List.Head;   -- Start at the beginning of the linked list
-- Search the linked list
-- Each iteration, check one node
loop
    exit when Location = null                     or else  -- Reached the end
              Key < Key_Of (Location.all.Info)  or else  -- Passed by
              Key = Key_Of (Location.all.Info);          -- Found it
    Location := Location.all.Next;       -- Move to the next node
end loop;
```

We need some additional logic to set the remaining two `out` parameters, `Found` and `Pred_Loc`. We know that `Found` is true when `Location` designates a node containing `Key`. The following assignment statement carries out this logic:

```
Found := Location /= null  and then  Key = Key_Of (Location.all.Info);
```

This statement uses the short-circuit logical operator `and then` to ensure that we do not dereference `Location` when it is `null`.

How do we set the value of `Pred_Loc`? In an array-based list, determining the location (index) of the previous list element is a trivial operation—simply subtract one from the index of the current list element. Given a pointer to a node in a linked list, we cannot figure out the location of its predecessor. The links in a linked list go in only one direction—to the successor of the current node.

A solution to this problem is to move `Pred_Loc` down the list at the same time we are moving `Location` down the list. As `Location` moves along the list, searching for a key, the access variable, `Pred_Loc`, trails behind by one node. Using this second access variable complicates our search loop slightly. We initialize `Location` to `List.Head` as we did before and `Pred_Loc` to `null`. Then, inside the loop, we advance both pointers. As Figure 7.12 shows, the process resembles the movement of an inchworm. `Pred_Loc` (the tail of the inchworm) catches up with `Location` (the head), and then `Location` advances. Here's the code for the revised search loop:

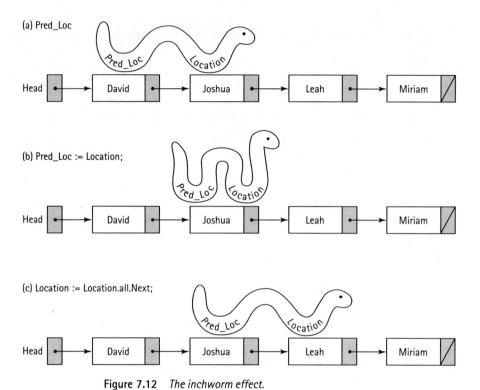

Figure 7.12 *The inchworm effect.*

```
-- Final version
Location := List.Head;    -- Start at the beginning of the linked list
Pred_Loc := null;         -- No predecessor for 1st element in the list
-- Search the linked list
-- Each iteration, check one node
loop
   exit when Location = null                       or else  -- Reached the end
             Key < Key_Of (Location.all.Info) or else  -- Passed by
             Key = Key_Of (Location.all.Info);            -- Found it
   Pred_Loc := Location ;              -- Move inchworm's tail
   Location := Location.all.Next;      -- Move inchworm's head
end loop;

Found    := Location /= null  and then  Key = Key_Of (Location.all.Info);
```

The `Retrieve` *and* `Modify` *Operations* The basic algorithms for procedures `Retrieve` and `Modify` are identical to the sequential list versions given earlier in the chapter. This time our search returns a designator to the node containing the desired element rather than an array index.

Retrieve
    Search Linked List
    if Found then
        Element := Location.all.Info
    else
        raise KEY_ERROR
    end if

Modify
    Search Linked List
    if Found then
        Location.all.Info := Element
    else
        raise KEY_ERROR
    end if

The Insert Operation To insert a new element into the linked list, we use the general algorithm developed for the sequential list implementation.

Insert (version 1)
    Find the place where the new element belongs
    Create space for the new element
    Put the new element into the list

The first task is simple: We call `Search_Linked_List`. Of course, we do not expect to find the new element's key in the list. If we do, we need to raise `DUPLICATE_KEY`. The results of the search for Leah are illustrated in Figure 7.13(a).

The second task is to create space for the new element. In the sequential version of `Insert`, we had to move all the data elements down one slot, from the insertion location to the end of the list, to make room for the new element. A major advantage to a linked list implementation is that all this data movement can be avoided, because the space for the new element does not come out of the existing structure. Instead we create space dynamically at run time by asking the system to allocate some free memory space, using the allocator `new`. We then can put the value of `Element` into the `Info` part of the new node.

Create space for the new element
    New_Space   :=   new Node_Type   — *get the space*
    New_Space.all.Info :=   Element   — *assign the new element*

The result of these two assignments is illustrated in Figure 7.13(b).

(a) Find the place where the new node belongs (Insert Leah)

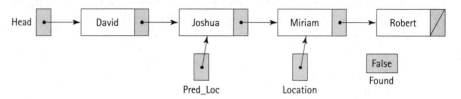

(b) Create space for the new element

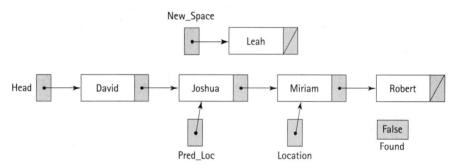

(c) Put the new element in the list

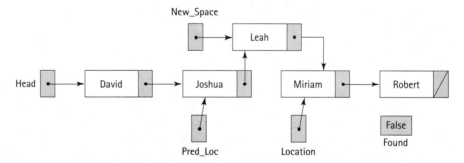

Figure 7.13 *Inserting into the middle of the list.*
(a) Find the place where the new node belongs. (Insert Leah.)
(b) Create space for the new element.
(c) Put the new element in the list.

The last task of the insert algorithm is to put the new element in the list. To complete the insertion, we must manipulate the access variables to link the new node into its appropriate position in the list. As shown in Figure 7.13(c), we need to change two pointers to link Leah into the list. We need to set Joshua's `Next` field to designate our new node and set our new node's `Next` field to designate Miriam's node. The following code accomplishes this step:

Put the new element into the (middle of the) list

```
Pred_Loc.all.Next   := New_Space;   -- Link the previous node to the new node
New_Space.all.Next  := Location;    -- Link the new node to the successor node
```

The insertion illustrated in Figure 7.13 was made in the middle of a linked list. There are three additional cases to consider: (1) inserting into an empty list; (2) inserting before the first node in the list; and (3) inserting after the last node in the list. Figure 7.14 illustrates these three cases.

In the first case, we merely need to set Head (the external pointer to the list) to designate the new node (Figure 7.14[a]). Because the new node is the last node in the linked list, we need to set its Next field to null. The second case is similar (Figure 7.14[b]). We set Head to designate our new node and set the new node's Next field to designate the node that was originally the first node in the linked list. Both of these cases require us to change the value of Head.

The third additional case, adding a new node after the last node in the list, is similar to inserting a node in the middle of a list—we need to change the Next field of the predecessor node (Figure 7.14[c]). The new node is the last node in the linked list, so we need to set its Next field to null.

Two of our insert situations require a change to the list's external pointer and two require a change of the Next field in the node designated by Pred_Loc. Using this observation, we can code the following algorithm to handle all four cases:

Insert (version 2)
```
    Search_Linked_List                               -- Find the insert location
    New_Space              :=  new Node_Type         -- Create Space for the new element
    New_Space.all.Info     :=  Element               -- Put Element into the new node
    if the list is empty or inserting at the beginning of the list
        New_Space.all.Next :=  Head
        Head               :=  New_Space
    else                                             -- Inserting at middle or at the end
        New_Space.all.Next :=  Location
        Pred_Loc.all.Next  :=  New_Space
    end if
```

How do we know if the list is empty or if we are inserting at the beginning of the list? In both of these cases, the value of Pred_Loc returned from Search_Linked_List is null.

There is one further refinement we can make to this algorithm. We can supply an initial value for a node when we allocate memory for it. We can use this feature to eliminate the need for the local variable New_Space and to reduce the size of our procedure, as shown in the final version of our insert algorithm.

Insert (final version)
```
    Search_Linked_List
    if Pred_Loc = null                               -- Inserting at the beginning (empty or not)
        Head := new Node_Type'(Info => Element, Next => Head)
    else                                             -- Inserting at middle or at the end
        Pred_Loc.all.Next := new Node_Type'(Info => Element, Next => Location)
    end if
```

454 | Chapter 7: Key-Ordered Lists

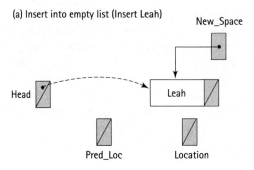

(a) Insert into empty list (Insert Leah)

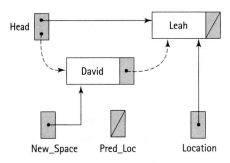

(b) Insert at beginning of list (Insert David)

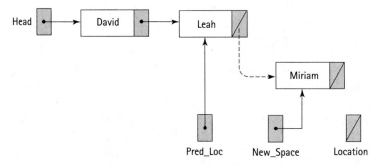

(c) Insert at end of list (Insert Miriam)

Figure 7.14 *Three additional insert cases. Solid arrows show the values of pointers just after obtaining memory for the new node. Dashed arrows show the values of pointers after the insert operation is complete.*

The Delete Operation The last operation specified for our list class is the deletion of an element with a given key. The basic tasks for the delete algorithm are the following:

Delete
    Find the element in the list
    Remove the element from the list

Procedure `Search_Linked_List` gives us a designator to the node we wish to delete, as well as one that designates its predecessor, if there is one.

The second task, to remove the element from the list, has two parts. First we must "unlink" the deleted element from the list; then we dispose of its node space. When unlinking the deleted element, we must pay attention to the node's position in the list.

We consider the same four cases we did for inserting: (1) deleting the only list element, leaving the list empty; (2) deleting the first node; (3) deleting a "middle" node; and (4) deleting the last node. Figure 7.15 illustrates these four cases. In the first two cases we change the external pointer `Head`. In the last two cases we change the `Next` field of the node designated by `Pred_Loc`. Here is the algorithm:

Delete
    Search_Linked_List
    if Pred_Loc = null   *-- Deleting the first node (and possibly only node) in the list*
        Head := Location.all.Next;
    else   *--Deleting a middle or last node in the list*
        Pred_Loc.all.Next := Location.all.Next
    end if
    Recycle memory designated by Location

All the algorithms we developed in this section neglected to handle the exceptions described in the key-ordered list specification. Body 7.3 contains the implementation of all the operations complete with exception generation.

Body 7.3   **Unbounded Key-Ordered List: Implements Specification 7.4**

```
with Unchecked_Deallocation;
package body Unbounded_List is

   -- Instantiate procedure for recycling node memory
   procedure Free is new Unchecked_Deallocation (Object => Node_Type,
                                                 Name   => Node_Ptr);

   -- Local procedure
   ----------------------------------------------------------------------
   procedure Search_Linked_List (List     : in  List_Type;
                                 Key      : in  Key_Type;
                                 Found    : out Boolean;
                                 Pred_Loc : out Node_Ptr;
```

456 | Chapter 7: Key-Ordered Lists

(a) Delete the only node in the list. (Delete David.)

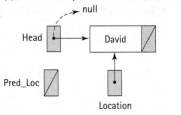

(b) Delete the first node in the list. (Delete David.)

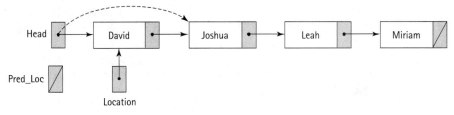

(c) Delete a "middle" node in the list. (Delete Leah.)

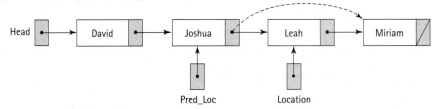

(d) Delete the last node in the list. (Delete Miriam.)

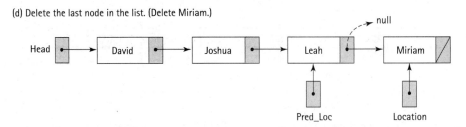

Figure 7.15 *Deleting from a linked list. Solid arrows show the values of pointers just after the search. Dashed arrows show the values of pointers after the delete operation is complete.*

```ada
                         Location : out Node_Ptr) is
-- Purpose        : Searches for the location of Key in the List
-- Preconditions  : The nodes in List are in ascending order
-- Postconditions : If Key is in List
--                      Found is True
--                      Location designates the element with Key
--                      Pred_Loc designates the predecessor of the node
--                              designated by Location.  If Location
--                              designates the first node in the list,
--                              Pred_Loc is null.
--                  else
--                      Found is False
--                      Location designates the node that would follow a node
--                              containing Key.  If Key's node would follow
--                              the last node in the list, Location is null.
--                      Pred_Loc designates the predecessor of the node
--                              designated by Location.  If Location
--                              designates the first node in the list,
--                              Pred_Loc is null.
begin
   Location := List.Head;   -- Start at the beginning of the linked list
   Pred_Loc := null;        -- No predecessor for 1st element in the list
   -- Search the linked list
   -- Each iteration, check one node
   loop
      exit when Location = null                    or else  -- Reached the end
               Key < Key_Of (Location.all.Info) or else  -- Passed by
               Key = Key_Of (Location.all.Info);          -- Found it
      Pred_Loc := Location ;              -- Move inchworm's tail
      Location := Location.all.Next;      -- Move inchworm's head
   end loop;
   Found := Location /= null  and then  Key = Key_Of (Location.all.Info);
end Search_Linked_List;


-- Operations defined in the specification
-------------------------------------------------------------------------------
procedure Clear (List : in out List_Type) is
   To_Recycle : Node_Ptr;    -- Designates a node for recycling
begin
   loop
      exit when List.Head = null;      -- Exit when list is empty
      To_Recycle := List.Head;         -- Unlink the
      List.Head  := List.Head.all.Next;  --    first node
      Free (To_Recycle);               -- Recycle the node
   end loop;
end Clear;
```

```ada
procedure Insert (List : in out List_Type;
                  Item : in     Element_Type) is
   Have_Duplicate : Boolean;
   Pred_Loc       : Node_Ptr;
   Location       : Node_Ptr;
begin
   Search_Linked_List (List     => List,
                       Key      => Key_Of (Item),
                       Found    => Have_Duplicate,
                       Pred_Loc => Pred_Loc,
                       Location => Location);
   if Have_Duplicate then
      raise DUPLICATE_KEY;
   elsif Pred_Loc = null then
      -- Add Item to the head of the linked list
      List.Head := new Node_Type'(Info => Item, Next => List.Head);
   else   -- Add at the middle or end of the linked list
      Pred_Loc.all.Next := new Node_Type'(Info => Item, Next => Location);
   end if;
exception
   when STORAGE_ERROR =>    -- Overflow when no storage available
      raise OVERFLOW;
end Insert;


procedure Delete (List : in out List_Type;
                  Key  : in     Key_Type) is
   Found    : Boolean;
   Pred_Loc : Node_Ptr;
   Location : Node_Ptr;
begin
   Search_Linked_List (List     => List,
                       Key      => Key,
                       Found    => Found,
                       Pred_Loc => Pred_Loc,
                       Location => Location);
   if not Found then
      raise KEY_ERROR;
   elsif Pred_Loc = null then
      -- Delete first element
      List.Head := Location.all.Next;
   else  -- Delete middle or last element
```

```ada
         Pred_Loc.all.Next := Location.all.Next;
      end if;
      Free (Location);       -- Recycle node memory
   end Delete;

   ----------------------------------------------------------------------
   procedure Modify (List    : in out List_Type;
                     Element : in     Element_Type) is
      Found    : Boolean;
      Pred_Loc : Node_Ptr;
      Location : Node_Ptr;
   begin
      Search_Linked_List (List     => List,
                          Key      => Key_Of (Element),
                          Found    => Found,
                          Pred_Loc => Pred_Loc,
                          Location => Location);
      if not Found then
         raise KEY_ERROR;
      else
         Location.all.Info := Element;
      end if;
   end Modify;

   ----------------------------------------------------------------------
   procedure Retrieve (List    : in   List_Type;
                       Key     : in   Key_Type;
                       Element :  out Element_Type) is
      Found    : Boolean;
      Pred_Loc : Node_Ptr;
      Location : Node_Ptr;
   begin
      Search_Linked_List (List     => List,
                          Key      => Key,
                          Found    => Found,
                          Pred_Loc => Pred_Loc,
                          Location => Location);
      if not Found then
         raise KEY_ERROR;
      else
         Element := Location.all.Info;
      end if;
   end Retrieve;

   ----------------------------------------------------------------------
```

```ada
function Full (List : in List_Type) return Boolean is
begin
   return False;
end Full;
```

```ada
function Empty (List : in List_Type) return Boolean is
begin
   return List.Head = null;
end Empty;
```

```ada
function Length (List : in List_Type) return Natural is
   Location : Node_Ptr;   -- Designates current node
   Count    : Natural;
begin
   Count := 0;
   Location := List.Head;
   loop
      exit when Location = null;
      Count := Count + 1;
      Location := Location.all.Next;
   end loop;
   return Count;
end Length;
```

```ada
procedure Traverse
     (List    : in out List_Type;
      Process : not null access procedure (Element : in out Element_Type)) is
   Location : Node_Ptr;    -- Designates current node
begin
   Location := List.Head;   -- Start with the first node in the linked list
   loop
      exit when Location = null;
      Process (Location.all.Info);   -- Call user's procedure to process info
      Location := Location.all.Next; -- Move to next node
   end loop;
end Traverse;
end Unbounded_List;
```

7.4 Analyzing the List Implementations

Now let's compare the sequential and linked implementations of the list class. Just as we compared stack and queue implementations, we look at several different factors: the length of the source code required to implement the solutions, the amount of memory required to store the structure, and the amount of "work" the solution does.

Complexity

The size of the source code of the declarations, procedures, and functions for each implementation is summarized in the table that follows. As you can see from the chart, the linked implementation takes about 14% more lines of code than the sequential implementation. That is not a significant difference. Deciding which design is easier to understand is very subjective. Which implementation seems simpler to you?

Comparison of Lines of Code

	Array Implementation	Linked Implementation
Declarations (private part)	6	12
Clear	4	10
Empty	4	4
Full	4	4
Length	4	13
Search	31	17
Insert	22	22
Delete	17	21
Modify	15	17
Retrieve	16	18
Traverse	8	12
Total	131	150

Space

Now let's compare the storage requirements. The array field of our list record takes the same amount of memory, no matter how many array slots actually are used, because we need to reserve space for the maximum possible. The linked implementation using dynamically allocated storage space requires only enough space for the number of elements actually in the list at run time. However, as we discussed in detail in Chapters 5 and 6, each node element is larger, because we must store the link (the Next field) as well as the user's data. At this point you should be able to determine formulas for calculating the storage requirements of each implementation.

Array-Based List Storage = 2 × (storage needed for one integer)
   + Max_Size × (storage needed for one element)

Linked List Storage = storage needed for one pointer
   + current list size × (storage needed for one node)

Node Storage = storage needed for one element + storage needed for one pointer

Big-O

We can compare the relative "efficiency" of the two implementations. Most of the operations are nearly identical in the two implementations. The `Full` and `Empty` functions in both implementations are clearly O(1). As in the stack and queue operations, `Clear` is an O(1) operation for a sequential list but becomes an O(N) operation for a linked list. The sequential implementation merely marks the list as empty, whereas the linked implementation must access each list element to recycle its dynamically allocated space. The `Traversal` operation processes each element in the list once. Traverse is O(N) for both list representations.

The local search procedures are based on different search algorithms. `Search_Array` uses the binary search algorithm developed in Chapter 1. Each iteration of this loop reduces the search area by half. The maximum number of times we can cut a list in half before it is empty is $\log_2 N$. The binary search is therefore $O(\log_2 N)$. `Search_Linked_List` uses a sequential search. Beginning at the first element, it examines one element after another until the correct element is found. Because it potentially must search through all the elements in a linked list, the algorithm is O(N). Sequential searches are often called linear searches.

The `Retrieve` and `Modify` procedures are virtually identical for the two implementations. They first call the search and then assign the output parameters. However, as we just saw, the two search algorithms have different growth rates. The array version of `Retrieve` and `Modify` are $O(\log_2 N) + O(1) = O(\log_2 N)$ whereas the linked versions are $O(N) + O(1) = O(N)$.

Both insert operations call the local search procedure to find the insertion position. Then they make space for the new element and fill it with the data. To make space for an element in an array requires the movement of all the elements that follow the insertion point. The number of elements to be moved by the array slice assignment statement ranges from 0, when we insert to the end of the list, to `List.Length`, when we insert to the beginning of the list. Here is a case where an assignment statement is not O(1), but O(N). So the growth rate for our array-based insertion algorithm is $O(\log_2 N) + O(N) = O(N)$. In this algorithm, the search is the "goldfish" (discussed in Chapter 5) and making space in the array is the "elephant."

The insertion part of the algorithm for the linked list representation simply requires the reassignment of a couple of pointers—an O(1) operation. This characteristic is one of the main advantages of linking. However, adding the linear search task to the insertion task gives us $O(N) + O(1) = O(N)$—the same Big-O approximation as for the sequential list! Doesn't the linking offer any advantage in efficiency? Remember that the Big-O evaluations are only rough approximations of the amount of work that an operation does. We'll look at some timing tests in the next section to see whether the linked list's insertion operation really is faster.

The `Delete` procedure is similar to `Insert`. Both delete operations call the local search procedure and then reclaim the space used by the deleted element. Reclaiming space in an array requires the same sort of data movement we used in the insert algorithm—an O(N) operation. The time to recycle the memory used by a node in the linked list does not depend on the number of elements in the list so it is an O(1) operation. Combining the two operations for each implementation shows that each is O(N).

This Big-O analysis does not mean that both implementations will take the same amount of time to execute, however. The sequential implementation requires a great deal of data movement for both `Insert` and `Delete`. Does all this data movement really make any difference? It doesn't matter too much when the list is very small. If there are many elements or the elements are large, however, the data movement starts to add up.

The table that follows summarizes the Big-O comparison of the list operations for sequential and linked implementations.

Big-O Comparison of Key-Ordered List Operations

	Array Implementation	Linked Implementation
Clear	$O(1)$	$O(N)$
Empty	$O(1)$	$O(1)$
Full	$O(1)$	$O(1)$
Length	$O(1)$	$O(N)$
Search	$O(\log_2 N)$	$O(N)$
Insert [Search + Place in List]	$O(N)$ $[O(\log_2 N) + O(N)]$	$O(N)$ $[O(N) + O(1)]$
Delete [Search + Remove]	$O(N)$ $[O(\log_2 N) + O(N)]$	$O(N)$ $[O(N) + O(1)]$
Modify [Search + Assignment]	$O(\log_2 N)$ $[O(\log_2 N) + O(1)]$	$O(N)$ $[O(N) + O(1)]$
Retrieve [Search + Assignment]	$O(\log_2 N)$ $[O(\log_2 N) + O(1)]$	$O(N)$ $[O(N) + O(1)]$
Traverse	$O(N)$	$O(N)$

Time

Let's look at an actual timed test case, with real numbers. The following table shows how long it takes one particular computer to insert and then delete 10,000 elements (a record containing an integer key and a 60-character string) in various orders. The test program ran three cases:

1. *Random inserts/deletes:* The test program inserted the elements in "random" order, then deleted them in the same order.

2. *End of list inserts/deletes:* The test program inserted elements with keys from 1 through 10,000, in order; then it deleted the elements in reverse order (10,000 through 1) so that insertions and deletions always took place at the end of the list.

3. *Front of list inserts/deletes:* The test program inserted elements in reverse order, from key 10,000 through 1; then it deleted the elements in order (1 through 10,000) so that insertions and deletions always took place at the beginning of the list.

Time for List Operations (Milliseconds)

	Array Implementation	Linked Implementation
Case 1: Random		
Insert	995.14	1259.35
Delete	1034.80	1041.89
Case 2: List End		
Insert	4.89	1346.88
Delete	4.30	1328.48
Case 3: List Front		
Insert	2224.82	6.16
Delete	2117.16	4.51

As you can see from the information in the table, the times for both implementations are about the same for random additions and deletions to the list (Case 1).

In Case 2, we eliminated the array implementation's data movement by inserting and deleting only at the end of the list. This case is a race between search algorithms. When searching for the last item in these lists, the binary search of the array requires $\log_2 N$ comparisons whereas the linear search of the linked list requires N comparisons. Because no elements are moved to make room at the end of the array, the create/free space task is O(1) for both implementations. The timing data show the expected difference between a binary and linear search of a large list.

In Case 3 we maximize the array implementation's data movement by inserting and deleting only at the front of the list. The linear search performed in the linked version takes only one comparison when the key value belongs at the front of the list. So it should come as no surprise that the linked version is so much faster in this case.

Other Factors to Consider

Choosing to use a sequential or linked implementation for a particular application depends greatly on what you want to do with the data stored in the list. We already have compared the operations that were specified in our key-ordered list package. With its binary search, the sequential implementation provides superior performance for retrieve and modify operations. But if your application is more involved with inserting and deleting, the linked version may provide better performance. If the maximum number of elements in the list cannot be predicted, a linked list is preferable, especially if the list elements for the application are large.

There are other operations that might be specified for an ordered list, some of which are better for one implementation than another. For instance, if the dominant activity in your application is to access the nth element in the list, or if you need to print out the elements in reverse order, a sequential list is preferable to a linked list.

7.5 Testing the List Operations

By means of a test driver, we can test the list package independently of the program that will use it. The simplest kind of test driver sets up a scenario that executes the various test cases. To make sure that you have tested all the necessary cases, you should make a test plan, listing all the list operations and the tests needed for each.

You can use the same test driver to test both the sequential and linked list implementations; you merely replace the package names and the list object declaration. Except for the `Full` function, you should get the same test results for both implementations.

Summary

We have seen how lists may be represented in a sequential or linked representation and how they may be implemented with static (an array) or dynamic variables. The list class specification at the beginning of this chapter didn't mention any of these design issues, so we were free to implement the abstract data structure list in many ways. There was nothing in the specification of this class to say that the list was sequential or linked, or that its elements were stored in statically or dynamically allocated storage.

We could specify a number of other operations for the list package. Some operations, such as one to find the preceding node in a list, are easy to implement for a sequential list but would be difficult to implement using a list that is linked in one direction (like the lists in this chapter). This operation would be simpler if the list had links going both forward and backward. We can think of many variations for representing a linked list in order to simplify the kinds of operations that are specified for the list: doubly linked lists, circular lists, or lists that are accessed from both the beginning and the end. We continue this discussion in Chapter 8.

The idea of linking the elements in a data structure is not specific to the type of list we have discussed in this chapter. In Chapters 5 and 6 we implemented stacks and queues as linked structures; we use this powerful tool to implement other data structures in this book.

Exercises

Logical Level

1. Give examples from the "real world" of unsorted lists, key-ordered lists that permit duplicate keys, and key-ordered lists that do not permit duplicate keys.
2. Describe how the individuals in each of the following groups of people could be uniquely identified; that is, what would make a good key value for each of the groups?
   a. Citizens of a country who are eligible to vote
   b. Members of a sports team
   c. Students in a school

d. Email users
e. Automobile drivers
f. Actors/actresses in a play
g. Cell phone owners
h. Nobel Peace Prize winners
i. Employees of a large corporation
j. Doctors who prescribe controlled drugs

3. Describe the operations of a key-ordered list at the logical level.
4. Define the following terms:
   a. Sorted list
   b. Key-ordered list
   c. Container class
   d. Constructor
   e. Destructor
   f. Transformer
   g. Observer
   h. Iterator
5. a. How are the lists described in this chapter similar to the stacks and queues described in the previous two chapters?
   b. How are the lists described in this chapter different from the stacks and queues described in the previous two chapters?
   c. If you were to use inheritance to relate lists, stacks, and queues, which class(es) would be on the general side of the inheritance relationship and which would be on the specialized side of the inheritance relationship?
6. Draw a Unified Modeling Language (UML) diagram of the generic key-ordered list class defined in Specification 7.1.
7. Discuss changes, if any, that would have to be made to the key-ordered list specification if nonunique (duplicate) keys are allowed in the list.
8. The generic procedure `Traverse` of our key-ordered list class has a formal parameter called `Process`. Procedure `Process` has a single parameter, `Element`. Discuss the virtues of changing the mode of parameter `Element` from `in out` to `in`. What are the virtues of leaving it mode `in out`?

Application Level

9. Given the following declarations:

```
type Credit_Rating_Type is (Poor, Fair, Good, Excellent);
type Company_String is String (1..20);
type Dollars        is delta 0.01 digits 8 range 0.00 .. 100_000.00;
```

```
type Account_Rec is
   record
      Account_Number  : Positive;
      Company_Name    : Company_String;
      Balance_Due     : Dollars;
      Credit_Rating   : Credit_Rating_Type;
   end record;
```
  a. Write a function called `Number_Of` that returns the `Account_Number` field of a parameter of type `Account_Rec`.
  b. Instantiate a package called `Account_List` for a key-ordered list class whose elements are `Account_Rec`s in ascending order by `Account_Number`.
  c. Write a function called `Name_Of` that returns the `Company_Name` field of a parameter of type `Account_Rec`.
  d. Instantiate a package for a key-ordered list class whose elements are `Account_Rec`s in ascending order by `Company_Name`.
  e. Instantiate a package for a key-ordered list class whose elements are `Account_Rec`s in descending order by `Company_Name`. Hint: You need only change a single character in the answer you wrote for part (d).
  f. We need a key-ordered list of `Account_Rec`s ordered alphabetically by `Company_Name` similar to what you created in part (d). This time, we need to be able to insert duplicate company names. We can, however, assume that companies with the same name have different account numbers. Write all of the necessary code to instantiate such a key-ordered list.

10. Rewrite the `Label` procedure given in the address book application developed in this chapter so that it prints labels sorted by ZIP code instead of by name. Hint: Instantiate a local key-ordered list package using the ZIP code as a key.

11. The types we used to model phone numbers in the address book application are valid for North America. Do some research on the web to learn how other countries organize their phone numbers. Then design a hierarchy of phone number classes that will handle phone numbers from all countries. Your solution need not have a complete hierarchy, but you should have enough information to convince yourself that your design can handle other phone number organizations.

Implementation Level

12. a. Explain the difference between a sequential and a linked representation of a list.
    b. Give an example of a problem for which a sequential list would be the better solution.
    c. Give an example of a problem for which a linked list would be the better solution.

13. *True or False.* If you answer false, correct the statement.
    a. An array is a random-access structure.
    b. A sequential list is a random-access structure.
    c. A linked list is a random-access structure.
    d. A sequential list is always stored in a static variable.
    e. The elements in a linked list can be stored in an array.
14. In relation to elaboration/execution time, what is meant by
    a. a static variable?
    b. a dynamic variable?

    Use the following declarations in Exercises 15–25:

```
type Node_Type;
type Node_Ptr is access Node_Type;
type Node_Type is
   record
      Info : Element_Type;     -- One element
      Next : Node_Ptr;         -- Link to next node in the list
   end record;

List : Node_Ptr;
A    : Node_Ptr;
B    : Node_Ptr;
Ptr  : Node_Ptr;
One_Node : Node_Type;
```

15. *True or False.* If you answer false, explain why.
    a. The space for the variable `Ptr` is dynamically allocated at run time.
    b. The space for `Ptr.all` is dynamically allocated at run time.
    c. `Ptr` is undefined until the `new` operator is used to assign it a value.
    d. After the declarations, `Ptr` is equal to `null`.
    e. After the statement `Ptr := new Node_Type`, `Ptr.all.Next` is `null`.
    f. Because `Ptr` accesses a record of type `Node_Type`, `Ptr` and `One_Node` take the same amount of space in memory.
    g. The declaration of `One_Node` is syntactically incorrect, because `Node_Type` records can only be allocated dynamically.

    Use the linked list pictured below in Exercises 16–19.

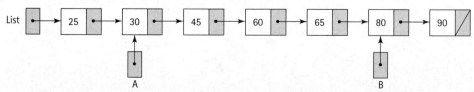

16. Give the values of the following expressions:
    a. `A.all.Info`
    b. `B.all.next.all.Info`
    c. `List.all.Next.all.Next.all.Info`
17. Do the following statements evaluate to true or to false?
    a. `List.all.Next  =  A`
    b. `A.all.Next.all.Info  =  60`
    c. `B.all.Next  =  null`
    d. `List.all.Info  =  25`
18. Decide whether the syntax in each of the following assignment statements is valid or invalid. If it is invalid, explain what is wrong.
    a. `List.all.Next := A.all.Next;`
    b. `List.all.Next := B.all.Next.all;`
    c. `List.all := B;`
    d. `B := A.all.Next.all.Info;`
    e. `A.all.Info := B.all.Info;`
    f. `List := B.all.Next.all.Next;`
    g. `B := B.all.Next.all.Next.all.Next;`
19. Write a statement to do each of the following:
    a. Make `List` designate the node containing 45.
    b. Make `B` designate the last node in the list.
    c. Make `List` designate an empty list. (Don't worry about memory leaks.)
    d. Set the `Info` value of the node containing 45 to 46.
20. Show what is written by the following segment of code:

    ```
    List := new Node_Type;
    Ptr  := new Node_Type;
    List.all.Info := 2;
    Ptr.all.Info  := 5;
    List := Ptr;
    Ptr.all.Info := 7;
    Put (Ptr.all.Info);
    Put (List.all.Info);
    ```

21. Show what is written by the following segment of code:

    ```
    List := new Node_Type'(Info => 10, Next => null);
    Ptr  := new Node_Type'(Info => 18, Next => null);
    Ptr  := new Node_Type;
    Ptr.all.Info := 20;
    Ptr.all.Next := List;
    ```

```
List := Ptr;
loop
   exit when Ptr = null;
   Put (Ptr.all.Info);
   New_Line;
   Ptr := Ptr.all.Next;
end loop;
```

22. Show what is written by the following segment of code:
    ```
    List := new Node_Type'(Info => 0, Next => null);
    for Count in 1..4 loop
       List := new Node_Type'(Info => Count, Next => List);
    end loop;
    Ptr := List;
    loop
       exit when Ptr = null;
       Put (Ptr.all.Info);
       New_Line;
       Ptr := Ptr.all.Next;
    end loop;
    ```

23. Show what is written by the following segment of code:
    ```
    List := new Node_Type'(Info => 5, Next => null);
    Ptr := List;
    for Count in 1..4 loop
       Ptr.all.Next := new Node_Type'(Info => Count, Next => List);
       Ptr := Ptr.all.Next;
    end loop;
    for Count in 1..6 loop
       Put (Ptr.all.Info);
       New_Line;
       Ptr := Ptr.all.Next;
    end loop;
    ```

24. Show what is written by the following segment of code:
    ```
    List := new Node_Type'(Info => 5, Next => null);
    Ptr := List;
    for Count in 1..4 loop
       Ptr.all.Next := new Node_Type'(Info => Count, Next => List);
       Ptr := Ptr.all.Next;
    end loop;
    for Count in 1..6 loop
       Put (Ptr.all.Info);
       New_Line;
       Ptr := Ptr.all.Next.all.Next;
    end loop;
    ```

25. Show what is written by the following segment of code, starting with the statement that follows the procedure:

    ```
    procedure Attach (Value : in      Natural;
                      Ptr   : in out  Node_Ptr) is
    begin
       Ptr := new Node_Type;
       Ptr.all.Info := Value;
    end Attach;

    Attach (Value => 2, Ptr => List);
    Attach (Value => 4, Ptr => List.all.Next);
    Attach (Value => 6, Ptr => List.all.Next.all.Next);
    Ptr := List;
    loop
       exit when Ptr = null;
       Put (Ptr.all.Info);
       New_Line;
       Ptr := Ptr.all.Next;
    end loop;
    ```

26. Procedure `Traverse` of our list package has a precondition that the user's supplied function (through parameter `Process`) cannot change the key of an element.
    a. Rewrite the specification of `Traverse` so that it has no preconditions but raises the exception KEY_ERROR if the user-supplied element processing procedure attempts to change the key of an element.
    b. Implement the body of this modified `Traverse`.
    c. When the body you wrote for part (b) raises KEY_ERROR, does it leave the original list unchanged? Consider the possibility that the user's supplied procedure may change only some of the key in the list. If necessary, rewrite comments in the specification you wrote for part (a).

27. The key-ordered list class is to be extended with a Boolean function, `Value_In_List`, which inputs a list and a key value and determines whether there is an element with this key in the list.
    a. Write the specification for this function as it would appear in either Specification 7.1 or Specification 7.4.
    b. Write the function body as it would appear in Body 7.2 (using the sequential implementation).
    c. Write the function body as it would appear in Body 7.4 (using the linked list implementation).
    d. Describe `Value_In_List` in terms of Big-O for each of the two implementations.

28. The key-ordered list class is to be extended with the function `Size`, which returns the number of elements in a list.

   a. Write the specification for this function as it would appear in either Specification 7.1 or Specification 7.4.
   b. Write the function body as it would appear in Body 7.2 (using the sequential implementation).
   c. Write the function body as it would appear in Body 7.4 (using the linked list implementation).
   d. Describe `Size` in terms of Big-O for each of the two implementations.

29. The key-ordered list class is to be extended with a procedure, `Merge_Lists`, with the following specification:

```
procedure Merge_Lists (List_1   : in out List_Type;
                      List_2    : in out List_Type;
                      New_List  :    out List_Type);
-- Purpose        : Merges two lists into a single list
--
-- Preconditions  : New_List is empty
--                  No key is present in both List_1 and List_2
--
-- Postconditions : List_1 and List_2 are empty
--                  New_List contains all the elements
--                     from List_1 and List_2
```

   a. Write the procedure body as it would appear in Body 7.2 (using the sequential implementation). You may not call the `Insert` operation in your merge body.
   b. Write the procedure body as it would appear in Body 7.2 (using the sequential implementation). This time, develop a solution that calls the `Insert` operation.
   c. Describe `Merge_Lists` in terms of Big-O for each of the two implementations from parts (a) and (b).
   d. Write the procedure body as it would appear in Body 7.4 (using the linked list implementation). You may not call the `Insert` operation in your merge body.
   e. Write the procedure body as it would appear in Body 7.4 (using the linked list implementation). This time, you should call the `Insert` operation in your merge body.
   f. Describe `Merge_Lists` in terms of Big-O for each of the two implementations from parts (d) and (e).

30. The key-ordered list class is to be extended with a procedure, Split_List, with the following specification:

```
procedure Split_List (Main_List : in out List_Type;
                      Split_Key : in      Key_Type;
                      List_1    :         out List_Type;
                      List_2    :         out List_Type);
-- Divides a list into two lists according to the key value of each
-- element.  All elements with keys less than Split_Key will be put
-- into List_1, all elements with keys greater than or equal to
-- Split_Key will be put into List_2.
--
-- Preconditions  : List_1 and List_2 are empty.
--
-- Postconditions : Main_List is empty
--                  List_1 contains all elements from Main_List with
--                      keys less than Split_Key
--                  List_2 contains all elements from Main_List with
--                      keys greater than or equal to Split_Key
```

    a. Write the procedure body as it would appear in Body 7.2 (using the sequential implementation).

    b. Write the procedure body as it would appear in Body 7.4 (using the linked list implementation).

    c. Describe the two algorithms you used for Split_List in terms of Big-O.

    d. Compare the two implementations of Split_List in terms of space requirements.

31. The key-ordered list class is to be extended by the addition of procedure Get_Element, which takes a key-ordered list and an integer, Position, and returns a copy of the element in the specified list position. For instance, if Position is 1, a copy of the first list element is returned; if Position is 12, a copy of the twelfth list element is returned. If Position is greater than the number of elements in the list, CONSTRAINT_ERROR is raised.

    a. Write the specification for procedure Get_Element as it would appear in either Specification 7.1 or Specification 7.4.

    b. Write the procedure body as it would appear in Body 7.2 (using the sequential implementation).

    c. Write the procedure body as it would appear in Body 7.4 (using the linked list implementation).

    d. Describe Get_Element in terms of Big-O for each of the two implementations.

32. The key-ordered list class is to be extended by the addition of procedure `Reverse_Traverse`, with the identical parameter profile (signature) as `Traverse`. As its name implies, this procedure processes the elements in the list in descending order by key.

   a. Write the specification for `Reverse_Traverse` as it would appear in either Specification 7.1 or Specification 7.4.

   b. Write the procedure body for `Reverse_Traverse` as it would appear in Body 7.2 (using the sequential implementation).

   c. Write the procedure body for `Reverse_Traverse` as it would appear in Body 7.4 (using the linked list implementation). Hint: Make use of the stack class.

   d. Compare the sequential and linked versions of `Reverse_Traverse`, in terms of code length, space requirements, and Big-O.

Programming Problems

33. Create a subclass of `Key_Ordered_List.List_Type`. Your class should extend the original key-ordered class with all of the operations described in Exercises 27 through 32.

    Write a complete test plan and test program to test the new operations in your list subclass.

34. Create a subclass of `Unbounded_List.List_Type`. Your class should extend the original key-ordered class with all of the operations described in Exercises 27 through 32.

    Write a complete test plan and test program to test the new operations in your list subclass.

35. The following is a specification of a subclass of `Unbounded_List.List_Type`. This extension of the unbounded key-ordered list class developed in this chapter provides an alternative mechanism to iterate through all of the elements of a list. This mechanism is based on the concept of the cursor. Like a cursor that indicates your current position in a document you are typing in a word processor, a list cursor indicates the current element in the list.

```
generic
package Unbounded_List.Cursor is

   type List_Type is new Unbounded_List.List_Type with private;

   CURSOR_CONSTRAINT_ERROR : exception;

   -------------------------------------------------------------------
   function Element (List : in List_Type) return Element_Type;
   -- Purpose        : Return a copy of an element in List
   -- Preconditions  : None
```

```
   -- Postconditions : A copy of the element designated by List's cursor
   --                  is returned
   -- Exceptions     : CURSOR_CONSTRAINT_ERROR is raised if the List's cursor
   --                                          is undefined

   ---------------------------------------------------------------------
   function Cursor_Defined (List : in List_Type) return Boolean;
   -- Purpose        : Checks whether the List's cursor is currently defined
   -- Preconditions  : None
   -- Postconditions : Returns True if the List's cursor is defined;
   --                  otherwise, returns False.


   ---------------------------------------------------------------------
   procedure First (List : out List_Type);
   -- Purpose        : Sets List's cursor to the first element in List
   -- Preconditions  : None
   -- Postconditions : List's cursor designates the first element in List.
   --                  If there is no first element, the List's cursor
   --                  is undefined.


   ---------------------------------------------------------------------
   procedure Next (List : in out List_Type);
   -- Purpose        : Sets List's cursor to the next element in List
   -- Preconditions  : None
   -- Postconditions : List's cursor designates the next element in List.
   --                  If the cursor originally designated the last element of
   --                  List, the List's cursor will be undefined
   -- Exceptions     : CURSOR_CONSTRAINT_ERROR is raised if the List's cursor
   --                                          is undefined

private
   type List_Type is new Unbounded_List.List_Type with
      record
         Cursor : Node_Ptr;
      end record;
end Unbounded_List.Cursor;
```

An application programmer can use the following code to process all of the elements in an instance of this subclass:

```
My_List.First;           -- Set cursor to first element
loop
   exit when not My_List.Cursor_Defined;
   My_Element := My_List.Element;     -- Retrieve the current element
   Process (My_Element);              -- Process the current element
   My_List.Next;                      -- Move to the next element
end loop;
```

Using this subclass, application programmers need not process all of the elements in a list. They can restart at the beginning whenever necessary.

You task is to

a. Implement the body of package `Unbounded_List.Cursor`.

b. Write a test plan to test the package `Unbounded_List.Cursor`.

c. Write a test program to implement your test plan.

36. Repeat the previous exercise for a sequential list implementation. This time you will have to write the specification of the subclass.

37. Your assignment is to track the corporate careers of some up-and-coming executives who are busily changing jobs, being promoted and demoted, and, of course, getting paid.

In this (admittedly unrealistic) version of the corporate world, people either belong to a company or are unemployed. The list of people the program must deal with is not fixed; initially there are none, and new people may be introduced by the JOIN command (see page 477).

Executives within a company are ordered according to a seniority system and are numbered from 1 to N (the number of people in the company) to indicate their rank: 1 is the lowest rank and N is the highest. A new employee always enters at the bottom of the ladder and hence will always start with a rank of 1. When a new person joins a company, the rank of everyone in the company is increased by one, and when an employee quits, the rank of employees above him or her in that company is decreased by one. Promotions can also occur and affect the ranks in the obvious way.

Naturally, salaries are based on rank. An employee's salary is Rank * $1000. Unemployed people draw $50 in unemployment compensation.

Input

From file COMPANY.TXT: The company names are listed one per line. There will be at most 20 companies. Company names are at most 10 characters and do not contain embedded blanks.

From the keyboard: Commands, as listed below. Person and company names are at most 10 characters and do not contain embedded blanks.

JOIN *<person> <company>*

> *<Person>* joins the specified *<company>*. This may be the first reference to this person, or he or she may be unemployed. The person will not currently belong to another company. Remember that when a person joins a company he or she always starts at the bottom.

QUIT *<person>*

> *<Person>* quits his or her job and becomes unemployed. You may assume that the person is currently employed.

CHANGE *<person> <company>*

> *<Person>* quits his or her job and joins the specified new *<company>*. You may assume that the person is currently employed.

PROMOTE *<person>*

> *<Person>* is moved up one step in the current company, ahead of his or her immediate superior. If the person has highest rank within the company, no change occurs.

DEMOTE *<person>*

> *<Person>* is moved one step down in the current company, below his or her immediate subordinate. If the person has lowest rank within the company, no change occurs.

PAYDAY

> Each person is paid his or her salary as specified above. (You must keep track of the amount each person has earned from the start of the program.)

EMPLOYEES *<company>*

> The current list of employees should be printed for the specified *<company>*. The employees must be printed in order of rank; either top to bottom or bottom to top is appropriate.

UNEMPLOY

> The list of unemployed people should be printed.

DUMP

> Print the employees in each company, as specified under the EMPLOYEES command above, then print the unemployed people. Label the output appropriately.

END

> Stop accepting commands.

Chapter 7: Key-Ordered Lists

Note that the CHANGE, PROMOTE, and DEMOTE commands do not tell you the person's current employer; you will have to search to find the person.

Output (to screen and file EMPLOY.OUT)

Echo print all commands, and print out a message that indicates what action has been taken. (For the EMPLOYEES and UNEMPLOY commands, print out the information specified in the Input section.)

After all the commands have been processed, print out one list consisting of all the people who have been mentioned in any command and the total amount of money they have accumulated. The list should be sorted by decreasing order of total salary accumulated.

Testing

Here is some sample data:

File COMPANY:

Apple

Microsoft

IBM

Dell

Google

NEC

XEROX

Commands from keyboard:

```
JOIN David XEROX       JOIN Bob Apple         QUIT David
JOIN Mario XEROX       JOIN Susan IBM         PROMOTE Marge
JOIN John Dell         JOIN Joshua Dell       PROMOTE Marge
JOIN Fred Dell         JOIN Max NEC           PAYDAY
JOIN Phil IBM          PAYDAY                 UNEMPLOY
CHANGE Fred NEC        EMPLOYEES IBM          EMPLOYEES IBM
JOIN Miriam Dell       EMPLOYEES Dell         EMPLOYEES XEROX
JOIN Sharon Microsoft  EMPLOYEES NEC          JOIN John Google
JOIN Harvey Dell       JOIN Tim IBM           JOIN Ralph Google
CHANGE Miriam Apple    DEMOTE Harvey          QUIT Phil
PAYDAY                 PROMOTE Max            JOIN Phil Google
EMPLOYEES Dell         DEMOTE Marge           DUMP
JOIN Marge Apple       CHANGE Marge IBM       CHANGE Marge Google
JOIN Lesley Microsoft  QUIT John              CHANGE Miriam Google
JOIN Sam Dell          PAYDAY                 CHANGE Fred Google
JOIN George NEC        QUIT Mario             CHANGE Susan Google
```

```
QUIT Tim              PROMOTE Fred          PROMOTE Bob
PAYDAY                DEMOTE Miriam         DEMOTE Bob
EMPLOYEES Google      JOIN Laszlo Dell      DEMOTE John
JOIN Mario XEROX      PROMOTE Laszlo        PAYDAY
JOIN David XEROX      CHANGE Joshua Google  DUMP
EMPLOYEES XEROX       PAYDAY                END
JOIN Tim Google       PROMOTE Sharon
PROMOTE Tim           DEMOTE Lesley
```

(This programming assignment was developed from an idea by Jim Bitner.)

Lists Plus

Goals for this chapter include that you should be able to
- implement a circular linked list.
- implement a doubly linked list.
- implement a linked list with a header node or a trailer node or both.
- implement a linked list in an array of records.
- implement a linked list in a direct file.
- discuss design issues for implementing lists with nonunique keys.

In Chapter 7 you saw how a useful data structure, the ordered list, can be represented as either a sequential or a linked structure. There are many variations of list structures: lists with restricted access (such as the stack and the queue) and lists with special requirements whose operations can be simplified by using different implementations of the linked list.

As we consider many possible implementations, note that the specifications of the class operations do not change. From the application programmer's perspective, the list (or stack or queue) is a logical structure that can be manipulated through a set of operations. It shouldn't matter to the application if we change the implementation. We repeat this point over and over because it may be the most important concept you will learn from this book. In this chapter we develop additional implementations of the key-ordered list class described by Specifications 7.1 and 7.4. Each implementation has advantages and disadvantages. No single implementation is best for all ordered list needs.

8.1 Circular Linked Lists

The linked list data structures that we implemented in Chapter 7 are characterized by a linear (line-like) relationship between the elements: Each element (except the first one) has a unique predecessor, and each element (except the last one) has a unique successor. The algorithm we developed in Chapter 7 for inserting into a linear linked list is O(1) for adding an element to the beginning of the list and O(N) for adding to the end of the list. These differences were confirmed by the insertion times found in our experiments.

Circular linked list   A linked list in which every node has a successor; the "last" element is succeeded by the "first" element.

It is not uncommon for the data we want to add to a list to already be in order. Sometimes people manually sort raw data before turning it over to a data entry clerk. Data produced by other programs is often in some order. With sorted input data, we always insert at the end of the list. It is ironic that the work done previously to order the data now results in maximum insertion times. However, we can improve the efficiency of inserting at the end of a list by using a **circular linked list**. Circular lists are good for applications that require access to both ends of the list.

In a circular linked list, the pointer in the Next field of the last node points back to the first node instead of containing null (Figure 8.1). We can start at any node in the list and traverse the whole list. Thus we can make our external pointer to the list point to any node and still be able to access every node in the list. In fact, a truly circular list may not have a first or a last node—just a ring of elements linked to each other.

Of course, we must now ensure that all of our list operations maintain this new property of the list: that after the execution of any list operation, the last node contin-

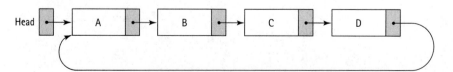

Figure 8.1   *A circular linked list.*

ues to point to the front node. A quick consideration of each of the operations should convince us that we could continue to efficiently support all of them except when an operation changes the first element on the list. Consider, for example, if we try to delete the first element. Our previous delete approach would simply change the external pointer to designate the second element on the list, effectively removing the first element. Now, however, we must also update the reference in the last element on the list, so that it points to the new first element. The only way to do that is to traverse the entire list to obtain access to the last element, and then make the change. A similar problem arises if we insert an item into the front of the list.

Inserting and deleting elements at the front of a list might be a common operation for some applications. Our linear linked list approach supported these operations very efficiently, but our first circular linked list approach does not. We can fix this problem by letting our external pointer designate the last element in the list rather than the first; now we have direct access to both the first and the last elements in the list. Tail designates the last node, and Tail.all.Next designates the first node in the list (Figure 8.2[a]). The Next field of the node in a list with only one element points to the element itself (Figure 8.2[b]). An empty circular list is represented by a null value for the external pointer to the list (Figure 8.2[c]).

We mentioned this type of list structure in Chapter 6, when we discussed circular linked queues. We let the external pointer, Queue.Rear, point to the rear node; Queue.Rear.all.Next then points to the front node. Let's look at how to implement the key-ordered list class (Specification 7.4) as a circular linked list. We develop some of the operations in detail; the rest are left as exercises.

Other than using the more descriptive field name Tail in place of Head, there is no need to change any of the private part declarations of Specification 7.4 to make the list circular, rather than linear. After all, the fields in the nodes are the same; only the value of the Next field of the last node has changed. How does the circular nature of the list change the implementation of the list operations? An empty circular list is one with a

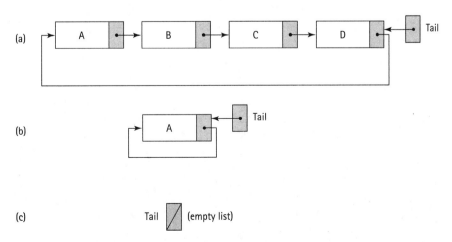

Figure 8.2 *Circular linked lists with the external pointer pointing to the rear element.*

null external pointer, so the `Empty` operation is not changed at all. However, using a circular list requires an obvious change in algorithms that traverse the list (`Traverse`, `Search`, and `Clear`, for instance). We no longer stop when the traversing pointer becomes `null`. Unless the list is empty, the pointer never becomes `null`. Instead we must look for the external pointer itself as a stop sign.

Traversing a Circular List

Let's write the body of the generic procedure `Traverse` that is described in Specification 7.4. We initialize a temporary pointer, `Location`, to the beginning of the list. Because `List.Tail`, the external pointer, designates the last element in the list, we must initialize `Location` to `List.Tail.all.Next`. We continue until Location comes full circle—when `Location = List.Tail`.

Traverse (first attempt)
```
    Location := List.Tail.all.Next        - - Start with "first" node
    loop
        Process (Location.all.Info)
        exit when Location = List.Tail
        Location := Location.all.Next
    end loop
```

We have used a midtest loop to delay checking if `Location = List.Tail` until after we have processed the element. If we had used a pretest loop

Traverse (second attempt)
```
    Location := List.Tail.all.Next        - - Start with "first" node
    loop
        exit when Location = List.Tail    - - Pretest loop fails to process last element in the list
        Process (Location.all.Info)
        Location := Location.all.Next
    end loop
```

we would have stopped before processing the last element. This problem is easy to spot in a list containing only one element—when `List.Tail` and `List.Tail.all.Next` are equal (see Figure 8.2[b]). In this case, `Location` is initialized to `List.Tail` and we exit the loop without processing the only element in the list. Therefore, we need to use a midtest looping structure with the check made after processing the element.

Because this midtest loop always processes one element, we have a problem when the list is empty (Figure 8.2[c]). The assignment of `List.Tail.all.Next` to `Location` raises CONSTRAINT_ERROR when `List.Tail` is null. We can resolve this problem by checking for this possibility ahead of time and avoiding the loop if the list is empty. Here is the Ada code for procedure `Traverse`:

```
procedure Traverse (List : in out List_Type) is
    Location : Node_Ptr;        -- Designates current node
```

```
begin
   if List.Tail /= null then      -- Don't do anything if List is empty
      Location := List.Tail.all.Next;   -- Start at beginning of list
      loop
         Process (Location.all.Info);   -- Call user's process procedure
         exit when Location = List.Tail;
         Location := Location.all.Next; -- Move to next node
      end loop;
   end if;
end Traverse;
```

Finding a List Element in a Circular List

The `Retrieve`, `Modify`, `Insert`, and `Delete` operations all require us to search the list. Again we write a local search procedure to simplify these other operations. Specification 8.1 describes the local search procedure for a circular linked list.

Specification 8.1 Circular Linked List Search

```
procedure Search_Circular_List (List     : in  List_Type;
                                Key      : in  Key_Type;
                                Found    : out Boolean;
                                Pred_Loc : out Node_Ptr;
                                Location : out Node_Ptr);

-- Purpose        : Searches for the location of Key in the List
-- Preconditions  : The nodes in List are in ascending order
--                  The List is circularly linked (List.Tail designates
--                      the last node).
-- Postconditions : If List is empty
--                      Found is False
--                      Location is null
--                      Pred_Loc is null
--                  elsif Key is in List
--                      Found is True
--                      Location designates the element with Key
--                      Pred_Loc designates the predecessor of the node
--                          designated by Location.
--                  else
--                      Found is False
--                      Location designates the node that would follow a
--                          node containing Key in the circular list.
--                      Pred_Loc designates the predecessor of the node
--                          designated by Location.
```

The `in` parameters for this procedure are an external pointer to the list and a key value to search for. The `out` parameters are a Boolean telling whether the key was found in the list, and two pointers to locate it.

Following the execution of the search procedure, if a matching key is found, Location points to the list node with that key and Pred_Loc points to its predecessor in the list (Figure 8.3[a]). Note that if Key is the smallest key in the list, Pred_Loc points to its physical predecessor—the last node in the circular list (Figure 8.3[b]). If Key is not in the list, Pred_Loc and Location point to the nodes that would be before and after it if the key were in the list (Figures 8.3[c] and 8.3[d]). If the list is empty, both pointers are returned as null (Figure 8.3[e]).

As we did in the previous chapter, we search the linked list looking for the key using the inchworm technique. We must modify the initialization of the two pointers and loop termination conditions for our circular list. For the circular list search, we initialize Location to point to the first node, and Pred_Loc to point to its predecessor. The predecessor is the last node in the list (Figure 8.4).

But wait a minute! Using this logic cannot give us the O(1) insertion at the end of the list that we wanted; it always starts the search at the beginning of the list. To optimize insertions at the end of the list we need to add a test before our loop to see if the key should go at the end of the list. And like the traversal operation we developed earlier, to prevent a CONSTRAINT_ERROR, we must check for an empty list before we begin our search loop. Here is the resulting search procedure:

```
procedure Search_Circular_List (List     : in List_Type;
                                Key      : in Key_Type;
                                Found    : out Boolean;
                                Pred_Loc : out Node_Ptr;
                                Location : out Node_Ptr) is
begin
   if List.Tail = null then        -- Is the list empty
      Found    := False;
      Location := null;
      Pred_Loc := null;
   elsif Key_Of (List.Tail.all.Info) < Key then -- Is Key greater than
      Found    := False;                        -- any Key in the list?
      Location := List.Tail.all.Next;  -- Goes between last and first node
      Pred_Loc := List.Tail;
   else   -- Search the list from the beginning
      Location := List.Tail.all.Next;  -- Start at the beginning of
      Pred_Loc := List.Tail;           -- the linked list
      -- Search the linked list
      -- Each iteration, check one node
      loop
         exit when Key < Key_Of (Location.all.Info) or else   -- Passed by
                   Key = Key_Of (Location.all.Info);          -- Found it
         Pred_Loc := Location;              -- Move inchworm's tail
         Location := Location.all.Next;     -- Move inchworm's head
      end loop;
      Found := Key = Key_Of (Location.all.Info);
   end if;
end Search_Circular_List;
```

8.1 Circular Linked Lists | 487

(a) The general case (Find John)

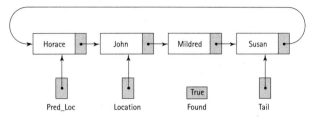

(b) Searching for the smallest list element (Find Horace)

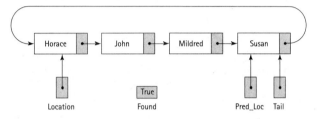

(c) Searching for element that isn't there (Find Kelly)

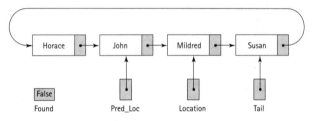

(d) Searching for element bigger than any in the list (Find Tom)

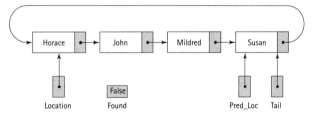

(e) Searching an empty list (Find Mildred)

Figure 8.3 *Searching a circular linked list.*

488 | Chapter 8: Lists Plus

```
Location := List.Tail.all.Next;
Pred_Loc := List.Tail;
```

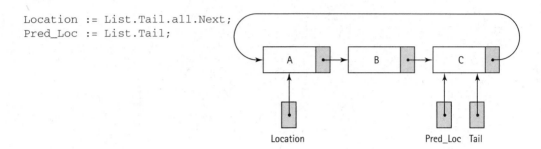

Figure 8.4 *Initializing for the search of a circular list.*

The loop in our search procedure executes until (1) we find the desired key, or (2) we have passed the spot in the list where the key should be. Why don't we need the third condition (we reach the "end" of the list) that we had in our original search of a linked list (in Chapter 7)? The check to see if Key comes after the last node prior to the loop in the circular list search ensures that we never go beyond the end of the list.

Inserting into a Circular List

The algorithm to insert an element into a sorted circular linked list is similar to that for the linear list insertion:

Insert
    Find the place where the new element belongs
    Create space for the new element
    Link the new element into the list

The first task is simple: We just call Search_Circular_List. If the search procedure finds an element with the same key of the element we wish to insert, the insert procedure should raise DUPLICATE_KEY. The second task, creating space for the new element, is the same: We use the allocator new.

Now we are ready to link the new element into the list. This node is linked after the node designated by Pred_Loc. If the list is empty, the search procedure returns null for Pred_Loc (Figure 8.3[e]); there is no predecessor to link the new node after. In this case we want to make List.Tail point to the new node (Figure 8.5[a]). Here is the algorithm:

Put Element into Empty List
    List.Tail := new Node_Type   *-- Get space*
    List.Tail.all.Info := Item   *-- Assign element*
    List.Tail.all.Next := List.Tail   *-- Link "last" to "first"*

8.1 Circular Linked Lists | 489

Once the list is no longer empty, the algorithm for linking an element into the list is the same at the beginning, the middle, and the end of the list; we link it between the nodes designated by `Pred_Loc` and `Location`. Figure 8.5 illustrates this algorithm for inserting into the "middle" (Figure 8.5[b]), the "beginning" (Figure 8.5[c]), and the "end" (Figure 8.5[d]). In all three cases, we set the `Next` field of the new node to point to the same node that `Location` points to and change the `Next` field of the node designated by `Pred_Loc` so that it points to our new node. Figure 8.5(d) indicates that there is one more pointer to change when we add a new node to the end of the list. The external pointer, `List.Tail`, now must designate the new "last" node. This special case occurs when the key we wish to add is greater than any other key in the list. Here is the algorithm for adding a node to a nonempty list:

Put Element into Nonempty List
    Pred_Loc.all.Next := new Node_Type'(Info => Item, Next => Location)
    if Key > Key of the last node in the list then
        List.Tail := List.Tail.all.Next
    end if

The procedure body with exceptions added is shown below:

```
procedure Insert (List : in out List_Type;
                  Item : in      Element_Type) is
   Have_Duplicate : Boolean;
   Pred_Loc       : Node_Ptr;
   Location       : Node_Ptr;
begin
   Search_Circular_List (List     => List,
                         Key      => Key_Of (Item),
                         Found    => Have_Duplicate,
                         Pred_Loc => Pred_Loc,
                         Location => Location);
   if Have_Duplicate then
      raise DUPLICATE_KEY;
   elsif Location = null then         -- Is the list empty?
      List.Tail     := new Node_Type;    -- Add first node to list
      List.Tail.all := (Info => Item, Next => List.Tail);
   else      -- Add at the middle or end
      Pred_Loc.all.Next := new Node_Type'(Info => Item, Next => Location);
      -- Did we add at end of list?
      if Key_Of (Location.all.Info) < Key_Of (Item) then
         List.Tail := List.Tail.all.Next;
      end if;
   end if;
exception
   when STORAGE_ERROR =>    -- Overflow when no storage available
      raise OVERFLOW;
end Insert;
```

490 | Chapter 8: Lists Plus

(a) Inserting into an empty list (Insert Horace)

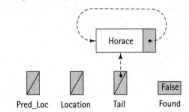

(b) Inserting into the middle of the list (Insert Kelly)

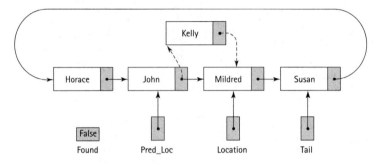

(c) Inserting at the beginning of the list (Insert Amy)

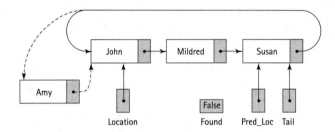

(d) Inserting at the end of the list (Insert Tom)

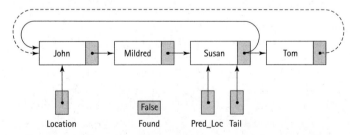

Figure 8.5 *Inserting into a circular linked list. Dashed arrows show the new values of pointers after the insert operation is complete.*

Deleting from a Circular List

To delete an element from the circular linked list, we use the same general algorithm that we developed in Chapter 7:

Delete
    Find the element in the list
    Remove the element from the list
    Recycle the memory used by the node

For the first task, we use our trusty helper, `Search_Circular_List`. On return from a call to this search procedure, `Location` points to the node we wish to delete, and `Pred_Loc` points to its predecessor in the list. To remove the node from the list, we reset its predecessor's `Next` field to jump over the node we are deleting.

```
Pred_Loc.all.Next := Location.all.Next;
```

That assignment statement works for at least the case of deleting from the middle of a list (Figure 8.6[a]). What kind of special cases do we have to consider? In the linear list version, we had to check for deleting the first (or first-and-only) element. From our experience with the insertion operation, we might surmise that deleting the smallest element (the first node) of the circular list is not a special case. Figure 8.6(b) shows that guess to be correct. However, deleting the only node in a circular list is a special case, as we see in Figure 8.6(c). The external pointer `List.Tail` must be set to `null` to indicate that the list is now empty. We can detect this situation by checking to see if `Pred_Loc` is equal to `Location` after the search; if so, the node we are deleting is the only one in the list.

We also might guess that deleting the largest list element (the last node) from a circular list is a special case. As Figure 8.6(d) illustrates, when we delete the last node, we first perform the general-case processing to unlink the node designated by `Location` from the list, then we reset the external pointer to point to its predecessor, which is designated by `Pred_Loc`. We can detect this situation by checking whether `Location` is equal to `List.Tail` after the search.

The complete procedure body for `Delete` with exceptions added is shown here:

```
procedure Delete (List : in out List_Type;
                  Key  : in      Key_Type) is
   Found    : Boolean;
   Pred_Loc : Node_Ptr;
   Location : Node_Ptr;
begin
   Search_Circular_List (List     => List,
                         Key      => Key,
                         Found    => Found,
                         Pred_Loc => Pred_Loc,
                         Location => Location);
```

(a) Deleting from the middle of the list (Delete John)

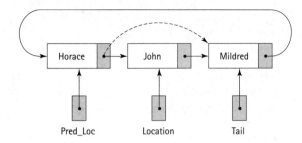

(b) Deleting from the beginning of the list (Delete Horace)

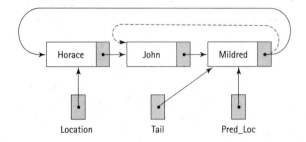

(c) Deleting the only element (Delete Susan)

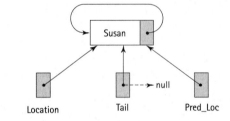

(d) Deleting from the end of the list (Delete Mildred)

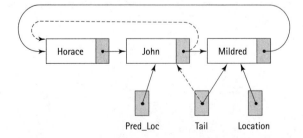

Figure 8.6 *Deleting from a circular linked list. Dashed arrows show the new values of pointers after the delete operation is complete.*

```
      if not Found then
         raise KEY_ERROR;
      elsif Pred_Loc = Location then    -- Deleting the only node in the list?
         Free (List.Tail);     -- Recycle the only node in the list
      else
         Pred_Loc.all.Next := Location.all.Next;   -- Unlink node
         if Location = List.Tail then       -- Deleting last element?
            List.Tail := Pred_Loc;          -- Change external pointer
         end if;
         Free (Location);   -- Recycle the memory used by the deleted node
      end if;
   end Delete;
```

Having worked through a number of the list operations in detail, we leave the implementation of the other operations specified for the circular list as exercises. The complete package for this circular linked list is available on the publisher's website for this book.

8.2 Doubly Linked Lists

We have discussed using circular linked lists to enable us to reach any node in the list from any starting point. Although this structure has advantages over a simple linear linked list, it is still too limited for certain types of applications. Suppose we want to be able to delete a particular node in a list, given only one pointer to that node (Location). This task involves changing the Next field of the node preceding the node designated by Location. As we saw in the previous chapter, however, given a pointer to a node, we cannot easily access its predecessor in the list.

Another task that is complex to perform on a linear linked list (or even a circular linked list) is traversing the list in reverse. For instance, suppose we have a list of student records, ordered by grade point average (GPA) from lowest to highest. The dean of students might want a printout of the students' records, ordered from highest to lowest, to use in preparing the dean's list.

In cases like these, where we need to be able to access the node that precedes a given node, a **doubly linked list** is useful. In a doubly linked list, the nodes are linked in both directions. As shown in Figure 8.7, each node of a doubly linked list contains three parts:

> **Doubly linked list** A linked list in which each node is linked to both its successor and its predecessor.

Info: The data stored in the node
Next: The pointer to the following node
Back: The pointer to the preceding node

A linear doubly linked list is pictured in Figure 8.8. Note that the Back field of the first node and the Next field of the last node contain a null value.

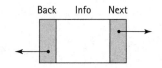

Figure 8.7 *A node for a doubly linked list.*

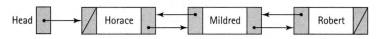

Figure 8.8 *A linear doubly linked list.*

Finding a List Element in a Doubly Linked List

In our search procedure, we no longer need to use the inchworm search to keep track of the current node's predecessor; instead we can get the predecessor to any node through its `Back` pointer, as shown here:

```
Pred_Loc := Location.all.Back;    -- Determine Location's predecessor
```

When searching a linear list like the one shown in Figure 8.8 for a key greater than any other in the list, our search loop terminates when `Location` becomes `null`. In this case `Location` does not designate a node and we cannot use the assignment statement `Pred_Loc := Location.all.Back` to determine a predecessor. To prevent `Location` from running off the end of the list, doubly linked lists are often implemented either as circular or with dummy nodes (the topic of the next section). Figure 8.9 shows a circular doubly linked list. If we do not make our doubly linked list either circular or with dummy nodes, we must use the inchworm search with `Pred_Loc` trailing along behind `Location` to search our list. The following declarations can be used in Specification 7.4 to declare such a list:

```
private

   type Node_Type;                         -- Incomplete type declaration
   type Node_Ptr is access Node_Type;      -- Access to a node
   type Node_Type is                       -- Complete type declaration
      record
         Info : Element_Type;              -- One element
         Next : Node_Ptr;                  -- Link to next node in the list
         Back : Node_Ptr;                  -- Link to previous node in the list
      end record;

   type List_Type is new Ada.Finalization.Limited_Controlled with
      record
         Tail : Node_Ptr;                  -- Pointer to the last node in the
      end record;                          -- circular doubly linked list

   overriding procedure Finalize (List : in out List_Type) renames Clear;

end Doubly;
```

8.2 Doubly Linked Lists

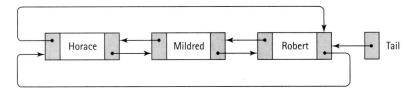

Figure 8.9 *A circular doubly linked list. Tail points to the last node of the list.*

Using a doubly linked circular list allows us to change the parameters of our local search procedure slightly. Specification 8.2 describes the local search procedure for a circular doubly linked list. Because we no longer need `Pred_Loc`, we return one access value, `Location`. If `Key` is found in the list, `Location` points to the node containing it; otherwise, `Location` points to the node that is the successor in the list. (We can easily get to the preceding node through the `Back` pointer.)

Specification 8.2   Circular Doubly Linked List Search

```
procedure Search_Circular_List (List     : in List_Type;
                                Key      : in Key_Type;
                                Found    : out Boolean;
                                Location : out Node_Ptr);
-- Purpose         : Searches for the location of Key in the List
-- Preconditions   : The nodes in List are in ascending order.
--                   The List is circular doubly linked (List.Tail designates
--                     the last node).
-- Postconditions  : If List is empty
--                       Found is False
--                       Location is null
--                   elsif Key is in List
--                       Found is True
--                       Location designates the element with Key
--                   else
--                       Found is False
--                       Location designates the node that would follow a
--                           node containing Key in the circular list.
```

The procedure shown below searches a circular doubly linked list; it implements Specification 8.2. The algorithm for this procedure is nearly identical to the algorithm we developed for the circular singly linked list in the previous section.

```
procedure Search_Circular_List (List     : in List_Type;
                                Key      : in Key_Type;
                                Found    : out Boolean;
                                Location : out Node_Ptr) is
```

```
                    -- Searches for the location of Key in the List
                begin
                    if List.Tail = null then         -- Is the list empty?
                        Found    := False;
                        Location := null;
                    elsif Key_Of (List.Tail.all.Info) < Key then   -- Is Key greater than
                        Found    := False;                         --    any in list?
                        Location := List.Tail.all.Next;  -- Goes between last and first node
                    else  -- Search the list from the beginning
                        Location := List.Tail.all.Next;  -- Start at the beginning
                        loop  -- Each iteration, one node is checked
                            exit when Key < Key_Of (Location.all.Info) or   -- Passed by
                                      Key = Key_Of (Location.all.Info);     -- Found it
                            Location := Location.all.Next;
                        end loop;
                        Found := Key = Key_Of (Location.all.Info);
                    end if;
                end Search_Circular_List;
```

Operations on a Doubly Linked List

The algorithms for the insertion and deletion operations on a doubly linked list are somewhat more complicated than those for operations on a singly linked list. The reason is clear: There are more pointers to keep track of in a doubly linked list.

For example, consider the Insert operation. To link the new node after a given node in a singly linked list, we need to change two pointers (see Figure 8.10[a]). The same operation on a doubly linked list requires four pointer changes (see Figure 8.10[b]).

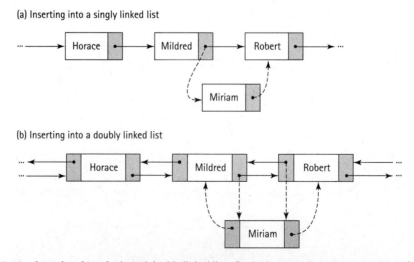

Figure 8.10 *Insertions into singly and doubly linked lists. Dashed arrows show the new values of pointers after the insert operation is complete.*

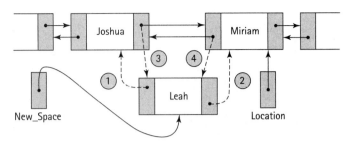

Figure 8.11 *Inserting a new node into a doubly linked list.*

To find the insertion place we call `Search_Circular_List`. On return, `Location` is `null` (if the list is empty) or designates the node that should *follow* the new node.

As usual, we allocate space for the new element using the `new` operator, and put the new element into the space. Now we are ready to link the new node into the list. Because of the complexity of the operation, it is important to be careful about the order in which you change the pointers. For instance, when inserting our new node before the node designated by `Location`, if we first change `Location.all.Back`, we lose our pointer to `Location`'s predecessor. One correct order for the pointer changes is illustrated in Figure 8.11. These four pointer changes are accomplished with the following assignment statements:

```
New_Space := new Node_Type'(Info => Item,
                            Back => Location.all.Back);        ①
                            Next => Location,                  ②

Location.all.Back.all.Next := New_Space;                       ③

Location.all.Back         := New_Space;                        ④
```

The `Insert` procedure for a circular doubly linked list complete with all special cases is as follows:

```
procedure Insert (List : in out List_Type;
                  Item : in     Element_Type) is
   Have_Duplicate : Boolean;
   Location       : Node_Ptr;
   New_Space      : Node_Ptr;
begin
   Search_Circular_List (List     => List,
                         Key      => Key_Of (Item),
                         Found    => Have_Duplicate,
                         Location => Location);
```

```
      if Have_Duplicate then
         raise DUPLICATE_KEY;
      elsif Location = null then        -- Is the list empty?
         List.Tail     := new Node_Type;    -- Add first node to list
         List.Tail.all := (Info => Item,
                           Next => List.Tail,
                           Back => List.Tail);
      else
         New_Space := new Node_Type'(Info => Item,
                                     Next => Location,
                                     Back => Location.all.Back);
         Location.all.Back.all.Next := New_Space;
         Location.all.Back          := New_Space;
         -- Did we add at end of list?
         if Key_Of (Location.all.Info) < Key_Of (Item) then
            List.Tail := New_Space;
         end if;
      end if;
   exception
      when STORAGE_ERROR =>    -- Overflow when no storage available
         raise OVERFLOW;
   end Insert;
```

One of the useful features of a doubly linked list is that we don't need a pointer to a node's predecessor in order to delete the node. Through the `Back` pointer field, we can alter the `Next` field of the preceding node to make it jump over the unwanted node:

```
Location.all.Back.all.Next := Location.all.Next;
```

Then we make the `Back` pointer of the succeeding node point to the preceding node:

```
Location.all.Next.all.Back := Location.all.Back;
```

The effect of these two statements is shown in Figure 8.12. Here is the version of procedure `Delete` for a circular doubly linked list that includes the special case of deleting the last node in the list:

```
procedure Delete (List : in out List_Type;
                  Key  : in     Key_Type) is
   Found    : Boolean;
   Location : Node_Ptr;
begin
   Search_Circular_List (List     => List,
                         Key      => Key,
                         Found    => Found,
                         Location => Location);
```

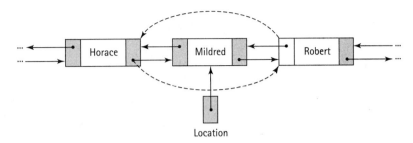

Figure 8.12 *Deleting from a doubly linked list. Dashed arrows show the new values of pointers after the Delete operation is complete.*

```
      if not Found then
         raise KEY_ERROR;
      elsif Location = Location.all.Next then   -- Deleting the only node?
         Free (List.Tail);      -- Recycle the only node in the list
      else
         Location.all.Back.all.Next := Location.all.Next;  -- Unlink the
         Location.all.Next.all.Back := Location.all.Back;  -- node
         if Location = List.Tail then        -- Deleting last element?
            List.Tail := Location.all.Back;
         end if;
         Free (Location);
      end if;
   end Delete;
```

Having worked through a number of the list operations in detail, we leave the implementation of the other operations specified for the list as exercises. The complete package for this circular doubly linked list is available on the publisher's website for this book.

8.3 Linked Lists with Dummy Nodes

In writing the insert and delete algorithms for linked lists, we saw that special cases arise when we are dealing with the first node of the list. And in writing the search algorithm, we found that we needed three different exit conditions (found the key, passed by the spot where it should be, and reached the end of the list). One way to simplify all three of these algorithms is to make sure that we never insert or delete at either end of the list. We can accomplish this simplification through the use of dummy nodes. A dummy node is a node in the linked list that does not contain list data. Dummy nodes simply act as placeholders.

A **header node** is a dummy node placed at the beginning of the list. Like any node, it is a record with `Info` and `Next` fields. However, the `Info` field contains no list data; it contains

> **Header node** Placeholder node at the beginning of a list; used to simplify list processing.

(a) A list containing three items

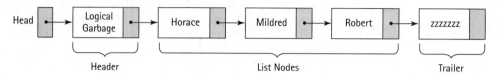

(b) An empty list

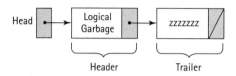

Figure 8.13 *A linked list with header and trailer nodes.*

> **Trailer node** Placeholder node at the end of a list; used to simplify list processing. The key of a trailer node must be greater than any valid key for the list.

logical garbage. A **trailer node** is a dummy node placed at the end of the list. The trailer node must contain an element whose key is greater than any valid key possible for the list. Figure 8.13(a) shows a list of three elements with a header node and a trailer node. Figure 8.13(b) shows an empty list with a header node and a trailer node. The keys in these lists are seven-character names. The trailer nodes in Figure 8.13 contain the key "zzzzzzz", a string that is greater than any valid name.

As usual, a new list implementation requires us to change the private part of our specification. This time we need to ensure that every list object is initialized with a header node and a trailer node. We can accomplish this initialization by overriding the controlled type's `Initialize` procedure with our own. Here is the private part with the necessary declarations:

```
private

   type Node_Type;
   type Node_Ptr is access Node_Type;
   type Node_Type is
      record
         Info : Element_Type;
         Next : Node_Ptr;
      end record;

   type List_Type is new Ada.Finalization.Limited_Controlled with
      record
         Head: Node_Ptr;
      end record;
```

8.3 Linked Lists with Dummy Nodes

```ada
      overriding procedure Initialize (List : in out List_Type);
      overriding procedure Finalize   (List : in out List_Type);

end Dummy;
```

`Finalize` is not just a new name for `Clear`, as in our previous classes. `Clear` makes a list empty. As you can see in Figure 8.13(b), an empty list for a list with header and trailer nodes contains two nodes. When such a list goes out of scope, we must recycle the memory used by the dummy nodes as well as that used by any data nodes. Here are the bodies of these two procedures:

```ada
procedure Initialize (List : in out List_Type) is
begin
   -- Create the Header node with logical garbage in the Info field
   List.Head := new Node_Type'(Info => Max_Element, Next => null);
   -- Create the Trailer node with maximum key in the Info field
   List.Head.all.Next := new Node_Type'(Info => Max_Element, Next => null);
end Initialize;
```

```ada
procedure Finalize (List : in out List_Type) is
   To_Recycle : Node_Ptr;         -- Designates a node for recycling
begin
   loop
      exit when List.Head = null;       -- When all nodes are gone
      To_Recycle := List.Head;          -- Unlink the
      List.Head  := List.Head.all.Next; --    first node
      Free (To_Recycle);                -- Recycle the node
   end loop;
end Finalize;
```

Procedure `Initialize` assigns the value `Max_Element` to the `Info` fields of both dummy nodes. Where do we get `Max_Element`? Its key must be greater than any possible for the list. Only the application programmer instantiating a package from our generic package knows what the keys and elements actually are. Therefore, he or she must supply us with an element whose key is greater than any possible key in the application. How can our package get `Max_Element` from the application programmer? We use a generic formal object. The application programmer supplies an actual value when he or she instantiates a sorted list package. Here is a portion of the generic package specification showing the additional generic parameter `Max_Element`:

```ada
with Ada.Finalization;
generic
   type Element_Type is private;        -- The type of element in the list
   type Key_Type is limited private;    -- The type of key
```

```
       Max_Element : in Element_Type;       -- An element with key greater than
                                            -- any legitimate element

  -- The user must supply a function that returns the Key of an Element
  with function Key_Of (Element : in Element_Type) return Key_Type;
  -- The user must supply functions for comparing Keys
  with function "=" (Left : in Key_Type; Right : in Key_Type) return Boolean;
  with function "<" (Left : in Key_Type; Right : in Key_Type) return Boolean;
package Unbounded_List is
```

As we stated at the beginning of this section, the use of dummy nodes eliminates the special cases for inserting and deleting at the ends of a linked list. We leave the implementation of these and the other operations specified for a linked list with header and trailer nodes as exercises. The complete package for a singly linked list with header and trailer nodes is available on the publisher's website for this book.

Depending on the particular application, you may want to use a header, a trailer, both, or neither. Header nodes simplify the insert and delete procedures by eliminating the special case of changing the external list pointer. The disadvantages of using a header node include slightly more complicated logic for initializing the search (we start with the second node rather than the first) and the extra memory used.

Trailer nodes simplify the search by eliminating one of the three exit conditions from our original search loop. The disadvantages of trailer nodes include use of extra memory and the selection of a key value that is greater than any possible in the list. A programmer using this version of our list class must be very careful to make sure that the key of Max_Element he or she supplies as a generic parameter is truly "larger" than any valid key. (Maybe there is someone named "zzzzzzz"!)

Doubly Linked Lists with Dummy Nodes

As we saw earlier, doubly linked lists are often circular so we do not run off the end when we search it with a single pointer rather than the inchworm approach. In the previous section you saw that dummy nodes are another way to handle the problem at the ends of a linked list. We can also use dummy nodes with doubly linked lists. Figure 8.14 shows a doubly linked list with header and trailer nodes.

Figure 8.15 illustrates another form of the doubly linked list with dummy nodes. This one combines a circular linked list and a single dummy node. The single dummy acts as both a header node and a trailer node. Remember that the information in a

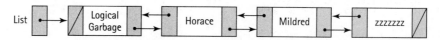

Figure 8.14 *A doubly linked list with header and trailer nodes.*

(a) List with three elements

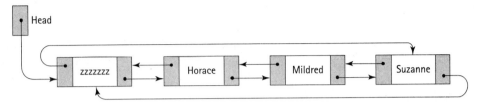

(b) List with one element

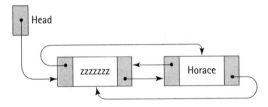

(c) Empty list

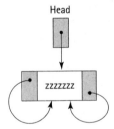

Figure 8.15 *A doubly linked list with a single dummy node.*

header node is never accessed (it is considered logical garbage) and the key of the trailer node must be greater than any valid key in the list. The algorithms to retrieve, modify, insert, and delete in this list are identical to those we developed for the circular doubly linked list. The search and traverse operations require different initialization and loop exit conditions. We start our search with the node after the header node and end it when we find the desired key or pass the spot where that key should be. Because the key of the trailer node is greater than any valid key in the list, we never go beyond the trailer node in our search. We leave the problem of initialization of this structure to Exercise 27.

8.4 The Linked List as an Array of Nodes

In Chapter 7 we said that the values in a linked list are not necessarily stored in dynamically allocated memory. They can also be stored in a static structure, the array. In this section we look at the details of how this implementation might work. The elements in the list can be stored in an array of nodes, with each node in the list consisting of a record with two fields, Info and Next. Unlike the sequential list implementation developed in Chapter 7, these records can be stored in any physical order in the array. Their logical order is specified explicitly through the value in their Next fields. The Next field should point out which node (array slot) comes next in the list. We don't need to use an Ada access type for this; we only need to know the index ("address" in the array) of the succeeding list element. See Figure 7.3(b) on page 428.

Why Use an Array?

We have seen that dynamic allocation has many advantages, so why would we even discuss using a static implementation instead? Remember that dynamic allocation is only one issue in choosing a linked implementation; another advantage is the efficiency of the insert and delete algorithms. Most of the algorithms that we have discussed for operations on a linked list can be used for either a static or a dynamic implementation. The main difference is the requirement that we manage our own free space in an array-based implementation. Sometimes, managing the free space ourselves gives us greater flexibility.

Another reason to use an array is that there are a number of programming languages (such as BASIC and COBOL) that do not have dynamic allocation or access types. You can still use linked lists if you are programming in one of these languages, using the techniques presented in this section.

Using access variables presents a problem when we need to save the information in a data structure between runs of a program. Suppose we want to write all the nodes in a list to a file and then use this file as input the next time we run the program. If the links are access values—containing memory addresses—they are meaningless on the next run of the program because the program may be placed somewhere else in memory the next time. We must save the user data part of each node in the file, and then rebuild the linked structure the next time we run the program (like we did in the address book application in Chapter 7). An array index, however, is still valid on the next run of the program. We can store the whole array, including the Next fields (indexes), and then read it back in the next time we run the program.

More importantly, there are times when dynamic allocation isn't possible or feasible, or when dynamic allocation of each node, one at a time, is too costly in terms of time—especially in real-time system software such as operating systems, air traffic control systems, and automotive systems. In such situations, an array-based linked approach provides the benefits of linked structures without the runtime costs.

How Is an Array Used?

Let's get back to our discussion of how a linked list can be implemented in an array. As we have said, the `Next` field of each node tells us the array index of the succeeding node. The beginning of the list is accessed through a "pointer" that contains the array index of the first element in the list. Figure 8.16 shows how a key-ordered list containing the elements David, Joshua, Leah, Miriam, and Robert might be stored in an array of records called `Nodes`. Do you see how the order of the elements in the list is explicitly indicated by the chain of `Next` indexes?

What goes in the `Next` field of the last list element? Its "null" value must be an invalid address for a real list element. Because the `Nodes` array indexes begin at 1, the value 0 is not a valid index into the array; that is, there is no `Nodes(0)`. Therefore, 0 makes an ideal value to use as a "null" address. We could use the literal value 0 in our programs:

```
loop
   exit when Location = 0
   .
   .
   .
```

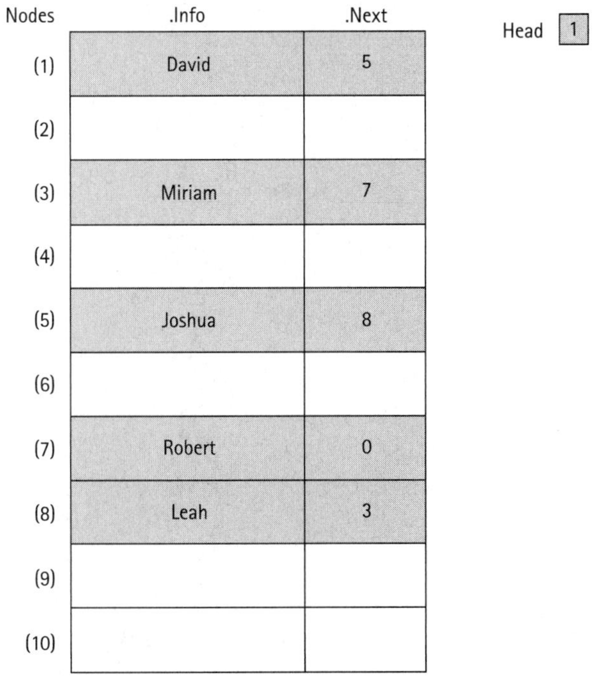

Nodes	.Info	.Next
(1)	David	5
(2)		
(3)	Miriam	7
(4)		
(5)	Joshua	8
(6)		
(7)	Robert	0
(8)	Leah	3
(9)		
(10)		

Head 1

Figure 8.16 *An ordered list stored in an array.*

but it is better programming style to declare a constant. We can't use the identifier `null`, however, because this is an Ada reserved word. We'll use the identifier `Nil` instead:

```
Nil : constant := 0;
```

When an array of records implementation is used to represent a linked list, the programmer must write routines to manage the free space available for new list elements. Where is this free space? Look again at Figure 8.16. All of the array elements that do not contain values in the list constitute free space. Instead of the built-in allocator `new`, which allocates memory dynamically, we must write our own function to allocate nodes from the free space. We call this function `New_Node`. To be consistent with Ada's `new` allocator, we can write two versions of `New_Node`—one where an initial value for the node is supplied, and one where it is not.

When elements are deleted from the list, we need to free the node space. We can't use `Unchecked_Deallocation`, because it only works for dynamically allocated space. We write our own procedure, `Free_Node`, to put a node back in the pool of free space.

We need a way to track the collection of nodes that are not being used to hold list elements. We can link this collection of unused array elements into a second list, a linked list of free nodes. Figure 8.17 shows the array `Nodes` with both the list of values and the list of free space linked through their `Next` fields. The list of values begins at `Head`, at index 1 (containing the value David). Following the links in the `Next` field, we see that the list continues with the array slots at index 5 (Joshua), 8 (Leah), 3

Nodes	.Info	.Next
(1)	David	5
(2)	Garbage	6
(3)	Miriam	7
(4)	Garbage	9
(5)	Joshua	8
(6)	Garbage	4
(7)	Robert	0
(8)	Leah	3
(9)	Garbage	10
(10)	Garbage	0

Head [1]
Free [2]

Figure 8.17 *An array with linked lists of values and free space.*

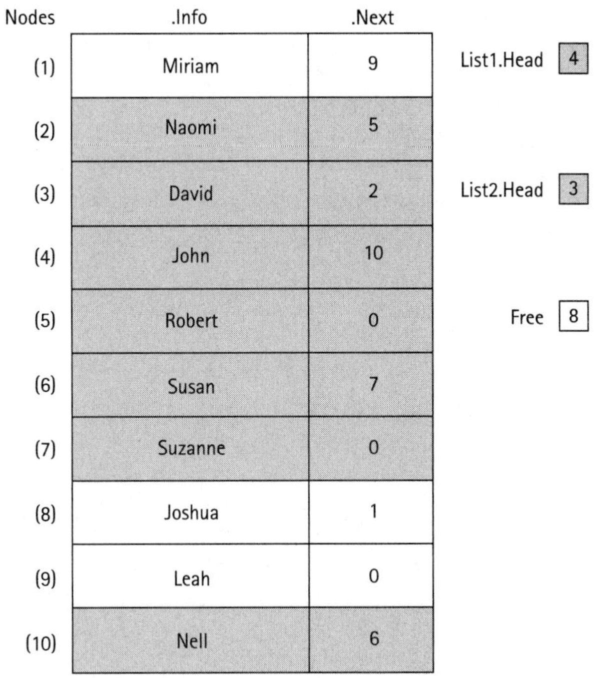

Nodes	.Info	.Next
(1)	Miriam	9
(2)	Naomi	5
(3)	David	2
(4)	John	10
(5)	Robert	0
(6)	Susan	7
(7)	Suzanne	0
(8)	Joshua	1
(9)	Leah	0
(10)	Nell	6

List1.Head 4
List2.Head 3
Free 8

Figure 8.18 *An array with three lists (including the free list).*

(Miriam), and 7 (Robert), in that order. The free list begins at `Free`, at index 2. Following the links in the `Next` field, we see that the free list also includes the array slots at index 6, 4, 9, and 10. You see two `Nil` values in the `Next` field column because there are two linked lists contained in the `Nodes` array. We can use one array to store many different linked lists. Figure 8.18 shows an array that contains two different lists. `List1` contains the values John, Nell, Susan, and Suzanne and `List2` contains the values David, Naomi, and Robert. The remaining three array slots in Figure 8.18 are linked in the free list.

Now let's look at how the list is declared. In the following variation of Specification 7.1, we have added the generic formal object `Max_Size`, so that the user may set the size of our storage array. `Max_Size` determines the combined number of elements that can be stored in all the list objects declared from this package. Having to specify this maximum size is a disadvantage of the array-based linked list not found in the access-based linked list. In the private part we enclose the external pointer in a record to allow us to assign an initial value of "empty" to every list object declared.

Specification 8.3   Array-Based Key-Ordered List

```
generic
   Max_Size : in Positive;        -- The storage for ALL list objects
```

```ada
      type Element_Type is private;        -- The type of element in the list
      type Key_Type     is limited private; -- The type of key

      -- The user must supply a function that returns the Key of an Element
      with function Key_Of (Element : in Element_Type) return Key_Type;
      -- The user must supply functions for comparing Keys
      with function "=" (Left : in Key_Type; Right : in Key_Type) return Boolean;
      with function "<" (Left : in Key_Type; Right : in Key_Type) return Boolean;
package Array_Based is


   -- Same list operations as Specification 7.4 (access-based key-ordered list)


private

   subtype Node_Ptr is Integer range 0..Max_Size;  -- Pointer to a node
   Nil : constant Node_Ptr := 0;
   type List_Type is
      record
         Head: Node_Ptr := Nil;    -- Initialize list to empty
      end record;

end Array_Based;
```

Most of the types for this implementation are completely hidden in this package body. The body also contains variables for the storage array, Nodes, and a pointer, Free, to the first node in the list of free nodes. These variables are accessed globally by the procedures in the package body, but because they are declared within the body, they are not available outside of the package body. Here are the types and variables declared in our package body:

```ada
package body Array_Based is

   subtype Index_Range is Node_Ptr range 1..Node_Ptr'Last;

   type Node_Type is
      record
         Info : Element_Type;
         Next : Node_Ptr := Nil;
      end record;

   type Node_Array is array (Index_Range) of Node_Type;

   -- Package Variables  (used globally in the package)
```

8.4 The Linked List as an Array of Nodes

```
Nodes   : Node_Array;    -- Storage array for the nodes
Free    : Node_Ptr;      -- Head of list of available nodes
   .
   .
   .
```

It only takes a little rearranging to convert the code used to implement the operations for an access-based linked list to an array-based linked list. With the array implementation, nodes are accessed through a pointer that is an array index rather than an access type. Compare the following two assignment statements to copy the information in the node to which `Location` "points":

```
Element := Location.all.Info;       -- Access-based linked list

Element := Nodes(Location).Info;    -- Array-based linked list
```

In the access-based linked list, the pointer is an access value that designates a node somewhere in memory. In the array-based linked list, the pointer is an index that selects a node somewhere in the array. The following table shows how the two implementations correspond.

Algorithm	Array of Nodes	Dynamic Storage
Allocate a node (with and without an initial value)	New_Node(Initial_Value) New_Node	new'(Initial_Value) new
Free a node	Free_Node(Ptr)	Free(Ptr)
Access Info	Nodes(Ptr).Info	Ptr.all.Info
Access Next	Nodes(Ptr).Next	Ptr.all.Next
Exit when no more elements	exit when Ptr = Nil	exit when Ptr = null

To show you how easy it is to change the implementation, let's look at the code for the insert procedure. First, here is the code for the access-based linked list:

```
-- Insert into an access-based linked list
Search_Linked_List (List     => List,
                    Key      => Key_Of (Item),
                    Found    => Have_Duplicate,
                    Pred_Loc => Pred_Loc,
                    Location => Location);
if Have_Duplicate then
   raise DUPLICATE_KEY;
elsif Pred_Loc = null then
   -- Add Item to the head of the linked list
```

```ada
      List.Head := new Node_Type'(Info => Item,  Next => List.Head);
else    -- Add at the middle or end of the linked list
      Pred_Loc.all.Next := new Node_Type'(Info => Item,  Next => Location);
end if;
```

And here is the "same" code for an array-based linked list:

```ada
-- Insert into an array-based linked list
Search_Linked_List (List     => List,
                    Key      => Key_Of (Item),
                    Found    => Have_Duplicate,
                    Pred_Loc => Pred_Loc,
                    Location => Location);
if Have_Duplicate then
   raise DUPLICATE_KEY;
elsif Pred_Loc = Nil then    -- Add at beginning
   List.Head := New_Node ((Info => Item,  Next => List.Head));
else    -- Add at the middle or end
   Nodes(Pred_Loc).Next := New_Node ((Info => Item,  Next => Location));
end if;
```

Changing the linked list operations that we coded in Chapter 7, this array-based implementation is so simple that much of the work to make this conversion can be accomplished through "search and replace" commands available in a program editor. That is exactly what we did to produce the implementation given in Body 8.1.

Body 8.1   Array-Based Linked List: Implements Specification 8.3

```ada
package body Array_Based is

   subtype Index_Range is Node_Ptr range 1..Node_Ptr'Last;

   type Node_Type is
      record
         Info : Element_Type;
         Next : Node_Ptr := Nil;
      end record;

   type Node_Array is array (Index_Range) of Node_Type;

   -- Package Variables   (used globally in the package)

   Nodes : Node_Array;      -- Storage array for the nodes
   Free  : Node_Ptr;        -- Head of list of available nodes

   -- Local procedures
```

8.4 The Linked List as an Array of Nodes

```
procedure Initialize_Memory is
-- Purpose         : Initializes memory management for the array of nodes
-- Preconditions   : None
-- Postconditions  : All nodes in the array Nodes are linked together
--                   into a list of available nodes.
begin
   Free := Nodes'First;
   -- Link all nodes together into the free list
   for Index in Nodes'First .. Nodes'Last - 1 loop
      Nodes(Index).Next := Index + 1;
   end loop;
   Nodes(Nodes'Last).Next := Nil;   -- Mark the end of free list
end Initialize_Memory;


function New_Node (Initial_Value : in Node_Type) return Node_Ptr is
-- Purpose         : Finds a free node in the array (memory allocation)
-- Preconditions   : None
-- Postconditions  : Unlinks an available node from the list of available
--                   nodes, sets its value to Initial_Value,
--                   and returns its index.
-- Exceptions      : OVERFLOW raised when the list of available nodes
--                   is empty
   Result : Node_Ptr;
begin
   if Free = Nil then
      raise OVERFLOW;
   else -- Get a node from the free list
      Result := Free;
      Free   := Nodes(Free).Next;       -- Unlink the free node
      Nodes(Result) := Initial_Value;   -- Assign the initial value
      return Result;
   end if;
end New_Node;


procedure Free_Node (X : in out Node_Ptr) is
-- Purpose         : Deallocates a node
-- Preconditions   : X is not Nil
-- Postconditions  : The node designated by X is added to the list
--                   of available nodes.
--                   X is set to Nil
begin
```

```
         Nodes(X).Next := Free;    -- Link the node
         Free := X;                 -- into the free list
         X    := Nil;               -- Set the user's pointer to Nil
      end Free_Node;

      --------------------------------------------------------------------

      procedure Search_Linked_List (List     : in  List_Type;
                                    Key      : in  Key_Type;
                                    Found    : out Boolean;
                                    Pred_Loc : out Node_Ptr;
                                    Location : out Node_Ptr) is
      -- Purpose         : Searches for the location of Key in the List
      -- Preconditions   : The nodes in List are in ascending order
      -- Postconditions  : If Key is in List
      --                       Found is True
      --                       Location designates the element with Key
      --                       Pred_Loc designates the predecessor of the node
      --                           designated by Location.  If Location
      --                           designates the first node in the list,
      --                           Pred_Loc is Nil.
      --                   else
      --                       Found is False
      --                       Location designates the node that would follow a node
      --                           containing Key.  If Key's node would follow
      --                           the last node in the list, Location is Nil.
      --                       Pred_Loc designates the predecessor of the node
      --                           designated by Location.  If Location
      --                           designates the first node in the list,
      --                           Pred_Loc is Nil.
      begin
         Location := List.Head;    -- Start at the beginning of the linked list
         Pred_Loc := Nil;          -- No predecessor for 1st element in the list
         loop  -- Each iteration, one node is checked
            exit when Location = Nil                        or else  -- Reached end
                     Key < Key_Of (Nodes(Location).Info) or else  -- Passed by
                     Key = Key_Of (Nodes(Location).Info);          -- Found it
            Pred_Loc := Location;                    -- Move inchworm's tail
            Location := Nodes(Location).Next;        -- Move inchworm's head
         end loop;
         Found := Location /= Nil  and then  Key = Key_Of (Nodes(Location).Info);
      end Search_Linked_List;

      -- Operations defined in the specification
      --------------------------------------------------------------------
```

```ada
procedure Clear (List : in out List_Type) is
   To_Recycle : Node_Ptr;        -- Designates a node for recycling
begin
   loop
      exit when List.Head = Nil;        -- Exit when list is empty
      To_Recycle := List.Head;             -- Unlink the
      List.Head := Nodes(List.Head).Next;  --    first node
      Free_Node (To_Recycle);           -- Recycle the node
   end loop;
end Clear;
```

```ada
procedure Insert (List : in out List_Type;
                  Item : in      Element_Type) is
-- OVERFLOW is raised by the call to New_Node when the free list is empty
   Have_Duplicate : Boolean;
   Pred_Loc       : Node_Ptr;
   Location       : Node_Ptr;
begin
   Search_Linked_List (List     => List,
                       Key      => Key_Of (Item),
                       Found    => Have_Duplicate,
                       Pred_Loc => Pred_Loc,
                       Location => Location);
   if Have_Duplicate then
      raise DUPLICATE_KEY;
   elsif Pred_Loc = Nil then      -- Add at beginning
      List.Head := New_Node ((Info => Item, Next => List.Head));
   else    -- Add at the middle or end
      Nodes(Pred_Loc).Next := New_Node ((Info => Item, Next => Location));
   end if;
end Insert;
```

```ada
procedure Delete (List : in out List_Type;
                  Key  : in     Key_Type) is
   Found    : Boolean;
   Pred_Loc : Node_Ptr;
   Location : Node_Ptr;
begin
   Search_Linked_List (List     => List,
                       Key      => Key,
                       Found    => Found,
                       Pred_Loc => Pred_Loc,
                       Location => Location);
```

```
        if not Found then
            raise KEY_ERROR;
        elsif Pred_Loc = Nil then
            -- Deleting first element is special case
            List.Head := Nodes(Location).Next;
        else
            -- Delete a middle or last element
            Nodes(Pred_Loc).Next := Nodes(Location).Next;
        end if;
        Free_Node (Location);      -- Recycle node memory
end Delete;
```

```
procedure Modify (List    : in out List_Type;
                  Element : in     Element_Type) is
    Found    : Boolean;
    Pred_Loc : Node_Ptr;
    Location : Node_Ptr;
begin
    Search_Linked_List (List     => List,
                        Key      => Key_Of (Element),
                        Found    => Found,
                        Pred_Loc => Pred_Loc,
                        Location => Location);
    if not Found then
        raise KEY_ERROR;
    else
        Nodes(Location).Info := Element;
    end if;
end Modify;
```

```
procedure Retrieve (List    : in     List_Type;
                    Key     : in     Key_Type;
                    Element :    out Element_Type) is
    Found    : Boolean;
    Pred_Loc : Node_Ptr;
    Location : Node_Ptr;
begin
    Search_Linked_List (List     => List,
                        Key      => Key,
                        Found    => Found,
                        Pred_Loc => Pred_Loc,
                        Location => Location);
    if not Found then
```

```ada
         raise KEY_ERROR;
      else
         Element := Nodes(Location).Info;
      end if;
end Retrieve;

-------------------------------------------------------------------------------
function Full (List : in List_Type) return Boolean is
begin
   return False;
end Full;

-------------------------------------------------------------------------------
function Empty (List : in List_Type) return Boolean is
begin
   return List.Head = Nil;
end Empty;

-------------------------------------------------------------------------------
function Length (List : in List_Type) return Natural is
   Location : Node_Ptr;    -- Designates current node
   Count    : Natural;
begin
   Count := 0;
   Location := List.Head;
   loop
      exit when Location = Nil;
      Count := Count + 1;
      Location := Nodes(Location).Next;
   end loop;
   return Count;
end Length;

-------------------------------------------------------------------------------
procedure Traverse
     (List    : in out List_Type;
      Process : not null access procedure (Element : in out Element_Type)) is
   Location : Node_Ptr;       -- Designates current node
begin
   Location := List.Head;
   loop
      exit when Location = Nil;
      Process (Nodes(Location).Info);    -- Call user's procedure to process
      Location := Nodes(Location).Next;  -- Move to next node
   end loop;
```

```
      end Traverse;

begin -- Package Initialization
   Initialize_Memory;   -- Link all of the nodes into the free list
end Array_Based;
```

Array Memory Management

Body 8.1 contains three additional local operations. These operations are necessary to manage the memory in the array in which all nodes are stored. We said earlier that we need to do our own memory management by writing the subprograms New_Node and Free_Node. The code for procedure Insert illustrates a call to function New_Node. New_Node returns a node "pointer" (the index of an entry in the array Nodes). The version of New_Node included in Body 8.1 has a parameter that is assigned as the initial value to the newly acquired node. Using our box-and-arrow pictures, let's see how the New_Node operation works. Figure 8.19 shows two linked lists, one containing the user's data (accessed through List.Head) and the other containing nodes that are not in use (accessed through Free).

As calls are made to New_Node, nodes are removed from the list of free nodes. Because the free list doesn't contain "real" data and isn't ordered in any way, we can take any node from it. The simplest approach is just to take the first element from the free list. Figure 8.20 illustrates how the function New_Node affects the free list. Figure 8.20(a) shows that Result is set to designate the first node in the free list. Then, as illustrated in Figure 8.20(b), this first node is removed from the free list. The algorithm for function New_Node is nearly identical to the algorithm we developed in Chapter 5 for the linked version of the stack procedure Pop. In fact, we could just consider the free "list" to be a linked *free-space stack*.

To better duplicate Ada's new operator for access types, we make one addition to the "pop" algorithm. We include a parameter containing the initial value we wish to assign to the newly obtained node. The complete code for procedure New_Node is given in Body 8.1.

Calls to Free_Node move nodes back into the list of available nodes. We could add them anywhere in the free list, but again the simplest approach is just to insert them at

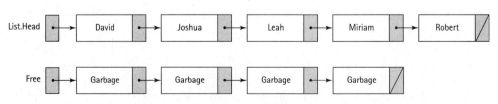

Figure 8.19 *The two lists.*

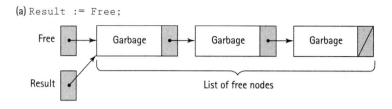

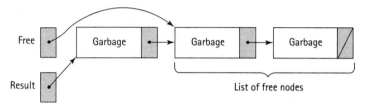

Figure 8.20 *The New_Node operation.*

the beginning of the list as if it were a stack. Figure 8.21 illustrates how the `Free_Node` operation affects the free list. In Figure 8.21(a), the recycled node is linked into the free list by setting its `Next` field to designate the current first node in the free list. The linking is completed in Figure 8.21(b), where `Free` is changed to make our recycled node the first node in the free list. Body 8.1 contains the complete code for function `Free_Node` (using the parameter name X to be consistent with the parameter name used by Ada's `Unchecked_Deallocation` procedure). This operation is just like the linked version of procedure `Push`, with X as the pointer to the node being returned to the free list.

But we're not finished. How did the nodes get into the free list in the first place? All of the nodes in the array should start out linked together in the list of free-space nodes, which is accessed through the pointer field, `Free`. The free nodes can be linked in any order, of course, but it is simplest to string them together sequentially, as illustrated in Figure 8.22. Procedure `Initialize_Memory` in Body 8.1 links all of the nodes in this sequential fashion.

We include a call to procedure `Initialize_Memory` at the end of our package body so that it is called whenever our package is elaborated. We first took advantage of this package initialization feature in the address book application in Chapter 7.

One final word of advice. When developing algorithms for array-based linked lists, use the box-and-arrow pictures that we always draw when working with linked lists (Figure 8.19) instead of array pictures (Figure 8.17). The box-and-arrow pictures include only the information necessary to manipulate the list. The unimportant details, such as where the nodes are physically stored, are not shown. As usual, choosing the correct level of abstraction makes problem solving easier.

(a) `Nodes(X).Next := Free;`

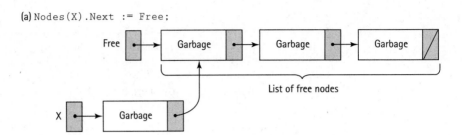

(b) `Free := X;`

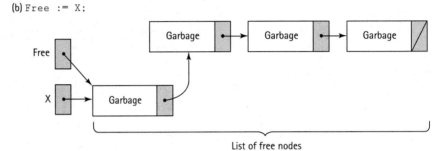

Figure 8.21 *The Free_Node operation.*

Nodes	.Info	.Next
(1)	Garbage	2
(2)	Garbage	3
(3)	Garbage	4
(4)	Garbage	5
(5)	Garbage	6
(6)	Garbage	7
(7)	Garbage	8
(8)	Garbage	9
(9)	Garbage	10
(10)	Garbage	0

List.Head 0
Free 1

Figure 8.22 *Initializing the free list to contain all the nodes in the array.*

8.5 Comparison of the Linked Implementations

We have presented five different linked implementations of a key-ordered list. Is the efficiency of insertion and deletion operations (in terms of Big-O) different in these variations? The following table compares them.

Big-O Comparisons of Insert and Delete Operations

	Linked List (Chapter 7)	Circular Linked List	Linked with Header and Trailer Nodes	Doubly Circular Linked List	Array-Based Linked List
Insert					
Random	O(N)	O(N)	O(N)	O(N)	O(N)
Beginning	O(1)	O(1)	O(1)	O(1)	O(1)
End	O(N)	O(1)	O(N)	O(1)	O(N)
Delete					
Random	O(N)	O(N)	O(N)	O(N)	O(N)
Beginning	O(1)	O(1)	O(1)	O(1)	O(1)
End	O(N)	O(N)	O(N)	O(N)	O(N)

The improvement here is for the circular lists where inserting at the end is O(1) rather than O(N). Remember that the array-based linked list implementation used the same algorithms developed in Chapter 7 so these two columns should be the same. Let's see what our experiments (described in Chapter 7) can tell us about these different implementations.

Time for Insert and Delete Operations (Milliseconds)

	Linked List (Chapter 7)	Circular Linked List	Linked with Header and Trailer Nodes	Doubly Circular Linked List	Array-Based Linked List
Insert					
Random	1259.35	1149.02	1144.79	1136.38	1185.91
Beginning	6.16	6.46	6.21	6.67	1.48
End	1346.88	6.33	1230.66	6.15	1669.52
Delete					
Random	1041.89	930.32	935.42	937.90	1041.30
Beginning	4.51	4.71	4.62	4.56	0.83
End	1328.48	1213.80	1211.69	1195.96	1652.61

These results are consistent with the Big-O analyses. But they do provide some interesting insights on the absolute efficiencies of the implementations. The array-based linked list is significantly faster than all of the dynamic implementations for insertions and deletions at the beginning of the list. Because these operations have insignificant search times (only a single key is checked), this observation suggests that our specialized memory management operations are more efficient than the general memory allocation provided by the Ada run-time system. The slightly longer times for inserting and deleting at the end of the list suggest that array indexing is slower than following an access value to gain access to a particular node. As always, experiments such as these are only valid for the particular compiler and hardware used.

8.6 The Linked List as a File of Nodes

We have stored the information for all of our data structures in memory, using either a static array or dynamic memory. There are times, however, when the amount of data is too large to fit in the computer's random access memory (RAM). For such applications, we must store the information in secondary memory—usually on magnetic disks. Keeping our list information on disk also means that it will be there the next time we run our program. Using binary files, it is not difficult to modify any of our list algorithms to use disk memory instead of RAM.

Direct Files

> **Direct file (random access file)** A binary file whose components can be accessed sequentially or randomly (in any order).
>
> **Sequential file** A binary file whose components can be accessed sequentially.
>
> **Binary file** A file data type whose components are stored using the internal binary representation of the machine.

Direct files, sometimes called random access files, are binary files. Sequential files, like the one used in the address book application in Chapter 7, are also binary files. A **binary file** is a file whose components are stored using the internal representation of the machine. The components of a binary file are not restricted to characters as a text file is. Because no data conversions are made, input and output with binary files are usually much faster than input and output with text files.

Figure 8.23 illustrates a direct file. A direct file is similar to an array. We can access any component in a direct file by specifying a component number much like we can access any array component by specifying an index. Like the array, the direct file is one of Ada's predefined classes. Because the direct file class is defined in the generic package `Direct_IO`, this type is used just like those we define; package `Direct_IO` contains a `File_Type` and functions and procedures for the operations on that type. Many of the operations, like `Open`, `Create`, and `Close`, are familiar from our work with text files. Three other operations are needed to implement a sorted list in a direct file. Procedure `Read` moves a copy of a file component into a variable; procedure `Write` moves a copy of a variable into a file component; and function `Size` returns the number of components in the file. Here are the declarations of these three operations and some associated types:

8.6 The Linked List as a File of Nodes

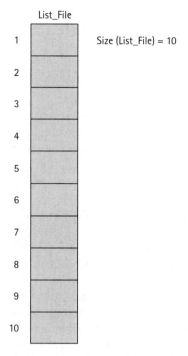

Figure 8.23 *A direct file containing 10 elements.*

```
-- Declarations found in package Ada.Direct_IO

type File_Type is limited private;          -- The direct file type

type    Count          is range 0..implementation_defined;
subtype Positive_Count is Count range 1..implementation_defined;

procedure Read (File : in  File_Type;       -- File to read from
                From : in  Positive_Count;  -- The component number
                Item : out Element_Type);   -- Contains copy of component

procedure Write (File : in File_Type;       -- File to write to
                 To   : in Positive_Count;  -- Where to write
                 Item : in Element_Type);   -- The value to write

function Size (File : in File_Type) return Count;
```

Because `Direct_IO` is a generic package, we must instantiate a separate package for each different element type for which we need a file. Here are two example instantiations:

```
package Number_IO is new Direct_IO (Element_Type => Integer);

package Node_IO   is new Direct_IO (Element_Type => Node_Type);
```

The first line instantiates a package for a direct file class whose components are integers. The second instantiates a package for a direct file class whose components are nodes. Once we have instantiated a package, we can declare file variables.

```
List_File : Node_IO.File_Type;    -- A direct file of Nodes
```

Arrays and files are very similar, but there are some important differences. We will discuss two of them. First, file element numbers are more restricted than array indexes. The index of an array can be any discrete type and start at any value. File element numbers are always type `Positive_Count` and the first element number in a file is always 1. Second, we do not have to declare a maximum size for a file. Although the index of the last component of an array is fixed by its declaration, the last element number in a file increases as elements are written to locations beyond the end of the file. A file may grow in size until there is no room left on the storage device. In this sense, a file is more like the dynamic memory we use to implement linked lists than a static array. Function `Size` returns the element number of the last element in the file.

The Abstract Level

The specification for a file-based implementation needs some additional information than those of the memory-based lists. Each file must have a name compatible with the computer's file system. The programmer using our file-based sorted list class must supply names; he or she knows the syntax rules for filenames on his or her particular computer and what filenames are most appropriate for the application. Each file-based linked list requires two files—one file to store the nodes (equivalent to the array) and another file to store bookkeeping information (including the external pointers for the node list and free list) between runs of the program. At the abstract level, there are two ways to handle the assignment of filenames. We *could* introduce a `Create` operation that includes filename parameters. We take a second approach. We declare our file-based list as an abstract data object (ADO) rather than an abstract data type (ADT). We include generic formal parameters for the filenames. The two filenames are supplied when the package is instantiated.

Because all files must be closed before our program terminates we need another "list" operation that is called before the program terminates. We include a `Close` operation in our specification. Specification 8.4 is the abstract-level view of our file-based linked list.

Specification 8.4   File-Based Key-Ordered List

```
generic

   List_File_Name    : in String;      -- Name of file for list
   Header_File_Name  : in String;      -- Name of file for bookkeeping info
```

```ada
    type Element_Type is private;           -- The type of element in the list
    type Key_Type     is limited private;   -- The type of key

    -- The user must supply a function that returns the Key of an Element
    with function Key_Of (Element : in Element_Type) return Key_Type;
    -- The user must supply functions for comparing Keys
    with function "=" (Left : in Key_Type; Right : in Key_Type) return Boolean;
    with function "<" (Left : in Key_Type; Right : in Key_Type) return Boolean;

package File_Based is

-- This package implements an ordered list ADO.  The list is physically stored
-- in two files.  The user supplies a filename without an extension.  The
-- list package creates two files with this name but with different extensions

-- Each element in the list has a unique key.

-- The elements in the list are ordered from smallest to largest using the "<"
-- function supplied as a generic parameter.  The key value of the predecessor
-- of an element is less than the key value of the element, which is less than
-- the key value of the successor of the element.

    DUPLICATE_KEY  : exception;
    KEY_ERROR      : exception;
    OVERFLOW       : exception;

-- Transformers

    -------------------------------------------------------------------------
    procedure Clear;
    -- Purpose        : Removes all elements from List.
    -- Preconditions  : None
    -- Postconditions : List is empty.

    -------------------------------------------------------------------------
    procedure Insert (Item : in Element_Type);
    -- Purpose        : Adds Item to List.
    -- Preconditions  : None
    -- Postconditions : List = original list + Item
    -- Exceptions     : OVERFLOW       If there is no room for Item.
    --                                 List is unchanged.
    --                  DUPLICATE_KEY  If an element already exists in the list
    --                                 with the same key as Item.
    --                                 List is unchanged.

    -------------------------------------------------------------------------
```

```
procedure Delete (Key   : in Key_Type);
-- Purpose        : Deletes the element containing Key from List.
-- Preconditions  : None
-- Postconditions : List = original list without element identified by Key
-- Exceptions     : KEY_ERROR  If there is no element with Key in List.
--                             List is unchanged.

-------------------------------------------------------------------------
procedure Modify (Element : in Element_Type);
-- Purpose        : Replace existing list element.
-- Preconditions  : None
-- Postconditions : List = original list with value of Element replacing
--                         like-keyed original element
-- Exceptions     : KEY_ERROR  If there is no element with the key of
--                             Element in List.  List is unchanged.

-- Observers

-------------------------------------------------------------------------
procedure Retrieve (Key     : in     Key_Type;
                    Element :    out Element_Type);
-- Purpose        : Gets a copy of the element that contains Key.
-- Preconditions  : None
-- Postconditions : Element = copy of element containing Key
--                  List is unchanged.
-- Exceptions     : KEY_ERROR  If there is no element with the
--                             Key in List.  List is unchanged.

-------------------------------------------------------------------------
function Empty return Boolean;
-- Purpose        : Tests whether List is empty (contains no elements)
-- Preconditions  : None
-- Postconditions : Empty = (List is empty)


-------------------------------------------------------------------------
function Full return Boolean;
-- Purpose        : Tests whether List is full.  List is full when
--                         no more elements can be inserted into it.
-- Preconditions  : None
-- Postconditions : Full = (List is full)


-------------------------------------------------------------------------
function Length return Natural;
-- Purpose        : Determines the number of elements in List.
-- Preconditions  : None
```

```
   -- Postconditions : Length = number of elements in List

-- Iterator

   ---------------------------------------------------------------------------
   procedure Traverse
          (Process : not null access procedure (Element : in out Element_Type));
   -- Purpose         : To process all the elements in List.
   -- Preconditions   : Procedure Process does not change the key of an element
   -- Postconditions  : Every element in List is passed to a call of
   --                   Procedure Process

   ---------------------------------------------------------------------------
   procedure Close;
   -- Purpose         : Saves list header information in a file.
   --                   Must be called before ending the program
   --                   or list will be lost.
   -- Preconditions   : Close was not previously called
   -- Postconditions  : Both list files are closed

end File_Based;
```

The generic formal parameters for this list package include two filenames. The package uses `List_File_Name` as the external filename of a file in which the list elements are stored and `Header_File_Name` as the external filename of a file in which list bookkeeping information is stored.

Because this package is an ADO rather than an ADT, there is no list type defined and the operations have no list parameter. Procedure `Close` must be called when the program is finished using the list. Failure to close the list will yield corrupted list files the next time the program is run.

The Implementation Level

Body 8.2 contains the code for our file-based linked list implementation of a key-ordered list. Because a direct file is so much like an array, it should not be surprising that the file-based list implementation is very similar to the array-based linked list implementation. The only significant difference is that we use input and output procedures to access individual nodes instead of array indexes. This difference usually results in longer procedures. For example, once the location of a node is known in an array-based list, it only takes a single assignment statement to modify the `Info` field of that node. It requires three statements to modify the `Info` field in a file-based list: (1) read a copy of the node from the file; (2) modify the copy; and (3) write the modified copy back to the file.

```
Read_Node (From => Location, Node => Local_Copy);         -- (1)
Local_Copy.Info := Element;                               -- (2)
Write_Node (To => Location, Node => Local_Copy);          -- (3)
```

In Body 8.2, we have declared `Node_Ptr` as a synonym for `Natural`. It would be more accurate if we made `Node_Ptr` a synonym for `Node_IO.Count` because our pointers are actually file element numbers. However, we must declare `Node_Ptr` before we can declare `Node_Type`, which we must declare before we instantiate package `Node_IO`. We saw a similar "chicken and egg" problem in Chapter 5. Our solution to the problem was the incomplete type. Because an incomplete type may be named only in the definition of an access type, this solution is not applicable here. Instead we use the two different types and use explicit type conversions to convert between them.

Five package variables are accessed globally by procedures in Body 8.2. `List_File` is the direct file in which the list elements and free elements are stored. `Count` is the number of elements currently in the list. `List` is a pointer to the first node in our linked list. `Free` is a pointer to the first node in a linked list of free nodes. This list of free nodes is stored in the same file as our list elements; they are intertwined in the file just as they were in the array. Finally, `Header_File` is a sequential file used to store the values of `Count`, `List`, and `Free` between program runs.

The actual reading and writing to the list file is done by two local procedures, `Read_Node` and `Write_Node`. There are two reasons why we chose to write these local procedures instead of calling `Node_IO.Read` and `Node_IO.Write` directly. First, because our pointers are type `Natural`, we must make explicit conversions between `Natural` and `Node_IO.Count` (the type used for the direct file indices). It is clearer if we limit these explicit type conversions to two places rather than using such conversions throughout the entire package body. Second, we can more easily add a node caching scheme to avoid multiple reading of the same node from the file (see Exercise 54).

Memory management is slightly more complicated in the file-based list than it was for the array-based list. The memory we are managing here is in the disk file rather than in an array. Procedure `Free_Node` uses the same algorithm as the array-based list; the node is added to a list of free nodes. In the array-based list, we initialized the list of free nodes by linking all of the nodes in the array. Because a file has no declared upper bound, we cannot link all of the file nodes. Instead we initialize the free list to empty and use the following algorithm to find an available node on the disk:

New_Node
    if the list of free nodes is empty then
        return the Size of the list plus 1
    else
        return the location of the first node on the free list
    end if

If there are no nodes on the free list, we extend the size of our file by one element. Nodes are added to the free list only when procedure `Free_Node` is called.

To minimize the number of disk reads (a time-consuming operation), we use the package variable `Count` to keep track of the number of elements in the list. `Count` is returned by function `Length`. `Count` is incremented each time a new element is added to the list and decremented each time an element is deleted from the list. Why can't we call `Node_IO.Size` to determine the number of elements in the list? `Node_IO.Size` returns the total number of nodes in the file. This total includes the nodes in the list and the nodes in the free list.

Procedure `Close` closes the direct file used to store the list nodes. This procedure also saves the values of three package variables (`Count`, `List`, and `Free`) that are needed the next time the program is run.

The sequence of statements at the end of the package body is executed whenever the package is elaborated. These statements initialize the list: The `List_File` and `Header_File` are opened (using the names supplied by the application programmer as generic objects) and the values of `Count`, `List`, and `Free` are read from `Header_File`. If these files do not yet exist, the open operation raises `NAME_ERROR`. The exception handler for `NAME_ERROR` then creates the `List_File` and initializes `Count`, `List`, and `Free` with values for an empty list.

Body 8.2   File-Based Linked List ADO: Implements Specification 8.4

```ada
with Direct_IO;
with Sequential_IO;
package body File_Based is

   subtype Node_Ptr is Natural;

   Nil : constant Node_Ptr := 0;

   type Node_Type is
      record
         Info : Element_Type;
         Next : Node_Ptr := Nil;
      end record;

   -- For input and output of list nodes
   package Node_IO is new Direct_IO (Element_Type => Node_Type);
   -- For input and output of bookkeeping information
   package Header_IO is new Sequential_IO (Element_Type => Integer);


   -- Package Variables   (used globally in the package)

   Header_File : Header_IO.File_Type;   -- Keep header info between runs
   List_File   : Node_IO.File_Type;     -- Storage file for the nodes
   Count       : Natural   := 0;        -- Size of the List
   List        : Node_Ptr := Nil;       -- The "head" pointer of the list
   Free        : Node_Ptr := Nil;       -- Head of list of available nodes

   -- Local procedures
```

```ada
procedure Read_Node (From : in  Node_Ptr;
                     Node : out Node_Type) is
-- Reads a node from the list file
begin
   Node_IO.Read (File => List_File,
                 Item => Node,
                 From => Node_IO.Positive_Count(From));
end Read_Node;

-------------------------------------------------------------------------------
procedure Write_Node (To   : in Node_Ptr;
                      Node : in Node_Type) is
-- Writes a node to the list file
begin
   Node_IO.Write (File => List_File,
                  Item => Node,
                  To   => Node_IO.Positive_Count(To));
end Write_Node;

-------------------------------------------------------------------------------
function New_Node return Node_Ptr is
-- Finds a free node in the file (memory allocation)
   Result : Node_Ptr;
   Node   : Node_Type;
begin
   if Free = Nil then   -- use next place in file
      return Node_Ptr (Node_IO.Size (List_File)) + 1;
   else -- Get a node from the free list
      Result := Free;
      -- Unlink the free node
      Read_Node (From => Result, Node => Node);
      Free   := Node.Next;
      return Result;
   end if;
end New_Node;

-------------------------------------------------------------------------------
procedure Free_Node (X : in out Node_Ptr) is
   Node : Node_Type;
-- Deallocates a node
begin
   -- Link the node into the free list
   Node.Next := Free;
   Free := X;
   Write_Node (To => Free, Node => Node);
```

```ada
      X      := Nil;     -- Reset pointer
end Free_Node;

---------------------------------------------------------------------------
procedure Search_Linked_List (Key      : in  Key_Type;
                              Found    : out Boolean;
                              Pred_Loc : out Node_Ptr;
                              Location : out Node_Ptr) is
-- Purpose        : Searches for the location of Key in the List
-- Preconditions  : The nodes in List are in ascending order
-- Postconditions : If Key is in List
--                      Found is True
--                      Location designates the element with Key
--                      Pred_Loc designates the predecessor of the node
--                          designated by Location.  If Location
--                          designates the first node in the list,
--                          Pred_Loc is Nil.
--                  else
--                      Found is False
--                      Location designates the node that would follow a node
--                          containing Key.  If Key's node would follow
--                          the last node in the list, Location is Nil.
--                      Pred_Loc designates the predecessor of the node
--                          designated by Location.  If Location
--                          designates the first node in the list,
--                          Pred_Loc is Nil.

   Node     : Node_Type;      -- Local copy of a list node
begin
   Location := List;          -- Start at the beginning of the linked list
   Pred_Loc := Nil;           -- No predecessor for 1st element in the list
   loop  -- Each iteration, one node is checked
      exit when Location = Nil; -- Reached the end
      Read_Node (From => Location, Node => Node);
      exit when Key < Key_Of (Node.Info) or   -- Passed by
                Key = Key_Of (Node.Info);     -- Found it
      Pred_Loc := Location;     -- Move inchworm's tail
      Location := Node.Next;    -- Move inchworm's head
   end loop;
   Found := Location /= Nil  and then  Key = Key_Of (Node.Info);
end Search_Linked_List;

-- Operations defined in the specification
---------------------------------------------------------------------------
procedure Clear is
```

```
      To_Recycle : Node_Ptr;          -- Designates a node for recycling
      Node       : Node_Type;
begin
   loop
      exit when List = Nil;           -- Exit when list is empty
      To_Recycle := List;
      -- Unlink the first node
      Read_Node (From => List, Node => Node);
      List := Node.Next;
      Free_Node (To_Recycle);         -- Recycle the node
   end loop;
end Clear;
```

```
procedure Insert (Item : in      Element_Type) is
   Have_Duplicate : Boolean;
   Pred_Loc       : Node_Ptr;        -- Pointer to predecessor
   Location       : Node_Ptr;        -- Pointer to successor
   New_Location   : Node_Ptr;        -- Pointer to available spot
   Node           : Node_Type;       -- A list node
begin
   Search_Linked_List (Key      => Key_Of (Item),
                       Found    => Have_Duplicate,
                       Pred_Loc => Pred_Loc,
                       Location => Location);
   if Have_Duplicate then
      raise DUPLICATE_KEY;
   elsif Pred_Loc = Nil then         -- Add at beginning
      New_Location := New_Node;
      Node := (Info => Item, Next => List);
      Write_Node (To => New_Location, Node => Node);
      List := New_Location;
   else    -- Add at the middle or end
      New_Location := New_Node;
      Node := (Info => Item, Next => Location);
      Write_Node (To => New_Location, Node => Node);
      -- Change the predecessor's Next field
      Read_Node (From => Pred_Loc, Node => Node);
      Node.Next := New_Location;
      Write_Node (To => Pred_Loc, Node => Node);
   end if;
   Count := Count + 1;
exception
   when Node_IO.USE_ERROR =>          -- Raised when disk is full
      raise OVERFLOW;
end Insert;
```

```ada
---------------------------------------------------------------------
procedure Delete (Key : in  Key_Type) is
   Found    : Boolean;
   Pred_Loc : Node_Ptr;
   Location : Node_Ptr;
   Next     : Node_Ptr;
   Node     : Node_Type;
begin
   Search_Linked_List (Key      => Key,
                       Found    => Found,
                       Pred_Loc => Pred_Loc,
                       Location => Location);
   if not Found then
      raise KEY_ERROR;
   elsif Pred_Loc = Nil then
      Read_Node (From => Location, Node => Node);
      List := Node.Next;            -- Delete first element
   else  -- Delete middle or last element
      -- Get the location of the successor of the node to delete
      Read_Node (From => Location, Node => Node);
      Next := Node.Next;
      -- Change the predecessor to point to the successor
      Read_Node (From => Pred_Loc, Node => Node);
      Node.Next := Next;
      Write_Node (To => Pred_Loc, Node => Node);
   end if;
   Free_Node (Location);                          -- Recycle node memory
   Count := Count - 1;
end Delete;

---------------------------------------------------------------------
procedure Modify (Element : in Element_Type) is
   Found    : Boolean;
   Pred_Loc : Node_Ptr;
   Location : Node_Ptr;
   Node     : Node_Type;
begin
   Search_Linked_List (Key      => Key_Of (Element),
                       Found    => Found,
                       Pred_Loc => Pred_Loc,
                       Location => Location);
   if not Found then
      raise KEY_ERROR;
   else
      Read_Node (From => Location, Node => Node);
      Node.Info := Element;
```

```
            Write_Node (To => Location, Node => Node);
         end if;
   end Modify;
```

```
procedure Retrieve (Key     : in     Key_Type;
                    Element :    out Element_Type) is
   Found    : Boolean;
   Pred_Loc : Node_Ptr;
   Location : Node_Ptr;
   Node     : Node_Type;
begin
   Search_Linked_List (Key      => Key,
                       Found    => Found,
                       Pred_Loc => Pred_Loc,
                       Location => Location);
   if not Found then
      raise KEY_ERROR;
   else
      Read_Node (From => Location, Node => Node);
      Element := Node.Info;
   end if;
end Retrieve;
```

```
function Empty return Boolean is
begin
   return List = Nil;
end Empty;
```

```
function Full return Boolean is
begin
   return False;
end Full;
```

```
function Length return Natural is
begin
   return Count;
end Length;
```

```
procedure Traverse
     (Process : not null access procedure (Element : in out Element_Type)) is
```

```ada
      Location : Node_Ptr;        -- Designates current node
      Node     : Node_Type;       -- Local copy of node from file
   begin
      Location := List;
      loop
         exit when Location = Nil;
         Read_Node (From => Location, Node => Node);
         Process (Node.Info);      -- Call user's procedure to process it
         -- Put possibly modified element back into list
         Write_Node (To => Location, Node => Node);
         Location := Node.Next;  -- Move to next node
      end loop;
   end Traverse;

   ----------------------------------------------------------------------

   procedure Close is
   begin
      Header_IO.Create (File => Header_File,
                        Name => Header_File_Name);
      Header_IO.Write (File => Header_File, Item => Count);
      Header_IO.Write (File => Header_File, Item => List);
      Header_IO.Write (File => Header_File, Item => Free);
      Header_IO.Close (Header_File);
      Node_IO.Close (List_File);
   end Close;

begin  -- Initialize the key-ordered list

   Node_IO.Open (File => List_File,
                 Mode => Node_IO.InOut_File,
                 Name => List_File_Name);
   Header_IO.Open (File => Header_File,
                   Mode => Header_IO.In_File,
                   Name => Header_File_Name);
   Header_IO.Read (File => Header_File, Item => Count);
   Header_IO.Read (File => Header_File, Item => List);
   Header_IO.Read (File => Header_File, Item => Free);
   Header_IO.Close (Header_File);
exception
   when Node_IO.NAME_ERROR =>  -- List files don't exist.
      -- Create node file.
      Node_IO.Create (File => List_File,
                      Mode => Node_IO.InOut_File,
                      Name => List_File_Name);
      -- Initialize empty list
```

```
        Count := 0;
        List  := Nil;
        Free  := Nil;

end File_Based;
```

Analysis of the File-Based List

Except for the `Length` operation, the Big-O of all operations in the file-based list are the same as those in the array-based linked list. However, Big-O says nothing about the actual amount of time the operations take. It simply describes how that time changes as the list size grows. $O(N)$ for a list means that the amount of time to carry out an operation is directly proportional to the size of the list. If we double the size, we double the time.

With a large list, the amount of time an $O(N)$ file-based operation takes may be significant. Most computer users would not tolerate the wait required to search a large file-based linked list. (Even we were too impatient to wait for the results of our timing tests when we used the file-based implementation of the key-ordered list.) In Chapter 10 we look at another linked structure, the binary search tree, whose search is $O(\log_2 N)$. The techniques introduced in this chapter for storing linked lists on disk can also be used to implement file-based trees.

8.7 Lists with Duplicate Keys

The lists we have discussed so far in this chapter and in Chapter 7 were all composed of elements with unique keys; that is, there were no duplicate keys in the list. For instance, a list of university students might be made up of elements of the following type:

```
type Student_Rec is
   record
      ID         : Positive;
      Last_Name  : Name_Str;
      First_Name : Name_Str;
      GPA        : GPA_Type;
   end record;
```

The list might be ordered according to student ID. In this case, there would be no duplicate keys in the list because each student has a unique ID number (Figure 8.24[a]). However, if the list was instantiated for assigning class rank, and GPA was the key on which the elements were ordered, there would almost certainly be some duplicate keys (Figure 8.24[b]). Duplicate keys are also possible if the list is to be ordered alphabetically by the students' names (Figure 8.24[c]).

When lists are not ordered according to a unique key, the operations specified for the list must be changed to reflect this situation. Some of the changes would be internal

(a) Ordered by ID (unique key)

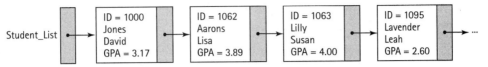

(b) Ordered by GPA (duplicate keys possible)

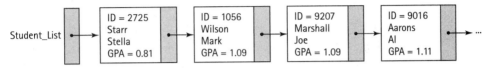

(c) Ordered by Last_Name/First_Name (duplicate keys possible)

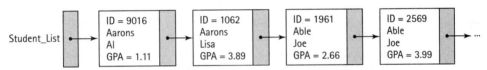

Figure 8.24 *Duplicate keys in a list.*

to the operation. For example, should the `Insert` operation insert a new element before or after elements already in the list that have the same key as the new one?

Other changes, however, must be reflected in the specifications of the operations themselves. For instance, what is returned by `Retrieve`, which searches a list for an element with a specific key, when the keys are not unique? Does it return the first element with the specified key, or a list of the elements that have this key? What is done by `Delete`, which takes a list and the key of the element to delete, if there are multiple elements with that key? Should they all be deleted? Should the procedure specification be changed to take a list and copy of the element (rather than just its key value), to make sure that the procedure deletes only a particular element? Similar questions can be raised for the `Modify` operation. These are no longer purely internal implementation issues, because the application programmer must understand the interfaces and the functions of the operations.

We will not tell you a single algorithmic answer to the problem of elements with duplicate keys, because the solution depends on how the list will be used. These are design choices that you, as the programmer, will have to make and to record in the specification of the list class. In the programs that you are writing now, you are probably wearing two hats: one as the application programmer using the list class and one as the list implementer. In many real-world programming situations, you will be using classes that another programmer has implemented. Good communications skills (and well-documented specifications) are essential for programmers who write "utilities" that other programmers use.

Summary

In this chapter we have looked at a number of variations on the linked list theme. Obviously, given the wide variety of applications that use lists, there are many interesting ways that a programmer can use this way of organizing data. All of the implementations are supported by a common method of development: As programmers, we determine the needs of the application and then decide on a physical representation for the data. Along with the declarations of the data type, we must provide a set of basic operations so that the user of the data type can create and access elements in the structure. For lists, these operations generally include procedures and functions to add, delete, and modify elements, traverse a list, and determine whether the list is empty. We don't expect—or allow—the application programmer to manipulate the data structure directly.

The idea of linking the elements in a list has been extended in this chapter to include circular lists, lists with header and trailer nodes, and doubly linked lists. The idea of linking the elements is a possibility to consider in the design of many types of data structures.

The dynamic allocation of the space for nodes in a linked structure allows the program to get just what it needs during execution. In a program where the amount of data to be stored is very unpredictable or may vary widely, the dynamic allocation of space has major advantages. An access variable provides efficient access to a node because it contains (among other information) the node's actual location in memory.

Although a linked list can be used to implement virtually any list application, its real strength is in applications that largely process the list elements in order. This is not to say that we cannot do "random access" operations on a linked list. Our List class specifications include operations that access elements in random order—for instance, procedures `Retrieve`, `Modify`, and `Delete` manipulate a particular element in the list. However, the only way to find an element is to search the list, beginning at the first element, and continuing sequentially to examine element after element. This search is O(N), because the amount of work required is directly proportional to the number of elements in the list. A particular element in a sequentially ordered list in an array, in contrast, can be found with a binary search, decreasing the search algorithm to $O(\log_2 N)$. For a large list, the O(N) sequential search can be quite time consuming. There is a linked structure that supports $O(\log_2 N)$ searches: the binary search tree. We discuss this data structure in detail in Chapter 10.

Linked lists are not synonymous with dynamic storage allocation. As we demonstrated in this chapter, we can also store linked lists in an array or in a direct file. We continue to use linked representations of data structures in the chapters that follow and typically implement them with dynamic storage allocation. A static implementation (with arrays and files) of these linked structures is also possible, however, and in some cases is desirable or necessary.

Exercises

1. Write a procedure, `Print_Reverse`, that takes the external pointer to a singly linked list and prints the elements in reverse order, using the following

approach: Traverse the list from first to last node, reversing the direction of each `Next` pointer, as illustrated below:

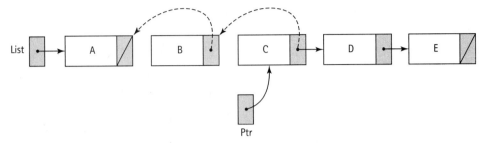

When you reach the end of the list, you have a linked list whose elements are in the reverse order from the original list. Now traverse this list, processing each element by printing the element and reinverting its `Next` pointer, as illustrated below:

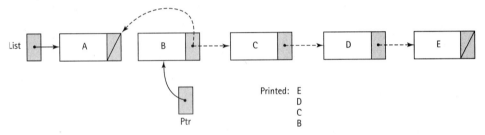

When you reach the (original) beginning of the list, the whole list is printed in reverse order, and the links are back to their original values.

2. a. What is the Big-O of the algorithm in the previous exercise?
   b. How many times is each node accessed?

Circular Linked Lists

3. What are the advantages of a circularly linked list over the simple linked list we developed in Chapter 7?
4. Are there any disadvantages to using a circularly linked list rather than a simple linked list?
5. What is the advantage of having the external pointer of a circularly linked list designate the last node in the linked list rather than the first node in the linked list?
6. Complete the procedure bodies for the remaining operations for the circular linked list in this chapter: `Clear`, `Empty`, `Full`, `Retrieve`, and `Modify`.
7. The key-ordered list class with a circularly linked implementation is to be extended with a procedure, `Merge_Lists`, with the following specification:

```
procedure Merge_Lists (List_1    : in out List_Type;
                       List_2    : in out List_Type;
                       New_List  :    out List_Type);
-- Purpose        : Merges two lists into a single list
--
-- Preconditions  : New_List is empty
--                  No key is present in both List_1 and List_2
--
-- Postconditions : List_1 and List_2 are empty
--                  New_List contains all the elements
--                       from List_1 and List_2
```

    a. Write the procedure body using a circularly linked list as described in this chapter. You may not call the `Insert` operation in your merge body.

    b. Describe `Merge_Lists` in terms of Big-O.

8. The key-ordered list class with a circularly linked implementation is to be extended with a procedure, `Split_List`, with the following specification:

```
procedure Split_List (Main_List : in out List_Type;
                      Split_Key : in     Key_Type;
                      List_1    :    out List_Type;
                      List_2    :    out List_Type);
-- Divides a list into two lists according to the key value of each
-- element.  All elements with keys less than Split_Key will be put
-- into List_1, all elements with keys greater than or equal to
-- Split_Key will be put into List_2.
--
-- Preconditions  : List_1 and List_2 are empty.
--
-- Postconditions : Main_List is empty
--                  List_1 contains all elements from Main_List with
--                       keys less than Split_Key
--                  List_2 contains all elements from Main_List with
--                       keys greater than or equal to Split_Key
```

    a. Write the procedure body using a circularly linked list as described in this chapter. You may not call the `Insert` operation in your merge body.

    b. Describe `Split_List` in terms of Big-O.

9. The key-ordered list class with a circularly linked implementation is to be extended by the addition of procedure `Get_Element`, which takes a key-ordered list and an integer, `Position`, and returns a copy of the element in the specified list position. For instance, if `Position` is 1, a copy of the first list element is returned; if `Position` is 12, a copy of the twelfth list element is returned. If `Position` is greater than the number of elements in the list, `CONSTRAINT_ERROR` is raised.

a. Write the specification for procedure `Get_Element` as it would appear in either Specification 7.1 or Specification 7.4.

b. Write the procedure body using a circularly linked list as described in this chapter.

c. Describe `Get_Element` in terms of Big-O.

10. The key-ordered list class with a circularly linked implementation is to be extended by the addition of procedure `Reverse_Traverse`, with the identical parameter profile (signature) as `Traverse`. As its name implies, this procedure processes the elements in the list in descending order by key.

    a. Write the specification for `Reverse_Traverse` as it would appear in either Specification 7.1 or Specification 7.4.

    b. Write the procedure body using a circularly linked list as described in this chapter. Hint: Make use of the stack class.

    c. Describe `Reverse_Traverse` in terms of Big-O.

Doubly Linked Lists

11. What are the advantages of a doubly linked list over the simple linked list we developed in Chapter 7?

12. Are there any disadvantages to using a doubly linked list rather than a simple linked list?

13. Using the circular doubly linked list below, give the expression corresponding to each of the following descriptions.

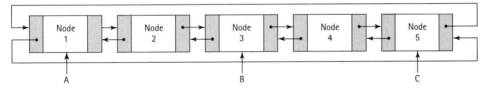

(For example, the expression for the `Info` field of Node 1, referenced from pointer A, would be `A.all.Info`.)

a. The `Info` field of Node 1, referenced from pointer C

b. The `Info` field of Node 2, referenced from pointer B

c. The `Next` field of Node 2, referenced from pointer A

d. The `Next` field of Node 4, referenced from pointer C

e. Node 1, referenced from pointer B

f. The `Back` field of Node 4, referenced from pointer C

g. The `Back` field of Node 1, referenced from pointer A

14. Complete the procedure bodies for the remaining operations for the circular doubly linked list in this chapter: `Clear`, `Empty`, `Full`, `Retrieve`, and `Modify`.

15. The Big-O of the delete procedure we developed for a circular linked list is O(1) for deleting the element at the beginning of the list and O(N) for deleting the element at the end of the list. Make the necessary changes to the search and/or delete procedures so that deletion of first and last elements is O(1).

16. The package `Ada.Containers.Doubly_Linked_Lists` in the standard library is a generic package with a set of operations to manage a doubly linked list. Read Section A.18.3 of the *Ada Reference Manual* to find the answers to the following questions:

    a. What is a cursor?

    b. Are the elements in a list defined in this package ordered by a key?

    c. Describe three ways to determine whether a list is empty.

    d. Write the declarations to instantiate a doubly linked list of unbounded-length strings and to declare a list object called `Roster` and a cursor variable called `Position`.

    e. Write three lines of code to insert the following three names into `Roster` in the given order:

    Smedley, Mildred

    Beasley, Horace

    Kramden, Ralph

    f. Using the cursor variable `Position`, write a loop to display all of the names in `Roster`.

    g. Use the procedure `Iterate` to display all of the names in `Roster`.

    h. What does it mean for an application to *tamper with cursors*?

    i. What does it mean for an application to *tamper with elements*?

    j. Does inserting a new element into a list tamper with cursers? Tamper with elements?

    k. Does updating an element in a list tamper with cursers? Tamper with elements?

17. The key-ordered list class with a circular doubly linked implementation is to be extended with a procedure, `Merge_Lists`, with the following specification:

    ```
    procedure Merge_Lists (List_1   : in out List_Type;
                           List_2   : in out List_Type;
                           New_List :    out List_Type);
    -- Purpose         : Merges two lists into a single list
    --
    -- Preconditions   : New_List is empty
    --                   No key is present in both List_1 and List_2
    --
    -- Postconditions  : List_1 and List_2 are empty
    ```

```
--                  New_List contains all the elements
--                        from List_1 and List_2
```
   a. Write the procedure body using a circular doubly linked list as described in this chapter. You may not call the `Insert` operation in your merge body.

   b. Describe `Merge_Lists` in terms of Big-O.

18. The key-ordered list class with a circular doubly linked implementation is to be extended with a procedure, `Split_List`, with the following specification:

```
procedure Split_List (Main_List : in out List_Type;
                      Split_Key :    in     Key_Type;
                      List_1    :        out List_Type;
                      List_2    :        out List_Type);
-- Divides a list into two lists according to the key value of each
-- element.  All elements with keys less than Split_Key will be put
-- into List_1, all elements with keys greater than or equal to
-- Split_Key will be put into List_2.
--
-- Preconditions  : List_1 and List_2 are empty.
--
-- Postconditions : Main_List is empty
--                  List_1 contains all elements from Main_List with
--                       keys less than Split_Key
--                  List_2 contains all elements from Main_List with
--                       keys greater than or equal to Split_Key
```

   a. Write the procedure body using a circular doubly linked list as described in this chapter. You may not call the `Insert` operation in your merge body.

   b. Describe `Split_List` in terms of Big-O.

19. The key-ordered list class with a circular doubly linked implementation is to be extended by the addition of procedure `Get_Element`, which takes a key-ordered list and an integer, `Position`, and returns a copy of the element in the specified list position. For instance, if `Position` is 1, a copy of the first list element is returned; if `Position` is 12, a copy of the twelfth list element is returned. If `Position` is greater than the number of elements in the list, `CONSTRAINT_ERROR` is raised.

   a. Write the specification for procedure `Get_Element` as it would appear in either Specification 7.1 or Specification 7.4.

   b. Write the procedure body using a circular doubly linked list as described in this chapter.

   c. Describe `Get_Element` in terms of Big-O.

20. The key-ordered list class with a circular doubly linked implementation is to be extended by the addition of procedure `Reverse_Traverse`, with the identical parameter profile (signature) as `Traverse`. As its name implies, this procedure processes the elements in the list in descending order by key.

a. Write the specification for `Reverse_Traverse` as it would appear in either Specification 7.1 or Specification 7.4.

b. Write the procedure body using a circular doubly linked list as described in this chapter.

c. Describe `Reverse_Traverse` in terms of Big-O.

Linked Lists with Dummy Nodes

21. Dummy nodes are used to simplify list processing by eliminating some "special case."

    a. What special case is eliminated by a header node in a linear linked list?

    b. What special case is eliminated by a trailer node in a linear linked list?

    c. Would dummy nodes be useful in implementing a linked stack? That is, would their use eliminate a special case? Explain your answer.

    d. Would dummy nodes be useful in implementing a linked queue with pointers to both head and rear elements? Explain your answer.

    e. Would dummy nodes be useful in implementing a circular linked queue? Explain your answer.

22. The element in a trailer node must have a key that is greater than any legitimate key in the list. Why doesn't the element in the header node have to have a key that is less than any legitimate key in the list?

23. Horace and Mildred are programmers for the local school district. One morning Horace commented to Mildred about the funny last name the new family in the district had: "Have you ever heard of a family named Zzuan?" Mildred replied, "Uh-oh; we have some work to do. Let's get going."

    a. Can you explain Mildred's response?

    b. How could Horace and Mildred solve the problem so it will not occur again?

24. Complete the procedure bodies for the remaining operations for the linked list with dummy nodes described in this chapter: `Search_Linked_List`, `Insert`, `Delete`, `Clear`, `Empty`, `Full`, `Retrieve`, and `Modify`.

25. In most of our previous collection classes we used the `Clear` operation to recycle the memory used by all the nodes making up the collection. Why can we not use the `Clear` operation to recycle all of the memory used by a linked list with dummy nodes?

26. In most of the previous controlled type subclasses we used the superclass's null `Initialize` operation. Why did we need to override the `Initialize` operation of the superclass `Ada.Finalization.Limited_Controlled` in our implementation of the key-ordered list using dummy nodes?

27. Write the body of overriding procedure `Initialize` for a doubly linked list with a single dummy node, as shown in Figure 8.15.

28. The key-ordered list class with a linked implementation with dummy nodes is to be extended with a procedure, Merge_Lists, with the following specification:

    ```
    procedure Merge_Lists (List_1   : in out List_Type;
                           List_2   : in out List_Type;
                           New_List :    out List_Type);
    -- Purpose       : Merges two lists into a single list
    --
    -- Preconditions : New_List is empty
    --                 No key is present in both List_1 and List_2
    --
    -- Postconditions : List_1 and List_2 are empty
    --                  New_List contains all the elements
    --                       from List_1 and List_2
    ```

    a. Write the procedure body using a linked implementation with dummy nodes as described in this chapter. You may not call the Insert operation in your merge body.

    b. Describe Merge_Lists in terms of Big-O.

29. The key-ordered list class with a linked implementation with dummy nodes is to be extended with a procedure, Split_List, with the following specification:

```
procedure Split_List (Main_List : in out List_Type;
                      Split_Key : in      Key_Type;
                      List_1    :    out List_Type;
                      List_2    :    out List_Type);
-- Divides a list into two lists according to the key value of each
-- element.  All elements with keys less than Split_Key will be put
-- into List_1, all elements with keys greater than or equal to
-- Split_Key will be put into List_2.
--
-- Preconditions  : List_1 and List_2 are empty.
--
-- Postconditions : Main_List is empty
--                  List_1 contains all elements from Main_List with
--                       keys less than Split_Key
--                  List_2 contains all elements from Main_List with
--                       keys greater than or equal to Split_Key
```

   a. Write the procedure body using a linked implementation with dummy nodes as described in this chapter. You may not call the Insert operation in your merge body.

   b. Describe Split_List in terms of Big-O.

30. The key-ordered list class with a linked implementation with dummy nodes is to be extended by the addition of procedure `Get_Element`, which takes a key-ordered list and an integer, `Position`, and returns a copy of the element in the specified list position. For instance, if `Position` is 1, a copy of the first list element is returned; if `Position` is 12, a copy of the twelfth list element is returned. If `Position` is greater than the number of elements in the list, CONSTRAINT_ERROR is raised.

   a. Write the specification for procedure `Get_Element` as it would appear in either Specification 7.1 or Specification 7.4.

   b. Write the procedure body using a linked implementation with dummy nodes as described in this chapter.

   c. Describe `Get_Element` in terms of Big-O.

31. The key-ordered list class with a linked implementation with dummy nodes is to be extended by the addition of procedure `Reverse_Traverse`, with the identical parameter profile (signature) as `Traverse`. As its name implies, this procedure processes the elements in the list in descending order by key.

   a. Write the specification for `Reverse_Traverse` as it would appear in either Specification 7.1 or Specification 7.4.

   b. Write the procedure body using a linked implementation with dummy nodes as described in this chapter. Hint: Make use of the stack class.

   c. Describe `Reverse_Traverse` in terms of Big-O.

32. The text edited by a line editor is represented by a doubly linked list of nodes, each of which contain an unbounded-length string. There is one external pointer (`Line_Ptr_Type`) to this list, which points to the "current" line in the text being edited. The list has a header node, which contains the string:

   –Top of File–

   and a trailer node, which contains the string:

   –Bottom of File–

   a. Draw a sketch of this data structure.

   b. Write the type declarations to support this data structure. Make your list class a subclass of `Ada.Finalization.Limited_Controlled`.

   c. Instantiate a procedure to recycle the memory for one node in the doubly linked list.

   d. Code the following operations on this structure:

```
overriding procedure Initialize (Line_Ptr : in out Line_Ptr_Type);
-- Purpose         : Initializes the doubly linked list
-- Preconditions   : Line_Ptr is null
-- Postconditions  : Line_Ptr designates the header node of an empty list
```

```
overriding procedure Finalize (Line_Ptr : in out Line_Ptr_Type);
-- Purpose        : Recycles all memory used by the doubly linked list
-- Preconditions  : Line_Ptr designates some node in the linked list
-- Postconditions : All nodes in the linked list have been recycled

procedure Go_To_Top (Line_Ptr : in out Line_Ptr_Type);
-- Purpose        : Makes the first line the current line
-- Preconditions  : Line_Ptr designates a node in the doubly linked list
-- Postconditions : If the doubly linked list is not empty, Line_Ptr
--                  designates the first line in the list.
--                  Else Line_Ptr designates the header node

procedure Go_To_Bottom (Line_Ptr : in out Line_Ptr_Type);
-- Purpose        : Makes the last line the current line
-- Preconditions  : Line_Ptr designates a node in the doubly linked list
-- Postconditions : If the doubly linked list is not empty, Line_Ptr
--                  designates the last line in the list.
--                  Else Line_Ptr designates the trailer node
```

    e. Describe `Go_To_Top` and `Go_To_Bottom` in terms of Big-O. How could the list be changed to make these operations O(1)?

    f. Code the `Insert_Line` operation, using the following declaration:

```
procedure Insert_Line (Line_Ptr : in out Line_Ptr_Type;
                       New_Line : in     String);
-- Purpose        : Inserts New_Line after the "current" line
-- Preconditions  : Line_Ptr does not designate the trailer node
-- Postconditions : A node containing a copy of New_Line is inserted
--                  into the linked list after the node designated
--                  by Line_Ptr
--                  Line_Ptr designates the new node
```

    g. Code the `Display_Text` operation, using the following declaration:

```
procedure Display_Text (Line_Ptr : in out Line_Ptr_Type);
-- Purpose        : Displays all of the text in the doubly linked list
-- Preconditions  : Line_Ptr designates some node in the linked list
-- Postconditions : The text in all of the nodes of the linked list from
--                  the first to the last node is displayed
--                  Line_Ptr designates the trailer node
```

33. Of the three variations of linked lists (circular, doubly linked, and with header and trailer nodes), which would be most appropriate for each of the following applications?

a. Search a list for a key and return the keys of the two elements that come before it and the keys of the two elements that come after it.

b. A text file contains integer elements, one per line, ordered from smallest to largest. You must read the values from the file and create an ordered linked list containing the values.

c. A list is short and frequently becomes empty. You want a list that is optimal for inserting an element into the empty list and deleting the last element from the list.

34. Figure 8.15 illustrates a doubly linked list with a single dummy node. Figure 8.15(c) shows an empty list for this implementation.

   a. Does this implementation require an overriding `Initialize` procedure to initialize a list to empty or can we supply default initial values in the `List_Type` record to accomplish the desired initialization?

   b. Write the code (the `List_Type` record or the specification and body of overriding procedure `Initialize`) necessary to initialize a list.

The Linked List As an Array of Nodes

35. What is the Big-O for initializing the free list in the array-based list package (procedure `Initialize_Memory`)? For the procedures `New_Node` and `Free_Node`?

36. Use the linked lists contained in the array pictured in Figure 8.18 to answer the following questions:

   a. What elements are in `List1`? (Give the `Info` of each.)

   b. What elements are in `List2`? (Give the `Info` of each.)

   c. What array positions (indexes) are part of the free-space list?

   d. What would the array look like after the deletion of 32 from `List1`?

   e. What would the array look like after the insertion of 17 into `List2`? Assume that before the insertion the array is as pictured in Figure 8.18.

37. An array of records (nodes) is used to contain a doubly linked list, with the `Next` and `Back` fields indicating the index of the linked nodes in each direction.

   a. Show how the array would look after it was initialized to an empty state, with all the nodes linked into the free-space list. (Note that the free-space nodes only have to be linked in one direction.)

	Nodes .Info	.Next	.Back
(1)			
(2)			
(3)			
(4)			
(5)			
(6)			
(7)			
(8)			
(9)			
(10)			

List.First ☐

Free ☐

b. Draw a box-and-arrow picture of a doubly linked list into which the following numbers were inserted into their proper places in the doubly linked list: 17, 4, 25.

c. Fill in the contents of the array below after the following numbers were inserted into their proper places in the doubly linked list: 17, 4, 25.

	Nodes .Info	.Next	.Back
(1)			
(2)			
(3)			
(4)			
(5)			
(6)			
(7)			
(8)			
(9)			
(10)			

List.First ☐

Free ☐

d. Show how the array in part (c) would look after 17 was deleted.

	Nodes		
	.Info	.Next	.Back
(1)			
(2)			
(3)			
(4)			
(5)			
(6)			
(7)			
(8)			
(9)			
(10)			

List.First ▢

Free ▢

38. What is an advantage of implementing a stack as an array-based linked list rather than as a sequential list stored in an array?

The Linked List As a File of Nodes

39. What is the Big-O for initializing the free list in the file-based list package?
40. Body 8.2 contains a package variable `Count` that is used to store the number of elements in the list. How does this value differ from what is returned by a call to the function `Node_IO.Size`?
41. The `Close` operation in our file-based list package saves the state of the list. Programmers often forget to call `Close` when they have finished with the list. Discuss how you could use a controlled type to automatically call `Close`. With this approach, we would eliminate the declaration of `Close` in the package specification.
42. We implemented the file-based linked list as an ADO rather than an ADT.
    a. What changes must be made to the types and subprogram parameters in the package declaration to convert this ADO to an ADT?
    b. What additional operation(s) must be included in the package declaration to convert this ADO to an ADT?
    c. What additional precondition must be added to all other list operations?

Lists with Duplicate Keys

43. Complete the following local search procedure for a sorted list that *can contain duplicate keys*. The list is implemented as a singly linked list with header and trailer nodes.

```
procedure Search_Linked_List (List     : in List_Type;
                              Key      : in Key_Type;
                              Found    : out Boolean;
                              Pred_Loc : out Node_Ptr;
                              Location : out Node_Ptr) is
-- Searches for the location of Key in the List
-- Preconditions  : The nodes in List are in ascending order.
--                  List has Header and Trailer Nodes
-- Postconditions : If Key is in List
--                     Found is True
--                     Location designates the first element with
--                                Key
--                     Pred_Loc designates the predecessor of the
--                                node designated by Location.
--                  else
--                     Found is False
--                     Location designates the node that would
--                                follow a node containing Key.
--                     Pred_Loc designates the predecessor of the
--                                node designated by Location.
```

44. The following is a declaration for an `Insert` operation for a sorted list that *can contain duplicate keys*.

```
procedure Insert (List : in out List_Type;
                  Item : in     Element_Type);
-- Insert Item into List
-- Preconditions  : None
-- Postconditions : Item is inserted into List.  If one or more
--                  elements with the key of Item are already in
--                  the list, Item is inserted after the last of
--                  these "duplicate" elements.
```

The list is implemented as a singly linked list with header and trailer nodes. Write the procedure body for this operation. You may call the search procedure whose specification was given in Exercise 43.

45. The following is a declaration for a `Retrieve` operation for a sorted list that *can contain duplicate keys*.

```
procedure Retrieve (List     : in      List_Type;  -- List to search
                    Key      : in      Key_Type;   -- Key to look for
                    Elements :     out List_Type); -- A list of all
                                                   --   elements with
                                                   --   the given Key
```

```
-- Retrieve all of the elements with the given Key.
-- Preconditions  : Elements is an empty list
-- Postconditions : Elements contains copies of all elements in List
--                  with the given Key.  If no element in List
--                  has the Key, the list Elements will be empty.
```

The list is implemented as a singly linked list with header and trailer nodes. Write the procedure body for this operation. You may call the search procedure whose specification was given in Exercise 43.

Programming Problems

46. After answering Exercise 16, use the package `Ada.Containers.Doubly_Linked_Lists` to create a new implementation of the address book ADO given in Chapter 7.

47. a. Implement a key-ordered list class using a linked list with only a trailer node (no header node). Include the same operations as available in the key-ordered list class defined by Specification 7.1.
    b. Complete a test plan for testing your key-ordered list.
    c. Write a test program that implements your test plan.

48. a. Implement a key-ordered list class using only a header node (no trailer node). Include the same operations as available in the key-ordered list class defined by Specification 7.4.
    b. Complete a test plan for testing your key-ordered list.
    c. Write a test program that implements your test plan.

49. Implement unbounded natural numbers with doubly linked lists of digits. Copy the four files `Big_Natural.ads`, `Big_Natural.adb`, `Big_Natural-IO.ads`, and `Big_Natural-IO.adb` from the publisher's website. The first two files are the specification and body for an unbounded natural number class. The second two files are for a child service package that provides input and output operations for unbounded natural numbers.

    Read through the specification of the unbounded natural number class. The private part of this package contains the declarations necessary to implement a big natural number as a doubly linked list of digits. Here is a picture of how the number 5739 would be stored:

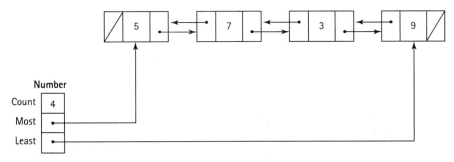

Your task is to complete the bodies of the 16 `Big_Natural` operations defined in the specification. Five of these operations are defined in the private part of the specification. Procedures `Insert_Most` and `Insert_Least` are used by the child service package for the input of unbounded natural numbers. Procedure `Initialize` should create a data structure with no nodes and a `Count` of zero. Procedure `Finalize` should recycle the memory used for all of the nodes used in the doubly linked list. Procedure `Adjust` should turn an alias of a doubly linked list into a copy of a doubly linked list. (See an example of an `Adjust` procedure that we wrote for the unbounded-length string class in Chapter 4.)

Other Requirements

a. Do not make local copies of big natural numbers.

b. The addition and subtraction operations should be O(N) where N is the number of digits in the larger number.

c. The relational operations should be O(1) when the numbers have different numbers of digits and O(N) when they contain the same number of digits. N is the number of digits in the number.

d. Use the algorithm for multiplication based on the method you learned in grade school using multiplications (one digit times multiple digits), left shifts, and additions. This algorithm is O(N × M + M), where N is the number of digits in the larger number and M is the number of digits in the smaller number.

```
    4821  ← number with more digits
 ×   385  ← number with less digits
   24105  ← 4821 × 5 shifted left 0 places
  385680  ← 4821 × 8 shifted left 1 place
 1446300  ← 4821 × 3 shifted left 2 places
 1856085
```

e. The `Shift_Left` and `Shift_Right` operations should be O(1).

f. Your big natural operations should have no memory leaks. Although procedure `Finalize` automatically recycles the entire linked list for a `Big_Natural` object that is no longer needed, it does not recycle individual nodes when you no longer need them. You need to recycle any such nodes yourself.

g. Write a test plan and test program to test your unbounded natural class.

50. Declare and implement an unbounded integer class with the same operations as the unbounded natural class of the previous question. Declare and implement a service package for input and output of unbounded integers with the same operations as the equivalent unbounded natural package.

51. Modify the postfix calculator program given in Chapter 5 (Program 5.1) so that it uses unbounded natural (or integer) numbers rather than standard integers.

52. Using a linked list implemented in an array of records to contain the queue elements, rewrite the First in, First out (FIFO) queue private declarations and the package body containing the operations specified in Chapter 6. Write a test plan and test program.

53. Implement the key-ordered list class as an array-based linked list with header and trailer nodes. Write a test plan and test program.

54. The file-based linked list package given in Body 8.2 reads the disk more than it needs to. For example, when we modify an element, the element is read from disk in the search procedure and then read again by the modify procedure.

    a. Find other examples in the package where elements are read from the disk multiple times.

    We can minimize the number of disk accesses by using a cache of nodes. A cache is a time-ordered collection of the most recently read nodes used by procedures `Read_Node` and `Write_Node`. This cache is stored in primary memory (RAM).

    Here is one way a cache might operate. When `Read_Node` is called, it first checks to see if the desired node is in the cache. If it is in the cache, it returns a copy; no disk access is done. If it is not in the cache, `Read_Node` reads it from the disk, saves a copy in the cache, and returns a copy to the caller. If the cache is full when adding a node, the oldest node is deleted to make room for the newest node. In our caching scheme, `Write_Node` always writes to the disk and adds a copy of the node to the cache. If that node is already in the cache, the old copy should be deleted and the new copy added.

    b. What sort of data structure is most appropriate for a cache?

    c. Write a generic package for a cache class that includes all the necessary operations needed to implement our descriptions of the cache-based `Read_Node` and `Write_Node` procedures. Think carefully about what operations to include. You should allow the user to specify a maximum cache size (as a discriminant on the cache type). The cache may be array-based or based on a linked list.

d. Write a test plan and program to test your cache class.
e. Rewrite the package body for the file-based sorted list. Instantiate a cache from your generic cache package. Rewrite procedures `Read_Node` and `Write_Node` to take advantage of the cache.
f. Write a test plan and program to test your file-based list with caching.

You may find that adding caching to the file-based sorted list does not improve its performance. Our Ada programs do not access the computer's disk directly. All input and output is actually performed by the computer's operating system. Our Ada programs do input and output by making requests of the operating system. Because many computer operating systems maintain their own disk caches, adding our own cache may actually slow down the read operations.

Programming with Recursion

Goals for this chapter include that you should be able to
- discuss recursion as another form of repetition.
- given a recursive routine:
    - determine whether the routine halts.
    - determine the base case(s).
    - determine the general case(s).
    - determine what the routine does.
    - determine whether the routine is correct and, if it is not, correct it.
- given a simple recursive problem:
    - determine the base case(s).
    - determine the general case(s).
    - design and code the solution as a recursive procedure or function.
- verify a recursive routine, according to the three-question method.
- decide whether a recursive solution is appropriate for a problem.
- compare and contrast dynamic storage allocation and static storage allocation in relation to using recursion.
- explain how recursion works internally by showing the contents of the run-time stack.
- replace a recursive solution with iteration and/or the use of a stack.
- explain why recursion may or may not be a good choice to implement for the solution of a problem.

This chapter introduces the topic of recursion—a unique problem-solving approach supported by many computer languages (Ada included). With recursion, you solve a problem by repeatedly breaking it into smaller versions of the same problem, until the problem is reduced to a trivial size that can be easily solved; then you repeatedly combine your solutions to the subproblems until you arrive at a solution to the original problem.

Although recursion can at first appear unwieldy and awkward, when applied properly it is an extremely powerful and useful problem-solving tool.

9.1 What Is Recursion?

You may have seen a set of gaily painted Russian matryoshka dolls that fit inside one another. Inside the first doll is a smaller doll, inside of which is an even smaller doll, inside of which is yet a smaller doll, and so on. A recursive algorithm is like such a set of Russian dolls. It reproduces itself with smaller and smaller versions of itself until a version is reached that can no longer be subdivided—that is, until the smallest doll is reached. The recursive algorithm is implemented by using a subprogram that makes **recursive calls** to itself, analogous to taking the dolls apart one by one. The solution often depends on passing larger and larger subsolutions back from the recursive calls, analogous to putting the dolls back together again.

> **Recursive call** A subprogram call in which the subprogram being called is the same as the one making the call.
>
> **Direct recursion** Recursion in which a subprogram directly calls itself.
>
> **Indirect recursion** Recursion in which a chain of two or more subprograms returns to the subprogram that originated the chain.

In Ada, any subprogram can call another subprogram. A subprogram can even invoke itself! When a subprogram calls itself, it is making a recursive call. The word *recursive* means "having the characteristic of coming up again, or repeating." In this case, a subprogram call is being repeated by the subprogram itself. This type of recursion is sometimes called **direct recursion**, because the subprogram directly calls itself. All of the examples in this chapter are of direct recursion. **Indirect recursion** occurs when subprogram A calls subprogram B, and subprogram B calls subprogram A; the chain of subprogram calls could be even longer, but if it eventually leads back to subprogram A, then it is indirect recursion.

Recursion is a powerful programming technique. However, you must be careful when using recursion. Recursive solutions can be less efficient than iterative solutions to the same problem. In fact, many of the examples used in this chapter are better suited to iterative methods. Still, many problems lend themselves to simple, elegant, recursive solutions and are exceedingly cumbersome to solve iteratively. Some programming languages, such as early versions of FORTRAN, BASIC, and COBOL, do not allow recursion. Other languages are especially oriented to recursive approaches—LISP is one of these. Ada lets us take our choice; we can implement both iterative and recursive algorithms in Ada.

9.2 The Classic Example of Recursion

Mathematicians often define concepts in terms of the process used to generate them. For instance, $n!$ (read "n factorial") is used to calculate the number of permutations of n elements. One mathematical description of $n!$ is

$$n! = \begin{cases} 1, & \text{if } n = 0 \\ n \times (n-1) \times (n-2) \times \ldots \times 1, & \text{if } n > 0 \end{cases}$$

Consider the case of 4!. Because $n > 0$, we use the second part of the definition:

$$4! = 4 \times 3 \times 2 \times 1 = 24$$

This description of $n!$ provides a different definition for each value of n, because the three dots stand in for the intermediate factors. That is, the definition of 2! is 2 × 1, the definition of 3! is 3 × 2 × 1, and so forth.

We can also express $n!$ with a single definition for any nonnegative value of n:

$$n! = \begin{cases} 1, & \text{if } n = 0 \\ n \times (n-1)!, & \text{if } n > 0 \end{cases}$$

This definition is *recursive*, because we express the factorial function in terms of itself.

Let's consider the recursive calculation of 4! intuitively. Because 4 is not equal to 0, we use the second half of the definition:

$$4! = 4 \times (4 - 1)! = 4 \times 3!$$

Of course, we can't do the multiplication yet, because we don't know the value of 3!. So we call up our good friend Sue Ann, who has a PhD in math, to find the value of 3!.

4! = 4 × 3!

Sue Ann has the same formula we have for calculating the factorial function, so she knows that

$$3! = 3 \times (3 - 1)! = 3 \times 2!$$

She doesn't know the value of 2!, however, so she puts you on hold and calls up her friend Max, who has an MS in math.

Max has the same formula Sue Ann has, so he quickly calculates that

$$2! = 2 \times (2 - 1)! = 2 \times 1!$$

But Max can't complete the multiplication because he doesn't know the value of 1!. He puts Sue Ann on hold and calls up his mother, who has a BA in math education.

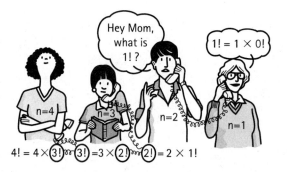

Max's mother has the same formula Max has, so she quickly figures out that

$$1! = 1 \times (1 - 1)! = 1 \times 0!$$

Of course, she can't perform the multiplication, because she doesn't have the value of 0!. So Mom puts Max on hold and calls up her colleague Bernie, who has a BA in English literature.

Bernie doesn't need to know any math to figure out that 0! = 1 because he can read that information in the first clause of the formula ($n! = 1$, if $n = 0$). He reports the answer immediately to Max's mother. She can now complete her calculations:

$$1! = 1 \times 0! = 1 \times 1 = 1.$$

She reports back to Max, who now performs the multiplication in his formula and learns that

$$2! = 2 \times 1! = 2 \times 1 = 2.$$

He reports back to Sue Ann, who can now finish her calculation:

$$3! = 3 \times 2! = 3 \times 2 = 6.$$

Sue Ann calls you with this exciting bit of information. You can now complete your calculation:

$$4! = 4 \times 3! = 4 \times 6 = 24.$$

9.3 Programming Recursively

Of course, the use of recursion is not limited to mathematicians with telephones. Computer languages such as Ada that support recursion give the programmer a powerful tool for solving certain kinds of problems by reducing the complexity or hiding the details of the problem.

We consider recursive solutions to several simple problems. In our initial discussion, you may wonder why a recursive solution would ever be preferred to an iterative, or nonrecursive, one because the iterative solution may seem simpler and more efficient. Don't worry. There are, as you will see later, situations in which the use of recursion produces a much simpler—and more elegant—program.

Coding the Factorial Function

A recursive function or procedure is one that calls itself. In the previous section Sue Ann, Max, Max's mom, and Bernie all had the same formula for solving the factorial function. When we construct a recursive Ada function Factorial for solving $n!$, we know where we can get the value of $(n - 1)!$ that we need in the formula. We already have a function for doing this calculation: Factorial. Of course, the actual parameter $(n - 1)$ in the recursive call is different than the parameter in the original call (n). (The recursive call is the one within the function.) As you will see, this different value of the parameter is an important and necessary consideration.

An Ada function for calculating $n!$ may be coded as follows. Subtype Natural is used for the parameter because the factorial function is only defined for values greater than or equal to zero, and subtype Positive is used for the result.

```
function Factorial (N : in Natural) return Positive is
   Result : Positive;
begin
   if N = 0 then                              -- line 1
      Result := 1;                            -- line 2
   else
      Result := N * Factorial (N-1);          -- line 3
   end if;
   return Result;                             -- line 4
end Factorial;
```

Notice the use of Factorial in line 3. Factorial is a recursive call to the function, with the parameter N-1.

Let's walk through the calculation of 4! using function Factorial. The original value of N is 4. The steps in the calculation are shown in Table 9.1. These steps are shown graphically in Figure 9.1.

Table 9.1 Walkthrough of Factorial (4)

Line	Action	Call Number
1	N is 4. Because N is not 0 the *else* branch is taken.	1
3	Result := 4 * Factorial (4 − 1)	
	First recursive call sends us to the beginning of the function with N = 3.	1
1	N is 3. Because N is not 0 the *else* branch is taken.	2
3	Result := 3 * Factorial (3 − 1)	2
	Second recursive call sends us to the beginning of the function with N = 2.	
1	N is 2. Because N is not 0 the *else* branch is taken.	3
3	Result := 2 * Factorial (2 − 1)	
	Third recursive call sends us to the beginning of the function with N = 1.	3
1	N is 1. Because N is not 0 the *else* branch is taken.	4
3	Result := 1 * Factorial (1 − 1)	
	Fourth recursive call sends us to the beginning of the function with N = 0.	4
1	N is 0. This time we take the *then* branch.	5
2	Result := 1	5
4	The Result, 1, is returned to the calling statement in the fourth recursive call.	5
3	Result := 1 * Factorial (0) = 1 * 1 = 1	4
4	The Result, 1, is returned to the calling statement in the third recursive call.	4
3	Result := 2 * Factorial (1) = 2 * 1 = 2	3
4	The Result, 2, is returned to the calling statement in the second recursive call.	3
3	Result := 3 * Factorial (2) = 3 * 2 = 6	2
4	The Result, 6, is returned to the calling statement in the first recursive call.	2
3	Result := 4 * Factorial (3) = 4 * 6 = 24	1
4	The Result, 24, is returned to the calling statement, the original nonrecursive call.	1

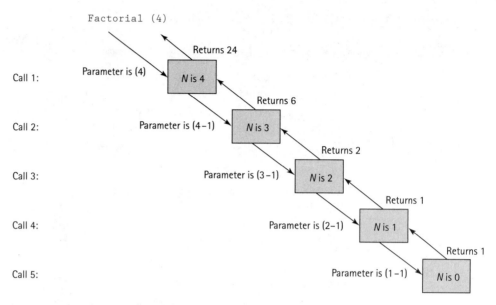

Figure 9.1 *Execution of Factorial (4).*

Comparison to the Iterative Solution

We have used the factorial algorithm to demonstrate recursion because it is familiar and easy to visualize. In practice, one would never want to solve this problem using recursion. The iterative solution is simpler and much more efficient because starting a new iteration of a loop is a faster operation than calling a function. For purposes of comparison, let's look at the recursive and iterative solutions to this problem side by side:

```
function Factorial (N : in Natural)
                    return Positive
is
   Result : Positive;
begin
   if N = 0 then
      Result := 1;
   else
      Result := N * Factorial (N-1);
   end if;
   return Result;
end Factorial;
```

```
function Factorial (N : in Natural)
                    return Positive
is
   Result : Positive;
begin
   Result := 1;
   for Count in 2..N loop
      Result := Count * Result;
   end loop;
   return Result;
end Factorial;
```

Iterative solutions tend to employ loops, whereas recursive solutions tend to have selection statements—either an `if` or a `case` statement. Recursive subprograms rarely contain loops. In fact, if you use a loop in the design of a recursive algorithm you have probably made an error in your design.

9.4 Verifying Recursive Procedures and Functions

The kind of walkthrough we did in the previous section to check the validity of a recursive function or procedure is time consuming, tedious, and often confusing. Furthermore, simulating the execution of `Factorial(4)` tells us that the function works if the parameter is 4, but it doesn't tell us whether the function is valid for all other nonnegative values. It would be useful to have a technique that would help us determine inductively whether a recursive algorithm works.

The Three-Question Method

We use the three-question method of verifying recursive procedures and functions. To verify that a recursive solution works, you must be able to answer yes to all three of these questions:

1. *The base-case question:* Is there a nonrecursive way out of the procedure or function, and does the routine work correctly for this "base" case?
2. *The smaller-caller question:* Does each recursive call to the procedure or function involve a smaller case of the original problem? By smaller we mean that it is closer to the base case. This guarantees that we ultimately reach the base case.
3. *The general-case question:* Assuming that the recursive call(s) works correctly, does the whole procedure or function work correctly?

Let's apply these three questions to function `Factorial`.

1. *The base-case question:* The base case occurs when $N = 0$. `Result` is then assigned a value of 1, which is the correct value of 0!, and no further (recursive) calls to `Factorial` are made. The answer is yes.
2. *The smaller-caller question:* To answer this question we must look at the parameters passed in the recursive call. In function `Factorial`, the recursive call passes $N - 1$. Each subsequent recursive call sends a decremented value of the parameter, until the value sent is finally 0. At this point, as we verified with the base-case question above, we have reached the base case, and no further recursive calls are made. The answer is yes.
3. *The general-case question:* In the case of a function like `Factorial`, we need to verify that the formula we are using actually results in the correct solution. Assuming that the recursive call `Factorial(N-1)` gives us the correct value of $(n - 1)!$, we give the assignment of $N * (N - 1)!$ to `Result`. This is the definition of a factorial, so we know that the function works for all positive integers. In answering the

first question, we have already ascertained that the function works for $N = 0$. (The function is defined only for nonnegative integers.) So the answer is yes.

Those of you who are familiar with inductive proofs recognize what we have done. Having made the assumption that the function works for $(n - 1)$, we can now show that applying the function to the next value, $(n - 1) + 1$, or n, results in the correct formula for calculating $n!$. Because we have also shown that the formula works for the base case, $n = 0$, we have inductively shown that it works for any integer argument $>= 0$.

9.5 Writing Recursive Procedures and Functions

The three questions we use to verify recursive procedures and functions can also be used as a guide for writing recursive subprograms. You can use the following approach to write any recursive routine:

1. Get an exact definition of the problem to be solved. (This, of course, is the first step in solving any programming problem.)
2. Determine the size of the problem to be solved on this call to the subprogram. On the initial call to the procedure or function, the size of the whole problem is expressed in the value(s) of the parameter(s).
3. Identify and solve the base case(s) in which the problem can be expressed nonrecursively. This ensures a yes answer to the base-case question.
4. Identify and solve the general case(s) correctly in terms of a smaller case of the same problem—a recursive call. This ensures yes answers to the smaller-caller and general-case questions.

In the case of `Factorial`, the definition of the problem is summarized in the definition of the factorial function. The size of the problem is the number of values to be multiplied: N. The base case occurs when $N = 0$, in which case we take the nonrecursive path. Finally, the general case occurs when $N > 0$, resulting in a recursive call to `Factorial` for a smaller case: `Factorial(N-1)`.

Writing a Boolean Function

Let's apply this approach to writing a function, `Value_In_Array`, that searches for a value in an array and returns a Boolean value indicating whether the value was found. The array is declared as

```
type Array_Type is array (Integer range <>) of Integer;
```

and the specification of our function is

```
function Value_In_Array (List  : in Array_Type;
                        Value : in Integer)    return Boolean;
-- Purpose         : Searches List for Value
-- Preconditions   : None
-- Postconditions  : Returns (Value exists in List)
```

9.5 Writing Recursive Procedures and Functions

We can decompose our problem into two smaller problems by deciding if `Value` is in the first position of the array or in the rest of the array.

Value in Array
    Result := (Value is in the first position of the array) or
           (Value is in the rest of the array)
    return Result

We can answer the first question (from our three-question method) just by comparing `Value` to `List(List'First)`. But how do we know whether `Value` is in the rest of the array? If only we had a function that would search the rest of the array. But we do have one! Function `Value_In_Array` searches for a value in an array. We simply need to start searching `List` at the second position, instead of the first (a smaller case). To do this, we need to pass the "rest of the array" to `Value_In_Array` as a parameter—a slice of the original array. Here is an assignment statement that illustrates that call:

```
Result := Value_In_Array (List  => List (List'First + 1 .. List'Last),
                          Value => Value);
```

By passing a slice beginning with the second element of the array, we have diminished the size of the problem to be solved by the recursive call. That is, searching the array from `List'First + 1` to `List'Last` is a smaller task (smaller by one array element) than searching from `List'First` to `List'Last`.

Finally, we need to know when to stop searching. In this problem we have two base cases: (1) when the value is found (return true), and (2) when the array contains no elements (return false). In either case we can stop making recursive calls to `Value_In_Array`. Here is the resulting function. Figure 9.2 shows an execution of this function.

```
function Value_In_Array (List  : in Array_Type,
                         Value : in Integer) return Boolean is
   Result : Boolean;
begin
   if List'Length = 0 then
      Result := False;       -- Base Case 2, empty array
   elsif Value = List(List'First) then
      Result := True;        -- Base Case 1, Value found
   else    -- General Case
      Result := Value_In_Array  -- General Case: search rest of List
                 (List  => List (List'First+1 .. List'Last),
                  Value => Value);
   end if;
   return Result;
end Value_In_Array;
```

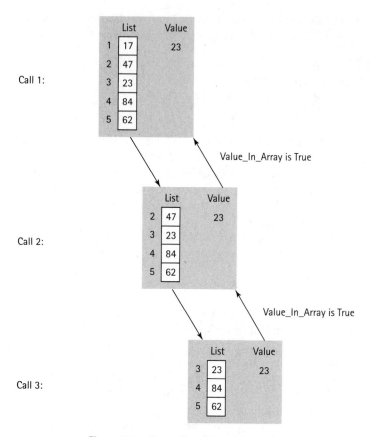

Figure 9.2 *Execution of Value_In_Array.*

Let's use the three-question method to verify this method.

1. *The base-case question:* One base case occurs when the value is found in the first position of the array; we return true and exit the function without any further calls to itself. A second base case occurs when the list is empty; we return false and exit the function without any further calls to itself. The answer is yes.
2. *The smaller-caller question:* The recursive call in the general case decreases the size of the list by one, making the search problem smaller by one element. We are guaranteed that eventually we will reach the second base case. The answer is yes.
3. *The general-case question:* Let's assume that the recursive call in the general case correctly tells us whether the value is found in the second through last elements in

the list. Then base case 1 gives us the correct answer of true if the value is found in the first element in the list, and base case 2 gives us the correct answer of false if the list contains no elements. Assuming that the recursive call works correctly, the whole method works, so the answer to this question is also yes.

Multiple Recursive Calls

Our two previous examples of recursion contain a single recursive call. Recursive algorithms can contain several different base cases and several different recursive calls. Let's look at such an algorithm. The following sequence of numbers is called the Fibonacci sequence:

$$1, 1, 2, 3, 5, 8, 13, 21, 34, 55, 89, \ldots$$

The numbers in this sequence are called Fibonacci numbers. Each Fibonacci number in this sequence is the sum of the two previous numbers. Fibonacci numbers are often found in nature. In fact, the sequence was first used by Leonardo Fibonacci of Pisa, a medieval mathematician, to determine the number of rabbits that would be produced in a hutch in *n* months starting with a single pair of newborn rabbits. Leonardo made the following assumptions in this problem:

1. Newborn rabbits become adults (are able to breed) one month after birth.
2. There are an equal number of male and female rabbits.
3. Each pair of adult rabbits produces one pair of newborn rabbits each month.
4. No rabbits die.

Figure 9.3 illustrates the pattern of reproduction in the hutch for 7 months. Each row of the figure traces one pair of rabbits through the months. For example, the first row traces the initial pair of rabbits. The pair is young during month 1 and adult in the remaining months. The ninth row traces the first pair of offspring of the initial pair. The number of rows under any given month is the number of pairs in the hutch that month. The monthly numbers are listed at the bottom of the figure.

The number of pairs of rabbits each month is equal to the number of pairs last month plus the number of pairs born this month (which is equal to the number of pairs 2 months previous). This is a Fibonacci sequence. To know how many rabbits are in the hutch after a year, we just determine the 13th Fibonacci number.

- *The base-case question:* The first number in the Fibonacci sequence is always 1. This number looks like a good base case. We can state it as
  $F_1 = 1$
- *The general-case question:* The value of the *n*th Fibonacci number is equal to the sum of the two previous Fibonacci numbers. We can state this relation as
  $F_n = F_{n-1} + F_{n-2}$
- *The smaller-caller question:* F_n is calculated from two smaller Fibonacci numbers, F_{n-1} and F_{n-2}. For example, F_5 is calculated from F_4 and F_3.

568 | Chapter 9: Programming with Recursion

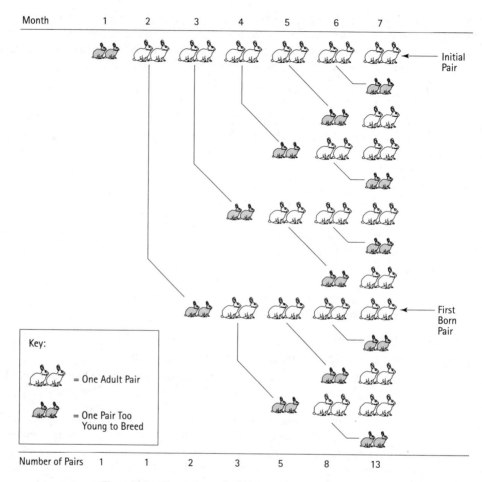

Figure 9.3 *The pattern of rabbit reproduction over 7 months.*

There is a problem in using our general case for calculating F_2. Calculating F_2 requires the value of the first Fibonacci number and the zeroth Fibonacci number, a number that is not defined. The solution to this problem is to add a second base case. Both the first and second Fibonacci numbers are 1. Here is a summary of our two base cases and general case containing two recursive calls:

Fibonacci
    if N is 1 or 2 then   -- *Two base cases*
        the result is 1
    else
        the result is Fibonacci (N-1) + Fibonacci (N-2)   -- *Two recursive calls*

And here is an Ada function to determine a particular Fibonacci number:

```
function Fibonacci (N : in Positive ) return Positive is
-- Determine the Nth Fibonacci number
   Result : Positive;
begin
   if N <= 2 then                                      -- Two base cases
      Result := 1;
   else
      Result := Fibonacci (N-1) + Fibonacci (N-2);     -- Two recursive calls
   end if;
   return Result;
end Fibonacci;
```

9.6 Using Recursion to Simplify Solutions—Three Examples

So far the examples we have looked at could just as easily (or more easily) have been written as iterative routines. There are, however, many problems in which using recursion simplifies the solution. At the end of the chapter, we talk more about choosing between iterative and recursive solutions.

Combinations

Our first example of a problem that is easily solved with recursion is the evaluation of another mathematical function, Combinations, which tells us how many combinations of a certain size can be made out of a total group of elements. For instance, if we have 20 different books to pass out to 4 students, we can easily see that—to be equitable—we should give each student 5 books. But, how many combinations of 5 books can be made out of a group of 20 books?

The optimal solution to our language translation case study in Chapter 3 involved combinations. We asked how many combinations of 2 languages, of 3 languages, of 4 languages, and so on we can make out of the group of 10 languages spoken.

There is a mathematical formula that can be used for solving this problem. Given that C is the total number of combinations, *group* is the total size of the group to pick from, *members* is the size of each subgroup, and *group* $\geq$ *members*,

$$C(\text{group}, \text{members}) = \begin{cases} \text{group}, & \text{if members} = 1 \\ 1, & \text{if members} = \text{group} \\ C(\text{group}-1, \text{members}-1) + C(\text{group}-1, \text{members}), & \text{if group} > \text{members} > 1 \end{cases}$$

Because this definition of C is recursive, it is easy to see how a recursive function could be used to solve the problem. There are two base cases: (1) the number of members is 1 and (2) the number of members is equal to the size of the group. The general case is defined by the third line of our definition of C. This line uses the definition of C twice in a sum. Each use involves a smaller number of *members* and/or a smaller *group* size. We have answered our three questions and are ready to write the Ada code. The resulting recursive function, Combinations, is as follows:

Chapter 9: Programming with Recursion

```
function Combinations (Group   : in Positive;
                      Members : in Positive) return Positive is
-- Returns the number of combinations of Members size that can be
-- made from the total group size.
   Result : Positive;
begin
   if Members = 1 then
      Result := Group;      -- Base Case 1
   elsif Members = Group then
      Result := 1;          -- Base Case 2
   else
      Result := Combinations (Group - 1, Members - 1) +
                Combinations (Group - 1, Members);
   end if;
   return Result;
end Combinations;
```

The processing of this function to calculate the number of combinations of three elements that can be made from a set of four is shown in Figure 9.4.

Returning to our original problem, we can now find out how many combinations of 5 books can be made from the original set of 20 books with the statements

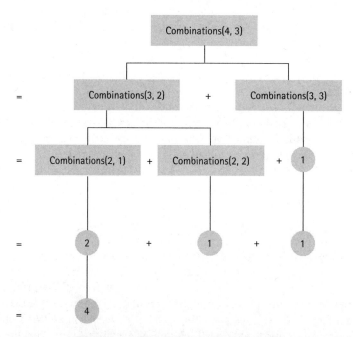

Figure 9.4 *Calculating combinations (4, 3).*

```
Put ("Number of combinations = ");
Put (Item => Combinations (Group => 20, Members => 5),
     Width => 1);
```

which output "Number of combinations = 15504". Did you guess that it would be that large a number? Recursive definitions can be used to define functions that grow quickly.

Recursive Processing of Linked Lists

Writing a recursive solution to a problem that is characterized by a recursive definition, like Combinations or Factorial, is fairly straightforward. In this section we look at a problem that has no recursive definitions; we must design our own recursive solution as we did for functions Value_In_Array and Fibonacci.

Let's look at a procedure that traverses a linked list. The following declarations define a simple linked list of nodes:

```
type Node_Type;
type Node_Ptr is access Node_Type
type Node_Type is
   record
      Info : Integer;
      Next : Node_Ptr;
   end record;
My_List: Node_Ptr;    -- External pointer to first node of list
```

By now you are probably protesting that this task is so simple to accomplish iteratively (loop, exit when Location = null) that it does not make any sense to write it recursively. So let's make the task more fun: Process the elements in the list in *reverse* order. This problem is much more easily and "elegantly" solved recursively.

What is the task to be performed? The algorithm is given at the top of page 572 and illustrated in Figure 9.5.

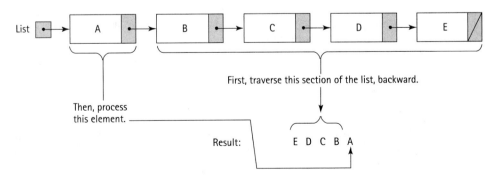

Figure 9.5 *Recursive Reverse_Traverse.*

Reverse Traverse
    Traverse the second through last elements in the list in reverse order
    Process the first element in the list

The second part of the task is simple. Because `List` points to the first node in the list, we can process it with the statement `Process (List.all.Info);`. The first part of the task—traversing all the other nodes in the list in reverse order—is also simple, because we have a routine that traverses lists in reverse order: We just call procedure `Reverse_Traverse` recursively. Of course, we have to adjust the parameter somewhat, to `Reverse_Traverse (List => List.all.Next)`. This call says "Traverse, in reverse order, the linked list pointed to by `List.all.Next`." This task, in turn, is accomplished recursively in two steps:

    Reverse_Traverse the rest of the list (third through last elements).
    Then Process the second element in the list.

And of course the first part of this task is accomplished recursively. Where does it all end? We need a base case. What is the simplest list to traverse? Although a list with only one element is easy to traverse, a list with no elements is even easier. The base case for nearly all recursive linked list algorithms is an empty list. The other recursive routines that we have written have been functions; the `Reverse_Traverse` operation is a procedure.

```
procedure Reverse_Traverse (List : in List_Type) is
-- Traverses List in reverse order.
begin
   if List = null then
      null; -- list is empty (do nothing)       -- Base case
   else
      Reverse_Traverse (List => List.all.Next);  -- General
      Process (Element => List.all.Info);        --   case
   end if;
end Reverse_Traverse;
```

To traverse (in reverse order) the whole linked list designated by `My_List`, we would use the following procedure call:

```
Reverse_Traverse (List => My_List);
```

Let's verify this procedure using the three-question method.

1. *The base-case question:* When `List = null`, we do nothing and return to the caller. The answer is yes.

2. *The smaller-caller question:* The recursive call passes the list designated by List.all.Next, which is one node smaller than the list designated by List. The answer is yes.
3. *The general-case question:* We assume that Reverse_Traverse (List => List.all.Next) correctly traverses the rest of the list in reverse order; this call, followed by the statement processing the value of the first element, gives us the whole list, traversed in reverse order. So the answer is yes.

How would you change procedure Reverse_Traverse (in addition to changing its name) to make it traverse the list in forward rather than reverse order?

Towers of Hanoi

One of your first toys may have been three posts with colored circles or disks of different diameters. If so, you probably spent countless hours moving the disks from one post to another. If we put some constraints on how the disks can be moved, we have an adult game invented by the French mathematician Edouard Lucas in 1883 called the Towers of Hanoi. When the game begins, all the disks are on the left post in order by size, with the smallest on the top. The object of the game is to move the disks, one at a time, to the right post. The catch is that a disk cannot be placed on top of one that is smaller in diameter. The center post can be used as an auxiliary post, but it must be empty at the beginning and the end of the game.

To get a feel for how this might be done, let's look at some sketches of what the configuration must be at certain points if a solution is possible. We use four disks. The beginning configuration is:

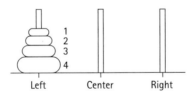

To move the largest disk (disk 4) to the right post, we must move the three smaller disks to the center post. Then disk 4 can be moved into its final place:

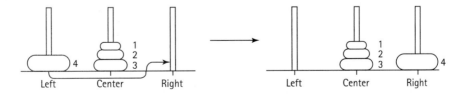

Let's assume that we can do this. Now, to move the next largest disk (disk 3) into place, we must move the two disks on top of it onto an auxiliary post (the left post in this case):

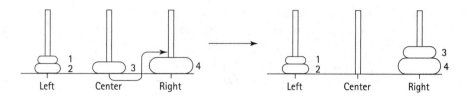

To get disk 2 into place, we must move disk 1 to another post, freeing disk 2 to be moved to its place on the right post.

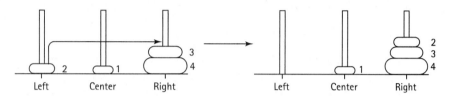

We can now move the last disk (disk 1) into its final place, finishing the game.

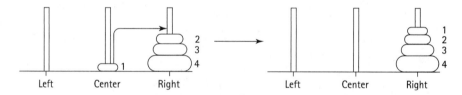

Notice that to free disk 4, we had to move three disks to another post. To free disk 3, we had to move two disks to another post. To free disk 2, we had to move one disk to another post. This sounds like a recursive algorithm: to free the nth disk, we have to move $n - 1$ disks. Each stage can be thought of as beginning again with three posts, but with one fewer disk each time.

Based on these pictures we developed the following general algorithm for moving n disks from one post (the source) to another post (the destination) using the remaining post as an intermediate.

To Get n Disks Moved from the Source Post to the Destination Post (version 1)
    Get $n - 1$ circles moved from the source post to the intermediate post
    Move nth circle from the source post to the destination post
    Get $n - 1$ circles moved from the intermediate post to the destination post

The first and third steps in this algorithm are recursive calls. Let's use the three-question method to verify this algorithm. The base-case question asks if there is a non-recursive way out of the procedure. Oops! There is no base case in our algorithm. How do we know when to stop the recursive process? The clue is in the expression "Get n Disks Moved." If we don't have any disks to move, we don't have anything to do. Therefore, when the number of disks equals zero, we do nothing (that is, we simply return). We need to add an *if* statement to test the number of disks.

Next, let's examine the smaller-caller question. Each of the two recursive calls involves one fewer disk. Therefore we are sure to eventually reach our base case of zero disks. Earlier we demonstrated that the three steps do indeed work to solve the problem. With all three questions now answered, we have verified our final version of the Towers of Hanoi algorithm.

To Get *n* Disks Moved from the Source Post to the Destination Post (final version)
    if $n > 0$ then
        Get $n - 1$ circles moved from the source post to the intermediate post
        Move *n*th circle from the source post to the destination post
        Get $n - 1$ circles moved from the intermediate post to the destination post

If you still find it hard to believe that such a simple algorithm works, we'll show you with an Ada program. We can't actually move disks, of course, but we can print out messages to do so. Our output for three disks should look like this:

```
Move a disk from left    to right
Move a disk from left    to center
Move a disk from right   to center
Move a disk from left    to right
Move a disk from center  to left
Move a disk from center  to right
Move a disk from left    to right
```

Here is the program that does it.

Program 9.1 Towers of Hanoi

```ada
with Ada.Text_IO;          use Ada.Text_IO;
with Ada.Integer_Text_IO;  use Ada.Integer_Text_IO;
procedure Towers_Of_Hanoi is

   type    Post_Type is (Left, Center, Right);
   package Post_IO   is new Ada.Text_IO.Enumeration_IO (Enum => Post_Type);

   -------------------------------------------------------------------------

   procedure Move_Disks (Disks        : in Natural;     -- Number of Disks
                         Source       : in Post_Type;   -- Source of Disks
                         Destination  : in Post_Type;   -- Destination of Disks
                         Intermediate : in Post_Type) is -- Intermediate post
   begin
      if Disks > 0 then  -- Do nothing if there are no disks to move

         -- Move N - 1 Disks from source to intermediate post
         Move_Disks (Disks        => Disks - 1,
                     Source       => Source,
                     Destination  => Intermediate,
                     Intermediate => Destination);
```

```
            -- Move one Disk from source to destination
            Put ("Move a disk from ");
            Post_IO.Put (Item => Source, Width => 6, Set => Lower_Case);
            Put (" to ");
            Post_IO.Put (Item => Destination, Width => 6, Set => Lower_Case);
            New_Line;

            -- Move N - 1 Disks from intermediate to destination post
            Move_Disks (Disks        => Disks - 1,
                        Source       => Intermediate,
                        Destination  => Destination,
                        Intermediate => Source);
        end if;
    end Move_Disks;

----------------------------------------------------------------------------

    Num_Disks : Positive;

begin
    -- Get data from user
    Put_Line ("Enter the number of Disks to move");
    Get (Num_Disks);
    New_Line;

    -- Print instructions to move the Disks
    Move_Disks (Disks        => Num_Disks,
                Source       => Left,
                Destination  => Right,
                Intermediate => Center);
end Towers_Of_Hanoi;
```

You can obtain a copy of this program from the publisher's website and try it yourself. Legend has it that there is a temple in Hanoi with 64 golden disks that monks are moving from one golden post to another according to the rules we described. It is claimed that when they move the last disk, the world will end. Should you want to run this program to obtain directions for the monks, be prepared to wait. This algorithm is $O(2^N)$. Sixty-four disks requires 18,446,744,073,709,551,615 moves. If your computer is fast enough to calculate and display 1 million moves per second, it will take about 58,494 years to display all the instructions. The monks, of course, move much slower than our computers.

9.7 A Recursive Version of Binary Search

In the application section of Chapter 1, we developed the binary search procedure that we used with the array-based implementation of our key-ordered list abstract data type (ADT). Let's review the algorithm:

Binary_Search
    if there is nothing remaining in the list to examine
        stop searching - value not in list
    else
        Examine the middle element in the array
        if the middle element contains the desired key then
            stop searching - value in list
        elsif the middle element is larger than the desired key then
            Search the first half of the array
        else (middle element is smaller than the key)
            Search the second half of the array
        end if
    end if

Though the procedure that we wrote in Chapter 1 was iterative, our thinking during its design was recursive. The solution is expressed in smaller versions of the original problem: If the answer isn't found in the middle position, search the appropriate half of the array (a smaller problem).

This problem has two different base cases (we find `Value` or we don't find `Value`) and two general cases (we search the left half or the right half of the list). Here is the recursive version of the procedure. Figure 9.6 shows its execution with an array containing five integers.

```
procedure Binary_Search (List     : in Array_Type;
                         Value    : in Element_Type;
                         Location : out Natural) is
-- Search List for Value;
-- return Location (an array index) if found,
-- otherwise return value of 0 in Location.

   Midpoint : Natural;    -- index of search area's midpoint

begin  -- Binary_Search
   if List'Length = 0 then
      Location := 0;                    -- Base Case 1
   else
      Midpoint := (List'First + List'Last) / 2;
```

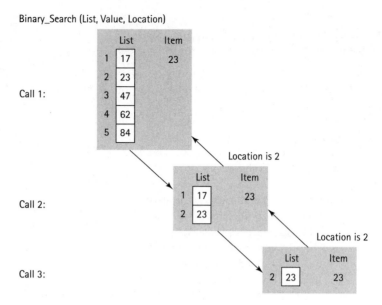

Figure 9.6 *Execution of Binary_Search.*

```
        if List (Midpoint) = Value then
            Location := Midpoint;         -- Base Case 2
        elsif List (Midpoint) > Value then
            -- Search first half of the list (General Case 1)
            Binary_Search (List     => List (List'First..Midpoint-1),
                           Value    => Value,
                           Location => Location);
        else
            -- Search second half of the list (General Case 2)
            Binary_Search (List     => List (Midpoint+1..List'Last),
                           Value    => Value,
                           Location => Location);
        end if;
    end if;
end Binary_Search;
```

How does this version of the code compare with the iterative version in Chapter 1? We'll look at the objective measures first: In terms of noncomment lines of code, the recursive version is nearly 25% shorter. The iterative version used four local variables, whereas the recursive version uses only one. Score one point for the recursive version. Timed execution experiments show that for one particular computer, the iterative binary search procedure runs about twice as fast as the recursive binary search procedure. Score one point for the iterative version.

The subjective measure asks: Which procedure is easier to write and to understand? We think that the recursive procedure wins this round—it works the way that we naturally think of the problem: divide and conquer. Therefore our final score is recursive version 2 points, iterative version 1 point.

9.8 Debugging Recursive Routines

Because of their nested calls to themselves, recursive subprograms can be confusing to debug. The most serious problem is the possibility that the method recurses forever. The typical symptom of this problem is the run-time system raising the exception STOR-AGE_ERROR telling us that the system has run out of space in the run-time stack, due to the level of recursive calls. (In the next section we look at how recursion uses the run-time stack.) Using the three-question method to verify recursive methods should help us avoid the problem of never finishing. If we can answer yes to the base-case and smaller-caller questions, we should be able to guarantee that the method eventually ends—theoretically, at least.

That does not guarantee, however, that the program does not fail due to lack of space. In the next section we discuss the amount of space overhead required to support recursive calls. And since a call to a recursive subprogram may generate many, many levels of calls to itself, it might be more than the system can handle.

One error that programmers often make when they first start writing recursive methods is to use a looping structure instead of a branching one. Because they tend to think of the problem in terms of a repetitive action, they inadvertently use a *loop* statement rather than an *if* statement. The main body of the recursive subprogram should always be a breakdown into base and recursive cases. Hence, we use a branching statement, not a looping statement. It's a good idea to double-check your recursive methods to make sure that you used an *if* or *case* statement to get a branching effect.

Recursive routines are good places to put debugger breakpoints during testing. Display the parameters and local variables, if any, at the beginning and end of the subprogram. Be sure to display the values of the parameters on the recursive call(s) to make sure that each call is trying to solve a problem smaller than the previous one.

The beauty of recursion is that it can easily be verified before the code is even entered. The best way to debug recursive routines is to design them so there are no bugs to find. That's what our three-question method is for.

9.9 How Recursion Works

In order to understand how recursion works and why some programming languages allow it and some do not, we have to take a detour and look at how languages associate places in memory with variable names. The association of a memory address with a variable name is called **binding**. The point in the compile/link/execute cycle when binding occurs is called the **binding time**. We want to stress that binding time refers to a point of time in a process, not the amount of clock time that it takes to bind a variable.

Programming languages are usually classified as having either static storage allocation or dynamic storage allocation. Static storage allocation associates variables with memory locations at compile or link time; dynamic storage allocation associates variables with memory locations at execution time. We know from our discussions of elaboration and access variables that Ada is a language that supports dynamic storage allocation. As we look at how static and dynamic storage allocation work, consider the following question: When are the parameters of a procedure bound to a particular address in memory? The answer to this question tells something about whether recursion can be supported.

> **Binding** The association of a memory address with a variable name.
>
> **Binding time** The point in the compile /link/ execute cycle when variable names are associated with addresses in memory.

Static Storage Allocation

As a program is being translated, the compiler creates a table called a *symbol table*. When a variable is declared, it is entered into the symbol table, and a memory location—an address—is assigned to it. For example, let's see how the compiler would translate the following Ada declarations:

```
Girls : Natural;
Boys  : Natural;
Kids  : Natural;
```

To simplify this discussion, we assume that integers take only one memory location. These three declarations cause three entries to be made in the symbol table:

Symbol	Address
Girls	0000
Boys	0001
Kids	0002

That is, at *compile time*,

> `Girls` is bound to address 0000.
>
> `Boys` is bound to address 0001.
>
> `Kids` is bound to address 0002.

Whenever a variable is used later in the program, the compiler searches the symbol table for its actual address, and substitutes that address for the variable name. After all, meaningful variable names are for the convenience of the human reader; addresses, however, are meaningful to computers. For example, the assignment statement,

```
Kids := Girls + Boys;
```

is translated into machine instructions that execute the following actions:

- Get the contents of address 0000.
- Add it to the contents of address 0001.
- Put the result into address 0002.

The object code (machine language instructions translated from the source program by the compiler) are stored in a different part of memory. Let's say that the machine instructions begin at address 1000. At the beginning of the program, control is transferred to address 1000. The instruction stored there is executed; then the instruction in 1001 is executed; and so on.

Where are the parameters of subprograms stored? With static storage allocation, the formal parameters of a subprogram are assumed to be in a particular place; for instance, the compiler might set aside space for the parameter values immediately preceding the code for each subprogram. The following procedure

```
procedure Count_Kids (Girl_Count : in Natural;
                      Boy_Count  : in Natural) is
   Total_Kids : Natural;
   .
   .
   .
```

has two parameters, `Girl_Count` and `Boy_Count`, as well as a local variable `Total_Kids`. Let's assume that the procedure's code begins at an address we'll call `Count_Kids`. The compiler leaves room for the two formal parameters and the local variable at addresses `Count_Kids - 1`, `Count_Kids - 2`, and `Count_Kids - 3`, respectively. The statement

```
Total_Kids := Girl_Count + Boy_Count;
```

in the body of the procedure would generate the following actions:

- Get the contents of address `Count_Kids - 1`.
- Add it to the contents of address `Count_Kids - 2`.
- Store the result in address `Count_Kids - 3`.

Figure 9.7 shows how a program with two subprograms might be arranged in memory when static storage allocation is used. The machine instructions for the main subprogram, procedure `Print_Total`, and procedure `Count_Kids` begin at locations 1000, 4400, and 9800, respectively. The formal parameters `Girl_Count` and `Boy_Count` are at addresses 9799 (`Count_Kids - 1`) and 9798 (`Count_Kids - 2`). The local variable `Total_Kids` is at address 9797 (`Count_Kids - 3`)

This discussion has been greatly simplified because, among other things, the compiler sets aside space not only for the parameters and local variables, but also for the return address (the location in memory of the next instruction to process, following the

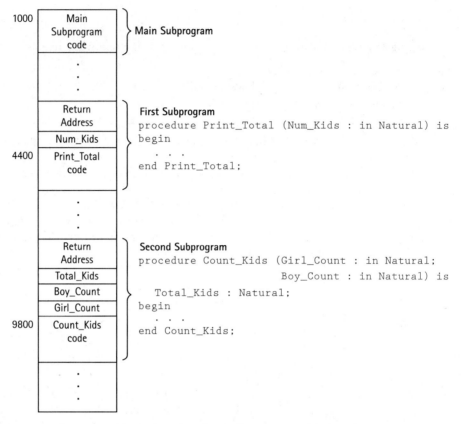

Figure 9.7 *Static allocation of space for a program with two subprograms.*

completion of the procedure) and the computer's current register values. However, we have illustrated the main point. The addresses of the procedure's formal parameters and local variables are bound to actual addresses in memory at compile time.

We can compare the static allocation scheme to one way of allocating seats in an auditorium where a lecture is to be held. A finite number of invitations are issued for the event, and the exact number of chairs needed are set up before the lecture. Each invited guest has a reserved seat. If anyone brings friends, however, there is nowhere for them to sit.

What is the implication of binding variables to memory locations before the program executes? Each parameter and local variable has but a single location assigned to it at compile time. (They are like invited guests with reserved seats.) If each call to a procedure is an independent event, there is no problem. But in the case of recursion, each recursive call is dependent on the state of the values in the previous call. Where is the storage for the multiple versions of the parameters and local variables generated by recursive calls? Because the intermediate values of the parameters and local variables must be retained, the recursive call cannot store its arguments in the fixed number of locations that were set up at compile time. The values from the previous recursive call would be overwritten and lost. Thus, a language that uses only static storage allocation cannot support recursion.

Dynamic Storage Allocation

The situation described previously is like a class of students that must share one copy of a workbook. Joe writes his exercise answers in the space provided in the workbook, then Mary erases his answers, and writes hers in the same space. This process continues until each student in the class writes his or her answers into the workbook, obliterating all the answers that came before. Obviously this situation is not practical. Clearly what is needed is for each student to read from the single copy of the workbook, and then write his or her answers on a separate piece of paper. In computer terms, what each invocation of a procedure needs is its own work space. Dynamic storage allocation provides this solution.

With dynamic storage allocation, variables are not bound to actual addresses in memory until run time. The compiler references variables not by their actual addresses, but by **relative addresses**, the offset from some other address known only at run time. Of particular interest to us, the compiler references the parameters and local variables of a procedure or function relative to some address known only at run time, not relative to the location of the subprogram's code.

Relative address The offset (number of memory locations) from some other address determined at run time.

Activation record A record used at run time to store information about a subprogram call, including the parameters, local variables, register values, and return address.

Let's look at a simplified version of how this might work in Ada. (The actual implementation depends on the particular machine and compiler.) When a subprogram is invoked, it needs space to keep its formal parameters, its local variables, and the return address (the address in the calling program to which the computer returns when the subprogram completes its execution). Just like students sharing one copy of a workbook, each invocation of a procedure or function needs its own work space. This work space is called an **activation record**. A simplified version of an activation record for function `Factorial` might have the following "declarations":

```
type Activation_Rec is
   record
      Return_To : Address_Type;        -- return address
      N         : Natural;             -- formal parameter
      Result    : Positive;            -- local variable
   end record;
```

Each call to a procedure or function, including recursive calls, generates a new activation record. Within the subprogram, references to the parameters and local variables use the values in the activation record. When the subprogram ends, the activation record is released. How does this happen? Your source code doesn't need to allocate and free activation records; the compiler adds a "prologue" to the beginning of each procedure and an "epilogue" to the end of each procedure. Execution of the prologue is what Ada calls *elaboration*. The following listings compare the source code for function Factorial with a simplified version of the "code" executed at run time. (Of course, the code executed at run time is in machine language, but we are listing the source code "equivalent" so that it makes sense to the reader.) In the prologue, memory is found for a new activation record and the values of the parameter N and return address (in the return address register, $Ra) are copied into the activation record. In the epilogue, the result is assigned to a result value register, the return address is assigned to the return address register ($Rv), the memory used by the activation record is released, and control is transferred back to the caller.

What happens to the activation record of one subprogram when a second subprogram is invoked? Consider a program whose main subprogram calls Proc1, which then calls Proc2. When the main subprogram begins executing, the "main" activation record is generated. (Because the main subprogram's activation record exists for the entire exe-

Run-Time Version of Factorial (Simplified)

What Your Source Code Says

```
function Factorial (N : in Natural) is
  Result : Positive;


begin
  if N = 0 then
    Result := 1;
  else
    Result := N *
           Factorial(N-1);
  end if;

  return Result;
end Factorial;
```

What the Run-Time System Does

```
-- Function Prologue (elaboration)
Get memory for a new Act record
Act.Return_To := $Ra;
Act.N         := N;
  if Act.N = 0 then
    Act.Result := 1;
  else
    Act.Result := Act.N *
               Factorial(Act.N - 1);
  end if
-- Function Epilogue
$Rv := Act.Result;
$Ra := Act.Return_To;
Release the memory used by Act;
    Act is now the previous Act record
Jump (goto) $Ra
```

cution of the program, the program's global data can be considered "static.") At the first procedure call an activation record is generated for Proc1:

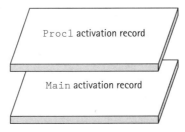

When Proc2 is called from within Proc1, its activation record is generated. Because Proc1 has not finished executing, its activation record is still around; just like the mathematicians with telephones, one waits "on hold" until the next call is finished:

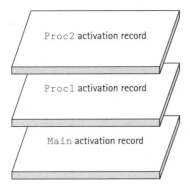

When Proc2 finishes executing, its activation record is released. But which of the other two activation records becomes the active one: Proc1's or Main's? Proc1's activation record is now active, of course. The order of activation follows the last-in-first-out (LIFO) rule. We know of a structure that supports LIFO access—the stack—so it should come as no surprise that the structure that keeps track of the activation records at run time is called the **run-time stack**.

Run-time stack A data structure that keeps track of activation records during the execution of a program.

When a procedure or function is invoked, its activation record is pushed onto the run-time stack. Each nested level of procedure calls adds another activation record to the stack. As each subprogram completes its execution, its activation record is popped from the stack. Recursive procedure or function calls, like calls to any other subprograms, cause a new activation record to be generated. The level of recursive calls in a program determines how many activation records for this subprogram are pushed onto the run-time stack at any one time.

Using dynamic allocation might be compared to another way of allocating seats in an auditorium where a lecture has been scheduled. A finite number of invitations is issued, but each guest is asked to bring his or her own chair. In addition, each guest can invite an unlimited number of friends, as long as they all bring their own chairs. Of course, if the number of extra guests gets out of hand, the space in the auditorium runs out, and there is not enough room for any more friends or chairs. Similarly, the level of recursion in a program must eventually be limited by the amount of memory available in the run-time stack.

Let's walk through function Factorial again, to see how its execution affects the run-time stack. Here is the function:

```
function Factorial (N : in Natural) return Positive is
   Result : Positive;
begin
   if N = 0 then
      Result := 1;
   else
      Result := N * Factorial (N-1);
   end if;
   return Result;
end Factorial;
```

Let's say that the main program is loaded in memory beginning at location 5000, and that the initial call to Factorial is made in a statement at memory location 5200. The machine language instructions for the Factorial function are loaded in memory at location 1000, with the recursive call made in the statement at location 1010. Figure 9.8 shows a simplified version of how this example program is loaded in memory. (These numbers have been picked arbitrarily, so that we have actual numbers to show in the Return_To address field of the activation record.)

When Factorial is called the first time from the statement in the main program at address 5200:

```
Answer := Factorial (4);
```

an activation record is pushed onto the run-time stack to hold four pieces of data: the return address (5200), the value that is returned from the function (Factorial), the formal parameter N (whose value is 4), and the local variable Result. This activation record is now on the top of the run-time stack:

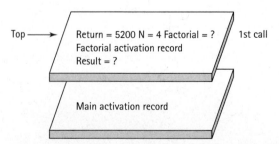

9.9 How Recursion Works

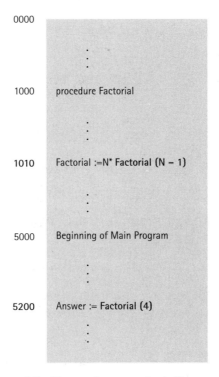

Figure 9.8 *The sample program loaded in memory.*

The code is now executed. Is N (the N value in the top activation record) equal to 0? No, it is 4, so the *else* branch is taken:

```
Factorial := N * Factorial(N - 1);
```

This time the function Factorial is called from a different place. It is called recursively from within the function, from the statement at location 1010. After the value of Factorial(N - 1) is calculated, we will return to this location to calculate the value returned from the function. A new activation record is pushed onto the run-time stack:

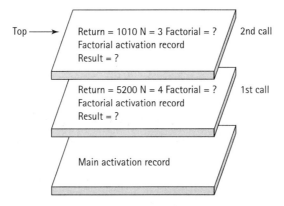

588 | Chapter 9: Programming with Recursion

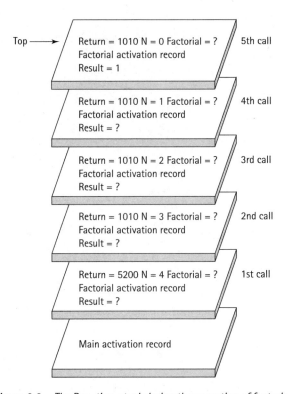

Figure 9.9 *The Run-time stack during the execution of factorial.*

Again the code is executed. Is N (the value in the top activation record) equal to 0? No, N = 3, so the *else* branch is taken:

```
Factorial := N * Factorial(N - 1);
```

So the function Factorial is again called recursively from the instruction at location 1010. This process continues until the situation looks as shown in Figure 9.9. Now, as the code is being executed, we again ask the question: Is N (the value of N in the top activation record) equal to 0? Yes. This time we take the *then* branch, storing the value 1 in Result (the Result in the top activation record, that is). The statement

```
return Result;
```

assigns the value of Result to Factorial. The fifth invocation of the function has executed to completion, and the value of Factorial in the top activation record is returned from the function. The run-time stack is popped to release the top activation record, leaving the activation record of the fourth call to Factorial at the top of the run-time stack. We don't restart the function from the beginning, however. As with any procedure or function call, we return to execute the instruction following the call to Factorial. This was the return address (location 1010) stored in the activation record.

The next instruction is where the returned value (1) is multiplied by the value of N in the top activation record (1) and the result (1) is stored in Result (the instance of Result in the top activation record, that is). The return statement assigns Result to Factorial. Now the fourth invocation of the function is complete, and the value of Factorial in the top activation record is returned from the function. Again the run-time stack is popped to release the top activation record, leaving the activation record of the third call to Factorial at the top of the run-time stack. We return to execute the instruction following the recursive call to Factorial.

This process continues until we are back to the first call and 6 has just been returned as the value of Factorial(N - 1). This value is multiplied by the value of N in the top activation record (that is, 4) and the result, 24, is stored in the Result field of the top activation record. The assignment of Result to Factorial by the return statement completes the execution of the initial call to function Factorial. The value of Factorial in the top activation record (24) is returned to the place of the original call, and the activation record is popped. This leaves the main activation record at the top of the run-time stack. The final value of Factorial is stored in the variable Answer, and the statement following the original call is executed.

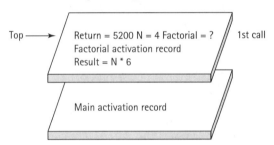

Recursion and Big-O

We made four recursive calls to our recursive function Factorial to calculate the factorial of 4. The number of recursive calls is the **depth of recursion**. Notice the relationship between the complexity of the iterative version of Factorial in terms of Big-O notation and the depth of recursion for the recursive version. Both are based on the parameter, N. Is it a coincidence that the depth of recursion is about the same as the number of iterations in the iterative version? No. Recursion is another way of doing repetition, so you would expect that the depth of recursion to be approximately the same as the number of iterations.

Depth of recursion The number of recursive calls used to complete an original call of a recursive subprogram.

Parameter Passing

The fact that the parameters for the recursive calls have to be passed in their activation records suggests that we should avoid passing large structures as parameters. But this is not the case. Ada parameter modes are designed to enable the compiler to minimize the amount of activation record storage needed for parameters.

Let's review Ada's three parameter modes. Mode `in` is used to pass information from the caller to the subprogram. Mode `out` is used to return results from the subprogram to the caller. And mode `in out` is used for the times we need a subprogram to modify values supplied by the caller; a value is passed in, changed, and returned. We select parameter modes based on the direction of information flow between the caller and the subprogram.

When you first studied subprogram parameters you may have learned that information is exchanged between actual and formal parameters by copying. This model is valid for scalar value parameters such as integers, floats, characters, and enumeration types. However, when a structured type like an array or record is passed, the entire structure is not copied. Instead, the subprogram is supplied with the address of the original data. The formal and actual parameters become synonyms for the same memory locations.[1] So when the subprogram changes the value of a formal structured parameter, it also changes the actual parameter. But even though the subprogram is manipulating the original data, the restrictions imposed by parameter modes are still enforced; a subprogram cannot modify an `in` mode parameter.

When designing the interface for a subprogram, you should not worry about *how* the information is actually transferred between the caller and the subprogram. Continue to select parameter modes based on the direction of information flow needed by the problem. The Ada compiler ensures that the parameters are passed in the most efficient way possible.

9.10 Removing Recursion

In cases where a recursive solution is not desirable, either because the language doesn't support recursion or because the recursive solution is deemed too costly in terms of space (multiple activation records) or time (on many computers, calling a subprogram takes more time than evaluating a loop termination condition), a recursive algorithm can be implemented as a nonrecursive procedure or function. There are two general techniques that are often substituted for recursion: iteration and stacking.

Iteration

As noted later in this chapter, function `Value_In_Array` is a poor use of recursion. However, it is simple to remove the recursion from this kind of subprogram—one in which the recursive call is in the last statement executed in the general case. Let's see how to replace this recursion with a loop.

The recursive solution has two base cases: One occurs if we find the value and the other occurs if we reach the end of the list without finding the value. The base cases

---

[1]This parameter-passing mechanism is often called *pass by reference*.

solve the problem without further executions of the function. In the iterative solution, the base cases become the terminating conditions of the loop:

```
loop
    exit when Index > List'Last  or else  Value = List(Index);
```

When the terminating conditions are met, the problem is solved without further executions of the loop body.

In the general case of the recursive solution, `Value_In_Array` is called to search the remaining, unsearched part of the list. Each recursive execution of the function processes a smaller version of the problem. The smaller-caller question is answered affirmatively because the slice of the array passed is one element smaller on every recursive call. Similarly, in an iterative solution, each subsequent execution of the loop body processes a smaller version of the problem. The unsearched part of the list is shrunk on each execution of the loop body by incrementing `Index`. Here is the iterative version of the function:

```
function Value_In_Array (List  : in Array_Type,
                         Value : in Integer)  return Boolean is
-- Purpose         : Searches List for Value using iteration
-- Preconditions   : None
-- Postconditions  : Returns True if Value is in List and False otherwise
    Index : Integer;
begin
    Index := List'First;  -- Start with first value in array
    loop
        exit when Index > List'Last or else Value = List (Index);
        Index := Index + 1;
    end loop;
    return Index <= List'Last  and then Value = List (Index);
end Value_In_Array;
```

Cases where the recursive call is in the last statement executed are called **tail recursion**. Note that the recursive call is not necessarily the last statement in the procedure. For instance, the recursive call in the following version of `Value_In_Array` is still tail recursion, even though it is not the last physical statement in the procedure:

> **Tail recursion** The case where a recursive subprogram contains a single recursive call that is the last statement executed in the subprogram.

```
function Value_In_Array (List  : in Array_Type,
                         Value : in Integer)  return Boolean is
```

```ada
   -- Purpose        : Searches List for Value using iteration
   -- Preconditions  : None
   -- Postconditions : Returns True if Value is in List and False otherwise
   Result : Boolean;
begin
   if List'Length /= 0 then
      if Value = List(List'First) then
         Result : = True;
      else        -- Search rest of List
         Result := Value_In_Array (List  => List (List'First+1..List'Last),
                                   Value => Value);
      end if;
   else
      Result := False;
   end if;
   return Result;
end Value_In_Array;
```

The recursive call is the last statement *executed* in the general case—thus it is tail recursion. Tail recursion is easily replaced by iteration to remove recursion from the solution.

Stacking

When the recursive call is *not* the last action executed in the general case of a recursive procedure, we cannot simply substitute a loop for the recursion. For instance, in procedure `Reverse_Traverse` we make the recursive call and then process the value in the current node. In cases like this, we must replace the stacking that was done by the system with stacking that is done by the programmer.

How would we write procedure `Reverse_Traverse` nonrecursively? As we traverse the list, we must keep track of the pointer to each node, until we reach the end of the list (when our traversing pointer equals `null`). When we reach the end of the list, we process the `Info` field of the last node. Then we back up and process again, back up and process, and so on, until we have printed the first list element.

We know of a data structure in which we can store pointers and retrieve them in reverse order: the stack. The general task for `Reverse_Traverse` is

Reverse_Traverse (iterative)
    -- Construct a stack of pointers (one pointer to each node in the list)
    Ptr := pointer to first node in list
    loop
        exit when Ptr is null
        Push Ptr onto the stack
        Advance Ptr
    end loop

-- Process the nodes in reverse order (last node first)
loop
    exit when Stack is empty
    Pop the stack to get Ptr (to previous node)
    Process (Ptr.all.Info)
end loop;

A nonrecursive `Reverse_Traverse` procedure may be coded as follows:

```
procedure Reverse_Traverse (List : List_Type) is
-- Prints out the elements in the list in reverse order.
-- This is a nonrecursive procedure.

   -- Instantiate a stack package for stacks of node pointers
   package Ptr_Stack is new Stack (Element => Node_Ptr);
   -- Local variables
   Stack : Ptr_Stack.Stack_Type;    -- Stack of pointers
   Ptr   : Node_Ptr;                -- Pointer to current node
begin
   -- Push pointers to all nodes onto the stack
   Ptr := List;    -- Start with first node
   loop   -- Each iteration, a pointer to a node is pushed
      exit when Ptr = null;   -- exit at end of list
      -- Push an alias that points to the current element
      Ptr_Stack.Push (Stack => Stack, Element=> Ptr);
      Ptr := Ptr.all.Next;    -- Advance Ptr to next node
   end loop;
   -- Retrieve pointers in reverse order and process elements
   loop   -- Each iteration, a pointer to a node is popped
      exit when Ptr_Stack.Empty (Stack);
      Ptr_Stack.Pop (Stack => Stack, Element => Ptr);
      Process (Ptr.all.Info);
   end loop;
end Reverse_Traverse;
```

Notice that the nonrecursive version of `Reverse_Traverse` is quite a bit longer than its recursive counterpart, especially if we consider the code for the stack package. This verbosity is caused by our need to stack and unstack the pointers explicitly. In the recursive version, we just called `Reverse_Traverse` recursively, and let the run-time stack keep track of the pointers. Notice also that the recursive version uses fewer local variables than the iterative version.

9.11 Deciding Whether to Use a Recursive Solution

There are several factors to consider in deciding whether to use a recursive solution to a problem. The main issues are the clarity and the efficiency of the solution. Let's talk about efficiency first. In general, a recursive solution is more costly in terms of both computer time and space. (This is not an absolute decree; it really depends on the computer and the compiler.) A recursive solution usually requires more "overhead" because of the nested recursive procedure or function calls, in terms of both time (the procedure prologues and epilogues must be run for each recursive call) and space (an activation record must be created). A call to a recursive routine may hide many layers of internal recursive calls. For instance, the call to an iterative solution to Factorial involves a single function invocation, causing one activation record to be put on the run-time stack. Invoking the recursive version of Factorial, however, requires $N + 1$ function calls and $N + 1$ activation records to be pushed onto the run-time stack. That is, the depth of recursion is $O(N)$. For some problems, the system just may not have enough space in the run-time stack to run a recursive solution.

Let's look at the data from two simple experiments. For the first experiment we created a linked list containing 100,000 integers. Then we measured the amount of CPU time it took to traverse this list with both a recursive procedure and an iterative procedure. In the second experiment we created an ordered array-based list containing 100,000 integers. Then we measured the amount of CPU time it took to search for the smallest value in the list—the worst case for a binary search. Because the binary search is so efficient, we repeated the search 10,000 times to obtain the times shown. Here are the results of these experiments:

Results (in milliseconds) of the Timed Implementation Comparisons

Procedure	Recursive Implementation	Iterative Implementation
Traversal	1.67	0.11
Binary search	0.73	0.34

The iterative traversal was nearly 15 times faster than the recursive traversal! This observation clearly demonstrates the amount of overhead of the recursive calls. Although the binary search results again show that the iterative version is faster, the difference is really not great enough to rule out using the recursive version. As usual, keep in mind that these results are valid only for the particular computer and Ada compiler used in the experiments.

Another problem to look for is the possibility that a particular recursive solution might just be inherently inefficient. Such inefficiency is not a reflection of how we choose to implement the algorithm; rather, it is an indictment of the algorithm itself. For instance, look back at function Combinations, which we discussed earlier in this chapter. The example of this function illustrated in Figure 9.4 [Combinations (4, 3)] seems straightforward enough. But consider the execution of Combinations (6, 4), as illustrated in Figure 9.10. The inherent problem with this function is that the same values are calculated over and over. Combinations (4, 3) is calculated in two different places, and Combinations (3, 2) is calculated in three places, as are Combinations (2, 1) and Combinations (2, 2). It is unlikely that we could solve a combinatorial problem of any large size using this procedure. The problem is that the program runs "forever"—or until it exhausts the capacity of the computer; it is an exponential-time

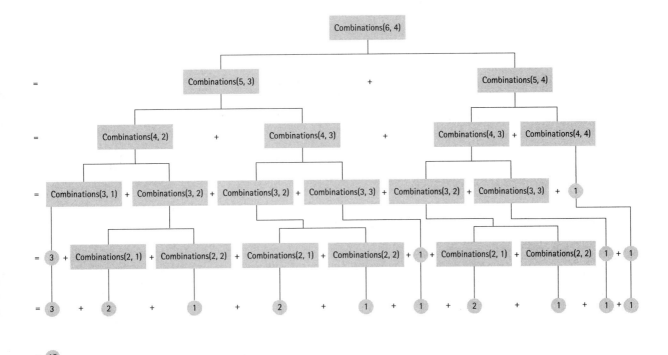

Figure 9.10 *Calculating Combinations (6, 4).*

[$O(2^N)$] solution to a linear time [$O(N)$] problem. Although our recursive function is very easy to understand, it is not a practical solution. In such cases an iterative solution must be sought.

The issue of the clarity of the solution is still a very important factor. For many problems a recursive solution is simpler and more natural for the programmer to write. The total amount of work required to solve a problem can be envisioned as an iceberg. By using recursive programming, the application programmer may limit his or her view to the tip of the iceberg. The system takes care of the great bulk of the work below the surface. Compare, for example, the recursive and nonrecursive versions of procedure Reverse_Traverse. In the recursive version we let the system take care of the stacking that we had to do explicitly in the nonrecursive procedure. Thus recursion is a tool that can help reduce the complexity of a program by hiding some of the implementation details.

To summarize, it is good to use recursion when:

- *The depth of recursive calls is relatively "shallow"—some fraction of the size of the problem.* For instance, the level of recursive calls in the Binary_Search procedure is $O(\log_2 N)$; this is a good candidate for recursion. The depth of recursive calls in the Factorial and Value_In_Array routines, however, is $O(N)$.
- *The recursive version does about the same amount of work as the nonrecursive version.* You can compare the Big-O approximations to determine this. For

instance, we have determined that the $O(2^N)$ recursive version of `Combinations` is a poor use of recursion, compared to an $O(N)$ iterative version. Both the recursive and iterative versions of `Binary_Search`, however, are $O(\log_2 N)$. The recursive version of `Binary_Search` is a good use of recursion.

- *The recursive version is shorter and simpler than the nonrecursive solution.* By this rule, `Factorial` and `Value_In_Array` are not good uses of recursive programming. They illustrate how to understand and write recursive procedures and functions, but they could more efficiently be written iteratively—without any loss of clarity in the solution. `Reverse_Traverse` is a better use of recursion. Its recursive solution is very simple to understand, and the nonrecursive equivalent is much less elegant.

In the next chapter we look at an inherently recursive structure where recursive algorithms are much simpler than their iterative counterparts.

The differences between recursive and iterative solutions suggest a good general programming strategy. First, develop and test a clearly understandable recursive solution to a problem. Then convert this recursive solution into a possibly less readable but more efficient iterative one using our two techniques for removing recursion.

Problem-Solving Case Study

Escape from a Maze

As a child, did you ever dream of playing in a maze? How fun and scary it would have been to get lost and then, just at sundown, find your way out. If you had thought about it, you might have come up with the idea of marking your path as you went along. If you were trapped, you could then go back to the last crossing and take the other path.

This technique of going back to the last decision point and trying another way is called *backtracking*. We illustrate this very useful problem-solving technique in the context of trying to get out of a maze.

Given a maze (like the one illustrated on the right side of Figure 9.11) and a starting point within it, you are to determine whether there is a way out. There is only one exit from the maze. You may move horizontally or vertically (but not diagonally) in any direction in which there is an open path, but you may not move in a direction that is blocked. If you move into a position where you are blocked on three sides, you must go back the way you came (backtrack) and try another path.

We write a program that uses this technique to escape from a maze, according to the following specifications.

Escape from a Maze

Purpose
This program uses a backtracking technique to escape from a maze.

Maze	(1)	(2)	(3)	(4)	(5)	(6)	(7)	(18)	(9)	(10)
(1)	O	O	+	F	+	O	O	+	+	+
(2)	O	+	+	O	+	O	+	O	O	O
(3)	O	O	O	O	O	O	+	O	+	O
(4)	+	+	+	+	+	O	+	+	O	O
(5)	O	O	O	+	O	O	O	+	O	+
(6)	O	+	O	+	O	+	+	+	O	+
(7)	O	+	O	+	O	O	O	+	O	O
(8)	+	+	O	+	+	+	O	+	+	O
(9)	O	+	O	O	O	O	O	+	+	O
(10)	O	+	O	+	+	O	+	O	O	O

Key to symbols
+ Trap (hedge)
O Open path
F Exit from maze

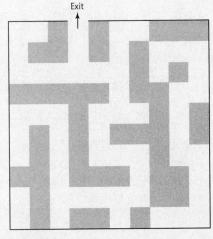

Key to Maze
☐ Open path
▨ Trap (hedge)

Figure 9.11 *Picture of a maze.*

Input

The input comes from two text files. The first, `maze.txt`, contains the original maze, represented as a square matrix of symbols, with one row of the matrix per input line. Each symbol is a character that indicates whether the corresponding maze position is an open path ('O'), a trap ('+'), or the finish ('F'). The size of the maze is 10 by 10 positions. Here is an example of the data that we might find in this file:

```
O  O  +  F  +  O  O  +  +  +
O  +  +  O  +  O  +  O  O  O
O  O  O  O  O  O  +  O  +  O
+  +  +  +  +  O  +  +  O  O
O  O  O  +  O  O  O  +  O  +
O  +  O  +  O  +  +  +  O  +
O  +  O  +  O  O  O  +  O  O
+  +  O  +  +  +  O  +  +  O
O  +  O  O  O  O  O  +  +  O
O  +  O  +  +  O  +  O  O  O
```

The second file, `start.txt`, contains a series of starting position coordinates. Each line contains a pair of values, representing the row and column of the starting position in the maze. We are to process each of these starting points until the end of the file is reached.

Output

For each starting position, print the following:

1. The maze with the starting point represented by a * symbol
2. A message that indicates the result of the escape:
   "HOORAY! I am free!" or "HELP! I am trapped!"
3. The number of positions tried before a solution was found

Processing Requirements

Begin processing each starting position at the specified coordinates, and continue moving until you find the way out or have no more moves to try. You may move horizontally or vertically into any position that is an open path ('O'), but not into any position that is blocked ('+'). If you move into the finish position ('F') you have exited the maze. Don't worry if the number of positions tried is greater than the number of positions in the maze; there may be positions that were duplicated during backtracking.

Assumptions

1. The two input files exist; all input is valid.
2. The starting position is not marked as a trap.

The Design

The maze is the major object in this problem. Because we need only one maze, we model it as an abstract data object (ADO). The maze ADO requires operations to (1) mark a position on the maze and (2) return the "symbol" value of a maze position.

From a logical perspective, the maze itself can be thought of as a two-dimensional grid of "positions" in the maze. Each position can be identified by its Row and Column numbers—values between 1 and 10, according to the specifications. Each position contains a Symbol that represents its contents: Open (an open path), Trap (a dead end), Finish (exit from the maze), or Start (the starting point for the escape attempt). The specifications tell us that the file input designates an open path by 'O', a trap by '+', and the finish by 'F'. When we print the maze, the starting point is to be marked with the character '*'. For convenience, in our illustrations, we use these characters to represent the contents of the maze positions. Figure 9.11 shows the logical picture of a maze.

The two maze operations can be specified as follows:

```
procedure Mark (Row    : in Row_Type;
                Column : in Column_Type;
                Symbol : in Symbol_Type);
-- Purpose         : Set the maze position of the specified
--                   Row and Column to the value of Symbol
-- Preconditions   : None
-- Postconditions  : Maze is updated to include modified Symbol value
--                   at the position specified by Row and Column
-- Exceptions      : SYMBOL_ERROR if Symbol is not a legal symbol
```

```
function Symbol_At (Row    : in Row_Type;
                    Column : in Column_Type) return Symbol_Type;
-- Purpose        : Returns the Symbol value at a maze position
-- Preconditions  : None
-- Postconditions : Symbol_At = symbol value of the maze position
--                  at Row and Column
```

Now that the maze operation's been fully specified, let's turn our attention to the overview of the processing with a top level design.

Escape
    loop
        exit when end of the Start File
        Get Maze from the Maze File
        Get Start Point from Start File
        Display Maze
        Try to Escape
        Display Results
    end loop

Using our maze ADO operations, we can describe much of the program's processing. In *Get Maze from the Maze File*, we input the original maze from `maze.txt` by reading the values, row by row, and calling `Mark` to put the appropriate symbols (`Open`, `Trap`, or `Finish`) into the specified positions in the maze. In *Get Start Point from Start File*, we mark a starting point by calling `Mark` to set the designated maze position to the Start symbol. *Display Maze* displays the maze row by row, using the `Symbol_At` function to retrieve the symbol value of each maze position. Displaying the results of the escape attempt merely involves a call or two to `Put_Line`. The designs for *Get Maze from the Maze File*, *Get Start Point*, *Display Maze*, and *Display Results* are straightforward, so let's go on to the interesting part of the problem: How do we get out of the maze?

Escape Processing Let's look more closely at the *Try to Escape* operation. It needs to know the position (`Row` and `Column`) of the starting point. It does some processing and then returns the results: whether the escape was successful and a count of how many moves we had to make in the escape attempt. Here is the procedure's specification:

```
procedure Try_To_Escape (Start_Row    : in  Row_Type;
                         Start_Column : in  Column_Type;
                         Free         : out Boolean;
                         Tries        : out Natural) is
-- Purpose        : To determine if it is possible to escape from a maze.
-- Preconditions  : The Maze ADO contains a valid maze.
-- Postconditions : Free = (there is a path from the Start to the Exit).
```

```
--          Tries is the number of positions in the Maze that
--          were tried in the escape attempt. Due to backtracking,
--          a position may be tried more than once.
```

What is this escape processing? Beginning at the starting point, we can move in any direction—up, down, right, or left—but only to an `Open` path ('O') or the `Finish` ('F'). Given the part of the maze shown in Figure 9.12, this means that we could move up or left, into an Open path. However, we cannot move down or right, where there are Traps ('+').

Let's say that we move to the left. Now we are facing the same kind of situation (see Figure 9.13). We can move in any direction where we are not trapped. Because the positions above and below the current position are blocked, we do not try these. To the right is the Start position ('*'). There's no use going back there, so we move again to the left.

Again we are in the same kind of situation (see Figure 9.14). We can move in any direction that is not blocked. There is a Trap to the left, so we don't move there. There are Open positions above and below and to the right. We just came from the position to the right, so it's not worth going back there. In fact, this is the same situation we faced in Figure 9.13, when we decided not to go back into the Start position. That time, because we saw the Start symbol in the maze position, we knew not to move into the spot. This time, however, it is just another Open position. How do we know not to go back?

If you were hiking in an uncharted area, you might mark your trail by breaking twigs or leaving stones in the path you had traveled. We can use that same idea here. We mark the trail

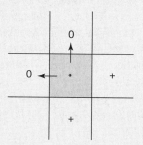

Figure 9.12   *The starting position.*

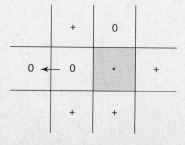

Figure 9.13   *After the first move.*

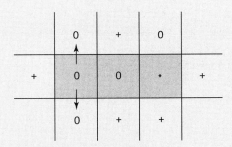

Figure 9.14 *After the second move.*

of positions that we've already tried by replacing the Open symbol with a special symbol, Tried. We use a little stone ('.') to depict the Tried symbol.

We have two choices in Figure 9.14: up or down. We decide to go up (see Figure 9.15). Now we face the usual choice with a modified restriction. We can go in any direction that is not blocked or already tried. Uh-oh! Our new position is blocked in all the untried directions. We are trapped.

But we don't know for sure that there is no way to get out of the maze. We only know that the path we tried doesn't get us there. We passed up a couple of Open positions (see Figures 9.12 and 9.14) as we were going along the path that led us into the dead end. We could go back to one of them and try another path from there. Even better, we can collect all these alternative paths as we pass them; then if we get trapped we can go back to the path most recently passed and resume the escape attempt.

A Stack-Based Solution This line of thinking leads us to the idea of using a data structure that we are already familiar with—the stack—to collect the alternative moves. Every time we enter a position, we put all the possible alternatives (Open positions adjacent to the current position) onto a stack. Then to move, we pop the top alternative off the stack. This move takes

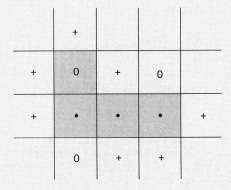

Figure 9.15 *After the third move, marking our trail.*

us to a new position, from which we push all of the alternative moves onto the stack, and so on. The following algorithm describes this solution:

Try To Escape -- *Stack Version*
    Tries := 0
    loop
        Increment Tries
        Push the positions (Row and Column) of all possible moves
            (up, down, left, or right positions that are marked
            as Open or Finish) onto Stack
        exit when Current Maze Position = Finish or the Stack is Empty
        Mark current position as Tried
        Pop new Current Position off the stack
    end loop;
    Free := Current Maze Position = Finish

A Recursive Solution This stack-based solution sounds as if it would work, but before we actually try it we notice something else in the discussion. Every time we made a move, we said, "Now we are facing the same situation. . . ." Every time we moved into a new position, we faced a version of the same problem that led us to call `Try_To_Escape` in the first place. This suggests a recursive solution to the problem; perhaps we can use recursion to let the system take care of the backtracking, instead of using a stack.

Let's look at the *general* case of a recursive version of the `Try_To_Escape` procedure. The general case is when the current position, on entering the procedure, is `Open`. Our current position is described by `Row` and `Column` numbers. What are the recursive calls that would solve the problem of escaping from the maze? We could `Try_To_Escape` up or down or right or left. Actually, we could `Try_To_Escape` in *all* of these directions. Here's a first pass at a recursive algorithm for `Try_To_Escape`:

Try To Escape -- *Recursive Version 1*
    Increment Tries
    if base case then
        Do something nonrecursive
    else (general case)
        Mark current position as Tried.
        Try_To_Escape (Row + 1, Column, Free, Tries)
        Try_To_Escape (Row - 1, Column, Free, Tries)
        Try_To_Escape (Row, Column + 1, Free, Tries)
        Try_To_Escape (Row, Column - 1, Free, Tries)
    end if

What is the base case? This is the case that can be solved nonrecursively, ensuring that the procedure eventually ends. The situations we might face when we enter procedure `Try_To_Escape` are summarized in the next table.

Try To Escape Processing

If the content of Current Position is	Then `Try_To_Escape` Should
`Tried`	Do nothing (return from procedure)
`Trap`	Do nothing (return from procedure)
`Finish`	Set `Free` to true (and return from procedure)
`Open` (or `Start`)	Execute general case

In addition, because a call to `Try_To_Escape` may cause `Free` to be set to true, a subsequent call may be made with `Free` already true. In this case, we don't want to do anything except exit the procedure. Let's summarize these conditions in a second draft of the `Try_To_Escape` algorithm.

Try To Escape -- *Recursive Version 2*
    Increment Tries
    Current_Position := Symbol_At (Row, Col)
    if Free then
        Do Nothing   -- *Base case, problem already solved*
    elsif Current_Position = Tried or Current Position = Trap then
        Do Nothing   -- *Base case, can't go this way*
    elsif Current_Position = Finish then
        Free := True   -- *Base case, found the exit*
    else   -- *General case, Current Position is Open*
        -- *mark this position so we don't try it again*
        Mark (Row, Column, Tried)
        -- *try all adjacent positions*
        Try_To_Escape (Row + 1, Column, Free, Tries)
        Try_To_Escape (Row - 1, Column, Free, Tries)
        Try_To_Escape (Row, Column + 1, Free, Tries)
        Try_To_Escape (Row, Column - 1, Free, Tries)
    end if;

Verifying the Recursive Design Let's use our three questions to verify that this recursive procedure works.

1. *The base-case question:* The base cases occur when the current position is not an `Open` path, in which case we should stop searching this path (do nothing), and when `Free` is already true on entrance to the procedure, in which case we already know the answer to the problem and can quit.

2. *The smaller-caller question:* We need to show here that the portion of the maze left to be processed is smaller on each recursive call. It is only the `Open` positions that are

processed. Each time we set the value of an `Open` position to `Tried`, the size of the maze that is left to process becomes "smaller" by one. We usually look at the parameters of the recursive calls to see how the size of the problem is changing. In this case, the maze is not a parameter; it is a globally accessible ADO.

For each recursive call, the `Row` and `Column` parameters are adjusted to guide the search for the finish into new paths adjacent to the current position. This observation, however, leads us to note a shortcoming of our design: As we increment and decrement the `Row` and `Column` parameters, what keeps us from going right off the edge of the maze? The design needs to be modified to account for the edges of the maze. We finish our proof and then come back to this problem.

3. *The general-case question:* Let's assume that a call to `Try_To_Escape` correctly tells us whether an escape can be made from a given position. If we can escape from some known position in the maze, then we can also escape from an Open position adjacent to that position. So if we check all the positions adjacent to the starting point (the four calls to `Try_To_Escape`) and find that any of them leads to an escape, then we know that we can escape from the starting point. The converse is also true: If none of the adjacent positions leads to the finish, then the starting point cannot lead to the finish. So the general case should solve the problem, assuming that the recursive calls do what they're supposed to do.

The Boundary Problem We noticed during our verification of the smaller-caller question that there isn't anything to keep us from going over the edges of the maze as `Row` and `Column` are incremented and decremented in the recursive calls. We can add explicit checks for the lower and upper bounds of the array index:

if (Row < 1) or (Row > 10) or (Column < 1) or (Column > 10) then
    Do nothing, just exit

Another way to handle this condition is to modify the data structure that supports the maze so that the existing conditions take care of the problem. We can add a "hedge" that borders the whole maze (another row on the top and bottom of the maze, and another column on the left side and right side of the maze), setting all of these border positions to the `Trap` symbol. Then if the current position is in the border, it is processed the same way as any other `Trap` position; that is, we just exit the recursive call to the procedure.

When do we add the boundary hedges to the maze? The specification does not include the `Trap` symbols for the boundary in the text file. We can make use of package initialization code to set up the hedges in the maze ADO.

The Implementation

Let's start with the maze ADO whose specification is given in Specification 9.1. Our design described the two operations. We must also declare the types of the operations' parameters. To prevent any confusion between row and column numbers, we use a different type for each. We use subtypes to document our separation of the actual maze from the boundary we added around it. There are four symbols used in the maze (`Open`, `Trap`, `Finish`, or `Tried`) represented by their single-character equivalents. Declaring constants for these characters helps make our program easier to read.

Specification 9.1   Maze ADO

```ada
package Maze is

-- This ADO models a maze.  Initially, all maze positions are marked as Trap

   subtype Symbol_Type is Character;

   Open   : constant Symbol_Type := 'O';
   Trap   : constant Symbol_Type := '+';
   Finish : constant Symbol_Type := 'F';
   Start  : constant Symbol_Type := '*';
   Tried  : constant Symbol_Type := '.';

   SYMBOL_ERROR : exception;   -- Raised if some character other than
                               -- the four above is used
   Maze_Size : constant := 10;

   -- Types for maze array
   type Column_Range is range 0..Maze_Size + 1;
   type Row_Range    is range 0..Maze_Size + 1;

   -- Subtypes for positions inside the boundary hedge
   subtype Internal_Column is Column_Range range 1..Maze_Size;
   subtype Internal_Row    is Row_Range    range 1..Maze_Size;

   -------------------------------------------------------------------------

   procedure Mark (Row    : in Internal_Row;
                   Column : in Internal_Column;
                   Symbol : in Symbol_Type);
   -- Purpose        : Set the maze position of the specified
   --                  Row and Column to the value of Symbol
   -- Preconditions  : None
   -- Postconditions : Maze is updated to include modified Symbol value at
   --                  the position specified by Row and Column
   -- Exceptions     : SYMBOL_ERROR if Symbol is not a legal symbol

   -------------------------------------------------------------------------

   function Symbol_At (Row    : in Row_Range;
                       Column : in Column_Range) return Symbol_Type;
   -- Purpose        : Returns the Symbol value at a maze position
   -- Preconditions  : None
```

```
--  Postconditions : Symbol_At = symbol value of the maze position
--                   at Row and Column
end Maze;
```

We've managed to get all the way through the design without tying ourselves down to a representation of the maze. Although we could probably think up more interesting structures to implement the maze, the most natural is a two-dimensional array of symbols. Using this representation, each maze operation takes only a single assignment statement. Is it worth encapsulating these one-liners in an ADO instead of just referencing an array in the calling program? There are several reasons for using the ADO. We could change the implementation (say to a linked list) with no change in the rest of the program. All of the related types (`Row_Range`, `Column_Range`, and `Symbol_Type`) are together. The encapsulation also allows us to check for symbol errors in a single place. Finally, we can use package initialization code to set up the borders of the maze. Body 9.1 contains the body of the maze ADO.

Body 9.1   Maze ADO: Implements Specification 9.1

```
package body Maze is

   type Maze_Type is array (Row_Range, Column_Range) of Symbol_Type;

   The_Maze : Maze_Type;    -- The maze "object"

----------------------------------------------------------------

   procedure Mark (Row    : in Internal_Row;
                   Column : in Internal_Column;
                   Symbol : in Symbol_Type) is
   begin
      if Symbol = Trap    or  Symbol = Open  or  Symbol = Tried  or
         Symbol = Finish  or  Symbol = Start then
         -- Mark the maze
         The_Maze (Row, Column) := Symbol;
      else
         raise SYMBOL_ERROR;
      end if;
   end Mark;

----------------------------------------------------------------

   function Symbol_At (Row    : in Row_Range;
                       Column : in Column_Range) return Symbol_Type is
   begin
      return The_Maze (Row, Column);
   end Symbol_At;

begin
   Initialize entire maze to traps
```

```
      The_Maze := (Row_Range => (Column_Range => Trap));
end Maze;
```

       Now let's move on to the implementation of our recursive escape algorithm. While converting our design to Ada, we discovered some housekeeping tasks that we ignored in our design. We need to initialize the counter `Tries` to zero. If we initialize it at the beginning of the recursive procedure, it is set to zero with every recursive call, obliterating the count from previous calls. One solution would be to initialize `Tries` before calling `Try_To_Escape`. Such a solution breaks procedural abstraction by dividing the work of the escape algorithm between the caller and the procedure. A better solution is for the `Try_To_Escape` procedure to do the necessary initialization and then call a second procedure to perform our recursive search for the exit.

       Our design of the escape algorithm also neglected the detail of assigning false to `Free`. The algorithm assumed that `Free` was initialized to false and only changes its value when it finds the exit. We can initialize `Free` at the same place we initialize `Tries`. The implementation of our escape program is given in Program 9.2.

Program 9.2 Escape from a Maze

```
with Ada.Integer_Text_IO;    use Ada.Integer_Text_IO;
with Ada.Text_IO;            use Ada.Text_IO;
with Maze;
procedure Escape is

   -- Instantiate I/O packages for maze row and column numbers
   package Column_IO is new Ada.Text_IO.Integer_IO (Maze.Internal_Column);
   package Row_IO    is new Ada.Text_IO.Integer_IO (Maze.Internal_Row);

   ----------------------------------------------------------------------

   procedure Get_Maze (Maze_File : in  Ada.Text_IO.File_Type) is
   -- Purpose        : Gets values for maze positions from Maze_File.
   -- Assumptions    : Data in the file is valid.
   -- Preconditions  : Maze_File is open and the reading marker is
   --                  positioned at the beginning of the file.
   -- Postconditions : The symbols in the Maze ADO are set to those in the file

      Symbol    : Maze.Symbol_Type;    -- A symbol for one maze position
   begin
      for Row in Maze.Internal_Row loop
         for Column in Maze.Internal_Column loop
            Get (File => Maze_File, Item => Symbol);
            Maze.Mark (Row, Column, Symbol);
         end loop;
      end loop;
   end Get_Maze;

   ----------------------------------------------------------------------
```

```ada
procedure Get_Start_Point (Start_File : in  Ada.Text_IO.File_Type;
                           Row        : out Maze.Internal_Row;
                           Column     : out Maze.Internal_Column) is
-- Purpose        : Gets the starting point and marks it on the maze.
-- Preconditions  : Maze_File is open.
--                  There is data remaining in Maze_File.
-- Postconditions : The starting point is returned.
--                  The starting point is marked on the Maze ADO.
begin
   Row_IO.Get    (File => Start_File, Item => Row);
   Column_IO.Get (File => Start_File, Item => Column);
   Maze.Mark (Row => Row, Column => Column, Symbol => Maze.Start);
end Get_Start_Point;

-------------------------------------------------------------------------------
procedure Display_Maze is
-- Purpose        : Displays the maze
-- Preconditions  : None
-- Postconditions : The symbols in the Maze ADO are displayed
begin
   for Row in Maze.Row_Range loop
      for Column in Maze.Column_Range loop
         Put (Item => Maze.Symbol_At (Row, Column));
      end loop;
      New_Line;
   end loop;
end Display_Maze;

-------------------------------------------------------------------------------
procedure Try_To_Escape (Start_Row    : in  Maze.Internal_Row;
                         Start_Column : in  Maze.Internal_Column;
                         Free         : out Boolean;
                         Tries        : out Natural) is
-- Purpose        : To determine if it is possible to escape from a maze.
-- Preconditions  : The Maze ADO contains a valid maze.
-- Postconditions : Free = (there is a path from the Start to the Exit).
--                  Tries is the number of positions in the Maze that
--                  were tried in the escape attempt. Due to backtracking,
--                  a position may be tried more than once.

   ----------------------------------------------------------------------------
   procedure Try (Row    : in     Maze.Row_Range;
                  Column : in     Maze.Column_Range;
                  Free   : in out Boolean;
                  Tries  : in out Natural) is
```

```ada
      -- This recursive routine does the work for Try_To_Escape
      use type Maze.Row_Range;
      use type Maze.Column_Range;
   begin
      Tries := Tries + 1;
      if not Free then            -- Do nothing if already free (base case)
         case Maze.Symbol_At (Row, Column) is
            when Maze.Finish =>    -- Base case that requires an action
               Free := True;
            when Maze.Trap   |     -- Remaining base cases require no action
                 Maze.Tried =>
               null;
            when Maze.Open  | Maze.Start  =>   -- General case
               Maze.Mark (Row, Column, Maze.Tried);
               Try (Row + 1, Column,     Free, Tries);
               Try (Row - 1, Column,     Free, Tries);
               Try (Row,     Column + 1, Free, Tries);
               Try (Row,     Column - 1, Free, Tries);
            when others      =>    -- Invalid symbol
               raise Maze.SYMBOL_ERROR;
         end case;
      end if;
   end try;

begin  -- Try_To_Escape
   Tries := 0;         -- Initialize the
   Free  := False;     -- out parameters
   Try (Start_Row, Start_Column, Free, Tries); -- Call the recursive search
end Try_To_Escape;

-------------------------------------------------------------------------
procedure Display_Results (Free : in Boolean;  Tries : in Natural) is
-- Purpose        : Display the results of the escape attempt.
-- Preconditions  : None
-- Postconditions : An appropriate message is displayed for the results
--                  of an escape attempt.  The number of positions
--                  tried in the attempt is displayed.
begin
   if Free then
      Put_Line ("HOORAY!  I am free!");
   else
      Put_Line ("Help!  I am trapped!");
   end if;
   Put ("Number of moves taken = ");
   Put (Item => Tries, Width => 1);
```

```ada
         New_Line;
      end Display_Results;

   ----------------------------------------------------------------------

      Maze_File  : Ada.Text_IO.File_Type;   -- File containing the maze
      Start_File : Ada.Text_IO.File_Type;   -- File containing starting positions

      Start_Column : Maze.Internal_Column;  -- Maze position
      Start_Row    : Maze.Internal_Row;     -- variables

      Free  : Boolean;              -- Result
      Tries : Natural;              -- Number of tries to escape

   begin
      Ada.Text_IO.Open (File => Maze_File,
                        Mode => Ada.Text_IO.In_File,
                        Name => "maze.txt");
      Ada.Text_IO.Open (File => Start_File,
                        Mode => Ada.Text_IO.In_File,
                        Name => "start.txt");
      -- Process all of the starting points in the start file
      -- Each iteration, try to escape from a starting point
      loop
         exit when End_Of_File (Start_File);
         Ada.Text_IO.Reset (Maze_File);  -- Set reading marker to beginning of file
         Get_Maze (Maze_File);           -- Get the maze
         Get_Start_Point (Start_File, Start_Row, Start_Column);
         Display_Maze;
         New_Line;
         Try_To_Escape (Start_Row, Start_Column, Free, Tries);
         Display_Results (Free, Tries);
         New_Line(3);
      end loop;
      Close (Maze_File);
      Close (Start_File);
   end Escape;
```

Testing the Program

In our first attempt at testing this program, we try out the input and output routines (Get_Maze, Get_Start_Point, Display_Maze) with sample files of data, commenting out the call to Try_To_Escape in the program. When we see that those procedures work correctly, we get up our nerve to try running the program with the recursive procedure Try_To_Escape restored. To ensure that we can trace its execution through all the recursive calls, we put debug `Put`s at the start of the recursive procedure `Try`, before any other statements:

```
Put ("Try_To_Escape entered with Row ");
Row_IO.Put (Item => Row, Width => 1);
Put (" and Column ");
Column_IO.Put (Item => Column, Width => 1);
Put_Line (" and Free " & Boolean'Image(Free));
```

Then we run the program using a variety of starting positions. The debugging output helps us to check whether the procedure is really solving the problem as we had expected. It does work, but we are really surprised at how many recursive calls have to be made. Sometimes `Tries` is larger than the total number of positions in the maze! We realize that we shouldn't be surprised, because we can come back to a position more than once, only to find that we have already been there (in these cases we exit immediately).

Looking through the debugging output, we realize that some of the calls are being made to `Try` even after we have determined that we are free. For instance, if `Free` is set to true on the first of the four recursive calls in the general case, we still make the other three recursive calls, exiting immediately because `Free` is true (one of the base cases). We can avoid these extra calls by putting a condition before the recursive calls in the general case rather than as a base case within procedure `Try`. Then we only make the call if we are not free.

```
-- in the general case
      .
      .
      .
   Try (the position above);
   if not Free then
      Try (the position below);
   end if;
   if not Free then
      Try (the position on the right);
   end if;
   if not Free then
      Try (the position on the left);
   end if;
```

We made this change to the `Try` procedure and ran the program again on the same input file. This time some (but not all) of the values of `Tries` are smaller. A comparison of the output values for the two versions of `Try` is shown in the next table. Note that if there is no escape, it doesn't help to make the calls to `Try` conditional—`Free` is never true. If we do escape, however, there is a noticeable difference between the two versions.

A Comparison of Output of the Two Versions of Procedure `Try_To_Escape`

Starting Coordinates		Result	Number of Moves to Determine Results	
Row	Column		Version 1	Version 2
1	2	Freed	33	20
10	1	Trapped	9	9
10	8	Trapped	65	65
7	6	Freed	121	108
1	7	Freed	125	115
8	7	Freed	121	106
7	9	Trapped	65	65
9	3	Freed	121	100
7	1	Freed	121	82
2	8	Trapped	65	65

The Recursive Solution vs. a Nonrecursive Solution

Well . . . was it worth recursing?

One of the criteria we mentioned for deciding whether to use a recursive solution to a problem was to ask if the recursive solution produced a shorter and simpler program. It just so happens that there's a nonrecursive solution to this same program; it uses the stacking algorithm discussed earlier to handle the backtracking.

Not counting the code for the stack package, the two versions have nearly the same number of executable lines of code. Of course, including the code from either of the stack packages we developed in Chapter 5, the stack version makes the total size of the nonrecursive version considerably larger. The nonrecursive version is also less clear; it takes some time to become convinced that all the pushing and popping really solves the problem of getting out of the maze. In this case we believe that the recursive solution is a good choice.

Summary

Recursion is a very powerful computing tool. Used appropriately, recursion can simplify the solution of a problem, often resulting in shorter, more easily understood source code. As usual, there are trade-offs: Recursive procedures are often less efficient, in terms of both time and space, due to the overhead of many levels of procedure calls. How expensive this cost is depends on the computer system and compiler.

A recursive solution to a problem must have at least one base case—that is, a case where the solution is derived nonrecursively. Without a base case, the procedure or function recurses forever (or at least until the computer runs out of memory). The recursive solution also has one or more general cases that include recursive calls to the procedure or function. The recursive calls must involve a "smaller caller." One (or more) of the actual parameter values must change in each recursive call to redefine the problem to be closer to the base case than it was on the previous call. Thus each recursive call leads the solution of the problem toward the base case(s).

A typical implementation of recursion involves the use of a stack. Each call to a subprogram generates an activation record to contain its return address, parameters, and local variables. The activation records are accessed in a last-in-first-out manner. Thus a stack is the choice of data structure. Recursion can be supported by systems and languages that use dynamic storage allocation. The procedure parameters and local variables are not bound to addresses until an activation record is created at run time. Thus multiple copies of the intermediate values of recursive calls to the program can be supported, as new activation records are created for them.

With static storage allocation, in contrast, a single location is reserved at compile time for each parameter and local variable of a procedure. There is no place to store intermediate values calculated by repeated nested calls to the same procedure. Therefore, systems and languages with only static storage allocation cannot support recursion.

When recursion is not possible or appropriate, a recursive algorithm can be implemented nonrecursively by using a looping structure and, in some cases, by pushing and popping relevant values onto our own stack. This programmer-controlled stack explicitly replaces the system's run-time stack. Although such nonrecursive solutions are often more efficient in terms of time and space, there is usually a trade-off in terms of the elegance of the solution.

In the case study, we developed a recursive solution to the problem of finding the way out of a maze. This problem was once included in a Pascal version of this book as a stack application. We said earlier that any recursive solution can be implemented using iteration or a stack. Our case study illustrates another way of looking at this idea: Any problem that uses a stack in its solution may be a good place to use a recursive algorithm.

Exercises

Basics

1. Explain what is meant by
   a. Base case
   b. General (or recursive) case
   c. Direct recursion
   d. Indirect recursion
2. Use the three-question method to verify the `Value_In_Array` function in this chapter.

3. If you have had a course in discrete mathematics, describe the three-question method of verifying recursive methods in relation to an inductive proof.

Intermediate

Use the following function in answering Exercises 4 and 5:
```
function Puzzle (Base  : in Natural;
                 Limit : in Natural) return Integer is
   Result : Integer;
begin -- Puzzle
   if Base > Limit then
      Result := -1;
   elsif Base = Limit then
      Result := 1;
   else
      Result := Base * Puzzle (Base + 1, Limit);
   end if;
   return Result;
end Puzzle;
```

4. Identify
   a. The base case(s) of function `Puzzle`.
   b. The general case(s) of function `Puzzle`.
5. Show what would be written by the following calls to the recursive function `Puzzle`.
   a. `Ada.Integer_Text_IO.Put (Item => Puzzle (14, 10));`
   b. `Ada.Integer_Text_IO.Put (Item => Puzzle (4, 7));`
   c. `Ada.Integer_Text_IO.Put (Item => Puzzle (0, 0));`
6. Given the following function:
```
function Fun (Num : in Num_Type) return Num_Type is
   Result : Num_Type;
begin
   if Num = 0 then
      Result := 0;
   else
      Result := Num + Fun (Num + 1);
   end if;
   return Result;
end Fun;
```

   a. Write a type declaration of `Num_Type` that allows this function to pass the smaller-caller test.
   b. Is `Fun(7)` a legal call, given your declaration of `Num_Type`? If so, what is returned from the function?

c. Is Fun(0) a legal call, given your declaration of Num_Type? If so, what is returned from the function?

d. Is Fun(-5) a legal call, given your declaration of Num_Type? If so, what is returned from the function?

e. Is Fun(-5.2) a legal call, given your declaration of Num_Type? If so, what is returned from the function?

7. For each of the following recursive subprograms, identify the base case(s), the general case(s), and explain what the subprogram does.

   a.
   ```
   function Power (Base     : in Integer;
                   Exponent : in Natural) return  Integer is
      Result : Integer;
   begin
      if Exponent = 0 then
         Result := 1;
      else
         Result : = Base * Power (Base, Exponent - 1);
      end if;
   end Power;
   ```

   b.
   ```
   function Factorial (Num : in Integer) return Integer is
      Result : Integer
   begin
      if Num > 0 then
         Result := Num * Factorial (Num - 1);
      elsif Num = 0 then
         Result := 1;
      else
         raise CONSTRAINT_ERROR;
      end if;
   end Factorial;
   ```

   c.
   ```
   procedure Sort (Data : in out Array_Type) is
      Maxi : Index_Type;
   begin
      if Data'Length > 1 then
         -- Find index of the largest element in array
         Maxi := Max_Position (Data);
         -- Exchange the values of the two array elements
         Swap (Data(Maxi), Data(Data'Last));
         Sort(Data => Data (Data'First .. Data'Last - 1));
      end if;
   end Sort;
   ```

d.
```
function Fun2 (N : in Integer) return Integer is
begin
    if N < 0 then
        return -1;
    elsif N < 10 then
        return 1;
    else
        return 1 + Fun2(N/10);
    end if;
end Fun2;
```

e.
```
function Fun3 (N : in Integer) return Integer is
begin
    if N < 0 then
        return -1;
    elsif N < 10 then
        return N;
    else
        return N rem 10 + Fun3 (N/10);
    end if;
end Fun3;
```

8. Fill in the blanks to complete the following function:

```
function Sum (Data : in Array_Type) return Integer is
-- Returns the sum of all the elements in the array Data
    Result : Integer;
begin
    if _____ then
        Result := _____;  --
Base case
    else -- General case
        Result :=
_____;
    end if;
    return Result;
end Sum;
```

9. Here are EBNF definitions that define a postfix expression (discussed in Chapter 5):

```
postfix_expression   ::=   operand operand operator

operator ::=    + | - | * | /

operand  ::=    postfix_expression | integer
```

a. Describe the indirect recursion in these EBNF definitions.

b. What is the base case?

10. You must assign the grades for a programming class. Right now the class is studying recursion, and they have been given this simple assignment: Write a recursive function Sum_Squares that takes a pointer to a linked list of integer elements and returns the sum of the squares of the elements. If the list is empty, return zero.

Example:

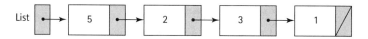

Sum_Squares(List) yields $(5 \times 5) + (2 \times 2) + (3 \times 3) + (1 \times 1) = 39$.

You have received quite a variety of solutions. Grade the procedures below, marking errors where you see them.

a.
```
function Sum_Squares (List : in List_Type) return Natural is
   Sum : Natural;
begin
   Sum := 0;
   if List /= null then
      Sum := (List.all.Info) ** 2 + Sum_Squares (List.all.Next);
   end if;
   return Sum;
end Sum_Squares;
```

b.
```
function Sum_Squares (List : in List_Type) return Natural is
   Sum : Natural;
   Ptr : List_Type;
begin
   Sum := 0;
   Ptr := List;
   loop
      exit when Ptr = null;
      Sum := Sum + (Ptr.all.Info) ** 2;
      Ptr := Ptr.all.Next;
   end loop;
   return Sum;
end Sum_Squares;
```

c.
```
function Sum_Squares (List : in List_Type) return Natural is
    Sum : Natural;
begin
    if List = null then
        Sum := 0;
    else
        Sum := (List.all.Info) ** 2 + Sum_Squares (List.all.Next);
    end if;
    return Sum;
end Sum_Squares;
```

d.
```
function Sum_Squares (List : in List_Type) return Natural is
    Sum : Natural;
begin
    if List.all.Next = null then
        Sum := (List.all.Info) ** 2;
    else
        Sum := (List.all.Info) ** 2 + Sum_Squares (List.all.Next);
    end if;
    return Sum;
end Sum_Squares;
```

e.
```
function Sum_Squares (List : in List_Type) return Natural is
    Sum : Natural;
begin
    if List = null then
        Sum := 0
    else
        Sum := Sum_Squares (List.all.Next) *
               Sum_Squares (List.all.Next);
    end if;
    return Sum;
end Sum_Squares;
```

11. Using the recursive function on page 569,
    a. Calculate the value of `Fibonacci(6)` by hand.
    b. What does this exercise tell you about the efficiency of the recursive solution? Would you call this a good use of recursion?
    c. Write a nonrecursive version of function `Fibonacci`.

12. The following is the declaration of a function that calculates an approximation of the square root of Num, starting with an approximate answer (Approx), within the specified tolerance (Tol). Float_Type is a subtype of Float.

    ```
    function Sqrt (Num    : in Float_Type;
                   Approx : in Float_Type;
                   Tol    : in Float_Type) return Float_Type;
    -- This function calculates an approximation of the
    -- square root of Num.

    -- Approx is an initial approximation of the square root of Num
    -- Tol is the desired tolerance of the result
    ```

    The function uses Newton's method, as defined below. The vertical bars indicate the absolute value.

    Sqrt (Num, Approx, Tol) =

    $$\begin{cases} \text{Approx}, & \text{if } |\text{Approx}^2 - \text{Num}| \leq \text{Tol} \\ \text{Sqrt (Num, (Approx}^2 + \text{Num}) / (2 \times \text{Approx}), \text{Tol}), & \text{if } |\text{Approx}^2 - \text{Num}| > \text{Tol} \end{cases}$$

    a. What limitations must be made on the values of the parameters, if this method is to work correctly? Write the subtype declaration for Float_Type to ensure that these limitations are met.
    b. Write a recursive version of function Sqrt.
    c. Write a nonrecursive version of function Sqrt.
    d. Write a driver to test the recursive and iterative versions of function Sqrt.

13. A procedure to search a list has the following declaration:

    ```
    procedure Search (List     : in  List_Type;   -- list to search
                      Value    : in  Integer;     -- value to search for
                      Location : out Loc_Type;    -- location of value
                      Found    : out Boolean);    -- search successful?
    ```

    a. Complete the procedure as a recursive search of an unordered linked list of integers. List is the external pointer to a linked list of nodes. Each node contains an integer (Info) and a pointer to the next node (Next). If the search is successful, Location designates the node containing Value and Found is true. If the search is not successful, Found is false and Location is not defined.
    b. Complete the procedure as a recursive search of an unconstrained, unordered array of integers, List. Location is a positive array index. If the search is successful, Location is the index of the array element containing Value and Found is true. If the search is not successful, Found is false and Location is not defined.

14. Given the following function:
    ```
    function Ulam (Num : in Integer) return Integer is
       Result : Integer;
    begin
       if Num < 2 then
          Result := 1;
       elsif Num rem 2 = 0 then
          Result := Ulam (Num / 2);
       else
          Result := Ulam (3* Num + 1);
       end if;
       return Result;
    end Ulam;
    ```
    a. What problems come up in verifying this function?

    b. How many recursive calls are made by the following initial calls:
    ```
    Ada.Integer_Text_IO.Put (Item => Ulam (7));
    Ada.Integer_Text_IO.Put (Item => Ulam (8));
    Ada.Integer_Text_IO.Put (Item => Ulam (15));
    ```

15. Using the recursive procedure `Reverse_Traverse` on page 572 as a model, write the recursive procedure `Traverse`, which traverses the elements in the list in order. Does one of these routines constitute a better use of recursion? If so, which one?

16. Remove the local procedure `Search_Linked_List` and write recursive implementations for `Retrieve`, `Modify`, `Insert`, and `Delete` for the unbounded key-ordered list in Body 7.3. You will discover that the recursive implementations are significantly shorter, that you do not need an external search procedure, and that, unlike the iterative versions, there are no special cases to consider.

Advanced

17. We want to count the number of paths possible to move in a two-dimensional grid from row 1, column 1 to row N, column N. Steps are restricted to going up or to the right, but not diagonally. The illustration on the following page shows three of many paths, if $N = 10$:

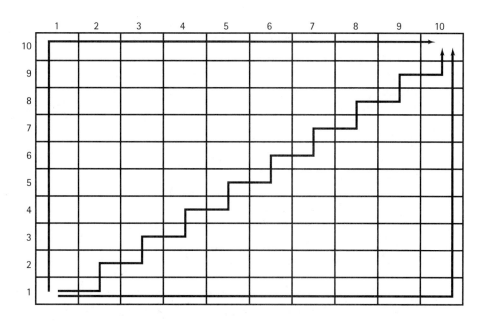

a. The following function, Num_Paths, is supposed to count the number of paths, but it has two problems. Debug the function.

```
function Num_Paths (Row : in Positive;     -- Starting Row
                    Col : in Positive;     -- Starting Column
                    N   : in Positive) return Positive is
   Result : Positive;
begin
   if Row = N then
      Result := 1;       -- Only one path to exit from here
   elsif Col = N then
      Result := Num_Paths + 1;
   else
      Result := Num_Paths (Row + 1, Col) *
                Num_Paths (Row, Col + 1);
   end if;
   return Result;
end Num_Paths;
```

b. After you have corrected the function, trace the execution of `Num_Paths` with $N = 4$ by hand. Why is this algorithm inefficient?

c. The efficiency of this operation can be improved by keeping intermediate values of `Num_Paths` in a global two-dimensional array of positive values. This keeps the function from having to recalculate values that it has already done. Design and code a version of `Num_Paths` that uses this approach.

d. Show an invocation of the version of `Num_Paths` in part (c), including any array initialization necessary.

e. How do the two versions of `Num_Paths` compare in terms of time efficiency? Space efficiency?

18. Explain what is meant by
    a. Run-time stack
    b. Binding time
    c. Tail recursion
    d. Binding

19. *True or False*. If false, correct the statement. Recursive procedures and functions . . .
    a. often have fewer local variables than the equivalent nonrecursive routines.
    b. generally use `loop`, `while`, or `for` statements as their main control structure.
    c. are possible only in languages with static storage allocation.
    d. should be used whenever execution speed is critical.
    e. are always shorter and clearer than the equivalent nonrecursive routines.
    f. must always contain a path that does not contain a recursive call.
    g. are always less "efficient," in terms of Big-O.

20. What data structure would you most likely see in a nonrecursive implementation of a recursive algorithm?

21. Explain the relationship between dynamic storage allocation and recursion.

22. What do we mean by binding time, and what does it have to do with recursion?

23. Given the following values in an array, `List`:

2	6	9	14	23	65	92	96	99	100
(1)	(2)	(3)	(4)	(5)	(6)	(7)	(8)	(9)	(10)

show the contents of the run-time stack during the execution of this call to Binary_Search:

`Binary_Search (List => List, Value => 99, Location => Location);`

Maze Case Study

24. What are the base case(s) and general case(s) of the `Try_To_Escape` procedure?

25. Describe a scheme to improve the efficiency of the escape attempt by marking the "original" maze with the results of previous attempts.

26. A very large maze (Max_Maze = 100) contains very few open paths relative to the number of trap positions. To save space, you decide to represent the maze ADO as an array of Max_Maze pointers, where each pointer accesses a list of Open or Finish path positions in one row, as illustrated below:

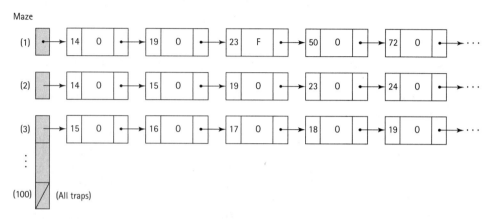

The numbers in these nodes are column numbers. From the drawing we can see that for row 1, columns 14, 19, 50, 72, ... are all open and that column 23 of this row contains the exit.

a. Write type declarations to support Maze_Type.

b. Describe algorithms for the revised Mark and Symbol_At operations.

c. Describe how this change of data representation affects the rest of program Escape.

Programming Problems

27. Modify the maze program so that if an escape route is found, the maze with the route marked with *'s is displayed.

28. Implement and test the revised maze ADO described in Question 26.

29. The determination of the area under a curve is necessary in many mathematical, science, and business applications. If you have taken calculus you know that the definite integral is a common method for determining this area. In this assign-

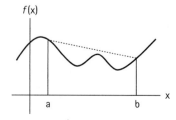

Figure 9.16 *Approximating the Area under a Curve with One Trapezoid.*

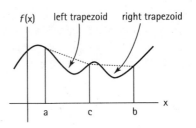

Figure 9.17 *Approximating the Area under a Curve with Two Trapezoids.*

ment you will learn a way to determine the area under a curve that does not require knowledge of calculus.

Figure 9.16 shows the plot of a function, $f(x)$. We would like to determine the area bounded by this function on the top, the x axis on the bottom, and the two vertical lines at $x = a$ and $x = b$. We can use a trapezoid to *approximate* this area. This trapezoid is defined by the two vertical lines at $x = a$ and $x = b$, the x axis, and the dotted line connecting the intersections of the two vertical lines with the function. In case you don't remember the formula for the area of a trapezoid from your geometry class, the area of the trapezoid in Figure 9.16 is calculated using the formula:

total area = $0.5 \times (f(a) + f(b)) \times (b - a)$ (An approximation of area under $f(x)$)

where $f(a)$ is the value of the function evaluated at a and $f(b)$ is the value of the function evaluated at b. You can obtain a better approximation of the area under the curve by adding a vertical line ($x = c$) halfway between a and b (as in Figure 9.17) to form two trapezoids. The area under the curve is then approximated by the sum of the areas of the two trapezoids. The area of each of these trapezoids is calculated with the formulas

left area = $0.5 \times (f(a) + f(c)) \times (c - a)$

right area = $0.5 \times (f(c) + f(b)) \times (b - c)$

The sum of the left area and the right area is a better approximation of the area under the curve than that made with a single trapezoid. We define the error of an approximation as the difference between that approximation and the actual area under the curve. Mathematicians have estimated that the error in the better approximation (the one that uses the left and right areas to calculate the area under the curve) is

estimate of error = (total area − (left area + right area)) / 3

Here is the declaration of a generic function to calculate the area under a curve, given the function that defines the curve ($f(x)$), the two endpoints (a and b), and the amount of error (epsilon) we are willing to accept:

```
-- Integrate is a generic subprogram for integrating a mathematical
-- function. It uses an adaptive trapezoidal rule method for integration.
-- It is adaptive in that the number of trapezoids used in a
-- particular region of the function is determined dynamically
-- to meet the given error criteria.
generic
    -- The floating point type used in the calculations
    type Real is digits <>;
function Integrate (F : not null access function (X : in Real) return Real;
                    A       : in Real;
                    B       : in Real;
                    Epsilon : in Real) return Real;

-- Determine an approximation of the integral of the function F in the
-- interval A to B
--
-- Parameters   F       - A pointer to the function to integrate
--              A       - The left endpoint of the integration interval
--              B       - The right endpoint of the integration interval
--              Epsilon - The maximum allowed absolute value of the error
-- Preconditions  : None
-- Postconditions : An approximation of the definite integral is returned
-- Exceptions     : STORAGE_ERROR raised if there is not enough memory to
--                  approximate the integral to the given error tolerance
```

Your first task is to complete the body of this generic integration function. Your integration function should calculate the area using one trapezoid and then calculate the area using two trapezoids (using the formulas given earlier). If the absolute value of the estimated error is less than the specified error, return the sum of the two trapezoids (the better approximation). This is the base case of a recursive algorithm.

If the error is not acceptable, call the function recursively for each half of the curve and return the sum of the two results. We are only calculating half of the area in each of these recursive calls, so the value for the acceptable error passed in to these two recursive calls must be half of what we would tolerate for the entire area.

Next, write a program that instantiates your generic integration function with a floating point type with 15 digits of precision; that prompts for and reads in values of A, B, and Epsilon; and that displays the results of the integrations of the following functions:

$$f(x) = 1$$
$$f(x) = x$$
$$f(x) = e^{-x^2}$$
$$f(x) = (1/3 - x)^{1/3}$$
$$f(x) = 4 / (1 + x^2)$$
$$f(x) = \sin(x) - 0.5 \cos(x)$$

The generic package `Ada.Numerics.Generic_Elementary_Functions` contains the mathematical functions `Exp` (for calculating *e* raised to a power), `**` (for raising a real number to a real power), `Sin`, and `Cos` that you will need to write these functions in Ada.

To check your results, search the web for an online calculator for definite integrals. Compare your answers to what you get from the calculator.

Binary Search Trees

Goals for this chapter include that you should be able to

- define and use the following terminology:

  - binary tree
  - binary search tree
  - root
  - leaf
  - parent
  - child
  - ancestor
  - descendant
  - level
  - height
  - subtree
  - perfect binary tree
  - complete binary tree

- given a binary tree, identify the order the nodes would be visited for preorder, inorder, and postorder traversals.

- define a binary search tree at the logical level.

- show what a binary search tree would look like after a series of insertions and deletions.

- implement the following binary search tree algorithms in Ada:

  - creating an empty tree
  - inserting an element
  - deleting an element
  - retrieving an element
  - modifying an element
  - counting the number of nodes
  - traversing a tree in preorder, inorder, and postorder.

- discuss the Big-O efficiency of a given binary search tree operation.

- describe an algorithm for balancing a binary search tree.

- show how a binary tree can be represented in an array, with implicit positional links between the elements.

We have discussed some of the advantages of using a linear linked list to store value-ordered information. One of the drawbacks of using a linear linked list is the time it takes to search a long list. A sequential search of (possibly) all the nodes in the whole list is an O(N) operation. In Chapter 1 we saw how a binary search could find an element in an ordered list stored sequentially in an array. The binary search is an $O(\log_2 N)$ operation. It would be nice if we could binary search a linked list, but there is no practical way to find the midpoint of a linked list of nodes. We can, however, reorganize the list's elements into a linked structure that is just perfect for binary searching: the binary search tree. The binary search tree provides us with a structure that retains the flexibility of a linked list while allowing quicker [$O(\log_2 N)$ in the average case] access to any node in the list.

This chapter introduces some basic tree vocabulary and then develops the algorithms and implementations of the operations needed to use a binary search tree. Our application uses a binary search tree to calculate the frequency of words in a text file.

10.1 Trees

Each node in a singly linked list may point to one other node: the one whose value follows it in the chain of nodes. Thus a singly linked list is a *linear* structure; each node in the list (except the last) has a unique successor. A **tree** is a nonlinear structure in which each node is capable of having many successor nodes, called *children*. Each of the children, being nodes in a tree, can also have many child nodes, and these children can also have many children, and so on, giving the tree its branching structure. The predecessor of a node in a tree is called the *parent* of that node. The "beginning" of the tree is a unique starting node called the **root**. The root node does not have a parent. Trees are useful for representing hierarchical relationships among data items. Figure 10.1 shows three example hierarchies. The first is an outline of the chapters, sections, and subsections of this textbook; the second represents the hierarchical relationship among Ada's scalar types; and the third represents a scientific classification of butterflies.

> **Tree** A structure with a unique starting node (the root), in which each node is capable of having many child nodes, and in which a unique path exists from the root to every other node.
>
> **Root** The top node of a tree structure; a node with no parent.

Trees are recursive structures. You can view any tree node as being the root of its own tree; such a tree is called a *subtree* of the original tree. For example, in Figure 10.1(b) the node labeled "discrete" is the root of a subtree containing all of the discrete data types. There is one more defining quality of a tree: Its subtrees are disjoint; that is they do not share any nodes. Another way of expressing this property is to say that there is a unique path from the root of a tree to any other node in the tree. This means that every node (except the root) has a unique parent. In the structure shown in Figure 10.2, this rule is violated any way you look at it: the subtrees of A are not disjoint; there are two paths from the root to the node containing D; and D has two parents. Therefore, this structure is not a tree.

Trees are useful structures. In this chapter we concentrate on a particular form of tree: the binary tree. We first introduce you to general binary trees and then concentrate on a particular type of binary tree: the binary search tree.

(a) A Textbook

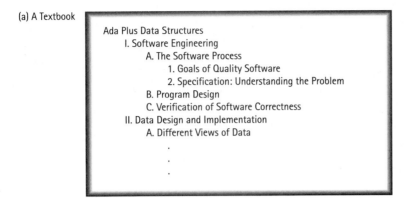

(b) Scalar Data Types

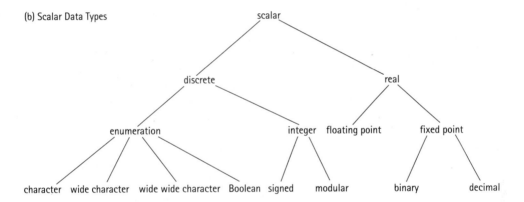

(c) Scientific Classificaitoin of Butterflies and Moths

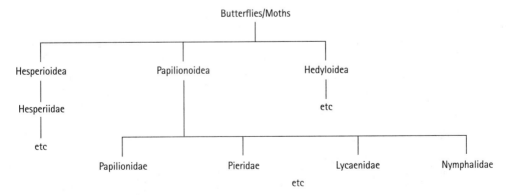

Figure 10.1 *Trees model hierarchical relationships.*

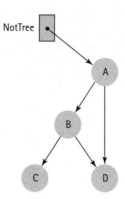

Figure 10.2 *A structure that is not a tree.*

Binary Trees

A **binary tree** is a tree in which each node is capable of having two children. Figure 10.3 depicts a binary tree. The root node of this binary tree contains the value A. Each node in the tree may have 0, 1, or 2 children. The child to the left of a node, if it exists, is called its *left child*. For instance, the left child of the root node in Figure 10.3 contains the value B. The child to the right of a node, if it exists, is its *right child*. The right child of the root node in Figure 10.3 contains the value C. The root node is the parent of the nodes containing B and C. If a node in the tree has no children, it is called a **leaf**. For instance, the nodes containing G, H, E, I, and J are leaf nodes.

Note that in Figure 10.3 each of the root node's children is itself the root of a smaller binary tree. The root node's left child, containing B, is the root of its *left subtree*, while the right child, containing C, is the root of its *right subtree*. In fact, any node in the tree can be considered the root node of a subtree. The subtree whose root node has the value B also includes the nodes with values D, G, H, and E. These nodes are the *descendants* of the node containing B. The descendants of the node containing C are the nodes with the values F, I, and J. A node is an *ancestor* of another node if it is the parent of the node, or the parent of some other ancestor of that node. (Yes, this is a recursive definition.) The ancestors of the node with the value G are the nodes containing D, B, and A. Obviously, the root of the tree is an ancestor of every other node in the tree.

> **Binary Tree** A tree in which each node is capable of having two child nodes, a left child node and a right child node.
>
> **Leaf** A tree node that has no children.
>
> **Level** The distance of a node from the root node.
>
> **Height** The number of levels in a tree.

The **level** of a node refers to its distance from the root. Therefore, in Figure 10.3 the level of the node containing A (the root node) is 0 (zero), the level of the nodes containing B and C is 1; the level of the nodes containing D, E, and F is 2; and the level of the nodes containing G, H, I, and J is 3.

The number of levels in a tree determines its **height**. The maximum number of nodes at any level is 2^L (where L is the level number). Often, however, levels do not contain the maximum number of nodes. For instance, in Figure 10.3, Level 2 could contain four nodes, but because the node containing C in Level 1 has only one child, Level 2

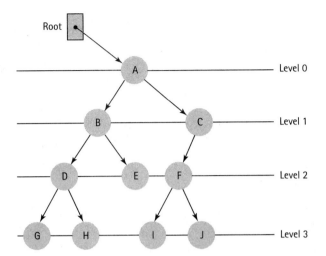

Figure 10.3 *A binary tree.*

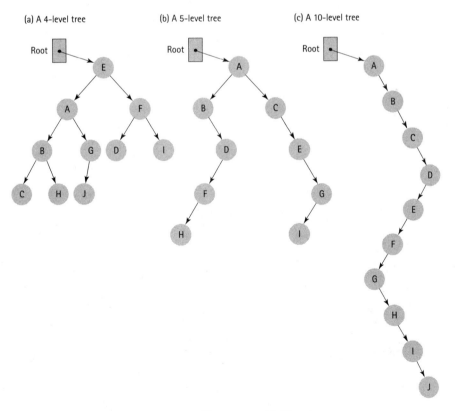

Figure 10.4 *Binary trees with 10 nodes.*

contains three nodes. Level 3, which could contain eight nodes, has only four. We could make many differently shaped binary trees out of the 10 nodes in this tree. A few variations are illustrated in Figure 10.4.

It is easy to see that the maximum number of levels in a binary tree with N nodes is N (Figure 10.4[c]). What is the minimum number of levels? If we fill the tree by giving every node in each level two children until we run out of nodes, the tree has $\lceil \log_2(N + 1) \rceil$ levels. The symbols $\lceil\ \rceil$ around the expression designate the ceiling function, which converts a real value to an integer value by selecting the next largest integer. For example, $\lceil 7.95 \rceil$ and $\lceil 7.05 \rceil$ are both 8. The following table shows the minimum tree height possible for various numbers of nodes.

Minimum Heights of Binary Trees

N	$\log_2(N + 1)$	$\lceil \log_2(N + 1) \rceil$
1	1.000	1
2	1.585	2
3	2.000	2
4	2.322	3
5	2.585	3
6	2.807	3
7	3.000	3
8	3.170	4
9	3.322	4
10	3.459	4
100	6.658	7
1000	9.967	10
10,000	13.288	14
100,000	16.610	17
1,000,000	19.932	20

The height of a tree is the critical factor in determining how efficiently we can search for elements. Consider the maximum-height tree in Figure 10.4(c). If we begin searching at the root node and follow the pointers from one node to the next, accessing the node with the value J (the farthest from the root) is an O(N) operation—no better than searching a linear list! On the other hand, given the minimum-height tree depicted in Figure 10.4(a), to access the node containing J, we only have to look at three other nodes—the ones containing E, A, and G—before we find J. Thus, if the tree is of minimum height, its structure supports O($\log_2 N$) access to any element.

However, the arrangement of the values in the tree pictured in Figure 10.4(a) does not lend itself to quick searching. Let's say that we want to find the value G. We begin searching at the root of the tree. This node contains E, not G, so we need to keep searching. But which of its children should we look at next, the right or the left? There is no special order to the nodes, so we have to check both subtrees. We could search the tree, level by level, until we come across the value we are searching for, but that is an $O(N)$ search operation, which can be accomplished more easily with a linear list.

Binary Search Trees

To support $O(\log_2 N)$ searching, we add a special property based on the relationship among the keys of the items in the binary tree. We put all the nodes with values smaller than the value in the root into its left subtree, and all the nodes with values larger than the value in the root into its right subtree. Figure 10.5 shows the nodes from Figure 10.4(a) rearranged to satisfy this property. The root node, which contains E, has two subtrees. The left subtree contains all the values smaller than E and the right subtree contains all the values larger than E.

Searching for the value G, we look first in the root node. G is larger than E, so we know that G must be in the root node's right subtree. The right child of the root node

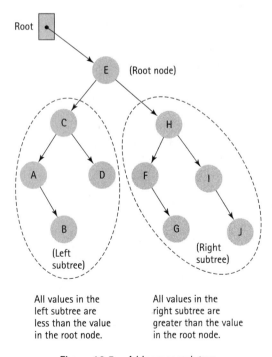

Figure 10.5 *A binary search tree.*

contains H. Now what? Do we go to the right or to the left? This subtree is also arranged according to the binary search property: The nodes with smaller values are to the left and the nodes with larger values are to the right. The value of this node, H, is greater than G, so we search to its left. The left child of this node contains the value F, which is smaller than G, so we reapply the rule and move to the right. The node to the right contains G; we have found the node we were searching for.

A binary tree with this special property is called a **binary search tree**. Like any binary tree, it gets its branching structure by allowing each node to have up to two child nodes. It gets its easy-to-search structure by maintaining the *binary search property*: The left child of any node (if there is one) is the root of the subtree that contains all of the values smaller than the node. The right child of any node (if there is one) is the root of the subtree that contains all of the values that are larger than the node. Like the key-ordered list of Chapter 7, the binary search tree may not contain duplicate keys.

> **Binary search tree** A binary tree in which the key value in every node is greater than the key values in its left subtree and less than the key values in its right subtree.

Four comparisons instead of up to 10 doesn't sound like such a big deal, but as the number of elements in the structure increases, the difference becomes impressive. In the worst case—searching for the last node in a linear linked list—you must look at every node in the list; on the average you must search half the list. If the list contains 1 million nodes, you must make 1 million comparisons to find the last node! If the 1 million nodes were arranged in a binary search tree of minimum height, you would never make more than 20 comparisons, no matter which node you were seeking!

Binary Tree Traversals

As with the list, to traverse a tree means to process all its nodes—for example, to display all of the values in the tree or to delete all the elements in the tree. What orders are possible? For linear lists, the most common orders are forward (from smallest to largest value) and backward (largest to smallest value). Other orders are also possible for linear lists. For example, we could process the odd elements (the first, third, fifth, and so on) and then process the even elements. Such a processing order is rare. Lists are almost always traversed forward or backward.

To traverse a linear linked list, we set a temporary pointer to the first node of the list and then follow the `next` field from one node to the other until we reach a node whose `next` field is `null`. Similarly, to traverse a binary tree, we initialize our pointer to the root of the tree. But where do we go from there—to the left or to the right? Do we process the root or the leaves first? The answer is "all of these." As with lists, there are many ways to traverse a tree.

Our traversal definitions depend upon the relative order in which we process a root and its subtrees. We define the three most common traversals here:

- *Preorder traversal:* Process the root, traverse the left subtree, traverse the right subtree.
- *Inorder traversal:* Traverse the left subtree, process the root, traverse the right subtree.

- *Postorder traversal:* Traverse the left subtree, traverse the right subtree, process the root.

Notice that the name given to each traversal specifies where the root itself is processed in relation to its subtrees. Also note that these are recursive definitions.

We can visualize each of these traversal orders by drawing a "loop" around a binary tree, as in Figure 10.6. Before drawing the loop, extend the nodes of the tree that have less than two children with short lines so that every node has two "edges." Then draw the loop from the root of the tree, down the left subtree, and back up again, hugging the shape of the tree as you go. Each node of the tree is "touched" three times by the loop (the touches are numbered in the figure): once on the way down before the left subtree is reached, once after finishing the left subtree but before starting the right subtree, and once on the way up, after finishing the right subtree. To generate a preorder traversal, follow the loop and visit each node the first time it is touched (before visiting the left subtree). To generate an inorder traversal, follow the loop and visit each node the second time it is touched (in between visiting the two subtrees). To generate a postorder

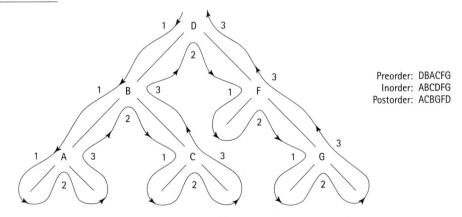

Figure 10.6 *Visualizing binary tree traversals.*

traversal, follow the loop and visit each node the third time it is touched (after visiting the right subtree). Use this method on the tree in Figure 10.7 and see if you agree with the listed traversal orders.

You may have noticed that an inorder traversal of a binary search tree visits the nodes in order from the smallest to the largest. Obviously, this would be useful when we need to access the elements in ascending key order; for example, to print a sorted list of the elements. There are also useful applications of the other traversal orders. For example, the preorder and postorder traversals can be used to translate infix arithmetic expressions into their prefix and postfix counterparts.

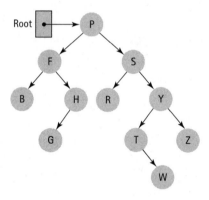

Inorder: B F G H P R S T W Y Z
Preorder: P F B H G S R Y T W Z
Postorder: B G H F R W T Z Y S P

Figure 10.7 *A binary search tree.*

10.2 The Logical Level

Now let's specify a binary search tree class. Our binary search tree specification is very similar to our key-ordered list specification. That is not surprising, because both are typically used to store and retrieve sorted data. The generic formal parameters are identical to those of our key-ordered list. We can easily change an application that uses one of these classes to the other without affecting the program.

Although we could define a binary search tree class with the exact same operations as our list, we have elected to show you a different approach to processing items in a container class. Our binary search tree specification includes the notion of a *current element*. One element in the tree is designated as the current element. The retrieve and modify operations operate on the current element.

The current element is not always defined. For example, an empty tree has no elements, so it cannot have a current element. Should we delete the current element, it is no longer defined. Our specification includes the Boolean function `Current_Defined`, which returns whether the current element is defined. `Modify` and `Retrieve` raise the exception `CURRENT_UNDEFINED` in an attempt to access an undefined current element. The current element is typically set through the search operation `Find`, which locates the tree element with a given key. The insert operation also sets the current element.

Using a current element improves the performance of changing an element in a container. To change an element we must retrieve it from the container, make our changes, and then put it back into the container. In our key-ordered list class our implementation must search the list twice to accomplish such a change: once when we call `Retrieve` and a second time when we call `Modify`. In our binary search tree class we search the tree once when we call `Find` to set the current element. Calls to `Retrieve` and `Modify` do not require searches because they operate on the previously located current element.

The container classes in the standard Ada library extend the idea of an implicit current element. Each of the container classes includes an explicit cursor type. Just as a cursor on the window of a word processing program marks the current location within the document, a cursor for a container class marks a specific element in the collection. The application programmer may create as many cursors as he or she desires.

Specification 10.1 supports all three of the traversal orders discussed in the previous section. We use a single traversal procedure with a parameter to identify which traversal order we desire.

Specification 10.1   Binary Search Tree

```ada
with Ada.Finalization;
generic

    type Element_Type is private;          -- The type of element in the list
    type Key_Type is limited private;      -- The type of key in the element

    -- The user must supply a function that returns the Key of an Element
    with function Key_Of (Element : in Element_Type) return Key_Type;
    -- The user must supply functions for comparing Keys
    with function "=" (Left : in Key_Type; Right : in Key_Type) return Boolean;
    with function "<" (Left : in Key_Type; Right : in Key_Type) return Boolean;

package Binary_Search_Tree is

-- This package implements a binary search tree.
-- Each element in the tree is identified by a unique key.

-- The tree class includes the notion of a current element in the tree.
-- The retrieve and modify operations are performed on the current node.
```

```ada
type Tree_Type is new Ada.Finalization.Limited_Controlled with private;

type Traversal_Order is (Inorder, Preorder, Postorder);

DUPLICATE_KEY     : exception;
KEY_ERROR         : exception;
OVERFLOW          : exception;
CURRENT_UNDEFINED : exception;

-- Transformers

-----------------------------------------------------------------------
procedure Clear (Tree : in out Tree_Type);
-- Purpose        : Removes all elements from Tree.
-- Preconditions  : None
-- Postconditions : Tree is empty.


-----------------------------------------------------------------------
procedure Insert (Tree : in out Tree_Type;
                  Item : in     Element_Type);
-- Purpose        : Adds Item to Tree.
-- Preconditions  : None
-- Postconditions : Tree = original Tree + Item
--                  Item becomes the current element
-- Exceptions     : OVERFLOW      If there is no room for Item.
--                  DUPLICATE_KEY If an element already exists in the tree
--                                with the same key as Item.
--                                Tree is unchanged in both cases.


-----------------------------------------------------------------------
procedure Delete (Tree : in out Tree_Type;
                  Key  : in     Key_Type);
-- Purpose        : Deletes the element with the given Key from Tree
-- Preconditions  : None
-- Postconditions : Tree = original Tree with the Key element removed
--                  If the element removed was the current element, the
--                  current element is not defined.
-- Exceptions     : KEY_ERROR  If Key is not found in Tree.
--                             Tree is unchanged.


-----------------------------------------------------------------------
procedure Modify (Tree    : in out Tree_Type;
                  Element : in     Element_Type);
-- Purpose        : Replace current element with Element.
-- Preconditions  : None
```

```
-- Postconditions : The current element is replaced by Element
-- Exceptions     : CURRENT_UNDEFINED  If the current element is not
--                                     defined.  Tree is unchanged.
--                  KEY_ERROR          If Element has a different key than the
--                                     current element.  Tree and current
--                                     element are unchanged.

-------------------------------------------------------------------------------
procedure Find (Tree : in out Tree_Type;
                Key  : in     Key_Type);
-- Purpose        : Searches Tree for Key
-- Preconditions  : None
-- Postconditions : If there is an element with Key in Tree, that element
--                  becomes the current element for the Tree.  If the Key
--                  is not found in Tree, the current element is undefined.


-- Observers

-------------------------------------------------------------------------------
function Current_Defined (Tree : in Tree_Type) return Boolean;
-- Purpose        : Determines whether a current element is defined
-- Preconditions  : None
-- Postconditions : Returns True if a current element is defined, otherwise
--                  returns False.

-------------------------------------------------------------------------------
function Empty (Tree : in Tree_Type) return Boolean;
-- Purpose        : Determines whether Tree is empty.
-- Preconditions  : None
-- Postconditions : Empty = (Tree is empty)

-------------------------------------------------------------------------------
function Full (Tree : in Tree_Type) return Boolean;
-- Purpose        : Determines whether Tree is full.
-- Preconditions  : None
-- Postconditions : Full = (Tree is full)

-------------------------------------------------------------------------------
function Size (Tree : in Tree_Type) return Natural;
-- Purpose        : Determines the number of elements in Tree.
-- Preconditions  : None
-- Postconditions : Size = number of elements in Tree

-------------------------------------------------------------------------------
```

```
procedure Retrieve (Tree     : in      Tree_Type;
                    Element  :     out Element_Type);
-- Purpose         : Get an element from Tree
-- Preconditions   : None
-- Postconditions  : Element is a copy of the current element of Tree.
-- Exceptions      : CURRENT_UNDEFINED  If the current element is not
--                                      defined.

-- Iterator
-----------------------------------------------------------------------------
procedure Traverse
      (Tree    : in out Tree_Type;
       Order   : in Traversal_Order;
       Process : not null access procedure (Element : in out Element_Type));
-- Purpose         : Process all the elements in Tree in the given Order
-- Preconditions   : Procedure Process does not change the key of an element
-- Postconditions  : Every element in Tree is passed to a call of
--                   procedure Process. Elements processed in the given Order.

private

   -- We fill this in later

end Binary_Search_Tree;
```

10.3 The Application Level

Problem: Our firm is planning to create some text analysis software, for example, software that automatically calculates the reading level of a document. As a first step, we've been assigned the task of creating a prototype word frequency generator. This generator is to be used to perform some preliminary text analysis during the planning stage of the project; if it works well it may be incorporated into the tools developed later.

The word frequency generator is to read a text file indicated by the user, and generate an alphabetical listing of the unique words that it contains, along with a count of how many times each word occurs. The output is to go to a text file, also indicated by the user. To allow the users to control the amount of useful output from the generator, based on the particular problem they are studying, the generator must allow the users to specify a minimum word size and a minimum frequency count. The generator should skip over words smaller than the minimum word size; the generator should not include a word on its output list if the word occurs fewer times than the minimum frequency count.

Discussion: Clearly, the desired output in this problem is a list of words with associated frequencies. Therefore, the first thing we must do is define a "word."

We discuss this question with our manager. What is a tentative definition of a word in this context? How about "something between two blanks"? Or better yet, a "character string between two blanks." That definition works for most words. However, all words before '.' and ',' would have the '.' and ',' attached. Also, words with quotes would cause a problem. Therefore, we settle on the following definition: A word is a string of alphabetical characters between markers where markers are all characters other than letters. Although we "lose" some words following this definition (for example, contractions such as "can't" are treated as two words, "can" and "t"), we decide that these small problems do not adversely affect our goals. Finally, our manager points out that all words should be transformed into lowercase characters for processing—"THE" and "the" represent the same word.

Brainstorming: As usual, the first step is to list objects that might be useful in solving the problem. Scanning the problem statement, we identify the following "nouns": word frequency generator, input text file, user, alphabetical listing, unique words, word count, output text file, minimum word size, minimum frequency count, and output list. That's 10 candidate objects. We realize that we need to use a data structure to store words—for now we just call it the word store and add that to our list, giving us 11 candidate objects.

Listing the verbs in a problem statement often helps identify the actions our program needs to take. In this case, however, we are clear on the actions needed: read in the words, determine their frequencies, and output the results. A quick scan of the problem statement reminds us that the results are to be sorted alphabetically and that some pruning of the data is required based on minimum thresholds for word size and word frequency.

Filtering: We have identified 11 candidate objects. A few of them can be discarded immediately: the word frequency generator is the entire program; minimum word size and minimum frequency count are input values. Some of the candidate objects (input text file, user, output text file, output list) are related to the user interface discussed next. The remaining four candidates are grouped as follows:

- *Unique words, word count:* These two are related because we need to have a word count for each unique word. The frequency is simply a `Natural` value. We decide to represent words as unbounded-length strings. Finally, we can create a record called `Freq_Rec` to hold a word-frequency pair.
- *Alphabetical listing, word store:* We realize that we can combine these objects by using a container that supports sorted traversals to hold our frequency records. The key-ordered list and binary search tree classes are both candidates for these objects. Given the topic of this chapter you should not be surprised at our choice of binary search tree.

Because this is a prototype we will not create a robust or graphical interface for this program. We will just prompt the user to enter the filenames and minimum values for word lengths and frequencies. For the same reason, we will not worry about checking input values for validity.

Here is the basic algorithm we developed for the frequency generator:

Frequency Generator
    Get user data (Input and Output file names, minimum word and frequency values)
    Prepare the files

```
loop
    exit when there is no data left in the input file
    Get one Line from the input file
    Process the words in the Line
end loop
Generate the report
Close the files
```

There are some steps that need further work before we can turn them into Ada code.

Process the Words in a Line
```
convert all letters in Line to lowercase
loop
    Take (remove) the first Word from Line
    if the length of Word ≥ Minimum word length then
        if Word is already in the binary search tree
            increment the Word's frequency
        else
            add the Word to the binary search tree
        end if
    end if
end loop
```

Generate the Report
```
Create headings
Traverse the binary search tree in inorder using a process procedure that displays one word
```

Here is the logic of the procedure we pass to our inorder traversal:

Process one Word (the process passed to the binary search tree traversal)
```
if the Word's frequency ≥ Minimum frequency then
    display the frequency and word
end if
```

We need to use a number of the string operations we studied in Chapter 4 to carry out the separation of words in the input line. This separation process is often called tokenizing. The string operation `Find_Token` is especially useful for this task. This operation requires three `in` parameters: the string we are searching, a set of characters for distinguishing between tokens and token separators, and a value to indicate whether the given set of characters is for the tokens or the separators. For our application we use the set of letters predefined in `Ada.Strings.Maps.Constants`. Our tokens are composed of characters `Inside` of this set. `Find_Token` returns the positions of the first and last characters of the token within the string. We use a slice operation to obtain a copy of the token and a delete operation to remove the token from the string.

Once we have a word that is not below our minimum length, we can search to see if it is already in the binary search tree. If it is, we need to retrieve its record, increment the frequency count, and return the modified record to the tree. If our word is not in the binary search tree, we set the frequency to one and insert it.

The generation of the report is simply a matter of calling the binary search tree traverse operation, passing in the desired order (inorder) and a pointer to a procedure to process one element of the tree. This processing procedure first checks to see if the frequency of the particular word is at least the minimum frequency before putting the information into the output file. Notice the nesting of our `Put_One_Word` procedure within the `Create_Report` procedure. The process procedure for the binary search tree iterator, `Traverse`, is restricted to a single parameter, a tree element. The nesting allows our element processing procedure to access the `Min_Freq` parameter of the enclosing procedure that we need to check our word against.

Program 10.1 shows the resulting program.

Program 10.1   Word Frequency Generator

```ada
with Binary_Search_Tree;
with Ada.Text_IO;                       use Ada.Text_IO;
with Ada.Text_IO.Unbounded_IO;          use Ada.Text_IO.Unbounded_IO;
with Ada.Integer_Text_IO;               use Ada.Integer_Text_IO;
with Ada.Strings.Unbounded;             use Ada.Strings.Unbounded;    use Ada.Strings;
with Ada.Characters.Handling;           use Ada.Characters.Handling;
with Ada.Strings.Maps.Constants;
procedure Word_Frequency is

-- This program creates a text file containing a word frequency list.
--
-- Input:   Name of text file with data
--          Name of output file for results
--          Minimum length of words to include in the frequency list
--          Minimum number of occurrences needed to include word in list

   -- Declarations for a binary search tree of word frequency records
   -----------------------------------------------------------------------
   type Freq_Rec is
      record
         Word : Unbounded_String;
         Freq : Natural;
      end record;

   function Word_Of (Element: in Freq_Rec) return Unbounded_String is
   begin
      return Element.Word;
   end Word_Of;
```

```ada
package Freq_Tree is new Binary_Search_Tree
                  (Element_Type =>  Freq_Rec,
                   Key_Type     =>  Unbounded_String,
                   Key_Of       =>  Word_Of,
                   "="          =>  Ada.Strings.Unbounded."=",
                   "<"          =>  Ada.Strings.Unbounded."<");
use Freq_Tree;
```

```ada
procedure Process_Words (Line     : in out Unbounded_String;
                         Min_Size : in     Positive;
                         Tree     : in out Freq_Tree.Tree_Type) is
-- Purpose        : Processes all the words in Line
-- Preconditions  : None
-- Postconditions : The frequency Tree is updated with all words of
--                  adequate size in Line.  All words are removed from Line

   Word    : Unbounded_String;   -- One word from Line
   First   : Natural;            -- Positions of the first and last
   Last    : Natural;            -- characters in a word within Line
   Element : Freq_Rec;           -- Element for the frequency tree

begin
   -- Convert all characters to lowercase using Ada.Characters.Handling
   Line := To_Unbounded_String (To_Lower (To_String(Line)));

   -- Process all the words in Line
   -- Each iteration, process one word
   loop
      -- Find the first word (a sequence of letters) in Line
      Find_Token (Source => Line,
                  Set    => Ada.Strings.Maps.Constants.Letter_Set,
                  Test   => Ada.Strings.Inside,
                  First  => First,
                  Last   => Last);
      exit when Last = 0;  -- All done when there are no words in Line
      -- Get a copy of the word
      Word := Unbounded_Slice (Source => Line,
                               Low    => First,
                               High   => Last);
      -- Remove the word from the Line
      Delete (Source => Line, From => 1, Through => Last);

      -- Only process words that are at or above the minimum size
      if Length (Word) >= Min_Size then
         -- Is Word already in our frequency tree?
```

```ada
            Tree.Find(Word);
            if Tree.Current_Defined then
               -- Increment the frequency in the word
               Tree.Retrieve (Element);
               Element.Freq := Element.Freq + 1;
               Tree.Modify (Element);
            else
               -- Add a new word to the tree
               Element.Word := Word;
               Element.Freq := 1;
               Tree.Insert (Element);
            end if;
         end if;

      end loop;
   end Process_Words;

   ----------------------------------------------------------------------------
   procedure Create_Report (File     : in out Ada.Text_IO.File_Type;
                            Min_Freq : in     Positive;
                            Tree     : in out Freq_Tree.Tree_Type) is
   -- Purpose         : Put frequency tree data into a text file
   -- Preconditions   : File is open for output
   -- Postconditions  : File contains an alphabetical listing of words and
   --                   frequencies of those words in Tree with frequencies
   --                   at or above Min_Freq.

      procedure Put_One_Word (Element : in out Freq_Rec) is
      begin
         if Element.Freq >= Min_Freq then
            Put (File => File, Item => Element.Freq, Width => 9);
            Put (File => File, Item => "  ");
            Put_Line (File => File, Item => Element.Word);
         end if;
      end Put_One_Word;

   begin
      Put_Line (File => File, Item => "Frequency  Word");
      Put_Line (File => File, Item => "---------  ----");
      New_Line (File);
      Tree.Traverse (Order => Inorder, Process => Put_One_Word'Access);
   end Create_Report;

   ----------------------------------------------------------------------------
   File_Name   : Unbounded_String;              -- Input and Output files
```

```ada
      Input_File  : Ada.Text_IO.File_Type;
      Output_File : Ada.Text_IO.File_Type;

      Min_Size  : Positive;                      -- Word filtering parameters
      Min_Freq  : Positive;

      Frequency_Tree : Freq_Tree.Tree_Type;      -- Words and their frequencies
      Line           : Unbounded_String;         -- One line from the input file

   begin
      -- Get the parameters for the run and prepare the two files
      Put_Line ("Enter the name of the text file you would like to analyze.");
      Get_Line (File_Name);
      Open (File => Input_File, Mode => In_File, Name => To_String(File_Name));
      New_Line;
      Put_Line ("Enter the name of the text file for the results.");
      Get_Line (File_Name);
      Create (File => Output_File, Name => To_String(File_Name));
      New_Line;
      Put_Line ("Enter the minimum word size.");
      Get (Min_Size);
      Put_Line ("Enter the minimum frequency to report.");
      Get (Min_Freq);

      -- Process all of the words in the input file
      -- Each iteration, process one line of the file
      loop
         exit when End_Of_File (Input_File);
         Get_Line (File => Input_File, Item => Line);
         Process_Words (Line, Min_Size, Frequency_Tree);
      end loop;
      Close(Input_File);

      -- Generate results file
      Create_Report (Output_File, Min_Freq, Frequency_Tree);
      Close (Output_File);

   end Word_Frequency;
```

Testing: This program should first be tested using small files, where it is easy for us to determine the expected output. We should test the program on a series of input files, with varying minimum word sizes and frequency counts. Here are the results of running the program on a text file version of the program itself. The minimum word size was set to 4 and the minimum frequency count was set to 5.

```
Frequency  Word
---------  ----
        5  begin
        5  characters
       16  element
       46  file
        6  first
       22  freq
       15  frequency
        5  from
        9  input
        6  item
        7  last
       33  line
        5  minimum
       11  name
        7  output
        9  process
        8  size
       11  string
        8  strings
       14  text
       28  tree
        9  type
       15  unbounded
       10  with
       32  word
       14  words
```

10.4 The Implementation Level

In this section we develop the algorithms for the binary search tree operations and implement them with a linked structure whose nodes are allocated dynamically. Here are the declarations for the private part of Specification 10.1:

```
private

   type Node_Type;                        -- Incomplete type declaration
   type Node_Ptr is access Node_Type;     -- Access to a node
```

```
   type Node_Type is                           -- Complete type declaration
      record
         Info  : Element_Type;    -- One element
         Left  : Node_Ptr;        -- Link to left child
         Right : Node_Ptr;        -- Link to right child
      end record;

   type Tree_Type is new Ada.Finalization.Limited_Controlled with
      record
         Root    : Node_Ptr;  -- Designates first node in the tree
         Current : Node_Ptr;  -- Designates the current node in the tree
      end record;

   overriding procedure Finalize (Tree: in out Tree_Type) renames Clear;

end Binary_Search_Tree;
```

Each node contains an element and two pointers that designate the left and right subtrees of the node. As we have done for all of our linked data structures, we have made `Tree_Type` a subclass of `Ada.Finalization.Limited_Controlled` to prevent memory leaks within applications using our class. `Tree_Type` has two pointers: one to the node that is the root of the binary search tree and one to the node that contains the current element in the tree. Figure 10.8 shows an example of a tree based on this implementation.

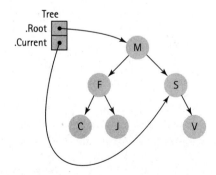

Figure 10.8 *A binary search tree whose current element is S.*

Simple Binary Search Tree Operations

A tree is empty if it has no nodes. In this case, the root is null. Our algorithm for empty is simply:

Empty
    return Tree.Root = null

We take the same approach with the full operation as we did with all of our data structures based on dynamically allocated nodes—simply return false.

Full
    return False

Our current element is designated by a pointer, so it is easy to determine whether there is a current element.

Current Defined
    return Tree.Current /= null

We have a pointer to the current node in the tree, so the retrieve and modify operations do not require a search. We simply access the node designated by Tree.Current. We do need to handle the case where the current element is not defined. Here are the algorithms:

Retrieve
    if Tree.Current = null
        raise CURRENT_UNDEFINED
    else
        Element := Tree.Current.all.Info
    end if

Modify
    if Tree.Current = null
        raise CURRENT_UNDEFINED
    else
        Tree.Current.all.Info := Element
    end if

The Ada implementations of these five operations are given in Body 10.1.

Recursive Binary Search Tree Operations

Because the binary search tree is inherently a recursive structure, we first implement the remaining algorithms using recursive solutions. In a later section we develop iterative `Insert` and `Delete` operations.

The `Size` Operation   When we developed function `Factorial` in Chapter 9 we said that we could determine the factorial of N if we knew the factorial of $N - 1$. The analogous statement here is, we can determine the number of nodes in the tree if we know the number of nodes in the left subtree and the number of nodes in the right subtree. This gives us the general case for our `Size` operation.

return 1 + Size (Left Subtree) + Size (Right Subtree)

Do you see where the 1 comes from? It is the root node.

What about the base case? We need a tree whose size is trivial to determine. The simplest tree is an empty tree. The size of an empty tree is zero. Here, then, is a recursive algorithm with our base and general cases:

Size
    if Tree is empty then
        return 0
    else
        return 1 + Size (Left Subtree) + Size (Right Subtree)
    end if

Let's use our three-question method to verify this recursive function:

1. *The base-case question:* The base case occurs when the tree is empty. `Size` is then assigned a value of 0, which is the correct value for a tree with no nodes, and no further (recursive) calls to `Size` are made. The answer is yes.

2. *The smaller-caller question:* To answer this question we must look at the parameters passed in the recursive call. There are two recursive calls in function `Size`. The first recursive call passes the left subtree and the second passes the right subtree. Each recursive call is made with a subtree that is *at least* one node smaller than the current tree. Eventually, the subtree passed will be an empty tree. At this point, as we verified with the base-case question above, we have reached the smallest case, and no further recursive calls are made. The answer is yes.

3. *The general-case question:* In the case of a function like `Size`, we need to verify that the formula we are using actually results in the correct solution. Assuming that the recursive call `Size (Left Subtree)` gives us the correct value of the size of the left subtree and the recursive call `Size (Right Subtree)` gives us the correct value of the size of the right subtree, we calculate the size of the tree as the sum of the sizes of its two subtrees plus one. This is correct for a nonempty tree. In answering the first question, we have already ascertained that the function works for an empty tree. So the answer is yes.

When developing recursive tree algorithms, novice programmers frequently choose to use a different base case: a tree with one node. Although this base case seems simple enough, it inevitably leads to more complicated algorithms than the empty tree base case. When using recursion, always search for the simplest base case. For lists and trees, this is the empty structure.

There is one additional problem to solve in order to translate our recursive `size` algorithm into Ada code. The following direct translation illustrates the problem:

```
-- Direct translation of the recursive size algorithm does not compile
function Size (Tree : in Tree_Type) return Natural is
begin
   if Tree.Root = null then                              -- This is a record type.
      return 0;
   else
      return 1 + Size (Tree.Root.all.Left)
             + Size (Tree.Root.all.Right);
   end if;                                               -- The actual parameters
end Size;                                                   passed in each call
                                                            are access values.
```

The problem is that the `Size`'s parameter `Tree` is a record with two fields, `Root` and `Current`. But our two recursive calls each pass a single access value that designates a child node. One solution is to write the recursive size algorithm as a procedure that accepts an access value parameter inside of the publicly accessible `Size` procedure. Here is the resulting code:

```
-- A valid implementation of the recursive size algorithm
function Size (Tree : in Tree_Type) return Natural is
   function Recursive_Size (Root : in Node_Ptr) return Natural is
   begin
      if Root = null then
         return 0;
      else
         return 1 + Recursive_Size (Root.all.Left)
                + Recursive_Size (Root.all.Right);
      end if;
   end Recursive_Size;
begin
   return Recursive_Size (Tree.Root);
end Size;
```

Here procedure `Size` calls `Recursive_Size`, passing only the pointer that designates the root of the tree. We take the same approach in translating our other recursive algorithms.

What is the Big-O of function `Size`? The recursive function makes two recursive calls for each node in the tree. So for a tree with N nodes, there are $2N$ calls made to calculate the size. Therefore `Size` is $O(N)$. With a slight change to our implementation, we can dramatically improve the performance of the size operation. We could add a third field to the record `Tree_Type` that contains a count of the number of nodes in the tree. This count is initialized to zero, incremented by procedure `Insert`, and decremented by procedure `Delete`. This revised function `Size` returns the value of the count with O(1) effort.

The `Find` Operation   The `Find` operation is used to set the current element. Earlier we described an algorithm to search a binary search tree for a particular value. When we look at a node, there are three possibilities:

1. The node contains the key for which we are searching; we are done.
2. The key for which we are searching is less than the key of the node; we need to search the left subtree of the node.
3. The key for which we are searching is greater than the key of the node; we need to search the right subtree of the node.

This looks like a good candidate for a recursive algorithm. We have already identified a base case and two general cases with smaller calls. There is only one thing missing. What happens when the key for which we are searching is not in the binary search tree? We need a second base case. As usual for recursive tree algorithms, this is the case when the tree we are searching is empty. Here is the algorithm that incorporates all of the cases:

Find
    if Root = null or else Key = Key of the Root node then
        Current := Root   *- - Two base cases (not found and found in root)*
    elsif Key < Key of the Root node then
        Find the Key in the left subtree
    else
        Find the Key in the right subtree
    end if

We must use the shortcut operator `or else` so we do not dereference a `null` pointer when the tree is empty. Can you see that the statement assigning `Root` to `Current` is valid for both base cases in this recursive search algorithm? When the tree is empty, `Root` is `null` and we make `Current` undefined by setting it to `null`. When the root node contains the desired key, `Current` is set to designate that node. The Ada implementation of this algorithm is given in Body 10.1. Notice that we have again nested the recursive algorithm within the `Find` procedure.

The `Insert` Operation   To create and maintain the information stored in a binary search tree, we must have an operation that adds new nodes into the tree. We use the following approach: A new node is always inserted into its appropriate position in the tree as a leaf. Figure 10.9 illustrates this approach by showing a series of insertions into an originally empty binary search tree.

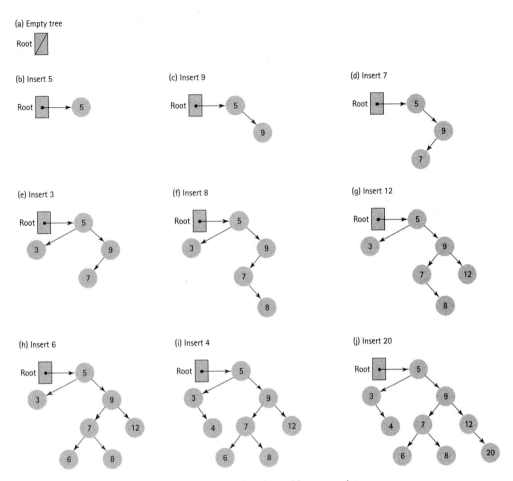

Figure 10.9 *Insertions into a binary search tree.*

Now let's develop an algorithm for the insert operation. From Figure 10.9 we see that the simplest insertion is the first one—inserting an item into an empty tree. As with nearly all recursive tree algorithms, the empty tree is a base case. The general case nearly always involves repeating the algorithm on one of the two child nodes that are each the root of a subtree. Here is our algorithm:

Insert
    if Tree is empty then
        Create a new (root) node containing the Item
    else
        Insert into the appropriate subtree
    end if

The appropriate subtree is determined by comparing the key of the `Item` to the key of the root node. If the `Item`'s key is smaller, we insert it into the left subtree; if the `Item`'s key is larger, we insert it into the right subtree.

Our specification for this operation indicates that the procedure should raise the exception `DUPLICATE_KEY` if a node with the same key as `Item` is in our tree. To accomplish this task, we can, as we did in procedure `Find`, check to see whether the root node contains the key of interest. If it does, we raise the exception. So like `Find`, `Insert` has two base cases and two general cases. Here is the Ada code:

```ada
procedure Insert (Tree : in out Tree_Type;
                  Item : in     Element_Type) is
   procedure Recursive_Insert (Root : in out Node_Ptr;
                               Key  : in     Key_Type) is
   begin
      if Root = null then
         -- Base case, inserting into an empty tree
         Root := new Node_Type'(Info => Item, Left => null, Right => null);
         Tree.Current := Root;  -- Inserted element is the current element
      elsif Key = Key_Of (Root.all.Info) then
         -- Base case, key already in tree
         raise DUPLICATE_KEY;
      elsif Key < Key_Of (Root.all.Info) then
         -- General case: Insert into left subtree
         Recursive_Insert (Root => Root.all.Left, Key => Key);
      else
         -- General case: Insert into right subtree
         Recursive_Insert (Root => Root.all.Right, Key => Key);
      end if;
   end Recursive_Insert;
begin
   Recursive_Insert (Root => Tree.Root, Key => Key_Of(Item));
end Insert;
```

Let's trace this procedure. Procedure `Insert` passes the root of the tree to procedure `Recursive_Insert`. In Figure 10.10(a), we want to insert an `Item` with the key value 13 into the tree whose root node is the node designated by `Root`. Because 13 is greater than 7, we know that the new node belongs in the root node's right subtree. We now have defined a smaller version of our original problem: We want to insert a node with the key value 13 into the tree whose root is designated by `Root.all.Right`. We call `Recursive_Insert` to insert `Item` into this right subtree.

Procedure `Recursive_Insert` begins its second execution, looking for the place to insert Item in the tree whose root is the node with the value 15 (Figure 10.10[b]). We compare the key of Item (13) with the key of the root (15); 13 is less than 15, so we know that Item belongs in the tree's left subtree. Again we have redefined a smaller version of the problem. We want to insert a node with the key value 13 into the tree whose root is designated by Root.all.Left.

Procedure Recursive_Insert begins its third execution. We compare the key of Item (13) to the key of the root node (10) (Figure 10.10[c]), and then call Recursive_Insert to insert Item into the correct subtree. This time it is the subtree designated by Root.all.Right.

At the beginning of the fourth execution of Recursive_Insert we find that Root is null. We have reached a base case. Figure 10.10(d) shows where we create the new node with the call:

Root := new Node_Type'(Info => Item, Left => null, Right => null);

We are now finished with our insertion.

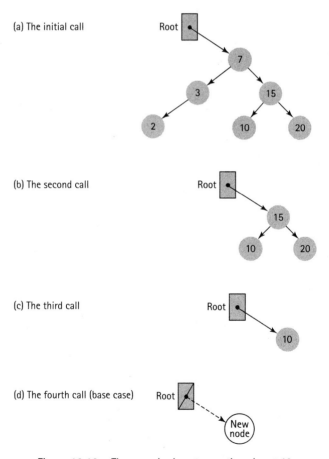

Figure 10.10 *The recursive insert operation—insert 13.*

656 | Chapter 10: Binary Search Trees

Wait a minute! How does this assignment statement link the new node to the existing tree? To understand this point, you must understand that in every recursive execution the formal parameter `Root` is actually an internal pointer. Consider the formal and actual parameters of our recursive call. The last recursive call (Figure 10.11[a]) is

```
Recursive_Insert (Root => Root.all.Right, Item => Item);
```

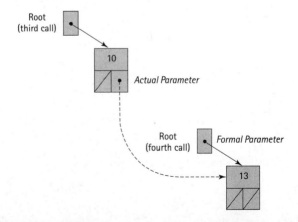

(a) Making the last (fourth) call to Insert

Root (third call) → [10]   `Insert (Root => Root.all.Right, Item => Item);`

(b) Beginning of the last execution of Insert

Root (fourth call) □

(c) Creation of a new node

Root (fourth call) → [13]   `Root := new Node_Type'(Info => Item, Left => null, right => null);`

(d) Copying back of the in out mode parameter

Root (third call) → [10]   *Actual Parameter*

Root (fourth call) → [13]   *Formal Parameter*

Figure 10.11 *The formal parameter* `Root` *copied to the actual parameter* `Root.all.Right`.

Root is an in out parameter. Therefore the value of Root.all.Right (null) is copied into Root when the procedure is called (Figure 10.11[b]). Next, the assignment statement changes the value of Root to one that designates the newly allocated node (Figure 10.11[c]). Now that the fourth execution of the procedure is complete we return to the caller. Because the formal parameter, Root, is mode in out, its value is copied back to the actual parameter (Figure 10.11[d]), linking the node with key 10 to the new node through its right pointer.

Insertion Order and Tree Shape Earlier in this chapter we showed that the height of a tree is the critical factor in determining how efficiently we can search for elements. Let's look at another example. Figure 10.12 illustrates how the same data, inserted in different orders, produce differently shaped trees. If the values are inserted in order (or reverse order), the tree is completely *skewed*. We call such a tree a *degenerate tree*. A random mix of values produces a shorter *bushy* tree. Because the height of the tree determines the maximum number of comparisons to locate an element in the tree, the tree's shape is very important. Obviously, minimizing the height of the tree maximizes the efficiency of searching it. In a later section we will present an algorithm to adjust a tree to make its shape more desirable.

The Delete Operation The Recursive_Delete procedure is given the external pointer to a binary search tree and the key of an element to delete. This operation finds and deletes the node containing that key from the tree. The operation raises the exception KEY_ERROR if no node in the tree contains the given key. From our experience with procedure Find, we know how to recursively search for a node with a given key. We can use a very similar algorithm for a recursive delete procedure.

```
procedure Recursive_Delete (Root : in out Node_Ptr;
                            Key  : in     Key_Type) is
begin
   if Root = null then                                      -- Base case
      raise KEY_ERROR;
   elsif Key = Key_Of (Root.all.Info) then                  -- Base case
      Delete_Root (Root);
   elsif Key < Key_Of (Root.all.Info) then                  -- General case
      Recursive_Delete (Root => Root.all.Left,  Key => Key);
   else                                                     -- General case
      Recursive_Delete (Root => Root.all.Right, Key => Key);
   end if;
end Recursive_Delete;
```

658 | Chapter 10: Binary Search Trees

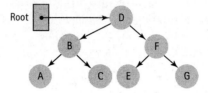

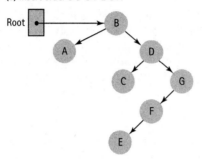

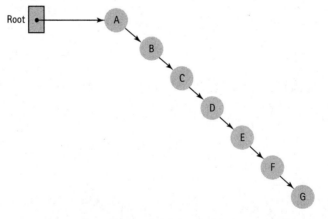

Figure 10.12 *The insert order determines the shape of the tree.*

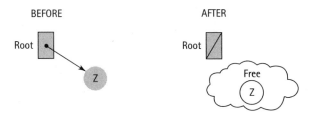

Figure 10.13 *Deleting a root node with no children.*

There is only one difference between this procedure and the one we developed for the recursive Find operation: We delete the root node instead of setting Current to designate it.

It is clear that the delete task will involve changing pointers of the parent of the node we wish to delete. Because our recursive algorithms pass Root as an in out mode parameter, the formal parameter Root is equivalent to the pointer in the parent that we must change (recall Figure 10.11).

We can break down the Delete_Root procedure into three cases, depending on the number of children the root node has:

1. *No children:* The root node is a leaf. As shown in Figure 10.13, deleting a root node with no children is simply a matter of setting Root to null and then deallocating the memory used by the node.

2. *One child:* The simple solution of setting Root to null will not suffice for removing a root node with children, because we don't want to lose all of its descendants from the tree. As illustrated in Figure 10.14, we want to make Root skip over the deleted node and point instead to the child of the node we intend to delete. We then deallocate the memory used by the unwanted node.

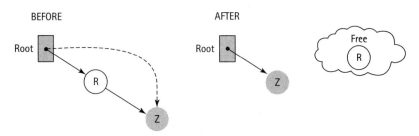

Figure 10.14 *Deleting a root node with one child.*

3. *Two children:* This case is the most complicated because we cannot make `Root` designate *both* of the deleted node's children. The arrangement of nodes in the binary tree must keep the search property intact. There are several ways to accomplish this removal. The method we use does not delete the root node but replaces its `Info` with the `Info` from another node in the tree so that the search property is retained. We then delete this other node.

What element could we replace the root element with that would maintain the search property? We can use either the element whose key immediately precedes it (the root's logical predecessor) or the element whose key immediately follows it (the root's logical successor).

We have elected to use the predecessor. We replace the root's `Info` with the `Info` of its logical predecessor—the node whose key is closest in value to, but less than, the key of the root node we wish to delete. The logical predecessor is the node in the left subtree with the largest key. For example, in Figure 10.15 the logical predecessor of H is E, the logical predecessor of S is P, and the logical predecessor of L is J.

After replacing the `Info` in our root node with the `Info` in the logical predecessor, we delete the logical predecessor. This replacement node is guaranteed to have either no children or just a left child (see nodes E, P, and J in Figure 10.15), so this is not a difficult task.

Figure 10.16 shows the deletion of a root node with two children. The logical predecessor of Q is P. After copying P into the root node, the original node containing P is unlinked from the tree by changing P's parent to designate P's only child. Finally, the memory used by the replacement node is reclaimed.

Here is the Ada code that implements these three cases. In this code, we have split the case of the root node with one child into two cases: having a right child and having a left child.

```ada
procedure Delete_Root (Root : in out Node_Ptr) is
-- Purpose       : Delete the root node from a tree
-- Preconditions : Root is not null
-- Postconditions: The node designated by Root is deleted.
--                 Tree remains a binary search tree

   To_Recycle : Node_Ptr;   -- For recycling nodes
   Pred_Ptr   : Node_Ptr;   -- Designates the root's logical predecessor
begin
   if Root.all.Left = null and Root.all.Right = null then
      -- Root node has no children
      Free (Root);                          -- Entire tree now empty
   elsif Root.all.Left = null then
      -- Root node has only a right child
      To_Recycle := Root;                   -- Save for later deallocation
      Root := Root.all.Right;               -- Unlink the root node
      Free (To_Recycle);                    -- Deallocate former root node
```

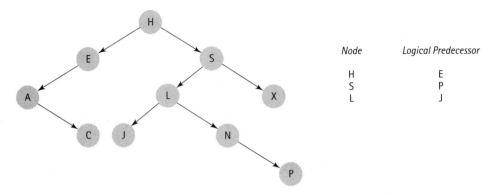

Figure 10.15 *The logical predecessors of nodes with two children.*

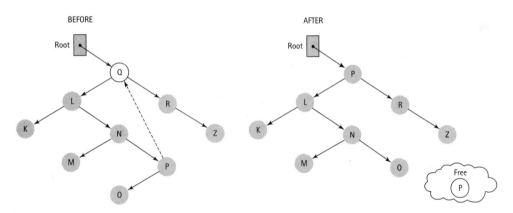

Figure 10.16 *Deleting a root node with two children.*

```
elsif Root.all.Right = null  then
    -- Root node has a left child
    To_Recycle := Root;                 -- Save for later deallocation
    Root := Root.all.Left;              -- Unlink the root node
    Free (To_Recycle);                  -- Deallocate former root node
else  -- Root node has two children
    -- Find and unlink the logical predecessor
    Find_And_Unlink_Max (Root    => Root.all.Left,
                         Max_Ptr => Pred_Ptr);
```

```
        Root.all.Info := Pred_Ptr.all.Info;  -- Copy Info from predecessor
        Free (Pred_Ptr);                     -- Deallocate predecessor
    end if;
end Delete_Root;
```

The first case, where the root node is a leaf, is straightforward. We simply free the memory used by the root node. Because `Root` is an `in out` parameter, null is copied back to the actual parameter.

When the root has a single child, that child becomes the new root. `Root` is changed to designate the non-null child. A different assignment statement is required depending on whether the child is a left child or a right child. In either case, the memory used by the original root node is deallocated.

When the root has two children we must find its logical predecessor. Recall that the logical predecessor of a node with two children is the node with the maximum key in the left subtree (see Figures 10.15 and 10.16). Procedure `Find_And_Unlink_Max` is

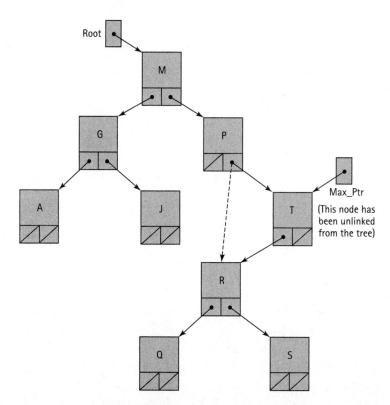

Figure 10.17 *Find_And_Unlink_Max.*

called to find the node in the root's left subtree with the maximum key value. This procedure returns a pointer to the maximum value node and unlinks it from the tree. `Delete_Root` then copies the information and deallocates the memory.

This only leaves procedure `Find_And_Unlink_Max`. This procedure finds the node in the given tree with the maximum key. The maximum value in any tree is in its rightmost node. To find it, we start at the root and keep moving down the right until the right child is null. For example, in Figure 10.17, we start at the root node, M, and move down the right links until we reach the node containing T, the largest key in the tree. Figure 10.17 also illustrates how the largest key node is unlinked from the tree. Its parent's pointer is changed so that it points to the largest key node's left child. If the largest key node has no left child, `null` is assigned.

Earlier we said that we are guaranteed that the logical predecessor of a root node with two children has no children or just a left child. Now you see why. The logical predecessor is the node with the maximum key in the left subtree. As we just showed, the node in a tree with the *maximum* key has no right child.

Here is the code for procedure `Find_And_Unlink_Max`:

```
procedure Find_And_Unlink_Max (Root    : in out Node_Ptr;
                               Max_Ptr :    out Node_Ptr) is
-- Purpose        : Finds and unlinks the node with the maximum key
--                  from a tree whose Root is given
-- Preconditions  : Root is not null
-- Postconditions : Max_Ptr designates the node containing the
--                  largest key in the tree rooted at Root
--                  The node designated by Max_Ptr is unlinked
--                  from the tree rooted at Root
begin
   if Root.all.Right = null then     -- Is there a right child?
      -- Base case, root contains the maximum key in Tree
      Max_Ptr := Root;               -- Return pointer to it
      Root    := Root.all.Left;      -- Unlink it from Tree
   else
      -- General case, keep looking in the right subtree
      Find_And_Unlink_Max (Root => Root.all.Right, Max_Ptr => Max_Ptr);
   end if;
end Find_And_Unlink_Max;
```

The base case for this recursive procedure is that the root has no right child. When we find the maximum key, we unlink it from the tree by changing `Root`. By changing the `in out` parameter `Root`, we change the corresponding actual parameter—the parent's pointer. The general case in this procedure is to search to the maximum node in the right subtree.

Examples of all these types of deletions are shown in Figure 10.18.

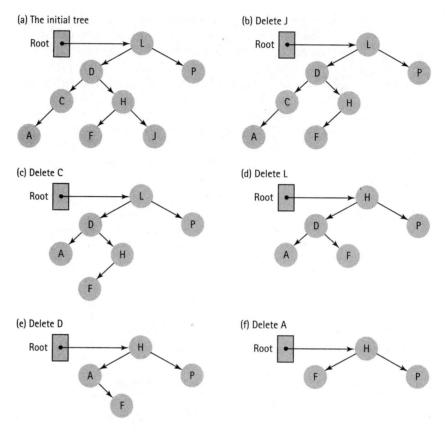

Figure 10.18 *Deletions from a binary search tree.*

The Traverse Operation We gave definitions for inorder, preorder, and postorder tree traversals earlier in the chapter. Let's look at them again:

- *Preorder traversal:* Process the root, traverse the left subtree, traverse the right subtree.
- *Inorder traversal:* Traverse the left subtree, process the root, traverse the right subtree.
- *Postorder traversal:* Traverse the left subtree, traverse the right subtree, process the root.

These recursive definitions are easily implemented as recursive procedures. Here, for example, is the Ada code for an inorder traversal:

```ada
procedure Inorder (Root: in Node_Ptr) is
begin
   if Root /= null then
      Inorder (Root => Root.all.Left);     -- Traverse Left subtree
      Process (Root.all.Info);             -- Process the root
      Inorder (Root => Root.all.Right);    -- Traverse Right subtree
   end if;
end Inorder;
```

The base case of this recursive procedure, like nearly all recursive tree procedures, is an empty tree. In a traversal, we do nothing when the tree is empty. We create the remaining two traversal procedures by reordering the three statements to change the order of processing the root node and traversing its subtrees. You can see in Body 10.1 how these three procedures are nested within the single traversal procedure defined in Specification 10.1.

The Clear Operation The Clear operation needs to recycle the memory used by each of the nodes in the tree. To delete all the elements we traverse the tree, deleting each node from the tree when we process it. Which traversal order should we use? Only a postorder traversal works. Using preorder or inorder would recycle the memory for the root node before recycling the memory for a subtree. But once the root is recycled, we have no way to access its subtrees—a large memory leak. You can see the code in Body 10.1.

Body 10.1   Binary Search Tree: Implements Specification 10.1

```ada
with Ada.Unchecked_Deallocation;
package body Binary_Search_Tree is

   -- Instantiate procedure for recycling node memory
   procedure Free is new Ada.Unchecked_Deallocation (Object => Node_Type,
                                                     Name   => Node_Ptr);

   ------------------------------------------------------------------------

   procedure Clear (Tree : in out Tree_Type) is
      procedure Recursive_Clear (Root : in out Node_Ptr) is
      begin
         if Root /= null then
            Recursive_Clear (Root.all.Left);
            Recursive_Clear (Root.all.Right);
            Free (Root);
         end if;
      end Recursive_Clear;
   begin
      Recursive_Clear (Tree.Root);   -- Recycle all nodes in Tree
```

```ada
         Tree.Current := null;           -- Current now undefined
      end Clear;


   ---------------------------------------------------------------------

   procedure Insert (Tree : in out Tree_Type;
                     Item : in     Element_Type) is
      procedure Recursive_Insert (Root : in out Node_Ptr;
                                  Key  : in     Key_Type) is
      begin
         if Root = null then
            -- Base case, inserting into an empty tree
            Root := new Node_Type'(Info => Item, Left => null, Right => null);
            Tree.Current := Root;    -- Inserted element is the current element
         elsif Key_Of (Item) = Key_Of (Root.all.Info) then
            -- Base case, key already in tree
            raise DUPLICATE_KEY;
         elsif Key_of (Item) < Key_Of (Root.all.Info) then
             -- General case:  Insert into left subtree
            Recursive_Insert (Root => Root.all.Left, Key => Key);
         else
            -- General case:  Insert into right subtree
            Recursive_Insert (Root => Root.all.Right, Key => Key);
         end if;
      end Recursive_Insert;
   begin
      Recursive_Insert (Root => Tree.Root, Key => Key_Of(Item));
   end Insert;


   ---------------------------------------------------------------------

   procedure Find_And_Unlink_Max (Root    : in out Node_Ptr;
                                  Max_Ptr :    out Node_Ptr) is
   -- Purpose       : Finds and unlinks the node with the maximum key
   --                 from a tree whose Root is given
   -- Preconditions : Root is not null
   -- Postconditions: Max_Ptr designates the node containing the
   --                 largest key in the tree rooted at Root
   --                 The node designated by Max_Ptr is unlinked
   --                 from the tree rooted at Root
   begin
      if Root.all.Right = null then       -- Is there a right child?
```

```ada
         -- Base case, root contains the maximum key in Tree
      Max_Ptr := Root;                 -- Return pointer to it
      Root    := Root.all.Left;        -- Unlink it from Tree
   else
         -- General case, keep looking in the right subtree
      Find_And_Unlink_Max (Root => Root.all.Right, Max_Ptr => Max_Ptr);
   end if;
end Find_And_Unlink_Max;
```

```ada
procedure Delete_Root (Root : in out Node_Ptr) is
-- Purpose        : Delete the root node from a tree
-- Preconditions  : Root is not null
-- Postconditions : The node designated by Root is deleted.
--                  Tree remains a binary search tree

   To_Recycle : Node_Ptr;    -- For recycling nodes
   Pred_Ptr   : Node_Ptr;    -- Designates the root's logical predecessor
begin
   if Root.all.Left = null and Root.all.Right = null then
         -- Root node has no children
      Free (Root);                         -- Entire tree now empty
   elsif Root.all.Left = null then
         -- Root node has only a right child
      To_Recycle := Root;                  -- Save for later deallocation
      Root := Root.all.Right;              -- Unlink the root node
      Free (To_Recycle);                   -- Deallocate former root node
   elsif Root.all.Right = null then
         -- Root node has a left child
      To_Recycle := Root;                  -- Save for later deallocation
      Root := Root.all.Left;               -- Unlink the root node
      Free (To_Recycle);                   -- Deallocate former root node
   else  -- Root node has two children
         -- Find and unlink the logical predecessor
      Find_And_Unlink_Max (Root    => Root.all.Left,
                           Max_Ptr => Pred_Ptr);
      Root.all.Info := Pred_Ptr.all.Info;  -- Copy Info from predecessor
      Free (Pred_Ptr);                     -- Deallocate predecessor
   end if;
end Delete_Root;
```

```ada
------------------------------------------------------------------------------
procedure Delete (Tree : in out Tree_Type;
                  Key  : in     Key_Type) is
   procedure Recursive_Delete (Root : in out Node_Ptr;
                               Key  : in     Key_Type) is
   begin
      if Root = null then                                   -- Base case
         raise KEY_ERROR;
      elsif Key = Key_Of (Root.all.Info) then               -- Base case
         Delete_Root (Root);
      elsif Key < Key_Of (Root.all.Info) then               -- General case
         Recursive_Delete (Root => Root.all.Left,  Key => Key);
      else                                                  -- General case
         Recursive_Delete (Root => Root.all.Right, Key => Key);
      end if;
   end Recursive_Delete;
begin
   if Tree.Current /= null and then key = Key_Of(Tree.Current.all.Info) then
      Tree.Current := null;
   end if;
   Recursive_Delete (Root => Tree.Root, Key => Key);
end Delete;


------------------------------------------------------------------------------
procedure Modify (Tree    : in out Tree_Type;
                  Element : in     Element_Type) is
begin
   if Tree.Current = null then
      raise CURRENT_UNDEFINED;
   end if;
   Tree.Current.all.Info := Element ;
end Modify;


------------------------------------------------------------------------------
procedure Find (Tree : in out Tree_Type;
                Key  : in     Key_Type) is
   function Recursive_Find (Root : in Node_Ptr;
                            Key  : in Key_Type) return Node_Ptr is
   begin
      if Root = null or else Key = Key_Of (Root.all.Info) then
         return Root;     -- Two base cases (not found and found in root)
```

```ada
      elsif Key < Key_Of (Root.all.Info) then
         -- General case (search Left subtree)
         return Recursive_Find (Root => Root.all.Left, Key => Key);
      else
         -- General case (search Right subtree)
         return Recursive_Find (Root => Root.all.Right, Key => Key);
      end if;
   end Recursive_Find;
begin
   Tree.Current := Recursive_Find (Tree.Root, Key);
end Find;

-------------------------------------------------------------------------------
function Current_Defined (Tree : in Tree_Type) return Boolean is
begin
   return Tree.Current /= null;
end Current_Defined;

-------------------------------------------------------------------------------
function Empty (Tree : in Tree_Type) return Boolean is
begin
   return Tree.Root = null;
end Empty;

-------------------------------------------------------------------------------
function Full (Tree : in Tree_Type) return Boolean is
begin
   return False;
end Full;

-------------------------------------------------------------------------------
function Size (Tree : in Tree_Type) return Natural is
   function Recursive_Size (Root : in Node_Ptr) return Natural is
   begin
      if Root = null then
         return 0;
      else
         return 1 + Recursive_Size (Root.all.Left)
                  + Recursive_Size (Root.all.Right);
      end if;
   end Recursive_Size;
```

```
begin
   return Recursive_Size (Tree.Root);
end Size;

-------------------------------------------------------------------------------
procedure Retrieve (Tree    : in    Tree_Type;
                    Element :    out Element_Type) is
begin
   if Tree.Current = null then
      raise CURRENT_UNDEFINED;
   end if;
   Element := Tree.Current.all.Info;
end Retrieve;

-------------------------------------------------------------------------------
procedure Traverse
   (Tree    : in out Tree_Type;
    Order   : in Traversal_Order;
    Process : not null access procedure (Element : in out Element_Type)) is

   ---------------------------------------
   procedure Inorder (Root: in Node_Ptr) is
   begin
      if Root /= null then
         Inorder (Root => Root.all.Left);     -- Traverse Left subtree
         Process (Root.all.Info);             -- Process the root
         Inorder (Root => Root.all.Right);    -- Traverse Right subtree
      end if;
   end Inorder;

   ---------------------------------------
   procedure Preorder (Root : in Node_Ptr) is
   begin
      if Root /= null then
         Process (Root.all.Info);             -- Process the root
         Preorder (Root => Root.all.Left);    -- Traverse Left subtree
         Preorder (Root => Root.all.Right);   -- Traverse Right subtree
      end if;
   end Preorder;

   ---------------------------------------
```

```
         procedure Postorder (Root : in Node_Ptr) is
         begin
            if Root /= null then
               Postorder (Root => Root.all.Left);     -- Traverse Left subtree
               Postorder (Root => Root.all.Right);    -- Traverse Right subtree
               Process (Root.all.Info);               -- Process the root
            end if;
         end Postorder;

      begin
         case Order is
            when Inorder   => Inorder (Tree.Root);
            when Preorder  => Preorder (Tree.Root);
            when Postorder => Postorder (Tree.Root);
         end case;
      end Traverse;

end Binary_Search_Tree;
```

Iterative Binary Search Tree Operations

The recursive Find, Insert, and Delete procedures we developed in the last section all used tail recursion; the recursive call is the last statement executed in the general case. As we discussed in Chapter 9, tail recursion can be converted to iteration without a programmer-defined stack. In this section we develop the iterative implementations of these three operations.

Searching a Binary Search Tree In the recursive versions of the Insert and Delete operations, we embedded the search function within the procedures that needed it. The other alternative is to have a general search procedure, as we did in Chapter 7 for the key-ordered list. Let's do that here. Procedure Search_Tree is given a pointer to the root node of a binary search tree and a key to find. If the key is in the tree, the search procedure returns a pointer (Location) to the node containing the key and a pointer (Parent) to that node's parent. These two access variables are the tree equivalents of Location and Pred_Loc that we used in Chapter 7 for our lists.

What do we do if we do not find an item with the given key, as in the case when we are inserting an element? For the key-ordered list search, we used a Boolean parameter to indicate the results of the search. For this search we use the Location parameter to give us this information. If the search is not successful, Location is set to null; otherwise, it designates the node containing the key. When we don't find the key, our search procedure returns a pointer to the node that would be its parent if we were to insert it now. Here is our local search procedure:

```ada
procedure Search_Tree (Root     : in  Node_Ptr;
                       Key      : in  Key_Type;
                       Parent   : out Node_Ptr;
                       Location : out Node_Ptr) is
-- Purpose        : Searches for the location of Key in a binary search tree
-- Preconditions  : None
-- Postconditions : If Key is in Tree
--                      Location designates the element with Key
--                      Parent designates the parent of the node
--                          designated by Location.  If Location designates
--                          the root node of the tree, Parent is null.
--                  else
--                      Location is null.
--                      If the tree is not empty then
--                          Parent designates the node in the tree that
--                          is logical parent of a node containing Key.
--                      else
--                          Parent is null.
begin
   Location := Root;    -- Initialize pointer
   Parent   := null;
   loop
      exit when Location = null  or else  Key = Key_Of (Location.all.Info);
      Parent := Location;                                   -- Move Inchworm tail
      if Key < Key_Of (Location.all.Info) then
         Location := Location.all.Left;                     -- Go to left subtree
      else
         Location := Location.all.Right;                    -- Go to right subtree
      end if;
   end loop;
end Search_Tree;
```

We initialize Location to the external pointer Root. Because the root has no parent, we initialize Parent to null. There are two exit conditions for our loop. If Location is null, we have run off the bottom of the tree and did not find Key. If the key of the node designated by Location is the key for which we are searching, our search was successful. As we did in the key-ordered list search, we use the "inchworm" method of moving the two external pointers down the tree.

The Insert Operation   The algorithm for the iterative Insert operation has the same three tasks that any insert operation must have:

Insert

Find the insertion place
Create a node to contain the new element
Link the new node into the structure

Creating a node is the same as in the recursive version of Insert—we use the allocator new. Finding the insertion point and linking the node into the structure are different, however.

Let's see how procedure Search_Tree can be used to perform the search for us. Suppose we want to insert an element with the key value 13 into the binary search tree pictured in Figure 10.19. In procedure Search_Tree, Parent is initialized to null and Location is initialized to designate the root of the tree (Figure 10.19[a]). Key (13) is greater than the key of the root node (7) so we move Location to the right, dragging Parent along behind it (Figure 10.19[b]). Now Key is less than the key of the node designated by Location (15), so we move Location to the left, with Parent following (Figure 10.19[c]). Key (13) is now greater than the node designated by Location (10), so Parent catches up, and Location moves to the right (Figure 10.19[d]). At this point Location is null, so we exit the loop and return with the pointers, as shown in Figure 10.19(d). Because Parent is trailing right behind Location, we can attach the new node to the node designated by Parent, as shown in Figure 10.19(e).

Figure 10.19 showed the case of adding a new node as a right child. Why was it not added as a left child? We need to compare the key of the new item to the key of the parent to see which side to attach the new node to. There is another check we need to make. When we insert the first node into an empty tree, there is no parent node to attach it to—procedure Search_Tree returns a null value for Parent. When inserting into an empty tree, we must change the external pointer that designates the root node. The following procedure includes all of the different cases for our nonrecursive Insert procedure:

```
procedure Insert (Tree : in out Tree_Type;
                  Item : in      Element_Type) is
-- Iterative version
Parent : Node_Ptr;   -- Designates new node's parent
Child  : Node_Ptr;   -- Needed for search; should return as null

begin
   -- Search for insertion place
   Search_Tree (Root     => Tree.Root,
                Key      => Key_Of (Item),
                Parent   => Parent,
                Location => Child);
   if Child /= null then      -- Does Tree already contain Key?
      raise DUPLICATE_KEY;
```

674 | Chapter 10: Binary Search Trees

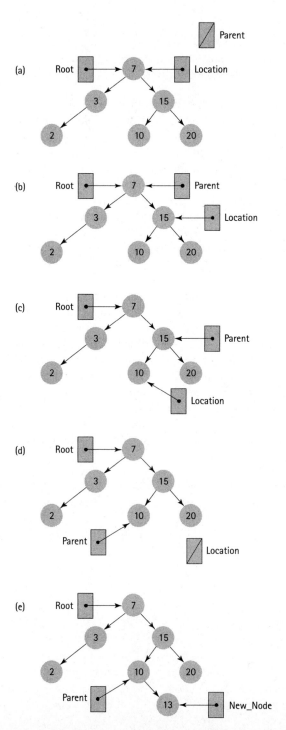

Figure 10.19 *Using procedure* `Search_Tree` *to find the insertion point.*

```ada
      else  -- Insert the new item
         if Parent = null then    -- Special case, empty tree
            Tree.Root := new Node_Type'(Info  => Item,
                                        Left  => null,
                                        Right => null);
            Tree.Current := Tree.Root;
         elsif Key_Of (Item) < Key_Of (Parent.all.Info) then
            -- Insert as left child
            Parent.all.Left := new Node_Type'(Info  => Item,
                                              Left  => null,
                                              Right => null);
            Tree.Current := Parent.all.Left;
         else
            -- Insert as right child
            Parent.all.Right := new Node_Type'(Info  => Item,
                                               Left  => null,
                                               Right => null);
            Tree.Current := Parent.all.Right;
         end if;
      end if;
end Insert;
```

The `Delete` *Operation* The same three cases exist for the nonrecursive `Delete` procedure that exist for the recursive version: deleting a node with no children, one child, or two children. We can use `Search_Tree` to locate the node that we need to delete as well as its parent node. In the recursive algorithm, we performed the actual deletion with procedure `Delete_Root`. This procedure takes a single parameter—a pointer that designates the subtree whose root node is deleted. We can use this same procedure if we can determine the place in the structure to pass to `Delete_Root`. That is, given `Location` and `Parent`, we must determine whether the node we want to delete is the root node of the left subtree or the right subtree. If it is the left subtree, we pass `Parent.all.Left` to `Delete_Root`, otherwise we pass `Parent.all.Right`.

```ada
procedure Delete (Tree : in out Tree_Type;
                  Key  : in     Key_Type) is
-- Iterative version
   Location : Node_Ptr;  -- Designates node to delete
   Parent   : Node_Ptr;  -- Designates parent of node to delete
begin
   -- Search for the node containing Key
   Search_Tree (Root     => Tree.Root,
                Key      => Key,
                Parent   => Parent,
                Location => Location);
```

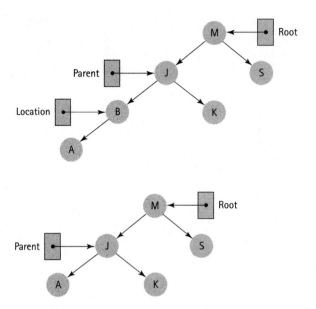

Figure 10.20 *Nonrecursive deletion of node B.*
(a) Pointers `Location` *and* `Parent` *are external to the tree.*
(b) Pointer `Parent` *is external to the tree, but* `Parent.all.Left` *is an internal pointer.*

```
      if Location = null then      -- Is the Key missing?
         raise KEY_ERROR;
      else  -- Delete the node containing Key
         if Parent = null then
            -- Delete the root node
            Delete_Root (Tree.Root);
         elsif Key < Key_Of (Parent.all.Info) then
            -- Delete the root node of the parent's left subtree
            Delete_Root (Root => Parent.all.Left);
         else
            -- Delete the root node of the parent's right subtree
            Delete_Root (Root => Parent.all.Right);
         end if;
      end if;
   end Delete;
```

It is very important to recognize the difference between passing `Location` to `Delete_Root` and passing either `Parent.all.Left` or `Parent.all.Right`. See Figure 10.20. If we pass `Location` to `Delete_Root`, the link in the parent node is not changed.

We can use the procedure `Delete_Root` we developed earlier; it contains no recursive calls. However, we used recursion in the procedure it calls to find a logical predecessor, `Find_And_Unlink_Max`. Because our recursive version uses tail recursion, it is not difficult to convert it to iteration. Here is an iterative version:

```
procedure Find_And_Unlink_Max (Root    : in out Node_Ptr;
                               Max_Ptr :    out Node_Ptr) is
-- Purpose        : Finds and unlinks the node with the maximum key
--                  from a tree whose Root is given
-- Preconditions  : Root is not null
-- Postconditions : Max_Ptr designates the node containing the
--                  largest key in the tree rooted at Root
--                  The node designated by Max_Ptr is unlinked
--                  from the tree rooted at Root
   Parent : Node_Ptr;   -- Parent of Current node
begin
   Max_Ptr := Root;   -- Start at the root
   loop
      exit when Max_Ptr.all.Right = null;
      Parent  := Max_Ptr;                 -- Move inchworm tail
      Max_Ptr := Max_Ptr.all.Right;       -- Move inchworm head
   end loop;
   -- Unlink the largest key node from the tree
   if Parent = null then
      Root := Max_Ptr.all.Left;           -- Change external tree pointer
   else
      Parent.all.Right := Max_Ptr.all.Left;   -- Change parent node
   end if;

end Find_And_Unlink_Max;
```

The logic to unlink the node from the tree is a little more complex than our recursive version. We use an `if` statement to see if the node with the largest key has a parent in the tree. If it doesn't, the node with the largest key is the root of the subtree and we have to change the external tree pointer to unlink it.

Recursion or Iteration

Now that we have looked at both the recursive and iterative versions of `Insert` and `Delete`, can we determine which is better? In Chapter 9 we gave some guidelines for determining when recursion is appropriate. Let's apply these to the use of recursion with binary search trees.

- *Is the depth of recursion relatively shallow?* Yes. The depth of recursion is dependent on the height of the tree. If the tree is bushy, the depth of recursion is closer to $O(\log_2 N)$ than to $O(N)$.
- *Is the recursive solution shorter or clearer than the nonrecursive version?* Yes. The recursive solutions are certainly shorter than the combination of the nonrecursive procedures plus the supporting procedure `Search_Tree`. Are they clearer? Once you accept the fact that in every recursive execution the `Tree` parameter is actually a pointer field *within* the tree, the recursive versions become very easy to understand. The iterative versions are filled with special

cases and `if` statements. And look at the complexity of the postconditions given for the local iterative procedure `Search_Tree`!
- *Is the recursive solution much less efficient than the nonrecursive version?* No. Both the recursive and nonrecursive versions of insert and delete are $O(\log_2 N)$ operations assuming a bushy tree and $O(N)$ for a degenerate tree. When the tree is bushy, our timing experiments (detailed in Table 10.2 in the next section) indicate that execution times of the recursive versions of `Insert` and `Delete` are noticeably but not significantly longer than their iterative counterparts. However, when the tree is degenerate, the recursive insertion was significantly slower than the iterative insertion.

We give the recursive versions of the `Insert` and `Delete` procedures an 'A'; they are good uses of recursion *when the trees are not degenerate*. The clarity they provide the programmer is worth the extra execution time required.

10.5 Comparing Binary Search Trees to Linear Lists

A binary search tree is an appropriate structure for many of the same applications discussed previously with other ordered list structures. The special advantage of using such a tree is that it facilitates searching, with the benefit of linking the elements. It provides the best features of both the sorted array-based list and linked lists: Like a sorted array-based list, it can be searched quickly, using a binary search. Like a linked list, it allows insertions and deletions without having to move data. Thus it is particularly suitable for applications in which search time must be minimized or in which the nodes are not necessarily processed in sequential order.

As usual, there is a trade-off. The binary search tree, with its extra pointer in each node, takes up more memory space than a singly linked list. In addition, the algorithms for manipulating the tree are somewhat more complicated. If all of the list's uses involve sequential rather than random processing of the elements, the tree is certainly not a good choice.

Suppose we have 100,000 customer records in a list. If the main activity in the application is to send out updated monthly statements to the customers, and if the order in which the statements are printed is the same as the order in which the records appear on the list, a linked list would be suitable. But suppose we decide to give out account information to the customers whenever they make a query at our secure website. If the data are kept in a linked list, the first customer on the list can be given information almost instantly, but the last customer has to wait while the other 99,999 records are examined. We need to examine about 10 records to find any customer in a binary search tree. When direct access to the records is a requirement, a binary search tree is a more appropriate structure.

Big-O and Execution Time Comparisons

To illustrate the difference between the operations that manipulate a linked list and a binary search tree, we ran a timed test. Before we tell you how the tests came out, let's describe the operations in terms of their Big-O approximations. Then we can see how well we would expect the operations to perform.

Finding the node to process, as we would expect in a structure dedicated to searching, is the most interesting operation to analyze. In the best case—if the order that the elements were inserted results in a minimum-height tree—we can find any node in the tree with at most $\lceil \log_2(N + 1) \rceil$ comparisons. We would expect to be able to locate a random element in such a tree much faster than finding an element in an ordered linear list. In the worst case—if the elements were inserted in order from smallest to largest or vice versa—the tree isn't really a tree at all; it is a linear list, linked through either the left or right pointers. In this case, the tree operations should perform much the same as the operations on a linked list. Therefore, if we were doing a worst-case analysis, we would have to say that the timing of the tree operations is identical to the comparable linked list operations. In the following analysis we assume that the items are inserted into the tree in random order, giving a bushy tree.

As we explained in the previous paragraph, the Find operation for a bushy tree is $O(\log_2 N)$. Once a we have found the element in the tree, the time required to Retrieve or Modify it is $O(1)$. The Insert operation requires us to work our way down from the root to a leaf. Once we are there, we get a new node and change a pointer. This search takes us down the entire height of the tree, so Insert is $O(\log_2 N)$ for a bushy tree.

The Delete operation consists of finding the node plus Delete_Root. In the worst case (deleting a node with two children), Delete_Root must find the replacement value, an $O(\log_2 N)$ operation. (Actually, the two tasks together add up to $\log_2 N$ comparisons, because if the delete node is higher in the tree, fewer comparisons are needed to find it, and more comparisons may be needed to find its replacement node; and vice versa.) Otherwise, if the deleted node has 0 or 1 child, Delete_Root is an $O(1)$ operation. So Delete, too, may be described as $O(\log_2 N)$. Notice that this analysis is true for both the recursive and iterative versions. Finding the node to process is $O(\log_2 N)$ whether the search is done using iteration or recursion.

The Traverse, Clear, and Size operations require a visit to every node in the tree, processing each element once. Thus, these are $O(N)$ operations. Empty, Full, and Current_Defined have no iteration or recursion and so are $O(1)$.

The orders of magnitude for the tree and list operations are compared in Table 10.1. Because we added the notion of a current element to our binary search tree specification, some of the operations of the tree are not directly comparable to those of the lists. The list Retrieve and Modify operations incorporate a search. With the tree, Retrieve and Modify act on the current element and therefore do not include a search. The Find operation is used to set the current element in a tree. The use of a current element provides a boost in performance in applications like our word frequency generator where we retrieved a copy of a word, incremented its frequency, and then modified the tree to incorporate this change. The notion of the current element allows us to accomplish this task with a single search. Performing the same update on one of our list implementations does two searches: one in the retrieve and a second in the modify. Of course, we could easily modify our linked list to incorporate the notion of a current element.

Table 10.1
Big-O Comparisons of Bushy Tree and List Operations

	Binary Search Tree	Array-Based Linear List	Linked List
Empty	O(1)	O(1)	O(1)
Full	O(1)	O(1)	O(1)
Clear	O(N)	O(1)	O(N)
Traverse	O(N)	O(N)	O(N)
Size	O(N)		
Find	O($\log_2 N$)		
Retrieve	O(1)*	O($\log_2 N$)	O(N)
Modify	O(1)*	O($\log_2 N$)	O(N)
Insert	O($\log_2 N$)	O(N)	O(N)
Delete	O($\log_2 N$)	O(N)	O(N)

*After using Find to set the current element

Now let's see how our timed experiments came out. For each structure (binary search tree and linked list) we inserted 10,000 elements (a record containing an integer key and a 60-character string) and then deleted them one by one. We ran three different test cases.

In the first test case, we inserted the elements in random order, to produce a bushy tree. We then deleted the elements one by one, in the same order in which they were inserted. As you can see in Table 10.2, the results were as expected: Both the tree insertions and deletions with random data were significantly faster than the comparable linear list operations. The recursive tree operations took a little more time than the iterative ones.

In the second test case, we inserted 10,000 elements with the keys in order, and then deleted them one by one in the same order. All inserts and deletes were at the head of the linear list, so its times were very fast. The tree produced from this data was essentially a linear list linked through the right child pointer. There is a great difference between the tree insertion and deletion times. New nodes are always added as leaves at the bottom of the degenerate tree. Deletions are always of the root node. So these great differences are expected. What is interesting in this data is the significantly greater amount of time required for the recursive version when compared to the iterative version. The overhead of recursion in *this set* of experiments is obvious. The depth of recursion in these highly skewed trees is great and the time required to push and pop the parameters and activation records on the system stack was significant.

In the third test case, we inserted elements with the keys in reverse order, and then deleted them one by one in reverse order. All inserts and deletes were at the end of the linear list, so its times were slow. We see the same difference between the times for tree insertions and deletions that we saw in the second test case. The tree here is again a linear structure, this time leaning in the opposite direction. The insertions to the "end" of the degenerate tree took slightly more time than to the end of the linked list. The deletions worked in reverse: The first (root with one child) element was always deleted from the tree [an O(1) operation], but the last node was always deleted from the list [an O(N) operation]. The timing results are as we would expect.

Table 10.2
Results of the Timed Implementation Comparisons (in milliseconds)

	Binary Search Tree		Linked List
	Recursive	*Iterative*	
Case 1: Random			
Insert	13.00	10.47	1,259.35
Delete	9.90	8.82	1,041.89
Case 2: In Order			
Insert	9,996.60	1,472.89	6.16
Delete	4.16	4.28	4.30
Case 3: In Reverse Order			
Insert	10,020.41	1,469.39	1,346.88
Delete	4.18	4.29	1,242.02

Remember, the results of these experiments are valid only for the system on which they were run. In fact, results from similar experiments made for the first edition of this textbook on a different computer using a different Ada compiler showed only a factor of two difference between the recursive and iterative tree algorithms. Only Big-O allows us to compare algorithms without regard to what computer system we run them on.

This exercise does illustrate an important point about binary search trees: The order in which the elements are inserted is critical in determining the efficiency of the tree operations. This order determines the shape of the tree—short and bushy (good) or tall and stringy (bad). The shorter the tree (fewer levels to search), the faster we can access random elements. The speed of operations that process every node, such as `Size` and `Traverse`, are unaffected by the shape. A short bushy tree, a tall stringy tree, or a linked list all take about the same time to traverse. However, there are space implications: The overhead from the recursive calls to traverse a tall, stringy tree may raise `STORAGE_ERROR` if the run-time stack overflows due to the large number of recursive calls required to reach the leaf nodes.

682 | Chapter 10: Binary Search Trees

10.6 Balancing a Binary Search Tree

In our Big-O analysis of binary search tree operations we assumed our tree was balanced. As we saw in the experimental results, the timings of a skewed tree can be much worse than those of a linked list. Therefore, a beneficial addition to our binary search tree class operations is an operation that balances the tree. The specification of the operation is:

```
procedure Balance (Tree : in out Tree_Type);
-- Purpose          : Restructures Tree for optimum performance
-- Preconditions    : None
-- Postconditions   : Tree is a minimum height tree
--                    The current element is not defined
```

It should not be invoked too often because, as you shall see, it has both a time and memory cost associated with it. It is up to the application to use the balance method appropriately. There are several ways to restructure a binary search tree. We use a simple approach:

Balance
    Copy the tree information into an ordered array
    Clear the tree
    Create a new balanced tree from the array data

We can use an inorder traversal to create an ordered array. Figure 10.21(a) shows a binary search tree that is not a minimum height tree. Figure 10.21(b) shows the sorted array created by an inorder traversal of the tree.

How do we convert the array back into a binary search tree with minimum height? Let's start with a simpler question. Which element in the array should we use as the root

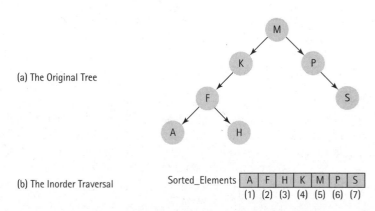

Figure 10.21 *Copying tree information into an array.*

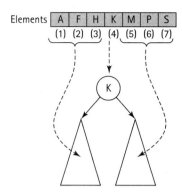

Figure 10.22 *Building a minimum height binary search tree from a sorted array. The middle element becomes the root, the slice to its left becomes the left subtree, and the slice to its right becomes the right subtree.*

in our new tree? Picking the middle element as the root will leave half of the remaining elements for the left subtree and half for the right subtree. Figure 10.22 illustrates this reasoning.

Once we have the root, we can take the same approach to create its left and right subtrees from the two array slices on either side of the middle array element. Here is the code that implements the entire tree balance algorithm:

```ada
procedure Balance (Tree : in out Tree_Type) is
   -- Declare an array the exact size of the tree
   type Element_Array is array (Positive range <>) of Element_Type;
   Sorted_Elements : Element_Array (1..Tree.Size);
   Index : Natural := 0;

   -------------------------------------------------------------------

   procedure Store_One_Element (Element : in out Element_Type) is
   begin
      Index := Index + 1;
      Sorted_Elements (Index) := Element;
   end Store_One_Element;

   -------------------------------------------------------------------

   function Array_To_Tree (Elements : in Element_Array) return Node_Ptr is
      Middle : Positive;    -- The middle element in the array Elements
   begin
      if Elements'Length = 0 then
         return null;       -- Base case, no elements is an empty tree
      else
         Middle := (Elements'First + Elements'Last) / 2;
         -- Return a tree with the middle element as the root, the elements
```

```ada
         -- before the middle as the left subtree, and the elements after
         -- the middle as the right subtree
         return new Node_Type'
              (Info  => Elements(Middle),
               Left  => Array_To_Tree (Elements (Elements'First..Middle-1)),
               Right => Array_To_Tree (Elements (Middle+1..Elements'Last)));
      end if;
   end Array_To_Tree;

begin -- Balance
   -- Copy the Tree into a sorted array of elements
   Tree.Traverse (Order   => Inorder,
                  Process => Store_One_Element'access);
   Tree.Clear;
   Tree.Root    := Array_To_Tree (Sorted_Elements);
   Tree.Current := null;
end Balance;
```

Procedure `Balance` first does an inorder traversal of the tree. `Traverse` calls procedure `Store_One_Element` for each node in the tree. This procedure puts a copy of the element into the next spot in the sorted array. Next the memory of the original tree is recycled. Finally, `Balance` calls the function `Array_To_Tree` to convert the sorted array into a minimum height binary search tree.

The recursive function `Array_To_Tree` returns a pointer to the root node of a minimum height binary search tree constructed from the array. The base case is an array that contains no elements—we return an empty tree. Otherwise we use our allocator `new` to obtain memory for one node. The middle array element is used as the new node's element. The new node's left pointer is assigned a value that designates the tree formed from the slice of the array to the left of the middle element. The new node's right pointer is assigned a value that designates the tree formed from the slice of the array to the right of the middle element. See Figure 10.22 again. How do we obtain these two trees? By calling `Array_To_Tree`, of course.

Earlier we said that our simple tree-balancing procedure came with time and memory costs. The extra storage is evident in Figure 10.21. We store all of the elements twice—in the tree and in the array. Let's look at where the time is used in this algorithm. The declaration of the array `Sorted_Elements` calls the tree's `Size` operation, which counts all the nodes in the tree. The inorder traversal goes through all of the nodes a second time. The `Clear` operation goes through the nodes a third time when it recycles the memory used by each node. The recursive `Array_To_Tree` calls the allocation operator `new` for each element in the array. The total time cost of balancing is $N + N + N + N$. Although the Big-O of balance is $O(N)$, the absolute running time is higher than our other $O(N)$ tree operations.

Other Approaches to Balancing

In the last section we looked at a method to restructure any binary search tree into a minimum height tree. However, it is difficult to know when an application should call procedure Balance. Another strategy is to let nature take its course (insert the values in the order in which they come), but *monitor* the shape of the tree and *intervene* if the shape deviates too much from a minimum height tree. Search trees that grow naturally until they get out of balance and are rebalanced are called **balanced trees**. In the following sections we give a very brief introduction to two approaches to balanced trees. We will not give the details of the algorithms for these tree variations. You can find them in more advanced texts.[1]

> **Balanced tree** A tree in which the shape of the tree is monitored during each insert and delete. A balancing intervention is made when the shape of the tree deviates too much from a minimum height tree.

AVL Trees Perhaps the most common balanced binary tree is the AVL tree, named for Georgii M. Adelson-Velskii and Evgenii M. Landis, the Russian scientists who first investigated them. An AVL tree is a binary search tree in which every node is *height balanced*. A node is height balanced if the heights of its left and right subtrees differ by no more than one. Figure 10.23 shows an AVL tree. Each node in this tree is height balanced.

Based on the heights of its subtrees, every node of an AVL tree is in one of three states:

1. *Balanced:* The heights of the node's two subtrees are equal.
2. *Leaning left:* The height of the node's left subtree is one greater than the height of its right subtree.
3. *Leaning right:* The height of the node's right subtree is one greater than the height of its left subtree.

Below each node in Figure 10.23 is an arrow that indicates the balance of that node. A left arrow indicates that the node is leaning left, a right arrow indicates that the node is leaning right, and a double arrow indicates that the node is balanced.

When an insertion into or a deletion from an AVL tree results in a node no longer being height balanced, a *portion* of the AVL tree is restructured to reestablish balance. For example, consider adding an element with a key of 12 to the AVL tree shown in Figure 10.23. The standard binary search insert will attach this node as a right child of the node with the key 10. After this insertion, the node with key 5 becomes unbalanced. This imbalance can be corrected by restructuring only the three nodes with keys 5, 10, and 12.

---

[1] N. Dale, H. Walker, *Abstract Data Types, Specifications, Implementations, and Applications* (Sudbury, MA: Jones and Bartlett, 1996) gives complete algorithms for all the trees mentioned in this section.

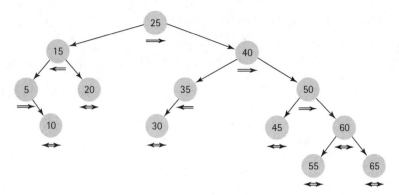

Figure 10.23 *An AVL tree. Arrows beneath each node indicate whether the node is balanced, left leaning, or right leaning.*

Balanced Multi-Way Trees A multi-way search tree is characterized by nodes containing multiple elements. There are many variations of multi-way search trees, including 2-3 Trees, B-Trees, B+-Trees, 2-3-4 Trees, and Red/Black Trees. Figure 10.24 shows a type of fifth-order multi-way search tree called a balanced multi-way search tree or B-Tree. Each node of a fifth-order multi-way tree can have as many as four elements and five children. The B-Tree in Figure 10.24 has a root node with two elements and three children. The leftmost child of the root node contains three elements and has four null children. The rightmost child contains the maximum number of elements (four) and has five null children. Notice that the left child contains all of the keys that are less than f, the middle child contains all of the keys that are between f and k, and the right child contains all of the keys that are greater than k.

B-Trees and B+-Trees are commonly used with applications that require searching for data within large files. Database systems are prime users of multi-way search trees. Because disk accesses take a great amount of time we need to minimize the number of accesses during a database search, so each node in these multi-way search trees may contain thousands of elements.

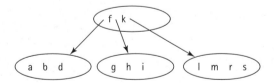

Figure 10.24 *A fifth-order B-Tree.*

10.7 A Nonlinked Representation of Binary Trees

Our discussion of the implementation of binary trees has so far been limited to a scheme in which the pointers from parent to children are *explicit* in the data structure. A field was declared in each node for the pointer to the left child and the pointer to the right child.

A binary tree can be stored in an array in such a way that the relationships in the tree are not physically represented by link fields, but are *implicit* in the algorithms that manipulate the tree stored in the array. The code is, of course, much less self-documenting, but we might save memory space because there are no pointers.

Let's take a binary tree and store it in an array in such a way that the parent–child relationships are not lost. We store the tree in the array level by level, left to right. Figure 10.25 illustrates this mapping.

To implement the algorithms that manipulate the tree, we must be able to find the left and right child of a node in the tree. Comparing the tree and the array in Figure 10.25, we see that

Tree(1)'s children are in Tree(2) and Tree(3).

Tree(2)'s children are in Tree(4) and Tree(5).

Tree(3)'s children are in Tree(6) and Tree(7).

Do you see the pattern? For any node Tree(Index), its left child is in Tree(Index * 2) and its right child is in Tree(Index * 2 + 1) (provided that these child nodes exist). Notice that the nodes in the array from Tree(Tree'Last / 2 + 1) to Tree(Tree'Last) are leaf nodes.

Not only can we easily calculate the location of a node's children, but we also can determine the location of its parent node. This task is not an easy one in a binary tree linked with pointers from parent to child nodes, but it is very simple in our implicit link implementation:

Tree(Index)'s parent is in Tree(Index / 2).

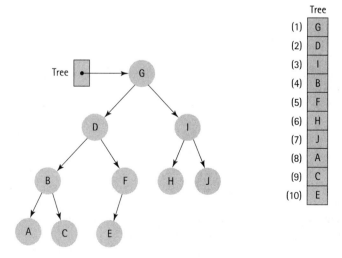

Figure 10.25 *A binary tree and its array representation.*

Because integer division truncates any remainder, `Index / 2` is the correct parent index for either a left or right child. Thus this implementation of a binary tree is linked in both directions: from parent to child, and from child to parent. We take advantage of this fact in the next chapter when we study heaps.

This tree representation works well for any binary tree that is perfect or complete. A **perfect binary tree** is a binary tree in which all of the leaves are on the same level and every nonleaf node has two children. The basic shape of a perfect binary tree is triangular:

> **Perfect binary tree** A binary tree in which all of the leaves are on the same level and every nonleaf node has two children.
>
> **Complete binary tree** A binary tree that is either perfect or perfect through the next-to-last level, with the leaves on the last level as far to the left as possible.

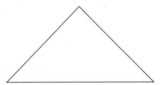

A **complete binary tree** is a binary tree that is either perfect or perfect through the next-to-last level, with the leaves on the last level as far to the left as possible. The shape of a complete binary tree is either triangular (if the tree is perfect) or something like the following:

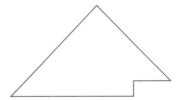

Figure 10.26 shows some examples of different types of binary trees.

The array-based representation is simple to implement for trees that are perfect or complete, because the elements occupy contiguous array slots. If a tree is not perfect or complete, however, we must account for the gaps where nodes are missing. To use the array representation, we must store a dummy value in those positions in the array in order to maintain the proper parent–child relationship. The choice of a dummy value depends on what information is stored in the tree. For instance, if the elements in the tree are positive integers, a negative value can be stored in the dummy nodes. Another approach is to store records that include a Boolean field in addition to the data. The Boolean field is used to mark the element as data or dummy.

Figure 10.27 illustrates a tree that is not complete and its corresponding array. Some of the array slots do not contain actual tree elements, however; they contain dummy values. The algorithms to manipulate the tree must reflect this situation. For example, to determine whether the node in `Tree(Index)` has a left child, you must

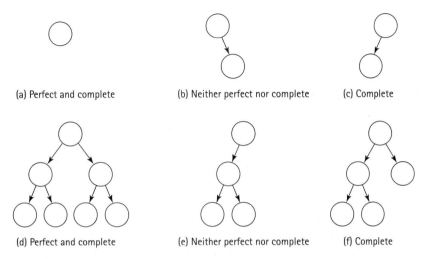

(a) Perfect and complete (b) Neither perfect nor complete (c) Complete

(d) Perfect and complete (e) Neither perfect nor complete (f) Complete

Figure 10.26 *Examples of different types of binary trees.*

check whether `Index * 2 <= Tree'Last`, and then check to see if the value in `Tree(Index * 2)` is a dummy value.

We have just seen how an array can be used to represent a binary tree. We can also reverse this process, creating a binary tree from the elements in an array. We can regard any one-dimensional array as representing the nodes in a tree, but the data values that happen to be stored in it may not match this structure in a meaningful way.

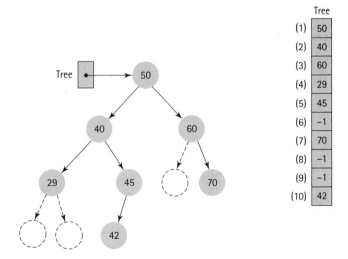

Figure 10.27 *A binary search tree stored in an array with dummy values.*

Summary

In this chapter we have seen how the binary tree may be used to structure ordered information to reduce the search time for any particular element. For applications where direct access to the elements in an ordered structure is needed, the binary search tree is a very useful class. If the tree is bushy, we can access any node in the tree with an $O(\log_2 N)$ operation. The binary search tree combines the advantages of quick random access (like a binary search of a sequential list) with the flexibility of a linked structure.

We also saw that the tree operations could be implemented very elegantly and concisely using recursion. This makes sense, because a binary tree is itself best defined as a recursive structure: Any node in the tree is the root of another binary tree. Each time we moved down a level in the tree, taking either the right or left path from a node, we cut the size of the (current) tree in half, a clear case of the smaller-caller. We also saw cases of iteration that replaced recursion (`Insert` and `Delete`).

We discussed a binary search tree balancing operation that uses traversals and arrays. We also mentioned that there are other types of trees, called balanced trees, that monitor their shape and modify it when necessary to maintain a bushy shape.

In this chapter we stored most of our tree values in dynamically allocated memory. We examined a way of storing trees in static arrays. We use this approach to implement the heap data structure in the next chapter.

Exercises

Trees

1. Binary tree levels:
   a. What does the level of a binary search tree mean in relation to the searching efficiency?
   b. What is the maximum number of levels that a binary search tree with 100 nodes can have?
   c. What is the minimum number of levels that a binary search tree with 100 nodes can have?

2. Which of these formulas gives the maximum total number of nodes in a tree that has N levels? (Remember that the root is Level 0.)
   a. $N^2 - 1$
   b. $2^{N+1} - 1$
   c. 2^N
   d. 2^{N+1}

3. Which of these formulas gives the maximum number of nodes in the Nth level of a binary tree?

a. N^2

b. 2^{N+1}

c. 2^N

d. $2^N - 1$

4. How many ancestors does a node in the Nth level of a binary search tree have?

5. How many different *binary trees* can be made from three nodes that contain the key values 1, 2, and 3?

6. How many different *binary search trees* can be made from three nodes that contain the key values 1, 2, and 3?

7. Draw all the possible binary trees that have four leaves and all the nonleaf nodes have two children.

8. Given the following tree:

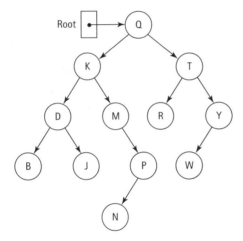

a. What are the ancestors of node P?

b. What are the descendants of node K?

c. What is the maximum possible number of nodes in the tree at the level of node W?

d. What is the maximum possible number of nodes in the tree at the level of node N?

e. What is the order in which the nodes are visited by an inorder traversal?

f. What is the order in which the nodes are visited by a preorder traversal?

g. What is the order in which the nodes are visited by a postorder traversal?

9. Given the following tree:

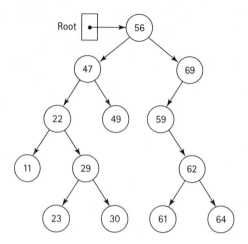

a. What is the height of the tree?
b. What nodes are on level 3?
c. Which levels have the maximum number of nodes that they could contain?
d. What is the maximum height of a binary search tree containing these nodes?
e. What is the minimum height of a binary search tree containing these nodes? Draw such a tree.
f. What is the order in which the nodes are visited by an inorder traversal?
g. What is the order in which the nodes are visited by a preorder traversal?
h. What is the order in which the nodes are visited by a postorder traversal?

10. *True or False.*

a. A preorder traversal of a binary search tree processes the nodes in the tree in the exact reverse order that a postorder traversal processes them.
b. An inorder traversal of a binary search tree always processes the elements in the same order, regardless of the way they are arranged within the binary search tree.
c. A preorder traversal of a binary search tree always processes the elements in the same order, regardless of the way they are arranged within the binary search tree.

11. Review the following binary search tree. The numbers shown are labels so that we can talk about the nodes. The numbers are not keys.

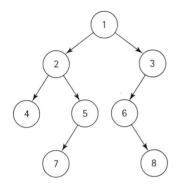

a. If we had not told you, how could you tell that the numbers shown are not the keys of the nodes in this binary search tree?

b. 4 2 7 5 1 6 8 3 is a traversal of the tree in which order?

c. 1 2 4 5 7 3 6 8 is a traversal of the tree in which order?

Logical Level

12. Describe the differences between our specifications of the key-ordered list class and the binary search tree class.

13. Why is procedure Find classified as a transformer operation?

14. How can we tell whether a call to procedure Find was able to find the key for which we are searching?

15. *True or False.*

    a. The binary search tree iterator Traverse can change the data stored in a binary search tree.

    b. The binary search tree iterator Traverse can change the shape of a binary search tree.

    c. The results of a call to the search tree iterator Traverse are undefined if the actual procedure supplied for the formal procedure Process changes the key of an element.

16. Draw a UML class diagram for the binary search tree defined by Specification 10.1.

17. Which procedures might raise the exception CURRENT_UNDEFINED? Under what circumstance will they raise this exception?

18. `Tree_Type` is a subclass of `Ada.Finalization.Limited_Controlled`, which means that we cannot make use of an assignment operator to create a copy of a binary search tree object. Describe two ways we could modify the binary search tree specification to allow an application to make copies of tree objects.

Application Level

19. Given the following declarations

```
type Credit_Rating_Type is (Poor, Fair, Good, Excellent);
type Company_String is String (1..20);
type Dollars          is delta 0.01 digits 8 range 0.00 .. 100_000.00;

type Account_Rec is
   record
      Account_Number : Positive;
      Company_Name   : Company_String;
      Balance_Due    : Dollars;
      Credit_Rating  : Credit_Rating_Type;
   end record;
```

   a. Write a function called `Number_Of` that returns the `Account_Number` field of a parameter of type `Account_Rec`.
   b. Instantiate a package called `Account_List` for a binary search tree class whose elements are `Account_Rec`s in ascending order by `Account_Number`.
   c. Write a function called `Name_Of` that returns the `Company_Name` field of a parameter of type `Account_Rec`.
   d. Instantiate a package for a binary search tree class whose elements are `Account_Rec`s in ascending order by `Company_Name`.
   e. We need a collection of `Account_Rec`s ordered alphabetically by `Company_Name` that is similar to what you created in part (d). This time, we need to be able to insert duplicate company names. We can, however, assume that companies with the same name have different account numbers. Write all of the necessary code to instantiate such a binary search tree.

20. Our word frequency application used a binary search tree to store information on words and their frequencies. We would like to know the greatest frequency in that tree. Complete the following function, assuming that it will be placed into the word frequency program. Hint: Use the iterator.

```
function Greatest_Frequency (Tree : in Freq_Tree.Tree_Type) return Natural is
-- Purpose        : Returns the highest frequency in Tree
-- Preconditions  : None
-- Postconditions : If Tree is empty, returns 0.  Otherwise, returns
--                  the highest frequency count in Tree
```

21. Our word frequency application used a binary search tree to store information on words and their frequencies. We would like to see all of the words that occurred with a particular frequency. Complete the following procedure, assuming that it will be placed into the word frequency program. Hint: Use the iterator.

```
procedure Words (Tree : in out Freq_Tree.Tree_Type;
                 Freq : in     Positive) is
-- Purpose        : Displays all words in Tree that occurred Freq times
-- Preconditions  : None
-- Postconditions : All words in Tree with a frequency of Freq are
--                  displayed in alphabetical order
```

22. Given the following declarations:

```
type Appraisal_Type is (Superior, Good, Fair, Warning, Pink_Slip);
type Dollars is delta 0.01 digits 8;
package Dollar_IO is new Ada.Text_IO.Decimal_IO (Dollars);

type Employee_Rec is
   record
      ID        : Positive;
      Salary    : Dollars;
      Appraisal : Appraisal_Type;
   end record;

function ID_Of (Employee : in Employee_Rec) return Positive is
begin
   Return Employee.ID;
end ID_Of;

package Emp_Tree is new Binary_Search_Tree (Element_Type => Employee_Rec,
                                            Key_Type     => Positive,
                                            Key_Of       => ID_Of,
                                            "<"          => "<",
                                            "="          => "=");
```

a. We need to be able to change the ID number of an employee. Complete the procedure Change_ID to change the ID number of an employee whose information is in the binary search tree.

```
procedure Change_ID (Employees : in out Emp_Tree.Tree_Type;
                     Old_ID    : in     Positive;
                     New_ID    : in     Positive) is
-- Purpose        : Change the ID number of an employee
-- Preconditions  : There is an employee with ID Old_ID
--                  There is no employee with ID New_ID
-- Postconditions : The ID number of the employee is changed
--                  from Old_ID to New_ID
```

b. Complete the following procedure to display all the employees who earn more than `Salary` dollars.

```
procedure Salaries (Employees : in out Emp_Tree.Tree_Type;
                    Salary    : Dollars) is
-- Purpose        : Displays the ID and Salary of the Employees who
--                  earn a salary greater than or equal to Salary
-- Preconditions  : None
-- Postconditions : The ID and Salary of all the Employees who
--                  earn at least Salary dollars.
--                  Employees are displayed in order by ID
```

c. Complete the procedure `Display`, which is given a binary search tree and appraisal value, and displays the IDs and salaries of every employee with that appraisal rating.

```
procedure Display (Employees : in out Emp_Tree.Tree_Type;
                   Appraisal : in     Appraisal_Type) is
-- Purpose        : Display the ID and Salary of the Employees
--                  with a given Appraisal
-- Preconditions  : None
-- Postconditions : The ID and Salary of all the Employees with
--                  the given Appraisal are displayed in order by ID
```

d. Complete the procedure `Give_Raises`, which is given a binary search tree of employee records and modifies the salary of every employee according to their last appraisal rating.

```
procedure Give_Raises (Employees : in out Emp_Tree.Tree_Type;
                       Appraisal : in     Appraisal_Type) is
-- Purpose        : Adjust Employees salaries
-- Preconditions  : None
-- Postconditions : All Employees have there salaries adjusted
--                  based upon their Appraisal
--                  Superior  raise current salary by 10%
--                  Good      raise current salary by  5%
--                  Fair      raise current salary by  3%
--                  Warning   no change
--                  Pink_Slip set salary to $0.00
```

23. Given the following declarations:

```
subtype Name_String is String (1..20);
type    Sex_Type    is (Male, Female);
type    Class_Type  is (Freshman, Sophomore, Junior, Senior, Grad);
type    GPA_Type    is digits 4 range 0.0..4.0;
```

```
type Student_Rec is
   record
      Last_Name  : Name_String;
      First_Name : Name_String;
      ID_Num     : Positive;
      Sex        : Sex_Type;
      Class      : Class_Type;
      GPA        : GPA_Type;
   end record;

function ID_Of  (Student : in Student_Rec) return Positive is
begin
   return Student.ID_Num;
end ID_Of;

package Student_Tree is new Binary_Search_Tree
                           (Element_Type => Student_Rec,
                            Key_Type     => Positive,
                            Key_Of       => ID_Of,
                            "<"          => "<",
                            "="          => "=");
```

- a. Write a procedure that takes an ID number and a binary search tree and either displays all of the corresponding student information (if the specified student is found) or prints "No student found with" and then the ID number.
- b. The dean wants to specially honor all of the students with a GPA of 4.0. Write a procedure that takes a binary search tree and prints the name of each student with a GPA of 4.0. The names can be printed in any order.
- c. A women's organization wants to select some graduating female students to receive awards. Write a procedure that is given a binary search tree and prints the name, GPA, and ID number of each of the women in the senior class, ordered from highest to lowest GPA.

Implementation Level

24. Use the three-question method to verify the recursive Find operation.
25. Use the three-question method to verify the recursive Insert operation.
26. Draw the binary search tree whose elements are inserted in the following order:
    50 72 96 94 107 26 12 11 9 2 10 25 51 16 17 95
27. Given the following binary search tree:

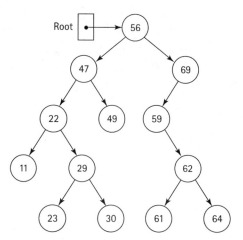

a. Trace the path that would be followed in searching for 61.
b. Trace the path that would be followed in searching for 28.
c. What would the binary search tree look like after each of the following changes? Use the original tree to answer each part; that is, ignore any changes you made in previous parts.
   i. Insert element with key 5.
   ii. Insert element with key 51.
   iii. Insert element with key 72.
   iv. Insert elements with keys 63, 77, 76, 48, 9, and 10 (in that order).
   v. Delete element with key 49.
   vi. Delete element with key 59.
   vii. Delete element with key 62.
   viii. Delete element with key 69.
   ix. Delete element with key 47.
   x. Delete element with key 56.
28. The key of the nodes in a binary search tree of animal names is a short character string.
   a. Show how such a tree would look after the following words were inserted (in the order indicated):

   "monkey" "canary" "donkey" "deer" "zebra" "yak" "walrus" "vulture" "penguin" "quail"

   b. Show how the tree would look if the same words were inserted in this order:

   "quail" "walrus" "donkey" "deer" "monkey" "vulture" "yak" "penguin" "zebra" "canary"

   c. Show how the tree would look if the same words were inserted in this order:

   "zebra" "yak" "walrus" "vulture" "quail" "penguin" "monkey" "donkey" "deer" "canary"

29. *True or False.* Invoking the delete procedure in this chapter might create a tree with more levels than the original tree had.

30. If you wanted to traverse a tree, writing all the elements to a file, and later (the next time you ran the program) rebuild the trees by reading and inserting, would an inorder traversal be appropriate? Why or why not?

31. If you wanted to traverse a tree, writing all the elements to a file, and later (the next time you ran the program) rebuild the trees by reading and inserting, which traversal would you choose so that the re-created tree is identical to the original?

32. a. One hundred integer elements are chosen at random and inserted into an ordered linked list and a binary search tree. Describe the efficiency of searching for an element in each structure, in terms of Big-O.

    b. One hundred integer elements are inserted in order, from smallest to largest, into an ordered linked list and a binary search tree. Describe the efficiency of searching for an element in each structure, in terms of Big-O.

33. When we deleted a node that had two children we replaced its element with the element that was its logical predecessor and then deleted that predecessor. We can use the logical successor in the same manner.

    a. Repeat the deletions in Exercise 27(c) using the logical successor rather than the logical predecessor.

    b. Using similar logic to the procedure `Find_And_Unlink_Max` that we used in the implementation of the binary search tree, write a procedure called `Find_And_Unlink_Min` that finds the node with the smallest key value in a tree and unlinks it from the tree. A pointer to the unlinked node should be returned as an `out` parameter.

    c. Modify the `Delete_Root` procedure from our implementation of the binary search tree so that it uses the logical successor (rather than the predecessor) of the value to be deleted in the case of deleting a node with two children. You should call the procedure `Find_And_Unlink_Min` that you wrote in part (b).

34. The following operation has been added to the specification of our binary search tree package. Write the body.

    ```
    function Height (Tree : in Tree_Type) return Natural;
    -- Preconditions  : None
    -- Postconditions : Return the number of levels in tree
    ```

    You will need to determine the larger of two natural numbers. Ada provides the attribute `'Max` for every scalar type. This attribute can be used to determine the larger of two values of that type. For example, the following statement puts a copy of the larger of the positive variables `Apple` and `Orange` into `Fruit`:

    ```
    Fruit := Positive'Max (Apple, Orange);
    ```

35. The following operation has been added to the specification of our binary search tree package:

```
procedure Ancestors
    (Tree    : in Tree_Type;
     Key     : in Key_Type;
     Process : not null access procedure (Element : in out Element_Type));
-- Purpose         : Process the ancestors of the node with the given Key
-- Preconditions   : Key exists in Tree
-- Postconditions  : Process is called for every ancestor of Key in Tree
```

    a. Write the body of procedure `Ancestors` that uses a nonrecursive algorithm. The ancestors should be processed from oldest to youngest; that is, process the parent before the child.

    b. How would you modify your answer to part (a) if you had to process the ancestors from youngest to oldest?

    c. Write the body of procedure `Ancestors` that uses a recursive algorithm. The ancestors should be processed from youngest to oldest.

36. The following operation has been added to the specification of our binary search tree package.

```
function Leaf_Count (Tree : in Tree_Type) return Natural;
-- Preconditions   : None
-- Postconditions  : Returns the number of leaves in Tree
```

    a. Write the body for function `Leaf_Count`.

    b. What is the Big-O of function `Leaf_Count`?

37. The following operation has been added to the specification of our binary search tree package. Write the body.

```
function Single_Child_Count (Tree : in Tree_Type) return Natural;
-- Preconditions   : None
-- Postconditions  : Returns the number of nodes in Tree with one child
```

38. The following operation has been added to the specification of our binary search tree package. Write the body. Make sure that you produce a copy and not an alias.

```
procedure Copy (Source : in  Tree_Type;
                Target : out Tree_Type);
-- Purpose         : Make a copy of a binary search tree
-- Preconditions   : None
-- Postconditions  : Target is a copy of Source
```

39. The following operation has been added to the specification of our binary search tree package. Write the body.

```
function Same_Shape (Left  : in Tree_Type;
                     Right : in Tree_Type) return Boolean;
-- Preconditions   : None
-- Postconditions  : Returns True if the two trees have the same shape
```

40. In Chapter 8 we discussed how a linked list could be stored in an array of nodes using index values as "pointers" and managing our list of free nodes. We can use these same techniques to store the nodes of a binary search tree in an array, rather than using dynamic storage allocation. Here are declarations that could be used to store a binary search tree in an array of nodes:

```
Max_Nodes : constant := 10;

type Node_Ptr is range 0..Max_Nodes;
Nil : constant Node_Ptr := 0;

type Node_Type is
   record
      Info  : Character;
      Left  : Node_Ptr := Nil;
      Right : Node_Ptr := Nil;
   end record;

subtype Index_Type is Node_Ptr range 1..Node_Ptr'Last;
type    Node_Array is array (Index_Type) of Node_Type;

Nodes : Node_Array;   -- Array storage for a binary tree and free list
Root  : Node_Ptr;     -- Pointer to the root node of a binary search tree
Free  : Node_Ptr;     -- Pointer to the first of a list of free nodes
```

    a. The picture below shows the value of the array and external pointers after inserting the following values into the binary search tree:

       Q L W F M R N S

	Nodes .Info	.Left	.Right
(1)	Q		
(2)	L		
(3)	W		
(4)	F		
(5)	M		
(6)	R		
(7)	N		
(8)	S		
(9)	garb	garb	10
(10)	garb	garb	0

Root: 1

Free: 9

The content of the boxes containing *garb* are undefined. As we did in Chapter 8, we use a linked stack to keep track of array nodes not currently in use. The free nodes are linked through their right child pointers. You can see in the picture that there are two free nodes in this linked stack.

Fill in the remaining 16 pointer values in the above picture. Hint: Draw a circle and arrow picture of the binary search tree you would obtain by inserting the elements in the given order. Once you know all the parent–child relationships, you can easily fill in the pointer values.

b. Fill in the following picture to show what happened to the previous picture after the insertion of H and the deletion of L.

41. Consider the following binary trees:
   a. Which satisfy the binary search tree property?
   b. Which are complete binary trees?
   c. Which are perfect binary trees?

(a)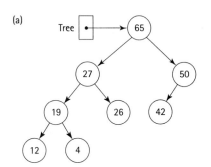

(a)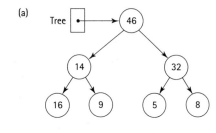

(c)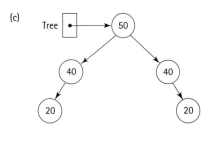

(d)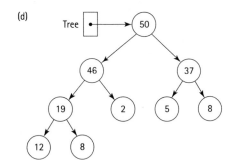

(e)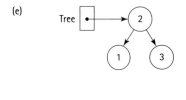

(f)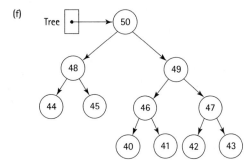

42. The elements in the following complete binary tree are to be stored in an array, as described in the chapter. Each element is a Natural value.

   a. Does this binary tree satisfy the binary search tree property?
   b. Show the contents of the array.

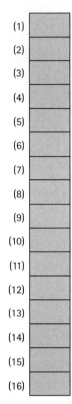
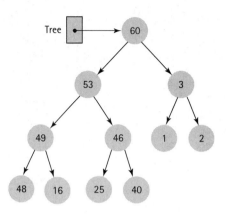

43. Given the array pictured below, draw the binary tree that can be created from its elements. (The elements are arranged in the array as discussed in the chapter.)

(1)	1
(2)	55
(3)	59
(4)	44
(5)	33
(6)	58
(7)	57
(8)	22
(9)	11
(10)	99

44. A binary tree is stored in an array called Tree, which is indexed from 1 to 100, as described in the chapter. The tree contains 85 elements. Mark each of the following statements as true or false, and explain your answers.

   a. Tree(43) is a leaf node.
   b. Tree(42) has only one child.
   c. The right child of Tree(13) is Tree(26).
   d. The subtree rooted at Tree(8) is a perfect binary tree with four levels.
   e. The tree has seven levels that are perfect, and one additional level that contains some elements.

Programming Problems

45. Add the new operations described in Exercises 34 through 39 to Specification 10.1. Add the bodies you wrote to Body 10.1. Prepare a test plan to test these operations and implement the test program.

46. a. Write a package declaration for a binary search tree abstract data object (ADO) that stores the tree nodes in a direct file. Be sure to include an operation that saves the tree information necessary to use the tree again the next time the program is run.
    b. Implement the package body for this ADO.
    c. Write a "dump" program that displays all of the components of the file produced by your ADO.
    d. Write a test plan for testing this ADO. You may use the dump program in your plan.

47. In an inorder traversal, we move as far to the left as we can, letting the run-time stack keep track of the nodes that we pass. When we reach a null tree, we back up, process the node, and move to the node's right child. The process then repeats itself. This algorithm can be implemented using a stack rather than using recursion. Write an iterative inorder traversal procedure. You may instantiate a stack from either of the packages developed in Chapter 5. (Hint: The traversal is finished when the stack is empty and the right child is null.)

Priority Queues, Heaps, and Graphs

Goals

Goals for this chapter include that you should be able to

- describe a priority queue at the logical level and discuss alternative implementation approaches.
- describe the shape and order properties of a heap, and implement a heap in a nonlinked tree representation in an array.
- compare the implementation of a priority queue using a heap, linked list, and binary search tree.
- define the following terms related to graphs:

  - directed graph
  - undirected graph
  - vertex
  - edge
  - path
  - complete graph
  - weighted graph
  - adjacency matrix
  - adjacency list

- implement a graph using an adjacency matrix to represent the edges.
- implement a graph using an adjacency list of edges.
- explain the difference between a depth-first and a breadth-first search and implement these searching strategies using stacks and queues for auxiliary storage.
- implement a shortest-paths operation, using a priority queue to access the edge with the minimum weight.

So far we have examined several basic classes in depth, discussing their uses and operations, as well as one or more implementations of each. As we have constructed these programmer-defined data structures out of the built-in types provided by our high-level language, we have noted variations that adapt them to the needs of different applications. In Chapter 10 we looked at how a tree structure, the binary search tree, facilitates searching data stored in a linked structure. In this chapter we will see how other branching structures are used to model a variety of applications.

11.1 Priority Queues

A priority queue is an abstract data type with an interesting accessing protocol. Only the *highest-priority* element can be accessed. "Highest priority" can mean different things, depending on the application. Consider, for example, a small company with one secretary. When employees leave work on the secretary's desk, which jobs get done first? The jobs are processed in order of the employee's importance in the company; the secretary completes the president's work before starting the vice president's, and does the marketing director's work before the work of the staff programmers. The *priority* of each job relates to the level of the employee who initiated it.

In a telephone answering system, calls are answered in the order in which they are received; that is, the highest-priority call is the one that has been waiting the longest. Thus a FIFO queue can be considered a priority queue whose highest-priority element is the one that has been queued the longest time.

Sometimes a printer shared by a number of computers is configured to always print the smallest job in its queue first. This way, someone who is printing only a few pages does not have to wait for large jobs to finish. For such printers, the priority of the jobs relates to the size of the job: shortest job first.

The Logical Level

The operations defined for the priority queue class include operations to enqueue items, dequeue items, and clear a priority queue, as well as to test for an empty or full priority queue. These operations are very similar to those specified for the FIFO queue discussed in Chapter 6. The Enqueue operation adds a given element to the priority queue. The Dequeue operation removes the highest-priority element from the priority queue and returns it. The difference is that the priority queue does not follow the "first in, first out" approach; the priority queue always returns the highest priority item from the current set of enqueued items, no matter when it was enqueued. What happens when there are items with the same priority in the queue? Say, for example, when the president has given the secretary two jobs to complete. In this case, we sometimes dequeue the item that has been in the queue the longest. Other times we simply return any of the items with the same priority. Specification 11.1 defines a priority queue class in which we take the latter approach to duplicate priorities.

Specification 11.1   Priority Queue

```ada
generic
   type Element_Type  is private;
   type Priority_Type is limited private;
   with function Priority_Of (Element : in Element_Type) return Priority_Type;
   with function ">" (Left : in Priority_Type; Right : in Priority_Type)
                     return Boolean;
package Priority_Queue is

   -- This package implements a Priority Queue.
   -- The priorities are ordered by the generic formal function ">"

   type Queue_Type (Max_Size : Positive) is tagged limited private;

   OVERFLOW  : exception;
   UNDERFLOW : exception;

   ------------------------------------------------------------------------
   procedure Clear (Queue : in out Queue_Type);
   -- Purpose        : Remove all elements from the queue
   -- Preconditions  : None
   -- Postconditions : Queue is empty; it contains no elements


   ------------------------------------------------------------------------
   procedure Enqueue (Queue : in out Queue_Type;
                      Item  : in     Element_Type);
   -- Purpose        : Adds Item to the rear of Queue
   -- Preconditions  : None
   -- Postconditions : Queue = original Queue with Item included
   -- Exceptions     : OVERFLOW  Raised on attempt to Enqueue an element onto
   --                            a full queue.  Queue is unchanged.


   ------------------------------------------------------------------------
   procedure Dequeue (Queue : in out Queue_Type;
                      Item  :    out Element_Type);
   -- Purpose        : Removes and returns the element with the highest
   --                  priority from Queue
   -- Preconditions  : None
   -- Postconditions : Queue = original Queue with highest priority element
   --                  priority from Queue.  Elements with equal priority
   --                  are not ordered.
   --                  Item  = highest priority element of original queue
   -- Exceptions     : UNDERFLOW  Raised on attempt to dequeue an element from
   --                             an empty Queue.  Queue remains empty.
```

```ada
  --------------------------------------------------------------------
  function Full (Queue : in Queue_Type) return Boolean;
  -- Purpose        : Tests whether a queue is full.  A queue is full when
  --                  no more elements can be enqueued into it
  -- Preconditions  : None
  -- Postconditions : Full = (no more elements can be enqueued into Queue)

  --------------------------------------------------------------------
  function Empty (Queue : in Queue_Type) return Boolean;
  -- Purpose        : Tests whether a queue is empty (contains no elements)
  -- Preconditions  : None
  -- Postconditions : Empty = (Queue is empty)

private

  -- We fill this in later

end Priority_Queue;
```

The generic formal parameters of this package are nearly identical to those of our key-ordered list and binary search tree packages. In a priority queue we are interested in the priority of a particular element. We do not need to have unique keys for elements in a priority queue.

The Application Level

In discussing FIFO queue applications in Chapter 6, we said that the operating system of a multiuser computer system may use job queues to save users' requests in the order in which they are made. Another way such requests may be handled is according to how important the job request is. That is, the head of the company might get higher priority than the lowly junior programmer. Or an interactive program might get higher priority than a job to print out a report that isn't needed until the next day. To handle these requests efficiently, the operating system may use a structure called a priority queue.

One of the authors had a recent experience with a priority queue. After an accident with a router in his wood shop he went to the emergency room of the local hospital to repair his mangled little finger. He was happy to see a nearly empty waiting room and called home to say that he would not be long. While waiting for his name to be called, several ambulances arrived with victims of a multi-car accident. Hospital emergency rooms see patients in priority queue order; the patient with the most severe injuries sees the doctor first. Needless to say, it was many hours before the author finally returned home.

Priority queues are also useful in sorting. Given a set of elements to sort, we can enqueue the elements into a priority queue, and then dequeue them in sorted order (from largest to smallest). We'll have a look at a version of such a sort in Chapter 12.

11.1 Priority Queues

Let's look in a little more detail at our example of a small company with a single secretary. He would like a program to help manage the work requests that other employees submit to him. These requests are prioritized in the following order:

President	*Highest Priority*
Vice presidents	
Managers	
Staff	*Lowest Priority*

We can use an enumeration type to represent these priorities:

```
type Title_Type is (Staff, Manager, Vice_President, President);
```

Notice that we have arranged these job titles from lowest to highest priority. A work request can be modeled as a record.

```
type Work_Request_Rec is
   record
      Name  : Name_String;        -- Name of person submitting the request
      Title : Title_Type;         -- Title of person submitting the request
      Work  : Description_Type;   -- Description of the work
   end record;
```

We have now defined the type of the element (Work_Request_Rec) for our priority queue and the type on which priorities are based (Title_Type). Our generic priority queue package also requires that we supply two functions. The first function returns the priority of an element. The priority of a work request is determined by the job title of the requestor. Here is a function that returns that information:

```
function Title_Of (Request : in Work_Request_Rec) return Title_Type is
begin
   return Request.Title;
end Title_Of;
```

The second function needed to instantiate a priority queue of work requests is one to determine whether one priority value is greater than another. In our application, a priority value is an enumeration type (Title_Type). Our declaration of Title_Type gives us all the relational operators for this type so we do not have to write the comparison function ourselves. Here, then, is the code to instantiate a priority queue class with work requests as queue elements and priority by job title:

```
-- Job queue giving the President highest priority
package Job_Queue is new Priority_Queue (Element_Type  => Work_Request_Rec,
                                         Priority_Type => Title_Type,
                                         Priority_Of   => Title_Of,
                                         ">"           => ">");
```

Now suppose someone in the company discovers that more profits are made when the staff's job requests are completed before the president's requests; that is, to maximize profits, we need to reverse our current priorities. We could make this change in our program by reversing the order of the values in the enumeration type Title_Type. But, what if the original order is required by other parts of our program. Reversing the declaration order might require us to make many changes elsewhere in the program. There is another way to reverse our priorities: Supply the "reverse" relational operator in the instantiation. Then our instantiation becomes:

```
-- Job queue giving the President lowest priority
package Job_Queue is new Priority_Queue (Element_Type  => Work_Request_Rec,
                                         Priority_Type => Title_Type,
                                         Priority_Of   => Title_Of,
                                         ">"           => "<");
```

This instantiation creates a priority queue whose highest priority element is the one with the lowest value of job title.

The Implementation Level

There are many ways to implement a priority queue. In any implementation, we want to access the element with the highest priority quickly and easily. Let's briefly consider some possible approaches:

An Unsorted List   Enqueing an item would be very easy. Simply insert it at the end of the array or the beginning of a linked list, an O(1) operation. However, dequeing would require searching through the entire list, an O(N) operation, to find the highest priority element.

An Array-Based Sorted List   Dequeing is very easy with this approach. Simply return the last (highest priority) element from the array and reduce the size of the list, an O(1) operation. Enqueing, however, would be more expensive: We have to find the place to enqueue the item [O($\log_2 N$) if we use a binary search] and reorganize the elements in the array after moving array elements to make room for the new element [O(N)].

A Pointer-Based Sorted List   Let's assume that the linked list is kept sorted from highest priority to lowest priority. Dequeing simply requires removing and returning the first list element. From our experience with a linked list–based stack, we know that this operation requires only a few steps and is O(1). But enqueing again is O(N) because we must search the list one element at a time to find the insertion location.

A Binary Search Tree For this approach the enqueue operation would be implemented as a standard binary search tree insert operation. We know that this operation can vary between $O(\log_2 N)$ if the tree is bushy and $O(N)$ if the tree is degenerate. To dequeue, we must find the node with the highest priority and remove it from the search tree. We can use the `Find_And_Unlink_Max` procedure that we developed for deleting a node with two children to accomplish this task. This procedure's performance depends on the height of the tree, so our dequeue operation may also vary between $O(\log_2 N)$ and $O(N)$. Because we cannot have duplicate "keys" in a binary search tree, this approach to implementing a priority queue is restricted to those applications where each element has a unique priority.

A Heap In the next section we present an implementation of a priority queue based on a data structure called the heap. The heap guarantees $O(\log_2 N)$ for both enqueue and dequeue, even in the worst case.

The following table summarizes the efficiency of these different implementations.

Comparison of Priority Queue Implementations

	Enqueue	Dequeue
Unsorted list	$O(1)$	$O(N)$
Sorted list	$O(N)$	$O(1)$
Binary search tree		
Bushy	$O(\log_2 N)$	$O(\log_2 N)$
Degenerate	$O(N)$	$O(N)$
Heap	$O(\log_2 N)$	$O(\log_2 N)$

11.2 Heaps

The Logical Level

A heap is a binary tree that satisfies two properties, one concerning its shape and the other concerning the order of its elements. The *shape property* is simple: A heap must be a complete binary tree.[1] The *order property* defines a relationship between the value of an element and the values of its children. There are two possible orders. A **max-heap** is one in which the value of each element in the tree is greater than or equal to the values of its children. A **min-heap** is one in which the value of each element

> **Max-heap** A complete binary tree, each of whose elements contains a value that is greater than or equal to the value of each of its children.
>
> **Min-heap** A complete binary tree, each of whose elements contains a value that is less than or equal to the value of each of its children.

---

[1] In case you've forgotten, a complete binary tree is a binary that is either perfect or perfect through the next-to-last level, with the leaves on the last level as far to the left as possible.

in the tree is less than or equal to the values of its children. In this book we deal exclusively with max-heaps. When we say *heap*, we are referring to a max-heap.

Don't confuse the *heap data structure* with the *heap region of memory* we discussed in the context of dynamic memory allocation. These two concepts are not related.

Figure 11.1 shows two binary trees containing the values 'A' through 'J' that fulfill both the shape and order properties. Notice that the placement of the values differs in the two trees, but the shape is the same: a complete binary tree of 10 elements. Note also that the two heaps have the same root node. A group of values can be stored in a binary tree in many ways and still satisfy the order property of heaps. Because of the shape property, we know that the shape of all the heaps with a given number of elements are the same. We also know, because of the order property, that the root node always contains the largest value in the heap. This fact gives us a hint as to what this data structure might be good for. The special feature of heaps is that we always know where the maximum value is: It is in the root node.

Let's say that we want to remove the element with the largest value from a heap. The largest element is in the root node, so we can easily remove it, as illustrated in Figure 11.2(a). But this leaves a hole in the root position. We need to move one of the other elements to fill this hole. Because the heap's tree must be complete, we decide to fill the hole with the bottom rightmost element from the heap; now the structure satisfies the shape property (Figure 11.2[b]). However, the replacement value came from the bottom of the tree, where the smaller values are; the tree no longer satisfies the order property of heaps.

This situation suggests one of the basic heap operations: Given a complete binary tree whose elements, *other than the one in the root position*, satisfy the heap order property, repair the structure so that it is again a heap. This operation, called Reheap_Down, involves moving the element down from the root position until it ends up in a position where the order property is satisfied (see Figure 11.2[c]).

Now let's say that we want to add an element to the heap—where do we put it? The shape property tells us that the tree must be complete, so we put the new element in the next bottom leftmost place in the tree, as illustrated in Figure 11.3(a). Now the shape property is satisfied, but the order property may be violated. This situation illustrates the need for another basic heap operation. Given a complete binary tree whose elements, *other than the one in the last position*, satisfy the heap order property, repair the structure so that it is again a heap. To fix this structure, we need to float the last element up the tree until it is in its correct place (see Figure 11.3[b]). This operation is called Reheap_Up.

Although we have graphically depicted heaps as binary trees with nodes and links, it is very impractical to implement the heap operations using the usual linked tree representation. Our Reheap_Up operation needs to determine the parent of a given node. Parent determination is difficult with pointers. The shape property of heaps tells us that the binary tree is complete, so we know that it never has any holes in it. Thus we can easily store the tree in an array with implicit links. Recall from Chapter 10 that with this tree-to-array mapping, the index of a node's parent is the index of the node divided by two. Figure 11.4 shows how the values in a heap would be stored in this array representation. If a heap with N elements is implemented in this way, the shape property says

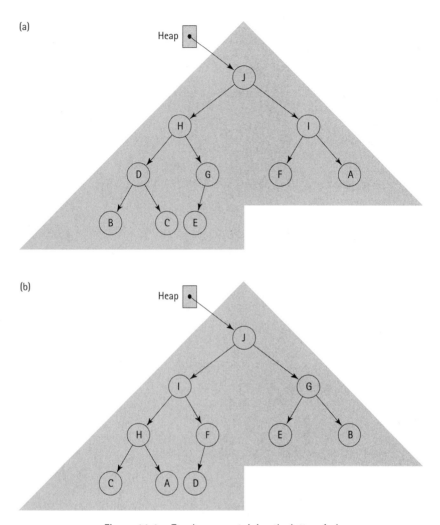

Figure 11.1 *Two heaps containing the letters A–J.*

that the heap elements are stored in N consecutive slots in the array, with the root element in the first slot and the last leaf node in the Nth slot.

Specification 11.2 contains the specifications of the two heap restoration operations. Most of the generic formal parameters of this package serve the same function as those in our generic key-ordered list and binary search tree packages. But unlike those two packages, we have not encapsulated the declaration of a heap *type* in our package. Instead, we have made the type for the heap a generic formal array parameter. The user of this package is responsible for declaring an array type for `Heap_Array`. Because the details of the heap array type are declared by the user, our heap package is not an abstract data type (ADT). It is simply a service package that supplies two operations for unconstrained one-dimensional arrays. Our heap package contains no insert, delete, tra-

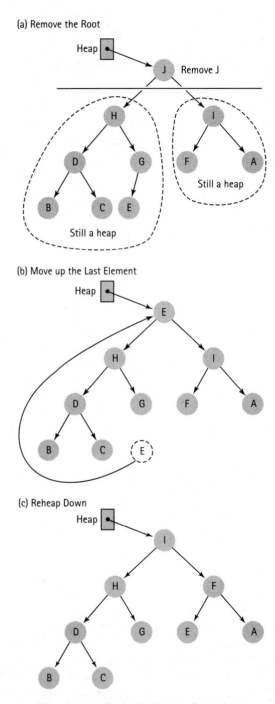

Figure 11.2 *Removing the root from a heap.*

11.2 Heaps

(a) Add as a Leaf

(b) Reheap Up

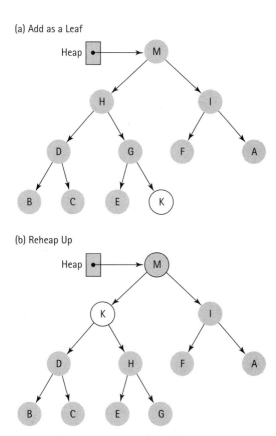

Figure 11.3 *Adding an element to a heap.*

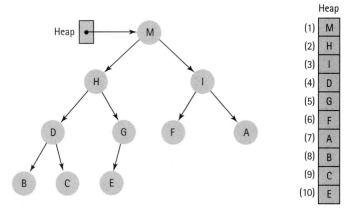

Figure 11.4 *Heap values in an array representation.*

verse, or other operations common with lists and trees. Heaps are seldom used alone. Like arrays, heaps are used as building blocks for higher level classes. They are most commonly used to implement priority queues (discussed in the next section) and efficient sorting procedures (Chapter 12).

Specification 11.2   Heap

```ada
generic
   type Element_Type is private;
   type Key_Type    is limited private;
   type Heap_Array  is array (Positive range <>) of Element_Type;
   with function Key_Of (Element : in Element_Type) return Key_Type;
   with function ">" (Left : in Key_Type; Right : in Key_Type) return Boolean;
package Heap is

-- This package implements a Heap, a binary tree that satisfies
-- two properties:
--    1. Shape Property : A heap must be a complete binary tree.
--    2. Order Property : The key of every node is greater than or equal to
--                        the keys of its children. This order is based on
--                        the formal generic ">" function.

-- The keys of the elements in a heap need not be unique.

   -----------------------------------------------------------------------
   procedure Reheap_Down (Heap : in out Heap_Array);
   -- Purpose        : Restores the order property to Heap.
   -- Preconditions  : The order property of heaps is violated only
   --                  by the first element of Heap.
   -- Postconditions: The order property applies to all elements of Heap.

   -----------------------------------------------------------------------
   procedure Reheap_Up (Heap : in out Heap_Array);
   -- Purpose        : Restores the order property to Heap.
   -- Preconditions:   The order property of heaps is violated only
   --                  by the last element of Heap.
   -- Postconditions: The order property applies to all elements of Heap.

end Heap;
```

The Application Level

Our application example for the heap is an implementation of the priority queue. A heap is an excellent way to implement a priority queue. Here are the appropriate private part declarations for Specification 11.1 to implement a heap-based priority queue:

```
private   -- for the priority queue of Specification 11.1

   -- An unconstrained array of priority queue elements
   type Queue_Array is array (Positive range <>) of Element_Type;

   type Queue_Type (Max_Size : Positive) is tagged limited
      record
         Count : Natural := 0;
         Items : Queue_Array (1..Max_Size);
      end record;

end Priority_Queue;
```

We keep the number of elements in a priority queue in Count. The elements are stored in the first Count slots of array Items. Because of the heap order property, we know that the largest element is in the root—that is, in the first array slot.

Let's look first at the Dequeue operation. The root element is returned to the caller. After we remove the root, we are left with two subtrees, each of which satisfies the heap property (review Figure 11.2). Of course, we cannot leave a hole in the root position, because that violates the shape property. Because we have removed an element, there are now Count - 1 elements left in the priority queue, stored in array slots 2 through Count. If we fill the hole in the root position with the bottom element, array slots 1 through Count - 1 contain the heap elements. The heap shape property is now intact, but the order property may be violated. The resulting structure is not a heap, but it is almost a heap—all of the elements, *other than the one in the root position*, satisfy the order property. This is an easy problem to correct, because we have a heap operation to do exactly this task: Reheap_Down. Here is our algorithm for Dequeue.

Dequeue
    Item := root element of heap
    Copy last leaf element into the root position
    Decrement Count
    Reheap Down

The Enqueue operation involves adding an element in its "appropriate" place in the heap. Where is this place? If the new element's priority is larger than the current root element's priority, we know that the new element belongs in the root. But that's not the typical case; we want a more general solution. To start, we can put the new element at the bottom of the heap, in the next available leaf position (review Figure 11.3). Now the array contains elements in the first `Count + 1` slots, preserving the heap shape property. The resulting structure is probably not a heap, but it's almost a heap—all of the elements, *other than the one in the last position*, satisfy the order property. This problem is easy to solve, using the `Reheap_Up` operation. Here is our algorithm for `Enqueue`:

Enqueue
    Increment Count
    Put Item in next available leaf position
    Reheap Up

The Ada code for all the priority queue operations is given in Body 11.1.

Body 11.1   Priority Queue: Implements Specification 11.1

```ada
with Heap;
package body Priority_Queue is

   -- Instantiate a heap service package using the declarations from the
   -- priority queue's generic formal parameters and private part.

   package Queue_Heap is new Heap (Element_Type => Element_Type,
                                   Key_Type     => Priority_Type,
                                   Heap_Array   => Queue_Array,
                                   Key_Of       => Priority_Of,
                                   ">"          => ">");
   use Queue_Heap;

   -------------------------------------------------------------------------

   procedure Enqueue (Queue : in out Queue_Type;
                      Item  : in     Element_Type) is
   begin
      if Queue.Count = Queue.Max_Size then
        raise OVERFLOW;
      else
         -- Put Item in the next free array slot
         Queue.Count               := Queue.Count + 1;
         Queue.Items(Queue.Count)  := Item;
         -- At this point, the heap order property applies to Items(1..Count-1)
         -- It is violated only by the last leaf node.  Fix it.
         Reheap_Up (Heap => Queue.Items(1..Queue.Count));
      end if;
   end Enqueue;

   -------------------------------------------------------------------------
```

```ada
   procedure Dequeue (Queue : in out Queue_Type;
                      Item  :    out Element_Type) is
begin
   if Queue.Count = 0 then
      raise UNDERFLOW;
   else
      Item := Queue.Items(1);    -- Return the root element
      -- Move the last leaf element into the root position
      Queue.Items(1) := Queue.Items(Queue.Count);
      Queue.Count    := Queue.Count - 1;
      -- At this point the heap order property applies to Items(2..Count).
      -- It is violated only by the root node.  Fix it.
      Reheap_Down (Heap => Queue.Items(1..Queue.Count));
   end if;
end Dequeue;

-------------------------------------------------------------------------

function Full (Queue : in Queue_Type) return Boolean is
begin
   return Queue.Count = Queue.Max_Size;
end Full;

-------------------------------------------------------------------------

function Empty (Queue : in Queue_Type) return Boolean is
begin
   return Queue.Count = 0;
end Empty;

-------------------------------------------------------------------------

procedure Clear (Queue : in out Queue_Type) is
begin
   Queue.Count := 0;
end Clear;
end Priority_Queue;
```

The heap instantiation is the most revealing aspect of the priority queue implementation. The `Queue_Array`, defined to hold the queue elements, is treated as a heap. What the heap specification calls a *key*, our application calls a *priority*. The queue body simply passes on its generic parameters to the heap.

The Implementation Level

Now we are ready to implement the two heap operations. The order property says that the key of any parent node in the heap is greater than or equal to the keys of its children. This means that for every *nonleaf* node, `Heap(Index)`,

```
Key_Of (Heap(Index))  >=  Key_Of (Heap(Index * 2))
```

and, if there is a right child

```
Key_Of (Heap(Index))  >=  Key_Of (Heap(Index * 2 + 1))
```

We've specified two operations to fix heaps that violate this order property at one end or the other. Now let's look at these operations in more detail.

When the `Reheap_Down` procedure is called, there are two possibilities. If the value of the root node, `Heap(1)`, is greater than or equal to the values of its children, the order property is still intact and we don't have to do anything. Otherwise we know that the maximum value of the tree is in either the root node's left child, `Heap(2)`, or the right child, `Heap(3)`. One of these values must be swapped with the smaller value in the root. Now the subtree rooted at the node that was swapped is a heap—except (possibly) for *its* root node. We apply the same process again, asking whether the value in this node is greater than or equal to the values in its children. We test smaller and smaller subtrees of the original heap, moving our original root node down until

1. the root of the current subtree is a leaf node; or
2. the value in the root of the current subtree is greater than or equal to the values of both its children.

The algorithm for this procedure is given below and illustrated with an example in Figure 11.5. With each call, `Heap'First` is the index of the root node that (possibly) violates the heap order property.

Reheap_Down
    -- Check for Base Case 1: Heap(Root) is a leaf
    if Heap(Root) is not a leaf node then
        -- Root is not a leaf so find the child with the larger key
        Max_Child := index of child with larger key
        -- Check for Base Case 2: Order property intact
        if Key_Of (Heap(Max_Child)) > Key_Of (Heap(Root)) then
            Swap the values in the root and larger child   *-- General case*
            Reheap_Down (Heap => Heap with root at Max_Child)
        else
            do nothing   *-- Base case, order intact*
        end if
    else
        do nothing   *-- Base case, a leaf node*
    end if

This is a recursive algorithm. In the general case, we swap the values in the root node with its largest child, and then repeat the process. On the recursive call, we pass

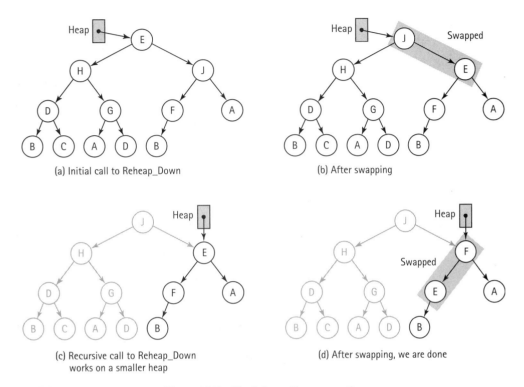

Figure 11.5 *The Reheap_Down operation.*

the subtree whose root is Max_Child; this shrinks the size of the tree still to be processed, satisfying the smaller-caller question. There are two base cases: (1) if Heap(Root) is a leaf, and (2) if the heap order property is already intact. In either of these cases, we do nothing.

How do we determine whether the root node is a leaf? We make use of another property of our mapping of a complete tree into an array (Figure 11.4). Elements with indices between Heap'First and Heap'Last / 2 have children. Elements with indices between Heap'Last / 2 + 1 and Heap'Last are leaves. So if the index of our (current) root is less than or equal to Heap'Last / 2, we know it is not a leaf.

To determine Max_Child (the index of the child with the larger key), we first check to see whether the current root node has only a single child. If so, it will be a left child (because the tree is complete), and we set Max_Child to its index. Otherwise we compare the values of the two child nodes and set Max_Child to the index of the node that has the larger value. The complete procedure Reheap_Down is given in Body 11.2.

The converse operation, Reheap_Up, takes a leaf node that violates the order property of heaps and moves it up until its correct position is found. We compare the value of the bottom node with the value of its parent node. If the parent's value is smaller, the order property is violated, so the two nodes are swapped. Then we examine the parent, repeating the process until

1. the current node is the root of the heap; or
2. the value in the current node is less than or equal to the value of its parent node.

The algorithm for this procedure is given below and illustrated in Figure 11.6.

Reheap_Up

```
-- Check for Base Case 1: Heap(Bottom) is the root
if Heap(Bottom) is not the root node then
    -- Bottom is not the root. Determine its parent
    Parent := Index of parent of Heap(Bottom)
    -- Check for Base Case 2: Order property intact
    if Key_Of (Heap(Bottom)) > Key_Of (Heap(Parent)) then
        Swap Heap(Bottom) and Heap(Parent)              -- General case
        Reheap_Up (Heap => Heap with Parent as new Bottom)
    else
        do nothing                                       -- Base case, order intact
    end if;
else
    do nothing                                           -- Base case, root node
end if
```

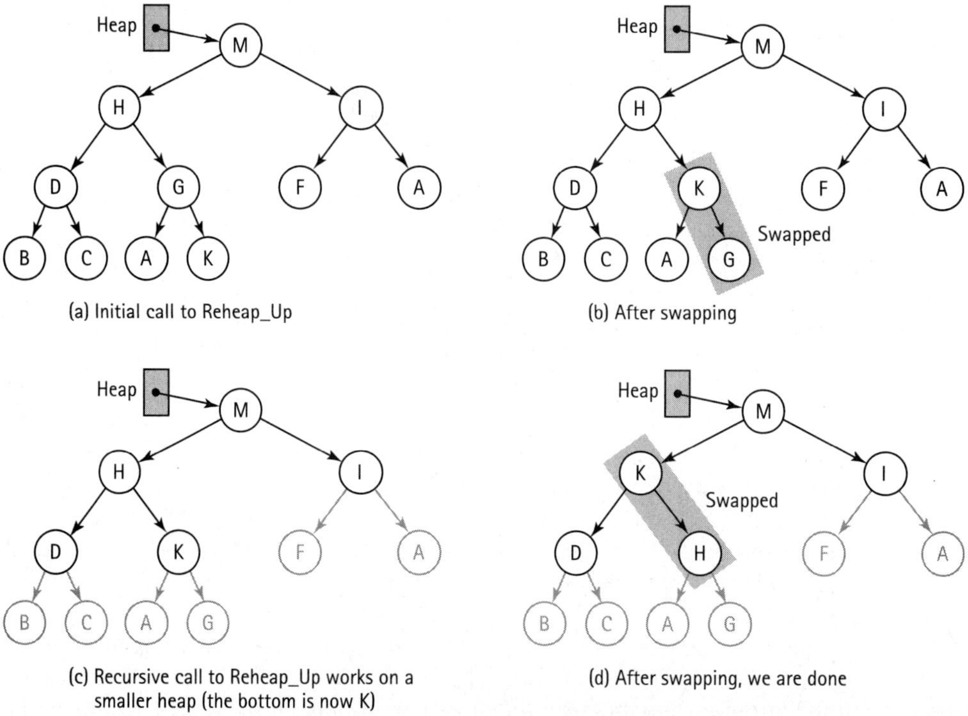

(a) Initial call to Reheap_Up

(b) After swapping

(c) Recursive call to Reheap_Up works on a smaller heap (the bottom is now K)

(d) After swapping, we are done

Figure 11.6 *The Reheap_Up operation.*

This is also a recursive algorithm. In the general case, we swap the (current) "bottom" node with its parent and invoke the procedure again. On the recursive call, we specify Parent as the bottom node; this shrinks the size of the tree still to be processed, so the smaller-caller question can be answered affirmatively. There are two base cases: (1) if we have reached the root node, or (2) if the heap order property is satisfied. In either of these cases, we exit the procedure without doing anything.

It is easy to determine whether the current node is the root node; the index of the root node is Heap'First. How do we find the parent node so that we can test the heap order property? This task is not easy in a binary tree linked together with pointers from parent to child nodes, but, as we saw earlier, it is very simple in our implicit link implementation: If a node is not the root, the index of the node's parent is the node's index divided by 2.

Body 11.2 contains the code for Reheap_Up.

Body 11.2 Heap: Implements Specification 11.2

```
package body Heap is


procedure Swap (Left : in out Element_Type; Right : in out Element_Type) is
-- Swaps the values of two variables
   Temp : Element_Type;
begin
   Temp  := Left;
   Left  := Right;
   Right := Temp;
end Swap;
pragma Inline(Swap);


function Larger_Child (Heap : in Heap_Array) return Positive is
-- Purpose        : Find the larger child of the root node of Heap
-- Preconditions  : The root node has at least a left child
-- Postconditions : Returns the index of the larger child of the
--                  root node of Heap

   Left_Child  : Positive;  -- Index of the left child node
   Right_Child : Positive;  -- Index of the right child node
begin
   Left_Child  := Heap'First * 2;
   Right_Child := Heap'First * 2 + 1;
   if Right_Child > Heap'Last then  -- Does the root node have a right child?
      return Left_Child;  -- There is no right child, left child is "larger"
```

```ada
      else   -- Pick the greater of the two children
         if Key_Of (Heap(Left_Child)) > Key_Of (Heap(Right_Child)) then
            return Left_Child;
         else
            return Right_Child;
         end if;
      end if;
   end Larger_Child;

------------------------------------------------------------------------

   procedure Reheap_Down (Heap : in out Heap_Array) is
      Root      : Positive;   -- Index of the root node
      Max_Child : Positive;   -- Index of child with larger key
   begin
      Root := Heap'First;
      -- Check for Base Case 1: Heap(Root) is a leaf
      if Root <= Heap'Last / 2 then
         -- Root is not a leaf so find the child with the larger key
         Max_Child := Larger_Child (Heap);
         -- Check for Base Case 2: Order property intact
         if Key_Of (Heap(Max_Child)) > Key_Of (Heap(Root)) then
            -- General Case: Swap and reheap
            Swap (Heap(Root), Heap(Max_Child));
            Reheap_Down (Heap => Heap(Max_Child..Heap'Last));
         end if;
      end if;
   end Reheap_Down;

------------------------------------------------------------------------

   procedure Reheap_Up (Heap : in out Heap_Array) is
      Bottom : Positive;   -- Index of the bottom node in the heap
      Parent : Positive;   -- Index of the parent of Bottom
   begin
      Bottom := Heap'Last;
      -- Check for Base Case 1: Heap(Bottom) is the root
      if Bottom > Heap'First then
         -- Bottom is not the root. Determine its parent
         Parent := Bottom / 2;
         -- Check for Base Case 2: Order property intact
         if Key_Of (Heap(Bottom)) > Key_Of (Heap(Parent)) then
            -- General Case: Swap and reheap
            Swap (Heap(Parent), Heap(Bottom));
```

```
            Reheap_Up (Heap => Heap(Heap'First..Parent));
         end if;
      end if;
   end Reheap_Up;
end Heap;
```

11.3 Introduction to Graphs

Binary trees provide a very useful way of representing relationships in which a hierarchy exists. That is, a node is pointed to by at most one other node (its parent), and each node points to at most two other nodes (its children). If we remove the restriction that each node can have at most two children, we have a general tree, as pictured in Figure 11.7.

If we also remove the restriction that each node may have only one parent node, we have a data structure called a **graph**. A graph is made up of a set of nodes called **vertices** and a set of lines called **edges** (or **arcs**) that connect the nodes.

The set of edges describes relationships among the vertices. For instance, if the vertices are the names of cities, the edges that link the vertices could represent roads between pairs of cities. Because the road that runs between Houston and Austin also runs between Austin and Houston, the edges in this graph have no direction. This is called an **undirected graph**.

However, if the edges that link the vertices represent flights from one city to another, the direction of each edge is important. The existence of a flight (edge) from Houston to Austin does not assure the existence of a flight from Austin to Houston. A graph whose edges are directed from one vertex to another is called a **directed graph**, or **digraph**.

From a programmer's perspective, vertices represent whatever is the subject of our study: people, houses, cities, courses, and so on. However, mathematically, vertices are the abstract

> **Graph** A data structure that consists of a set of nodes and a set of edges that relate the nodes to each other.
>
> **Vertex** A node in a graph.
>
> **Edge (arc)** A pair of vertices representing a connection between two nodes in a graph.
>
> **Undirected graph** A graph in which the edges have no direction.
>
> **Directed graph (digraph)** A graph in which each edge is directed from one vertex to another (or the same) vertex.

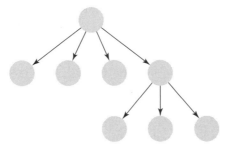

Figure 11.7 *A general tree.*

concept upon which graph theory rests. In fact, there is a great detail of formal mathematics associated with graphs. In other computing courses, you may analyze graphs and prove theorems about them. This textbook introduces the graph as an abstract data type, teaches some basic terminology, discusses how a graph might be implemented, and describes how algorithms that manipulate graphs make use of stacks, queues, and priority queues.

Formally, a graph is defined as follows:

$$G = (V, E)$$

where

V is a finite, nonempty set of vertices.

E is a set of edges (pairs of vertices).

The set of vertices is specified by listing them in set notation, within { } brackets. The following set defines the four vertices of the graph pictured in Figure 11.8(a):

$$V(Graph1) = \{A, B, C, D\}$$

The set of edges is specified by listing a sequence of edges. Each edge is denoted by writing the names of the two vertices it connects in parentheses, with a comma between them. For instance, the vertices in Graph1 in Figure 11.8(a) are connected by the four edges described below:

$$E(Graph1) = \{(A,B), (A,D), (B,C), (B,D)\}$$

Because Graph1 is an undirected graph, the order of the vertices in each edge is unimportant. The set of edges in Graph1 can also be described as follows:

$$E(Graph1) = \{(B,A), (D,A), (C,B), (D,B)\}$$

If the graph is a digraph, the direction of the edge is indicated by which vertex is listed first. For instance, in Figure 11.8(b), the edge (5, 7) represents a link from vertex 5 to vertex 7. However, there is no corresponding edge (7, 5) in Graph2. Note that in pictures of digraphs, the arrows indicate the direction of the relationship.

If two vertices in a graph are connected by an edge, they are said to be **adjacent**. In Graph1 (Figure 11.8[a]), vertices A and B are adjacent, but vertices A and C are not. If the vertices are connected by a directed edge, then the first vertex is said to be adjacent to the second, and the second vertex is said to be adjacent from the first. For example, in Graph2 (in Figure 11.8[b]), vertex 5 is adjacent to vertices 7 and 9, while vertex 1 is adjacent from vertices 3 and 11.

Adjacent vertices   Two vertices in a graph that are connected by an edge.

(a) Graph1 is an undirected graph.

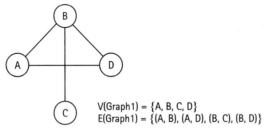

V(Graph1) = {A, B, C, D}
E(Graph1) = {(A, B), (A, D), (B, C), (B, D)}

(b) Graph2 is a directed graph.

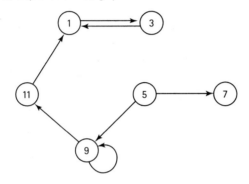

V(Graph2) = {1, 3, 5, 7, 9, 11}
G(Graph2) = {(1, 3), (3, 1), (5, 7), (5, 9), (9, 11), (9, 9), (11, 1)}

(c) Graph3 is a directed graph.

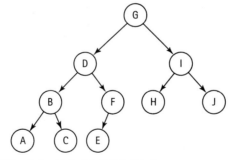

V(Graph3) = {A, B, C, D, E, F, G, H, I, J}
G(Graph3) = {(G, D), (G, J), (D, B), (D, F), (I, H), (I, J), (B, A), (B, C), (F, E)}

Figure 11.8 *Some examples of graphs.*

The picture of Graph3 in Figure 11.8(c) may look familiar; it is the tree we looked at earlier in connection with a nonlinked representation of a binary tree. A tree is a special case of a directed graph, in which each vertex may be adjacent from only one other vertex (its parent node) and one vertex (the root) is not adjacent from any other vertex.

A **path** from one vertex to another consists of a sequence of vertices that connect them. For a path to exist, there must be an uninterrupted sequence of edges from the first vertex, through any number of vertices, to the second vertex. For example, in Graph2, there is a path from vertex 5 to vertex 3, but not from vertex 3 to vertex 5. Note that in a tree, such as Graph3 (Figure 11.8[c]), there is a unique path from the root to every other node in the tree.

> **Path** A sequence of vertices that connects to nodes in a graph.
> **Complete graph** A graph in which every vertex is directly connected to every other vertex.
> **Weighted graph** A graph in which each edge carries a value.

A **complete graph** is one in which every vertex is adjacent to every other vertex. Figure 11.9 shows two complete graphs. If there are N vertices, there will be $N \times (N - 1)$ edges in a complete directed graph and $N \times (N - 1) / 2$ edges in a complete undirected graph.

A **weighted graph** is a graph in which each edge carries a value. Weighted graphs can be used to represent applications in which the *value* of the connection between the vertices is important, not just the existence of a connection. For instance, in the weighted graph pictured in Figure 11.10, the vertices represent cities and the edges indicate the Air Busters Airlines flights that connect the cities. The weights attached to the edges represent the air distances between pairs of cities.

To see whether we can get from Denver to Washington, we look for a path between them. If the total travel distance is determined by the sum of the distances between each pair of cities along the way, we can calculate the travel distance by adding the weights attached to the edges that constitute the path between them. Note that there may be multiple paths between two vertices. Later in this chapter, we talk about a way to find the shortest path between two vertices.

The Logical Level

We have described a graph at the abstract level as a set of vertices and a set of edges that connect some or all of the vertices one to another. What kind of operations are defined on a graph? In this chapter we specify and implement a small set of useful graph operations. Many other operations on graphs can be defined; we have chosen operations that are useful in the graph applications described later in the chapter.

Specification 11.3 describes a weighted digraph. Most of the generic formal parameters of this package are similar to those we used in our list and binary search tree packages. `Vertex_Type` describes the information the user wants to store in every vertex. A key of type `Key_Type` uniquely identifies each vertex in the graph. Because we need to assign values of type `Key_Type` in the package body, we have not declared it as limited.

(a) Complete directed graph.

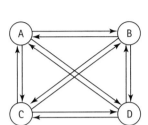

(b) Complete undirected graph.

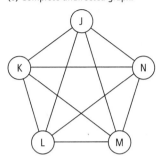

Figure 11.9 *Two complete graphs.*

From your experience with lists and trees and our general discussions of graphs, the purpose of the transformers `Clear`, `Add_Vertex`, and `Add_Edge` and the observers `Retrieve` and `Weight_Of` should already be clear.

The remaining operations have no counterparts in the packages we developed for lists and binary trees. Procedure `Get_Adjacent_Vertices` returns a collection of the keys of the vertices adjacent to a given vertex. For example, using the graph shown in Figure 11.10, the list of vertex keys returned for Denver consists of Chicago and Atlanta. `Clear_All_Marks`, `Mark_Vertex`, and `Marked` are used by applications to traverse the vertices of a graph. Our key-ordered list and binary search tree classes included traverse operations. These classes have standard traversal orders. There are many different orders in which to traverse a graph. The order for traversing a graph usually depends on the particular application. The vertex marking operations provide a mechanism for applications to create their own traversals without repeating a vertex. Recall in the maze application of Chapter 9 how we marked squares as visited. An application may mark vertices in a similar fashion. We look at some graph traversals in the next section.

Specification 11.3   Weighted Digraph

```
with Queue;
generic
   type Vertex_Type is private;
   type Key_Type    is private;
   type Weight_Type is private;
   with function Key_Of (Vertex : in Vertex_Type) return Key_Type;
   with function "=" (Left : in Key_Type; Right : in Key_Type) return Boolean;
package Graph is
```

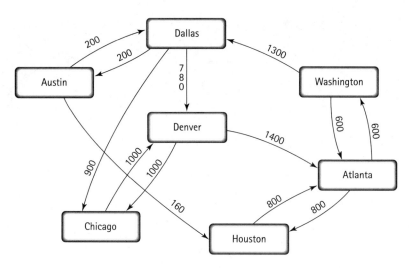

Figure 11.10 *A weighted graph.*

```ada
-- A graph consists of a set of vertices and a set of weighted
-- edges that connect some or all of the vertices one to another.

   type Graph_Type (Max_Vertices : Positive) is tagged limited private;

   -- Additional types for graph operation parameters

   -- An edge is described by a pair of vertex keys
   type Edge_Type is
      record
         From : Key_Type;
         To   : Key_Type;
      end Record;

   -- A queue class whose elements are Keys
   package Key_Queue is new Queue (Element_Type => Key_Type);

   -- Exceptions
   VERTEX_ERROR : exception;
   EDGE_ERROR   : exception;
   OVERFLOW     : exception;

   ------------------------------------------------------------------
   procedure Clear (Graph : in out Graph_Type);
   -- Purpose         : Makes a graph empty.
   -- Preconditions   : None
   -- Postconditions  : V(Graph) = empty
   --                   E(Graph) = empty
```

```
-------------------------------------------------------------------------------
procedure Add_Vertex (Graph  : in out Graph_Type;
                      Vertex : in     Vertex_Type);
-- Purpose        : Add Vertex to the Graph
-- Preconditions  : None
-- Postconditions : V(Graph) = V(Graph) + Vertex
-- Exceptions     : VERTEX_ERROR is raised if a vertex already exists
--                      in Graph with the same key of Vertex
--                  OVERFLOW is raised if Graph has no more room
--                      for an additional vertex

-------------------------------------------------------------------------------
procedure Add_Edge (Graph  : in out Graph_Type;
                    Edge   : in     Edge_Type;
                    Weight : in     Weight_Type);
-- Purpose        : Add Edge with specified Weight to Graph
-- Preconditions  : None
-- Postconditions : E(Graph) = E(Graph) + Edge
-- Exceptions     : VERTEX_ERROR is raised if one or both of the vertices
--                      defining Edge do not exist in the Graph

-------------------------------------------------------------------------------
procedure Retrieve (Graph  : in  Graph_Type;
                    Key    : in  Key_Type;
                    Vertex : out Vertex_Type);
-- Purpose        : Gets a copy of the Vertex with the given Key
-- Preconditions  : None
-- Postconditions : Vertex is a copy of the Graph vertex with the given Key
-- Exceptions     : VERTEX_ERROR is raised if there is no vertex with the
--                      given Key in Graph

-------------------------------------------------------------------------------
function Weight_Of (Graph : in Graph_Type;
                    Edge  : in Edge_Type) return Weight_Type;
-- Purpose        : Gets the weight associated with Edge
-- Preconditions  : None
-- Postconditions : Weight = weight associated with Edge
-- Exceptions     : VERTEX_ERROR is raised if one or both of the vertices
--                      defining Edge do not exist in Graph
--                  EDGE_ERROR is raised if Edge does not exist in Graph

-------------------------------------------------------------------------------
```

```
            procedure Get_Adjacent_Vertices (Graph    : in  Graph_Type;
                                             Key      : in  Key_Type;
                                             Adj_Keys : out Key_Queue.Queue_Type);
            -- Purpose        : Returns a queue of the keys of all the vertices adjacent
            --                   to the node with the given Key
            -- Preconditions  : None
            -- Postconditions : Adj_Keys contains the keys of all the vertices that are
            --                   adjacent to the vertex with the given Key
            -- Exceptions:      VERTEX_ERROR is raised if there is no vertex with the
            --                      given Key in the Graph
            --                  Key_Queue.OVERFLOW if there are more adjacent nodes
            --                      than Adj_Keys.Max_Size

            ---------------------------------------------------------------------
            procedure Clear_All_Marks (Graph : in out Graph_Type);
            -- Purpose        : Clears the marks from all vertices in Graph
            -- Preconditions  : None

            -- Postconditions: All vertices in Graph are marked as not visited

            ---------------------------------------------------------------------
            procedure Mark_Vertex (Graph : in out Graph_Type;
                                   Key   : in     Key_Type);
            -- Purpose        : Marks the vertex with the given Key
            -- Preconditions  : None
            -- Postconditions : The vertex with the given Key is marked
            -- Exceptions:      VERTEX_ERROR is raised if there is no vertex with the
            --                      given Key in the Graph

            ---------------------------------------------------------------------
            function Marked (Graph : in Graph_Type;
                             Key   : in Key_Type)      return Boolean;
            -- Purpose        : Determines whether the vertex with
            --                   the given key is marked
            -- Preconditions  : None
            -- Postconditions : Marked = (Vertex with Key is marked)
            -- Exceptions     : VERTEX_ERROR is raised if there is no vertex with the
            --                      given Key in the Graph

private

   -- We fill this in later

end Graph;
```

The Application Level: Graph Traversals

The graph specification given in the last section included only the most basic operations. It did not include any traversal operations. As you might imagine, there are many different orders in which we can traverse a graph. As a result, we consider the traversal algorithms a graph application rather than an operation. The basic operations given in our specification allow us to *implement* different traversals independent of how the graph itself is actually implemented.

In Chapter 10, we discussed the postorder tree traversal, which goes to the deepest level of the tree and works up. This strategy of going down a branch to its deepest point and moving up is called a *depth-first* strategy. Another systematic way to visit each vertex in a tree is to visit each vertex on level 0 (the root), then each vertex on level 1, then each vertex on level 2, and so on. Visiting each vertex by level in this way is called a *breadth-first* strategy. With graphs, both depth-first and breadth-first strategies are useful. We outline both algorithms within the context of the airline example.

Depth-First Searching One question we can answer with the graph in Figure 11.10 is "Can I get from city X to city Y on my favorite airline?" This is equivalent to asking "Does a path exist in the graph from vertex X to vertex Y?" Using a depth-first strategy, let's develop an operation that finds a path from Start_Vertex to End_Vertex.

We need a systematic way to keep track of the cities as we investigate them. With a depth-first search, we examine the first vertex that is adjacent from Start_Vertex; if this is End_Vertex, the search is over; otherwise, we examine all the vertices that are adjacent from this vertex. Meanwhile, we need to store the other vertices that are adjacent from Start_Vertex. If a path does not exist from the first vertex, we come back and try the second, third, and so on. Because we want to travel as far as we can down one path, backtracking if the End_Vertex is not found, a stack is a good structure for storing the vertices. Here is the algorithm we use:

Depth First Search
    Push Start_Vertex onto Stack
    loop
        Pop Vertex from Stack
        if Vertex /= End_Vertex
            Push all of the adjacent vertices onto the stack
        end if
        exit when Vertex = End_Vertex or Stack is empty
    end loop
    return (Vertex = End_Vertex)

Let's apply this algorithm to the sample airline route graph in Figure 11.10. We want to fly from Austin to Washington. We initialize our search by pushing our starting city onto the stack (Figure 11.11[a]). At the beginning of the loop we pop the current

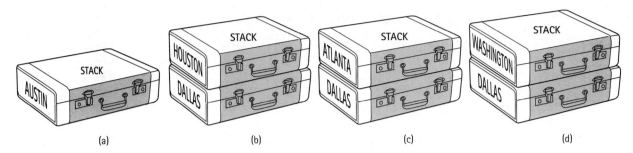

Figure 11.11 *Using a stack to store the routes.*

city, Austin, from the stack. The places we can reach directly from Austin are Dallas and Houston; we push both these vertices onto the stack (Figure 11.11[b]). At the beginning of the second iteration we pop the top vertex from the stack—Houston. Houston is not our destination, so we resume our search from there. There is only one flight out of Houston, to Atlanta; we push Atlanta onto the stack (Figure 11.11[c]). Again we pop the top vertex from the stack. Atlanta is not our destination, so we continue searching from there. Atlanta has flights to two cities: Houston and Washington.

But we just came from Houston! We don't want to fly back to cities that we have already visited; this could cause an infinite loop. We have to take care of cycling in this algorithm just as we did in the maze problem in Chapter 9. There we marked a square as having been visited by putting a little stone in the square. Here we must mark a city as having been visited so that it is not investigated a second time. Now you see the usefulness of our vertex marking operations. Let's assume that we have marked the cities that have already been tried, and continue our example. Houston has already been visited, so we ignore it. The second adjacent vertex, Washington, has not been visited so we push it onto the stack (Figure 11.11[d]). Again we pop the top vertex from the stack. Washington is our destination, so the search is complete. The path from Austin to Washington, using a depth-first search, is illustrated in Figure 11.12.

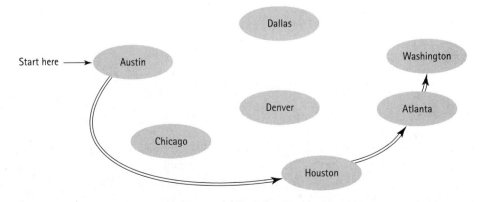

Figure 11.12 *The depth-first search.*

This search is called a depth-first search because we go to the deepest branch, examining all the paths beginning at Houston before we come back to search from Dallas. (The maze problem also used a depth-first search.) When you have to backtrack, you take the branch closest to where you dead-ended; that is, you go as far as you can down one path before you take alternative choices at earlier branches.

Before we look at the source code of the depth-first search operation, let's talk a little more about "marking" vertices on the graph. Before we begin the search, any marks in the vertices must be cleared to indicate they are not yet visited; this is the purpose of our graph package's procedure Clear_All_Marks. As we visit each vertex during the search, we mark it by calling Mark_Vertex. Before we process each vertex we can ask, "Have we visited this vertex before?" The answer to this question is returned by function Marked. If we have already visited this vertex, we ignore it and go on.

Now let's look at the Ada code for this search. First, here are the declarations necessary to instantiate a graph package for our airline example. Each vertex in our graph contains the name of the city. The weight of each edge is the number of miles between the two cities.

```
Max_Cities : constant := 10;
subtype City_String is String (1..10);
subtype Miles_Type  is Natural;

function Identity (City : in City_String) return City_String is
begin
   return City;
end Identity;

package Air_Routes is new Graph (Vertex_Type => City_String,
                                 Key_Type    => City_String,
                                 Weight_Type => Miles_Type,
                                 Key_Of      => Identity,
                                 "="         => "=");
```

Procedure Depth_First_Search is given a graph, a starting city, and an ending city. Because marking the graph changes it, parameter Graph must be declared as in out. This procedure uses the depth-first strategy to determine if there is a path from the starting city to the ending city. Note that there is nothing in the procedure listed in Body 11.3 that depends on the implementation of the graph. The procedure is implemented as a graph application; it uses the graph class (including the mark operations), without knowing how the graph is represented.

Body 11.3   Depth First Search

```
procedure Depth_First_Search (Graph      : in out Air_Routes.Graph_Type;
                              Start_City : in     City_String;
                              End_City   : in     City_String;
                              Found      : out    Boolean) is
```

```ada
-- Determine if a path exists in Graph from Start_City to End_City

   -- Stack stores city names for later LIFO retrieval
   package City_Stack is new Stack (Element_Type => City_String);
   Cities : City_Stack.Stack_Type (Max_Size => Max_Cities);

   -- Queue stores vertices adjacent to the current vertex
   Neighbors : Air_Routes.Key_Queue.Queue_Type (Max_Size => Max_Cities);

   City     : City_String;      -- Current city
   Neighbor : City_String;      -- Adjacent city

begin
   Graph.Clear_All_Marks;
   Cities.Push (Start_City);

   loop
      Cities.Pop (City);
      if City /= End_City then
         -- If city has not been visited, visit it
         if not Graph.Marked (City) then
            -- Mark vertex as visited
            Graph.Mark_Vertex (City);
            -- Get the vertices adjacent to City
            Graph.Get_Adjacent_Vertices (Key      => City,
                                         Adj_Keys => Neighbors);
            -- Push all adjacent vertices not yet visited
            loop
               exit when Neighbors.Empty;
               Neighbors.Dequeue (Neighbor);
               if not Graph.Marked (Neighbor) then
                  Cities.Push (Neighbor);
               end if;
            end loop;
         end if;
      end if;
      exit when City = End_City  or  Cities.Empty;
   end loop;
   Found := City = End_City;
end Depth_First_Search;
```

Breadth-First Searching A breadth-first search looks at all possible paths at the same depth before it goes to a deeper level. In our flight example, a breadth-first search checks all possible one-stop connections before checking any two-stop connections. For most travelers, this is the preferred approach for booking flights.

When we come to a dead end in a depth-first search, we back up as little as possible. We try another route from a recent vertex—the route on top of our stack. In a breadth-first search, we want to back up as far as possible to find a route originating from the earliest vertices. The stack is not the right structure for finding an early route. It keeps track of things in the order opposite of their occurrence—the latest route is on top. To keep track of things in the order in which they happened, we use a FIFO queue. The route at the front of the queue is a route from an earlier vertex; the route at the back of the queue is from a later vertex.

To modify the search to use a breadth-first strategy, we change all the calls to stack operations to the analogous FIFO queue operations. Searching for a path from Austin to Washington, we first enqueue all the cities that can be reached directly from Austin: Dallas and Houston (Figure 11.13[a]). Then we dequeue the front queue element. Dallas is not the destination we seek, so we enqueue all the adjacent cities that have not yet been visited: Chicago and Denver (Figure 11.13[b]). (Austin has been visited already, so it is not enqueued.) Again we dequeue the front element from the queue. This element is the other "one-stop" city, Houston. Houston is not the desired destination, so we continue the search. There is only one flight out of Houston, and it is to Atlanta. Because we haven't visited Atlanta before, it is enqueued (Figure 11.13[c]).

Now we know that we cannot reach Washington with one stop, so we start examining the two-stop connections. We dequeue Chicago; this is not our destination, so we put its adjacent city, Denver, into the queue (Figure 11.13[d]). Now this is an interesting situation: Denver is in the queue twice. Should we mark a city as having been visited when we put it in the queue or after it has been dequeued, when we are examining its outgoing flights? If we mark it only after it is dequeued, there may be multiple copies of the same vertex in the queue (so we need to check to see if a city is marked after it is dequeued).

An alternative approach is to mark the city as having been visited before it is put into the queue. Which is better? It depends on the processing. You may want to know whether there are alternative routes, in which case you would want to put a city into the queue more than once.

Back to our example. We have put Denver into the queue in one step and removed its previous entry at the next step. Denver is not our destination, so we put its adjacent cities that we haven't already marked (only Atlanta) into the queue (Figure 11.13[e]). This processing continues until Washington is put into the queue (from Atlanta), and is finally dequeued. We have found the desired city, and the search is complete. This search is illustrated in Figure 11.14.

The source code for the breadth-first search procedure is given in Body 11.4. It is identical to the depth-first search, except for the replacement of the stack with a FIFO queue.

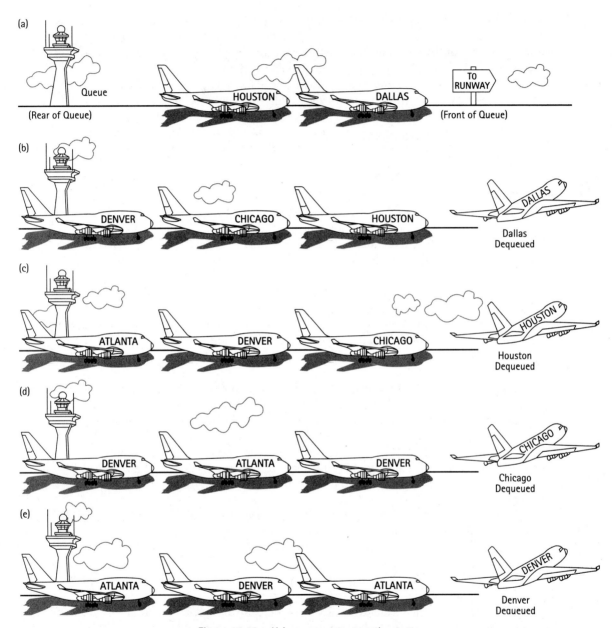

Figure 11.13 *Using a queue to store the routes.*

11.3 Introduction to Graphs

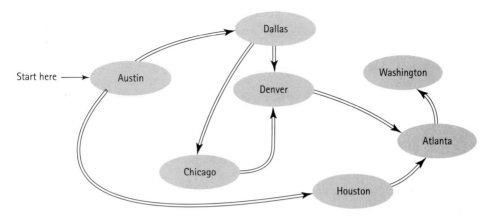

Figure 11.14 *The breadth-first search.*

Body 11.4   Breadth First Search

```
procedure Breadth_First_Search (Graph      : in out Air_Routes.Graph_Type;
                                Start_City : in     City_String;
                                End_City   : in     City_String;
                                Found      : out    Boolean) is
-- Determine if a path exists in Graph from Start_City to End_City

   -- Queue stores city names for later FIFO retrieval
   Cities : Air_Routes.Key_Queue.Queue_Type (Max_Size => Max_Cities);

   -- Queue stores vertices adjacent to the current vertex
   Neighbors : Air_Routes.Key_Queue.Queue_Type (Max_Size => Max_Cities);

   City     : City_String;       -- Current city
   Neighbor : City_String;       -- Adjacent city

begin
   Graph.Clear_All_Marks;
   Cities.Enqueue (Start_City);

   loop
      Cities.Dequeue (City);
      if City /= End_City then
         -- If city has not been visited, visit it
         if not Graph.Marked (City) then
```

```
               -- Mark vertex as visited
               Graph.Mark_Vertex (City);
               -- Get the vertices adjacent to City
               Graph.Get_Adjacent_Vertices (Key      => City,
                                            Adj_Keys => Neighbors);
               -- Push all adjacent vertices not yet visited
               loop
                  exit when Neighbors.Empty;
                  Neighbors.Dequeue (Neighbor);
                  if not Graph.Marked (Neighbor) then
                     Cities.Enqueue (Neighbor);
                  end if;
               end loop;
            end if;
         end if;
         exit when City = End_City  or  Cities.Empty;
      end loop;
      Found := City = End_City;
   end Breadth_First_Search;
```

The Single-Source Shortest Paths Problem We know from the two search operations above that there may be multiple paths from one vertex to another. Suppose that we want to find the shortest path from Austin to each of the other cities that Air Busters serves. By "shortest path" we mean the path whose edge values (weights), added together, have the smallest sum. Consider the following two paths from Austin to Washington:

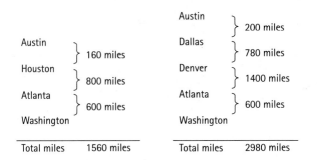

Clearly the first path is preferable, unless you want to collect frequent-flyer miles.

Let's develop an algorithm that displays the shortest path from a designated starting city to *every other* city in the graph—this time we are not searching for a path between a starting city and an ending city. As in the two graph searches described earlier, we need an auxiliary structure for storing cities that we process later. By retrieving the city that was most recently put into the structure, the depth-first search tries to keep going "forward." It tries a one-flight solution, then a two-flight solution, then a three-flight solution, and so on. It backtracks to a fewer-flight solution only when it reaches a dead end.

By retrieving the city that had been in the structure the longest time, the breadth-first search tries all one-flight solutions, then all two-flight solutions, and so on. The breadth-first search finds a path with a minimum number of flights.

But a minimum *number* of flights does not necessarily mean the minimum *total distance*. Unlike the depth-first and breadth-first searches, this *shortest path traversal* must use the number of miles (edge weights) between cities. We want to retrieve the city that is closest to the current city—that is, the city connected with the minimum edge weight. If we consider minimum distance to be the highest priority, then we know the perfect structure in which to store the neighboring cities—the priority queue. Our algorithm can use a priority queue whose elements are flights (edges) with their distances from the *starting city* as the priority.

The algorithm for the shortest path traversal is similar to those we used for the depth-first and breadth-first searches. There are two major differences.

1. We use a priority queue rather than a FIFO queue or stack.
2. We stop only when there are no more cities to process; there is no destination.

The code for the Shortest_Paths procedure is given in Body 11.5. The first set of declarations in this body creates a priority queue whose elements are flight records. Each flight record contains the origin and destination of one flight as well as the total number of miles from the starting city (the parameter Start_City) to the destination of this particular flight. In order to give highest priority to shorter distances, our priority queue instantiation uses the less-than operator as an actual parameter for comparing priorities.

Body 11.5   Shortest Paths

```
procedure Shortest_Paths (Graph      : in out Air_Routes.Graph_Type;
                          Start_City : in     City_String) is
-- Determine the shortest paths from Start_City to every other city in Graph

   -- Create a priority queue of flight records
   type Flight_Rec is
      record
         Route : Air_Routes.Edge_Type;  -- This flight's start and end cities
         Total : Miles_Type;            -- The total miles from starting city
      end record;                       --  to the destination of this flight

   function Distance_From_Start (Flight : in Flight_Rec) return Miles_Type is
   begin
      return Flight.Total;
   end Distance_From_Start;

   package P_Queue is new Priority_Queue (Element_Type  => Flight_Rec,
                                          Priority_Type => Miles_Type,
                                          Priority_Of   => Distance_From_Start,
                                          ">"           => "<");
```

```ada
        PQ : P_Queue.Queue_Type (Max_Size => 2 * Max_Cities);


        -- Queue stores vertices adjacent to the current vertex
        Neighbors : Air_Routes.Key_Queue.Queue_Type (Max_Size => Max_Cities);

        Flight        : Flight_Rec;     -- Current flight information
        Current_City  : City_String;    -- Current city (Destination of Flight)
        Previous_City : City_String;    -- The city we came from (Origin of Flight)
        Next_City     : City_String;    -- A city we go to after Current City
        Distance      : Miles_Type;     -- Miles from Start_City to Current_City
    begin
        Graph.Clear_All_Marks;
        Put_Line ("   Shortest Path from " & Start_City);
        New_Line;
        Put_Line ("Last City      Destination    Distance");
        Put_Line ("-----------------------------------");

        -- Initialize priority queue with starting city
        Flight.Route := (From => Start_City, To => Start_City);
        Flight.Total := 0;
        PQ.Enqueue (Flight);

        loop
            -- Exit when all cities have been visited
            exit when PQ.Empty;
            -- Get the flight whose destination is closest to Start_City
            PQ.Dequeue (Flight);
            Current_City  := Flight.Route.To;
            Previous_City := Flight.Route.From;
            Distance      := Flight.Total;    -- Miles traveled from Start_City
            -- If the city hasn't been visited, visit it
            if not Graph.Marked (Current_City) then
                -- Mark the city as visited
                Graph.Mark_Vertex (Current_City);

                -- Display the current flight cities and accumulated miles
                Put (Previous_City & "    ");
                Put (Current_City & "    ");
                Put (Item => Distance, Width => 6);
                New_Line;

                -- Get the vertices adjacent to City
                Graph.Get_Adjacent_Vertices (Key      => Current_City,
                                             Adj_Keys => Neighbors);
```

```
            -- Enqueue flights to all unmarked adjacent cities
            loop
                exit when Neighbors.Empty;
                Neighbors.Dequeue (Next_City);  -- Name of adjacent city
                if not Graph.Marked (Next_City) then
                    -- Set up the flight to Next_City
                    Flight.Route := (From => Current_City,  To => Next_City);
                    -- The distance from Start_City to Next_City is the sum of the
                    -- distance from Start_City to Current_City and the distance
                    -- between Current_City and Next_City.
                    Flight.Total := Distance + Graph.Weight_Of (Flight.Route);
                    PQ.Enqueue (Flight);
                end if;
            end loop;
        end if;
    end loop;
end Shortest_Paths;
```

The output from this procedure is a table of city pairs (edges), showing the total distance from `Start_City` to each of the other vertices in the graph, as well as the last vertex visited before the destination. If `Graph` contains the information shown in Figure 11.10, the procedure call

```
Shortest_Paths (Graph => Graph, Start_City => "Washington");
```

prints out the following table:

```
Shortest Path from Washington

Last City       Destination  Distance
----------------------------------------
Washington      Washington         0
Washington      Atlanta          600
Washington      Dallas          1300
Atlanta         Houston         1400
Dallas          Austin          1500
Dallas          Denver          2080
Dallas          Chicago         2200
```

The shortest-path distance from Washington to each destination is shown in the two columns to the right. For example, our flights from Washington to Chicago total 2200 miles. The left-hand column shows which city immediately preceded the destination in the traversal. Let's figure out the cities on the shortest path from Washington to

Chicago. We see from the left-hand column that the next-to-last vertex in the path is Dallas. Now we look up Dallas in the Destination (middle) column: The vertex before Dallas is Washington. The whole path is Washington-Dallas-Chicago.

The Implementation Level

Now that we have seen three applications that used our graph class, let's look at how we might implement it. As we have done in the past we present two solutions, one based on arrays and the other on linked lists.

An Array-Based Implementation An obvious way to represent V(Graph), the set of vertices in the graph, is with an array of elements. A simple way to represent E(Graph), the set of edges in a graph, is by using an **adjacency matrix**, a two-dimensional array of edge values (weights). We use the following declarations for the private part of Specification 11.3 to implement a weighted digraph:

Adjacency matrix For a graph of *N* nodes, an *N* by *N* table that shows the existence (and weights) of all edges in the graph.

```
private

   type Vertex_Rec is
      record
         Info   : Vertex_Type;         -- Information declared by user
         Marked : Boolean := False;    -- Has the Vertex been visited?
      end record;

   type Edge_Rec is
      record
         Weight  : Weight_Type;        -- Weight assigned to the edge
         Defined : Boolean := False;   -- Is this edge in the graph?
      end record;

   type Vertex_Array is array (Positive range <>) of Vertex_Rec;
   type Matrix_Type  is array (Positive range <>,
                               Positive range <>) of Edge_Rec;

   type Graph_Type (Max_Vertices : Positive) is tagged limited
      record
         Num_Vertices : Natural := 0;
         Vertices     : Vertex_Array (1..Max_Vertices);
         Edges        : Matrix_Type (1..Max_Vertices, 1..Max_Vertices);
      end record;

end Graph;
```

At the bottom of these declarations you can see that a graph consists of a count of vertices, a one-dimensional array of Vertex_Rec, and a two-dimensional array of Edge_Rec. The one-dimensional array provides space for the graph's vertices. Each Vertex_Rec contains the information for one vertex and a Boolean value used to mark the vertex as it is visited during a traversal. The two-dimensional array provides space for all possible edges. For a digraph with N nodes, there may be up to N^2 edges. Each Edge_Rec contains a weight and a Boolean value to indicate whether this edge exists in the graph.

Figure 11.15 depicts the implementation of the graph of Air Busters flights between seven cities. (A drawing of this graph is found in Figure 11.10, page 732). The names of the cities are contained in the one-dimensional array Graph.Vertices. For simplicity, we omit from the figure the Boolean fields needed to mark vertices as "visited" during a traversal. Although the city names in Figure 11.15 are shown in alphabetical order, there is no requirement that the elements in this array be ordered.

The edges in Figure 11.15 are shown in the two-dimensional array with either their weight (mileage between cities) or a dot to indicate that there is no edge (flight) between two vertices (cities). There are no city names stored in the two-dimensional array. We use the array indices to match an edge to its two vertices. For example, the value in Graph.Edges(2,4) tells us that there is a 200-mile flight from city 2 to city 4. Using

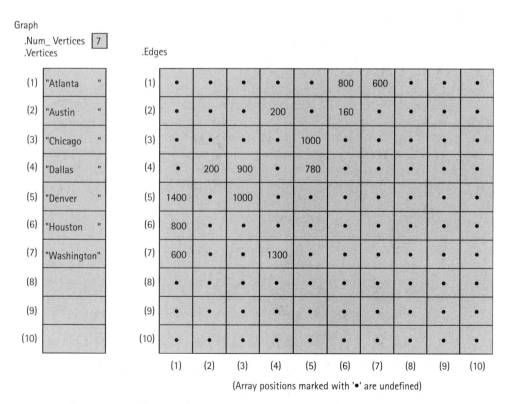

Figure 11.15 *Graph of flight connections between cities (matrix representation).*

these two index values and referring back to the one-dimensional array, we can determine that this flight is from Austin to Dallas. The value in Graph.Edges(4,2) tells us that there is also a 200-mile flight from Dallas to Austin.

Now let's look at how the graph operations given in Specification 11.3 would be implemented using these declarations. The Clear procedure sets Graph to its empty state. Simply by setting the Num_Vertices field to zero, we indicate that there are no vertices or edges.

The Add_Vertex procedure puts Vertex in the next free space in the Graph.Vertices array. Since the new vertex has no edges defined yet, we also initialize the Defined field of all the array elements in the appropriate row and column in the Graph.Edges matrix to false.

To add an edge to the graph, we must first locate the From vertex and To vertex given in the record parameter Edge that define the edge we want to add. To index the correct matrix slot, we need the index in the Graph.Vertices array that corresponds to each vertex. Once we know the indexes, it is a simple matter to set the weight of the edge in the matrix and set the Defined field to true. Here is the algorithm:

Add Edge
    From_Index   := Index of Edge.From in Graph.Vertices
    To_Index   := Index of Edge.To in Graph.Vertices
    Graph.Edges (From_Index, To_Index).Weight := Weight
    Graph.Edges (From_Index, To_Index).Defined := True

This algorithm requires us to search the array of vertices twice—once for From_Index and once for To_Index. We write a search function, Index_Of, that is given the key of a vertex and returns its location (Index) in Graph.Vertices. The specification and implementation of this local function are given at the beginning of Body 11.6.

Procedure Retrieve returns the information associated with the vertex with the given Key. We again use function Index_Of to find the desired vertex in Graph.Vertices. Once it is found, its Info field is returned.

The Weight_Of function returns the weight of an Edge. To implement this function, we first use our search function Index_Of to find the indexes of the two vertices (given by the To and the From fields of the edge record); then we return the value from the appropriate slot in the Graph.Edges matrix.

The three graph operations Clear_All_Marks, Mark_Vertex, and Marked all modify or examine the Marked field in the vertices in the array of vertices, Graph.Vertices. Clear_All_Marks traverses the one-dimensional array, setting every Marked field to false. We use our search function, Index_Of, to locate the particular vertex to check or modify.

The last graph operation that we specified is Get_Adjacent_Vertices. This procedure returns a collection of vertex keys for which there are edges from the designated vertex; that is, it returns a collection of all the vertices that you can get to from this vertex. Using an adjacency matrix to represent the edges, it is a simple matter to determine which nodes are adjacent to Vertex. We merely loop through the appropriate row in `Graph.Edges`; whenever a `Defined` value is found, we add another vertex key to the collection. The complete package body for the adjacency matrix implementation of `Graph` is given in Body 11.6.

Body 11.6   Weighted Digraph: Implements Specification 11.3

```
package body Graph is

-------------------------------------------------------------------------
function Index_Of (Graph : in Graph_Type;
                   Key   : in Key_Type) return Positive is
-- Purpose        : Returns the index of the vertex in Graph.Vertices
--                  with the given Key
-- Preconditions  : None
-- Postconditions : if there is an element in Graph with the given Key
--                     The index of it in Graph.Vertices is returned
--                  else
--                     Graph.Num_Vertices + 1 is returned
   Index : Positive;
begin
   Index := 1;
   loop
      exit when Index > Graph.Num_Vertices or else
                Key = Key_Of (Graph.Vertices(Index).Info);
      Index := Index + 1;
   end loop;
   return Index;
end Index_Of;

-------------------------------------------------------------------------
procedure Clear (Graph : in out Graph_Type) is
begin
   Graph.Num_Vertices := 0;
end Clear;

-------------------------------------------------------------------------
procedure Add_Vertex (Graph  : in out Graph_Type;
                      Vertex : in     Vertex_Type) is
   Index : Positive;   -- Location for new Vertex
begin
   Index := Index_Of (Graph, Key_Of (Vertex));   -- Find if its key is already
   if Index <= Graph.Num_Vertices then           -- in the Graph
      raise VERTEX_ERROR;
   elsif Index > Graph.Max_Vertices then         -- Any more room?
      raise OVERFLOW;
```

```ada
      else
         Graph.Vertices(Index).Info    := Vertex;   -- Add the new vertex to the
         Graph.Vertices(Index).Marked  := False;    -- end of the array
         Graph.Num_Vertices := Index;
         -- Initialize the adjacency matrix to indicate no edges
         for Row in 1..Graph.Num_Vertices loop      -- The row
            Graph.Edges(Row, Index).Defined := False;
         end loop;
         for Col in 1..Graph.Num_Vertices loop      -- The column
            Graph.Edges(Index, Col).Defined := False;
         end loop;
      end if;
   end Add_Vertex;

   -----------------------------------------------------------------------------
   procedure Add_Edge (Graph : in out Graph_Type;
                       Edge  : in     Edge_Type;
                       Weight : in    Weight_Type) is
      From_Index : Positive;
      To_Index   : Positive;
   begin
      From_Index := Index_Of (Graph, Edge.From);   -- Location of From vertex
      To_Index   := Index_Of (Graph, Edge.To);     -- Location of To vertex
      -- Do both vertices exist?
      if From_Index > Graph.Num_Vertices or To_Index > Graph.Num_Vertices then
         raise VERTEX_ERROR;
      else
         -- Update the adjacency matrix with the new edge
         Graph.Edges(From_Index, To_Index).Weight  := Weight;
         Graph.Edges(From_Index, To_Index).Defined := True;
      end if;
   end Add_Edge;

   -----------------------------------------------------------------------------
   procedure Retrieve (Graph  : in  Graph_Type;
                       Key    : in  Key_Type;
                       Vertex : out Vertex_Type) is
      Index : Positive;
   begin
      Index := Index_Of (Graph, Key);              -- Find the vertex's location
      if Index > Graph.Num_Vertices then
         raise VERTEX_ERROR;                       -- Vertex does not exist
      else
         Vertex := Graph.Vertices(Index).Info;     -- Return information
      end if;
   end Retrieve;
```

```ada
function Weight_Of (Graph : in Graph_Type;
                    Edge  : in Edge_Type) return Weight_Type is
   From_Index : Positive;
   To_Index   : Positive;
begin
   From_Index := Index_Of (Graph, Edge.From);  -- Find the location of
   To_Index   := Index_Of (Graph, Edge.To);    -- the two vertices in Edge
   -- Check to make sure that both vertices exist in Graph
   if From_Index > Graph.Num_Vertices or
      To_Index   > Graph.Num_Vertices then
         raise VERTEX_ERROR;
   elsif Graph.Edges(From_Index, To_Index).Defined then
      return Graph.Edges(From_Index, To_Index).Weight;
   else
      raise EDGE_ERROR;
   end if;
end Weight_Of;


procedure Get_Adjacent_Vertices (Graph    : in  Graph_Type;
                                 Key      : in  Key_Type;
                                 Adj_Keys : out Key_Queue.Queue_Type) is
   From_Index : Positive;
begin
   From_Index := Index_Of (Graph, Key);  -- Locate the vertex with the given Key
   if From_Index > Graph.Num_Vertices then
      raise VERTEX_ERROR;               -- Vertex does not exist
   else
      Adj_Keys.Clear;  -- Initialize queue of adjacent vertex keys
      -- Go through the From_Index row of the matrix
      for To_Index in 1..Graph.Num_Vertices loop
         -- Is there an edge from From_Index to To_Index?
         if Graph.Edges(From_Index, To_Index).Defined then
            -- Add the key of the To end of the edge to the list
            Adj_Keys.Enqueue(Item => Key_Of (Graph.Vertices(To_Index).Info));
         end if;
      end loop;
   end if;
end Get_Adjacent_Vertices;
```

```
procedure Clear_All_Marks (Graph : in out Graph_Type) is
begin
   for Index in 1..Graph.Num_Vertices loop
      Graph.Vertices(Index).Marked := False;
   end loop;
end Clear_All_Marks;


procedure Mark_Vertex (Graph : in out Graph_Type;
                      Key   : in      Key_Type) is
   Index : Positive;
begin
   Index := Index_Of (Graph, Key);   -- Find location of vertex with Key
   if Index > Graph.Num_Vertices then
      raise VERTEX_ERROR;
   else
      Graph.Vertices(Index).Marked := True;
   end if;
end Mark_Vertex;


function Marked (Graph : in Graph_Type;
                 Key   : in Key_Type)    return Boolean is
   Index : Positive;
begin
   Index := Index_Of (Graph, Key);   -- Find location of vertex with Key
   if Index > Graph.Num_Vertices then
      raise VERTEX_ERROR;
   else
      return Graph.Vertices(Index).Marked;
   end if;
end Marked;

end Graph;
```

Linked Implementations The advantages to representing the edges in a graph with an adjacency matrix are its speed and simplicity. Given the indexes of two vertices, determining the existence (or the weight) of an edge between them is an O(1) operation. The problem with adjacency matrices is that their use of space is $O(N^2)$, where N is the maximum number of vertices in the graph. If the maximum number of vertices is large, adjacency matrices may waste a lot of space. In the past, we have tried to save space by allocating space as we need it at run time, using linked structures. We can use a similar approach to implementing graphs. Adjacency lists are linked lists, one per vertex, that

Adjacency list A linked list that identifies all the vertices to which a particular vertex is connected. Each vertex has its own adjacency list.

identify the vertices to which each vertex is connected. There are several ways to implement adjacency lists. Figures 11.16 and 11.17 show two different adjacency list representations of the graph in Figure 11.10.

In Figure 11.16, the list of vertices is stored in an array. Each component of this array contains a pointer to a linked list of edge nodes. Each node in these linked lists contains an index number, a weight, and a pointer to the next node in the adjacency list. Let's look at the adjacency list for Denver. The first node in the list indicates that there is a 1400-mile flight from Denver to Atlanta (the vertex whose index is 1) and a 1000-mile flight from Denver to Chicago (the vertex whose index is 3).

No arrays are used in the implementation illustrated in Figure 11.17. The list of vertices is implemented as a linked list. Now each node in the adjacency lists contains a pointer to the vertex information rather than the index of the vertex. Because there are so many of these pointers in Figure 11.17, we have used text to describe the vertex that each pointer designates rather than draw them as arrows.

The advantage of adjacency lists over the adjacency matrix is the savings in memory. The price we pay for this memory is the extra time it takes to access a particular edge value. With the matrix, the two array indices allow us to access edge information directly. To access this information in an adjacency list, we must search the list. We leave the declarations for a graph based on adjacency lists and the implementation of the graph operations as exercises.

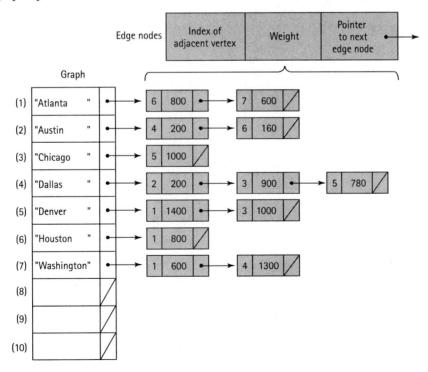

Figure 11.16 *Graph of flight connections between cities using array storage for vertices and adjacency lists for edges.*

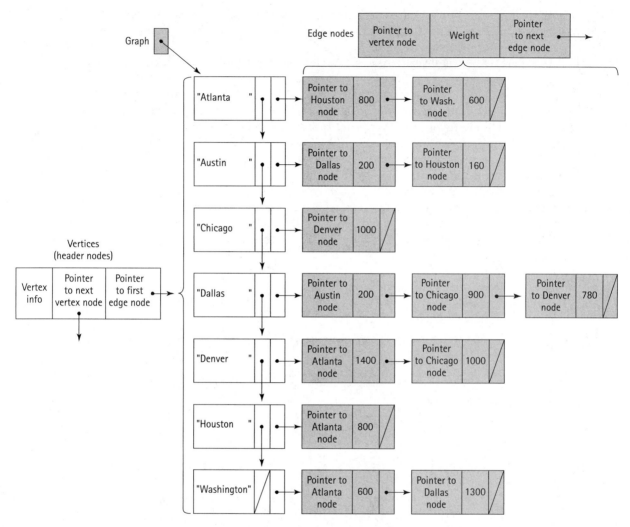

Figure 11.17   *Graph of flight connections between cities using a linked list for vertices and adjacency lists for edges.*

Summary

In this chapter we have discussed three structures: priority queues, heaps, and graphs. When we dequeue an element from a priority queue, that element has the highest priority in the collection. We discussed how we could use several different data structures to implement a priority queue. We used the heap to create an elegant implementation of the priority queue. A heap is a binary tree with two properties: The shape property states that the heap must be a complete binary tree. The order property states that for every node in the tree, the value stored in that node is greater than or equal to the values stored in each of its children.

Graphs are the most complex structure we studied. They are very versatile and are a good way to model many real-world objects and situations. Because there are many different types of applications for graphs, there are all kinds of variations and generalizations of their definitions and implementations. Many useful algorithms for manipulating and traversing graphs have been discovered. They are generally covered in detail in advanced computer science courses on algorithms.

Exercises

Priority Queues

1. Why would it not be fairer for a hospital emergency room to schedule patients like a FIFO queue rather than like a priority queue?
2. Have you ever gone shopping for an item or two at your local supermarket and found yourself waiting in the checkout line behind people with full shopping carts? If only we lined up based on the number of items we were buying. What is the major disadvantage of converting the checkout line from a FIFO queue to a priority queue based on the number of items (smaller number of items gets higher priority)?
3. Describe two examples of real-world situations that use priority queues. Do not repeat the examples given in this chapter.
4. A student record contains a name (a fixed-length string of 20 characters), a GPA (a float value between 0.0 and 4.0), and the number of days of class missed.
   a. Write the necessary Ada code to instantiate a priority queue of student records. Students with higher GPAs are to have higher priority.
   b. Write the necessary Ada code to instantiate a priority queue of student records. Students with fewer missed class days are to have higher priority.
5. Draw a UML class diagram for the priority queue defined by Specification 11.1.
6. A stack is implemented using a priority queue. Each element is time-stamped (with the time obtained from a call to `Ada.Calendar.Clock`) as it is put into the stack.
   a. What is the highest-priority element?
   b. Write the necessary Ada code to instantiate a suitable priority queue from the package developed in this chapter.
   c. Implement the `Push` and `Pop` operations, using the specifications in Chapter 5.
   d. Compare these `Push` and `Pop` operations to the ones implemented in Chapter 5, in terms of Big-O.
   e. Is this priority queue–based solution a reasonable way to implement a stack?

7. A FIFO queue is implemented using a priority queue. Each element is time-stamped (with the time obtained from a call to Ada.Calendar.Clock) as it is put into the queue.
   a. What is the highest-priority element?
   b. Write the necessary Ada code to instantiate a suitable priority queue from the package developed in this chapter.
   c. Implement the FIFO Enqueue and Dequeue operations, using the specifications in Chapter 6.
   d. Compare these Enqueue and Dequeue operations to the ones implemented in Chapter 6, in terms of Big-O.
   e. Is this priority queue-based solution a reasonable way to implement a FIFO queue?
8. A priority queue is implemented as a linked list, ordered from largest to smallest element.
   a. Write the declarations in the private part of the priority queue package declaration needed for this implementation.
   b. Write the Enqueue operation (from the chapter specification), using this implementation.
   c. Write the Dequeue operation (from the chapter specification), using this implementation.
   d. What are the Big-Os of your two operations?
9. A priority queue is implemented as a binary search tree.
   a. Write the declarations in the private part of the priority queue package declaration needed for this implementation.
   b. Write the Enqueue operation (from the chapter specification), using this implementation.
   c. Write the Dequeue operation (from the chapter specification), using this implementation.
   d. What are the Big-Os of your two operations?
10. A priority queue is implemented as a sequential array-based list. The highest priority item is in the first array position, the second highest priority is in the second array position, and so on.
    a. Write the declarations in the private part of the priority queue package declaration needed for this implementation.

b. Write the Enqueue operation (from the chapter specification), using this implementation.

c. Write the Dequeue operation (from the chapter specification), using this implementation.

d. What are the Big-Os of your two operations?

Heaps

11. Which of the following trees are heaps?

(a)
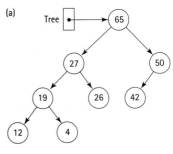

(b)
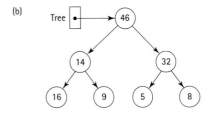

(c)
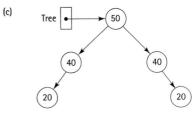

(d)
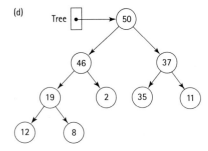

(e)
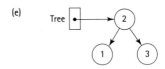

(f)
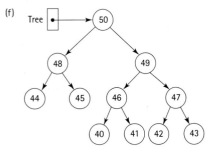

12. Draw a tree that satisfies both the binary search property and the order property of heaps.

13. Given the array pictured below:

(1)	1
(2)	55
(3)	59
(4)	44
(5)	33
(6)	58
(7)	57
(8)	22
(9)	11

    a. Draw the binary tree that can be created from its elements.
    b. Why is this tree not a heap?
    c. What procedure call(s) can be used to make the tree into a heap?

14. Given the array pictured below:

(1)	72
(2)	55
(3)	59
(4)	44
(5)	33
(6)	58
(7)	57
(8)	22
(9)	11
(10)	37

    a. Draw the binary tree that can be created from its elements.
    b. Why is this tree not a heap?

15. A minimum heap has the following order property: The value of each element is less than or equal to the value of each of its children. How can we instantiate a minimum heap package from the maximum heap package we developed in this chapter?

16. We created recursive versions of the heap operations in this chapter.
    a. Write a nonrecursive version of `Reheap_Down`.
    b. Write a nonrecursive version of `Reheap_Up`.
    c. Describe the nonrecursive versions of these operations in terms of Big-O.

17. Why is it not practical to implement a heap with the usual linked tree representation where each vertex is a record containing an information field and two explicit pointers to the left and right children?

18. A priority queue containing characters is implemented as a heap stored in an array. The precondition states that this priority queue cannot contain duplicate elements. There are 10 elements currently in the priority queue. What values might be stored in array positions 8–10 so that the properties of a heap are satisfied?

(1)	Z
(2)	F
(3)	J
(4)	E
(5)	B
(6)	G
(7)	H
(8)	?
(9)	?
(10)	?

19. A priority queue is implemented as a heap:

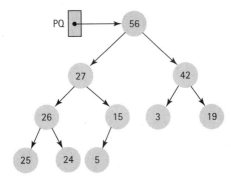

a. Show how the heap above would look after this series of operations:

```
PQ.Enqueue (28);
PQ.Enqueue (2);
PQ.Enqueue (40);
PQ.Dequeue (X);
PQ.Dequeue (Y);
PQ.Dequeue (Z);
```

b. What would the values of X, Y, and Z be after the series of operations in part (a)?

20. A priority queue of varying length strings is implemented using a heap. The heap contains the following 10 elements:

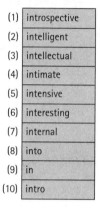

(1)	introspective
(2)	intelligent
(3)	intellectual
(4)	intimate
(5)	intensive
(6)	interesting
(7)	internal
(8)	into
(9)	in
(10)	intro

a. What feature of these strings is used to determine their priority in the priority queue?

b. Show how this priority queue is affected by adding the string "interviewing". You will need to add an 11th element to the array.

21. a. Instantiate a bounded-length string package from `Ada.Strings.Bounded` for a bounded-length string with a bound of 50 characters.

b. Using the bounded-length string class from part (a), write the necessary Ada code to instantiate a priority queue that satisfies the requirements of Exercise 20.

Graphs

22. Given the following description of an undirected graph:

Employee Graph = (V, E)

V(Employee Graph) = {Susan, Darlene, Mike, Fred, John, Sander, Lance, Jean, Brent, Fran}

E(Employee Graph) = {(Susan, Darlene), (Fred, Brent), (Sander, Susan), (Lance, Fran), (Sander, Fran), (Fran, John), (Lance, Jean), (Jean, Susan), (Mike, Darlene), (Brent, Lance), (Susan, John)}

a. Draw a picture of Employee Graph.

b. Draw Employee Graph, implemented as an adjacency matrix. Store the vertex values in alphabetical order.

c. Using the adjacency matrix for Employee Graph from part (b), describe the path from Susan to Lance
   i. using a breadth-first strategy.
   ii. using a depth-first strategy.
d. Which one of the following phrases best describes the relationship represented by the edges between the vertices in Employee Graph?
   i. "Works for"
   ii. "Is the supervisor of"
   iii. "Is senior to"
   iv. "Works with"

23. Given the following description of an undirected graph:

    Zoo Graph   = (V, E)
    V(Zoo Graph)   = {dog, cat, animal, vertebrate, oyster, shellfish, invertebrate, crab, poodle, monkey, banana, dalmation, dachshund}
    E(Zoo Graph)   = {(vertebrate, animal), (invertebrate, animal), (dog, vertebrate), (cat, vertebrate), (monkey, vertebrate), (shellfish, invertebrate), (crab, shellfish), (oyster, shellfish), (poodle, dog), (dalmation, dog), (dachshund, dog)}

    a. Draw a picture of Zoo Graph.
    b. Draw the adjacency matrix for Zoo Graph. Store the vertices in alphabetical order.
    c. To tell if one element in Zoo Graph has relation X to another element, you look for a path between them. Show whether the following statements are true, using the picture or adjacency matrix.
       i. Dalmation X dog
       ii. Dalmation X vertebrate
       iii. Dalmation X poodle
       iv. Banana X invertebrate
       v. Oyster X invertebrate
       vi. Monkey X invertebrate
    d. Which of the following phrases best describes relation X in the previous question?
       i. "Has a"
       ii. "Is a kind of"
       iii. "Is a generalization of"
       iv. "Eats"

24. Given the following directed graph:

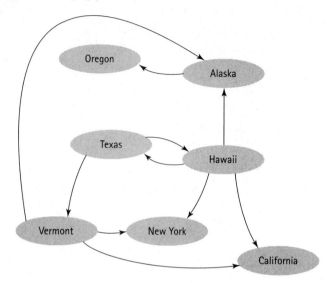

a. Describe the graph pictured above, using the formal graph notation.

V(State Graph) =

E(State Graph) =

b. Is there a path from Oregon to any other state in the graph?
c. Is there a path from Hawaii to every other state in the graph?
d. From which state(s) in the graph is there a path to Hawaii?
e. Show the adjacency matrix that would describe the edges in this graph. Store the vertices in alphabetical order.

25. Draw a UML class diagram for the weighted digraph defined by Specification 11.3.

26. Classify each of the operations in Specification 11.3 as a constructor, observer, transformer, or iterator.

27. Figure 11.13 shows the contents of the queue during part of the breadth-first search of Austin to Washington. Draw the queue for the remaining iterations of the search loop.

28. Download from the publisher's website the two files for the weighted digraph (Specification 11.3 and Body 11.6) and the file `searches.adb` containing a demonstration of the three searches (Bodies 11.3, 11.4, and 11.5). The search demonstration program builds the graph shown in Figure 11.10.

a. Add the line `Put_Line (City);` just after the city is popped in the loop in the depth-first search and just after the city is dequeued in the breadth-first search. These additions will display the cities visited during each of the searches.

b. Compile and run the program and record the order in which the cites are visited in the depth-first and breadth-first searches for flights from Austin to Washington.

c. The eight city names were added to the graph in alphabetical order. Reorder the calls to `Add_Vertex` so that the cities are added in reverse alphabetical order.

d. Rerun the program and compare the order in which the cities are visited to what you recorded in part (b). If they are different, give an explanation.

e. Was there any differences in the table produced for the shortest path operation in your two runs?

29. Fill in the following table with the Big-O for each of the graph operations in Body 11.6. N is the number of vertices in the graph.

Operation	Big-O
`Index_Of` (**search**)	_____
`Clear`	_____
`Add_Vertex`	_____
`Add_Edge`	_____
`Retrieve`	_____
`Weight_Of`	_____
`Get_Adjacent_Vertices`	_____
`Clear_All_Marks`	_____
`Mark_Vertex`	_____
`Marked`	_____

30. Our implementation of a weighted digraph (Body 11.6) stores the vertices *unordered* in a one-dimensional array. This approach makes adding a new vertex easy—just place it into the next available array location. If the vertices were ordered in the array, we could use a binary search to locate a vertex and speed up several graph operations.

a. When we insert a new vertex into an ordered structure, we must make room for it in the one-dimensional array of vertices and we must make room for a new row in the adjacency matrix. Both of these tasks require shuffling array values down (recall how in Chapter 7 we inserted a new element into a sequential list). Because we stored the adjacency matrix in a two-dimensional array, making room for a new row requires a pair of nested loops. Assuming that `Index` is the row for our new vertex, write the two loops to open up the space in the two-dimensional array.

b. Fill in the table from Exercise 29 with the Big-Os of the graph operations, assuming that the vertices are ordered in a one-dimensional array.

c. In Chapter 7 we used an assignment statement with slices to make room for a new element in a sequential list. Two-dimensional arrays do not have slicing operations. Slicing is available with an array of arrays. Change the declarations for the adjacency matrix from a two-dimensional array to an array of arrays. Then rewrite your solution to part (a) making use of this change. You need only one loop and an assignment statement with slices.

d. Will the code you wrote for part (c) execute faster than the code you wrote for part (a)?

e. Does the code you wrote for part (c) have a better Big-O than the code you wrote for part (a)?

31. Here are three Boolean operations we could add to Specification 11.3:

```
function Full (Graph : in Graph_Type) return Boolean;
-- Returns True if no more vertices can be added to Graph

function Empty (Graph : in Graph_Type) return Boolean;
-- Returns True if Graph contains no vertices

function Has_Edge (Graph : in Graph_Type;
                   Edge  : in Edge_Type) return Boolean;
-- Returns True if Edge exists in Graph
```

Write the bodies of these three functions as if you were including them in Body 11.6, which uses an adjacency matrix to implement the weighted digraph.

32. Here are two transformer operations we could add to Specification 11.3:

```
procedure Delete_Edge (Graph : in out Graph_Type;
                       Edge  : in      Edge_Type)
-- Purpose         : Removes Edge from Graph
-- Preconditions   : None
-- Postconditions  : Edge is removed from Graph
-- Exceptions      : VERTEX_ERROR is raised if one or both of the vertices
--                   defining Edge do not exist in Graph
--                   EDGE_ERROR is raised if Edge does not exist in the Graph

procedure Delete_Vertex (Graph : in out Graph_Type;
                         Key   : in      Edge_Type)
-- Purpose         : Removes the vertex identified by Key from Graph
-- Preconditions   : None
-- Postconditions  : The vertex identified by Key is not in Graph
--                   All edges that have this vertex as an end are removed
--                   from Graph
-- Exceptions      : VERTEX_ERROR is raised if there is no vertex in Graph
--                   identified by Key
```

Write the bodies of these three procedures as if you were including them in Body 11.6, which uses an adjacency matrix to implement the weighted digraph.

33. The `Depth_First_Search` operation can be implemented without a stack by using recursion.
    a. Name the base case(s). Name the general case(s).
    b. Write the algorithm for a recursive depth-first search.
34. The following undirected graph's vertices are single character values.

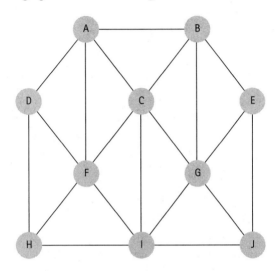

The graph is to be implemented as an adjacency matrix indexed by the characters 'A' through 'Z', using the following declarations:

```
subtype Alpha_Type  is Character range 'A'..'Z';
type    Vertex_Array is array (Alpha_Type) of Boolean;
type    Matrix_Type  is array (Alpha_Type, Alpha_Type) of Boolean;

type Graph_Type is
   record
      Vertices : Vertex_Array := (others => False);
      Edges    : Matrix_Type  := (others => (others => False));
   end record;


Alpha_Graph : Graph_Type;
```
    a. Show the contents of `Alpha_Graph`, given the graph pictured above. (You only need to show the portions of the two arrays that are in use.)
    b. Specify and implement an `Add_Vertex` operation for this graph.
    c. Specify and implement an `Add_Edge` operation for this graph.
    d. Specify and implement a `Delete_Vertex` operation for this graph.
    e. Specify and implement a `Delete_Edge` operation for this graph.

35. Modify the declarations for the private part of Specification 11.3 (given on page 746) to use the data structure of the weighted digraph depicted in Figure 11.16.

36. Modify the declarations for the private part of Specification 11.3 (given on page 746) to use the data structure of the weighted digraph depicted in Figure 11.17.

Programming Problems

37. Write a program to schedule the jobs submitted to a college's computer center printer. Your program should read all of the print requests from a file. Each print request consists of the requestor's title (Administrator, Professor, Student) and the size (in bytes) of the print job. Enqueue each print request into a priority queue where student jobs have high priority, professor jobs have medium priority, and administrative jobs have low priority. Within each of these three groups, smaller jobs go before larger jobs. Thus a student job to print 12,434 bytes has a higher priority than a student job to print 52,198 bytes. After enqueuing all of the print requests in the file, dequeue them all and display the job characteristics of each (Title and Size).

38. Implement the weighted digraph specified in Specification 11.3 using the data structure depicted in Figure 11.16. Write a test plan and test program to test your implementation.

39. Implement the weighted digraph specified in Specification 11.3 using the data structure depicted in Figure 11.17. Write a test plan and test program to test your implementation.

Sorting and Searching Algorithms

Goals for this chapter include that you should be able to

- design and implement the following sorting algorithms:

    - straight selection sort
    - bubble sort
    - short bubble sort
    - insertion sort
    - merge sort
    - quick sort
    - heap sort
    - radix sort

- compare the efficiency of the sorting algorithms, in terms of Big-O and space requirements.

- discuss other considerations: sorting small numbers of elements, stability, sorting on multiple keys, and sorting arrays of pointers to either dynamically allocated objects or objects in another array.

- discuss the performances of the following search algorithms:

    - sequential search of an unordered list
    - sequential search of an ordered list
    - binary search

- design and implement a high-probability ordered list.

- define the following terms:

    - hash function
    - collisions
    - linear probing
    - quadratic probing
    - clustering
    - double hashing
    - buckets
    - direct chaining
    - coalesced chaining
    - division method
    - multiplication method
    - folding

- design and implement an appropriate hashing function for an application.

- design and implement a collisions-resolution algorithm for a hash table.

- discuss the efficiency considerations for searching, in terms of Big-O.

- discuss the efficiency considerations for hashing, in terms of expected number of probes.

Chapter 12: Sorting and Searching Algorithms

At many points in this book, we have gone to great trouble to keep lists of elements in sorted order: student records sorted by ID number, integers sorted from smallest to largest, words sorted alphabetically. One goal of keeping sorted lists, of course, is to facilitate searching. Given an appropriate data structure, a particular list element can be found faster if the list is sorted.

In this chapter we directly examine strategies for sorting and searching, two tasks that are fundamental to a variety of computing problems. Perhaps more computer time is spent sorting and searching than on any other task. So it is important that we examine these topics in some detail.

12.1 Sorting

Putting an unordered list of data items into order—sorting—is a very common and useful operation. Whole books have been written about various sorting algorithms, as well as algorithms for searching an ordered list to find a particular element. The goal is to come up with better, more efficient sorts. Because sorting a large number of elements can be extremely time consuming, a good sorting algorithm is very desirable.

How do we describe efficiency? We pick an operation central to most sorting algorithms: the operation that compares two values to see which is smaller. In our study of sorting algorithms, we relate the number of comparisons to the number of elements in the list (N) as a rough measure of the efficiency of each algorithm. The number of swaps made is another measure of sorting efficiency. In the exercises, we ask you to analyze the sorting algorithms developed in this chapter in terms of moving data. When the items we are sorting are very large, data movement efficiency may be a more important measure of sorting efficiency than number of comparisons.

Another efficiency consideration is the amount of memory space required. In general, memory space is not a very important factor in choosing a sorting algorithm. We look at only two sorts in which space would be a serious consideration. The usual time versus space trade-off applies to sorts—more space often means less time, and vice versa.

Because processing time is the factor that applies most often to sorting algorithms, we have considered it in detail here. Of course, as in any application, the programmer must determine goals and requirements before selecting an algorithm and starting to code.

We first discuss the straight selection sort, the bubble sort, and the insertion sort. You probably wrote at least one of these three simple sorts in your first course. Then we examine three more complex (but more efficient) sorting algorithms: merge sort, quick sort, and heap sort.

We implement each of these six sorting algorithm as a generic procedure using the declarations given in Specification 12.1. Finally, we look at the radix sort, a completely different approach to sorting.

Specification 12.1   Sort

```
generic
   type Element_Type is private;
```

```
   type Array_Type   is array (Positive range <>) of Element_Type;
   with function "<" (Left : in Element_Type; Right : in Element_Type)
                  return Boolean;
procedure Sort (Values : in out Array_Type);
-- Purpose        : Sorts the elements in Values from smallest to largest
--                  as determined by function "<"
-- Preconditions  : Only one of our sorts (Heap Sort) has preconditions
-- Postconditions : The elements in Values are in order by function "<"
```

12.2 O(N^2) Sorts

In this section we present three "simple" sorts, so called because they use an unsophisticated brute force approach. Such approaches are not very efficient, but they are easy to understand and to implement. Nearly every experienced programmer has a favorite that they can code off the top of their head.

All of these simple sorts are based on dividing the array into a part that is sorted and a part that is not sorted. We use the variable Current to mark the boundary between the two portions, as illustrated in Figure 12.1.

Straight Selection Sort

If you were handed a list of names and asked to put them in alphabetical order, you might use this general approach:

1. Find the name that comes first in the alphabet, and write it on a second sheet of paper.
2. Cross the name out on the original list.
3. Continue this cycle until all the names on the original list have been crossed out and written onto the second list, at which point the second list is sorted.

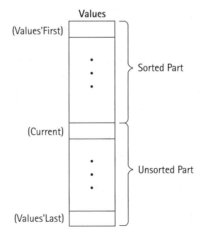

Figure 12.1 Current *partitions the array into sorted and unsorted parts.*

This algorithm is simple to translate into a computer program, but it has one drawback: It requires space in memory to store two complete lists. Although we have not talked much about memory space considerations, this duplication is clearly wasteful. A slight adjustment to this manual approach does away with the need to duplicate space, however. As you cross a name off the original list, a free space opens up. Instead of writing the minimum value on a second list, you can exchange it with the value currently in the position where the crossed-off element would go.

Because of this algorithm's simplicity, it is usually the first sorting method that students learn. Therefore, we go straight to the algorithm.

Selection Sort
```
Current := Values'First          -- entire array is currently unsorted
loop
    exit when the unsorted part of the array contains zero or one element
    Find the smallest value in the unsorted portion of the array
    Swap the Current item with the smallest one in the unsorted portion of the array
    Increment Current to shrink the size of the unsorted portion of the array
end loop
```

We use the variable `Current` to mark the beginning of the unsorted part of the array. We start out by setting `Current` to the index of the first array position. That means that the unsorted part of the array is `Values(Current..Values'Last)`, which is, of course, the entire array.

The main sort processing occurs in a loop. In each iteration of the loop body, the smallest value in the unsorted part of the array is swapped with the value in the `Current` location. After the swap, `Current` is in the sorted part of the array, so we shrink the size of the unsorted part by incrementing `Current`.

Because we removed the smallest value from the unsorted part, we know that every value in the unsorted part is greater than (or equal to, if duplicates are permitted) any value in the sorted part of the array. This fact helps us to determine the exit condition for our loop. When the unsorted array consists of just a single element, the entire array is sorted. In order for our algorithm to handle the degenerate case of sorting an empty array, we must also exit when there are no elements in the array.

How do we know when there is only one element left in the unsorted part of the array? When `Current` < `Values'Last`, the unsorted part of the array, contains *more* than one value. When `Current` = `Values'Last`, the unsorted part contains one element. We know that this value is greater than (or equal to) any value in the sorted part. So the value in `Values(Values'Last)` is in its correct place, and we are done.

Figure 12.2 traces the four iterations of the loop in our selection sort algorithm required to sort an array of five elements.

Now all we have to do is to locate the smallest value in the unsorted part of the array. Let's write a function to do this task. Function `Min_Index` is given an unconstrained array of elements and returns the index of the smallest value in this array.

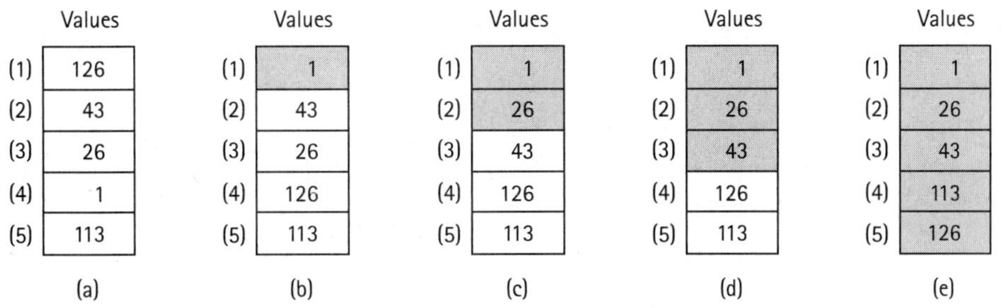

	Values		Values		Values		Values		Values
(1)	126	(1)	1	(1)	1	(1)	1	(1)	1
(2)	43	(2)	43	(2)	26	(2)	26	(2)	26
(3)	26	(3)	26	(3)	43	(3)	43	(3)	43
(4)	1	(4)	126	(4)	126	(4)	126	(4)	113
(5)	113	(5)	113	(5)	113	(5)	113	(5)	126
	(a)		(b)		(c)		(d)		(e)

Figure 12.2 *Example of straight selection sort. (The sorted elements are shaded.)*

Min_Index
    Min := Unsorted'First
    for Index in Unsorted'First + 1 .. Unsorted'Last loop
        if Unsorted(Index) < Unsorted(Min) then
            Min := Index
        end if
    end loop
    return Min

Trace this algorithm on the data in Figure 12.2(a). Did you come up with a result of 4?

Now that we know where the smallest unsorted element is, we swap it with the element at index `Current`. We can use the same `Swap` procedure we used in the heap package body we developed in Chapter 11. Body 12.1 contains the complete code for procedure `Selection_Sort`.

Body 12.1   Selection Sort: Implements Specification 12.1

```
procedure Selection_Sort (Values : in out Array_Type) is

   ------------------------------------------------------------------------
   procedure Swap (Left : in out Element_Type; Right : in out Element_Type) is
   -- Swaps the values of two variables
      Temp : Element_Type;
   begin
      Temp  := Left;
      Left  := Right;
      Right := Temp;
   end Swap;

   ------------------------------------------------------------------------
   function Min_Index (Unsorted : in Array_Type) return Positive is
   -- Purpose         : Finds the smallest element in Unsorted
```

```ada
   -- Preconditions  : Unsorted'Length > 0
   -- Postconditions : Min_Index = index of smallest element in Unsorted
      Min : Positive;
   begin
      Min := Unsorted'First;
      for Index in Unsorted'First + 1 .. Unsorted'Last loop
         if Unsorted(Index) < Unsorted(Min) then
            Min := Index;
         end if;
      end loop;
      return Min;
   end Min_Index;

   pragma Inline (Swap, Min_Index); -- See section on efficiency considerations

   -------------------------------------------------------------------------
   Current  : Positive;   -- Index that separates sorted from unsorted parts
   Smallest : Positive;   -- Index of smallest element in the unsorted part
begin
   Current := Values'First;
   loop  -- Each iteration, one element is moved to the correct spot
      exit when Current >= Values'Last;  -- Exit when 0 or 1 elements remain
      -- Find the index of the smallest unsorted element
      Smallest := Min_Index (Unsorted => Values(Current..Values'Last));
      -- Put the smallest element into the correct spot
      Swap (Values(Current), Values(Smallest));
      -- Shrink the unsorted part of the array
      Current := Current + 1;
   end loop;
end Selection_Sort;
```

Analyzing Straight Selection Sort Now let's try measuring the amount of "work" required by this algorithm. We describe the number of comparisons as a function of the number of elements in the array. To be concise, in this discussion we refer to `Values'Length` as N.

The comparison operation is in the `Min_Index` function. We know from the loop in the `Selection_Sort` procedure that function `Min_Index` is called $N - 1$ times. Within the function, the number of comparisons varies, depending on the size of the unsorted array parameter `Unsorted`:

```ada
for Index in Unsorted'First + 1 .. Unsorted'Last loop
   if Unsorted(Index) < Unsorted(Min) then
      Min := Index;
   end if;
end loop;
```

In the first call to Min_Index, Unsorted'First is 1 and Unsorted'Last is Values'Last, so there are $N - 1$ comparisons; in the next call there are $N - 2$ comparisons, and so on, until in the last call, there is only one comparison. The total number of comparisons is

$$(N - 1) + (N - 2) + (N - 3) + \ldots + 1 = N(N - 1)/2$$

To accomplish our goal of sorting an array of N elements, the selection sort requires $N(N - 1)/2$ comparisons. Note that the particular arrangement of values in the array does not affect the amount of work done at all. Even if the array is in sorted order before the call to Selection_Sort, the procedure still makes $N(N - 1)/2$ comparisons. The following table shows the number of comparisons required for arrays of various sizes. Note that doubling the array size roughly quadruples the number of comparisons.

Number of Comparisons Required to Sort Arrays of Different Sizes Using Selection_Sort

Number of Elements	Number of Comparisons
10	45
20	190
100	4,950
1000	499,500
10,000	49,995,000

How do we describe this algorithm in terms of Big-O? If we express $N(N - 1)/2$ as $1/2N^2 - 1/2N$, it is easy to see. In Big-O notation we only consider the term $1/2N^2$, because it increases fastest relative to N. (Remember the elephants and goldfish?) Further, we ignore the constant, $1/2$, making this algorithm $O(N^2)$. This means that, for large values of N, the computation time is approximately proportional to N^2. Looking back at the previous table, we see that multiplying the number of elements by 10 increases the number of comparisons by more than a factor of 100. That is, the number of comparisons is multiplied by approximately the square of the increase in the number of elements. Looking at this chart makes us appreciate why sorting algorithms are the subject of so much attention. Using Selection_Sort to sort a list of 1000 elements requires almost a half million comparisons!

The identifying feature of a selection sort is that on each pass through the loop, one element is put into its proper place. In the straight selection sort, each iteration finds the smallest value in the unsorted portion of the array and puts it into its correct place. If we had made the local function find the largest value instead of the smallest, the algorithm would have sorted in descending order. We could also run the loop in reverse, putting the elements into the end of the array first. All of these are variations on the straight selection sort. The variations do not change the basic way the minimum (or maximum) element is found.

Bubble Sort

The bubble sort uses a different scheme for finding the minimum value. Each iteration puts the smallest unsorted element in its correct place, but it also makes changes in the location of the other elements in the array. The first iteration puts the smallest element in the array in the first array position. Starting with the last array element we compare successive pairs of elements, swapping whenever the bottom element of the pair is smaller than the one above it. In this way the smallest element "bubbles up" to the top of the array. The next iteration puts the smallest element in the unsorted part of the array into the second array position, using the same technique.

The basic algorithm for the bubble sort is as follows:

Bubble Sort

    Current := Values'First   — *entire array is currently unsorted*
    loop
        exit when the unsorted part of the array contains zero or one element
        "Bubble up" the smallest element in the unsorted part of the array,
            causing intermediate swaps as necessary
        Increment Current to shrink the size of the unsorted portion of the array
    end loop

The structure of the loop is much like that of Selection_Sort. The unsorted part of the array is Values(Current..Values'Last). Current begins at Values'First, and we loop until Current reaches Values'Last, with Current incremented in each iteration. On entrance to each iteration of the loop body, the values in Values(Values'First..Current - 1) are already sorted, and all the elements in the unsorted part of the array are greater than or equal to the sorted elements.

As you look at the example in Figure 12.3, note that in addition to putting one element in its proper place, each iteration causes some intermediate changes in the array.

The inside of the loop body is different from the selection sort. Each iteration of the loop "bubbles up" the smallest values in the unsorted part of the array to the Current position. The algorithm for the bubbling task is as follows:

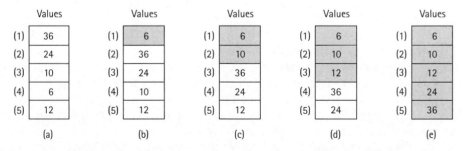

Figure 12.3 *Example of bubble sort. (The sorted elements are shaded.)*

Bubble Up
```
for Index in reverse Unsorted'First + 1 .. Unsorted'Last loop
    if Unsorted(Index) < Unsorted(Index - 1) then
        Swap Unsorted(Index)) with Unsorted(Index - 1)
    end if
end loop
```

A snapshot of this algorithm is shown in Figure 12.4. The code for procedure `Bubble_Sort` is given in Body 12.2.

Body 12.2   Bubble Sort: Implements Specification 12.1

```
procedure Bubble_Sort (Values : in out Array_Type) is

-------------------------------------------------------------------------------
procedure Swap (Left : in out Element_Type; Right : in out Element_Type) is
-- Swaps the values of two variables
    Temp : Element_Type;
begin
    Temp  := Left;
    Left  := Right;
    Right := Temp;
end Swap;
```

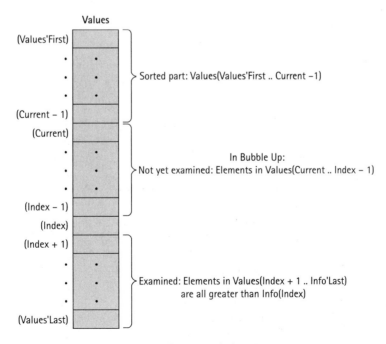

Figure 12.4   *Snapshot of a bubble sort.*

```ada
   procedure Bubble_Up (Unsorted : in out Array_Type) is
   begin
      -- Each iteration, the order of one adjacent pair of elements is fixed
      for Index in reverse Unsorted'First + 1 .. Unsorted'Last loop
         if Unsorted(Index) < Unsorted(Index - 1) then
            Swap (Unsorted(Index), Unsorted(Index - 1));
         end if;
      end loop;
   end Bubble_Up;

   pragma Inline (Swap, Bubble_Up);  -- See section on efficiency considerations
```

```ada
   Current : Positive;   -- Index that separates sorted from unsorted parts
begin
   Current := Values'First;
   loop  -- Each iteration, one element is bubbled up to the correct spot
      exit when Current >= Values'Last;   -- Exit when 0 or 1 elements remain
      -- Bubble up the smallest unsorted element
      Bubble_Up (Unsorted => Values(Current..Values'Last));
      -- Shrink the unsorted part of the array
      Current := Current + 1;
   end loop;
end Bubble_Sort;
```

Analyzing Bubble Sort   To analyze the work required by `Bubble_Sort` is easy. It is the same as for the straight selection sort algorithm. The comparisons are in `Bubble_Up`, which is called $N - 1$ times. There are $N - 1$ comparisons the first time, $N - 2$ comparisons the second time, and so on. Therefore, `Bubble_Sort` and `Selection_Sort` require the same amount of work, in terms of the number of comparisons. `Bubble_Sort` does more than just make comparisons, though; `Selection_Sort` has only one data swap per iteration, but `Bubble_Sort` may do many additional data swaps.

What is the purpose of these intermediate data swaps? By reversing out-of-order pairs of data as they are noticed, the procedure might get the array in order before $N - 1$ calls to `Bubble_Up`. However, this version of the bubble sort makes no provision for stopping when the array is completely sorted. Even if the array is already in sorted order when `Bubble_Sort` is called, this procedure continues to call `Bubble_Up` (which changes nothing) $N - 1$ times.

We could quit before the maximum number of iterations if `Bubble_Up` returns a Boolean flag to tell us when the array is sorted. Within `Bubble_Up`, we can set the out parameter Sorted to true; then in the loop, if any swaps are made, we reset Sorted to false. If no elements have been swapped, we know that the array is already in order. Now the bubble sort needs to make only one extra call to Bubble_Up when the array is in order. This version of the bubble sort is shown in Body 12.3.

Body 12.3   Short Bubble Sort: Implements Specification 12.1

```
procedure Short_Bubble_Sort (Values : in out Array_Type) is

   ------------------------------------------------------------------
   procedure Swap (Left : in out Element_Type; Right : in out Element_Type) is
   -- Swaps the values of two variables
      Temp : Element_Type;
   begin
      Temp  := Left;
      Left  := Right;
      Right := Temp;
   end Swap;

   ------------------------------------------------------------------
   procedure Bubble_Up (Unsorted : in out Array_Type;
                        Sorted   :    out Boolean) is
   begin
      Sorted := True;   -- Start out optimistic
      -- Each iteration, the order of one adjacent pair of elements is fixed
      for Index in reverse Unsorted'First + 1 .. Unsorted'Last loop
         if Unsorted(Index) < Unsorted(Index - 1) then
            Swap (Unsorted(Index), Unsorted(Index - 1));
            Sorted := False;   -- Found an element out of order
         end if;
      end loop;
   end Bubble_Up;

   pragma Inline (Swap, Bubble_Up);  -- See section on efficiency considerations

   ------------------------------------------------------------------
   Current : Positive;   -- Index that separates sorted from unsorted parts
   Sorted  : Boolean;
begin
   Current := Values'First;
   Sorted  := False;
   loop  -- Each iteration, one element is bubbled up to the correct spot
      exit when Sorted or Current >= Values'Last;
```

```
      -- Bubble up the smallest unsorted element
      Bubble_Up (Unsorted => Values(Current..Values'Last),
                 Sorted   => Sorted);
      -- Shrink the unsorted part of the array
      Current := Current + 1;
   end loop;
end Short_Bubble_Sort;
```

The analysis of `Short_Bubble_Sort` is more difficult. Clearly, if the array is already sorted, the first call to `Bubble_Up` tells us so. In this best case scenario, `Short_Bubble_Sort` is O(N); only $N - 1$ comparisons are required for the sort. What if the original array is actually sorted in descending order before the call to `Short_Bubble_Sort`? This is the worst possible case: `Short_Bubble_Sort` requires as many comparisons as `Bubble_Sort`, not to mention the "overhead"—setting, resetting, and testing the `Sorted` flag. Can we calculate an average case? In the first call to `Bubble_Up`, when `Current` is 1, there are `Values'Last` - 1 comparisons; on the second call, when `Current` is 2, there are `Values'Last` - 2 comparisons. The number of comparisons in any call to `Bubble_Up` is `Values'Last` - `Current`. If we let N indicate `Values'Last` and K indicate the number of calls to `Bubble_Up` executed before `Short_Bubble_Sort` finishes its work, the total number of comparisons required is

$$\underset{\text{1st call}}{(N-1)} + \underset{\text{2nd call}}{(N-2)} + \underset{\text{3rd call}}{(N-3)} + \ldots + \underset{K\text{th call}}{(N-K)}$$

A little algebra[1] changes this to

$$(2KN - K^2 - K)/2$$

In Big-O notation, the term that is increasing the fastest relative to N is $2KN$. We know that K is between 1 and $N - 1$. On the average, over all possible input orders, K is proportional to N. Therefore $2KN$ is proportional to N^2; that is, the short bubble sort algorithm is also $O(N^2)$.

Insertion Sort

In Chapter 7 we created a sorted list by inserting each new element into its appropriate place in an array. We can use a similar approach for sorting an array. The principle of

---

[1]For those of you who want to see the algebra:
$= (N - 1) + (N - 2) + \ldots + (N - K)$
$= KN - (\text{sum of 1 through } K)$
$= KN - (1/2 K(K + 1))$ [as we saw in Chapter 5]
$= KN - (1/2 K^2 + 1/2 K)$
$= (2KN - K^2 - K)/2$

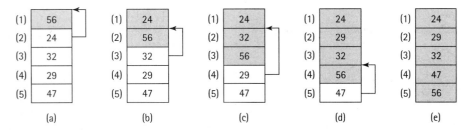

Figure 12.5 *An example of an insertion sort.*

the insertion sort is quite simple: Each successive element in the unsorted portion of the array is inserted into its proper pace in the sorted portion. Figure 12.5 illustrates this process, which we describe in the following algorithm:

Insertion Sort
  Current := Values'First + 1   - - *Sorted part has one element at start*
  loop
    Exit when there are no elements left in the unsorted portion
    Search the sorted portion of the array for the insertion Location of the Current element
    Make room for the Current value by moving array elements down
    Insert the Current value into Values(Location)
    Shrink the unsorted part of the list by incrementing Current
  end loop

Compare the middle three statements in the loop body to those in the `Insert` operation of our sequential implementation of a key-ordered list in Chapter 7.

We can search the sorted part of the array with a binary search or a sequential search. For simplicity, we choose to use a sequential search. Exercise 11 asks you to implement an insertion sort with a binary search. In all our previous sequential searches, we started with the first element of our sorted array. This time there is reason to start our search at the end. Searching in the reverse direction is faster when the array passed to the insertion sort is already in order. Let's demonstrate this with an example. Figure 12.6 shows the third iteration of the insertion loop for an array whose values were already in order. We are looking for the position in which to insert the current element, 30. Searching from beginning to end requires us to go through the entire sorted

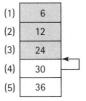

Figure 12.6 *The insert location is always after the last element in a sorted array.*

array before discovering that 30 belongs after the last element in the sorted part of the array. By starting our search at the end, we find the location immediately.

In Chapter 7 we described two methods for moving a block of array elements. We can move them with a loop or, using array slices, with a single assignment statement. We prefer the assignment method because array slice assignment usually executes faster than a loop.

There are two other minor details that we must address. Our algorithm initializes `Current` to the index of the second array element. As in the selection and bubble sorts, `Current` marks the first element of the unsorted part of the array. In those sorts we started with an "empty" sorted part. Here we begin with a sorted part containing one element. A list containing one element is sorted. Moving the elements down destroys the current value. For example, in Figure 12.5(c) we have determined that the current element, 29, belongs between 24 and 32. Moving elements 32 and 56 down overwrites 29 with 56. Therefore, before we move the elements down, we make a copy of the current element. Body 12.4 contains the complete insertion sort procedure.

Body 12.4   Insertion Sort: Implements Specification 12.1

```
procedure Insertion_Sort (Values : in out Array_Type) is

   ------------------------------------------------------------------
   function Insert_Location (Sorted : in Array_Type;
                             Value  : in Element_Type) return Positive is
   -- Purpose        : Find the location in Sorted where we should insert Value
   -- Preconditions  : Sorted'Length > 0
   -- Postconditions : Returns the Index where Value should go in Sorted

      Index : Natural;

   begin
      Index := Sorted'Last;    -- Search from end to beginning
      loop
         exit when Index < Sorted'First or else Sorted(Index) < Value;
         Index := Index - 1;
      end loop;
      return Index + 1;
   end Insert_Location;

   pragma Inline (Insert_Location);   -- See section on efficiency considerations

   ------------------------------------------------------------------
   Current : Positive;       -- Index that separates sorted from unsorted parts
```

```
      Location : Positive;           -- Insert location
      Value    : Element_Type;       -- Copy of Values(Current)
   begin
      Current := Values'First + 1;   -- Sorted part has one element at start
      loop  -- Each iteration, the first element in the unsorted part of the
            -- array is inserted into the sorted part of the array
         exit when Current > Values'Last;  -- Exit when no elements remain
         -- Find where in the sorted array to insert the current element
         Location := Insert_Location (Sorted => Values(Values'First .. Current-1),
                                      Value  => Values(Current));
         -- Make a copy of Values(Current)
         Value := Values(Current);
         -- Open up a space for the element by sliding all below it down
         Values(Location + 1 .. Current) := Values(Location .. Current - 1);
         -- Insert the current value
         Values(Location) := Value;
         -- Shrink the unsorted part of the array
         Current := Current + 1;
      end loop;
   end Insertion_Sort;
```

Analyzing Insertion Sort All of the comparisons in this sort are made in the search procedure. If the array elements are already ordered, each call to the search makes only one comparison. Because we call the search procedure $N - 1$ times, the number of comparisons for sorting an array whose elements are already in order is $N - 1$. Insertion sort is very efficient when the array is already sorted.

Now let's look at the worst case—one comparison is made the first time the search is called, two comparisons the second time, three comparisons the third time, and so on. $N - 1$ comparisons are made the last time the search is called. The number of comparisons in the worst case is

$$1 + 2 + 3 + \ldots + (N - 2) + (N - 2) + (N - 1) = N(N - 1)/2$$

The maximum number of comparisons is made only when the elements in the array are in reverse order. On the average, for a randomly ordered array, we search just half of the sorted part before finding the insert location. Therefore, for a randomly ordered array the total number of comparisons is closer to $N(N - 1)/4$. Because this value is half the number of comparisons made by selection sort and bubble sort, we might expect insertion sort to be faster in an array of mixed up values. The timing tests listed in the summary of this chapter support this observation.

Even though an insertion sort may be faster than the selection or bubble sorts, all are on the order of N^2; they are all too time-consuming for sorting large arrays. Thus, there is a need for sorting methods that work better when N is large.

12.3 O($N \log_2 N$) Sorts

Considering how rapidly N^2 grows as the size of the array gets larger, can't we do better? We note that N^2 is a lot larger than $(1/2N)^2 + (1/2N)^2$. If we could cut the array into two pieces, sort each segment, and then merge the two back together, we should end up sorting the entire array with a lot less work. An example of this approach is shown in Figure 12.7.

The idea of "divide and conquer" has been applied to the sorting problem in different ways, resulting in a number of algorithms that can do the job much more efficiently than O(N^2). We look at three of these sorting algorithms here—merge sort, quick sort, and heap sort. As you might guess, the efficiency of these algorithms is achieved at the expense of the simplicity seen in the straight selection, bubble, and insertion sorts.

Merge Sort

The merge sort algorithm is taken directly from the idea in the previous section:

Merge Sort
    Cut the list in half
    Sort the left half
    Sort the right half
    Merge the two sorted halves into one sorted list

Merging the two halves is an O(N) task. We merely go through the sorted halves, comparing successive pairs of values (one in each half) and putting the smaller value into the next slot in the final solution. Even if the sorting algorithm used for each half is O(N^2), we should see some improvement over sorting the whole list at once.

Actually, because merge sort is itself a sorting algorithm, we might as well use it to sort the two halves. That's right—we can make `Merge_Sort` a recursive procedure and let it call itself to sort each of the two subarrays:

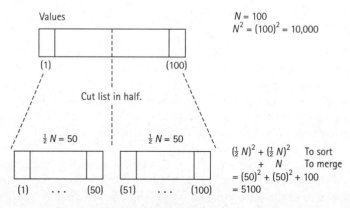

Figure 12.7 *Rationale for divide-and-conquer sorts.*

Merge_Sort--Recursive (general case)
    Cut the list in half
    Merge_Sort the left half
    Merge_Sort the right half
    Merge the two sorted halves into one sorted list

This is the general case, of course. What is the base case, the case that does not involve any recursive calls to `Merge_Sort`? If the "half" to be sorted doesn't have more than one element, we can consider it already sorted and just return. Here is our algorithm with this base case:

Merge_Sort--Recursive
    -- Check for the base case
    if the array Values contains more than one element then
        Cut the array in half *-- General Case*
        Merge_Sort the left half of Values
        Merge_Sort the right half of Values
        Merge the two sorted halves into one sorted list
    else
        Do Nothing   *-- Base Case*
    end if

Cutting the array in half is simply a matter of finding the midpoint between the first and last indexes:

```
Middle := (Values'First + Values'Last) / 2;
```

Then, in the smaller-caller tradition, we can make the recursive calls to `Merge_Sort`:

```
Merge_Sort (Values => Values(Values'First .. Middle);
Merge_Sort (Values => Values(Middle + 1  .. Values'Last);
```

So far this is pretty simple. Now we only have to merge the two halves and we're done.

Merging the Sorted Halves Obviously all the serious work is in the merge step. Let's first look at the general algorithm for merging two sorted arrays, and then we can look at the specific problem of our subarrays.

To merge two sorted arrays, we compare successive pairs of elements, one from each array, moving the smaller of each pair to the "final" array. We can stop when one array runs out of elements, and then move all the remaining elements (if any) from the other array to the final array. Figure 12.8 illustrates the general algorithm.

We use a similar approach in our specific problem, in which the two "arrays" to be merged are actually slices of the original array (Figure 12.9). Just as in the previous example, when we merged `Right` and `Left` into a third array, we will need to merge

784 | Chapter 12: Sorting and Searching Algorithms

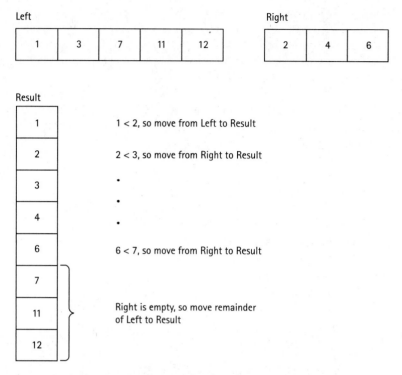

Figure 12.8 *Strategy for merging two sorted arrays.*

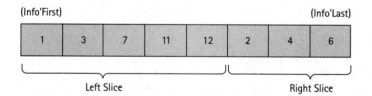

Figure 12.9 *Two array slices.*

our two slices into another array, temporarily. After the merge step, we copy the now-sorted elements back into the original array. The whole process is shown in **Figure 12.10**.

Let's specify a function, `Merge`, to do this task:

```
function Merge (Left  : in Array_Type;
                Right : in Array_Type) return Array_Type;
   -- Purpose          : Merge two sorted arrays into a single sorted array.
   -- Preconditions    : Left is sorted. Right is sorted.
   -- Postconditions   : A sorted array containing all the elements in Left
   --                    and Right is returned.
```

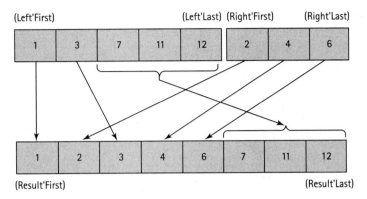

Figure 12.10 *Merging sorted halves.*

Here is the algorithm for function `Merge`:

Merge
```
    Left_Index    := Left'First
    Right_Index   := Right'First
    Result_Index  := Result'First
    loop
        exit when Left or Right runs out of elements
        if Left(Left_Index) < Right(Right_Index) then
            Result(Result_Index) := Left(Left_Index)
            Increment Left_Index
        else
            Result(Result_Index) := Right(Right_Index)
            Increment Right_Index
        end if
        Increment Result_Index
    end loop
    if there are any elements remaining in Left then
        Copy remaining elements in Left to Result
    else
        Copy remaining elements in Right to Result
    end if
    return Result
```

As we said, most of the work is in the merge task. The actual `Merge_Sort` procedure, given in Body 12.5, is short and simple.

Body 12.5 Merge Sort: Implements Specification 12.1

```
procedure Merge_Sort (Values : in out Array_Type) is
```

```ada
   function Merge (Left  : in Array_Type;
                   Right : in Array_Type) return Array_Type is
      Left_Index   : Positive;
      Right_Index  : Positive;
      Result_Index : Positive;
      Result       : Array_Type (1 .. Left'Length + Right'Length);
   begin
      -- Initialize array indexes
      Left_Index   := Left'First;
      Right_Index  := Right'First;
      Result_Index := Result'First;
      loop      -- Each iteration one element is moved into Result
         -- Exit when one array is "empty"
         exit when Left_Index  > Left'Last or
                   Right_Index > Right'Last;
         if Left(Left_Index) < Right(Right_Index) then
            Result(Result_Index) := Left(Left_Index);        -- Copy from Left
            Left_Index := Left_Index + 1;
         else
            Result(Result_Index) := Right(Right_Index);      -- Copy from Right
            Right_Index := Right_Index + 1;
         end if;
         Result_Index := Result_Index + 1;
      end loop;

      -- Copy any remaining elements
      if Left_Index <= Left'Last then    -- Still elements remaining in Left?
         Result(Result_Index..Result'Last) := Left(Left_Index..Left'Last);
      else
         Result(Result_Index..Result'Last) := Right(Right_Index..Right'Last);
      end if;
      return Result;
   end Merge;

   pragma Inline (Merge);    -- See section on efficiency considerations

   ----------------------------------------------------------------------
   Middle : Positive;    -- Middle index of array Values
begin
   -- Base Case:  Check for empty array or single element array
   if Values'Length > 1 then
      Middle := (Values'First + Values'Last) / 2;           -- Divide the array in half
      Merge_Sort (Values(Values'First .. Middle));          -- Sort the left half
      Merge_Sort (Values(Middle + 1 .. Values'Last));       -- Sort the right half
```

```
   -- Merge the two sorted halves back into the original array
   Values := Merge (Left  => Values(Values'First .. Middle),
                    Right => Values(Middle + 1 .. Values'Last));
  end if;
end Merge_Sort;
```

Analyzing Merge Sort We already pointed out that sorting two half-lists is less work than sorting one whole list. How much less work is it? The bulk of the work occurs in the merge processing. In the Merge function we make comparisons on each element in the two arrays. Because the combined number of elements in the two arrays is N, this is an O(N) operation. So the Merge function is O(N).

Now, how many times is the Merge function called? It is called in procedure Merge_Sort after the array has been divided in half and each of those halves has been sorted (using Merge_Sort, of course). In each of the recursive calls, one for the left half and one for the right, the array is divided in half again, making four pieces. Each of these pieces is similarly subdivided. At each level the number of pieces doubles (see Figure 12.11). We can keep dividing the array in half $\log_2 N$ times. (This is just like the binary search algorithm in Chapter 1.)

Each time the array is divided, we perform the O(N) Merge function to put it back together again. This gives us a product of $N \times \log_2 N$. Thus the whole algorithm is O($N \log_2 N$). As the table on the next page shows, for large values of N, O($N \log_2 N$) is a big improvement over O(N^2).

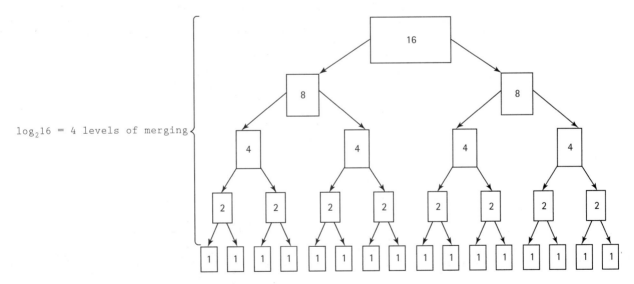

Figure 12.11 *Analysis of procedure* Merge_Sort *with N = 16.*

Comparing $N \log_2 N$ and N^2

N	$\log_2 N$	$N \log_2 N$	N^2
32	5	160	1024
64	6	384	4096
128	7	896	16,384
256	8	2048	65,536
512	9	4,608	262,144
1024	10	10,240	1,048,576
2048	11	22,528	4,194,304
4095	12	49,152	16,777,216

The disadvantage of Merge_Sort is that it requires an auxiliary array (the local variable Result) that, in the last merge, is as large as the original array to be sorted. If the array is large and space is a critical factor, this sort may not be an appropriate choice. Next we discuss two sorts that move elements around in the original array and do not need an auxiliary array.

Quick Sort

Like merge sort, quick sort is a divide-and-conquer algorithm. The name comes from the fact that quick sort can generally sort a list of data elements faster than any of the other common sorts. Our timing experiments presented later support this claim.

If you were given a large stack of final exams to sort by name, you might use the following approach: Pick a splitting value, say L, and divide the stack of tests into two piles, A–L and M–Z. (Note that the two piles may not necessarily contain the same number of tests.) Then take the first pile and subdivide it into two piles, A–F and G–L.

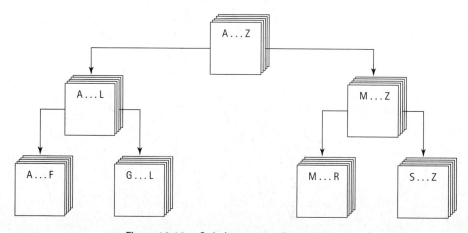

Figure 12.12 *Ordering exams using quick sort.*

The A-F pile can be further broken down into A-C and D-F. This division process goes on until the piles are small enough to be easily sorted. The same process is applied to the M-Z pile.

Eventually all the small sorted piles can be stacked one on top of the other to produce an ordered set of tests. (See Figure 12.12.)

This strategy is based on recursion—on each attempt to sort the stack of tests, the stack is divided, and then the same approach is used to sort each of the smaller stacks (a smaller case). This process goes on until the small stacks do not need to be further divided (the base case). Here is the top-level algorithm for quick sort:

Quick Sort
    if Values contains more than one element then
        Split Values into two portions
        Quick Sort the left portion
        Quick Sort the right portion
    end if

An obvious difference between the quick sort algorithm and the merge sort algorithm is the absence of a step to combine the two sorted portions—the merge. Because some sorting is done by each split (see Figure 12.12), the elements are already in their proper positions when we reach the base case of the recursive call.

Splitting the Array: The Logical Level Splitting the array is the easy part of the merge sort; we simply split the array in half. In quick sort, we split the array so that all of the elements in the left portion are less than all of the elements in the right portion. Separating these two portions is an element we call the *split value*. Some programmers call it the *pivot value*. More formally, after the array Values has been split into two portions, the elements in the array satisfy the following three assertions:

- All elements in Values(Values'First .. Split_Index - 1) < Split Value
- Values(Split_Index) = Split Value
- All elements in Values(Split_Index + 1 .. Values'Last) ≥ Split Value

How do we select the split value? One simple solution is to use the first value in the array as the splitting value (Figure 12.13[a]). We'll show another solution later. The Split procedure moves the split value to the correct position in the array (Split_Index) and moves some of the other elements so that all the elements less than the split value are on the left side of the array and all those greater than or equal to the split value are on the right (Figure 12.13[b]). Note that we don't know the value of Split_Index until the splitting process is complete.

Our recursive calls to Quick_Sort use Split_Index to reduce the size of the problem in the general case. The left portion of the array is sorted by the call

Quick_Sort (Values => Values(Values'First .. Split_Index - 1));

and the right portion of the array is sorted by the call

Quick_Sort (Values => Values(Split_Index + 1 .. Values'Last));

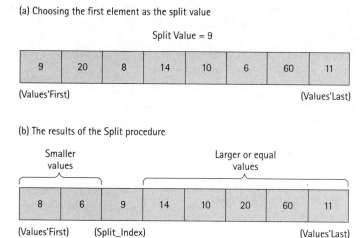

Figure 12.13 *Results of procedure* `Split`.

Let's verify our quick sort algorithm with the three-question method.

1. *Is there a nonrecursive base case?* Yes. When `Values'Length <= 1`, `Quick_Sort` does nothing.
2. *Does each recursive call involve a smaller case of the problem?* Yes. `Split` divides the segment into two not necessarily equal pieces, and each of these smaller pieces is then quick sorted. Note that even if the split value is the largest or smallest value in the segment, the two pieces are still smaller than the original one: If the split value is smaller than *all* the other values in the segment, then the left portion of the array, `Values(Values'First..Split_Index - 1)`, is a null array and the right portion, `Values(Split_Index + 1..Values'Last)`, contains one less element (the split value) than the original array.
3. *Assuming that the recursive calls succeed, does the whole procedure work?* Yes. We assume that `Quick_Sort(Values(Values'First..Split_Index - 1))` actually sorts the first `Split_Index - 1` elements, whose values are less than or equal to the split value. `Values(Split_Index)`, containing the split value, is in its correct place. We also assume that `Quick_Sort(Values(Split_Index + 1..Values'Last))` has correctly sorted the rest of the list, whose values are all greater than the split value. So we know that the whole list is sorted.

Splitting the Array: The Implementation Level   In good top-down fashion, we have shown that our algorithm works if procedure `Split` works. Now we must develop our splitting algorithm. We must find a way to get all of the elements less than the split value on one side of `Split_Index` and the elements greater than or equal to the split value on the other side.

12.3 O($N\log_2 N$) Sorts | 791

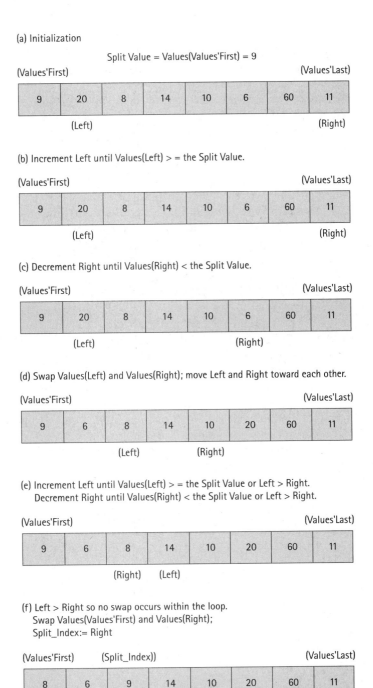

Figure 12.14 Trace of procedure `split`.

We do this by moving two indices, `Left` and `Right`, toward the middle of the array from the ends, looking for elements that are on the wrong side of the split point (Figure 12.14). Initially `Left` identifies the second element in the array and `Right` identifies the last element in the array. (See Figure 12.14[a].)

We start out by moving `Left` toward the middle, comparing `Values(Left)` to the split value. If `Values(Left)` is greater than the split value, we keep incrementing `Left`; otherwise we leave `Left` where it is and begin moving `Right` toward the middle. (See Figure 12.14[b].)

Now `Values(Right)` is compared to the split value. If it is greater than or equal to the split value, we continue decrementing `Right`; otherwise we leave `Right` in place. (See Figure 12.14[c].) At this point it is clear that `Values(Left)` and `Values(Right)` are each on the wrong side of the array. Note that the elements to the left of `Values(Left)` and to the right of `Values(Right)` are not necessarily sorted; they are just on the correct side with respect to the split value. To put `Values(Left)` and `Values(Right)` into their correct sides, we merely swap them, then increment `Left` and decrement `Right`. (See Figure 12.14[d].)

Now we repeat the whole cycle, incrementing `Left` until we encounter a value that is greater than or equal to the split value, then decrementing `Right` until we encounter a value that is less than the split value. (See Figure 12.14[e].)

When does the process stop? When `Left` and `Right` meet each other. They meet at the `Split_Index`. This location is where the split value belongs, so we swap `Values(Values'First)`, which contains the split value, with the element at `Values(Split_Index)` (Figure 12.14[f]). `Split_Index` is returned from the procedure, to be used by `Quick_Sort` to set up the two recursive calls.

Body 12.6 contains our code that implements the quick sort algorithm. We recommend that you spend some time walking through the `Split` procedure with different sized arrays containing values in different orders. Do you see why we initialized `Left` to `Values'First + 1` rather than `Values'First`? And what special case requires us to use `or else` rather than `or` in the exit statements of the first inner loop?

Body 12.6   Quick Sort: Implements Specification 12.1

```ada
procedure Quick_Sort (Values : in out Array_Type) is

   ----------------------------------------------------------------

   procedure Swap (Left : in out Element_Type; Right : in out Element_Type) is
   -- Swaps the values of two variables
      Temp : Element_Type;
   begin      Temp  := Left;
      Left  := Right;
      Right := Temp;
   end Swap;

   ----------------------------------------------------------------

   function ">=" (Left : in Element_Type; Right : in Element_Type)
              return Boolean is
```

```ada
begin
   return not (Left < Right);
end ">=";


-------------------------------------------------------------------------------
procedure Split (Values      : in out Array_Type;
                 Split_Index :    out Positive) is
   Left  : Positive;
   Right : Positive;
begin
   Left  := Values'First + 1;
   Right := Values'Last;
   loop  -- Each iteration, two out of place values are swapped
      -- Left to right search
      loop  -- Each iteration on element is inspected
         -- Exit when searches cross or find an element on wrong side
         exit when Left > Right   or else
                   Values(Left) >= Values(Values'First);
         Left := Left + 1;
      end loop;
      -- Right to left search
      loop  -- Each iteration on element is inspected
         -- Exit when searches cross or find an element on wrong side
         exit when Left > Right   or
                   Values(Right) < Values(Values'First);
         Right := Right - 1;
      end loop;
      -- Exit outer loop when searches cross
      exit when Left > Right;
      -- Swap the two values on the wrong side of the split value
      Swap (Values(Left), Values(Right));
      Left  := Left  + 1;
      Right := Right - 1;
   end loop;
   -- Move the split value into its proper location
   Swap (Values(Values'First), Values(Right));
   -- Return the index of the value that divides the two portions
   Split_Index := Right;
end Split;

pragma Inline (Swap, ">=", Split); -- See section on efficiency


-------------------------------------------------------------------------------
Split_Index : Positive;
```

```
begin
   if Values'Length > 1 then
      Split (Values, Split_Index);
      Quick_Sort (Values(Values'First .. Split_Index - 1));
      Quick_Sort (Values(Split_Index + 1 .. Values'Last));
   end if;
end Quick_Sort;
```

Our quick sort algorithm uses the "$>=$" operator to compare array elements. However, as you can see in Specification 12.1, the application programmer supplies only the "$<$" operator as a generic formal function. Rather than complicate the code of `Split` with the necessary Boolean transformations or add another generic formal function to our generic declaration, we use the application programmer-supplied function to write our own "$>=$" operator.

What happens if our splitting value is the largest or the smallest value in the segment? The algorithm still works correctly, but because of the lopsided splits it is not quick (we discuss the performance of quick sort in the next section).

Is this situation likely to occur? That depends on how we choose our splitting value and on the original order of the data in the array. If we use `Values(Values'First)` as the splitting value and the array is already sorted, then *every* split is lopsided. One side contains no elements, while the other side contains all but one of the elements (the split value). Thus our `Quick_Sort` is not a quick sort. This splitting algorithm favors an array in random order.

It is not unusual, however, to want to sort an array that is already in nearly sorted order. If this is the case, a better splitting value would be the middle value,

```
Values ((Values'First + Values'Last) / 2)
```

This value can be swapped with `Values(Values'First)` at the beginning of the `Split` procedure.

There are many other splitting algorithms; we have only discussed the most basic. You'll probably encounter others in future courses, other books, computer science journals, or someone else's programs.

Analyzing Quick Sort The analysis of `Quick_Sort` is very similar to that of `Merge_Sort`. On the first call, every element in the list is compared to the dividing value, so the work done is $O(N)$. The array is divided into two parts (not necessarily halves), which are then examined.

Each of these pieces is then divided in two, and so on. If each piece is split approximately in half, there are $O(\log_2 N)$ splits. At each split, we make $O(N)$ comparisons. So when each split divides the list nearly in half, `Quick_Sort` is an $O(N \log_2 N)$ algorithm, which is quicker than the $O(N^2)$ sorts we discussed at the beginning of this chapter.

But `Quick_Sort` isn't always quicker. Note that there are $\log_2 N$ splits only if each split divides the segment of the array approximately in half. As we've seen, `Quick_Sort` is sensitive to the order of the data.

What happens if the array is already sorted when `Quick_Sort` is called? If we use the first element as the split value, the splits are very lopsided, and the subsequent recursive calls to `Quick_Sort` sort a segment of no elements and a segment containing all the elements except the split value. This situation produces a sort that is not at all quick. In fact, there will be $N - 1$ splits; in this case `Quick_Sort` is $O(N^2)$.

Such a situation is very unlikely to occur by chance. By way of analogy, consider the odds of shuffling a deck of cards and coming up with a sorted deck. On the other hand, in some applications you may know that the original array is likely to be sorted or nearly sorted. In such cases you would want to use the middle element as the split value rather than the first value.

What about space requirements? Quick sort does not require an extra array as merge sort does. But because our quick sort algorithm is recursive, the space is used on the system stack for local variables, parameters, and return addresses. Usually this stack space is insignificant when compared to the space used by an array of "large" elements.

Heap Sort

In each iteration of the straight selection sort, we searched the unsorted portion of the array for the smallest element and put it in its correct place in the sorted portion of the array. Another way to write a selection sort is to find the maximum value in the array and swap it with the last array element, then find the next-to-largest element and put it in its place, and so on. Most of the work in this sorting algorithm comes from searching the unsorted part of the array in each iteration, looking for the maximum value.

In Chapter 11 we discussed the *heap*, a data structure with a very special feature—we always know where to find its greatest element. Because of the order property of heaps, the maximum value of a heap is in the root node. We can take advantage of this situation by using a heap to help us sort. The general approach of heap sort is as follows:

1. Take the root (maximum) element off the heap, and put it in its place.
2. Reheap the remaining elements. (This puts the next-largest element in the root position.)
3. Repeat until there are no more elements.

The first part of this algorithm sounds a lot like the straight selection sort. What makes the heap sort fast is the second step: finding the next-largest element. Because the shape property of heaps guarantees a binary tree of minimum height, we make only $O(\log_2 N)$ comparisons in each iteration, as compared with $O(N)$ comparisons in each iteration of the selection sort.

Building a Heap By now you are probably protesting that we are dealing with an unsorted array of elements, not a heap. Where does the original heap come from? Before we go on, we'll have to convert the unsorted array, `Values`, into a heap.

Let's take a look at how the heap relates to our array of unsorted elements. In Chapter 11 we saw how heaps can be represented in an array with implicit links. Because of the shape property, we know that the heap elements take up consecutive positions in the array. In fact, the unsorted array of data elements already satisfies the shape property of heaps. Figure 12.15 shows an unsorted array and its equivalent tree.

We also need to make the unsorted array elements satisfy the order property of heaps. First let's see if there's any part of the tree that already satisfies the order property. All of the leaf nodes (subtrees with only a single node) are heaps. In Figure 12.16(a) the subtrees whose roots contain the values 19, 7, 3, 100, and 1 are heaps because they are root nodes.

Now let's look at the first *nonleaf* node, the one containing the value 2 (Figure 12.16[b]). The subtree rooted at this node is not a heap, but it is almost a heap—all of the nodes *except the root node* of this subtree satisfy the order property. We know how to fix this problem. In Chapter 11 we developed a heap utility procedure, Reheap_Down, that can be used to correct this exact situation. Given a tree whose elements satisfy the order property of heaps except (perhaps) at the root node, Reheap_Down rearranges the nodes, leaving the (sub)tree as a heap.

We apply this procedure to all the subtrees on this level, then we move up a level in the tree and continue reheaping until we reach the root node. After Reheap_Down has been called for the root node, the whole tree should satisfy the order property of heaps. Here is the process expressed as an algorithm:

Build Heap
    for Index going from first nonleaf node up to the root node loop
        Reheap_Down (Heap => Values (Index .. Values'Last))
    end loop

We know where the root node is stored in our array representation of heaps—it's in Values(1). Where is the first nonleaf node? Because half the nodes of a complete binary tree are leaves (prove this yourself), the first nonleaf has the index of Values'Last / 2.

This heap-building process is illustrated in Figure 12.16; the changing contents of the array are shown in Figure 12.17.

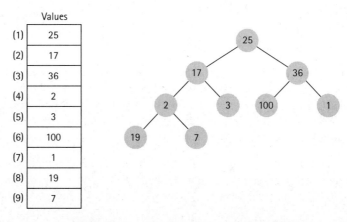

Figure 12.15 *An unsorted array and its tree.*

12.3 O($N\log_2 N$) Sorts | 797

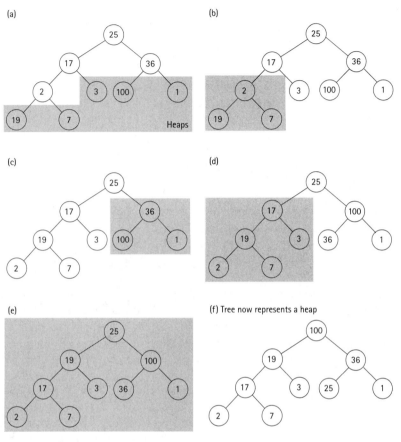

(a) Each leaf independently satisfies the two heap properties.
(b) Reheap down to fix the heap rooted at 2.
(c) Reheap down to fix the heap rooted at 36.
(d) Reheap down to fix the heap rooted at 17.
(e) Reheap down to fix the heap rooted at 25.
(f) Tree now represents a heap.

Figure 12.16 *The heap-building process.*

	(1)	(2)	(3)	(4)	(5)	(6)	(7)	(8)	(9)
Original Info	25	17	36	2	3	100	1	19	7
After ReapDown Index = 4	25	17	36	19	3	100	1	2	7
After Index = 3	25	17	100	19	3	36	1	2	7
After Index = 2	25	19	100	17	3	36	1	2	7
After Index = 1	100	19	36	17	3	25	1	2	7

Tree is a heap.

Figure 12.17 *Changing contents of the array.*

Because our heap storage scheme requires that the root node be at location 1, heap sort has the following precondition:

`-- Preconditions:   Values'First must be 1`

Although our other sorts could sort an array with arbitrary starting and ending index values, the starting index of the array for heap sort must be 1.

Sorting the Heap   Now that we are satisfied that we can turn the unsorted array of elements into a heap, let's take another look at the sorting algorithm.

We can easily access the largest element from the heap we just created—it's in the root node. In our array representation of heaps, that is `Values(1)`. This value belongs in the last-used array position `Values(Values'Last)`, so we can just swap the values in these two positions. Because `Values(Values'Last)` now contains the largest value in the array (its correct sorted value), we want to leave this position alone. Now we are dealing with a set of elements, from `Values(1)` through `Values(Values'Last - 1)`, that is almost a heap. We know that all of these elements satisfy the order property of heaps, except (perhaps) the root node. To correct this condition, we call our heap operation, `Reheap_Down`, for this smaller heap.

At this point we know that the next-largest element in the array is in the root node of the heap. To put this element in its correct position, we swap it with the element in `Values(Values'Last - 1)`. Now the two largest elements are in their final correct positions, and the elements in `Values(1)` through `Values(Values'Last - 2)` are almost a heap. So we call `Reheap_Down` again, and now the third-largest element is in the root of the heap.

This process is repeated until all of the elements are in their correct positions; that is, until the heap contains only a single element, which must be the smallest item in the array, in `Values(1)`. This is its correct position, so the array is now completely sorted from the smallest to the largest element. Notice that at each iteration the size of the unsorted portion (represented as a heap) gets smaller and the size of the sorted portion gets larger. At the end of the algorithm, the size of the sorted portion is the size of the original array.

The heap sort algorithm, as we have described it, sounds like a recursive process. Each time we swap and reheap a smaller portion of the total array. Because it uses tail recursion, we can code the repetition just as clearly using a simple `for` loop. The node sorting algorithm is as follows:

Sort Nodes
    for Index in last node up to next-to-root node loop
        Swap Root node with Values(Index);
        Reheap_Down (Heap => Values(1..Index - 1)
    end loop

Procedure `Heap_Sort`, given in Body 12.7, first builds the heap and then sorts the nodes, using the algorithms just discussed.

Body 12.7   Heap Sort: Implements Specification 12.1

```ada
with Heap;
procedure Heap_Sort (Values : in out Array_Type) is

   -- functions needed to instantiate a heap
   -------------------------------------------------------------------
   function Identity (Element : in Element_Type) return Element_Type is
   begin
      return Element;
   end Identity;

   function ">=" (Left : in Element_Type; Right : in Element_Type)
                 return Boolean is
   begin
      return not (Left < Right);
   end ">=";

   package Element_Heap is new Heap (Element_Type => Element_Type,
                                     Key_Type     => Element_Type,
                                     Heap_Array   => Array_Type,
                                     Key_Of       => Identity,
                                     ">"          => ">=");
   use Element_Heap;

   -------------------------------------------------------------------
   procedure Swap (Left : in out Element_Type; Right : in out Element_Type) is
   -- Swaps the values of two variables
      Temp : Element_Type;
   begin      Temp  := Left;
      Left  := Right;
      Right := Temp;
   end Swap;

   pragma Inline (Swap);   -- See section on efficiency considerations

   -------------------------------------------------------------------
begin
   -- Build the original heap from the unsorted elements
   for Index in reverse 1 .. Values'Last / 2 loop
      Reheap_Down (Heap => Values(Index..Values'Last));
   end loop;
```

```ada
-- Sort the elements in the heap by swapping the root (current largest) with
-- the last unsorted value, then reheaping the remaining part of the array.
for Index in reverse 2 .. Values'Last loop
   Swap (Values(1), Values(Index));
   Reheap_Down (Heap => Values(1 .. Index - 1));
end loop;
end Heap_Sort;
```

Analyzing Heap Sort The code for procedure `Heap_Sort` is very short—only a few lines of new code plus procedure `Reheap_Down`, which we developed in Chapter 11. These few lines of code, however, do quite a bit. All of the elements in the original array are rearranged to satisfy the order property of heaps, moving the largest element up to the top of the array, only to put it immediately into its place at the bottom.

Let's consider the loop that turns an unsorted array into a heap. We loop through $N/2$ times. Each iteration calls procedure `Reheap_Down`. In Chapter 11 we determined that `Reheap_Down` has $O(\log_2 N)$ comparisons. Multiplying these comparisons by the number of iterations our loop means our initial heap building $O(N \log_2 N)$.[2]

The analysis of the sorting loop is similar. We loop through $N - 1$ times, swapping elements and reheaping. Sorting our heap is therefore also $O(N \log_2 N)$. Adding the comparisons for the conversion of the unsorted array to those for sorting the heap shows that `Heap_Sort` has $O(N \log_2 N)$ comparisons.

Note that, unlike the quick sort algorithm, the heap sort's efficiency is not affected by the initial order of the elements. Procedure `Heap_Sort` is just as efficient in terms of space as `Quick_Sort`; only one array is used to store the data.

12.4 Radix Sort

We have placed radix sort in its own section because, unlike all of the other sorting algorithms we discussed in this chapter, radix sort is not a *comparison sort*. Radix sort doesn't compare two keys in the array. Therefore, we cannot analyze the amount of work done in terms of comparisons. In fact, the only thing that radix sort has in common with the other sorts is that it is given an unordered array and returns it ordered.

The idea behind radix sort is to divide the values into as many sublists as there are possible alternatives for each *position* in the key. For example, if the key is an integer number, each position is a digit and has 10 possibilities: 0..9. If the key is a string of letters and case is not important, then each position has 26 possibilities: 'a'..'z'. The number of possibilities is called the *radix*. After subdividing the items into radix sublists, we combine them back into one list and repeat the process. If we begin with the least significant position in the key, regroup the items in order, and repeat the process as many times as there are positions in the key, moving to next most significant position each time, the array is ordered when we finish.

---

[2]Robert W. Floyd found a method for converting an array into a heap using a merge procedure called *heapify* that is $O(N)$. Using heapify does not alter the Big-O of heap sort—heapify is the goldfish to the elephant-sized sorting loop.

Let's illustrate the algorithm by sorting three-digit positive integers. We divide these integers into 10 sublists based on the least significant digit (the units position). Let's create an array of queues to hold the sublists.

```
-- Instantiate a queue package for integer elements
package Int_Queue is new Unbounded_Queue (Element_Type => Integer);

type Queue_Array is array (0..9) of Int_Queue.Queue_Type;

Queues : Queue_Array;      -- An array of 10 queues
```

All items with 0 in the units position are enqueued into Queues(0); all items with a 1 in the units position are enqueued into Queues(1); and so on. After the first pass through the array, we collect the sublists with those in Queues(0) first and those in Queues(9) last.

This algorithm is illustrated in Figures 12.18 and 12.19; only the keys are shown. Look at the keys after each pass; the digits in the column that correspond to the pass number are ordered (Figure 12.18). Likewise, the digits in the pass number position are the same as the index of the queue that it is in (Figure 12.19).

Let's first write the algorithm for radix sort that matches our example:

Radix Sort
    for Position in 1..3 loop   *-- From units to hundreds column*
        for Index in Values'Range   *-- For each item in array Values*
            Which_Queue := Digit at Position in the key of Values(Index)
            Enqueue (Queue => Queues(Which_Queue),
                   Item   => Values (Index))
        end loop
        Collect Queues
    end loop

Original order	Order after 1st pass	Order after 2nd pass	Order after 3rd pass
762	800	800	001
124	100	100	100
432	761	001	124
761	001	402	402
800	762	124	432
402	432	432	761
976	402	761	762
100	124	762	800
001	976	976	976
999	999	999	999

Figure 12.18 *Key fields after each pass.*

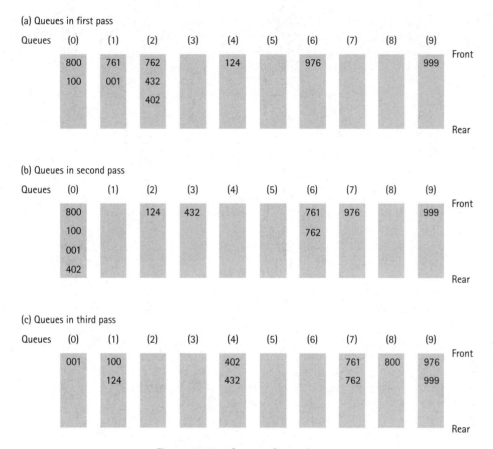

Figure 12.19 *Queues after each pass.*

Each iteration of the outer loop in this algorithm corresponds to one pass in Figures 12.18 and 12.19. In the first pass we use the units digit of our integer key to determine in which queue to enqueue the element. In the second pass we use the tens digit and in the third pass we use the hundreds digit. Next we need to expand the Collect Queues step of the algorithm. This is where we collect the elements from all of the queues. We put them back into Values.

```
Collect Queues
    Values_Index := Values'First
    for Queue_Index in 0..9 loop
        loop
            exit when Queue_Empty (Queues(Queue_Index))
            Dequeue (Queue => Queues (Queue_Index),
                     Item  => Values (Values_Index))
            Values_Index := Values_Index + 1
        end loop
    end loop
```

The outer loop in this algorithm goes through our 10 queues. The inner loop takes all the elements from a queue and puts them back into the array Values.

The Implementation Level

Now that we understand the algorithm, let's look at how we can make it general. What generic formal parameters are necessary to implement a generic radix sort? As with all our sorts, we need a type for the elements we are sorting (Element_Type) and a type for the array in which they are stored (Array_Type).

For our radix sort algorithm, we must know the number of different positions in the key. We use a generic formal object called Num_Positions to supply this information. Like we did in our example, let's number these positions starting with 1 (the least significant position) to Num_Positions (the most significant position).

We divide the key into Num_Positions subkeys. Because we work with subkeys of an element's key, we need a type for a subkey. This type must be supplied by the user; let's call it Subkey_Type. Because we use the portions of a key as indices in our array of queues, Subkey_Type must be a discrete type. We have a type for a portion of a key. Do we need a type for the entire key? No. Nowhere in our algorithm do we use the entire key.

In our other generic sorts, we had two generic formal functions. One of these ("<") is used to compare two key values. Radix sort does not compare key values so we don't need the user to supply such a function. The second generic formal function returns the key of a given element. Again, radix sort does not work with the entire key. However, it does work with portions of the key, values of type Subkey_Type. So we need the user to supply a function that returns a subkey for a given element. Because each element has Num_Positions subkeys, we need to also supply the position of the subkey we want as a parameter. Specification 12.2 is our declaration for a generic radix sort.

Specification 12.2   Radix Sort

```
generic
   Num_Positions : in Positive;      -- Number of positions in each element's key
   type Element_Type is private;
   type Array_Type   is array (Positive range <>) of Element_Type;
   type Subkey_Type is (<>);
   with function Subkey_Of (Element  : in Element_Type;
                            Position : in Positive) return Subkey_Type;
procedure Radix_Sort (Values : in out Array_Type);
-- Purpose        : Sorts the elements in Values from smallest to largest
--                    as determined by function "<"
--                  Lowest value of Position is least significant subkey
--                  Highest value of Position is most significant subkey
-- Preconditions  : None
-- Postconditions : Elements in Values are in ascending order by key
```

And here are the declarations necessary to instantiate a radix sort for our example (sorting an array of three digit non-negative integers):

```ada
subtype Element_Type  is Integer range 0..999;
type    Element_Array is array (Positive range <>) of Element_Type;
subtype Digit_Type    is Integer range 0..9;

function Digit_Of (Number   : in Element_Type;
                   Position : in Positive) return Digit_Type;

procedure Sort is new Radix_Sort (Num_Positions => 3,
                                  Element_Type  => Element_Type,
                                  Array_Type    => Element_Array,
                                  Subkey_Type   => Digit_Type,
                                  Subkey_Of     => Digit_Of);
```

Before we go on to the body of the radix sort procedure, let's implement the body of function `Digit_Of`. This function is given a three-digit number and a position. It returns the digit at the given position. This task was simple to do by hand in our example. How do we do it in Ada? We use the / and `rem` operators. Let's calculate a few positions and look for a pattern. Assume the Number is 749.

Digit at position 1:   (Number / 1)   rem 10 = 9
Digit at position 2:   (Number / 10)   rem 10 = 4
Digit at position 3:   (Number / 100) rem 10 = 7

Here is the resulting function:

```ada
function Digit_Of (Number   : in Element_Type;
                   Position : in Positive) return Digit_Type is
begin
   return (Number / 10 ** (Position - 1)) rem 10;
end Digit_Of;
```

Body 12.8 implements our radix sort algorithm.

Body 12.8   Radix Sort: Implements Specification 12.2

```ada
with Unbounded_Queue;
procedure Radix_Sort (Values : in out Array_Type) is

   -- Instantiate a queue package for Elements
   package Radix_Queue is new Unbounded_Queue (Element_Type => Element_Type);
```

```ada
    -- An array of queues for the sublists
    type Queue_Array is array (Subkey_Type) of Radix_Queue.Queue_Type;
    ------------------------------------------------------------------------
    procedure Collect_Queues (Values :    out Array_Type;
                              Queues : in out Queue_Array) is
    -- Purpose         : Transfers all the elements from the Queues into Values
    -- Preconditions   : The total number of elements in Queues = Values'Length
    -- Postconditions  : Values contains the elements in Queues with the
    --                   elements taken in order from Queues(Queues'First)
    --                   to Queues(Queues'Last).
    --                   All queues are empty.
        Values_Index : Positive;   -- Index for array Values
    begin
        Values_Index := Values'First;
        -- Each iteration, one queue is emptied, its elements moved to Values
        for Queue_Index in Queues'Range loop
            loop   -- Each iteration one element is dequeued into Values
                exit when Radix_Queue.Empty (Queues(Queue_Index));
                Radix_Queue.Dequeue (Queue => Queues(Queue_Index),
                                     Item  => Values(Values_Index));
                Values_Index := Values_Index + 1;
            end loop;
        end loop;
    end Collect_Queues;

    ------------------------------------------------------------------------

    Queues      : Queue_Array;
    Which_Queue : Subkey_Type;
begin
    -- Each iteration sort the items by one subkey
    for Position in 1..Num_Positions loop
        -- Each iteration, put a value into the appropriate subgroup
        for Index in Values'Range loop
            -- Determine which queue to place the Index'th element
            Which_Queue := Subkey_Of (Element  => Values(Index),
                                      Position => Position);
            -- Enqueue the element
            Radix_Queue.Enqueue (Queue => Queues(Which_Queue),
                                 Item  => Values(Index));
        end loop;
        -- Combine the information in all the queues
        Collect_Queues (Values, Queues);
    end loop;
end Radix_Sort;
```

Analysis of Radix Sort

We said earlier that we cannot use the number of comparisons as a basis for analyzing the amount of work done in radix sort because there are no comparisons. We can, however, analyze the number of times each item is processed and use this measure for the amount of work done. Each item in `Values` is processed `Num_Positions` times. If we use N for the number of elements and K for the number of positions, this processing is $O(KN)$. Although we cannot directly compare radix sort with the other sorts, we can say that the "shorter" the key, the better radix sort performs in comparison with the other sorts.

What about space requirements? Our `Radix_Sort` procedure requires space for at least two copies of each element: one place in the array and one space in a queue. If the queues are array-based, the amount of space is prohibitive because there must be room in each queue for every element. If the queues are linked, additional space for N pointers is required.

12.5 Efficiency Considerations

When N Is Small

As we have stressed throughout this chapter, our analysis of efficiency has been based on the number of comparisons made by a sorting algorithm. This number gives us a rough estimate of the computation time involved. The other activities that accompany the comparison (swapping, keeping track of Boolean flags, and so forth) contribute to the "constant of proportionality" of the algorithm.

In comparing Big-O evaluations, we ignored constants and smaller-order terms, because we wanted to know how the algorithm would perform for large values of N. In general, an $O(N^2)$ sort requires few extra activities in addition to the comparisons, so its constant of proportionality is fairly small. On the other hand, an $O(N \log_2 N)$ sort may be more complex, with more overhead and thus a larger constant of proportionality. This situation may cause anomalies in the relative performances of the algorithms when the value of N is small. In this case N^2 is not much greater than $N \log_2 N$, and the constants may dominate instead, causing an $O(N^2)$ sort to run faster than an $O(N \log_2 N)$ sort.

Eliminating Calls to Procedures and Functions

You may have seen versions of some of the sorting procedures developed in this chapter written without local subprograms. Instead, the statements of the local subprograms are written right in the body of the sort procedure. For example, we could replace every occurrence of

```
Swap (Values(Index_1), Values(Index_2));
```

when we wanted to swap two items with the in-line expansion:

```
Temp_Value      := Values(Index_1);
Values(Index_1) := Values(Index_2);
Values(Index_2) := Temp_Value;
```

Similarly, in `Selection_Sort` we coded the operation to find the minimum element as a nested function, `Min_Index`, and in `Bubble_Sort` we coded a nested procedure, `Bubble_Up`. We could expand all of these subprograms in-line right in the sort procedure bodies.

Coding these operations as procedures and functions makes the code simpler to write and to understand, avoiding more complicated nested loop structures. Why would a programmer give up the readability we get from procedural abstraction? The answer usually given is that by eliminating the extra overhead of subprogram calls the program will run slightly faster. Although it may improve the running time, writing the code for these local procedures directly in-line does not affect the Big-O of the algorithm; only the constants of proportionality are changed.

Because we believe that a programmer's time is valuable, we prefer to write our programs with an emphasis on clarity. This choice usually means that each different level module in our algorithm design is coded as a separate subprogram. However, with Ada, this does not necessarily mean that our programs run slower than those written with fewer subprograms. Ada provides a mechanism called **pragmas**, which we can use to direct the compiler to make certain changes to our program when it translates it into machine language. Annex L of the *Ada Language Reference Manual* describes nearly 50 pragmas. We discuss one pragma that is relevant here: pragma `Inline`.

> **Pragma** A statement that directs the Ada compiler to make certain changes to our program when it translates it into machine language.

Pragma `Inline` directs the Ada compiler to substitute a copy of the subprogram body for every call of the subprograms it names. For example, the statement

```
pragma Inline (Swap, Min_Index);
```

written just after these two subprograms in procedure `Selection_Sort` directs the Ada compiler to substitute the three assignment statements in procedure `Swap` for every call to that procedure and the six statements in function `Min_Index` for every call to that function. These substitutions are made in the machine code produced by the compiler, not in our Ada source code. As a result of the elimination of procedure calls, pragma `Inline` gives us efficiency of in-line code while maintaining the procedural abstraction so important for a person reading or modifying the code. Using pragma `Inline` does not impose any restrictions on how we write a subprogram. We can use whatever names we desire for formal parameters and local variables.

Programmers using a source-level debugger must often pay a price for the increase in efficiency achieved through pragma `Inline`. By copying the code in-line, the Ada source program no longer "matches" the machine language program created by the compiler. Your debugger may no longer permit you to step through the in-lined subprograms or set breakpoints within them. We recommend that you only include pragma `Inline` after you have successfully completed the debugging and testing of a particular program unit.

Removal of Recursion

The recursive sorting procedures, `Merge_Sort` and `Quick_Sort`, have a similar situation: They require the extra overhead involved in executing the recursive calls. You may want to avoid this overhead by coding nonrecursive versions of these procedures.

Because the recursion in these sort procedures is not tail recursion, removing recursion requires stacking (see Chapter 9).

If the recursive calls are less efficient, why would anyone ever decide to use a recursive version of a sort? The decision involves a choice between types of efficiency. Up until now, we have only been concerned with minimizing computer time. Although computers are becoming faster and cheaper, it is not at all clear that computer programmers are following that trend. Therefore, in some situations programmer time may be an important consideration in choosing a sort algorithm and its implementation. In this respect, the recursive version of `Quick_Sort` is more desirable than its nonrecursive counterpart, which requires the programmer to simulate the recursion explicitly.

12.6 More Sorting Considerations

We can instantiate procedures from the generic sort procedures developed in this chapter to solve a wide variety of sorting problems. In the following sections, we look at instantiation techniques for solving some common sorting problems.

Sorting in Descending Order

All of our sorting procedures order the array elements in ascending order. Given a little time, we could rewrite any of them to order the elements in descending value. But instead of writing one generic procedure to sort into ascending order and another to sort into descending order, we can make use of the same "trick" we used with our generic priority queue: Associate the ">" operator with the procedure's formal generic parameter "<". Here, for example, are the declarations for instantiating a descending order heap sort to sort an array of integers:

```
type Int_Array is array (Positive range <>) of Integer;

procedure Descending_Sort is new Heap_Sort (Element_Type => Integer,
                                            Array_Type   => Int_Array,
                                            "<"          => ">");
```

Stability

The stability of a sorting algorithm is based on what it does with duplicate values. Of course, the duplicate values all appear consecutively in the final order. For example, if we sort the list A B B A, we get A A B B. But is the relative order of the duplicates the same in the final order as it was in the original order? If that property is guaranteed, we have a **stable sort**.

> **Stable sort** A sorting algorithm that preserves the original order of duplicates.

Stability is not important when sorting scalar types. If instead we sort more complex objects, the stability of a sorting algorithm can become more important. We may want to preserve the original order of objects considered identical by the comparison operation.

Suppose the items in our array are student objects with instance values representing their names, ZIP codes, and identification numbers. The list may normally be sorted by the unique identification numbers. For some purposes we might want to see a listing in order by name. In this case the comparison would be based on the name field. To sort by ZIP code, we would sort on that instance field.

If the sort is stable, we can get a listing by ZIP code, with the names in alphabetical order within each ZIP code, by sorting twice: the first time by name and the second time by ZIP code. A stable sort preserves the order of the elements when there is a match. The second sort, by ZIP code, produces many such matches, but the alphabetical order imposed by the first sort is preserved.

Of the sorts that we have discussed in this book, only the heap sort and quick sort algorithms are inherently unstable. Radix sort is based on stability. The stability of the other sorts depends on what the code does with duplicate values. In some cases, stability depends on whether we use a "<" or a "<=" comparison in some crucial comparison statement. In the exercises, you are asked to examine the code for the other sorts as we have coded them and determine whether they are stable.

Of course, if you directly control the comparison operation used by your sort procedure, you can allow more than one variable to be used in determining a sort order. So another, more efficient approach to sorting our students by ZIP code and name is to define an appropriate "<" function for determining sort order. We'll look at an example of this approach in the next section.

Multiple Keys

In our illustrations of the various sorts, we showed examples of sorting integers. In reality, one is more likely to be sorting arrays of records that contain several fields of information, ordering the records according to one or more fields in the record. We mentioned one approach to sorting on multiple keys in the previous section. By invoking a stable sort once for each key field, we effectively sort the data by multiple keys. Using our generic sort specifications, we need to instantiate a different sort for each key and then call these sorts in the desired order.

We can also use a single instantiation of a generic sort procedure to sort on multiple keys. We use the following declarations to illustrate how our generic sort procedures may be used to sort on any combination of fields:

```
subtype Name_String    is String (1..10);
subtype Address_String is String (1..30);
subtype City_String    is String (1..15);
subtype State_String   is String (1..2);
subtype Zip_String     is String (1..5);

type Name_Rec is
   record
      First : Name_String;
      Last  : Name_String;
   end record;
```

```ada
      type Mailing_Label_Rec is
        record
           Name    : Name_Rec;
           Address : Address_String;
           City    : City_String;
           State   : State_String;
           Zip     : Zip_String;
        end record;

      -- Types for an array of club members
      type Label_Array is array (Positive range <>) of Mailing_Label_Rec;
```

Now suppose we want to send out meeting notices to all of the members of the Geology Club. Because we get a discount if all of our mail is sorted by ZIP code, we would like to sort this list in ascending order by ZIP code. However, to make it easier for a club volunteer to locate a particular member's envelope in the large pile, we also want to sort the labels alphabetically by name within each ZIP code. To accomplish this task, we write a function to compare two mailing label records based on our sorting criteria:

```ada
function "<" (Left : in Mailing_Label_Rec; Right : in Mailing_Label_Rec)
           return Boolean is
begin
   if Left.Zip < Right.Zip then
      return True;
   elsif Left.Zip > Right.Zip then
      return False;
   -- if the zip codes are the same, we need to compare the names
   elsif Left.Name.Last < Right.Name.Last then
      return True;
   elsif Left.Name.Last > Right.Name.Last then
      return False;
   else  -- Same last name, check the first name
      return Left.Name.First < Right.Name.First;
   end if;
end "<";
```

This function first compares the *primary sort key* (the ZIP code) and, if the ZIP codes are the same, goes on to compare the *secondary sort keys* (the last name and first name). We can now instantiate a sort to order the mailing labels by these keys:

```ada
procedure Label_Sort is new Quick_Sort (Element_Type => Mailing_Label_Rec,
                                        Array_Type   => Label_Array,
                                        "<"          => "<");
```

Sorting Pointers

Sorting large records using a sort that swaps array elements may require a lot of computer time just to move sections of memory from one place to another every time we make a swap. This move time can be reduced by setting up an array of pointers (either access values or array indices) to the records and then sorting the pointers instead of the actual records. This scheme is illustrated in Figure 12.20.

Note that after the sort the records are still in the same physical arrangement, but they may be accessed in order through the sorted array of pointers. Here are the declarations to instantiate a procedure to sort an array of access values designating mailing label records.

```
type Label_Ptr is access Mailing_Label_Rec;

type Access_Array is array (Positive range <>) of Label_Ptr;

function "<" (Left : in Label_Ptr; Right : in Label_Ptr) return Boolean is
begin
   return Left.all.Zip < Right.all.Zip;
end "<";

procedure Sort_Zip is new Some_Sort (Element_Type => Label_Ptr,
                                    Array_Type   => Access_Array,
                                    "<"          => "<");
```

A similar scheme may be extended to allow us to keep a large array of data sorted on more than one key. The array `Employee_Data` shown in Figure 12.21 contains employee data sorted by employee identification number. The two arrays `Name_Order` and `Salary_Order` contain indices of elements in the `Employee_Data` array. These

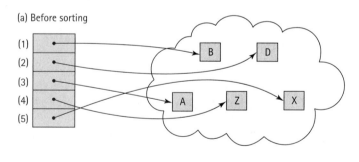

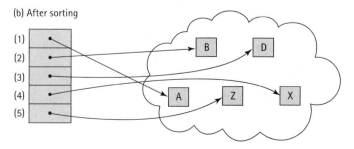

Figure 12.20 *Sorting arrays with access values.*

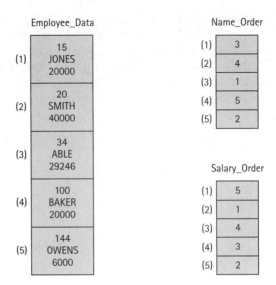

Figure 12.21 *Data sorted on more than one key.*

indices in the array `Name_Order` are sorted by employee name while the indices in the array `Salary_Order` are sorted by employee salaries. In Exercise 43 we ask you to instantiate sort procedures to order each of these arrays of pointers.

12.7 Summary—Sorting

We have not attempted in this chapter to give every known sorting algorithm. We have presented a few of the popular sorts, of which many variations exist. It should be clear from this discussion that no single sort is best for all applications. The simpler, generally $O(N^2)$ sorts work as well, and sometimes better, for fairly small values of N. Because they are simple, these sorts require relatively little programmer time to write and maintain. As you add features to improve sorts, you also add to the complexity of the algorithms, increasing both the work required by the routines and the programmer time needed to maintain them.

Another consideration in choosing a sort algorithm is the order of the original data. If the data are already ordered (or almost ordered), insertion sort is $O(N)$, whereas some versions of a quick sort are $O(N^2)$.

As always, the first step in choosing an algorithm is to determine the goals of the particular application. This step usually narrows down the options considerably. After that, knowledge of the strong and weak points of the various algorithms assists you in making a choice.

Table 12.1 summarizes the key comparison made by the sorts discussed in this chapter, in terms of Big-O.

Table 12.1 Big-O Comparison of Sorting Algorithms

Sort	Order of Magnitude		
	Best Case	Average	Worst Case
Simple Sorts			
Selection sort	$O(N^2)$	$O(N^2)$	$O(N^2)$
Bubble sort	$O(N^2)$	$O(N^2)$	$O(N^2)$
Short bubble sort	$O(N)$	$O(N^2)$	$O(N^2)$
Insertion sort	$O(N)$	$O(N^2)$	$O(N^2)$
Divide-and-Conquer Sorts			
Merge sort	$O(N \log_2 N)$	$O(N \log_2 N)$	$O(N \log_2 N)$
Quick sort	$O(N \log_2 N)$	$O(N \log_2 N)$	$O(N^2)$
Heap sort	$O(N \log_2 N)$	$O(N \log_2 N)$	$O(N \log_2 N)$

To make it perfectly clear that there really is a difference between an $O(N^2)$ sort and an $O(N \log_2 N)$ sort, we ran some timed tests. We used an array of 20,000 elements. Each element contained a five-digit positive integer key and a 20-character string. We executed each of the sorts in this chapter three times using the same data for each sort. First we sorted an array of mixed-up records, then an array of records already in order, and finally an array of records in reverse order. The results of the tests are summarized in Table 12.2.

Table 12.2 Timed Experiments of Sorting Procedures (times in milliseconds)

Sort	Mixed Up	In Order	Reverse Order
Simple Sorts			
Selection sort	1,532.51	1,519.05	1,574.51
Bubble sort	4,954.17	1,208.36	7,528.46
Short bubble sort	5,036.21	0.15	7,662.29
Insertion sort	1,153.44	0.52	2,260.36
Divide-and-Conquer Sorts			
Merge sort	21.43	16.06	15.61
Quick sort (first element split value)	7.33	1,774.20	1,653.66
Quick sort (middle element split value)	8.79	4.41	5.09
Heap sort	31.57	31.65	29.25
Radix sort	104.92	106.61	105.11

Perhaps the only unexpected results are those from the two bubble sorts. Although they have the same Big-Os as the selection and insertion sorts, their times in these experiments are significantly greater. To calculate Big-O in the sorts we counted the number of key comparisons made. Another factor that affects sorting time is the number of swaps. Data movement becomes more important as the size of an element increases. Bubble sort has many more swaps than our other sorting algorithms. Bubble sort requires $N - 1$ swaps to move the smallest value from the last position in the array to its correct position at the beginning. Selection sort needs only one swap to move the smallest value into place. It is also interesting to note that the additional order checking done by the short bubble sort resulted in longer sort times than the standard bubble sort for both random and reverse ordered data. Perhaps the lesson here is to avoid bubble sort. If you suspect that your data are already partially ordered, insertion sort gives nearly the same performance as short bubble sort.

These Big-O comparisons and timing experiments can help us choose the best sort for our problem. The simple sorts are easy to write and useful when N is small. Of these, insertion sort provides the best performance and bubble sort the worst. Quick sort lives up to its name as the quickest of the divide-and-conquer sorts. However, because it is sensitive to the initial order of the data, there is always a possibility that for some data its timing may be closer to $O(N^2)$. If your application cannot tolerate this possibility, use the merge sort or heap sort. Merge sort may be a little faster than heap sort, but it requires twice as much memory.

12.8 Searching

As we have seen throughout the text, for each particular structure used to hold data, the operations that allow access to elements in the structure must be defined. In some cases access is limited to the elements in specific positions in the structure, such as the top element in a stack or the front element in a queue. Often, when data are stored in a list or a table, we want to be able to access any element in the structure.

Sometimes the retrieval of a specified element can be performed directly. For instance, the fifth element of the list stored sequentially in an array-based list called `List` is found in `List.Values(5)`. Often, however, you want to access an element according to some key value. For instance, if a list contains student records, you may want to find the record of the student named Mildred Smedley or the record of the student whose ID number is 203557. In cases like these, some kind of *searching technique* is needed to allow retrieval of the desired record.

For each of the search techniques we review or introduce, we write a procedure that is given an array or external pointer to a linked structure and a key for which to search. The procedure returns the location of the element with the desired key and a Boolean value indicating whether the key was in the list. If the key is not in the list, the returned location is undefined. Because the search procedures return an index or pointer into the data structure, they are not seen by the application programmer who is using the class.

They are designed as auxiliary procedures to be used by any class operation that requires a search.

Linear Searching

We cannot discuss efficient ways to find an element in a list without considering how the elements were inserted into the list. Therefore, our discussion of search algorithms is related to the issue of the list's Insert operation. Suppose that we want to insert elements as quickly as possible, and we are not as concerned about how long it takes to find them. We would put the element into the last slot in an array-based list or the first slot in a linked list. These are O(1) insertion algorithms. The resulting list is sorted according to time of insertion, not key value.

To search this list for the element with a given key, we must use a simple sequential search. Beginning with the first element in the list, we search for the desired element by examining each subsequent item's key until either the search is successful or the list is exhausted. Here is the algorithm for an array-based unordered list:

Linear Search   (unordered data)
    Location := Values'First
    loop
        exit when Location > Values'Last or else Key = Key_Of (Values(Location))
        Index := Index + 1
    end loop
    Found := Location <= Values'Last

Based on the number of comparisons, it should be obvious that this search is $O(N)$, where N represents the number of elements. In the worst case, in which we are looking for the last element in the list or for a nonexistent element, we have to make N key comparisons. On the average, assuming that there is an equal probability of searching for any item in the list, we make $N/2$ comparisons for a successful search; that is, on the average we have to search half of the list.

High-Probability Ordering

The assumption in the previous paragraph of equal probability for every element in the list is not always valid. Sometimes certain list elements are in much greater demand than others. This observation suggests a way to improve the search. We can put the most-often-desired elements at the beginning of the list. Using this scheme, you are more likely to make a hit in the first few tries, and rarely do you have to search the whole list.

If the elements in the list are not static or if you cannot predict their relative demand, you need some scheme to keep the most frequently used elements at the front of the list. One way to accomplish this goal is to move an element to the front of the list each time we search for it. Of course, there is no guarantee that this element is later frequently used. If the element is not retrieved again, however, it drifts toward the end of the list as other elements are moved to the front. This scheme is easy to implement for linked lists, requiring only a couple of pointer changes, but it is less desirable for lists kept sequentially in arrays, because of the need to move all the other elements down to make room at the front.

A second approach, which causes elements to move toward the front of the list gradually, is appropriate for either linked or sequential list representations. As each element is accessed, it is swapped with the element that precedes it. Over many list retrievals, the most frequently desired elements tend to be grouped at the front of the list. To implement this approach, we only need to modify the end of the linear search algorithm to exchange the found element with the one before it in the list (unless it is the first element):

```
if Found and Location > Values'First then
    -- If the found element isn't already at the top, move it up in the list
    Swap (Values(Location), Values(Location - 1))
    Location := Location - 1
end if;
```

In the original version of the linear search algorithm, we would pass the array `Values` as an `in` mode parameter. In this version, however, `Values` must be passed as an `in out` mode parameter, because it is actually changed by the search operation. This change should be documented; it is an unexpected side effect of searching the list.

Keeping the most active elements at the front of the list does not affect the worst case; if the search value is the last element or is not in the list, the search still takes N comparisons. This is still an $O(N)$ search. The *average* performance on successful searches should be better, however.

Lists in which the positions of elements are changed by searching for them are called *self-organizing* or *self-adjusting* lists. The improvement in searching such lists depends on the assumption that some elements in the list are used much more often than others. If this assumption is not applicable, a different ordering strategy is needed to improve the efficiency of the search technique.

Key Ordering

If a list is ordered according to the key value, we can write more efficient search routines. To support a key-ordered list, we must either insert the elements in order, as the `Insert` operations we presented in Chapters 7 and 8 did, or we must sort the list before searching it, as we discussed in this chapter. [Note that constructing an ordered list by inserting the elements in order is an $O(N^2)$ process, because each insertion is $O(N)$]. If we insert each element in the next free slot, and then sort the list with a "good" sort, the process is $O(N \log_2 N)$.

If the list is sorted, a sequential search no longer needs to search the whole list to discover that an element does not exist. It only needs to search until it has passed the element's logical place in the list—that is, until an element with a larger key value is encountered. The `Search_Linked_List` procedure in Chapter 7 implemented this search technique.

One advantage of sequentially searching an ordered list is the ability to stop searching before the list is exhausted if the element does not exist. Again, the search is O(N)– the worst case, searching for the largest element, still requires N comparisons. The average number of comparisons for an unsuccessful search is now N/2, however, instead of a guaranteed N.

The advantage of sequential searching is its simplicity. The disadvantage is its performance: In the worst case you have to make N comparisons. If the list is sorted and stored in an array, however, you can improve the search time to a worst case of $O(\log_2 N)$ by using a binary search. However, efficiency is improved at the expense of simplicity.

Binary Searching

We know of a way to improve searching from O(N) to $O(\log_2 N)$. If the data elements are ordered and stored sequentially in an array, we can use a binary search. The binary search algorithm improves the search efficiency by limiting the search to the area where the element might be. The binary search algorithm takes a divide-and-conquer approach. It continually pares down the area to be searched until either the element is found or the search area is gone (the element is not in the list). We developed the `Binary_Search` procedure in Chapter 1, used it to implement procedure `Search_Array` in Chapter 7, and converted it to a recursive procedure in Chapter 9.

The binary search, however, is not guaranteed to be faster for searching very small lists. Notice that even though the binary search generally requires fewer comparisons, each comparison involves more computation. When N is very small, this extra work (the constants and smaller terms that we ignore in determining the Big-O approximation) may dominate. Although fewer comparisons are required, each involves more processing. For instance, in one assembly language program, the linear search required 5 time units per comparison, whereas the binary search took 35. For a list size of 16 elements, therefore, the worst-case linear search would require 5 × 16 = 80 time units. The worst-case binary search requires only four comparisons, but at 35 time units each, the comparisons takes 140 time units. In cases where the number of elements in the list is small, a linear search is certainly adequate and sometimes faster than a binary search.

As the number of elements increases, however, the disparity between the linear search and the binary search grows very quickly. Look back at the table on page 788 to compare the rates of growth for the two algorithms.

Note that the binary search discussed here is appropriate only for list elements stored in a sequential array-based representation. We cannot use a binary search to find an element in a linked list. After all, how can you efficiently find the midpoint of a linked list? However, you already know of a structure that allows you to perform a binary search on a linked data representation, the binary search tree. The operations used to search a binary tree were discussed in Chapter 10.

Interpolation Searching

Do you use a binary search when you look up someone in a telephone directory? No, you typically don't open the phone book in the middle. Instead you estimate where in the book the name should be and open it to that point. For example, if you were looking for the phone number of Mildred Smedley, you would open the phone book closer to the end rather than at the middle. This search is called an interpolation search. The number of comparisons needed for the average interpolation search is $O(\log_2(\log_2 N))$. But the number of comparisons needed for the worst case is $O(N)$. The difficult part of designing an interpolation search is determining how to calculate an estimate of a value's location. We leave that problem for a more advanced course.

12.9 Hashing

So far, we have succeeded in paring down our $O(N)$ search to $O(\log_2 N)$ by keeping the list ordered sequentially with respect to the key value. That is, the key of the first element is less than (or equal to) the key of the second element, which is less than the key of the third, and so on. Can we do better than that? Is it possible to design a search of $O(1)$; that is, one that takes the same search time to find any element in the list?

This goal is not an impossible dream. Suppose we would like to keep a list of repair records for 100 notebook computers. Each computer is assigned a unique ID number between 501 and 600. If we store the repair records in an array that is indexed from 501 to 600, we can directly access any computer's repair record through the array index. There is a one-to-one correspondence between the element keys and the array index; in effect, the array index functions as the key for each element.

In practice, however, this perfect relationship between the key value and the location of an element is not easy to establish or maintain. Consider a small company that uses its 100 employees' five-digit ID number as the primary key field. Now the range of key values is from 00000 to 99999. Obviously it is impractical to set up an array of 100,000 elements, of which only 100 are needed, just to make sure that each employee's element is in a perfectly unique and predictable location.

What if we lower the array size down to the size that we actually need (an array of 100 elements) and just use the last two digits of the key field to identify each employee? For instance, the element of employee 53374 is in `Employee_List(74)`, and the element of employee 81235 is in `Employee_List(35)`. Note that the elements are not ordered according to the value of the key field as they were in our earlier discussion; the position of employee 81235's record precedes that of employee 53374 in the array, even though the value of its key is larger. Instead, the elements are ordered with respect to *some function of the key value*.

This function is called a **hash function**, and the search technique we discuss in this section is called **hashing**. The data structure is often called a **hash table**. In the case of the employee list, the hash function is `Key rem 100`. The key, `ID_Num`, is divided by 100, and the remainder is used as an index into the array of employee elements, as illustrated in Figure 12.22.

The output of the hash function tells us where to *look* for a particular element—information we need to

Hash function A function used to manipulate the key of an element to identify its location in the list.

Hashing The technique used for ordering and accessing elements in a list in a relatively constant amount of time by manipulating the key to identify its location in the list.

Hash table The data structure used to store and retrieve elements using hashing.

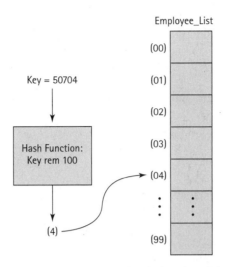

Figure 12.22 *Using a hash function to determine the location of the element in an array.*

retrieve the element from the hash table or to insert it into the table in the first place. Specification 12.3 defines a hash table abstract data object (ADO) with three operations. We need to supply three parameters to instantiate this generic package: the size of the hash table, the type of element stored in the hash table, and a function that returns an element's numeric key.

Specification 12.3   Hash Table

```
generic
   Table_Size : in Positive;
   type Element_Type is private;
   with function Key_Of (Element : in Element_Type) return Natural;
package Hash_Table is

-- This ADO implements a Hash Table
-- Each element in the Hash Table has a unique Natural key

   DUPLICATE_KEY : exception;
   KEY_ERROR     : exception;
   OVERFLOW      : exception;

   -------------------------------------------------------------------

   procedure Insert (Item : in Element_Type);
   -- Purpose        : Adds Item to the Hash Table.
   -- Preconditions  : None
   -- Postconditions : Hash Table = Hash Table + Item
```

```
--   Exceptions      : OVERFLOW        If there is no room for Item.
--                                     Hash table is unchanged.
--                    DUPLICATE_KEY    If an element already exists in the Hash
--                                     Table with the same key as Item.
--                                     Hash Table is unchanged.

-------------------------------------------------------------------------------

function Contains (Key : in Natural) return Boolean;
-- Purpose        : Determines whether an element exists in the Hash Table
--                  with the given Key
-- Preconditions  : None
-- Postconditions : Returns True if there is an element with Key in Hash
--                  Table.  Otherwise False is returned.

-------------------------------------------------------------------------------

procedure Retrieve (Key  : in   Natural;
                    Item : out  Element_Type);
-- Purpose        : Retrieve the element with the given Key from Hash Table
-- Preconditions  : None
-- Postconditions : Item is the element in the Hash Table with the given Key
-- Exceptions     : KEY_ERROR If there is no element in the Hash Table with
--                  the given Key

end Hash_Table;
```

Figure 12.23(a) shows an array whose elements—records for the employees with the key values (unique ID numbers) 12704, 31300, 49001, 52202, and 65606—were added using the `Insert` procedure from Specification 12.3. Note that procedure `Insert` does not fill the array positions sequentially. Because we have not yet inserted any elements

(a) Hashed		(b) Ordered by key	
(00)	31300	(00)	12704
(01)	49001	(01)	31300
(02)	52202	(02)	49001
(03)	Empty	(03)	52202
(04)	12704	(04)	65606
(05)	Empty	(05)	Empty
(06)	65606	(06)	Empty
(07)	Empty	(07)	Empty
⋮	⋮	⋮	⋮

Figure 12.23 *Comparing hashed and key-ordered lists of identical elements.*

whose keys produce the hash values 3 and 5, the array slots (3) and (5) are logically "empty." This is different from the approach we used in Chapter 7 to create a key-ordered list. In Figure 12.23(b), the same employee records have been inserted into a key-ordered list using the `Insert` operation from Chapter 7. Note that, unless the hash function was used to determine where to insert an element, the hash function is useless for finding the element.

Handling Collisions

By now you are probably objecting to this scheme on the grounds that it does not guarantee unique addresses. ID number 01234 and ID number 91234 both "hash" to the same array index: 34. The problem of avoiding these **collisions** is the biggest challenge in designing a good hash function. A good hash function *minimizes collisions* by spreading the elements uniformly throughout the array. We say "minimizes collisions," because it is extremely difficult to avoid them completely.

Assuming that there will be some collisions, where do you store the elements that produce them? We briefly describe several popular collision-handling algorithms in the next sections. For each, the scheme that is used to find the place to store an element determines the method subsequently used to retrieve it.

> **Collision** The condition resulting when two or more keys produce the same hash location.
>
> **Linear probing** Resolving a hash collision by sequentially searching a hash table beginning at the location returned by the hash function.

Open Addressing Open addressing is a group of techniques used to resolve collisions directly within the hash table. When a collision occurs, we check other positions in the hash table until an empty position is found. Methods for probing a hash table for empty positions include linear probing, quadratic probing, and double hashing.

Linear Probing A simple approach to resolving collisions is to store the colliding element in the next available space. This technique is known as **linear probing**. In the situation in Figure 12.24, we want to add the employee element with the key ID number 77003. The hash function returns 3. But there is already an element stored in this array slot, the record for Employee 50003. We increment our hash index to 4 and examine the next array slot. Slot 4 is also in use, so we increment the index again. This time we find a slot that is empty, so we store the new element in location 5.

What happens if the key hashes to the last index in the array and that space is in use? We can consider the array as a circular structure and continue looking for an empty slot at the beginning of the array. This situation is similar to our circular array-based queue in Chapter 6. There we used the `rem` operator when we incremented our index. We can use similar logic here.

How do we know whether an array slot is "empty"? We include a parallel array, `Status`, to indicate the status of each slot in the list. Each element in this array is given an initial value of `Empty`. All the declarations for our hash table are given in Body 12.9.

822 | Chapter 12: Sorting and Searching Algorithms

Both the hash table array and the status array are indexed from `0` to `Table_Size - 1`. As with all ADOs, these package variables are global to the operations that use them.

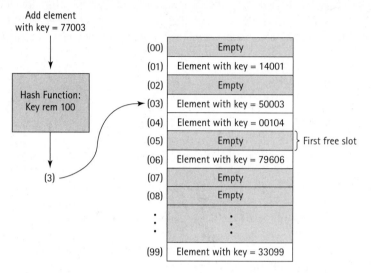

Figure 12.24 *Handling collisions with linear probing.*

Body 12.9   Hash Table: Implements Specification 12.3

```
package body Hash_Table is

    type    Status_Type is (Empty, Used);
    subtype Index_Range is Natural range 0 .. Table_Size - 1;
    type    Hash_Table_Array is array (Index_Range) of Element_Type;
    type    Status_Array     is array (Index_Range) of Status_Type;

Hash_Table : Hash_Table_Array;                               -- The hash table
Status     : Status_Array := (Index_Range => Empty);         -- Hash_Table is empty

-------------------------------------------------------------------------
function Search (Key : in Natural) return Index_Range is
-- Purpose        : Uses a hash function and linear probing to find
--                  the location of Key in Hash_Table
-- Preconditions  : None
-- Postconditions : If there is an element with Key in Hash_Table
--                      Returns the index of the element in the Hash_Table
--                  elsif the Hash_Table is full
--                      Returns the index of an arbitrary element in the
--                      Hash_Table
--                  else
```

```ada
      --                    Returns the first Location of the probe sequence
      --                    for which an empty element was found
      Location : Index_Range;
      Count    : Natural;
   begin
      Location := Key rem Table_Size;    -- Simple division hash function
      Count := 1;
      loop
         exit when Status(Location) = Empty           or else
                   Key = Key_Of (Hash_Table(Location)) or else
                   Count = Table_Size;
         Location := (Location + 1) rem Table_Size;   -- Linear probing
         Count    := Count + 1;
      end loop;
      return Location;
   end Search;

   ------------------------------------------------------------------------
   procedure Insert (Item : in Element_Type) is
      Location : Index_Range;
   begin
      Location := Search (Key_Of (Item));    -- Search Hash_Table for Key
      if Status(Location) = Empty then
         -- Found a spot in Hash_Table for Item
         Hash_Table(Location) := Item;
         Status(Location)     := Used;
      elsif Key_Of (Item) = Key_Of (Hash_Table(Location)) then
         raise DUPLICATE_KEY;
      else
         raise OVERFLOW;
      end if;
   end Insert;

   ------------------------------------------------------------------------
   function Contains (Key : in Natural) return Boolean is
      Location : Index_Range;
   begin
      Location := Search (Key);
      return Status(Location) = Used   and then
             Key = Key_Of (Hash_Table(Location));
   end Contains;

   ------------------------------------------------------------------------
   procedure Retrieve (Key  : in  Natural;
                       Item : out Element_Type) is
```

```
      Location : Index_Range;
   begin
      Location := Search (Key);
      if Status(Location) = Used       and then
         Key = Key_Of (Hash_Table(Location)) then
         Item := Hash_Table(Location);
      else
         raise KEY_ERROR;
      end if;
   end Retrieve;

end Hash_Table;
```

Function `Search` contains the hash function and linear probing logic to locate an element in the hash table. This local function is called by all three of our hash table operations. `Search` uses our simple hash function to calculate the location of the element with the given `Key`. The loop that follows the hashing of the key implements linear probing collision resolution. If the location calculated by the hash function contains the desired element, we exit this loop before completing the first iteration. Otherwise we check successive slots (linear probing) in the array until we

1. find the element with the given `Key`,
2. find an empty slot in the hash table, or
3. have checked every slot in the hash table.

Notice the use of `rem Table_Size` in the calculation of the next location to probe to wrap from the end of the array to the beginning. `Count` keeps track of how many probes we have made into the hash table. When it equals the hash table size, we have probed all of the slots in the array.

The desired result when procedure `Insert` calls function `Search` is the discovery of an empty slot in the hash table. In this case we insert our element into the hash table and change that slot's status to `Used`. If the location returned by `Search` is not empty it contains either an element with the same key as the one we wish to insert or an element with some arbitrary key. The latter result indicates that the hash table is full—`Search` checked all of the slots in the array without finding our key or an empty slot.

Function `Contains` returns a result based on whether `Search` located an element with the desired key. Procedure `Retrieve` uses the same logic as `Contains`, but either returns a copy of the element or raises a `KEY_ERROR` exception.

The basic technique of linear probing is to add 1 to the hash index to calculate a new hash index. Our `Search` function in Body 12.9 used the formula

Location := (Location + 1) rem Table_Size.

A more general version of linear probing adds a value other than 1 using a formula of the form

Location := (Location + *increment*) rem Table_Size

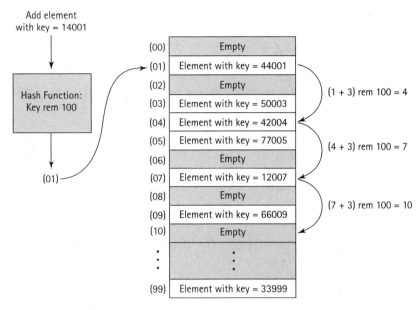

Figure 12.25 *Linear probing with an increment of 3.*

Figure 12.25 shows an example of using this formula with an increment of 3 to insert an element. Suppose that we want to add a record with the key 14001 to the hash table. The original hash function (Key rem 100) returns the hash address (01), but this array slot is in use; it contains the record with the key 44001. To determine the next array slot to try, we add 3 to the results of the first hash address (keeping in mind we might need to wrap around to the beginning of the array): (1 + 3) rem 100 = 4. The array slot at index (04) is also in use, so we reapply the formula until we get an available slot. Each time, we use the address computed from the previous hash address as input to the formula. The second application gives us (4 + 3) rem 100 = 7; this slot is in use. The third application gives us (7 + 3) rem 100 = 10; the array slot at index (10) is empty, so the new element is inserted there.

Using an increment other than 1 presents a potential problem. When searching for an empty slot, can we be sure that we have checked every slot in the array? Can you see that picking an increment of 2 would check only half of the slots in our array of 100? It turns out that the formula checks all possible array slots as long as *increment* and *table size* are relatively prime—that is, if the largest number that divides both of them evenly is 1. So the formula

Location := (Location + 3) rem 100

used in the linear probing illustrated in Figure 12.25 would check all 100 array slots. Although 100 is not a prime number, 3 and 100 are relatively prime; they have no common factor larger than 1.

Clustering One problem with linear probing is that it results in a situation called **clustering**. A good hash function results in a uniform distribution of indexes throughout the array's index range. Initially, therefore, records are inserted throughout the array, each slot equally likely to be filled. Over time, however, after a number of collisions have been resolved, the distribution of records in the array becomes less and less uniform. The records tend to cluster together, as multiple keys begin to compete for a single address.

Consider the hash table in Figure 12.26. Only an element whose key produces the hash address 8 would be inserted into array slot (08). However, any records with keys that produce the hash addresses 3, 4, 5, 6, or 7 would be inserted into array slot (07). That is, array slot (07) is five times as likely as array slot (08) to be filled. Clustering results in inconsistent efficiency of insertion and retrieval operations.

Using an increment other than 1 does not eliminate clustering (although the clusters are not always visually apparent in a figure). For example, in Figure 12.25, any record with a key value that produces the hash address 1, 4, 7, or 10 would be inserted in the slot at index (10).

> **Clustering** The tendency of elements to become unevenly distributed in the hash table, with many elements clustering around a single hash location.
>
> **Quadratic probing** Resolving a hash collision by using the square of the number of times we have probed the table to determine the next location.

Quadratic Probing In linear probing, we add a constant (usually 1) in each successive application of the rehash function. Another approach, called **quadratic probing**, makes the calculation of the next location dependent on how many times the probe formula has been applied. To use quadratic probing in function `Search` in Body 12.9, substitute the following assignment statement to calculate the next location:

```
Location := (Location + Count ** 2) rem Table_Size;  -- Quadratic Probing
```

The first application of the formula adds 1 to the hash location, the second application adds 4, the third application adds 9, and so on. By increasing the distance jumped with each probe, we lessen the chances that clashes at adjacent locations will probe the same spots in the table while searching for an opening.

Quadratic probing may help to reduce clustering, but it does not necessarily examine every slot in the array in its search for an empty slot. For example, if `Table_Size` is a power of 2 (512 or 1024, for example), relatively few array slots are examined. However, if `Table_Size` meets the two criteria, quadratic probing does examine every slot in the array:

- `Table_Size` is a prime number
- `Table_Size` = $4 \times K + 3$, where K is some integer

Double Hashing With both linear and quadratic probing, any two keys that happen to hash to the same index are sent to the same place when a collision is discovered. This behavior is a consequence of both of these probing techniques—we add the same value to the index to calculate the next hash address. Wouldn't it be nice if when two values hash to the *same* index we would send them to *different* places in search of an open slot

	(00)	Empty
	(01)	Element with key = 14001
Order of Insertion:	(02)	Empty
14001	(03)	Element with key = 50003
00104	(04)	Element with key = 00104
50003	(05)	Element with key = 77003
77003	(06)	Element with key = 42504
42504	(07)	Empty
33099	(08)	Empty
⋮	⋮	⋮
	(99)	Element with key = 33099

Figure 12.26 *A hash table with linear probing.*

in the hash table? A method of collision resolution known as **double hashing** does just that. Double hashing requires two different hash functions:

- A hash function that computes a hash address from a key
- A hash function that computes an increment from a key

The first hash function uses the key to calculate a valid array index. The second hash function uses the key to calculate an increment value between 1 and Table_Size - 1. Here is a version of procedure Search that uses double hashing:

> **Double hashing** Resolving a collision through a second hash function. The first function computes a hash address from the key. The second hash function computes the increment for use in the general linear probing formula.

```
function Search (Key : in Natural) return Index_Range is
   -- Double Hashing Version
   subtype Increment_Range is Index_Range range 1..Table_Size - 1;

   Location  : Index_Range;
   Count     : Natural;
   Increment : Increment_Range;
begin
   Location  := Key rem Table_Size;              -- Simple division hash function
   Increment := 1 + Key rem (Table_Size - 2);    -- Second division hash function
   Count := 1;
   loop
      exit when Status(Location) = Empty                 or else
                Key = Key_Of (Hash_Table(Location))      or else
                Count = Table_Size;
      Location := (Location + Increment) rem Table_Size;    -- Double hashing
```

```
            Count    := Count + 1;
        end loop;
        return Location;
    end Search;
```

This search procedure incorporates a commonly used hash function pair for double hashing:

Location := Key rem Table_Size

Increment := 1 + Key rem (Table_Size - 2)

For a table size of 100, the keys 47201 and 36101 both hash to location (01). The increment for key 47201 is 64 and the increment for key 36101 is 38. So although both keys hash to the same initial location, the table locations searched during collision resolution are very different. The probe sequence for each of these two keys is

Key	Probe Sequence
47201	01 65 29 93 57 ...
36101	01 39 77 15 53 ...

As we did with quadratic probing, we must question whether this probing scheme checks all possible slots in the array for an empty slot. For the hash function pair we used, it can be shown that if both `Table_Size` and `Table_Size - 2` are prime numbers, then an exhaustive search of the table is assured.

Chaining Another alternative for handling collisions is to allow multiple element keys to hash to the same location. We look at three common approaches.

Buckets The simplest approach to chaining is to let each computed hash address contain slots for multiple elements, rather than just a single element. Each of these multi-element locations is called a **bucket**. Figure 12.27 shows a hash table implemented as an array of arrays. Each row in this data structure is a bucket. Each bucket can contain up to three elements. Using this approach, we can allow collisions to produce duplicate entries at the same hash address, up to a point. When the bucket becomes full, we must again deal with handling collisions.

> **Bucket** A collection of elements associated with a particular hash location.
>
> **Direct chaining** A hash collision resolution method based on storing elements in linked lists (chains) external to the hash table. Each hash table entry is an external pointer to a linked list.

Direct Chaining Direct chaining (also called *external chaining*) avoids the problem of filling the bucket by storing the elements *outside* of the hash table. In direct chaining, our hash table array contains pointers rather than elements. Each pointer designates the first node of a linked list of elements. The elements in a particular

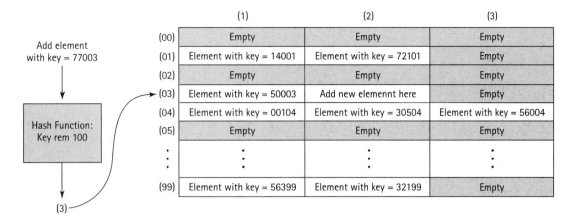

Figure 12.27 *Handling collisions by hashing with buckets.*

linked list are those whose keys hashed to the same slot. Each of these linked lists is called a *chain*. Figure 12.28 illustrates the direct chaining approach to resolving collisions.

Here are algorithms for inserting and retrieving elements from a hash table based on direct chaining:

Insert (into hash table using direct chaining)
    Hash the Key to determine the index in hash table array
    Add the element to the *front* of the linked list designated by the array entry

Retrieve (from hash table using direct chaining)
    Hash the Key to determine the index in hash table array
    Search the linked list designated by the array entry
    Return the element found in the linked list

Neither of these algorithms includes the logic for handling the exceptions defined in Specification 12.3.

A variation of this approach is to use an array of nodes rather than an array of pointers. Each component of the array is the first node of the chain. This alternative is more efficient when most of the chains contain single nodes.

Coalesced Chaining Coalesced chaining is a variation of chaining that stores the linked lists for each hash index within the hash table itself. The hash table is an array of nodes with the next field of each node containing the index of the next node in the linked list.

> **Coalesced chaining** A variation of chaining that stores the linked lists for each hash index within the table itself.

Here is the algorithm for adding an element to a hash table that uses coalesced chaining:

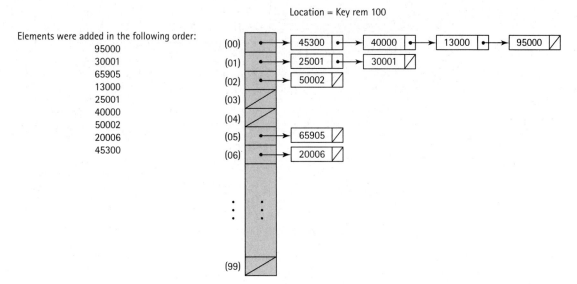

Figure 12.28 *Handling collisions through direct chaining*

Insert (into hash table using coalesced chaining)
    Hash the key to determine the index of hash table array
    if there is no node currently stored in the hash table at that index
        Add the element to the array at that index
    else -- *there is a node currently stored at the index, we need to find another spot*
        Starting at index 0, find the first available unused location in the hash table array
        Store the element at the available location found
        Link the element to the *end* of the linked list that starts at the hash index
    end if

With coalesced chaining, nodes are added to the *end* of the linked list. With direct chaining, nodes are added to the *front* of the linked list.

Figure 12.29 shows a hash table based on coalesced chaining. This figure illustrates the reason behind the name of this collision resolution technique. Searching the hash table for the element with key 5601, we first go to the array entry at index (1). When we do not find our element, we follow the link to the array entry at index (3) where we do find it. Now let's search for the element with key 9408. We start at index (8) and follow the links through indices (0), (1), (3), and (4). Notice that the list starting at index (1) and the list starting at index (8) joined together.

A popular variation of coalesced chaining makes use of additional elements in the hash table. We might, for example, declare an array of 120 elements for a table size of 100. The extra 20 elements are called the *cellar*. When a collision occurs, memory is located at the last available location in the array. Until 20 elements have collided, all of the chains are stored within the cellar. Not until the 21st collision occurs will we actu-

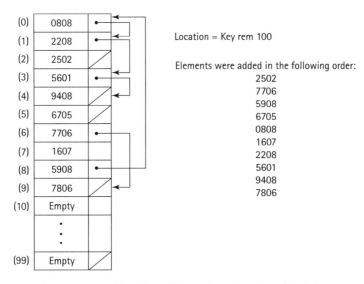

Figure 12.29 *Handling collisions through coalesced chaining.*

ally begin to coalesce our chains within the hash table proper. Exercise 63 investigates the use of a cellar in coalesced chaining.

Performance of Hashing

Given all of the work to resolve collisions, does hashing actually obtain the O(1) search times we claimed? We measured the performance of stacks, queues, lists, and trees in terms of N, the number of elements in the data structure. The performance of hashing techniques is best measured in terms of the **load factor** of the hash table. The load factor of a hash table is the fraction of the slots that are used. The load factor ranges from 0.0 for an empty hash table to 1.0 for a hash table in which every slot is used.

> **Load factor** The fraction of the slots in a hash table that are used.

The higher the load factor, the greater the chance of a collision when inserting a new element into a hash table. An element that required multiple probes to find an empty slot also requires multiple probes to retrieve it. Using probability theory, it is possible to calculate the number of probes we would expect to make into a hash table to find an item. The expected number of probes increases as the load factor of the table increases. Figure 12.30 shows the expected number of probes as a function of load factor.

The good news from these calculations is that if you make your table size large enough so that it is never more than half full, you can expect to *average* only 1.5 probes per search no matter what collision resolution method you use. This expectation is not guaranteed. Although unlikely, it is possible that some particular set of elements could hash to locations requiring up to N probes.

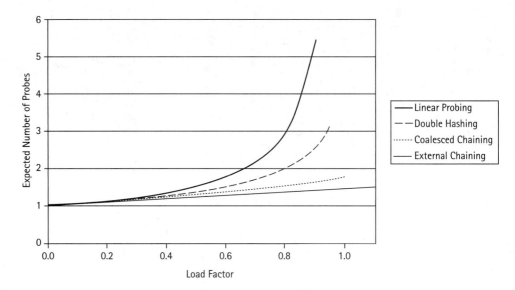

Figure 12.30 *Expected number of probes for successful searches in a hash table.*

Should the memory required for a load factor less than 0.5 be beyond that available for the application, it is more appropriate to use one of the chaining techniques. Notice that the curve for external chaining in Figure 12.30 goes beyond a load factor of 1.0. Because we are storing our elements outside of the array we can add an arbitrary number of nodes to each chain. Of course, the longer the chain, the more probes we would expect to find a particular element.

Deleting Elements

We have discussed the insertion and retrieval of elements in a hash table, but we have not mentioned how to delete an element from the table. As you might expect, the algorithm to delete an element from a hash table depends upon the collision resolution technique used to insert elements into the hash table.

All we need to do to delete an element from a hash table that uses direct chaining to resolve collisions is to delete the node from the chain. The process is more complicated when coalesced chaining is used. In this case we must detach the node from all of the coalesced lists that include the node.

Deleting an element from a hash table that uses one of the open addressing techniques for resolving might at first seem to be as easy as setting the status of the slot to `Empty`. A review of the `Search` procedure in Body 12.9 shows the problem. In the loop, the detection of an empty slot ends the search. If procedure `Delete` "empties" the slot occupied by a deleted element, we may terminate a subsequent search prematurely.

Let's look at an example. In Figure 12.31, suppose we delete the element with the key 77003 by setting the status of array slot (05) to `Empty`. A subsequent search for the

Figure 12.31

Location = key rem 100		
	(00)	Empty
	(01)	Element with key = 14001
Order of Insertion:	(02)	Empty
14001	(03)	Element with key = 50003
00104	(04)	Element with key = 00104
50003	(05)	Element with key = 77003
77003	(06)	Element with key = 42504
42504	(07)	Empty
33099	(08)	Empty
	⋮	⋮
	(99)	Element with key = 33099

Figure 12.31 *Deleting an element from a hash table with linear probing.*

element with the key 42504 would begin at location (04). The record in this slot is not the one we are looking for, so we increment the location to (05). The status of this slot, which formerly was occupied by the record that we deleted, is now Empty, so we terminate the search. We haven't really finished searching, however—the record that we are looking for is in the next slot.

One solution to this problem is to create a third status value, Deleted, to use in slots that were occupied by deleted records. A status of Deleted means that this slot is currently free, but the slot was previously occupied.

With this change, we must modify both the insertion and retrieval operations to process slots correctly. The insertion algorithm treats a slot that has status Empty or Deleted the same; the search for an available slot for the new element ends. A status of Empty halts the search in procedure Retrieve, but a status of Deleted does not.

This solution corrects the search problem, but generates another: After many deletions, the search "path" to a record may travel through many array slots with status Deleted. This may cause the efficiency of retrieving an element to deteriorate.

These problems illustrate that hash tables, in the forms that we have discussed, are not the most effective data structure for implementing tables whose elements may be deleted. These structures are more suited to applications where the necessary operations are limited to insertion and fast retrieval.

Choosing a Good Hash Function

The calculations of the expected number of probes shown in Figure 12.30 to find an element in a hash table assume that the hash function produces a random distribution of locations for the keys we hash. Therefore, one property of a good hash function is that it produces a random distribution of locations. Short computation time is another important property of a good hash function. If it takes more time to calculate the index than to search half the list, we might as well use a linear or binary search.

To design a good hash function, you need to know something about the distribution of keys. Imagine a company whose employee elements are ordered according to a company ID six digits long. There are 500 employees, and we decide to use a chained approach to handling collisions. We set up 100 chains (expecting an average of five elements per chain) and use the hash function

```
Location := ID_Num rem 100;
```

That is, we use the last two digits of the six-digit ID number as our index. The planned hash scheme is shown in Figure 12.32(a). Figure 12.32(b) shows what happened when the hash scheme was implemented. How could the distribution of the elements have come out so skewed? It turns out that the company's ID number is a concatenation of three fields:

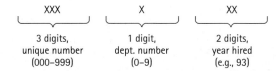

The hash scheme depended solely on the year hired to produce unique addresses. Because the company was founded in 1993, all the elements were crowded very disproportionately into a small subset of the hash addresses. A search for an employee element, in this case, is nearly O(N). Although this is an exaggerated example, it illustrates the need to understand as completely as possible the domain and predicted values of keys in a hash scheme.

Let's see if we can find a hash function that distributes the employees more evenly in our hash table. The first three digits of the company ID number provide a unique value for each employee. Let's take the two rightmost digits from this group of three digits. The following hash function does the job:

```
Location := (ID_Num / 1000) rem 100;
```

By selecting the appropriate divisors for our two integer division operators, "/" and `rem`, we can extract any sequence of digits from an integer. The challenge in any hashing application is in determining which, if any, digits to extract to increase the likelihood of a random distribution.

Division Methods This method of hashing a numeric key uses the two integer division operators,"/" and `rem`. The hash function developed for our fictitious company in the previous section and the hash function used in Body 12.9 are both examples of the division method. These functions are typically very fast to compute. Division method hash functions all rely on a division by the table size to produce a remainder that is in the range of the index of the hash table array.

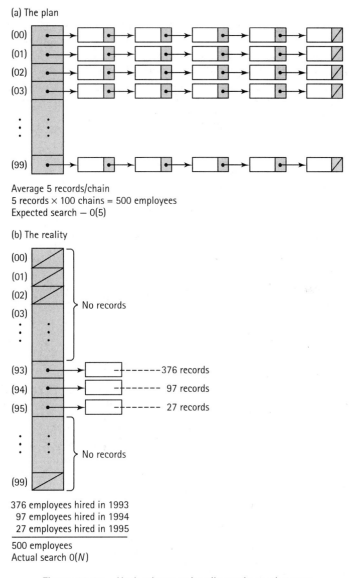

Figure 12.32 *Hash scheme to handle employee elements.*

In practice, the division method usually gives good results and is, perhaps, the most widely used method. However, it can perform poorly when the keys and divisor have common factors. This problem can be avoided by selecting a divisor that is a prime number. So although our examples used a table size of 100 so you could easily carry out the hashing, we would never select this value for a real application based on the division method.

As you will see in the following sections, the division method is commonly used in conjunction with other techniques for transforming keys into hash table indexes.

Multiplication Methods There are several hash methods based on multiplication. Perhaps the simplest is digit extraction from the square of the number. Let's look at how we might hash the five-digit key 53124 to a three-digit hash table index. Squaring this five-digit number gives a ten-digit number. Here is the mathematics carried out by hand:

```
    53124
   ×53124
   212496
   106248
    53124
   159372
   265620
  2822159376
```

Now we can use division to extract the middle three digits (shown shaded) to calculate the location in our hash table.

```
Location := (ID_Num ** 2 / 10000) rem 1000;   -- transforms 53124 to 215
```

There is good reason to pick the middle digits in our product. These middle digits involve subproducts of all the digits in the original key. The rightmost digits of the product are independent of the leftmost digits in the original key. Selecting these digits as our hash index would produce collisions between keys that differ only in their leftmost digits. Similarly, selecting the leftmost digits of our product would produce collisions between keys that differ only in their rightmost digits. A change of nearly any digit in the key will change the middle digits of the product.

Another multiplying method uses some real constant, A, where A is greater than 0.0 and less than 1.0. The formula used is

$$\text{Location} = \lfloor \text{Table Size} \times \text{Fractional Part of (Key} \times A) \rfloor \quad 0.0 < A < 1.0$$

where $\lfloor \ \rfloor$ indicates the floor function. This formula works best when

- The table size is some power of 2.
- A is an approximation of an irrational number not too close to 0.0 or 1.0.

Knuth[3] suggests that $(\sqrt{5} - 1) / 2$, the reciprocal of the golden ratio,[4] is a good choice for A. Here is Ada code that implements the formula:

---

[3] D.E. Knuth, *The Art of Computer Programming*, 2nd ed. (Volume 3, *Sorting and Searching*). (Addison Wesley Longman, 1998).

[4] M. Livio, *The Golden Ratio: The Story of Phi, the World's Most Astonishing Number*. (Broadway Books, 2003).

```
-- The reciprocal of the golden ratio:   (Square Root(5) - 1) / 2
A : constant := (2.2360679774997896964091736687313 - 1.0) / 2.0;

Key_Times_A := Float(Key) * A;
Fraction    := Key_Times_A - Float'Floor(Key_Times_A);
Location    := Index_Range (Float'Floor(Float(Table_Size) * Fraction));
```

For clarity we have used three separate assignment statements to hash the key. First, we convert `Key` to a floating point number and calculate its product with the constant `A`. Second, we use the floor attribute and a subtraction to calculate the fractional part of this product. Finally, we calculate the product of the table size and the fraction from the previous calculation, find its floor, and convert it to an integer index. Because there is a relationship between the golden ratio and the Fibonacci numbers, this method is sometimes called *Fibonacci hashing*.

Folding Methods Folding involves breaking the key into several pieces and recombining them in a different way to form a smaller number, which we use as the hash address. Let's look at an example. Suppose we want to hash the six-digit key

$$123456$$

We break this key into three pieces: 12, 34, 56. Finally, we combine these three pieces through addition to get the final result.

$$\begin{array}{r} 12 \\ 34 \\ \underline{56} \\ 102 \end{array}$$

Folding the key has compressed it from six digits to three digits. The sum of three two-digit numbers may range from 0 to 297. This suggests we use a table size of 298 for this hash function. Should we want to use a smaller table size, we could apply an appropriate division method (`Sum rem Table_Size`).

In addition to choosing how big the pieces we use should be, we have options for combining them. With addition, the sum generally has more digits than the pieces. In our example, the sum of our two-digit numbers was a three-digit number. Replacing addition with *exclusive or* avoids the expansion due to carries. You may recall from Chapter 2 that we can use the `xor` operator (and any other logical operator) with Ada's modular types. The logical operators act on the individual bits of the modular number. By converting our integer pieces into some modular type, it is no more difficult to `xor` than to add.

String Keys We have used integer keys in all of our previous hashing examples. In many applications, the key of an element is a string. Creative programmers have devised many clever hash functions for strings. They usually apply a variation of folding to convert a string to a hash table index. Here is a simple hashing of a string key:

```
Sum := 0;
-- Fold a string key by single characters
for Index in Key'Range loop
   Sum := Sum + Character'Pos(Key(Index));
end loop;
Location := Sum rem Table_Size;
```

Notice the use of the `'Pos` attribute to convert each character to an integer. Because the character positions range from 0 to 255, the upper bound of `Sum` in this loop is `Key'Length * 255`. If our key has 10 characters, its folded value can be no greater than 2550. If your application requires a larger hash table, you can fold pairs of characters. To do this we multiply the position of the first character of each pair by 256 to shift it to the left. If, for example, the string contains "Hello Mildred", the first pair of characters would fold to

```
Character'Pos('H') * 256 + Character'Pos('e') =   72 * 256 + 101  =  18,533
```

The following loop folds pairs of characters in a string key. Characters at odd indexes in the `Key` are shifted whereas characters at even indexes are not.

```
Sum := 0;
-- Fold a string key by pairs of characters
for Index in Key'Range loop
   Sum := Sum + Character'Pos(Key(Index)) * 256 ** (Index rem 2);
end loop;
Location := Sum rem Table_Size;
```

Perfect Hash Functions Finally, we should mention that if you know all of the possible keys ahead of time, it is possible to determine a perfect hash function. A **perfect hash function** is one that produces no collisions for a defined set of keys. Perfect hash functions guarantee an O(1) search. A **minimal perfect hash function** is a perfect hash function that maps its set of keys to a set of consecutive hash table locations. Hashing the defined keys with a minimal perfect hash function results in a hash table with a load factor of 1.0—one with no empty slots.

> **Perfect hash function** A hash function that produces no collisions for a defined set of keys.
>
> **Minimal perfect hash function** A perfect hash function that maps the defined set of keys to a hash table with a load factor of 1.0.

In general, it takes a great deal of effort to discover a perfect hash function, so perfect hash functions are usually reserved for those applications in which we need a quick search of a static set of keys. Let's look at an example. One of the first things a compiler must do when it processes an identifier in a program is to determine whether it is a reserved word or a programmer-defined word. One way to accomplish this task is to search a list of the reserved words. If that search is successful, the identifier is a reserved word. We can use a hash table to store that list of words for quick searching.

Ada 2005 has 72 reserved words. John Trono of Saint Michael's College has created the following minimal perfect hash function for this set of words[5]:

```
Number_Of_Reserved_Words : constant := 72;
subtype Index_Range is Natural range 0 .. Number_Of_Reserved_Words - 1;

function Hash (Word : in String) return Index_Range is
-- A minimal perfect hash function for Ada's 72 reserved words
-- Preconditions : Word contains only lowercase characters
--                 Word contains at least one character
begin
    return (Table_1 (Word (107 rem Word'Length + 1)) +
            Table_2 (Word (108 rem Word'Length + 1)) +
            Word'Length) rem Number_Of_Reserved_Words;
end Hash;
```

The expressions (107 rem Word'Length + 1) and (108 rem Word'-Length + 1) evaluate to two different positions within Word. The letters at these two positions are used as indices into two tables of Natural values. Figure 12.33 shows the values in each of these tables. The two values taken from the tables are added to the length of Word and the sum is divided by the hash table size. The remainder of this division is the index in the hash table in which the reserved word is stored.

Let's apply this hash function to the reserved word generic, which has a length of 7.

	Table_1				Table_2	
a	41	n	14	a	3	n	42
b	33	o	11	b	4	o	1
c	35	p	14	c	8	p	60
d	28	q	2	d	17	q	0
e	42	r	12	e	68	r	51
f	9	s	56	f	8	s	20
g	14	t	0	g	34	t	18
h	1	u	0	h	0	u	5
i	21	v	71	i	32	v	42
j	0	w	30	j	0	w	11
k	22	x	0	k	26	x	7
l	32	y	0	l	15	y	0
m	65	z	0	m	35	z	0

Figure 12.33 *Tables for John Trono's minimal perfect hash function for Ada 2005 reserved words.*

---

[5]J.A. Trono, Optimal Table Lookup for Reserved Words in Ada, *Ada Letters*, Volume 26, Number 1, pp. 29–34, April 2006.

$$\begin{aligned}
\text{Table\_1 (Word (107 rem 7 + 1))} &= \text{Table\_1 (Word (3))} &= \text{Table\_1 ('n')} &= 14 \\
\text{Table\_2 (Word (108 rem 7 + 1))} &= \text{Table\_2 (Word (4))} &= \text{Table\_2 ('e')} &= 68 \\
& & \text{length} &= 7 \\
& & \text{sum} & \ 89 \\
& & \text{sum rem 72} & \ 17
\end{aligned}$$

The final result, 17, is the index of the hash table where `generic` is stored. See if you can hash your favorite reserved word. Figure 12.34 shows the hash table after all 72 reserved words are inserted.

This minimal perfect hash function certainly requires a good deal of array access and computation. Perhaps it might take less time to use a binary search to search an ordered list of reserved words than it does to calculate the location in the hash table. To test this possibility, we ran some experiments. We created both an ordered list of reserved words and the hash table given in Figure 12.34. Then we searched for each of the 72 reserved words. We repeated these searches 100,000 times. Here are the times we measured for these 7.2 million searches:

Timed Experiments of Searching for Reserved Words

John Trono's minimal perfect hash function	2,260 milliseconds
Binary search	5,920 milliseconds

The hash function, in these experiments, is more than twice as fast as the binary search. However, the amount of effort required to create this minimal perfect hash function was not trivial. As we said earlier, perfect hash functions are most suited to data sets that rarely change.

Ada's Support for Hashing Ada provides the function `Ada.Strings.Hash`, which computes a modular integer value from a fixed-length string. This modular integer

0	exit	12	of	24	renames	36	then	48	in	60	synchronized
1	overriding	13	record	25	protected	37	until	49	goto	61	function
2	reverse	14	requeue	26	select	38	all	50	use	62	abs
3	new	15	or	27	end	39	procedure	51	begin	63	others
4	out	16	with	28	separate	40	delay	52	tagged	64	type
5	at	17	generic	29	when	41	while	53	range	65	access
6	null	18	is	30	do	42	else	54	case	66	mod
7	digits	19	exception	31	aliased	43	if	55	delta	67	abort
8	body	20	array	32	limited	44	task	56	entry	68	package
9	accept	21	elsif	33	loop	45	not	57	declare	69	terminate
10	constant	22	xor	34	and	46	raise	58	subtype	70	private
11	interface	23	for	35	pragma	47	rem	59	abstract	71	return

Figure 12.34 *Minimal perfect hash table of Ada 2005 reserved words.*

value is used in two container classes provided under Ada.Containers: sets and maps. The set operations we discussed in Chapter 4 are a subset of those provided in Ada.Containers.Hashed_Sets. The hashed implementation of sets is not restricted to discrete elements as we were in Chapter 4.

Summary—Searching

Searching, like sorting, is a topic that is closely tied to the goal of efficiency. We speak of a sequential search as an O(N) search, because it may require up to N comparisons to locate an element. (N refers to the number of elements in the list.) Binary searches are considered to be O($\log_2 N$) and are appropriate for arrays, provided they are sorted. A binary search tree may be used to support binary searches on a linked structure. The goal of hashing is to produce a search that approaches O(1). Because of collisions of hash addresses, some searching or rehashing is usually necessary. A good hash function minimizes collisions and distributes the elements randomly throughout the table. There is no single "best" hash function. Determining the properties of a hashing solution (array size and hash function) are very application dependent.

You can find packages in public or private Ada repositories that implement every sorting and searching method we have discussed. Why, then, have we devoted so much space to a discussion of well-known sorting and searching algorithms? First, it is important to be familiar with several of the basic sorting and searching techniques. These are tools that you use over and over again in a programming environment, and you need to know which ones are appropriate solutions to different problems. You may have to choose from several packages, each using a different sorting or searching algorithm. To choose wisely, you need to understand the advantages and disadvantages of each method. Second, a review of sorting and searching techniques has given us another opportunity to reexamine a measuring tool—the Big-O approximation—that helps us determine how much work is required by a particular algorithm. Both building and measuring tools are needed to construct sound program solutions.

Exercises

Simple Sorts

1. Instantiate a sort from Specification 12.1 that sorts an array of floating point numbers
   a. in ascending order.
   b. in descending order.
2. Multiple choice: How many comparisons are needed to sort an array containing 100 elements using selection sort if the array values were already sorted?
   a. 10,000
   b. 9900

c. 4950

d. 99

e. None of these

3. Determine the Big-O for selection sort based on data movements (swaps) rather than the number of comparisons
   a. for the best case.
   b. for the worst case.

4. In what case(s), if any, is the selection sort $O(\log_2 N)$?

5. In what case(s), if any, is the insertion sort $O(N)$?

6. How many comparisons would be needed to sort an array containing 100 elements using insertion sort
   a. in the best case.
   b. in the worst case.

7. Why does short bubble sort take longer than bubble sort to sort an array of elements that are in random order?

8. Show the contents of the array

43	7	10	23	18	4	19	5	66	14
(1)	(2)	(3)	(4)	(5)	(6)	(7)	(8)	(9)	(10)

   after the fourth iteration of
   a. selection sort
   b. bubble sort
   c. insertion sort

9. A sorting procedure is called to sort a list of 100 integers that have been read from a file. If all 100 values are zero, what would the execution requirements (in terms of Big-O) be if the sort used was
   a. bubble sort?
   b. short bubble sort?
   c. selection sort?
   d. insertion sort?

10. Given the array:

26	24	3	17	25	24	13	60	47	1
(1)	(2)	(3)	(4)	(5)	(6)	(7)	(8)	(9)	(10)

   Tell which simple sorting algorithm produced the following results after four iterations:

a.

1	3	13	17	26	24	24	25	47	60
(1)	(2)	(3)	(4)	(5)	(6)	(7)	(8)	(9)	(10)

b.

1	3	13	17	25	24	24	60	47	26
(1)	(2)	(3)	(4)	(5)	(6)	(7)	(8)	(9)	(10)

c.

3	17	24	25	26	24	13	60	47	1
(1)	(2)	(3)	(4)	(5)	(6)	(7)	(8)	(9)	(10)

11. The insertion sort developed in this chapter uses a sequential search to find the insertion location in the sorted part of the array.

   a. Rewrite procedure `Insertion_Sort` using a binary search instead of the sequential search.

   b. In terms of comparisons, what is the Big-O for this version of `Insertion_Sort`?

   c. In terms of data movements, is there any difference between this version of `Insertion_Sort` and the one presented in the chapter?

12. The following procedure sorts an array of integer values into ascending order:

    ```
    type Int_Array is array (Positive range <>) of Integer;

    procedure Integer_Sort is (Values : in out Int_Array) is
       Result       : Int_Array (Values'Range);
       Result_Index : Natural;
    begin
       Result_Index := Result'First - 1;
       for Value in Integer'First .. Integer'Last loop
          for Values_Index in Values'Range loop
             if Values(Values_Index) = Value then
                Result_Index := Result_Index + 1;
                Result(Result_Index) := Values(Values_Index);
             end if;
          end loop;
       end loop;
       Values := Result;
    end Integer_Sort;
    ```

    a. Explain why `Integer_Sort` is an O(N) sort.

    b. Would this O(N) procedure sort an array of 10 integers faster than the O(N^2) sorts discussed in this chapter? Explain your answer.

O($N\log_2 N$) Sorts

13. A merge sort is used to sort an array of 1000 test scores in descending order. Which of the following statements is true?
    a. The sort is fastest if the original test scores are ordered from smallest to largest.
    b. The sort is fastest if the original test scores are in completely random order.
    c. The sort is fastest if the original test scores are ordered from largest to smallest.
    d. The sort is the same, no matter what the order of the original elements.
14. Show how the values in the array in Exercise 8 would be arranged immediately before the execution of procedure `Merge` in the original (nonrecursive) call to `Merge_Sort`.
15. Use the three-question method to verify the `Merge_Sort` procedure.
16. Determine the Big-O of `Merge_Sort` based on the number of elements moved rather than on the number of comparisons
    a. for the best case.
    b. for the worst case.
17. In what case(s) is quick sort $O(N^2)$?
18. Which is true about quick sort?
    a. A recursive version executes faster than a nonrecursive version.
    b. A recursive version has fewer lines of code than a nonrecursive version.
    c. A nonrecursive version takes more space on the run-time stack than a recursive version.
    d. It can only be programmed as a recursive procedure.
19. Use the three-question method to verify the `Quick_Sort` procedure.
20. Determine the Big-O of `Quick_Sort` based on the number of elements moved rather than on the number of comparisons
    a. for the best case.
    b. for the worst case.
21. Study the Ada code for procedure `Quick_Sort`.
    a. In procedure `Split`, why was `Left` initialized to `Values'First + 1` rather than `Values'First`?
    b. Why was `or else` used rather than `or` in the exit statements of the first inner loop in procedure `Split`?
22. Show how the values in the array in Exercise 8 would be arranged immediately after the execution of the first call to procedure `Split` in the original (nonrecursive) call to `Quick_Sort`.
23. a. Modify the `Split` procedure in `Quick_Sort` so that the split value is the middle value in the array rather than the first value. Hint: First swap the first and middle elements and then use the same logic.

b. Show how the values in the array in Exercise 8 would be arranged immediately after the execution of the first call to the modified procedure Split in the original (nonrecursive) call to Quick_Sort.

24. Quick sort works best for large randomly ordered lists, but when the sublists become small, it might be more efficient to call another sort. Modify procedure Quick_Sort to make the recursive calls only when the number of elements to be sorted on that call is greater than a constant called Limit; otherwise, it calls procedure Insertion_Sort.

25. a. The first loop in procedure Heap_Sort creates a heap out of an unsorted array. Show how the array in Exercise 8 would look after this loop is executed with that array.

   b. Show how the array would look after four iterations of the second loop in procedure Heap_Sort.

26. Why does the heap sort have the precondition that Values'First is equal to 1?

27. A sorting procedure is called to sort a list of 100 integers that have been read from a file. If all 100 values are zero, what would the execution requirements (in terms of Big-O) be if the sort used was

   a. merge sort?
   b. quick sort (with the first element used as the split value)?
   c. heap sort?

28. A large list is ordered from smallest to largest when a sort is called. Which of the following sorts would take the longest time to execute and which would take the shortest time?

   a. Selection sort
   b. Bubble sort
   c. Insertion sort
   d. Merge sort
   e. Quick sort (with the first element as the split value)
   f. Heap sort

29. A very large array of elements is to be sorted. The program is to be run on a computer with limited memory. Which sort would be a better choice: heap sort or merge sort? Why?

30. *True or False?* Explain your answer.

   a. Merge sort requires more space to execute than heap sort.
   b. Quick sort (using the first element as the split value) is better for nearly sorted data than heap sort.
   c. The efficiency of heap sort is not affected by the order of the elements on entrance to the procedure.

31. Write the necessary declarations to instantiate a radix sort to sort an array of part names. Each part name has 10 characters. This sort should consider equivalent upper- and lowercase letters to be the same.

32. What simple change can be made to the radix sort algorithm developed in this chapter to convert it from one that sorts in ascending order to one that sorts in descending order?

More Sorting Considerations

33. For small values of N, the number of steps required for an $O(N^2)$ sort might be less than the number of steps required for a sort of lower degree. For each of the following pairs of mathematical functions f and g below, determine a value N such that if $n > N$ then $g(n) > f(n)$. This value represents the cutoff point, above which the $O(N^2)$ function is always larger than the other function.

   a. $f(n) = 4n$ $g(n) = n^2 + 1$
   b. $f(n) = 3n + 20$ $g(n) = \frac{1}{2}n^2 + 2$
   c. $f(n) = 4 \log_2 n + 10$ $g(n) = n^2$

34. Give arguments for and against using nested procedures (such as `Swap`) to encapsulate code in a sorting procedure. Assume that your programming language does not support the in-lining of code as we did with pragma `Inline`.

35. Assuming your Ada compiler does not support pragma `Inline`, write a version of `Selection_Sort` that does not make any procedure calls.

36. What is meant by the statement that programmer time is an efficiency consideration? Give an example of a situation in which programmer time is used to justify the choice of an algorithm, possibly at the expense of other efficiency considerations.

37. We said that heap sort is inherently unstable. Explain why.

38. Is `Integer_Sort`, given in Exercise 12, a stable sort?

39. Identify one or more correct answers: Reordering an array of pointers to list elements, rather than sorting the elements themselves, is a good idea when

   a. the number of elements is very large.
   b. the individual elements are large.
   c. the sort is recursive.
   d. there are multiple keys on which to sort the elements.

40. Write a procedure `Sort_Linked` that uses the selection sort algorithm to sort the elements in an unordered linked list. Do not change any links in the list. Just swap the elements in the nodes.

41. Given the following declarations:

    ```
    type Suit_Type   is (Club, Diamond, Heart, Spade);
    type Number_Type is (Two, Three, Four, Five, Six, Seven, Eight,
                         Nine, Ten, Jack, Queen, King, Ace);
    type Card_Type is
       record
          Suit   : Suit_Type;
          Number : Number_Type;
       end record;
    ```

```
type    Card_Array is array (Positive range <>) of Card_Type;
subtype Deck_Array is Card_Array (1..52);
```

a. Write the necessary declarations to instantiate a sort procedure from Specification 12.1 that can be used to sort a deck of cards in order by card numbers. Ignore the cards' suit.

b. Write a "<" function that is given two cards of Card_Type and returns true if the first is less than the second. Use the card suit as the primary key and the card number as the secondary key for this comparison.

c. Write the necessary declarations to instantiate a sort procedure from Specification 12.1 that can be used to sort a deck of cards in order by suit (primary key) and number (secondary key). Use the function you wrote for part (b).

42. Given the following declarations:

```
Max_Students : constant := 1000;

subtype Name_String is String (1..20);
type    Class_Type  is (Freshman, Sophomore, Junior, Senior);
subtype GPA_Type is Float range 0.0 .. 4.0;

type Name_Type is
   record
      First_Name : Name_String;
      Last_Name  : Name_String;
   end record;

type Student_Type is
   record
      Student_Name  : Name_Type;
      Student_ID    : Positive;
      GPA           : GPA_Type;
      Hours_Earned  : Natural;
      Class         : Class_Type;
      Zip_Code      : Positive;
   end record

type Student_Array is array (Positive range <>) of Student_Type;

type Student_List (Max_Size : Positive) is
   record
      Num_Students : Natural := 0;
      Students     : Student_Array (1..Max_Size);
   end record;

Students : Student_List (Max_Size => Max_Students)
```

a. The list of student records is sorted according to the Student_ID field as the primary key. For some types of processing, we need to order the student data according to a secondary key, Student_Name. To save space, we decide to keep an array of index pointers ordered on the name field.

   i. Write the necessary declarations for a list of index pointers.

   ii. Write the code to initialize the list of index pointers so the first value is 1, the second is 2, ... , and the last is Students.Num_Students.

b. Write the necessary declarations (including any comparison functions) necessary to instantiate a quick sort procedure to sort the array in the list of pointers you declared for part (a) so that they designate the student records in ascending order.

c. Write a sample call of the procedure you instantiated that sorts the list of index pointers you declared in part (a).

d. Write a procedure to display the names and GPAs of all the elements in the list Students alphabetically by name. The parameters to this procedure should be Students and the list of index pointers you sorted in parts (b) and (c). Both parameters should not be changed by the procedure.

43. Figure 12.21 shows the use of auxiliary arrays to provide alternative ordering of data. Given the following declarations for the arrays in Figure 12.21:

```
subtype Name_String is String (1..15);

type Employee_Rec is
   record
      ID     : Positive;
      Name   : Name_String;
      Salary : Positive;
   end record;

subtype Index_Range is Positive range 1..5;
type    Employee_Array is array Positive range <>) of
Employee_Rec;
type    Pointer_Array  is array Positive range <>) of
Index_Range;

-- The arrays
Employee_Data : Employee_Array (Index_Range);
Name_Order    : Pointer_Array  (Index_Range);
Salary_Order  : Pointer_Array  (Index_Range);
```

And given the following function to compare two names in the global array Employee_Data:

```
function Smaller_Name (Left : in Index_Range; Right : in Index_Range)
                                                      return Boolean is
   -- This function accesses the array Employee_Data globally
begin
   return Employee_Data(Left).Name < Employee_Data(Right).Name;
end Smaller_Name;
```

a. Complete the instantiation of the following procedure to sort the pointers in an array so that they are ordered by the names that they reference in the global array Employee_Data:

```
procedure Name_Sort is new Sort (Element_Type => _____;
                                 Array_Type   => _____;
                                 "<"          => _____);
```

b. Write a function and instantiation to sort the pointers in an array so that they are ordered by the salaries that they reference in the global array Employee_Data.

Searching

44. A data file contains the following integers:

    14 27 95 12 26 5 33 15 9 99

    a. Data_List is an array of 10 integers. Show what Data_List would look like if it were loaded sequentially with the integers from the file (the first number in the first slot, the second in the second slot, and so on).

    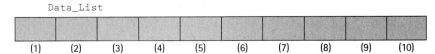

    b. Ordered_List is an array of 10 integer positions. Show what Ordered_List would look like if it were loaded with the integers from the file and then the elements were sorted from smallest to largest.

    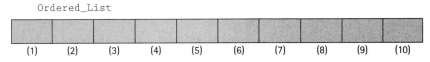

    c. Tree is a binary search tree of integer elements. Draw a picture that shows what Tree would look like if the integers from the file were inserted into the tree in the order in which they were read into the file.

d. Fill in the following table, showing the number of comparisons needed either to find the value or to determine that the value is not in the indicated structure based on the given search algorithm.

Value	Linear Search of Data_List	Linear Search of Ordered_List	Binary Search of Ordered_List	Search of Tree
15				
17				
14				
5				
99				
100				
0				

45. If you know the index of an element stored in an array of N unordered elements, which of the following best describes the order of the algorithm to retrieve the element?
    a. $O(1)$
    b. $O(\log_2 N)$
    c. $O(N)$
    d. $O(N^2)$

46. The element being searched for is not in an array of 100 elements. What is the *maximum* number of comparisons needed in a sequential search to determine that the element is *not* there
    a. if the elements are completely unordered?
    b. if the elements are ordered from smallest to largest?
    c. if the elements are ordered from largest to smallest?

47. The element being searched for is in an array of 100 elements. What is the *average* number of comparisons needed in a sequential search to determine the position of the element
    a. if the elements are completely unordered?
    b. if the elements are ordered from smallest to largest?
    c. if the elements are ordered from largest to smallest?

48. The element being searched for is not in an array of 100 elements. What is the *average* number of comparisons needed in a sequential search to determine that the element is *not* there
    a. if the elements are completely unordered?
    b. if the elements are ordered from smallest to largest?
    c. if the elements are ordered from largest to smallest?

49. Choose the answer that correctly completes the following sentence: The elements in an array may be ordered by highest probability of being requested in order to reduce

   a. the average number of comparisons needed to find an element in the list.
   b. the maximum number of comparisons needed to detect that an element is not in the list.
   c. the average number of comparisons needed to detect that an element is not in the list.
   d. the maximum number of comparisons needed to find an element that is in the list.

50. Your cell phone allows you to organize your list of names in any order you like. You search for a name by scrolling through the list. Here are a number of approaches for organizing and searching your phone's list of names:

Order of List of Names	Search Technique
Alphabetically	Linear search
Alphabetically	Binary search
Alphabetically	Interpolation search
By time of entry into list	Linear search
By time of entry into list	Binary search
By probability of searching for the name	Linear search
By probability of searching for the name	Binary search

   a. Indicate which, if any, of these approaches are impossible due to either the order of the list or the limitations of the cell phone.
   b. Of those that are possible, which approach will give you the quickest *average* search time?

Hashing

51. Given the following keys to be hashed into an array:

    66 47 87 90 126 140 145 153 177 285 393 395 467

    a. Hash the keys in the order given into the array below. Use *Key rem Table Size* for hashing and linear probing (with an increment of 1) for resolving collisions.

    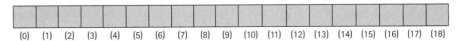

b. Hash the keys in the order given into the array below. Use *Key rem Table Size* for hashing and linear probing (with an increment of 3) for resolving collisions.

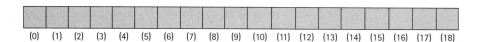

c. Hash the keys in the order given into the array below. Use *Key rem Table Size* for hashing and quadratic probing for resolving collisions.

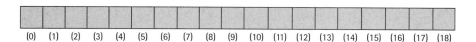

d. Hash the keys in the order given into the array below. Use *Key rem Table Size* for hashing and double hashing using *Key rem (Table Size − 2)* for resolving collisions.

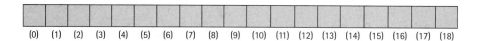

52. a. What is the load factor of the hash tables of Exercise 51 after all the data values are inserted?

    b. Use the graph in Figure 12.30 to estimate the expected number of probes to find a value in the hash table of Exercises 51(a) and 51(c).

53. a. Does the choice of a linear probing increment of 3 for the hash table size in Exercise 51(b) guarantee that all slots in the hash table will be examined for an empty slot during an insert? Explain why or why not.

    b. Does the hash table size in Exercise 51(c) guarantee that all slots in the hash table will be examined for an empty slot during an insert? Explain why or why not.

    c. Does the hash table size in Exercise 51(d) guarantee that all slots in the hash table will be examined for an empty slot during an insert? Explain why or why not.

54. a. Find the smallest hash table size that is greater than 1000 and guarantees that quadratic probing will examine all slots in the hash table for an empty slot during an insertion.

    b. Find the smallest hash table size that is greater than 1000 and guarantees that double hashing (using the two hash functions we described for double hashing) will examine all slots in the hash table for an empty slot during an insertion.

55. Given the following hash table created using *Key rem Table Size* for hashing and linear probing (with an increment of 1) for resolving collisions:

266	134				158	121		47	28	68	107	126	71	374	376	448	
(0)	(1)	(2)	(3)	(4)	(5)	(6)	(7)	(8)	(9)	(10)	(11)	(12)	(13)	(14)	(15)	(16)	(17)	(18)

How many probes are needed to determine whether each of the following keys are in the hash table?

a. 47 _____
b. 448 _____
c. 374 _____
d. 120 _____
e. 128 _____
f. 180 _____

56. Given the following hash table created using *Key rem Table Size* for hashing and linear probing (with an increment of 3) for resolving collisions:

266	134	376			158	121		47		68	28	374	71	107		448	126
(0)	(1)	(2)	(3)	(4)	(5)	(6)	(7)	(8)	(9)	(10)	(11)	(12)	(13)	(14)	(15)	(16)	(17)	(18)

How many probes are needed to determine whether each of the following keys are in the hash table?

a. 47 _____
b. 448 _____
c. 374 _____
d. 120 _____
e. 128 _____
f. 180 _____

57. Given the following hash table created using *Key rem Table Size* for hashing and quadratic probing for resolving collisions:

266	134				158	121		47	28	68	107	126	71	376	448		374
(0)	(1)	(2)	(3)	(4)	(5)	(6)	(7)	(8)	(9)	(10)	(11)	(12)	(13)	(14)	(15)	(16)	(17)	(18)

How many probes are needed to determine whether each of the following keys are in the hash table?

a. 47 _____
b. 448 _____
c. 374 _____
d. 120 _____

e. 128 _____

f. 180 _____

58. Given the following hash table created using *Key rem Table Size* for hashing and double hashing and using *Key rem (Table Size − 2)* for resolving collisions:

126	28		266			158	121		47		68	107	374	71	376	134	448
(0)	(1)	(2)	(3)	(4)	(5)	(6)	(7)	(8)	(9)	(10)	(11)	(12)	(13)	(14)	(15)	(16)	(17)	(18)

How many probes are needed to determine whether each of the following keys are in the hash table?

a. 47 _____

b. 448 _____

c. 374 _____

d. 120 _____

e. 128 _____

f. 180 _____

59. A hash table with 10 slots (indexed from 0 to 9) uses buckets to resolve collisions. Each hash bucket contains four elements. Draw a picture to illustrate the resulting hash table after inserting the following values. Use *Key rem Table Size* for hashing.

    66 47 87 90 126 140 145 153 177 285 393 395 467

60. Redo Exercise 59 using hash table slots with buckets that hold three elements. If a bucket is full, use the next (sequential) bucket that contains a free spot. This approach combines buckets and linear probing.

61. Redo Exercise 59 using a hash table with direct (external) chaining.

62. Redo Exercise 59 using a hash table with coalesced chaining.

63. Redo Exercise 59 using a hash table with coalesced chaining and a cellar. The array for the hash table consists of 10 slots (indexed from 1 to 9) and a cellar of 10 slots (indexed from 10 to 19). When you collide in the hash table, put the element in the bottommost open slot in the cellar and link it into the chain.

64. *True or False.*

    a. When a hash function is used to determine the placement of elements in an array, the order in which the elements are added does not affect the resulting array.

    b. When hashing is used, increasing the size of the array usually reduces the number of collisions.

    c. If we use buckets in a hashing scheme, we do not have to worry about collision resolution.

    d. If we use chaining in a hashing scheme, we do not have to worry about collision resolution.

e. The hashing approach described in this chapter may be used with elements stored in files.

f. The goal of a successful hashing scheme is an O(1) search.

65. A hash table can be stored in a direct access file as well as in an array. Discuss how chaining could be used to resolve collisions for a hash table stored in a direct access file.

66. Nine elements have been inserted into the following hash table, using a hash function to determine the insertion place. The linear probing method of collision resolution has been used.

51	34		20	3	4	38	7			28	11					
(0)	(1)	(2)	(3)	(4)	(5)	(6)	(7)	(8)	(9)	(10)	(11)	(12)	(13)	(14)	(15)	(16)

a. What is the hash function? Hint: It is a simple, commonly used hash function.

b. For each element in the hash table, show the result of the hash function and the number of places that had to be searched to find the insertion place.

c. Which of the following are possible insertion orders that would have produced the table above? (There may be more than one correct answer.)

   i. 51 34 20 3 38 4 7 28 11
   ii. 51 20 34 3 4 38 28 11 7
   iii. 28 11 7 51 34 20 3 4 38
   iv. 7 28 11 51 34 3 4 38 20

67. A hash table contains 1000 slots, indexed from 1 to 1001. The elements stored in the table have keys that range in value from 1 to 99,999. Which, if any, of the following hash functions would work correctly? (There may be more than one correct answer.)

   a. Key rem 1000
   b. Key rem 1001
   c. (Key - 1) rem 1001
   d. ((Key + 1) rem 1000)
   e. (Key rem 1001) + 1

68. A hash function works by cubing the integer key and then extracting the rightmost four digits. Does this approach make use of all of the digits in the key in determining the location? Explain your answer.

69. Using the formula

$$\text{Location} = \lfloor \text{Table Size} \times \text{Fractional Part of } (\text{Key} \times A) \rfloor$$

with a table size of 17 and $A = (\sqrt{5} - 1)/2$, hash the following integer keys:

9512 3431 20 3

70. The folding method example in this chapter hashed the key 123456 to the index 102. What is another key that hashes to this index?

71. When we used folding to hash 123456 to 102, we used addition to combine the pieces. We mentioned that the `xor` operator is another way to combine pieces in a folding hash function. Why can't we use the normal `or` operator to combine pieces?

72. The simplest method we showed for hashing a string used `Character'Pos` to convert each character in the string to an integer. These integers were summed and the result divided by the table size. The remainder of this division was used as the location for the string in the hash table. Assuming that the strings are English words, indicate whether the following changes would or would not improve this method of hashing strings.

    a. Instead of adding up the integer versions of all the characters, only add up the consonants.

    b. Only add up the integer versions of the odd-indexed elements in the string.

    c. Only add up the integer versions of the vowels in the string.

    d. Only use the integer version of the first letter in the string.

    e. Only use the integer versions of the first five characters in the string.

    f. Only use the integer versions of the last five characters in the packed array.

73. Use the minimal perfect hash function for Ada 2005 reserved words discussed in this chapter to hash the name *mildred*. With what reserved word does *mildred* clash?

Programming Problems

74. Implement and test an insertion sort procedure that sorts a linked list of values. Optional: Make the procedure a generic procedure.

75. Implement and test a quick sort procedure that sorts a doubly linked list of values. Optional: Make the procedure a generic procedure.

76. Download the program `Sort_Times` and the generic sort procedures `Selection_Sort`, `Bubble_Sort`, `Short_Bubble_Sort`, `Insertion_Sort`, `Merge_Sort`, `Quick_Sort`, `Quick_Sort_Middle`, `Heap_Sort`, and `Radix_Sort` from the publisher's website. Read over, compile, and link the program `Sort_Times`.

    a. With no other applications running, run program `Sort_Times` with small numbers of elements. Record the data displayed for each sorting algorithm. Are there any runs in which an $O(N^2)$ sort performed better than an $O(N \log_2 N)$ sort?

    b. With no other applications running, run program `Sort_Times` 10 times with the number of elements varying from 2000 to 20,000 in increments of 2000. Record the number of elements sorted and the times for each of the sorting algorithms in a spreadsheet. Prepare an *XY* scatter plot using the number of elements sorted as the *X* axis and time as the *Y* axis. Can you tell by the shapes of each plot which algorithms are O(N^2) and which are O($N\log_2 N$)?

c. Modify program Sort_Times by changing the number of characters in Data_String. Compile, link, and run the program for 10,000 elements. Use data sizes of 1, 10, 20, 30, and 40. Record the data size used and the times for each of the sorting algorithms in a spreadsheet. Prepare an *XY* scatter plot using the data size as the *X* axis and time as the *Y* axis. Describe the effect of data size on the various sorting algorithms.

77. The object of this assignment is twofold. First, you are to compare the relative performance of different searching algorithms on the same data set. Second, you are to compare the performance of the same algorithm on data sets of different sizes.

Download the program Sort_Times from the publisher's website. Determine how this program times the different sorting algorithms.

Using Sort_Times as a model, write a program to determine the timing behaviors of the following searches:

Linear search of an unordered list

Linear search of an ordered list

Binary search

Run your program for various size lists, record the results in a spreadsheet, prepare *XY* scatter plots, and comment on the resulting graphs.

78. Modify Specification 7.4 (Unbounded_List) and its body so that the elements are stored in order by search probability rather than key. Modify procedure Search_Linked_List so that a successful search for an element moves that element one place closer to the head of the linked list. Prepare a test plan and test program to test your revised package.

79. Modify the search function in Body 12.9 so that it displays the value of Count (the number of probes needed to find an element's location) before returning.

   a. Write a program that instantiates a hash table ADO with positive elements and a table size of 19 and inserts the following values:

   66   47   87   90   126   140   145   153   177   285   393   395   467

   Record the number of probes for each key and calculate the total number of probes for all keys.

   b. Change the increment of the linear probing used in the search function in Body 12.9 from 1 to 3. Rerun the program you wrote for part (a). Record the number of probes for each key and calculate the total number of probes for all keys.

   c. Change the collision resolution method used in the search function in Body 12.9 from linear probing to quadratic probing. Rerun the program you wrote for part (a). Record the number of probes for each key and calculate the total number of probes for all keys.

d. Change the collision resolution method used in the search function in Body 12.9 from linear probing to double hashing. Rerun the program you wrote for part (a). Record the number of probes for each key and calculate the total number of probes for all keys.

80. Modify the search function in Body 12.9 so that it displays the value of Count (the number of probes needed to find an element's location) before returning.

   a. Write a program that instantiates a hash table ADO with positive elements and a table size of 19 and inserts the following values:

   66   47   87   90   126   140   145   153   177   285   393   395   467

   Record the number of probes for each key and calculate the total number of probes for all keys.

   b. Change the hash function used in the search function in Body 12.9 to one that uses Fibonacci hashing. Rerun the program you wrote for part (a). Record the number of probes for each key and calculate the total number of probes for all keys.

   c. Change the hash function used in the search function in Body 12.9 to one that uses folding. Rerun the program you wrote for part (a). Record the number of probes for each key and calculate the total number of probes for all keys.

81. Modify Body 12.9 so that it uses direct (external) chaining to resolve collisions. Include a statement that displays the number of probes needed to find an element's location.

   Write a program that instantiates a hash table ADO with positive elements and a table size of 19 and inserts the following values:

   66   47   87   90   126   140   145   153   177   285   393   395   467

   Record the number of probes for each key and calculate the total number of probes for all keys.

82. Modify Body 12.9 so that it uses coalesced chaining to resolve collisions. Include a statement that displays the number of probes needed to find an element's location.

   Write a program that instantiates a hash table ADO with positive elements and a table size of 19 and inserts the following values:

   66   47   87   90   126   140   145   153   177   285   393   395   467

   Record the number of probes for each key and calculate the total number of probes for all keys.

83. Modify Body 12.9 so that it uses coalesced chaining with a cellar that is 50% of the size of the hash table to resolve collisions. Include a statement that displays the number of probes needed to find an element's location.

   Write a program that instantiates a hash table ADO with positive elements and a table size of 19 and inserts the following values:

   66   47   87   90   126   140   145   153   177   285   393   395   467

Record the number of probes for each key and calculate the total number of probes for all keys.

84. Add a delete operation to Specification 12.3. Make the necessary additions and modifications to Body 12.9. Write a test plan and test program for this modified hash table package.
85. A hash table can be stored in a direct access file as well as in an array. Modify the hash table ADO defined in Specification 12.3 so it uses a file rather than an array. Implement your specification, and write a test plan and test program for this file-based hash table. Use a hash function of your choice and linear probing to resolve collisions.

Glossary

Absolute error The difference between the real number and the model number used to represent it

Abstract class A class that may have no direct instances. You cannot create an object of an abstract class.

Abstract data object (ADO) See singleton class

Abstract data type (ADT) A data type whose properties (domain and operations) are specified independently of any particular implementation

Abstraction A model of a complex system that includes only the details essential to the perspective of the viewer of the system

Acceptance testing The process of testing the system in its real environment with real data

Access type variable A variable that provides access to an object of a designated type

Activation record A record used at run time to store information about a subprogram call, including the parameters, local variables, register values, and return address

Adjacency list A linked list that identifies all the vertices to which a particular vertex is connected. Each vertex has its own adjacency list.

Adjacency matrix For a graph of N nodes, an N by N table that shows the existence (and weights) of all edges in the graph

Adjacent vertices Two vertices in a graph that are connected by an edge

Algorithm A logical sequence of discrete steps that describes a complete solution to a given problem computable in a finite amount of time and space

Alias One of several access variables that designate the same object

Allocator An operation that creates space for an object during the execution of a program

Anonymous type A type that does not have a specific name

Assertion A statement that is true or false but not both

Association A relationship between two classes

Balanced tree A tree in which the shape of the tree is monitored during each insert and delete. A balancing intervention is made when the shape of the tree deviates too much from a minimum height tree.

Base type   The type from which the operations and values for a subtype are taken

Big-O notation   A notation that expresses computing time as a term in a function that increases most rapidly relative to the size of a problem

Binary file   A file data type whose components are stored using the internal binary representation of the machine

Binary search tree   A binary tree in which the key value in every node is greater than the key values in its left subtree and less than the key values in its right subtree

Binary tree   A tree in which each node is capable of having two child nodes, a left child node and a right child node

Binding   The association of a memory address with a variable name

Binding time   The point in the compile-link-execution cycle when variable names are associated with addresses in memory

Bit mask   A pattern of binary values that is combined with some value using bitwise or, and, or `xor` to set, clear, or change specific bits in the value

Black-box testing   Testing a program or operation based on the possible input values, treating the code as a "black-box"

Bounded-length string   A varying-length string with a fixed maximum number of characters. A bounded-length string has a current length and a maximum length.

Branch   A code segment that is not always executed; for example a case statement has as many branches as there are case alternatives

Bucket   A collection of elements associated with a particular hash location

Casting   See explicit type conversion

Child package   A package that is conceptually part of its parent. Subclasses are implemented as child packages

Circular linked List   A linked list in which every node has a successor; the "last" element is succeeded by the "first" element

Class wide type   a type consisting of the set of all types in an inheritance hierarchy

Clear (white)-box testing   Testing a program or operation based on covering all of the branches or paths of the code

Clustering   The tendency of elements to become unevenly distributed in the hash table, with many elements clustering around a single hash location

Coalesced chaining   a variation of direct chaining that stores the linked lists for each hash index within the table itself

Collision   The condition resulting when two or more keys produce the same hash location

Complete binary tree   A binary that is either perfect or perfect through the next-to-last level, with the leaves on the last level as far to the left as possible

Complete graph   A graph in which every vertex is directly connected to every other vertex

Composite data type   A data type whose elements are composed of multiple data items

Concrete class   A class that may have instances

Constructor An operation used to create new values of a class

Consultation an implementation mechanism in which an object forwards an operation to another object

Container class A class that consists of a collection of components organized by a data structure

Controlled type A tagged type that provides the programmer with explicit control over initialization, assignment, and finalization of objects

Data The representation of information in a manner suitable for communication or analysis by humans or machines

Data abstraction The separation of a data type's logical properties from its implementation

Data encapsulation The hiding of the representation of data from the applications that use the data at a logical level; a programming language feature that enforces information hiding

Data structure A collection of data elements whose logical organization reflects a structural relationship among the elements. A data structure is characterized by accessing operations that are used to store and retrieve the individual data elements.

Data type A category of data characterized by the supported elements of the category (its domain) and the supported operations on those elements

Debugging The process of removing known errors

Depth of recursion The number of recursive calls used to complete an original call of a recursive subprogram

Dereferencing The process of accessing the data in an object designated by an access variable

Deskchecking Tracing an execution of a design or program on paper

Destructor An operation used to destroy the structure of an instance

Digraph See directed graph

Direct chaining A hash collision resolution method based on storing elements in linked lists (chains) external to the hash table. Each hash table entry is an external pointer to a linked list.

Direct file (random access file) A binary file whose components can be accessed sequentially or randomly (in any order)

Direct recursion Recursion in which a subprogram directly calls itself

Directed graph (Digraph) A graph in which each edge is directed from one vertex to another (or the same) vertex

Discrete (ordinal) data type A scalar data type in which each value (except the first) has a unique predecessor and each value (except the last) has a unique successor

Discriminant A special field in a record declaration that allows us to use the record declaration for different kinds or sizes of objects

Double hashing Resolving a collision through a second hash function. The first function computes a hash address from the key. The second hash function computes the increment for use in the general linear probing formula.

Doubly linked list A linked list in which each node is linked to both its successor and its predecessor

Dynamic allocation Creation of storage space in memory for a variable during run time

Dynamic dispatching the automatic selection at execution time of the appropriate operation in a class hierarchy

Dynamic verification Verifying a program by executing it with a set of test data

Edge A pair of vertices representing a connection between two nodes in a graph

Elaboration The run-time processing of a declaration. Allocation of memory space for variables and initialization of variables are two common elaboration activities.

Empty set The set with no members

Exception Associated with an unusual, often unpredictable event, detectable by software or hardware, that requires special processing. The event may or may not be erroneous.

Explicit type conversion The conversion of a value from one type to another type. Also called *casting.*

Extension aggregate An aggregate used to specify a value for a type that is a record extension by specifying a value for the ancestor of the type, followed by associations for any components not determined by the ancestor

External pointer A pointer outside of a linked list that designates a node in that list

Fixed-length string A string that contains a fixed (constant) number of characters

Functional domain The set of valid input data for a program or operation

General access type Access types whose values can designate the elements of any storage pool, as well as aliased objects created by declarations (named objects)

Generic formal parameter A parameter defined in a generic unit declaration. Used to customize a generic unit for a specific problem.

Generic unit A template for a package or subprogram

Graph A data structure that consists of a set of nodes and a set of edges that relate the nodes to each other

Hash function A function used to manipulate the key of an element to identify its location in the list

Hash table Term used to describe the data structure used to store and retrieve elements using hashing

Hashing The technique used for ordering and accessing elements in a list in a relatively constant amount of time by manipulating the key to identify its location in the list

Header node Placeholder node at the beginning of a list; used to simplify list processing

Heap See max-heap and min-heap

Height The number of levels in a tree

Incomplete type declaration A type declaration that gives only the name of the type

Indefinite type a type for which we cannot declare an object without an initial value or explicit constraint

Indirect recursion Recursion in which a chain of two or more subprograms returns to the subprogram that originated the chain

Information hiding The practice of hiding the details of a module with the goal of controlling access to the details from the rest of the system

Inspection A verification method in which one member of a team reads the program or design line by line and the other points out errors

Instance An individual entity with its own identity. An object is an *instance* of a class.

Instance A package or subprogram created from a generic unit

Instantiation A declaration that creates an instance of a generic unit

Integration testing Testing that is performed on combined program modules that already have been independently tested

Internal pointer A pointer within a node that designates the next node in the linked list

Iterator An operation that allows us to process all of the components of a data structure

Key Field in a record whose values are used to determine the logical order of records in a list

Key-ordered list A list in which the elements are records and are ordered according to the value of a key field of each element

Leaf A tree node that has no children

Length The number of characters in a string

Level The distance of a node from the root node

Linear probing Resolving a hash collision by sequentially searching a hash table beginning at the location returned by the hash function

Linked list A collection of data where each item in the collection includes an access value that designates the next item in the collection

Load factor The fraction of the slots in a hash that are used

Loop invariant Assertion of what must be true at the start of each loop iteration and on exit from the loop

Max-heap A complete binary tree, each of whose elements contains a value that is greater than or equal to the value of each of its children

Min-heap A complete binary tree, each of whose elements contains a value that is less than or equal to the value of each of its children

Minimal perfect hash function A perfect hash function that maps the defined set of keys to a hash table with load factor of 1.0

Model number A real number that is represented exactly

Node A record containing data and an access value that designates another node

Null An access value literal that designates no object

Null procedure A procedure that has no effect

Observer An operation that returns an observation on the state of an object

Ordinal data type See discrete data type

Overloading The repeated use of a subprogram name with different parameter profiles

Overriding The replacement of a superclass's operation with one defined for the subclass

Package A group of logically related entities that may include types and subtypes, objects of those types and subtypes, and subprograms with parameters of those types and subtypes

Package body The implementation of a package

Package specification The visible portion of a package; specifies what resources are supplied by the package

Parameter profile The distinguishing features of a subprogram—whether the subprogram is a procedure or function, the number of parameters, the type of each parameter, and, if it is a function, the type of the result. Sometimes called the subprogram's signature.

Path A combination of branches that might be traversed during a single execution of a program or operation

Path testing A testing technique whereby the tester tries to execute all possible paths in a program or operation

Perfect binary tree A binary tree in which all of the leaves are on the same level and every nonleaf node has two children

Perfect hash function A hash function that produces no collisions for a defined set of keys

Pool-specific access type Access types whose values can designate only the elements of their associated storage pool

Postcondition Assertions that describe what results are expected at the exit of an operation, assuming that the preconditions were true

Pragma A statement that directs the Ada compiler to make certain changes to our program when it translates it into machine language

Precondition Assertions that must be true on entry into an operation for the postconditions to be guaranteed

Primitive operation An operation for a type that is declared in the same package specification as the type and has a parameter or a return value of the type

Private type A type used to encapsulate the attributes (data) of a class

Quadratic probing Resolving a hash collision by using the square of the number of times we have probed the table to determine the next location

Queue A structure in which elements are added to the rear and removed from the front; a "first in, first out" (FIFO) structure

Random access file See direct file

Recursive call A subprogram call in which the subprogram being called is the same as the one making the call

Regression testing Reexecution of program tests after modifications have been made in order to ensure the program still works correctly

Relative address The offset (number of memory locations) from some other address determined at run time

Relative error The absolute error divided by the true value of the real number

Requirements A statement of what is to be provided by a computer or software product

Robustness   The ability of a program to recover following an error; the ability of a program to continue to operate within its environment

Root   The top node of a tree structure; a node with no parent

Run-time stack   A data structure that keeps track of activation records during the execution of a program

Scalar data type   A data type in which the values are ordered and each value is atomic

Sequential file   A binary file whose components can be accessed sequentially

Signature   See parameter profile

Singleton class   A class for which there is only one object. Also called an abstract data object (ADO).

Software engineering   The discipline devoted to the design, production, and maintenance of computer programs that are developed on time and within cost estimates, using tools that help to manage the size and complexity of the resulting software products

Software process   A standard, integrated set of software engineering tools and techniques used on a project by an organization

Software specification   A detailed description of the function, inputs, processing, outputs, and special requirements of a software product. It provides the information needed to design and implement the product.

Sorted list   A list in which the elements are ordered by their value

Stable sort   A sorting algorithm that preserves the original order of duplicates

Stack   A structure in which elements are added and removed from only one end; a "last in, first out" (LIFO) structure

Static verification   Verifying a program without executing it

Stub   A special procedure or function that can be used in top-down testing to stand in for a lower level operation

Tail recursion   The case where a recursive subprogram contains a single recursive call that is the last statement executed in the subprogram

Test driver   A program that sets up the testing environment by declaring and assigning initial values to variables, then calls the operation to be tested

Test plan   A document showing the test cases planned for a program, class, or operation; their goals, inputs, expected outputs, and criteria for success

Testing   The process of executing a program with data sets designed to discover errors

Trailer node   Placeholder node at the end of a list; used to simplify list processing. The key of a trailer node must be greater than any valid key for the list.

Transformer   An operation that changes the internal state of an object

Tree   A structure with a unique starting node (the root), in which each node is capable of having many child nodes, and in which a unique path exists from the root to every other node

Type declaration   The association of a type identifier with the definition of a new data type

Unbounded-length string   A varying-length string with no bound on the number of characters

Undirected graph A graph in which the edges have no direction

Unit testing Testing a class or operation by itself

Universal set The set containing all the values of a component type

Validation The process of determining the degree to which a software product fulfills its intended purpose

Varying-length string A string in which the number of characters can change

Verification The process of determining the degree to which a software product fulfills its specification

Vertex A node in a graph

Walk-through A verification method in which a team performs a manual simulation of the program or design

Weighted graph A graph in which each edge carries a value

White-box testing See clear-box testing

Index

A

Absolute errors, 93
   floating point numbers and, 96
Abstract classes, 127, 128–130, 131
Abstract data objects, 124, 154, 522
   maze modeled as, 598
Abstract data types, 18, 153, 154, 206, 522
   defined, 82, 112
   graphs as, 728
Abstraction, 3, 8–9, 23, 62
Abstract level, sets and, 164–169
abstract reserved word, 130
Acceptance testing, 33
'**Access** attribute, 412
   examples for use of, 377
Access-based linked list, code for insert procedure, 509–510
Accessor operations, 83
Access types, 235–236, 256
   exceptions and, 240
   general, 375–378
   unbounded-length strings and, 234–255
Access type variable, 235
Access values
   keeping track of, *298*
   sorting arrays with, 811, *811*
Access variables
   with initial values of null, *236*
   with non-null access values, *236*
   obtaining locations to assign to, 377
   string objects designated by, *241*
Activation record, 583
Actual array types, rules for matching formal array types with, 189
Ada, 2. *See also* Ada's built-in types
   arithmetic expressions written in, 279
   composite types built in, 79
   controlled types in, 247
   dynamic allocation of space in, 235
   exceptions managed in, 32
   generic units in, 164
   hashing support with, 840–841
   large program development with, 108
   parameter modes in, 590
   primary module mechanisms in, 9
   recursive and iterative algorithms in, 557
   short-circuit operators in, 448
Ada 2005, reserved words in, 839, *839*
Ada.Calendar.Clock function, 425
Ada.Calendar package, 109
Ada.Calendar.Year function, 425
Ada.Containers.Hashed_Sets package, 164
Ada.Containers.Ordered_Sets package, 164
Ada.Containers package, 405
Ada.Direct_IO package, 109
Ada.Finalization.Controlled type, 381
Ada.Finalization.Limited_Controlled type

extension of, 309
   List_Type and extension of, 441
   Tree_Type as subclass of, 648
Ada.Finalization package, 246, 247
Ada Language Reference Manual, 221, 222, 226, 807
Ada library, container classes in, 405
Ada.Numerics.Discrete_Random, 170
Ada.Numerics.Float_Random, 170
Ada package, 109
Ada's built-in types, 88–107
   composite types, 97–104
   relationships among, *89*
   scalar types, 89–96
   subtypes, 105–107
Ada.Sequential_IO package, 109
Ada.Strings.Bounded.Generic_Bounded_Length
     package, 223, 224, 225, 226, 231, 256
Ada.Strings.Bounded package, 214, 221
Ada.Strings.Fixed package, 215, 216, 221, 256
Ada.Strings.Hash package, 840
Ada.Strings.Map package, 285
Ada.Strings.Maps.Constants package, 219, 642
Ada.Strings.Maps package, 164, 217–218
Ada.Strings package, 215
Ada.Strings.Unbounded package, 214, 215, 226, 256
Ada.Strings.Wide_Bounded package, 225
Ada.Text_IO.File_Type package, Rouses Point Hump
     Yard program and, 350, 352
Ada.Text_IO package, 109, 111, 124
   declarations for Put procedures in, 127
Ada.Text_IO.Unbounded_IO package, 226
Ada.Unchecked_Deallocation procedure, 256
Add_Edge transformer, graphs and, 731
Addition, of set elements, 166
Address Book ADO: Implements Specification 7.2,
     Body 7.1 of, 419–424
Address Book ADO (Specification 7.2), 414–417
Add_Vertex procedure, 748
Add_Vertex transformer, graphs and, 731
Adelson-Velskii, Georgii M., 685
Adjacency lists, 752–753
   adjacency matrices *vs.*, 753
   for edges, *753, 754*
Adjacency matrices, 746
   adjacency lists *vs.*, 753
Adjacent vertices, 728
Adjust operation, 405
Adjust procedure, 247, 250, 253, 254, 256
ADOs. *See* Abstract data objects
ADTs. *See* Abstract data types
Air routes
   storage of, in queues, *740*
   storage of, in stacks, *736*
Algorithms, 3
   for adding edge to graph, 748
   for adding to sequential list, 433
   analysis of, 317
   for array-based unordered list, 815
   for base case for **Merge_Sort**–Recursive, 783
   Big-O notation and comparison of, 319
   for binary search, 54–57
   for bubble sort, 774
   for bubbling up, 775
   for build heap, 796
   competing, comparing work done by, 317–318
   for **Delete** operation, 657
   for deleting from sequential list, 434–435
   for depth-first search, 735
   for **Dequeue** operation, 719
   for **Enqueue** operation, 720
   for **Find** operation, 652
   for frequency generator, 641–642
   greedy, 202
   for heap sort, 798
   for inserting/retrieving elements from hash table
     based on direct chaining, 829
   for insertion sort, 74–75, 779
   for **Insert** operation, 653
   for iterative **Insert** operation, 672–673
   for **Merge** function, 785
   for merge sort, 782
   for **Min_Index**, 771
   for quick sort, 789
   for radix sort, 801
   recursive, 556
   recursive tree, developing, 651
   for **Reheap_Down** procedure, 722
   for **Reheap_Up** operation, 724

for Rouses Point Hump Yard program, 351
for selection sort, 770
for shortest path traversal, 743
for tree balancing, 683–684
Algorithm Sum1, 321
Algorithm Sum2, analysis of, 321–322
aliased reserve word, 376
Alias(es), 238, 256, 376
    access types used in application level and, 377, 382
    simple unbounded-length string class and, 244–246
.all form
    array designation and, 242
    dereferencing field in designated records and, 300
Allocating memory, 236–237
Allocator, 236
all optional word, use of, 411
Alphabetizing names application
    algorithm for, 227
    implementation of, 227–230
    problem description, 226–227
    for strings, 226–230
Ambiguities, in interfaces, 16
Ancestor, 630
and operator, 91, 92
and then operator, 169, 448, 449
Angle brackets, in declarations, 183
Annotations, 38
Append operation, binary transformers and, 406
Application (or user) level, 83. *See also* Implementation level; Logical level
    for abstract data types, 142–144
    for binary search trees, 640–647
    for FIFO queues, 348–355
    for graph traversals, 735–737, 739, 742–743, 745–746
    for heaps, 719–721
    for key-ordered lists, 413–426
    for priority queues, 710–712
    for sets, 169–172
    for stacks, 279–290
    for strings, 226–230
A_Ptr pool-specific access type, 376

Arcs, in graphs, 727
Arithmetic expressions, writing in Ada, 279
Arithmetic operators, for some discrete types, 183
Array aggregates, 98
Array-based implementation, for graph class, 746
Array-Based Key-Ordered List (Specification 8.3), 507–508
Array-based linked list, code for insert procedure, 510
Array-Based Linked List: Implements Specification 8.3, Body 8.1 for, 510–516
Array-based linked lists, Big-O comparison of **Insert** and **Delete** operations in, 519*t*
Array-based lists, 712
Array_Based package body, 508, 510
Array-based Queue: Implements Specification 6.1, Body 6.1 of, 361–362
Array-based sorted list, 712
Array-Based Stack: Implements Specification 5.1, Body 5.1 of, 293
Array_Example package, example instantiation of, 189
Array implementations
    comparing, 362
    comparing lines of code between linked implementation and, 461*t*
Array indexes, 177, 504
Array of nodes, dynamic storage and, 509*t*
Array representations, heap values in, *717*
Arrays, 97–98
    copying tree information into, *682*
    with linked lists of values and free space, *506*
    memory management for, 516–517
    ordered list stored in, *505*
    reasons for using, 504
    with three lists, *507*
    unsuccessful searches of, *431*
    using, 505–516
Array Search (Specification 7.3), 430
Array slices, two, *784*
Array storage, for vertices, *753*
Array_to_Tree function, 684
Array_Type, 100
Array types, 188–190
Array wrap-around, 360

Assertions
    defined, 38
    program design and, 38–39
Assignment operation (:=), 100, 313
Assignment operators, 92, 183
    private types and, 190
Associations, 153
ATM. *See* Automated teller machine
Atomic types, 82
Attributes, 88, 134
AUnit, 51
Automated teller machine, scenario for developing software for, 7–8
Automatic range checking, programmer-defined subtypes and, 105
AVL trees, with nodes that are balanced, left leaning, or right leaning, 685, *686*

B

Back field, in linear doubly linked list, 494, *494*
Back pointer field, doubly linked lists and, 498
Backtracking, 596
Backus-Naur form, 179
Balanced trees, 690
    defined, 685
Balance procedure, 685
Balancing binary search tree, 682–686
    AVL trees, 685
    multi-way search trees, 686
Base case, for **Merge_Sort**, 783
Base-case question, 563
    applying to multiple recursive calls, 567
    avoiding endless recursive routines with, 579
    single recursive calls and, 566
    Towers of Hanoi algorithm and, 574
    for verifying Escape from Maze recursive design, 603
    for verifying recursive function, 650
    for verifying **Reverse_Traverse** procedure, 572
Base type, 105
BASIC, 504, 557
BCD. *See* Binary coded decimal
Big-O approximations
    of recursive versions *vs.* nonrecursive versions, 595–596
    sorting and searching techniques and, 841
Big-O comparisons
    binary search trees *vs.* linear lists, 678–681
    of **Bubble_Sort** and **Selection_Sort**, 776–777, 778
    of bushy trees and list operations, 679, 680t
    for heap sort, 800
    of **Insert** and **Delete** operations, in various implementations of key-ordered lists, 519t
    for insertion sort, 781
    of key-ordered list implementations, 462–463, 463t
    for merge sort, 787–788
    for merge sort, comparing $N \log_2 N$ and N^2, 788t
    of queue operations, 373t
    for quick sort, 794–795
    relative efficiency of queue implementations in terms of, 372–373
    for **Short_Bubble_Sort**, 778
    for sort arrays using **Selection_Sort**, 772–773, 773t
    of sorting algorithms, 813t
    of Sum1 and Sum2, 322
Big-O notation
    array implementation comparisons and, 362
    defined, 318
    efficiency of stack operations and, 323–324
    family laundry analogy and, 322–323
    height of tree and, 632–633
    recursion and, 589–590
Binary coded decimal, 96n2
Binary files, 520
    for address book, 425
Binary search algorithm, 54–57, 430
Binary_Search algorithm
    execution of, *578*
    recursive version of, 577–579
Binary searching
    efficiency with, 817
    timed experiment of searching for reserved words and, 840t
Binary search operation, testing (problem-solving case study), 53–62

Binary_Search procedure, 817
  level of recursive calls in, 595
Binary Search Procedure: Implements Specification 3.4, Body 3.5 of, 198–199
Binary search property, 634
Binary Search Tree: Implements Specification 10.1, Body 10.1 of, 665–671
Binary search tree insert operation, implementing priority queue and, 713
Binary_Search_Tree package body, 665
Binary search trees, 628, *633*, 633–634
  balancing, 682–686
  comparing priority queue implementations with, 713*t*
  with current element S, *648*
  defined, 634
  deletions from, *664*
  insertions into, *653*
  linear lists compared with, 678–681
  recursion or iteration?, 677–678
  searching, 671–672
  simple operations for, 649
  storage of, in array with dummy values, *689*
Binary search tree specification
  application level, 640–647
  implementation level, 647–678
  logical level, 636–640
Binary Search Tree (Specification 10.1), 637–640
Binary transformers, 406
Binary trees, 628, 630–633, *631*. *See also* Heaps
  array representation for, *687*
  complete, 688, *689*, 713n1
  defined, 630
  examples of different types of, 688, *689*
  implicit link implementation with, 687
  minimum heights of, 632*t*
  nonlinked representation of, 686–689
  perfect, 688, *689*
  with 10 nodes, *631*
Binary tree traversals, 634–636
  common, 634–635
  visualizing, *635*
Binding, 580
Binding time, 580

Bingo basket, CRC card for, *136*
Bingo_Basket package, 139, 171
Bingo Basket Singleton Class, 170–171
Bingo Basket Singleton Class: Implements Specification 2.12, 170–171
Bingo Basket Singleton Class (Specification 2.12), 139
Bingo caller, CRC card for, *138*
Bingo Caller: Implements Specification 2.14, Body 2.9 of, 145–146
Bingo_Caller package, 141–142
Bingo_Caller package body, 145–146
Bingo Caller Singleton Class (Specification 2.14), 141–142
Bingo card, *133*
  CRC card for, *136*
Bingo Card Class (Specification 2.13), 140–141
Bingo Cards: Implements Specification 2.13, Body 2.10 of, 146–152
Bingo_Cards package, 140–141
Bingo_Cards package body, 146–152
Bingo Games—How Long Should They Take? (problem-solving case study), 132–152
  approach taken in, 132–133
  Bingo Basket Singleton class, 139
  Bingo Caller, 145–146
  Bingo Caller Singleton class, 141–142
  Bingo Card class, 140–141
  Bingo cards, *133*, 146–152
  Bingo Games Simulation, 142–144
  Bingo Number Definitions, 138
  design, 133–135, 137
  logical level, 137
Bingo Game Simulation, 142–144
  Body 2.8 of, 142–144
Bingo Number Definitions (Specification 2.11), 138
Bingo Number Set, 167–168, 175–177
Bingo Number Set: Implements Specification 3.1, Body 3.2 of, 175–177
Bingo_Number_Set class, 171
Bingo_Number_Set operations, example expressions using, 169
Bingo_Number_Set package, 167
Bingo Number Set (Specification 3.1), 167–168
Bingo_Numbers package, 138

Bingo_Set package, 181
Bingo simulation
    initial class diagram for, *135*
    revised class diagram for, *137*
Bit masks, 92
Bitwise operations, 91
Black-box testing, 48
Blank_Set constant, 285
Booch, Grady, 11
Boolean expressions, for details of comparisons between two subarrays, 233
Boolean function, writing, 564–567
Boolean type, 106
Boolean values, 172
Bottom-up stepwise refinement, 11
Bottom-up testing, 50–51
Boundaries, 39
Bounded FIFO queue (Specification 6.1), 345–347
Bounded-length string operations, implementations for, 233–234
Bounded-length strings, 214, 221–225, *232*, 256
    catenation operations for, 224
    catenations of fixed-length strings and, 233–234
    conversion between fixed-length strings and, 222
    implementation of, 231–234
Bounded Stack (Specification 5.1), 276–277
Bounded Stack with an Additional Operation (Specification 5.3), 311
Bounded_String private type, 232
Bounded time, O(1), 319–320
Box-and-arrow pictures
    design of algorithms that manipulate linked lists and, 365
    developing algorithms for array-based linked lists and, 517
B+-Trees, 686
B_Ptr general access type, 376
Braces, empty sets indicated with, 165
Brackets, in set notation, 728
Brainstorming, 24, 26, 30
    binary search tree specification and, 641
Brakes_On procedure, 380
Branches, 48–49
    checking out, *49*

Branching statements, recursive routines and, 579
Breadth-First Search, Body 11.4 of, 741–742
Breadth-first searching, 739–742, *741*
Break point, 51
B-trees
    fifth-order, *686*
    uses for, 686
Bubble sort, 768, 774–778
    algorithm for, 774
    analyzing, 776–777, 778
    in Big-O comparison, 813*t*
    examples of, *774*
    snapshot of, *775*
    timed experiments on, 813*t*
Bubble_Sort, Big-O comparison between **Selection_Sort** and, 776–777, 778
Bubble Sort: Implements Specification 12.1, Body 12.2 of, 775–776
Bubble_Sort procedure, code for, 775–776
Bubble_Up, 776, 777
Bubbling up algorithm, 775
Buckets, 828
Budget, quality software completed within, 6
Bugs, origin of, 34–37
Bushy trees, 657, 690
    Big-O comparisons of list operations and, 679, 680*t*
    comparing priority queue implementations with, 713*t*
    depth of recursion and, 677
    Find operation for, 679
Butterflies and moths, scientific classification of, *629*

C

Cardinality, 135
Case studies. *See* Problem-solving case studies
Casting. *See* Explicit type conversion
Catenation, of bounded-length string and fixed-length string, 233–234
Catenation operations, for combining bounded-length strings, 224
Chaining
    buckets, 828
    coalesced, 829–831

direct, 828–829
Chains, 829
Character_Mapping type, 217
Character type, 92
Character types, 78
Child packages, 22, 109
Children, 628
    of binary trees, 630
    deleting root node with no children, 659, *659*
    deleting root node with one child, 659, *659*
    deleting root node with two children, 660, *661*
Circular doubly linked list, with tail pointing to last node of list, *495*
Circular Doubly Linked List Search (Specification 8.2), 495–496
Circular linked lists, *482*, 482–493
    Big-O comparison of **Insert** and **Delete** operations in, 519*t*
    defined, 482
    deleting from, 491, *492*, 493
    description of, 482–484
    empty, 483
    with external pointer pointing to rear element, 483, *483*
    finding list element in, 485–486, 488
    initializing for search of, *488*
    inserting into, 488–489, *490*
    searching, *487*
    traversing, 484–485
Circular Linked List Search (Specification 8.1), 485
Circular linked queue design, 370
C language, 98
C++ language, 2, 98
'**Class** attribute, 104
Class diagrams, 12
Classes, 153
    in Ada, 9
    in baking problem, 15
    container, 404–405
    filtering, 24
    identifying in object-oriented systems, 23–25
    in object-oriented design, 14–18
    private types and encapsulation of, 313

Classes, Responsibilities, and Collaborations (CRC) cards. *See* CRC cards
Class-wide types, 378–381, 382
    defined, 379
Clear_All_Marks graph operation, 731, 737, 748
Clear operation, 146, 275, 303
    Big-O comparison of key-ordered list implementations and, 462
    Big-O comparison of queue implementations and, 372
    Big-O comparisons of bushy tree and list operations, 679, 679*t*
    encapsulation and, 313
    linked lists and, 445
    queues and, 345
    recursive binary search trees and, 665
    sequential lists and, 429, 430
    for unbounded-length queue class, 381
Clear (or white) box testing, 48
Clear procedure, 292, 309
    Graph set to empty state and, 748
Clear transformer, graphs and, 731
Clock arithmetic, 91
Close operation, 522
Close procedure, 527
Clustering, 826
Coalesced chaining, 829–831
    collision handling through, *831*
COBOL, 96, 98, 504, 557
Code. *See also* Algorithms
    for **Bubble_Sort** procedure, 775–776
    for **Heap_Sort** procedure, 799–800
    for **Reheap_Up** procedure, 725
    for **Selection_Sort** procedure, 771–772
Code inspections, 63
Code segment, 255
Cohesive modules, 10
Cohesive responsibilities, examples of, 24
Collect Queues step, in radix sort algorithm, 802
Collision, defined, 821
Collision handling
    through coalesced chaining, *831*
    through direct chaining, *830*
Collision handling algorithms, 821–831

buckets, 828
chaining, 828–831
clustering, 826
coalesced chaining, 829–831
direct chaining, 828–829
double hashing, 826–828
linear probing, 821–822, *822*, 824–825
open addressing, 821
quadratic probing, 826
Color_Type package, 178
Combinations function
calculating, 594, *595*
calculating combinations (4,3), *570*
solving with recursion, 569–571
Communication skills, importance of, 535
Comparison of strings, 223–224
Compile-time errors, 35–36
Complete binary trees, 688, *689*, 713n1
Complete graphs, 730, *731*
Complexity
comparing, for different implementations, 316, *316*
controlling, during design process, 8–12
defined, 315
of list implementations, 461
of queue implementations, 371, 371*t*
Component selector, uses of, 97–98
Composite data types, 79, 153
Composite types, 97–104
access of, 240–248
arrays, 97–98
records, 98–102
tagged records, 103–104
unstructured, 98
Composition, UML diagram of, *79*
Composition associations, 153
Computation time, short, good hash function and, 833–834
Computer science, theoretical, analysis of algorithms in, 317
Concrete class, 129
Congestions problems, queueing theory and, 348
Constant of proportionality, of algorithm, 806
constant optional word, use of, 411

CONSTRAINT_ERROR, 106, 240, 448, 484, 486
Construct_Date function, 405
Construct_Date operation, 17
Construct operation, 146
Constructors, 17, 83, 119, 121, 405
Constructors package, 119
Consultation, 424
Container classes, 404–405
implicit current elements and, 637
Contains function, linear probing and, 824
Controlled procedures, overriding, 247–248
Controlled tagged type, 247
Controlled types, 247, 256
eliminating chances of memory leaks with, 255
Controlled unbounded-length string class, 246–250
Conversion, between fixed-length and bounded-length strings, 222
Copy constructor, 83, 405
Correctness, designing for, 37–45
Count observer, 406
Count search operation, 221
Course string variable, 376
Cover_Number operation, 146
CRC cards, 3, 23, 26, 404
for Bingo basket, *136*
for Bingo caller, *138*
for Bingo card, *136*
blank, *13*
for Entry, *29*
for identifying classes, 24, 25
information on, 12
with initial responsibilities, *28*
Create operation, 522
Cryptography, 91
Cubic time, $O(N^3)$, 320
Currencies, floating point numbers used for, 96
Current Defined binary search tree operation, 649
Current_Defined function, 637
Current element, binary search tree specification and, 636–637
CURRENT_UNDEFINED exception, 637
Current variable
bubble sort and, 774
insertion sort and, 780

marking unsorted part of array and, 770
for partitioning array into sorted and unsorted parts, 769, *769*
Cyclomatic (McCabe's) complexity, basis of, 315

D
Data, 78
　order of, and choosing sort algorithms, 812
Data abstraction, 79–82, 153
Data abstraction packages, 109, 112–115
Data coverage, 47–48
Data encapsulation, 3, 81, 153
Data levels, 83–84
Data structure, 18, 82–83, 153
　library as, 84–88
Data types, 78–79, 153. *See also* Ada's built-in types
　relationships between abstract data types, data structures, classes, and Ada constructs, *154*
Date class, 15–16, 82, 92
　is-a relationship and, 20
　package body for, 18
　UML class diagram for, *17*
Date objects, 15
Date_Type type, 17, 18
Day_Is operation, 17
Debugging, 32, 33
　with a plan, 51–52
　recursive routines, 579
　testing *vs.*, 33
Decimal equivalents, of 8-bit binary number, *80*
Decimal numbers, representation of, on binary computer, 96n2
Declarations
　package, 108, 110, 153
　subtype, 105
Deferred constant, 169
Definition packages, 109, 110
Degenerate trees, 657, 681
　comparison of priority queue implementations with, 713*t*
Delegation, 424n2
Deleted status, hash tables and, 833
Delete operation

Big-O comparisons of bushy tree and list operations, 679, 679*t*
circular lists and, 485, 491, *492*, 493
iterative version of, 675–678
linked lists and, 455
recursive version of, 657–663, 677–678
sequential lists and, 434–435, *436*
Delete procedure, doubly linked lists and, 498–499, *499*
Delete_Root procedure, 675, 676
　Ada code for implementation of three cases for, 660–662
　three cases for, 659–660
Delete string operation, as transformer, 405
Delivery, in software process, 2
delta, 188
Demonstration of the Extended Stack Class (Program 5.2), 312–313
Depth First Search, Body 11.3, 737–738
Depth-first searching, 735–738, *736*
Depth-first strategy, 735
Depth of recursion, 589
Dequeueing, array-based sorted lists and, 712
Dequeue operation, 345, *366*
　algorithm for, 719
　Big-O comparison of queue implementations and, 372
　fixed-front design and, 357
　floating-front design and effects of, *358*
　priority queue and, 708
　as transformer, 405
Dequeue procedure, UNDERFLOW exception and, 347, 354
Dereferencing, 235, 237–238
Derived classes, 134
Descendants, 630
Design
　of good hash functions, 834
　review activities, 45–46
　visualizing, 12
Designating object, with access variable, 235
Design errors, specifications and, 34–35
Design example
　brainstorming, 26, 30

enhancing CRC cards with additional information, 30–31, *31*
    filtering stage, 26–27
    first scenario walk-through, 27–30
    initial responsibilities, 27
Deskchecking, 45
Deskchecking programs, checklist for, *46*
Dewey decimal system, 84, 86
Diagrams, 12
Diesel Locomotive (Specification 2.10), 132
Difference, between sets, 165, 206
Digit_Of function, 804
digits, 188
Digits of precision, 94
Digraphs. *See* Directed graphs
Direct access, 97
Direct chaining, 828–829
    collision handling through, *830*
Directed graphs (digraphs), 727, *729*
    complete, *731*
Direct files
    defined, 520
    with 10 elements, *521*
Direct_IO package, 520, 522
Direct recursion, 556
Discrete data types, 79
Discrete Set: Implements Specification 3.2, 184–186
Discrete_Set package, 179–181
Discrete_Set package body, 184–186
Discrete Set (Specification 3.2), 179–181
Discrete types, 183, 206
Discriminants, 100
    in declarations of stack objects, 291
    using records with, 102
Divide-and-conquer algorithms
    merge sort, 782
    quick sort, 788
Divide-and-conquer sorts
    in Big-O comparison, 813*t*
    rationale for, 782, *782*
    timed experiments on, 813*t*
Division methods, good hash functions and, 834–836
Domain, of modular integer type, 91
Dot notation, 300

Dot_Size, 103, 104
Double hashing, 826–828
Doubly circular linked lists, Big-O comparison of **Insert** and **Delete** operations in, 519*t*
Doubly linked lists, 493–499
    defined, 493
    description of, 493–494
    with dummy nodes, 502–503
    finding list element in, 494–496
    with header and trailer nodes, *502*
    inserting new node into, *497*
    insertions into, *496*
    operations on, 496–499
    with single dummy node, *503*
Draw operation, 170
Drop parameter, 216, 222
Dummy nodes
    doubly linked lists with, 502–503
    linked lists with, 499–503
Dummy values, binary search tree stored in array with, *689*
DUPLICATE_KEY exception, 424, 434, 451, 488, 654
Duplicate keys, lists with, 534–535, *535*
DUPLICATE_NAME exception, 424
Duration type, 95
Dynamic allocation, 303, 504
Dynamic dispatching, 380, 382
Dynamic storage
    array-based lists in, 427, *427*
    array of nodes and, 509*t*
    linked lists in, 428, *428*
    sequential lists in, 427, *427*
Dynamic storage allocation, 294, 362
    recursion and, 583–589, 613
Dynamic verification, 37

E

EBNF. *See* Extended Backus-Naur Form
Edge_Rec, 747
Edges
    adding to graphs, 748
    graph of flight connections between cities using adjacency lists for, *753*, *754*
    in graphs, 727, 728

Efficiency
    with binary searching, 817
    eliminating calls to procedures and functions
        and, 806–807
    height of tree and, 632
    recursive solutions and, 594
    removal of recursion and, 807–808
    searching tied to, 841
    sorting, 768
    with sorting and searching algorithms, 806–812
    when N is small, 806
8-bit binary number, some decimal equivalents of, *80*
Elaboration, 234, 584
Electronic address book, 413–414
    implementation of, 418–424
    program data and retained data for, *419*
    specification for, 413–418
Elementary_Functions package, 111
Element observer, 406
Elements
    heterogeneous collections of, 375–381
    homogeneous collections of, 344, 375
Elements field, 315
Element_Type, test driver for queue operations and, 374, 375
Element_Type formal private type, 191
Element_Type generic formal parameter, 181
Elephant discussion, algorithm analysis and, 318, 462
Empty binary search tree operation, 649
Empty circular lists, 483
Empty function, 292, 303
    queues and, 345
Empty lists, inserting into, *454*
Empty operation, 355
    Big-O comparison of key-ordered list implementations and, 462
    Big-O comparison of queue implementations and, 372
    Big-O comparisons of bushy tree and list operations, 679, 679*t*
    floating-front design and, 359
    linked lists and, 444
    sequential lists and, 429, 430
    for stacks, 275

testing queue operations and, 374
Empty queues, *359*, *365*, 366
Empty_Set deferred constant, 169
Empty sets, 165, 172, 174
Empty stacks, *292*, *297*, 309
Empty trees
    creating, 649
    inserting items into, 653
Encapsulation, 108, 116–127
    of data, 153
    sequential lists and, 437
    stacks and, 313–314
Enqueue operation, 345, 719
    algorithm for, 720
    Big-O comparison of queue implementations and, 372
    with dashed arrow showing value of pointer after operation is complete, *366*
    fixed-front design and, 356
    floating-front design and effects of, *358*
    priority queue and, 708
    as transformer, 405
Enqueue procedure, OVERFLOW exception and, 348
Enumeration_IO package, 178
Enumeration types, 88, 92–93
Enum type, 178
Equality operators, 183
Equality testing, 100
    private types and, 190
Equality testing operators (=) and (/=), 92, 313
Errors
    compile-time, 35–36
    debugging, 51–52
    run-time, 36–37
    writing reusable components and, 278
Escape from a Maze case study, 596–612
    assumptions, 598
    boundary problem, 604
    comparison of output of versions of procedure Try_To_Escape, 612*t*
    design, 598–604
    Escape from Maze program, 607–610
    escape processing, 599–601, *600*, *601*
    implementation, 604–605

input, 597
Maze ADO, 605
Maze ADO: Implements Specification 9.1, 606
output, 598
picture of a maze, *597*
processing requirements, 598
recursive solution, 602–603
specifications, 596
stack-based solution, 601–602
testing Escape from Maze program, 610–611
verifying recursive design, 603–604
Escape from a Maze (Program 9.2), 607–610
testing, 610–612
Euro type, 96
Evaluate function, 285
Evidence, in top-down debugging plan, 52
Examiner. *See* SPARK Examiner
Exception handlers, 32
Exceptions
access types and, 240
handling, 31–32
postconditions and, 279
stacks and, 277–279
Execution time comparisons, Big-O and, binary search trees *vs.* linear lists, 678–681
Exhaustive testing, 47–48
Explicit type conversion, 90
Exponential time, $O(2^N)$, 320
Exposed implementation, encapsulated implementation *vs.*, *116*
Extended Backus-Naur Form, 411
Extended Stack: Implements Specification 5.3, Body 5.3 of, 312
Extended Stack class, demonstration of, 312–313
Extended_Stack_Type type, declaration of, 312
Extension aggregate, 104, 249
External chaining, 828
External pointer, 299

F

Factorial function, 650
calls to iterative solutions to, 594
coding, 560
depth of recursive calls in, 595

problem definition summarized in definition of, 564
recursive calculations and, 557–559
run-time stack and, 586–589
run-time stack during execution of, *588*
run-time version of (simplified), 584
sample program loaded in memory, *587*
for solving $n!$, 560
three-question method applied to, 563–564
Family laundry analogy, Big-O notation and, 322–323
Feet_Ops package, 187
Fibonacci function, 569
Fibonacci hashing, 837
Fibonacci numbers, 567–569
Fibonacci sequence, 567
Fields, in records, 98
FIFO (First In, First Out) queues, 344, *344*, 708, 710
application level, 348–355
breadth-first searching and, 739
comparing implementations of, 370–374
implementation level, 355–370
logical level, 344–348
testing operations and, 374–375
as "waiting lines," 348
Fifth-order B-Tree, *686*
File-Based Key-Ordered List (Specification 8.4), 522–525
File-Based Linked List ADO: Implements Specification 8.4, Body 8.2 of, 527–533
File-based lists, analysis of, 534
File_Based package, 523, 527
Filtering, binary search tree specification and, 641
Filtering classes, 24
Finalize operation, 405
Finalize procedure, 247, 250, 252, 254, 256, 309
Find_And_Unlink_Max procedure, *662*, 662–663
code for, 663
iterative version of, 676–677
Find operation
Big-O comparisons of bushy tree and list operations, 679, 679*t*
for bushy trees, 679
current element and, 637
recursive binary search trees and, 652

Find_Token observer, 406
Find_Token operation, 285
Find_Token string operation, in parameters for, 642
'First discrete attribute, 183, 186, 190
Fixed-front design, 356–357
Fixed-length strings, 214, 215–221, 256
    catenation of bounded-length strings and, 233–234
    conversion between bounded-length strings and, 222
    implementation of, 231
Fixed point types, 95–96
Floating-front design, 357, 359–361
Floating point types, 93–95
Float type, 94, 107
Floyd, Robert W., 800n2
Folding methods, good hash functions and, 837
for loops, in Ada, 43
Formal array types, rules for matching actual array types with, 189
FORTRAN, 98, 557
Forward slash (/) operator
    good hash functions and, 834
    implementing body of function Digit_Of and, 804
Free list, initializing, to contain all nodes in array, *518*
Free_Node operation, array memory management and, 516, 517, *518*
Free_Node procedure, 506, 526
Free pointer, 508
Free procedure, 239, 243, 245, 303
Free-space stack, 516
Freight train manifests, 349–350
Frequency generator, algorithm for, 641–642
Front indicator, floating-front design and, 357
Fruit_Set package, 181
Full binary search tree operation, 649
Full function, 303
Full operation, 275, 294, 355
    Big-O comparison of key-ordered list implementations and, 462
    Big-O comparison of queue implementations and, 372
    Big-O comparisons of bushy tree and list operations, 679, 679*t*

    floating-front design and, 359
    linked lists and, 444
    queues and, 345
    sequential lists and, 429
    testing queue operations and, 374
Full queues, 360, *360*
Function &, tracing a call to, 253, *253*
Functional decomposition, 13–14
    in stepwise refinement, 11
Functional design, for baking a cake, *14*
Functional domain, 47
Functions
    eliminating calls to, 806–807
    order of magnitude of, 318

G

Garbage collection, 238
    memory leak problem and, 246
Gauss, C. F., 91
General access types, 375–378
    defined, 376
General Access Types (Program 6.2), 377–378
    variables in, *378*
General-case question, 563
    applying to multiple recursive calls, 567
    single recursive calls and, 566–567
    for verifying Escape from Maze recursive design, 604
    for verifying recursive function, 650
    for verifying Reverse_Traverse procedure, 573
General Public Licenses, 51
Generic Binary Search (Specification 3.4), 195–196
Generic_Elementary_Functions package, 111
Generic formal parameter, 177
Generic formal parameter type, 206
Generic formal private types, 199
Generic formal subprograms, 191–193
Generic formal types, 183–191
Generic packages, 206
    extending classes defined in, 311
Generic Selection Sort (Specification 3.3), 191
Generic subprograms, 181
Generic units, 146, 164
    defined, 177

EBNF definitions for declaration of, including packages and subprograms, 181–182
programming for reuse and, 177–193
well-designed, reuse of, 207
Get_Adjacent_Vertices graph operation, 731, 748
Get procedure, 108
Global variables, 255
Going parameter, 219
examples with values supplied for, 218
Golden ratio, hash function and reciprocal of, 836–837
Goldfish discussion, algorithm analysis and, 318, 462
Graph
complete package body, for adjacency matrix implementation of, 749–752
declaring as in out, 737
Graph.Edges, 747, 748
Graphs, 154, 754, 755
adjacent vertices in, 728
complete, 730, *731*
defined, 728
description of, at abstract level, 727
directed, 727, *729*
edges added to, 748
undirected, 727, *729*
vertices added to, 748
weighted, 730, *732*
Graph traversals, 731
application level, 735
breadth-first searching, 739–742
depth-first searching, 735–738, *736*
single-source shortest paths problem, 742–746
Graph.Vertices procedure, 748
Gregorian calendar, 17
Growth, comparison of rates of, 320*t*

H

Halstead's complexity measures, basis of, 315
Hardware, 3
Hashed lists, comparing key-ordered lists and, for identical elements, *820*
Hash functions, 818
choosing, 833–841

determining location of element in array with, 819, *819*
perfect, 838–840
Hash index, linear probing and, 824
Hashing, 818–841
Ada's support for, 840–841
collision handling algorithms and, 821–831
Fibonacci, 837
performance of, 831–832
of string keys, 837–838
Hash scheme, for handling employee elements, *835*
Hash Table: Implements Specification 12.3, Body 12.9 of, 822–824
Hash tables, 818, 824
deleting elements from, 832–833
deleting elements from, with linear probing, *833*
expected number of probes for successful searches in, *832*
with linear probing, *827*
load factor of, 831
locating elements in, 824
Hash Table (Specification 12.3), 819–820
Header_File, 527
Header_File_Name, 525
Header nodes, 499
doubly linked list with, *502*
Heap: Implements Specification 11.2, Body 11.2 of, 725–727
Heap_Array, 715
Heap building
changing contents of array, *797*
process for, *797*
unsorted array and its tree, *796*
Heap data structure, heap region of memory *vs.*, 714
Heapify procedure, 800n2
Heap package body, 725
Heaps, 255, 713–727, 754, 795
application level, 719–721
building, 795–798
comparing priority queue implementations with, 713*t*
elements added to, 714, *717*
implementation level, 721–725
logical level, 713–715, 718

roots removed from, 714, *716*
two, containing letters A-J, *715*
Heapsort, 320
Heap Sort: Implements Specification 12.1, Body 12.7 of, 799-800
Heap_Sort procedure
  code for, 799-800
  efficiency of, 800
Heap sorts, 768, 795-800
  algorithm for, 798
  analyzing, 800
  in Big-O comparison, 813*t*
  building a heap, 795-798
  general approach with, 795
  inherent instability of, 809
  timed experiments on, 813*t*
Heap (Specification 11.2), 718
Heap storage, for unnamed objects, 375
Heap values, in array representations, *717*
Height, 630, 657
  depth of recursion and, 677
  minimum, of binary trees, 632*t*
Height balanced nodes, in balanced binary trees, 685
Heterogeneous collections, 375-381
  class-wide types, 378-381
  general access types, 375-378
Hierarchical relationships, tree models for, 628, *629*
High-level design, in software process, 2
High-probability ordering, 815-816
Holiday_Date class, 20
Holiday_Date subclass, 21
Homogeneous collection of elements, 344, 375, 404
Hypothesis, in top-down debugging plan, 52

I

Ideaware, 3
Identity constant, 217
Identity function, code for, 410
if statements, recursive routines and, 579
if-then statement, 49
Implementation level, 83. *See also* Application level; Logical level
  for abstract data types, 144-145
  for binary search trees, 647-678
  in Bingo Games case study, 144-145
  for FIFO queues, 355-370
  for graphs, 746-753
  for heaps, 721-727
  for key-ordered lists, 426-460
  for priority queues, 712-713
  of radix sort, 803-805
  sets and, 172-177
  splitting the array and, 790, 792, 794
  for stacks, 290-314
  for strings, 230-255
Implementation of design, in software process, 2
Implementation of package, separating declaration of package from, 108
Inchworm effect, with linked lists, 449, *450*
Inchworm technique
  doubly linked lists and, 495
  searching linked lists with, 486
Incomplete type declarations, 306-307
Indefinite types, 379
  common uses of, 380
Index function, 218, 227
  specification of, 219
Index_Non_Blank search operation, 221
Index observer, 406
Index_Of function, 748
Indirect recursion, 556
Inequality operator (/=), 169
Infinite loops, 240
Infix notation, 279
Info fields, 315
  header nodes and, 499
  linked lists and, 504
Information hiding, 3, 9-10, 23, 62, 108
Inheritance, 153
  object-oriented design and, 14, 19-23
  overriding and, 127
  tagged records and, 103
  UML class diagram for, 21
Inheritance associations, in UML diagram, 153
Initialize_Memory procedure, 517
Initialize operation, 405
Initialize procedure, 250, 252, 256, 309
  calling, 247

linked lists with dummy node and, 500, 501
Inline pragma, 807
in membership test, 169
in mode, 590
in operator, membership tests and, 107
Inorder traversal, 634, 636, 664
    ordered array and, 682
in out mode, 590
    parameters, 119
    use of, 411, 412
in parameter, circular lists and, 485
Insertion order, tree shape and, 657
Insertion Sort: Implements Specification 12.1, Body 12.4 of, 780–781
Insertion_Sort procedure, 780–781
Insertion sorts, 320, 768, 778–781
    algorithm for, 74–75, 779
    analyzing, 781
    in Big-O comparison, 813*t*
    example of, *779*
    timed experiments on, 813*t*
Insert operation, 779
    Big-O comparisons of bushy tree and list operations, 679, 679*t*
    for bushy tree, 679
    circular lists and, 485, 488–489, *490*
    doubly linked lists and, 496
    iterative version of, 672–675, 677–678
    linear searching and, 815
    recursive–insert 13, *655*
    recursive version of, 652–657, 677–678
    sequential lists and, 432–434, *434*
Insert procedure, hash function and, 820, 821
Insert string operation, as transformer, 405
Inspections, 45
Instances, 129, 177
Instantiation, 178
Integer data type, 80, 81
Integer division operators, good hash functions and, 834–836
Integer_Ops package body, 186–187
Integer_Ops template, 187
Integers, black box representing, *81*
Integers list (example), 410

Integer type, 90, 105, 107
Integer types, 78, 79, 186–187
Integration testing, 49, 50
Interfaces
    in Ada, 10
    ambiguities in, 16
Interfaces package, 109
Internal pointer, 299
Interpolation searching, 817–818
Intersection, of sets, 165, 206
INVALID_EXPRESSION exception, 285
Invalid postfix expressions, 284–285
Inventory record list (example), 409–410
Irrelevant classes, 134
is abstract, after operation, 130
is-a relationship, 20
Iteration, recursion and, 590–592
Iterative binary search tree operations, nonrecursive deletion of node B, *676*
Iterative binary search trees operations, 671–677
    Delete operation, 675–677
    Insert operation, 672–675
    searching a binary search tree, 671–672
Iterative implementations, results of timed implementation comparisons between recursive implementations and, 594*t*
Iterative solution, recursive solution *vs.*, 562–563
Iterators, 83, 406
    using, 411–413

J
Java, 2
Justify parameter, 216

K
KEY_ERROR exception, 432, 657
Key_Of function, 430
Key-ordered List Class (Specification 7.1), 406–409
Key-ordered list operations, Big-O comparison of, for sequential and linked implementations, 463*t*
Key_Ordered_List package body, 437
Key-ordered lists, 403–465
    application level, 413–426

Big-O comparisons of **Insert** and **Delete** operations in, 519*t*
comparing hashed lists and, for identical elements, *820*
as container classes, 404
defined, 404
implementation level, 426–460
logical level, 404–413
other factors to consider in use of, 464
sample package instantiations, 409–411
Key ordering, 816–817
Keys
data sorted on more than one key, *812*
defined, 404
multiple, 809–810
Key_Type type, 730
Knuth, D. E., 836

L

Landis, Evgenii M., 685
'**Last** discrete attribute, 183, 186, 189
Leaf, 630
Left child, 630
Left leaning nodes, in AVL trees, 685, *686*
Left subtree, 630
Length, of characters in a string, 214
'**Length** array attribute, 190, 234
LENGTH_ERROR exception, 222
Length field, 118
Length function, 222
Length observer, 406
Length operation
linked lists and, 445
sequential lists and, 429, 430
Length_Range subtype, 232
Length record field, 234
Leonardo Fibonacci of Pisa, 567
Letter_Set package, 181
Levels, of binary tree, 630, 632
Library data structure, 84–88
collection of books ordered in different ways, *85*
communication between application level and implementation level, *87*
Life-cycle verification activities, 64*t*

LIFO (last in, first out), 325
for stack, 290
stack structure and, 274
Limited controlled types, procedures with, 309
limited private designation, 239
Limited private types, 313
Linear doubly linked list, *494*
Linear linked lists, traversing, 634
Linear probing, 821–822, 824–825
collision handling with, *822*
deleting element from hash table with, *833*
hash table with, *827*
with increment of 3, 825, *825*
Linear searches, 430
Linear searching, 815
Linear time, $O(N)$, 320
Linked implementations
comparing lines of code between array implementations and, 461*t*
for graphs, 752–753
Linked list as file of nodes, 520–534
abstract level, 522–525
analysis of file-based list, 534
direct files, 520–522
implementation level, 525–534
Linked lists, 299, *441*
as array of nodes, 504–518
Big-O comparison of **Insert** and **Delete** operations in, 519*t*
binary search trees compared with, 678–681
Delete operation and, 455
deleting from, *456*
with dummy nodes, 499–503
Empty, **Full**, and **Clear** operations, 444–445
finding list elements in, 445–446
with header and trailer nodes, *500*
implementation of, 441–460
implementation of stack as, 294, 297–303, 306–311
inchworm effect and, 449, *450*
inserting into empty list; inserting at beginning of list; inserting at end of list, *454*
inserting into middle of, *452*, 453
Insert operation and, 451–453

Length operation and, 445
   recursive processing of, 571–573
   Retrieve and **Modify** operations and, 451
   searching, *447*
   in static and dynamic storage, 428, *428*
   Traverse operation and, 445
   for vertices, *754*
Linked List Search (Specification 7.5), 446
Linked lists with header and trailer nodes, Big-O comparison of **Insert** and **Delete** operations in, 519*t*
Linked nodes
   stack of, *309*
   stacks composed of, 299, *299*
Linked queue representation, *363*
Linked stacks
   basic algorithms for operations in, 306
   pushing new elements onto, 300–301, *301*
Linked structures, queues implemented as, 362–370
LISP, recursive approaches and, 557
List class, comparing sequential and linked implementations of, 460–464
List elements
   finding in circular lists, 485–486, 488
   finding in doubly linked lists, 494–496
List_File, 527
List implementations, analyzing, 460–464
List operations
   Big-O comparisons of bushy trees and, 679, 680*t*
   testing, 465
Lists, 154
   adjacency, 752–753
   duplicate keys with, 534–535, *535*
   as homogeneous collection of elements, 404
   key-ordered, 816–817
   self-organizing, 816
   sorted, 404
List.Tail, 484, 488, 489, 491
List_Type, three variables of, *101*
Load factor, 831
Load field, 118
Load operation, 170
Location of object, access variable and, 238

Location parameter, iterative binary search trees and, 671, 672, 673
Location pointer, circular list and, 484
Location variable
   circular lists and, 486, 489, 491
   doubly linked lists and, 493, 497
   linked lists and, 445, 446, 448, 449
   list operations and declaration of, 431, 432, 433, 434, 435, 437
Locomotive: Implements Specification 2.9, 131
Locomotive class, UML diagram of, *129*
Locomotives.Diesel package, 132
Locomotives package, 130–131
Locomotives (Specification 2.9), 130–131
Locomotive_Type 'Class, 379
Locomotive types, array of pointers to, *381*
Logarithmic time, $O(\log_2 N)$, 320
Logical operators, 91
   use of, with modular integers, 92
Logical (or abstract) level, 83. *See also* Application level; Implementation level
   for abstract data types, 137–142
   for binary search trees, 636–640
   in Bingo Games case study, 137
   for FIFO queues, 344–348
   for graphs, 730–731
   for heaps, 713–715, 718
   for key-ordered lists, 404–413
   for priority queues, 708–710
   for splitting the array, 789–790
   for stacks, 274–279
   for strings, 215–226
Loop invariants, 41–45
Loops
   error-free, 41
   invalid postfix expressions and, 284
   postfix evaluations and, 282–283
loop statements, recursive routines and, 579
Low-level design, in software process, 2
Lucas, Edouard, 573
Lukasiewicz, Jan, 279n1

M

Maintenance, in software process, 2

Mantissa, 93
Many-to-many association, 135
Mapping parameter, examples with values supplied for, 218
Marked graph operation, 731, 748
Mark_Vertex graph operation, 731, 737, 748
Matrices, adjacency, 746
Matrix representation, for graphing flight connections between cities, *747*
Max_Child, determining, 723
Max_Element value, linked lists with dummy node and, 501–502
Max-heaps, 713, 714
Maximum absolute error, 94, 95
Maximum relative error, 94, 95
Max_Length constant, 222, 232
Max_Size discriminant, 277, 291, 294
   array-based key-ordered lists and, 507
   sequential lists and, 430
Max_Size field, 315
Maze, picture of, *597*
Maze ADO: Implements Specification 9.1, Body 9.1 of, 606
Maze ADO (Specification 9.1), 605–606
Maze package, 605
maze.txt file, 597
Mega FLOPS (Millions of FLoating point OPerations per Second), 96
Members, of sets, 164
Membership operators, in expressions, 107
Membership sets, 206
Membership tests, 106
   examples of, 165
Memory
   allocating, 236–237
   organization of, 255
   simple unbounded-length string class and leaks in, 244–246
   unchecked deallocation of, 238–239
   use of, in running program, *255, 375*
Memory leaks, 238, 256
   access types used in application level and, 381, 382
   controlled types and, 255

   preventing, 309
Memory management array, 516–517
Memory space, sorting and, 768
Merge function, 784, 787
   algorithm for, 785
Mergesort, 320
Merge Sort: Implements Specification 12.1, Body 12.5 of, 785–787
Merge_Sort procedure, 785
   analysis of, 787–788
   analysis of with $N = 16$, *787*
   coding nonrecursive versions of, 807
   disadvantages with, 788
   as recursive procedure, 782–783
Merge sorts, 768
   algorithm for, 782
   analyzing, 787–788
   in Big-O comparison, 813*t*
   merging sorted halves, 783–784, *785*
   timed experiments on, 813*t*
Metric-based testing, 49
Min-heaps, 713
Minimal perfect hash function, 838
   for Ada 2005 reserved words, *839*
Minimal perfect hash table, with Ada 2005 reserved words, *840*
Minimizing Translations case study, 200–206
   greedy solution, 202
   optimal solution, 201
   Translations program, 202–206
Min_Index function, 770
Model numbers, 93
Modifiability, abstraction, information hiding and, 10
Modify binary search tree operation, 649
Modifying software, 4–5
Modify operation
   Big-O comparison of key-ordered list implementations and, 462
   Big-O comparisons of bushy tree and list operations, 679, 679*t*
   circular lists and, 485
   current element and, 637
   linked lists and, 451
   sequential lists and, 432, *433*

mod operator, 186, 359n1
Modular arithmetic, 91
Modular design, 62
Modular integers, logical operators used with, 92
Modular integer types, 91–92
Modules, 9
    as abstraction tool, 10
Modulus, 91
Month_Is operation, 17
Move procedure
    specification of, 216
    use of, for copying fixed-length strings, 216–217
Multiple keys, sorting and, 809–810
Multiple recursive calls, 567–569
    pattern of rabbit reproduction over 7 months and, *568*
Multiplication method, good hash functions and, 836–837
Multi-way search trees, balanced, 686
Mutators, 83, 405–406
My_Car record variable, 99–100
My_Set array variable, 172
My_Stack.Extended child generic package, 312
My_Stack package, 312
My_Strings package, 418

N

N, size of, exponential time in relation to, 320t
Named variables, 255
NAME_ERROR exception, 425, 527
Natural subtype, 105, 560
Negative subtype, 105
N-element arrays, initializing to zero in every element in, 321
Nesting, for address book operations, 424
new allocator, 255, 303
new allocator operator, size of designated object established by, 243
New_Node function, 506
New_Node operation, array memory management and, 516, *517*
new operator, 256
    general access types and, 375
New_Space variable, 453

Next field, 315
    doubly linked lists and, 498
    header nodes and, 499
    linear doubly linked lists and, 494, *494*
    linked lists and, 504
Nil identifier, 506
$N \log_2 N$, 320
$n!$ (n factorial), recursive calculations and, 557–559
Node_IO, 526
Node_Ptr access type, 306, 526
Nodes, 298
    child, 628
    height balanced, in AVL trees, 685
    linked list as array of, 504–518
    linked list as file of, 520–534
    linked lists of, 363
    parent, 628
    single, 299, *299*
Node sorting algorithm, 798
Nodes storage array, 508
Node_Type type, 306, 526
Noise, algorithm analysis and, 318
Nonempty circular lists, inserting elements into, 489
Non-tree structure, *630*
not in membership test, 169
not null optional words, use of, 411
not operator, membership tests and, 107
Nouns
    objects as, 24
    in problem statements, 641
Null access value literal, 235
Null_Bounded_String constant, 232
Null procedures, overriding, 247
null reserved word, 366, 370, 506
Null strings, 219
null value, 239, 303
Num_Positions subkeys, 803
N value, work done by operations, described in terms of, 319. *See also* Big-O notation

O

Object Management Group, 12n2
object.method syntax, 277, 311
Object.Operation form, 19

Object operations, syntax forms for, 19
Object-oriented classes, reuse and, 6
Object-oriented design, 3, 14–31, 62, 153
    classes in, 14–18
    design choices, 25–26
    design example, 26–31
    first scenario walk-through, 27–30
    identification of classes and, 23–25
    inheritance and, 14, 19–23
    initial responsibilities, 27
    methodology, 23
    objects in, 14, 18–19
Objects
    construction of, in Ada, 405
    in object-oriented design, 14, 18–19
Object type, 239
Observers, 17, 83, 98
    forms of, 406
One-dimensional arrays, 97
One-to-many association, 135
One-to-one association, 135
$O(N \log_2 N)$ sorts, 782–800
    heap sort, 795–800
    merge sort, 782–788
    quick sort, 788–795
$O(N^2)$ sorts, 769–781
    bubble sort, 774–778
    insertion sort, 778–781
    simplicity of, 812
    straight selection sorts, 769–773
OOD. *See* Object-oriented design
Open addressing
    double hashing, 826–828
    linear probing, 821–822, 824–825
    quadratic probing, 826
Operands, 281
Operation, in software process, 2
Operational scenarios, 7
Operation symbols, enclosure of, in quotation marks, 168
Operation terminology, 127–130, 131
Operator precedence rules, 279
Ordered list, storage of, in array, *505*

Order property, for heaps, 713, 714, 719, 722, 754, 795, 796
Orders of magnitude, common, 319–321. *See also* Big-O notation
Ordinal data types, 79
or else operator, 169, 652
or else short-circuit operator, 448
or operator, 91, 92
out mode, 590
out parameter, circular lists and, 485, 489
OVERFLOW exception, 277, 285, 294, 348, 354, 355
Overloading, 127, 128, 169
Overriding, 127
overriding reserved word, 128
Overwrite string operation, as transformer, 406

P
Package body, 16, 108, 121, 124, 126–127
    EBNF definition of, 425
Package declarations, 108, 110, 153
Packages, 108
    in Ada, 9
    data abstraction, 112–115
    defined, 16, 110
    kinds of, 109–115
    service, 110–112
Package specifications, 16
Padding, adding to records, 315
Padding characters, in fixed-length strings, 215, 216
Pad parameter, 216
Parameter passing, 589–590
Parameter profiles, 127
Parent packages, 22
Parents, 628
Pass by reference mechanism, 590n1
Path, 49, 730
Path testing, 49
PATTERN_ERROR, 219
Perfect binary trees, 688, *689*
Perfect hash functions, 838–840
Peso type, 96
Phone book, binary search of, 55
Pi (π), approximation of, 94
Pivot value, 789

Plotable_Point_Type, 103, 104
Pointer-based sorted lists, 712
Pointer references, 313
Pointers
    array of, to different locomotive types, *381*
    sorting, 810–812
Pointer variable, 235
Pointing to an object, 235
Point_Type, 103, 104
Pool-specific access types, 382
    defined, 376
Poor responsibilities, examples of, 25
Pop operation
    complete algorithm for, 302–303
    effect of, *275*
    effect of, on stacks, 294, *296*
    encapsulation and, 313
    exception UNDERFLOW and, 277, 285
    first attempt at algorithm for, 301
    for stacks, 275
    as transformer, 405
Popped_Element, 302, 303
Popping, last element in stacks, *305*
Popping elements, from stacks, 294
Popping the stack, *304*
'Pos discrete attribute, 183
Positive subtype, 105, 560
Postconditions, 39–40
    exceptions and, 279
    library data structure, 87
    in Linked List Search (Specification 7.5), 446
Postfix Evaluation (Program 5.1), 285–289
Postfix expressions
    calculator for evaluation of, *280*
    evaluating, 279–289
    invalid, *284*, 284–285
    with multiple operators and results from evaluation of, *289*
    results of, *280*
Postorder traversal, 635, 636, 664
Pragmas, 807
Preconditions, 39–40
    library data structure, 87
'Pred attribute for enumeration types, 92

'Pred discrete attribute, 183, 186
Predicate, 406n1
Pred_Loc access variable
    circular lists and, 486, 491
    linked lists and, 449, 453, 455
Pred_Loc parameter, 671
Preorder traversal, 634, 635, 636, 664
Primary sort keys, 810
Primitive operations, 119
    dynamic dispatching and, 380
Print_Manifest, 354
Print queue, 348
Priority Queue: Implements Specification 11.1, Body 11.1 of, 720–721
Priority_Queue package body, 720
Priority queues, 154, 708–713, 754
    application level, 710–712
    implementation level, 712–713
    logical level, 708
    work request example, 711–712
Priority Queue (Specification 11.1), 709–710
Private declarations, 118
private keyword, 17
Private types, 117–119, 190–191
    in ADT packages, 199
    enforcing information hiding and, 17
    limited, 313
    using, to encapsulate classes, 313
Problem analysis, in software process, 2
Problem solving, with recursion, 556
Problem-solving case studies
    Bingo Games—How Long Should They Take?, 132–152
    Escape from a Maze, 596–612
    Minimizing Translations, 200–206
    Reusable Binary Search Procedure, 193–200
    Testing a Binary Search Operation, 53–62
Procedures, eliminating calls to, 806–807
Processing time, sorting and, 768
Process parameter, declaration of, 411
Product function, 45
Program design, 8–32
    abstraction, 8–9
    exceptions, 31–32

functional decomposition, 13–14
information hiding, 9–10
object-oriented design, 14–31
stepwise refinement, 10–12
visual aids, 12
Programming by contract, 40
Programs
    Demonstration of the Extended Stack class, 312–313
    General Access Types, 377–378
    Postfix Evaluation, 285
    Rouses Point Hump Yard, 352–354
    Sort Names, 228–230
    Towers of Hanoi, 575–576
    Translations, 202–206
    Word Frequency Generator, 643–647
Program testing, 47–51
    bottom-up and top-down testing, 50–51
    code coverage, 48–49
    data coverage, 47–48
    test plans, 50
Program validation
Program verification, 63
Proper subsets, 166
Pseudocode, 13
Public declarations, 118
Push operation
    effect of, *275*
    effect of, on stack, 294, *295*
    encapsulation and, 313
    exception **OVERFLOW** and, 277, 285
    for stacks, 275
Push operator, as transformer, 405
Put calls, 51
Put_List procedure, 102
Put procedure, 108, 127

Q

Quadratic probing, 826
Quadratic time, $O(N^2)$, 320
Quality software, goals of, 4–6
Quartic time, $O(N^4)$, 320
Queue_Array, 721
Queue.Front access value, 366

Queue implementations
    complexity of, 371, *371*
    considerations related to selection of, 374*t*
    space requirements for, 371–372, *372*
    time and, 373
Queueing theory, 348
Queue is package body, 361
Queue operations
    effects of, *346*
    testing, 374–375
Queue overflow, 347
Queue package, 345–247
Queue.Rear access variable, 366, 370
Queues, 154
    bad design for, *369*
    as container classes, 404
    defined, 344
    empty, *359*, *365*, 366
    full, 360, *360*
    implementation of, as linked structures, 362–370
    implementation of, as static arrays, 355–362
    with one element, *365*
    operations on, 345–348
    routes stored in, *740*
    wrapping around, *358*, 359
Queue_type record, 370
Queue underflow, 347
Quicksort, 320
Quick Sort: Implements Specification 12.1, Body 12.6 of, 792–794
Quick sort algorithm, splitting value and, 794
Quick_Sort operation, analysis of, 794–795
Quick_Sort procedure, coding nonrecursive versions of, 807
Quick sorts, 768, 788–795
    analyzing, 794–795
    in Big-O comparison, 813*t*
    inherent instability of, 809
    ordering exams with, *788*
    splitting the array: implementation level, 790, 792, 794
    splitting the array: logical level, 789–790
    timed experiments on, 813*t*
    top-level algorithm for, 789

Quiz_Ops package, 187
Quiz_Score_Type, 187
Quotation marks, operator symbols enclosed in, 168

R

Radix Sort: Implements Specification 12.2, Body 12.8 of, 804–805
Radix_Sort procedure, space requirements for, 806
Radix sorts, 768, 800–806
    algorithm for, 801
    analysis of, 805–806
    description of, 800
    implementation level, 803–805
    key fields after each pass, *801*
    queues after each pass, *802*
    stability of, 809
    timed experiments on, 813*t*
Radix Sort (Specification 12.2), 803–804
Railroad Car ADO: Implements Specification 2.8, Body 2.6 of, 126
Railroad Car ADO (Specification 2.8), 125
Railroad car class, UML diagram of, *121*
Railroad_Car package body, 122, 126
Railroad Cars: Implements Specification 2.4, Body 2.2, 114
Railroad Cars: Implements Specification 2.6, Body 2.4 of, 122
Railroad Cars (encapsulated version) (Specification 2.6), 117–118
Railroad Cars (exposed version) (Specification 2.4), 112–114
Railroad_Cars package, 112–114, 117–118, 125
Railroad_Cars.Tanker package, 114–115, 120–121, 127
Railroad_Cars.Tanker package body, 123–124
Raise statements, 32
RAM. *See* Random access memory
Random access files, 520
Random access memory, 520
Random number generators, 170
Range, 94
'Range array attribute, 190
range integer type, 186
Ranges, subtype, 106

Readability, programmer-defined subtypes and, 105
Read_Node, 526
Real numbers, in programs, 93
Real types, 93, 188
Rear indicator, floating-front design and, 357, 359
Record discriminants, 100–102
Record objects, Ada syntax for, 300
Records, 98–102
    padding added to, 315
    tagged, 103–104
Recursion
    Big-O and, 589–590
    classic example of, 557–559
    combinations and, 569–571
    depth of, 589
    description of, 556–557
    direct, 556
    dynamic storage allocation and, 583–589, 613
    how it works, 579–590
    indirect, 556
    iteration and, 590–592
    processing of linked lists and, 571–573
    removal of, 590–593, 807–808
    stacking and, 592–593
    static storage allocation and, 580–583, 613
    tail, 591, 798
    Towers of Hanoi and, 573–576
    using to simplify solutions-three examples, 569–576
Recursive algorithm, for Reheap_Down procedure, 722
Recursive binary search tree operations, 650–665
    Clear operation, 665
    Delete operation, 657–663
    Find operation, 652
    Insert operation, 652–657
    Size operation, 650–652
    Traverse operation, 664–665
Recursive calls, 556
    to Merge_Sort, 783
    multiple, 567–569
    single, 564–567

Recursive implementations, results of timed implementation comparisons between interative implementations and, 594t
Recursive_Insert procedure, 654, 655
Recursive procedures and functions
    multiple recursive calls, 567–569
    trade-offs with, 612
    verifying, 563–564
    writing, 564–569
    writing a Boolean function, 564–567
Recursive programming, 560–563
    coding factorial function, 560
    comparison to iterative solution, 562–563
    execution of **Factorial (4)**, *562*
    walkthrough of **Factorial (4)**, 561*t*
Recursive routines, debugging, 579
Recursive solutions
    deciding upon use of, 593–596
    iterative solutions *vs.*, 562–563
Red/Black Trees, 686
Redundant classes, 134
Referencing an object, 235
Regression testing, 33
Reheap_Down operation, 714, 719, *723*
    algorithm for, 722
    heap building and, 796, 798, 800
Reheap_Up operation, 714, 720, 723, *724*
    algorithm for, 724
    code for, 725
Relational operators, 92, 183
Relative address, 583
Relative error, 93
Reliability, with encapsulation, 313
rem operator, 359n1
    good hash functions and, 834
    implementing body of function **Digit_Of** and, 804
Removal
    of recursion, 590–593, 807–808
    of set elements, 166
Replace_Slice procedure, 228
Replace_Slice string operation, as transformer, 406
Requirements, 4
Requirements definition, in software process, 2

Reserved words, timed experiments in searching for, 840*t*
Responsibilities
    cohesive, 24
    initial, 27
    poor, 25
Retrieve binary search tree operation, 649
Retrieve observer, graphs and, 731
Retrieve operation
    Big-O comparison of key-ordered list implementations and, 462
    Big-O comparisons of bushy tree and list operations, 679, 679*t*
    circular lists and, 485
    current element and, 637
    linked lists and, 451
    sequential lists and, 432, *432*
Retrieve procedure, 748
Reusability
    abstraction, information hiding and, 10
    of quality software, 5–6
Reusable Binary Search procedure case study, 193–200
    Binary Search Procedure, 198–199
    Generic Binary Search, 195–198
    private types and generic formal private types, 199–200
Reuse, 23
    programming for: generic units, 177–193
Reverse Polish notation, 279n1
Reverse_Traverse procedure, 572–573
    recursive, *571*
    writing nonrecursively, 592–593
Right child, 630
Right leaning nodes, in AVL trees, 685, *686*
Right subtree, 630
Robustness, 36
Root.all.Right parameter, formal parameter root copied to, *656*
Root formal parameter, 656
    copying to actual parameter **Root.all.Right**, *656*
Root node, 630
    deleting with no children, 659, *659*
    deleting with one child, 659, *659*

deleting with two children, 660, *661*
Roots, 628
    removal of, from heaps, 714, *716*
Round-trip gestalt design, in stepwise refinement, 11
Rouses Point hump yard, 349, *349*
Rouses Point Hump Yard (Program 6.1), 352–354
RPN. *See* Reverse Polish notation
Run-time errors, 36–37
Run-time stacks, 290, 585–589, 613
    during execution of **Factorial**, *588*

S

save operation, for address book ADO, 425, 426
Scalar data types, 78, 153
    hierarchical relationship among, 628, *629*
Scalar types, 89–96
    enumeration types, 92–93
    fixed point types, 95–96
    floating point types, 93–95
    modular integer types, 91–92
    real types, 93
    signed integer types, 90–91
Scaled integers, 96n2
Scenarios, 7
Scientific notation, 94
Search_Array procedure, 430, 817
Search_Circular_List procedure, 485, 488, 491, 497
Search function, linear probing and, 824
Searching, 814–818
    binary, 817
    high-probability ordering, 815–816
    interpolation, 817–818
    key ordering, 816–817
    linear, 815
    sequential, 817
    summary of, 841
Searching strings, 217–221
Searching techniques, 814
Search_Linked_List procedure, 451, 455
    key ordering and, 816
Search procedure, double hashing used with, 827–828
Search_Tree procedure, 671
    iterative binary search tree and, 673
    using to find insertion point, *674*

Secondary sort keys, 810
Selection_Sort, Big-O comparison between **Bubble_Sort** and, 776–777, 778
Selection Sort: Implements Specification 3.3, Body 3.4 of, 192–193
Selection_Sort: Implements Specification 12.1, Body 12.1 of, 771–772
Selection sorts, 320
    in Big-O comparison, 813*t*
    timed experiments on, 813*t*
Selector operations, 83
Self-adjusting lists, 816
Self-organizing lists, 816
Sequential Array-Based List: Implements Specification 7.1, Body 7.2 of, 437–440
Sequential files, 520
Sequential lists
    Delete operation and, 434–435
    deleting from, *436*
    encapsulation and, 437
    finding list elements, 430–432
    with five elements, *429*
    implementation of, 428–440
    inserting into, *434*
    Insert operation and, 432–434
    Retrieve and **Modify** operations and, 432
    in static and dynamic storage, 427, *427*
    Traverse operation and, 435–437
Sequential searching, advantages/disadvantages with, 817
Service packages, 109, 110–112
Set members, 164
Set notation, vertices specified by listing them in, 728
Set operations, examples of, *174*
Sets, 154, 163–207, 206
    abstract level of, 164–169
    abstract view of, 164–165
    application level and, 169–172
    difference between, 165, 206
    empty, 165, 172, 174
    implementation level and, 172–177
    intersection of, 165, 206
    membership, 206
    operations with, 165–166

postfix evaluation program and, 285
specification for, 166–169
storage of, as array of Booleans, *173*
union of, 165, 206
universal, 165
Set specification, 166
Bingo Number Set, 167–168
Set_Throttle procedure, 380
Shape property, for heaps, 713, 714–715, 719, 754, 795
Short_Bubble_Sort, analysis of, 778
Short Bubble Sort: Implements Specification 12.1, Body 12.3 of, 777–778
Short bubble sorts
in Big-O comparison, 813*t*
timed experiments on, 813*t*
Short-circuit operators, 169, 448
Shortest Paths, Body 11.5 of, 743–745
SI Base Units (Specification 2.2), 110
SI Conversions: Implements Specification 2.3, Body 2.1, 111–112
SI Conversions (Specification 2.3), 111
Signature, 127
Signed integer types, 90–91
Significant characters, in fixed-length strings, 215
Simple sorts, timed experiments on, 813*t*
Simple unbounded-length string class, 243–246
Single nodes, 299, *299*
Single-source shortest paths problem, 742–746
Single stepping, 51
Singleton classes, 124–127
Singly linked lists, insertions into, *496*
SI_Units.Base package, 110, 111
SI_Units.Base.String_Conversions package, 111
SI_Units package (Specification 2.1), 110
Size observer operation, 406
Size operation
Big-O comparisons of bushy tree and list operations, 679, 679*t*
recursive binary search trees and, 650
Size procedure, Big-O of, 651–652
Skewed trees, 657, 680, 682
Slice observer, 406
Slices, 98

Smaller-caller question, 563
applying to multiple recursive calls, 567
avoiding endless recursive routines with, 579
iteration and, 591
single recursive call and, 566
Towers of Hanoi algorithm and, 575
for verifying Escape from Maze recursive design, 603–604
for verifying recursive function, 650
for verifying **Reverse_Traverse** procedure, 573
Software, 3
quality, goals of, 4–6
Software crisis/challenge, 63
Software process, 2–8
defined, 3
Software specification, 4
in software process, 2
Sort algorithms, choosing, 812
Sorted arrays
building minimum height binary search tree from, *683*
insert location after last element in, *779*
merging, 783–784, *784*
Sorted lists, 404
comparison of priority queue implementations with, 713*t*
Sorting, 768–769
in descending order, 808
priority queues and, 710
summary of, 812–814
Sorting algorithms, Big-O comparison of, 813*t*
Sorting arrays, with access values, 811, *811*
Sorting pointers, 810–812
Sorting procedures, timed experiments of, 813*t*
Sort Names (Program 4.1), 228–230
Sort (Specification 12.1), 768–769
Space
efficient use of, 315
recursive solutions and, 594
Space character, in **Ada.Strings.Map** package, 285
Space requirements
comparison of, for two stack implementations, 316
for **Heap_Sort** procedure, 800

for list implementations, 461
for queue implementations, 371–372
for quick sorts, 795
for radix sorts, 806
SPARK Examiner, 38, 39, 107, 354
Specification errors, cost of, based on discovery time, *35*
Specifications
    design errors and, 34–35
    understanding the problem and, 6–7
    well-documented, 535
    writing detailed, 7–8
Split_Index
    splitting the array: implementation level and, 789, 790, 792
    splitting the array: logical level and, 789
split procedure, trace of, *791*
Splitting the array
    implementation level, 790, 792, 794
    logical level, 789–790
Split value, 789
Stability, 808–809
Stable sorts, 808–809
Stack class, extending, 311–313
Stack.Extended package, 311
Stack.Extended package body, 312
Stack implementations
    comparison of lines of code for, 316*t*
    comparison of space requirements for, *316*
Stacking
    recursion and, 592–593
    removing recursion and, 808
Stack operations
    Big-O comparison of, 323–324, 324*t*
    time for, *317*
Stack overflow, 277, 303
Stack package, 276–277
Stacks, 154, 255
    application level, 279–290
    array implementation of, containing three elements, *291*
    comparing implementations for, 314–324
    composed with linked nodes, 299, *299*
    as container classes, 404

    description of, 274
    effect of **Push** operation on, 294, *295*
    empty, *292*, *297*, 309
    encapsulation and, 313–314
    exceptions and, 277–279
    implementation level, 290–314
    implementation of, as linked list, 294, 297–303, 306–311
    implementation of, as static array, 290–294
    of linked nodes (controlled implementation), *309*
    logical level, 274–279
    operations on, 274–277
    popping, *304*
    popping last element in, *305*
    real-life, *274*
    routes stored in, *736*
    run-time, 585–589, 613
    space efficiency and, 315
Stack storage, for named objects, 375
Stack_Type declaration, 277, 309
Stack underflow, 277, 303
    checking for, 294
Standard package, functions for comparing integer values predefined in, 410
start.txt file, 597
Statement coverage, 48
Static allocation of space, for program with two subprograms, *582*
Static arrays
    queues implemented as, 355–362
    stacks implemented as, 290–294
Static storage
    array-based lists in, 427, *427*
    linked lists in, 428, *428*
    sequential lists in, 427, *427*
Static storage allocation, recursion and, 580–583, 613
Static verification, 37
Stepwise refinement, 10–12
STORAGE_ERROR exception, 240, 255, 303, 376, 579
Straight selection sorts, 768, 769–773
    analyzing, 772–773
    example of, *771*
String classes, observers in, 406
String keys, simple hashing of, 837–838

String objects, access variables and designation of, *241*
Strings, 154, 213-256
    application level and, 226-230
    bounded-length, 214, 221-225, 256
    classes of, 214, 256
    fixed-length, 214, 215-221, 256
    implementation level and, 230-255
    logical level and, 215-226
    null, 219
    postfix evaluation program and, 285
    searching, 217-221
    terminology, 214
    unbounded-length, 214, 226, 256
String type, 79, 105
Structs, 98
Structured composite types, 82
Stubs, 50-51
Subclasses, 19, 153
    for extending stack class, 311
Subkey_Type, 803
Subprogram calls, eliminating extra overhead of, 806-807
Subprograms, 206
    designing interfaces for, 590
    recursion and, 556, 579
    signature of, 127
Subsets, 166, 206
    proper, 166
Subtrees, 628
Subtype declarations, sample, 105
Subtype ranges, 106
Subtypes, 105-107
    examples of those declared as subsets of programmer-defined types and subtypes, 106
    programmer-defined, 105
    types *vs.*, 107
'**Succ** attribute, 92
'**Succ** discrete attribute, 183, 186
Sum function, 45
Summary operations, 83
Superclasses, 19, 153
Swapping, 806
    bubble sort and, 776, 777
    selection sort and, 770, 771
    sorting pointers and, 810-812
    sorting time and, 814
    values of two integer variables, 186-187
Swap procedures, instantiation of, 190
Swap_Values generic procedure, 190-191
Symbol table, 580*t*
Syntax
    of allocator, 236
    for dereferencing record object, 300
    errors, 23, 35, 36
    forms, for invoking object operations, 19
    shorthand, for designated arrays, 242
System package, 109

T

Tables, 12
tagged keyword, 103
Tagged records, 103-104
Tagged types, 119, 246, 247, 277
    advantages with, in class implementation, 311
    declaring access types for designation of, 378
Tail recursion, 591, 798
Tank car class, UML diagram of, *121*
Tank Cars: Implements Specification 2.7, 123-124
Tank Cars (encapsulated version) (Specification 2.7), 120-121
Tanker Cars: Implements Specification 2.5, 115
Tanker Cars (exposed version) (Specification 2.5), 114-115
Tare field, 118
TDD. *See* Test-driven development
Template class, 181
Test-driven development, 50
Test drivers, 50-51, 465
Testing, 32
    debugging *vs.*, 33
    queue operations, 374-375
    in software process, 2
Testing a binary search operation (problem-solving case study), 53-62
    binary search, 54-57
    binary search algorithm, 54
    debugger data on binary search test case 5, *61*

searching, 54
test driver, 58, 60
test plan, 57–58
test plan for binary search operation, *59*
Testing list operations, 465
Testing phase, software changes during, 5
Test parameter, 219
Test plans, 49, 50, 465
Three-question method
    avoiding endless recursive routines with, 579
    multiple recursive calls and, 567
    quick sort algorithm verified with, 790
    recursive procedures and function verified with, 563–564
    Towers of Hanoi algorithm verified with, 574–575
    for verifying Escape from Maze recursive design, 603–604
    for verifying recursive procedures and functions, 563–564, 650
    writing Boolean function and, 566–567
Time
    binding, 580
    for **Insert** and **Delete** operations for different key-ordered lists, 519*t*
    key-ordered list operations and, 463–464, 464*t*
    for queue operations, 373, 373*t*
    for stack operations, *317*
Timed experiments, of sorting procedures, 813*t*
Timed implementation comparisons, for binary search tree and linked list, 680–681, 681*t*
Time efficiency, algorithm choices and, 317–318
Timeliness, quality software and, 6
Tokenizing, 642
Top-down debugging plan, 52
Top-down stepwise refinement, 11, 23
Top-down testing, 50–51
Top field, 315
Top variable, 290
To_Recycle variable, 366
To_Set constructor, 285
To_String procedure, 252
Towers of Hanoi, description of, 573–575
Towers of Hanoi (Program 9.1), 575–576
Trailer nodes, 500–502

defined, 500
doubly linked list with, *502*
linked list with, *500*
Transformers (or mutators), 21, 83, 98, 119, 405–406
Translate string operation, as transformer, 406
Translations (Program 3.1), 202–206
Traveling salesman problem, 320
Traverse operation
    Big-O comparison of key-ordered list implementations and, 462
    Big-O comparisons of bushy tree and list operations, 679, 679*t*
    circular lists and, 484–485
    linked lists and, 445
    recursive binary search trees and, 664–665
    sequential lists and, 435, 437
Traverse procedure, 411, 412, 413
Traversing graphs, 731
    application level, 735
Tree balancing algorithm, 683–684
Tree information, copying into array, *682*
Trees, 154
    balanced, 690
    bushy, 657, 690
    defined, 628
    degenerate, 657
    as directed graphs, 730
    empty, 649
    height of, 657
    skewed, 657
Tree shape, insert order and, 657, *658*
Trees model hierarchical relationships, *629*
Tree_Type subclass, pointers for, 648
Trial and error, in design process, 26
Trim procedure, 227
Trim string operation, as transformer, 405
Trono, John
    minimal perfect hash function by, and timed experiments in searching for reserved words, 840*t*
    tables for minimal perfect hash function for Ada 2005 reserved words by, 839, *839*
Try_To_Escape procedure, comparing output for two versions of, 612*t*

2-3 Trees, 686
2-3-4 Trees, 686
Type declarations, 89
    for freight train manifests, 350
    incomplete, 306–307
Types
    of discriminants, 100
    subtypes *vs.*, 107
Type variables, 235

U

UML. *See* Unified Modeling Language
UML class diagrams, 12, 26
    alternative, of generic stack class and exceptions raised by, *278*
    associations in, 153
    composition shown by, *79*
    for **Date** class, *17*
    of generic queue class and exceptions it raises, *348*
    of generic set class and three instances, *178*
    of generic stack class and exceptions raised by, *278*
    inheritance shown with, 21
    of Locomotive class, *130*
    of railroad car and tank car classes, 121
    of set class, *166*
    showing is-a relationships between kinds of railroad locomotives with, *129*
Unbounded Key-Ordered List: Implements Specification 7.4, Body 7.3 of, 455, 457–460
Unbounded Key-Ordered List (Specification 7.4), 441–444
Unbounded-length strings, 214, 226, 256
    access types and, 234–255
Unbounded-Length Strings Based on Controlled Types (Specification 4.1), 248–249
Unbounded Queue: Implements Specification 6.2, Body 6.2 of, 367–369
Unbounded Queue Class (Specification 6.2), 363–365
Unbounded_Queue package, 363
Unbounded_Queue package body, 367
Unbounded Stack: Implements Specification 5.2, Body 5.2 of, 310–311
Unbounded Stack (Specification 5.2), 307–309
Unbounded_Strings: Implements Specification 4.1, Body 4.1 of, 251–252
Unbounded_Strings package, 248, 251–252
Unbounded_String_Type, declaring as private type, 249
Unchecked_Deallocation procedure, 238, 239, 302, 303
Unconstrained record types, 102n3
Unconstrained string objects, access variables and designation of, *243*
UNDERFLOW exception, 277, 285, 347, 354, 355
Undirected graphs, 727, *729*
    complete, *731*
Unified Modeling Language, 3, 79
Union, of sets, 165, 206
Unique keys, 404
Unit testing, 47
Universal set, 165
Universal_Set deferred constant, 169
Unordered collections, 172
Unsigned integer types, 91
Unsorted array, and tree, *796*
Unsorted lists, 712
    comparison of priority queue implementations with, 713*t*
Unstructured composite types, 82, 98
User scenarios, walkthroughs of, 27–30

V

Vague classes, 134
'**Val** discrete attribute, 183
Validation, 33
Value, lists ordered by, 404
Value_In_Array function, 591
    execution of, *566*
    writing, 564–567
Value_In_Array routine, depth of recursive calls in, 595
Value length, 428
Values, pushing new, onto linked stack, 301
Verbs
    operations as, 24
    in problem statements, 641

Verification
  dynamic, 37
  in software process, 2
  static, 37
  techniques, 63
Verification of software correctness, 32–53
  debugging with a plan, 51–52
  designing for correctness, 37–45
  design review activities, 45–46
  origin of bugs, 34–37
  practical considerations, 52–53
  program testing, 47–51
Verifying recursive procedures and functions, three-question method and, 563–564
Vertex_Key, 730
Vertices
  adjacent, 728
  graph of flight connections between cities using array storage for, *753*
  graph of flight connections between cities using linked list for, *754*
  in graphs, 727, 728
Vertices_Rec, 747
Visual aids, 12

W

Walkthroughs, 45
  of **Factorial (4)**, 561*t*
  first scenario, 27–30

Weighted digraph, implementing, 746
Weighted Digraph: Implements Specification 11.3, Body 11.6 of, 749–752
Weighted Digraph (Specification 11.3), 731–734
Weighted graphs, 730, *732*
Weight function, for class Locomotive, 130
Weight_Of function, 748
Weight_Of observer, graphs and, 731
White-box testing. *See* Clear-box testing
Whole_Number_Type, 187
Wide_Character type, 92
Winner operation, 146
with null record clause, subclass implementation and, 312
Word Frequency Generator (Program 10.1), 643–646
  testing, 646–647
Write_Node, 526
Writing
  detailed specifications, 7–8
  programs to wrong specifications, 34–35
  recursive procedures and functions, 564–569

X

xor operator, 91, 92

Y

Year_Is operation, 17